LEARNING
IN SOCIAL SETTINGS

LEARNING
IN SOCIAL SETTINGS

*New Readings in
the Social Psychology
of Education*

Matthew B. Miles
Teachers College
Columbia University

W. W. Charters, Jr.
University of Oregon

Sponsored by the
Society for the
Psychological Study
of Social Issues

ALLYN AND BACON, INC.
Boston

Contents

Introduction   1

1. EDUCATIONAL ENVIRONMENTS   11

Roger G. Barker, Paul V. Gump,
Wallace V. Friesen, Edwin P. Willems
   *The ecological environment: student participation in non-
       class settings*   12

Saul Pilnick, Albert Elias, Neale W. Clapp
   *The Essexfields concept: a new approach to the social treat-
       ment of juvenile delinquents*   44

David G. Winter, Richard Alpert, David C. McClelland
   The classic personal style   58

C. Robert Pace
   Differences in campus atmosphere   77

2. INSIDE THE CLASSROOM   93

Philip W. Jackson, Henriette M. Lahaderne
   Inequalities of teacher-pupil contacts   94

Don R. Thomas, Wesley C. Becker, Marianne Armstrong
*Production and elimination of disruptive classroom behavior
by systematically varying teacher's behavior*   105

O. J. Harvey, Misha Prather, B. Jack White,
James K. Hoffmeister
Teachers' beliefs, classroom atmosphere and student behavior   122

Jacob S. Kounin, Paul V. Gump, James J. Ryan, III
Explorations in classroom management   135

Richard A. Schmuck
*Some relationships of peer liking patterns in the classroom to
pupil attitudes and achievement*   151

3. THE RACE PROBLEM   169

Robert D. Hess, Virginia C. Shipman
*Early experience and the socialization of cognitive
modes in children*   170

Robert A. Dentler
Equality of educational opportunity—a special review   189

Henry S. Dyer
School factors and equal educational opportunity   200

John H. Litcher, David W. Johnson
*Changes in attitudes toward Negroes of white elementary
school students after use of multi-ethnic readers*   217

Irwin Katz
Experiments on Negro performance in bi-racial situations   225

Robert L. Crain
School system acquiescence to pressures for desegregation   241

4. ASPIRATIONS AND THE SCHOOL   269

James S. Coleman
The adolescent subculture and academic achievement   270

Denise Kandel, Gerald S. Lesser

    *Relative influence of parents and peers on the educational
    plans of adolescents in the United States and Denmark*   283

Buford Rhea

    Institutional paternalism in high school   308

5.   EDUCATIONAL PROCEDURES   319

Norma D. Feshbach, Geraldine Devor

    Teaching styles in four-year-olds   320

W. Victor Beez

    *Influence of biased psychological reports on teacher
    behavior and pupil performance*   328

Sarane S. Boocock, James S. Coleman

    Games with simulated environments in learning   336

Richard de Charms, Gerald H. Moeller

    Values expressed in American children's readers, 1800-1950   358

Melvin L. De Fleur, Lois B. De Fleur

    *The relative contribution of television as a learning
    source for children's occupational knowledge*   371

6.   EDUCATION AS PERSONAL CHANGE   389

Urie Bronfenbrenner

    *Soviet methods of character education: some implications
    for research*   390

David C. McClelland

    Toward a theory of motive acquisition   414

Matthew B. Miles

    *Changes during and following laboratory training: a
    clinical-experimental study*   436

Sara K. Winter, Jeffery C. Griffith, David A. Kolb

    Capacity for self-direction   458

M. Brewster Smith

*Explorations in competence: a study of Peace Corps
teachers in Ghana*   469

7. COLLEGE CONSEQUENCES   491

Alberta Engvall Siegel, Sidney Siegel

Reference groups, membership groups, and attitude change   492

Richard Flacks

*The liberated generation: an exploration of the roots of
student protest*   501

Theodore M. Newcomb, Richard Flacks, Donald P. Warwick

Group norms and creative individualism: a case study   524

David Gottlieb

Processes of socialization in American graduate schools   556

8. THE PEOPLE WHO EDUCATE   569

Thomas J. Johnson, Rhoda Feigenbaum, Marcia Weiby

*Some determinants and consequences of the teacher's
perception of causation*   570

Sam D. Sieber, David E. Wilder

*Teaching styles: parental preferences and professional
role definitions*   584

Bruce J. Biddle, Howard A. Rosencranz, Edward Tomich,
J. Paschal Twyman

Shared inaccuracies in the role of the teacher   600

Wayne K. Hoy

The influence of experience on the beginning teacher   615

Edwin M. Bridges, Wayne J. Doyle, David J. Mahan

*Effects of hierarchical differentiation on group productivity,
efficiency, and risk-taking*   625

Gerald H. Moeller, W. W. Charters, Jr.
*Relation of bureaucratization to sense of power
among teachers* 638

Richard O. Carlson
Succession and performance among school superintendents 657

9. CHANGING THE SCHOOLS 671

Richard O. Carlson
The adoption of educational innovations 672

Neal Gross, Joseph B. Giacquinta, Marilyn Bernstein
Failure to implement a major organizational innovation 691

Richard A. Schmuck
Helping teachers improve classroom group processes 707

Index of Persons 737

Index of Subjects 743

INTRODUCTION

In 1963, the Society for the Psychological Study of Social Issues[1] sponsored the publication of *Readings in the Social Psychology of Education,* edited by W. W. Charters, Jr. and N. L. Gage. That volume was the first of its kind: an effort to bring together a wide range of empirical work by social psychologists involved in the study of educational settings. The editors wrote:

> Social psychology is the study of interaction among persons, and of the psychological and collective phenomena which cause and result from such interaction. The social psychology of education studies interaction and its social products in the context of educational settings and issues.
>
> Until a decade or two ago, educators were wont to lament what seemed to be a lack of concern on the part of social psychologists with educational issues and settings. Social psychologists seemed to turn up everywhere—in distant early-warning stations in the Arctic and submarines under the Atlantic, in executive training programs and jury rooms, in German concentration camps and the Kingdom of Father Divine—everywhere except in the schools. But this neglect seems well on its way to being remedied, as the selections gathered in this volume will, we hope, attest. Indeed, the editors and the sponsoring society hope that the present volume will further the application of social psychological theory and method to pressing educational issues.

These comments proved prophetic (or at least accurately prognostic). Research in the social psychology of education has developed vigorously in

1. The Society for the Psychological Study of Social Issues (a division of the American Psychological Association), consists of more than two thousand psychologists and allied scientists concerned with the psychological aspects of important societal problems. The Society's members share a conviction that such problems deserve the concentrated attention of social psychologists. Such problems, they believe, can profitably be subjected to the kind of rigorous scrutiny that is so often reserved for physical and biological phenomena and for noncontroversial human affairs.

The Society is governed by Kurt Lewin's dictum that "there is nothing so practical as a good theory." In various ways, the Society seeks to bring theory and practice together on human problems of the group, the community, and the nation, as well as the increasingly important ones that transcend national boundaries. The Society has sponsored volumes on civilian morale, industrial conflict, mass communications, the American college, peace, research methods, social psychology, the problems of developing nations, and the social psychology of education.

the past six years; even by 1966 it was clear that the Society should sponsor a revision of the first volume.

During these few years, energy devoted to the study and improvement of the American educational system has also increased radically. Research and development centers, conferences on educational innovation, dozens of new curricula, increasingly sophisticated hardware, regional educational laboratories, workshops to train "change agents" have all proliferated. The militancy of teachers, the powerful pressures of black parents for relevance, and the revolutionary interventions of students have made it clear that an enterprise involving about 35 per cent of all Americans on any given working day is, after all, important.

As we write, several other books dealing with the social psychology of education are also appearing. Backman and Secord's *A Social Psychological View of Education* (Harcourt Brace, 1968), Guskin and Guskin's *A Social Psychology of Education* (Addison-Wesley, 1969), and Johnson's *The Social Psychology of Education* (Holt, Rinehart and Winston, 1970) are thoughtful efforts to provide an integrative view of this domain. Any of them could be profitably used in conjunction with this volume for teaching purposes.

It may be useful to review the approach we have taken in preparing this book.

Scope. We took as our domain the social-psychological literature with *direct* bearing on educational systems and processes. Our delineation of the domain was like that in the earlier volume.

In 1963, the editors wrote:

> The book was not intended to be a general reader in social psychology for educators. It was to be a book in the social psychology of education. A moment's thought will make this basic distinction clear. The former orientation, social psychology for educators, would open the door to a much wider variety of matter—anything in social psychology that had explicit *or implicit* significance for education. Many topics relate implicitly to educational process; many of them have been the focus of social psychological research. Thus, family fertility patterns, processes of decision-making in state legislatures, and labor-management strife in the community all have a distinct bearing upon the operation of the schools. But we did not want to go so far afield. To have done so would have been easier, but it would have made our book less convincing and less useful.
>
> The latter orientation, the social psychology of education, requires that the selections have explicit and direct connections with education. Schools, teachers, pupils, school board members, school achievement, and so on had to be involved directly in the research, not by analogy or by extrapolation.
>
> In short, we tried to admit only contributions of a uniquely social psychological character, contributions which embodied an immediate and intimate conception of the interaction of persons with their social environments.
>
> Further, we chose to restrict the selections to those with specific and explicit relevance to the educational institution and to persons functioning within it.

In the 1969 volume, we have essentially maintained this definition of the scope of the "social psychology of education." We have given slightly more attention to educative environments on the edge of the formal educational system—parent-child interaction, adult learning in sensitivity training groups, treatment centers for delinquents, the mass media. Our choice of title, however, indicates that we feel a social psychology of education must concern itself fundamentally with the functioning of persons in settings meant to encourage learning.

Substantively, we guided our search for relevant studies via two lists. The first, made up of social-psychological topics, was slightly expanded from the list used in the 1963 volume:

SOCIAL PSYCHOLOGICAL TOPICS

1. Social aspects of perception, including interpersonal perception.
2. Social aspects of cognitive processes, including problem solving, intelligence, memory.
3. Social aspects of motivation (excluding attitudes).
4. Personality development, self, and self concept.
5. Language and stereotypes.
6. Mass communication and public opinion.
7. Modes of face-to-face communication.
8. Modes of interpersonal influence.
9. Attitude formation and change.
10. Multiple-group membership, reference group.
11. Role, role conflict, role set.
12. Ideology, value systems, national character.
13. Socialization—child and adult, professionalization.
14. Social stratification.
15. Division of labor, occupations, social psychology of work.
16. Small group structure.
17. Small group process.
18. Leadership.
19. Group conflict, segregation, discrimination, prejudice.
20. Formal organizations, bureaucracies.
21. Planned change and innovation processes.

The second list, of educational settings, was also revised and expanded from the earlier version:

EDUCATIONAL SETTINGS

A. Teacher-pupil relationship (including parent-child).
B. Classroom group.
C. Student society of the school, culture.
D. Informal social organization of adults in the school.
E. Formal organizational aspects of schools.
F. Community in relation to education and the school.

G. School in the urban setting.

H. Profession of education.

I. University and college settings as cultures, as organizations.

J. Adult learning settings outside of schools and colleges (includes training laboratories, industrial training and development, treatment settings with an "habilitative," educative emphasis).

Each article examined in the scanning/selection process described below was coded (often multiply) for topic and setting; entering items in a 21 x 10 grid allows us to see where clusters of gaps, existed, in a general way. These topics and settings do not, of course, define the scope of the volume, and we had less method in our madness than this description implies. However, the coding did serve well to guide our search (and our filing and retrieval of materials).

Inclusion criteria. Most of the criteria used in 1963 still seemed relevant. We quote:

1.   EMPIRICAL GROUNDING. Reports of investigations in which data were generated or collected, variables were measured and interrelated, factors were manipulated and their effects observed—or summary reviews and critical analyses of such investigations—were consistently given preference over programmatic statements, descriptive surveys, insightful commentaries, and the like. In so doing, the editors intended the volume to adhere to the orientation of the Society, which maintains that social psychology is an empirical social science and that social issues can best be resolved in the light of the findings of empirical research.

In 1969, this remains our first criterion. In view of the greater volume and quality of original research reports, we have been able to reduce our dependence on review articles in favor of specific studies.

2.   METHODOLOGICAL SOUNDNESS . . . one purpose of our volume is to encourage students to apply empirical methods to the investigation of educational issues, and above all, to place their faith in the power of accurate, objective knowledge. Hence, we wanted to display social psychology at its methodological best.
. . . In many cases, the choices were hard. Practicing researchers are the first to recognize that any study, no matter how impeccable its design, is open to criticism, reinterpretation, and refutation in the light of new knowledge or new perspectives. . . .
Nevertheless, we applied the standards of 1962 to the best of our knowledge and judgment. The criterion of methodological soundness was applied primarily to eliminate those investigations in which the errors were obvious, important, and not open to serious debate.
Accurate, objective knowledge may be achieved in many ways, of course, and one of our objectives in presenting our selections is to display a variety of methodologies and approaches.
. . . The ways to the understanding of social issues are manifold, and we have endeavored to slight as few of them as possible.

This criterion, too, still stands. Dubious methodology, by 1969 standards, made us omit many articles. We kept pieces in which the methods made us feel confident about the findings, *and* we searched for studies which were methodologically inventive: Feshbach and Devor's studies of four-year-olds teaching three-year-olds, Johnson, Feigenbaum and Weiby's laboratory study in which teachers "taught" non-existent learners, Barker and Gump's ecological analyses, DeFleur and DeFleur's cartoon test for assessing how TV affects children's role stereotypes.

Our third criterion, interestingly enough, did not appear explicitly in 1963.

3. URGENCY, RELEVANCE. Given the educational and social crises facing us today, we felt that priority should be given to articles that had special bearing on "where it's at." This led us to include pieces (if they had data and if the methods were solid) which dealt with schooling and child-rearing in the ghetto, teacher power, educational change processes, college revolts, prejudice reduction, and intensive methods of human relations training. Including such studies (though they may be wrongly formulated in the light of the next few years' history, and may become dated, like some early studies of school desegregation in the 1963 volume) seemed crucial to us. We could not avoid the central social issues of our time and still subtitle our book "New Readings in the Social Psychology of Education."

The next criterion also appeared in 1963:

4. THEORETICAL SIGNIFICANCE. Another criterion, which could not be enforced consistently, was that the research be couched in terms of constructs that went beyond the immediate operational definitions of the variables involved. In some studies, data were reported as if they were sufficient unto themselves, without regard to their connection with general social psychological concepts, such as role, norm, attitude, reference group, cognitive dissonance, or whatever. Such studies had to meet the other criteria to an exceptionally high degree before their excessive specificity to a single circumstance was overlooked.

It is our impression that such exceptions to the criterion were far fewer in 1969 than in 1963, which is an encouraging sign. Social psychologists and educators have echoed the Lewinian dictum on the practicality of good theory for so long now that they not only believe it but even act on it.

And again from 1963:

5. READABILITY. Not the least of the criteria was the readability of the research report. Profusion of jargon, turgidity of style, obscurity in the development of argument, excessive resort to technicalities of statistics and method—all served to repel us from selections that might otherwise have met the requirements.

. . . Too often, it seems, social psychological reports fail to give any impression that one is reading about human beings. Readability, however, is a two-sided affair. The reader must be willing and able to meet

the author half way. Recognizing our fallibility in estimating the level
of understanding of potential readers, we nevertheless have tried to
minimize the difficulties in communication and, particularly, those imposed by poor writing.

We found in 1969 that we developed an associated informal criterion
called "bounce." Articles which had liveliness, interest, or non-typical
approach more often than not caught our eye.

There were two additional criteria used for this volume, altered somewhat from the first edition's.

6. REPRESENTATIVENESS AND RANGE. We tried to be sure that many
different lines of significant effort in the social psychology of education
were included, from operant conditioning to cognitive theory, and from
action research to environmental measurement. We should not like to
pretend that the final set of selections is exhaustive, or that there are not
important lacunae. We did feel, however, that the reader deserved a
broad-scale look at how educational phenomena can be studied social-
psychologically.

7. STATUS AS A CLASSIC. Some studies, either in the first volume or
conducted since its publication had, we felt, the kind of basal simplicity and fruitfulness which ordinarily starts a whole new line of
work. One man's classics are another man's chestnuts, but we did want
to include such selections as Coleman's article on peer cultures, McClelland's analysis of the acquisition of motives, Pace and Stern's campus
culture work, Barker and Gump's ecological views on the effects of
school size, and several other studies which had a similarly charismatic
quality. Without exception, however, the "classics" had to meet the
prime inclusion criteria outlined above.

The selection process. An early task was a thorough review of the articles
in the first edition. In this we were aided by the comments and criticisms
of many unnamed users of the book, a few of whom had taken the pains
to evaluate the contents systematically with their students, and more
directly by the suggestions of several social psychologists with an active
interest in the study of educational issues. Fred Kerlinger, Richard Bloom,
Wilbur Brookover, Paul Secord, Carl Backman, and Paul Torrance all read
the original volume and made suggestions for items to be retained, dropped,
or added.

We concentrated our search efforts on the literature produced since 1961,
the approximate cut-off date of the search made for the first edition. We
scanned through a total of thirty-five psychological, sociological, educational, and associated journals; read innumerable papers from professional
meetings; retrieved vigorously from ERIC (Educational Resources Information Center) clearing houses; and looked at many books. The general
pool of articles seen as possible candidates for inclusion totaled about 450.
The initial scanning process was carried out primarily by Lois Steinberg,
with the aid of Mary Chase and Thomas M. Stephens, along with other

members of a reading seminar on the social psychology of education at Teachers College.

The pool of items was winnowed down by Miles and Steinberg to 90; these, plus thirty-eight articles in the original book, and about 50 additional items which emerged during the selection process were reduced, via the editors' face-to-face discussion and generally incessant correspondence, to the final total of forty-two articles.

It is of considerable note to us that the new book is just that. Only four of the thirty-eight articles in the 1963 book survived our attentions; much interesting and useful work has been done in these past seven years.

Responsibilities. N. L. Gage began the process of defining the new book and selecting items with us; his keen sense of the problems of methodological and theoretical clarity in any particular study was invaluable. As the project proceeded, however, he felt that his other commitments precluded his doing enough work on the book to permit him to leave his name on the title page. He remains in our eyes, nonetheless, an honored co-editor.

The order in which the remaining two co-editors are listed reflects the division of work between us. While interaction was close and constant, Miles was the prime mover of the enterprise and shouldered the main burden of the administrative and editorial tasks. Final decisions on the selections and all other major issues were jointly made.

Our thanks go to Tamara Safford and Judy Martinez for the essential functions of obtaining permissions, running down references, keeping hundreds of Xeroxes in quick-access storage, and coping with myriad other details. Betty Miles was responsible for the bulk of the copy editing, that ordinarily thankless job which requires both intelligence and care.

We should like to acknowledge the support of the Department of Psychology at Teachers College, which provided Miles with released time from other duties during 1967-1968. The Educational Policy Research Center at Stanford Research Institute was generous with office space, Xeroxing, and secretarial support during 1968-69.

The final review of the manuscript, a step taken for all SPSSI-sponsored volumes, was carried out by Paul Secord; we should like to express our gratitude for his help.

Uses of the book. In the 1963 volume, the editors wrote:

> Under terms of the [SPSSI] Council directive, *Readings in the Social Psychology of Education* is intended to encourage as well as to service the growing interest among educators in social psychological theory and research. It is designed primarily as a set of supplementary readings for undergraduate and graduate students in a variety of education courses, including those on the social foundations of education, educational psychology, measurement and evaluation, supervision, curriculum, school administration, guidance, public relations, and, of course, the social psychology of education. This intent—namely, to offer something for a wide variety of education courses—reflects our conviction and that of the sponsoring society that social psychological phenomena pervade educational problems.

These uses still seem appropriate. However, a new one has emerged in the intervening years. A growing number of social psychologists do not think of themselves as "educators," but are fascinated by the special problems of educational environments. For such researchers and their graduate students, this volume can serve as a useful reference, stimulator, and source book.

We also believe the book can be helpful in the improvement of educational practice. In the Foreword to the 1963 volume, Goodwin Watson wrote:

> A persistent problem for any civilization which tries to make extensive use of scientific research is the gap between the scientist and the practitioner. . . .
>
> The root of the difficulty is that, while the scientist is seeking answers to questions about what is true, the practitioner is trying to cope with a life-situation. Scientific research tests hypotheses; management operates to get things done. When the research report is presented, the operator says, "Very interesting, but so what? How does this help me?" When the practical man asks for help on his complicated problems, the scientific adviser screens out all but the one facet on which he has some data or which fits into his theory. He assumes that if more and more research were done on more and more of these theoretical facets of the complex practical issue, wisdom would emerge. The harried operator doubts that this piecemeal attack on specific questions will ever produce an integrated procedure. In any case he knows he can't wait for generations of research; he must act next week.

Watson then proceeded to discuss the role of the "middlemen"—the engineers.

> . . . who take the confirmed hypotheses and established relationships from the pure scientist and develop the handbooks of formulas, tables, and techniques needed for putting scientific knowledge to practical use. We have learned not to ask the theoretical physicist, the mathematician, or the metallurgist how to build our bridges. Yet, without the basic research, the applied engineering tasks could never be done.

In 1963, few "educational engineers" existed, and Watson had to content himself with some thoughtful commentary on how educational practitioners could fruitfully use the book—both as a set of findings to be translated into action terms, and as a set of methods for carrying out similar inquiries at the local school system level.

Today, however, the educational scene is much better supplied with "engineers." Extensive development efforts are under way in the Research and Development Centers, the Regional Educational Laboratories, the dozens of industrial and business firms involved in the educational market, the major curriculum reform groups, and a wide variety of non-profit enterprises such as the Educational Research Council of America, Educational Services, Inc., and Educational Facilities Laboratories. More and more we have come to understand that educational problems must be solved by retrieving available information (e.g., from social psychology), by designing alternative solutions, trying them out, and revising them until a workable piece of "educational technology" (as repellent as that phrase once seemed) has been produced.

This book can serve educational "developers" as a source of valid principles from which specific educational products and procedures can be derived; it also contains a range of newly-available technologies, from T-group training to games and in-service education models. Developers also need imaginative, straightforward research methods to test the quality of their products; they can find a wide range of such methods in these pages.

Organization of the volume. In 1963, the editors wrote:

> No single, internally consistent, articulated theoretical system underlies the organization of this volume. This is a fact for which the editors do not apologize. Social issues are singularly resistant to attempts to shape them according to the conceptual schemes of social psychologists. Rather, they cut across such arrangements with utter abandon. The editors believe that the concrete problems of education must be viewed from diverse perspectives if they are to be resolved. In any event, this volume brings together a set of empirical studies, chosen according to the criteria outlined above, irrespective of their conceptual unity.

One consequence of this viewpoint, which we still hold, is that the studies are grouped into sections primarily for convenience—perhaps even to carry out something like an educational ritual. Many alternative approaches to sectioning could have been taken.

In any case, our experience has been that when a book of readings is used in a college or university class—or in an educational development organization—it is not used section by section, but article by article. The book's users most often need to go straight to specific studies.

Accordingly, we have developed what we came to call "micro-introductions" for each article. In them we take the reader by the elbow for a brief moment, trying to say whatever we think is important about the particular piece at hand—its place in the context of similar research, its theoretical slant, its methodologically interesting features, its weaknesses, its uniqueness, or its relation to other studies, in or out of the present book.

This is perhaps enough prologue, except for some editorializing about the state of social psychology and education. Making this collection did impress us considerably in several respects:

1. The social psychologist is no longer an alien in educational environments. The range and extent of thoughtful studies is substantial.
2. Social-psychological notions remain, in our view, especially productive in understanding the processes and outcomes of individuals' transactions with their educational environments. With Backman and Secord (1968, p. 32) we hold that:

The contemporary view of the relation of abilities and personality traits to educational achievement . . . elevates social psychological processes to a position of major importance. Our view is that the educational performance of an individual at any stage is a function not only of his previous experiences with objects and ideas in his environment but also of his previous interactions with persons. Futher, contemporary social processes prevailing during the assessment of his academic performance acquire significance. Traditional educational psychology has in the past given little attention to these matters.

3. Research in the social psychology of education is being produced by youthful scholars. For example, the principal author of one of our selections, David Winter, was a college undergraduate at the time the study was made. While we have not constructed an age distribution of the volume's contributors, we are impressed by what appears to be a sparsity of authors in their forties and fifties and beyond, and by the comparatively small representation of the Grand Old Men of social psychology. Students who use this book should be heartened by the fact that they need cross no generation gap before they, too, can contribute significantly to social-psychological understanding of educational issues.

4. That understanding has grown, but it is still limited. We need to know radically more, and in more depth, about almost every conceivable educational problem. What are the central factors blocking the learning of ghetto children? How can they be overcome? Can we develop a coherent model of educational change processes? What processes underlie "affective learning"? Do mass media transform belief systems? If so, how? Can two million teachers learn to change their teaching styles (assuming that seems indicated)? What is a good model of community power struggle centered around the schools? If students had substantially more influence in schools, what would happen? This book was satisfying to produce, because it suggests we are closer to some useful answers to questions of this sort than we were even six years ago.

M. B. M.

W. W. C.

1. EDUCATIONAL ENVIRONMENTS

It is almost platitudinous to say, along with social psychologists, that the external environment is an important determinant of a person's behavior. As obvious as the statement seems, it nevertheless harbors some severe theoretical and definitional problems. What exactly do we mean by a person's "environment"? Can it be defined and measured independently of the behavior it is supposed to determine? If not, we are in trouble, for our statement then runs the risk of being tautological.

Roger Barker and his colleagues at the University of Kansas have grappled with both the theoretical problems and the task of systematically describing the environmental contexts in which behavior occurs. A key concept in their descriptive system is *behavior setting*. The technical procedures they have developed for identifying the relevant behavior settings for groups of people are elaborate and relatively expensive at present, but the study of human environments is still in its infancy.

The present selection was taken from the report of a series of studies in which Barker and his associates applied their tools to an important educational issue: how large should a high school be? Choosing schools markedly different in size, their first task was to describe the schools in terms of the effective environments — the behavior settings — literally available to students. Thus, they converted the gross variable of school size into psychologically meaningful characterizations. In the process, they showed that larger high schools provided students with greater *numbers* of behavior settings, as one would expect, but not with commensurately greater *varieties* of settings. Next they turned to an examination of student participation in the settings offered by the high schools, and here the study findings were both surprising and instructive, as the reader will see.

The Ecological Environment:
Student Participation
In Non-Class Settings*

Roger G. Barker, Paul V. Gump,
Wallace V. Friesen, Edwin P. Willems

The Ecological Environment

The idea is expressed in many forms that the child, the school, and the community are parts of a complex, interdependent system, and hence that problems of education do not begin and end at the school door. And the view is widespread that, insofar as the school is concerned, it is the whole school that enters into the educational process, not only the individual pupil and his teachers. However, these undoubted truths have been without adequate conceptualization or empirical support, and so have had little effect upon the theory and practice of education. The intention of the studies reported here is to investigate these problems within a broad ecological context.

The Inside-Outside Problem

One of the obvious characteristics of human behavior is its variation. Every day a person's life is marked by wide fluctuations in almost every discriminable attribute of his behavior: in the intelligence he exhibits, in the speed with which he moves, in the emotion he expresses, in the loudness with which he speaks, in the goals he pursues, in his friendliness, his humor, his energy, his anxiety. Even geniuses think ordinary thoughts much of the time; they, too, have to count their change and choose their neckties. Continuous records of the behavior of children show that the ever changing aspects of the child's stream of behavior is one of its most striking features: trouble and well-being, quietude and activity, success and failure, dominance and submission, correct answers and wrong answers, interests and boredom occur in bewildering complexity (Barker, 1963; Wright, 1967). Laymen know of this dimension of human variation from their own experiences and observations; novelists, dramatists, and biographers have described it. But it is not prominent in scientific psychology.

* Adapted from R. G. Barker and P. V. Gump, *Big School, Small School*. Stanford: Stanford University Press, 1964. Chapters 1, 2, 6, 8, and 12. Used by permission of the authors and publisher.

Scientific psychology has been more concerned with another dimension of behavior variability, namely, differences *between* individuals. It is one of the great achievements of psychology that in spite of the variation of every individual's behavior, methods have been devised for identifying and measuring individual behavior constants. An important part of scientific psychology is concerned with the great number of behavior constants that have been measured and with the relations between them.

It is unfortunate that these accomplishments have not been accompanied by equal progress in studying naturally occurring, individual behavior variation.

The general sources of intra-individual behavior variation are clear. A person's behavior is connected in complicated ways with both his inside parts (his neurons, his muscles, his hormones, for example) and his outside context (the school class where he is a pupil, the game in which he is a player, the street on which he is a pedestrian). The *psychological person* who writes essays, scores points, and crosses streets stands as an identifiable entity between unstable interior parts and exterior contexts, with both of which he is linked, yet from both of which he is profoundly separated. The separation comes from the fact that the inside parts and the outside contexts of a person involve phenomena that function according to laws that are different from those that govern his behavior. Brain lesions, muscle contraction, and hormone concentration are not psychological phenomena. In the present state of our understanding, they involve laws that are utterly incommensurate with those of psychology. The same is true of the environment with which a person is coupled. The school class where he is a pupil the game in which he plays, and the street where he walks all function according to laws that are alien to those that govern his own behavior. This is the inside-outside problem which Allport his discussed (Allport, 1955).

The outside context which constitutes the *ecological environment* is the focus of this research. The ecological environment consists of those naturally occurring phenomena (1) outside a person's skin, (2) with which his molar actions are coupled, but (3) which function according to laws that are incommensurate with the laws that govern his molar behavior (Barker, 1960). The ecological environment differs from the psychological environment (or life space) and from the stimulus, as the following discussion will make clear.

The fact that behavior varies under the influence of the alien, incommensurate outside contexts of the psychological person places psychology in a serious dilemma. How is a unified science to encompass such diverse phenomena? Neither physics, nor astronomy, nor botany has to cope with psychological inputs to the systems with which they deal. How can psychology hope to cope with nonpsychological inputs? This is our problem, and it is the reason why "the whole school" (an outside, nonpsychological phenomenon) is, as yet, little more than a slogan.

The Tautological Problem

In order to study environmental-behavior relations on any level, the environment and the behavior must be described and measured independently; otherwise one becomes entangled in a tautological circle from which there is no escape. Thus, for example, three children who were each observed an entire day were found to interact with 571, 671, and 749 different objects; the total numbers of interactions with these objects were 1,882, 2,282, and 2,490, and each of these interactions had a number of attributes (Schoggen, 1951; Barker and Wright, 1955). But these objects did not constitute the ecological environments of the children, for the behavior of the children provided the sole criterion for identifying and describing the objects.

This confronts us with the essence of the ecological environment in its relation to people. One can easily conceive of the problems of students of light perception if they had no physical description of light, or only a physical description of light at the precise point of contact with the receptor. To understand this point of intersection, it is essential to know the *structure* of light, for the point of intersection takes part of its characteristics from the total wave, quanta, or matrix of which it is a part, and this cannot be known from the points of *contact*, i.e., the stimulus, alone.

This is a general problem in science. When we are concerned with the outside context of any entity, whether a behaving person, a supporting beam, or a word in a sentence, this context cannot be described in terms of the points of contact with the entity alone. The properties of the points depend upon the structure of which they are parts. Take the word "brought" in the succeedingly more inclusive contexts in which it occurs (from R. L. Stevenson, *The Pavilion on the Links*):

brought
were brought under
provisions were brought under cover
fresh provisions were brought under cover of darkness

The immediate points of contact between the word "brought" and its context are clearly insufficient to define this context; the properties of the contact points "were" and "under" depend upon the total sentence; in fact, "were" and "under" are not the context of the word "brought"; the whole sentence is the context. The contexts of all words in Stevenson's writings, and in all meaningful writings, occur in organized units that are larger than the preceding and succeeding connecting words.

Figure 1 illustrates another example. The supporting beam (a, b) and its momentary context are shown in the succeeding diagrams. The instantaneous behavior of the beam can be completely described in terms of the internal and external structural arrangements and forces existing for

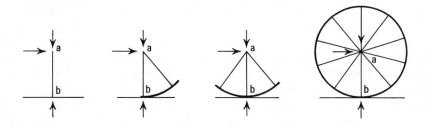

Figure 1.   The Context of a Supporting Beam; an Example.

it at a particular instant without regard for what is outside of points *a* and *b*. However, if more than an infinitely small time interval is involved, more is required: it is essential to know the structural and dynamic contexts of the intersection points *a* and *b*. The properties of contact point *b*, in this case, can be defined in terms of its position on the rim of a wheel of a certain diameter and motion, and the properties of point *a* by its position as the center of the wheel. Knowing, for example, that *b* is on the rim of a wheel moving forward at 50 miles an hour tells us immediately that there will be a cyclical change in the forward movement of *b* between zero and 100 miles an hour, with corresponding changes in the strength and direction of the forces and in the behavior of the beam.

This is true of the ecological environment of persons, too. A person's momentary behavior is completely determined by his life space, but if we wish to understand more than the immediate cross-section of the ongoing behavior stream, knowledge of the ecological environment is essential. For example, giving and receiving love between mother and child is an important variable in some theories of psychological development. From the developmental viewpoint, such an exchange takes part of its significance from the total context of the mother's and the child's life. It is important to know the larger ecological situation within which this type of contact occurs, because this is often, technically, the only way to understand what actually happens at the momentary intersection between the person and the ecological environment. But, more important, knowledge of the ecological context is essential, because development is not a momentary phenomenon (in fact most behavior in which we are interested is not momentary), and the *course* of the life space can only be known within the ecological environment in which it is embedded.

The Problem of Structure

The most primitive and simple thing we know about the ecological environment is that it has structure; it has parts with stable relations between them. One task is to describe this structure.

It is clear that structure cannot be discovered by observing a single part, such as the point of intersection of the environment with a particular person, or by considering the parts separately, one by one. For example, a complete description of a player's behavior in a ball game, or the complete statistics of all the plays occurring in the game, do not reveal the game of baseball. It is the rules of the game, and the arrangements of things and people according to the rules, that constitute the essential, unitary ecological environment of the players; it is these that shape the life space of each player. By dealing with such contexts in terms of their discriminable parts, and processing them by probability statistics, we destroy what we are searching to discover. This approach has the value of a filing system, or of a concordance; but we cannot understand a book from its concordance. By these methods, the structure of the context is dismantled and rearranged; the structure is destroyed.

This does not mean, of course, that such investigations are without value. Important information about one level of a functioning system can be obtained when the system is dismantled. All sciences have structure-destroying methods and make valuable use of them. Essential components of the brain can be determined by excising and mascerating brain tissue and analyzing it by physical and chemical techniques, even though this ignores or destroys the brain's macro-structure.

But most sciences have, also, special nondestructive techniques for studying the structure of their phenomena. X-ray analysis, and electrical, magnetic, and resonance techniques are instances. A primary concern of geologists, oceanographers, cytologists, mineralogists, geneticists, and astronomers is precisely with the naturally occurring, unrearranged structure of things: from chromosomes to the solar system and beyond. So it is important for psychology to discover tender-minded nondestructive techniques for preserving intact naturally occurring behavior and its ecological environment.

Ecological Units

An initial practical problem of ecological research is to identify the natural units of the phenomenon studied. The essential nature of the units with which ecology deals is the same, whether they are physical, social, biological, or behavioral units (a) they occur without feedback from the investigator; they are self-generated; (b) each unit has a time-space locus; (c) an unbroken boundary separates an internal pattern from a differing external pattern. By these criteria, an electron, a person, and a waterfall are ecological units. This is true also of most towns and cities; and within a city, it is true of a particular school, of the geometry lesson within the school, and of student Joe Doakes raising his hand to ask to recite. On the other hand, a square mile in the center of a city is not an ecological unit, since it is not self-generated; neither are the Republican voters of the city or the school system, since they have no continuously bounded time-space loci.

Our work is in behavioral ecology, and we are concerned with molar behavior and the ecological contexts in which it occurs. The problem can be illustrated by an example (from Barker *et al.*, 1961):

> Anne Matson was 10 years and 11 months of age and in the sixth grade of the Midwest public school. It was 2:09 P.M. and time for the daily music lesson with Miss Madison. The first five minutes of the record, made at the time (March 8, 1951), reported Anne's behavior as follows:
>
>> Mrs. Nelson said in a business-like manner, "All right, the class will pass."
>> Anne picked up her music book from her desk.
>> She stood.
>> She motioned urgently to her row, indicating that they should follow her around the front of the room.
>> The class filed out, carrying their music books.
>> Anne walked quickly to the music room; she was near the end of the single-file line.
>
> 2:10 The children seated themselves in a semicircle across the front of the music room.
>> Anne sat with Opal Bennet directly on her right and Rex Graw on her left. Alvin Stone was one seat over from Rex.
>> Miss Madison, the music teacher, said briskly, "All right, let's open our books to page 27."
>> Anne watched Miss Madison solemnly.
>> Anne licked her finger.
>> She turned to the correct page.
>> Miss Madison asked the class, "How would you conduct this song?"
>> Immediately Anne raised her hand, eager to be called on.
>
> 2:11 Miss Madison called on Ellen Thomas to show how she would conduct this song.
>> Ellen waved her right arm in three-quarter rhythm.
>> Miss Madison watched Ellen critically.
>> With her hand still part way in the air, Anne watched earnestly.
>> Someone in the class objected that Ellen's beat wasn't quite right.
>> Persistently, Anne put her hand up higher, wishing to be called on.
>> Miss Madison called on Stella Townsend.
>> Anne put her hand down, disappointment showing in her facial expression.
>> Intently she watched Stella demonstrate the pattern for conducting the song.
>> Miss Madison called on Opal Bennet.
>> Anne didn't raise her hand.
>>> (There was really no opportunity for hand-raising.)
>> She turned toward her right.
>> With interest she watched Opal demonstrate the way to lead the song.

Miss Madison demonstrated how three-quarter time should be led.

Anne watched with an interested expression.

2:12   She started to practice, moving her arms in the demonstrated pattern.

Some of the other children also started practicing.

Miss Madison said pedagogically, "All right, let's all do it together."

She stood sideways in a business-like way so that the children could see her hands.

She led the children as they all practiced conducting three-quarter time.

Anne let her fingers hang loosely in a consciously graceful manner.

With restraint and enjoyment she moved her arm up, down, and across in the correct pattern.

2:13   Miss Madison said, "Now we want one person to get up in front of the class and conduct."

Anne immediately raised her hand very eagerly straight up into the air.

On her face was a look of expectancy.

She held her hand in the air until Miss Madison called on Ellen Thomas.

Anne exchanged looks with Opal Bennet, apparently communicating about something of private significance.

She held her book up several inches off her lap expectantly.

She was sitting quite straight.

Miss Madison started the music on the piano.

Ellen started to conduct.

Anne sang the first few notes of the song.

Miss Madison stopped playing.

She showed Ellen how to begin the first beat.

As Miss Madison made the correction, Anne smiled sympathetically at Ellen.

Ellen smiled back.

Miss Madison resumed playing and Ellen conducted.

Anne sang.

2:14   Anne glanced alternately at her book and at Ellen, who was conducting.

She sang heartily and seemed to enjoy it a great deal.

This is an example of the dependent variable with which we are concerned, namely, a child's behavior. What are the *ecological contexts* of such behavior?

There are an infinite number of discriminable phenomena external to any individual's behavior. In the case of Anne Matson during the music class there were, for example, her neighbors Opal and Rex, the music book, the song on page 27, the piano, the fifth- and sixth-grade classroom across the hall, the cool overcast day, the town of Midwest, the country of U.S.A.; there were Anne's hand, the windows of the room, Andrea French sitting five seats away, Ellen's smile, and so on without limit. With which of these innumerable exterior phenomena was Anne's behavior linked? And were these phenomena related only via their links with Anne, or did they have a stable independent structure; were they an ecological assembly of units independent of Anne and her behavior?

It would appear that students of molar behavior might profitably emulate students of perception and look at the ecological environment of the behavior with which they are concerned, entirely aside from its connection with behavior. It is, in fact, one of the primary intentions of the present research to advance the science—for which we as yet have no name—that stands with respect to molar behavior as the physics of light and sound stands with respect to vision and hearing. For students of education this means that schools must be studied as carefully as the behavior of the individual children within them.

An analogy may help to make the problem clear.

If a novice, an Englishman for example, wished to understand the environment of a first baseman in a ball game, he might set about to observe the interactions of the player with his surroundings. To do this with utmost precision he might view the first baseman through field glasses, so focused that the player would be centered in the field of the glasses, with just enough of the environment included to encompass all his contacts with the environment, all inputs and outputs: all balls caught, balls thrown, players tagged, etc. Despite the commendable observational care, however, this method would never provide a novice with an understanding of "the game" which gives meaning to a first baseman's transactions with his surroundings, and which in fact, constitutes the environment of his baseball-playing behavior. By observing a player in this way, the novice would, in fact, fragment the game and destroy what he was seeking. So, he might by observations and interviews construct the player's life space during the game: his achievements, aspirations, successes, failures, and conflicts; his judgments of the speed of the ball, of the fairness of the umpire, of the errors of his teammates. But this would only substitute for the former fragmented picture of "the game" the psychological consequences of the fragment, and thus remove the novice even further from the ecological environment he sought. Finally, the novice might perform innumerable correlations between the first baseman's achievements (balls caught, players tagged, strikes and hits made, bases stolen, errors, etc.) and particular attributes of the ecological environment involved (speed of balls thrown to him, distance of throw, weight of bat, curve of balls, etc.). But he could never arrive at the phenomena known as a baseball game by this means.

It would seem clear that a novice would learn more about the ecological environment of a first baseman by blotting out the player and observing the game around him. This is what the student of light and sound does with elaborate instrumentation, and it is the approach we have taken in the present studies.

It is not easy, at first, to leave the person out of observations of the environment of molar behavior. Our perceptual apparatus is adjusted by our long training with the idiocentric viewing glasses of individual observa-

tions, interviews, and questionnaires to see *persons* whenever we see behavior. But with some effort and experience the extra-individual assemblies
of behavior episodes, behavior objects, and space that surround persons can
be observed and described. Their nonrandom distribution and bounded
character are a crucial aid. If the reader will recall a school class period,
some of the characteristics of an environmental unit will be clearly
apparent:

1. It is a natural phenomenon; it is not created by an experimenter for
    scientific purposes.

2. It has a space-time locus.

3. A boundary surrounds a school class.

4. The boundary is self-generated; it changes as the class changes in
    size and in the nature of its activity.

5. The class is objective in the sense that it exists independent of any-
    one's perception of it, *qua* class; it is a preperceptual ecological
    entity.

6. It has two sets of components: (*a*) behavior (reciting, discussing,
    sitting) and (*b*) nonpsychological objects with which behavior
    is transacted, e.g., chairs, walls, a blackboard, and paper.

7. The unit, the class meeting, is circumjacent to its components; the
    pupils and equipment are *in* the class.

8. The behavior and physical objects that constitute the unit school
    class are internally organized and arranged to form a pattern that
    is by no means random.

9. The pattern within the boundary of a class is easily discriminated
    from that outside the boundary.

10. There is a synomorphic relation between the pattern of the be-
    havior occurring within the class and the pattern of its nonbehav-
    ioral components, the behavior objects. The seats face the teacher's
    desk, and the children face the teacher, for example.

11. The unity of the class is not due to the similarity of its parts at any
    moment; for example, speaking occurs in one part and listening in
    another. The unity is based, rather, upon the interdependence of
    the parts; events in different parts of a class period have a greater
    effect upon each other than equivalent events beyond its boundary.

12. The people who inhabit a class are to a considerable degree inter-
    changeable and replaceable. Pupils come and go; even the teacher
    may be replaced. But the same entity continues as serenely as an
    old car with new rings and the right front wheel now carried as
    the spare.

13. The behavior of this entity cannot, however, be greatly changed
    without destroying it: there must be teaching, there must be study,
    there must be recitation.

14. A pupil has two positions in a class; first, he is a component of the
    supra-individual unit, and second, he is an individual whose life
    space is partly formed within the constraints imposed by the very
    entity of which he is a part.

This entity stands out with great clarity; it is a common phenomenon of everyday life. We have called it a K-21 *behavior setting*.[1] We have made extensive studies of K-21 behavior settings and found much evidence that they are stable extra-individual units with great explanatory power with respect to the behavior occurring within them (Barker and Wright, 1955; Barker, 1968).

According to the theory of behavior settings, a person who inhabits and contributes behavior to one of them is a component part, a fixture of a behavior setting. As such, he is anonymous and replaceable, and his behavior is subject to the nonpsychological laws of the superordinate unit. At the same time, however, every inhabitant of a behavior setting is a unique person subject to the laws of individual psychology, where his own private motives, capacities, and perceptions are the causal variables. This is the classical inside-outside paradox, involving in this case persons who are governed by incommensurate laws on different levels of inclusiveness.

One of the sticking points of social and educational psychology is how to account for the consensus, the norms, and the uniformities associated with school classes, business offices, and church services, for example, and at the same time account for the individuality of the members. This problem cannot be resolved by either individual or group psychology. It requires a different conceptual treatment, the unnamed science mentioned earlier. Below, we shall sketch the theory that has guided this research, and which appears to account for one small facet of this inside-outside paradox.

Theory of Behavior Settings

In order to make the discussion more concrete, sample behavior settings from the high schools in which most of the research was done are listed. These are presented in groups of similar settings from different schools.

Biology and Health Classes, Mr. Campbell (Malden)
Chemistry, Biology, Physics Classes, Mr. Johnson (Midwest)
Physics, Biology, General Science Classes, Miss Smith (Vernon)
Physiology Class, Miss Williams (Walker)
Chemistry Classes, Mr. Jones (Capital City)

Vocal Music Classes, Miss Harris (Malden)
Vocal Music Groups, Miss North (Midwest)
Vocal Music Groups, Miss West (Vernon)

1. The reader will find that the behavior settings which are identified and described in the schools and towns we have studied usually appear to be reasonable, common-sense parts. It must be emphasized, however, that the identification and enumeration of K-21 behavior settings is a highly technical task. It is essential that the operations for identifying K-21 behavior settings, which are presented in detail in Barker (1968, pp. 34-91), be followed by investigators making use of them. The essential technical problem is to identify a single part as *one* or as *more than one* K-21 behavior setting; e.g., is the school office a single K-21 behavior setting or is it two K-21 behavior settings: the school principal's office and the secretary's office? K-values are ratings of *interdependence* of parts; those with values above 21 are defined as separate K-21 behavior settings.

Vocal Music Group, Mr. Field (Walker)
Girls' Chorus Classes, Mr. McGregor (Capital City)

Basketball, Boys' A and B Teams and Girls' Team at Home (Malden)
Basketball, Boys' A and B Teams and Girls' Team at Home (Midwest)
Basketball, Boys' A and B Teams at Home (Vernon)
Basketball, Boys' A and B Teams and Girls' Team at Home (Walker)
Basketball, A Team at Home (Capital City)

After-Game Dance at Legion Hall (Malden)
Dance following Football Game (Midwest)
Sock Hop (Vernon)
Student Council Dance after Game (Walker)
Varsity Dance after Game (Capital City)

High School Principal, Office (Malden)
Grade and High School Principal, Office (Midwest)
High School Principal and School Superintendent, Office (Vernon)
High School Principal, Office (Walker)
High School General Office (Capital City)

Home Economics Class to the City (Malden)
Drama Club to "My Fair Lady" (Midwest)
Constitution Class Tours State Capitol (Vernon)
Band Attends U.S. Navy Band Concert (Walker)
Science Students to Math, Science Day at University (Capital City)

Behavior settings such as these are organized assemblies of behavior episodes, physical objects, spaces, and durations. Few things can be clearer in terms of direct experience than their coercive power over individuals; no one dances in Mr. Johnson's chemistry class and no one carries out chemistry experiments at the Sock Hop. Despite this, behavior settings have largely escaped the attention of behavioral scientists. We have to look to novelists, dramatists, and pictorial artists for descriptions of them. It is interesting to note, however, that there is evidence of a concern by town planners, highway engineers, human factors scientists, industrial designers, and architects, for example, for a science of behavior settings.

Despite the primitive state of knowledge regarding behavior settings, studies have provided a first step toward an understanding of them (Barker and Wright, 1955; Barker, 1960; Barker and Barker, 1961; Barker, 1968). According to the theory developed, a setting is a homeostatic system with controls that maintain the setting intact and operating at a stable functional level under widely varying conditions. These forces have multiple, independent origins, and this is one reason for the stability of settings. Some of the controls reside within the setting itself; in a school class, there are the time schedule, the "rules," the arrangement of the room. Some controls involve input and feedback circuits which couple the setting with exterior conditions; the whole school has its independent schedule and regulations and ways of requiring conformity by the individual class. Other controls involve feedback loops linking the setting with its inhabitants and other of its interior components; the maturity of the pupils and the textbook are examples of interior controls.

There is for every homeostatic level of a behavior setting an optimal number of elements in its internal, medium manifold. The Baseball Game calls for the behavior of 20 participants, 18 players, and two officials; in Midwest, the setting First Grade Academic Activities is believed to do best with the behavior of 23 inhabitants—22 pupils and one teacher. However— and this is crucial—the homeostatic mechanisms of a setting operate to maintain the setting intact and its functional level essentially unchanged when there is a decrease in the number of its interior units below the optimal level; the same pattern and strength of forces is distributed among fewer persons. There are, in Allport's terms, fewer junction points, or encounters, but the same number of forces and events (1955). Each point is therefore the focus of more forces and the locus of more events. Accordingly, the fewer available persons are pressed more strongly to produce the same number and variety of behavior units, and fewer behavior units are pressed to produce the same number and variety of achievements.

A setting is a place where most of the inhabitants can satisfy a number of personal motives, where they can achieve multiple satisfactions; a setting contains opportunities. Furthermore, different people achieve a different cluster of satisfactions in the same setting. The unity of a behavior setting does not arise from similarity in the motives of the occupants. In the setting Baseball Game, for example, the pitcher will experience a complex system of social-physical satisfactions, depending upon what kind of person he is; his mother in the bleachers will at the same time have quite a different set of satisfactions; and the coach will have still others. But unless these and other inhabitants of the setting Baseball Game are at least minimally satisfied, they will leave the game, or will not return on another occasion, and the setting will cease. In other words, a setting exists only when it provides its occupants with the particular psychological conditions their own unique natures require. Heterogeneity in the personal motives of the individual inhabitants of a setting contributes to the stability of the setting.

Settings impose obligations upon their occupants too. These arise via the intrinsic structure of the setting and the inhabitants' perception thereof. If the inhabitants of a setting are to continue to attain the goals that bring them satisfactions, the setting must continue to function at a level that each occupant defines for himself. Every occupant of a setting, therefore, encounters two routes: One is the immediate, direct route to his goals; and the other route, the maintenance route, is toward maintaining the setting in such condition that the goals, and the routes to them, will remain intact. One common maintenance route is toward getting others to act along maintenance channels too. These interlacings strengthen greatly the total coercive power of a setting and homogenize, so to speak, the source of its forces.

It is the resultant of such adjustment circuits that keeps a setting on a quasi-stationary level, or moving toward a more satisfying level for the inhabitants. Sometimes, of course, the forces along the maintenance routes are too weak, and the setting deteriorates.

Some Dynamics of Individual Behavior

Let us return to the consequences of a reduction of the number of interior elements of a behavior setting below that required by the homeostatic mechanism of the setting. We shall apply the theory to the case of two high schools similar in all respects except number of students and staff. Here is the argument:

1. People (students and staff) provide the component media of behavior settings of a school.
2. The behavior settings are homeostatic systems with optimal media requirements at each homeostatic level.
3. The homeostatic mechanisms maintain the functional level of the setting when the inhabitants fall below the optimum number, within a limited range.
4. The behavior settings of small and large high schools are equivalent in all respects, except that
5. the settings of small high schools are more frequently below the optimal level with respect to number of inhabitants than those of large high schools; therefore
6. the inhabitants of small high schools in comparison with those of large high schools are pressed (*a*) by stronger forces; (*b*) in more varied directions.

The phenotypic expression of these predictions takes many forms, which have been presented in detail elsewhere (Barker, 1960).

To illustrate, here is one prediction:

1. Behavior consequences of the stronger forces acting upon students of small high schools, in comparison with those of large high schools. The former students will:

    1.1 *Expend greater effort.* Greater individual effort can take the form of "harder" work or longer hours. The greater effort is directed both toward the primary goals of the setting and along the maintenance routes. When the assistant yearbook editor leaves, with no one available for replacement, the editor proofreads all the galleys instead of half of them.

    1.2 *Engage in more difficult and more important tasks.* There is in most settings a hierarchy of tasks with respect to difficulty and importance. The inexperienced sophomore has to take the lead role in the play when the experienced senior becomes ill (Barker, 1960, p. 30).

Other predictions, for example, are: students of smaller high schools engage in a wider variety of activities; they assume more responsibilities, have a clearer sense of self-identity, feel more insecurity, and have more frequent success and failure experiences.

This theory guided the research we have done; two representative studies are described briefly below. The reader is referred to Barker and Gump (1964) for full details.

Study 1: Participation in Nonclass Settings**

It seems obvious that a school that brings together a large number of students can offer its pupils a richer array of activities than can a smaller school. Findings described in Barker and Gump (1964, ch. 4) indicate that larger schools did offer a more extensive group of class and nonclass settings. The extra richness was perhaps less than might have been expected; certainly it did not keep pace with increase in size. For example, when the smallest and largest schools were compared, *population* increased by a factor of 65, number of different *settings* by a factor of 8, and number of different *varieties* of settings by a factor of only 1.5.

On the other hand, we knew nothing about the relation between number of students, number and variety of behavior settings, and degree of participation of individual students in the array of activities the schools provided. This section reports an investigation of this problem, using as subjects high school Junior[2] students within the nonclass behavior settings of five schools. Nonclass settings were investigated because the most adequate field methods made use of the free decision of students with respect to entering or not entering, and of participation or not participating in behavior settings.

The particular purposes of the study are: (*a*) to describe similarities and differences in the richness of nonclass offerings in large and small schools; (*b*) to determine the extent to which such offerings were actually used by large vs. small school students; and (*c*) to compare the quality of participation in the settings of large and small schools.

One large and four small schools were investigated;[3] the large school, Capital City,[4] had an enrollment of 2,287; the smaller schools, Malden, Walker, Midwest, and Vernon, had enrollments of from 83 to 151. For many comparisons, the four smaller schools were pooled together and labeled Midwest County Schools.

** Carried out by Paul V. Gump and Wallace V. Friesen.

2. Juniors: Students in the 11th grade; modal age of 16 years.

3. All schools studied were located in eastern Kansas within a homogeneous economic, cultural, and political region; all schools met the standards of the same state authority.

4. Since only one school provided data for the high end of the size continuum, it was important that this school adequately represent other large schools. Capital City High was a community school, thereby providing a balanced subject population; it was a school with an "enviable reputation"; data on the number and variety of its behavior settings indicated that it compared favorably with the other large schools studied.

Offerings of the Schools

Behavior setting surveys of these schools supplied the basis for assessing the availability of activities. For the present study, the surveys included only settings that occurred in the three-month period from the opening of school until the middle of December and that were freely accessible to Junior students. Table 1 summarizes the surveys.

Table 1

NUMBER OF JUNIORS, NUMBER OF NONCLASS BEHAVIOR SETTINGS
AVAILABLE TO JUNIORS, AND RATIOS OF JUNIORS TO THE
SETTINGS FOR EACH SCHOOL

SCHOOL	NO. OF JUNIORS	NO. OF BS	JUNIOR/BS (P/D RATIO)
Walker	16	45	.36
Malden	18	41	.44
Midwest	21	54	.39
Vernon	36	54	.67
Midwest County average	22.7	48.5	.47
Midwest County total	91	194	
Capital City	794	189	4.20

One issue of the investigation was that of the richness of activity offerings in the large and small schools. There were 189 nonclass behavior settings usable by Juniors in the large school and an average of 48.5 in the small schools. If richness means numbers, then it is clear that the large school provided the greater richness of opportunity. However, two settings can be different in terms of independence and yet very similar in terms of kind. Clearly, if richness means diversity, a more discriminating measure than independence is required. This is provided by the concept of behavior setting *variety*, or differences in kind. What varieties (types) of non-class settings were available to Juniors in the Capital City and Midwest County schools? Across all schools, thirty-three such varieties, from "Athletic Contests, Indoors" to "Volunteer Work, Fund Raising" were identified.

Capital City High School provided its Juniors with 88 per cent, and the small schools with 66 per cent (mean) of the 33 behavior setting varieties that occurred in all the schools. The small schools provided approximately 75 per cent (mean) of the number of varieties offered by Capital City High.

What were the specific advantages offered by the large school's greater variety? Examples of settings in the varieties that were unique to Capital City High are as follows:

VARIETY NUMBER	EXAMPLES OF BEHAVIOR SETTINGS
18	School Nurse's Office
20	All City Debate Clinic
23	All City Orchestra Clinic
24A	Swimming Meet
57	Chess Club Meeting
69	Photographic Rooms

A number of these unique settings appear to be somewhat peripheral to life in school in that they were established for quite special groups.

In order to deal more economically with the varieties, the schools' behavior settings were coded into eleven larger categories or *supervarieties,* such as Required Assemblies, Athletics, and Outings. The results made it clear that although the large school had many more settings (mean, 189) than the small schools (mean, 49), the small schools dispersed their activities into nearly as many varieties and supervarieties of settings as the large school.

Students' Use of Behavior Settings

METHOD.   *Subjects.* The small school sample consisted of all 91 Juniors enrolled in four high schools of Midwest County. The large school sample contained 604 Juniors from Capital City High School. Of the 794 Juniors enrolled at Capital City High, there were 122 Juniors who were not at school or had schedule conflicts when we collected the data at Capital City; 64 were excluded because they were non-Caucasian (all of the Juniors in Midwest County were of the Caucasian race), and four subjects were rejected because of evidence on their questionnaire that cast serious doubt on the truth of their answers.

Procedure. The Juniors from each of the five schools indicated, on a list of their school's behavior settings, the ones they had entered during the preceding three months, and explained what they had done in the setting.

Coding and quality of participation. Each student's report of his actions in each setting was coded for the degree of importance and centrality of his position in that setting (cf. Barker, 1968). The categories were:

1. A customer, ordinary member, or part of an audience in a setting.
2. An active, responsible member in a setting which, by its nature, required that each member accept responsibility for contributing action. Examples: Basketball Practice, Junior Play Practice.
3. A performer at a low level; subject held an important or responsible position in a part of the setting that was not directly involved in the central activity. Examples: working at concession stands at Basketball Games, ushering at the Junior Class Play.
4. Performer in the central activity; subject was directly involved in the maintenance or control of the setting. Examples: players in Football Games, president of a Y-Teens Meeting.

   In this analysis, responses to a setting coded 1 and 2 will be combined
and defined as *entries*. Responses coded 3 and 4 will be combined and
defined as *performances, or setting performances*. When only Level 4 performances are discussed, they will be called *high-level performances*.
When entries or performances are combined (codes 1 through 4), they
will be referred to as *participations*.

RESULTS.   *Setting size*. The median number of Juniors in each setting at
Capital City High was over three times as great as the median number in
small school settings (see Table 2, line 1). Thus the prediction that the
large school settings would be relatively highly populated is verified.
   Participation in settings. Line 2, Table 2 indicates that on the average, the large school Juniors entered and participated, on some level, in
six or more settings than did the small school Juniors. The significance of
this differences was $p < .001$ (Chi-square median test).
   In line 3 of Table 2 it can be seen that the small school students participated in extracurricular settings just as frequently as did large school

Table 2

SIZE OF BEHAVIOR SETTINGS AND MEAN
PARTICIPATION OF JUNIORS

	WALKER	MALDEN	MIDWEST	VERNON	MIDWEST COUNTY (MEAN)	CAPITAL CITY
1. Median number of Juniors per behavior setting	11	13	8	11	11	36
2. Mean number of *nonclass* settings in which Juniors participated (includes Offices, Required Assemblies, Smoking Room)	30.2	26.4	26.7	24.7	26.4	32.9
3. Mean number of *extracurricular* settings in which Juniors participated (omits School Offices, Required Assemblies, Smoking Room)	22.4	18.3	18.1	19.5	19.4	18.4
4. Extracurricular participation scope: mean number of different super-varieties attended					6.5	5.4

students. The equality in this respect is somewhat misleading. The distributions of the per cent of Juniors who participated in different numbers of
extracurricular settings are presented in Figure 2. It is very clear from this
graph that the population of the large school was widely dispersed from the
mean; a relatively large proportion of students engaged in ten or fewer settings, while a small proportion participated in over 37 settings, more than
any small school student. This small portion of the large school sample
elevated the group mean. In contrast, nearly all small school students participated in ten or more settings, and only a small proportion of the sample
participated in an excessively large or small number of settings.

The small school students participated in a slightly greater number of
supervarieties of behavior settings than the large school students (Table
2, line 4) ($p < .001$). Thus, although the means would indicate a similar
number of extracurricular setting participations, the small school Juniors
participated in more *kinds* of these activities.

The data presented thus far have demonstrated that the students' participation in settings of the large school did not coincide with the larger
number and wider variety of settings offered. The small school students
participated in a higher proportion and a wider variety of the settings
available to them.

PENETRATION INTO SETTINGS.   Up to this point only the number and
range of participants have been presented. Nothing has been said about the
quality of these participations. The most central hypothesis of this in-

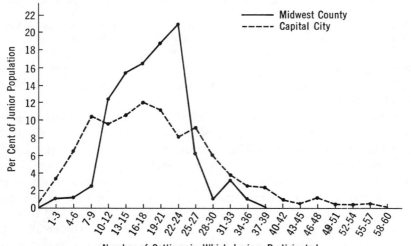

Figure 2.   Per Cent of Midwest County and Capital City School Juniors
Who Participated in Stated Numbers of Extracurricular Behavior
Settings.

vestigation was that the quality of participations would differ between large and small school students. It was predicted that small school students, in relation to those of the large school, would penetrate their settings more deeply and would occupy more positions of importance and responsibility. Data for the test of this hypothesis are displayed in Table 3 and in Figure 3. The table yields information on central tendency; the figure shows data on variance.

Table 3, line 1, indicates that the large school Juniors entered settings as audience persons or as members with much greater frequency than small school Juniors ($p < .001$). In contrast, line 2 demonstrates that the Juniors in the small schools held responsible positions twice as often as the

Table 3

PENETRATION QUALITY OF PARTICIPATIONS IN SETTINGS BY THE
JUNIORS AT MIDWEST COUNTY AND CAPITAL CITY HIGH SCHOOLS

	MEAN NUMBER OF SETTINGS IN WHICH JUNIORS PARTICIPATE AT DESIGNATED LEVELS	
LEVEL OF PARTICIPATION	MIDWEST COUNTY	CAPITAL CITY
1. Entry only: Levels 1 and 2	17.7*	29.4
2. Performance: Levels 3 and 4	8.7	3.5
3. High performance: Level 4 only	3.6	.6
4. Number of different supervarieties in which performances occurred	3.7	1.6

* The separate small schools are not presented in this table, since examination of the separate means revealed almost no differences between the four small schools.

large school Juniors ($p < .001$). Furthermore, line 3 indicates that small school Juniors held high-level performances six times as frequently as did large school Juniors ($p < .001$).

Figure 3 presents the distributions of the number of settings in which each subject of the two populations performed. Almost 30 per cent of the large school Juniors performed in no settings at all, while 2 per cent of the Juniors from the Midwest County schools failed to perform in any settings. Put another way, 42 per cent of the large school students performed in four or more settings, as compared to 80 per cent of the small school students. It is clear, then, that the large school Juniors had relatively superficial and inactive contact with their settings, while the small school Juniors were more actively contributing to the functioning of their settings.

Returning to Table 3, line 4, it can be seen that the variety of activities in which the Junior from the large school performed was less than half the variety in which small school Juniors held responsible positions when this is measured by supervarieties ($p < .001$). Not only did more small

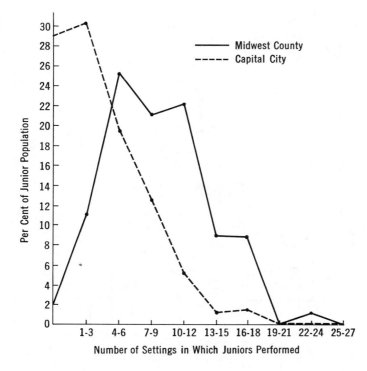

Figure 3. Per Cent of Midwest County and Capital City School
Juniors Who Performed in Stated Numbers of Behavior Settings.

school Juniors perform in a greater number of settings than did large school
Juniors, but they also held these responsible positions in twice as many
kinds of activity.

At this point it may be helpful to relate findings on performances to
the ecological factors from which they spring. According to the theory
utilized here, performance rates are higher in small schools than in large
schools because of the different relationship between number of persons
and number of settings in the two institutions. When many persons are
exposed to a limited number of settings, the performance opportunities
and obligations for any one person are reduced; when few persons are
exposed to relatively numerous settings, such opportunities and obligations
are increased. A graphic presentation of this relationship and of its outcome
in actual performances per student appears in Figure 4.

This study has demonstrated, then, that a large school provides a
somewhat larger number and wider variety of nonclass activities than a
small school. But in spite of specific large school advantages in the variety
of settings, the small school makes the same general kinds of activities
available to its students. Moreover, the small school provides a higher

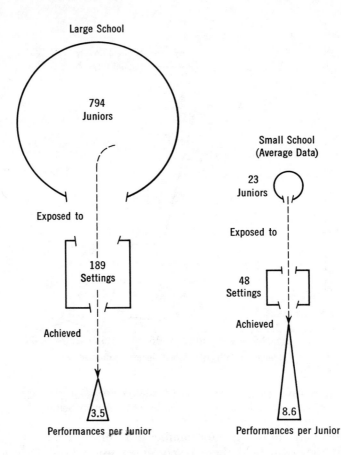

Figure 4.   Schematic Representation of Class Size, Number of Settings, and Performances Per Student.

proportion of settings to the number of students; this has the following consequences for the students' participation in activities:

(a) Small school students participate in the same *number* of settings commonly regarded as extracurricular as do large school students.

(b) Small school students participate in a wider *variety* of extracurricular activities than do the students in a large school.

(c) A much larger portion of small school students hold positions of importance and responsibility.

(d) Finally, small school students hold responsible and central positions in a wider variety of activities than do students in a large school.

Study 2: Forces toward Participation in Behavior Settings[*]

This study investigated the forces, "the real reasons for, or pulls toward" participating in voluntary school behavior settings as reported by students in large and small schools; second, it compared the reports of students who were relatively adequate academically (regular students) with the reports of students who were relatively unsuited for academic life (marginal students).

In Lewinian theory, the concept of *force* is defined as tendency to change, and has the conceptual properties of direction, strength, and point of application (Lewin, 1938, 1951). A number of empirical *symptoms* of tendency to change may be coordinated to the concept (Lewin, 1938). One of these symptoms is exemplified, with reference to the behavior setting Junior Class Play, by a student's statement, "My home-room teacher urged me strongly to go to the play." This statement reports that, at a particular point of application ("me"), there was a tendency to change ("go"), in a certain direction ("to the play"), with a designated strength ("strongly"). In this study, experiential symptoms of forces were secured by asking students, "What, if any, were for you real reasons for or pulls toward taking part in this activity?" (a precisely designated behavior setting).

Lewin (1951, p. 260) differentiated among three kinds of forces: (*a*) *own* forces, corresponding to the wishes, wills, and needs of the person himself (attractions), (*b*) induced forces, arising from the wishes and wills of some other person or persons, and (*c*) impersonal forces, arising from the impersonal environment. Here, induced and impersonal forces were combined into one class of *foreign* forces (pressures).

The *marginal students* of the study were those who had characteristics typical of students who drop out of high school without finishing the course of study, and the *regular students* were those who had characteristics typical of students who complete high school.

Method

CHOICE OF SCHOOLS AND STUDENTS. Junior students from the same schools involved in Study 1 above were subjects for the study. They had provided data in Study 1 three months previously.

The procedure for selecting marginal and regular students was entirely empirical. From a review of the literature on factors that characterize students who do not complete high school, and drawing especially on a study by Thomas (1954), the following cluster of five variables was chosen as predictive of this tendency to drop out of high school: (1) low IQ, (2) poor academic performance as indicated by grades, (3) father in a nonprofes-

[*] Carried out by Edwin P. Willems. The research is presented in more detail in a thesis (Willems, 1963).

sional occupation, (4) father who did not finish high school, and (5) mother who did not finish high school. These variables identified students who were presumably less suited for academic and school life; they were the marginal students of the present study. Regular students did not have these handicaps.

DATA COLLECTION.   In interviews, subjects, thinking of a particular behavior setting, were asked to give open-end "real reasons for or pulls toward attending this activity." These responses were coded as "own" or "foreign" forces. In addition, the responses were coded as to whether or not they showed "responsibility" to a behavior setting, other persons, or a group.

Subjects also responded to a Q-sort of 16 items for each behavior setting, measuring the extent to which "own" or "foreign" forces were involved in their participation.

The basic data were the number of "reasons or pulls" reported by each student toward taking part in designated behavior settings. Data were secured from 40 subjects (10 per cell in Figure 5) for the following classes of

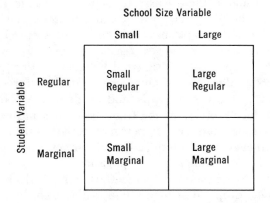

Figure 5.   Basic Design of the Study. School Size (Large vs. Small) and Kind of Student (Regular vs. Marginal) Were Studied for Their Association with Forces Toward Participation in Behavior Settings.

behavior settings in their respective schools: (a) five actual settings, i.e., behavior settings that had already occurred and that were equivalent across the schools, such as Basketball Game; (b) those settings of the five actual settings that the subject had entered during a three-and-a-half-month period; (c) one hypothetical setting (All-School Banquet), a setting that had not occurred in any school; and (d) the most meaningful setting, i.e., the school setting listed first by each subject among those that were especially attractive and worthwhile to him.

RESULTS.   Analyses of the open-ended responses to the five actual settings are provided in Figures 6 and 7.

Figure 6 shows the average numbers of attractions and pressures reported by the various subject groups: small school regular, small school marginal, large school regular, and large school marginal. Students of the small schools, where settings were relatively underpopulated, reported both more attractions ($p < .05$) and more pressures ($p < .001$) toward participation in the school settings than students from the large school; the small school advantage was greater in the case of pressures than in the case of attractions. Regular and marginal students within the small schools did not differ appreciably in either the number of pressures or the number of attractions reported; but within the large school, marginal students reported both fewer attractions and fewer pressures than regular students, and in the case of pressures the deficit was marked (the statistical interaction for pressures had an associated probability of less than .10).

We find here, as was found in Study 1, that the large school had a sizable group of "outsiders" not found in the small schools. One regular and three marginal students of the large school reported no pressure to participate, while all students of the small schools, regular and marginal alike, reported some pressures. It appears that the small school environments, made up of relatively underpopulated behavior settings, produced less discrimination between the two kinds of students we studied than the large school environment, made up of relatively overpopulated settings. According to the reports of the students, "everyone" in the small

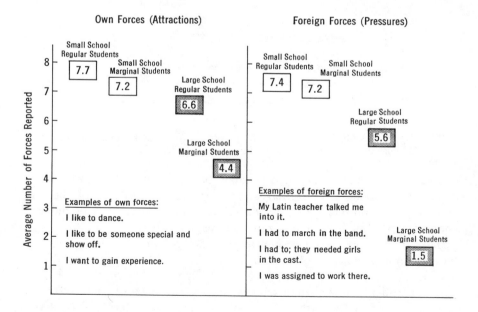

Figure 6. Mean Numbers of Forces Reported Toward Participation in Five Behavior Settings by Regular and Marginal Students in Large and Small Schools.

school felt that he had a chance at the rewards provided by the settings and that the settings, and the other persons in them, needed his contribution.

Figure 7 reveals the same relationship between the schools in the pattern of responsibility responses as in forces toward participation. Students of the small schools gave more responses indicative of acceptance of responsibility than did students of the large school ($p < .001$). Again, school size acted differentially, the difference between regular and marginal students being greater in the large than in the small schools; the statistical

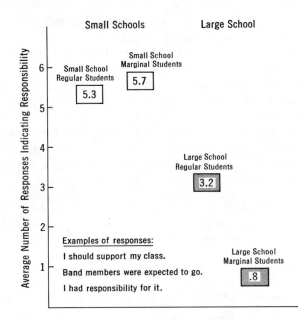

Figure 7. Mean Numbers of Responsibility Responses Reported by Regular and Marginal Students in Large and Small Schools.

interaction was significant at less than the .05 level. The large school produced outsiders. One regular and five marginal students of the large school reported no feelings of responsibility, while all students of the small schools reported at least one instance of responsibility.

The data on forces and responsibilities are relevant to the question of the comparative efficacy of personal variables and ecological variables in influencing behavior. The absence of differences between regular and marginal students in the small schools and the presence of such differences in the large school indicate that school size, as well as the kind of person, is a determinant of forces toward participation. The fact that marginal students of the small schools reported more forces than did the regular students of the large school is relevant too. In the large school the academically marginal student appeared to be truly an outsider, while in the small schools being marginal made no apparent difference on the experience of pressures, attractions, and responsibilities.

More detailed analysis showed that students in small schools, as compared with students in the large school:

> Reported more forces toward participation in all classes of setting, and for both open-end and card-sort data;
> Reported more attraction, and more pressures to participate;
> Reported a higher ratio of "foreign" to "own" forces (i.e., felt more pressure);
> Gave more "responsibility" responses;
> Were more likely to want to take part in a hypothetical behavior setting (95% vs. 50%).

It was also shown (see Table 4) that these reported forces, and the student's indication of his actual behavior (whether or not he had entered five specific settings, when queried in Study 1 three months previously), were positively correlated (all p's $<$ .005). These data provided a kind of validation of the number of reported "reasons" or "pulls" as a measure of forces toward participation. The open-ended data tend to correlate more strongly with actual behavior than the card-sort data, and foreign forces (pressures) tend to be more highly correlated to participation than own forces (attractions), especially in the case of performances.

Table 4

CORRELATIONS BETWEEN THE NUMBER OF SETTINGS
PARTICIPATED IN AND NUMBERS OF FORCES TOWARD ENTRY
INTO THE FIVE ACTUAL SETTINGS

BEHAVIOR SETTING DATA	OPEN-ENDED DATA			CARD-SORT DATA		
	OWN	FOREIGN	TOTAL	OWN	FOREIGN	TOTAL
No. of settings entered among the five actual settings	.61	.85	.87	.48	.58	.54
Participation data, Study 1						
Entries only	.49	.38		.12	.05	
Performances only	.30	.69		.48	.60	
Entries plus performances						
Total participation . . .	.53	.66	.67	.35	.38	.39

Note: In the table, Spearman rho's, corrected for ties, were computed for the first row; Pearson *r's* were computed for the other rows. Behavioral data for rows 2, 3, and 4 were obtained from Study 1 for the subjects of this study; scores were totals for the varieties of settings from which the five settings of this study were selected.

DISCUSSION.   Asch (1952) points out that the social order becomes "objectified" in the form of material objects and institutional relations, and that it is one of the important tasks of the psychologist to study how such stubborn environmental facts act upon and alter the behavior of persons. The studies reported in this article focus on one such stubborn fact, the ubiquitous, coercive behavior settings that students in high schools inhabit. The present investigation shows that the number of persons present in behavior settings not only alters overt behavior in predictable ways, but also determines, within limits, the nature of the psychological experience of students.

Results from this study yielded general support for the theory of the effects of behavior setting size, indicating that the theory is a powerful predictor from ecology to the experience and behavior of individual persons. Students from the small schools, where settings were relatively underpopulated, reported more own forces (attractions) and foreign forces (pressures) toward participation in behavior settings than did students from the large school. Furthermore, a sizable group of students emerged in the large school who experienced few, if any, forces toward participation. The small schools in the present study did not contain any such outsiders; all of the small school students reported experiencing many forces toward participation. Preselected marginal students in the small schools experienced as many forces as did regular students, while in the large school, the preselected marginals experienced very few forces, far fewer than the regular students.

Another important finding is that the responses of the small school students reflected more felt responsibility and obligation. Many persons feel that the development of a sense of responsibility is essential to good citizenship, and that it is one task of schools to encourage this sense of responsibility in students. The frequency of responsibility responses in this study followed the same pattern as the data on forces, with extreme differences between schools and the emergence of outsiders, persons in the large school who reported no felt responsibility.[5]

Pressures (foreign forces) varied more with school size than did attractions (own forces), and pressures correlated more highly with actual participation and involvement than did attractions. These findings suggest that self-generated pressures of behavior settings are more powerful than attractions in mediating the relationship between size and participation.

---

5. It is of interest to know what *satisfactions* were reported by students who were confronted with responsibilities in the large and small schools. Data reported in Barker and Gump (1964, ch. 7 and 9) show that Juniors from the small schools reported more satisfactions relating to the development of competence, to being challenged, to engaging in important actions, to being involved in group activities, and to achieving moral and cultural values; while large school Juniors reported more satisfactions dealing with vicarious enjoyment, with large entity affiliation, with learning about their school's persons and affairs, and with gaining "points" via participation. It was further predicted that these school differences would be causally related to differences in occupancy of important and responsible positions in school settings. This prediction was verified: the satisfactions reported were significantly influenced by the positions the student respondents occupied within settings, and most of the differences between large and small schools in this regard were eliminated when differences in setting position were held constant.

IMPLICATIONS. Quite apart from support for a particular theory, several implications stand out from the findings of this study, which impinge radically upon some commonly held ideas about psychological experience, motivation, and development.

First, it seems clear that school size is an important variable in the lives of students. On the basis of the present studies, effects of size seem to be facts of life which must be reckoned with. Not only is the overt behavior (participation) of students altered by school size, but their experience is altered as well. In Lewinian terms, not only are behavioral locomotions affected by size, but the very structure of the life space is altered. The data on the hypothetical setting were especially interesting in this regard. Here was a setting that no one had entered, because it had not occurred in any of the schools. Yet when students were asked to project ahead their experience of forces ("What would be real reasons for or pulls . . .?"), the students of the small schools expected more attractions, more pressures, and a greater proportion of pressures; and more of them definitely expected to enter the setting when it did occur.

Second, motivation is often seen as purely a function of the person. Attraction and sense of responsibility, especially, are often seen as such "inside-the-skin" variables. Yet, when similar persons were compared in different environments in the present study, attraction and felt responsibility were found to vary with the outside environment also. The data (Figures 6 and 7) offer some evidence on the question of the comparative influence of ecology and kind of person in determining the experience of forces. Within the limits of the methods used to identify and select regular and marginal students, one would expect, if the kind of person were more important than the ecology of the school, that similar groups of students would report similar experiences in different ecologies. Yet this was not the case. Marginal students from the small schools reported more forces than regular students from the large school. Marginal students from the large school were a group apart, a group of outsiders. These findings indicate that the academically marginal students had very different experiences in the two ecologies. In the small school, marginal characteristics made no difference; marginal students experienced almost as many forces toward participation as the nonmarginal students. In the large school, however, the marginal students experienced relatively very few attractions and pressures toward participation.

The correlations between forces and participation provide further evidence that ecology is a powerful factor in determining participation. The consistently high correlations between foreign forces and participation suggest that ecology was a powerful determinant of participation among the subjects of the present study.

Third, there are implications for developmental theory. If it is assumed that "the best way to learn is to *do*," or "the best way to learn responsibility is to have it," then the implications of the present study are clear. Individual students in small schools, with their relatively underpopulated settings, live under greater day-to-day attraction, pressure, and responsibility felt toward taking active part in the voluntary activities of their school environments. They are more motivated to take part.

Concluding Comments

The Issue of Method

The high schools of the United States provide a significant segment of the environment of the nation's adolescents. It is practically important, therefore, to study high schools as environments. How does one do this? These studies provide one answer.

The basic unit of the school environment is the behavior setting. To put it plainly: A school *is* its behavior settings. With this unit and associated measures it is possible to study the school in terms of its first-order reality for its inhabitants. The distinction between this approach and others is worth making explicit. For example, it is possible to study schools in terms of such variables as the social class of students, the training of teachers, and the extent of curricular offerings; but students do not respond directly to these variables. Students respond to the sectors of the school environment in which they live. The effects of social class and of other variables may impinge upon events within behavior settings, but students react to them as they are transformed within behavior settings. Differences in social class, for example, may have quite dissimilar consequences in small and large settings.

Behavior settings can enter research in three ways. First, they can be used as *sampling units*. If one wishes to know what happens in one kind of school as opposed to another, it is necessary that these schools be sampled in a representative and equitable fashion. A behavior setting survey maps the school environment; once the map is developed, decisions about areas from which to take measurements can be made with confidence. This "situational sampling" is as important as person sampling and is an essential aspect of environmental research.

Second, the number, kind, and organization of settings can be viewed as sets of *dependent variables*. If one is interested in the effects of consolidation, one can observe what this move does to the behavior settings of the schools involved: what happens, for example, to after-school settings when all students must ride the bus? Or, one can study effects of variation in educational philosophy upon the behavior settings of schools: how do secular versus religious, public versus private, American versus European schools differ in the number, kind, and interrelation of settings?

In the third place, behavior settings can be used as the *independent variables*. The target of such investigation is the response of the inhabitants of behavior settings to the settings. One aspect of school behavior settings was selected in the present effort, namely, population. There are, however, certainly other behavior-coercive properties of settings: e.g., the number of "performance niches" they contain, the amount of interdependence they require, the specific types of effort they demand, the kinds of human beings they include. Variations in setting qualities have implications for educational strategy. School learning occurs at the mutual boundary between the school and the individual student; this boundary is located in the school's behavior settings. Educators wish to create good schools, and this means to create settings consonant with their educational goals. The attainment of this consonance requires methods of identifying and characterizing settings and methods of describing the behavior that is responsive to setting contexts.

The Issue of Size

A basic problem for the immediate future is to investigate the degree to which the relations we have discovered between school size, school settings, and student participation are inevitable. Not only the present research, but all other research known to us, indicates that the negative relationship between institutional size and individual participation is deeply based and difficult, if not impossible, to avoid. It may be easier to bring specialized and varied behavior settings to small schools than to raise the level of individual participation in large schools. Furthermore, the current method of broadening educational offerings by moving hundreds of bodies to a central spot may be both unnecessary and old-fashioned. Already a technical revolution with respect to teaching devices and educational facilities is upon us. Self-teaching machines, taped school courses, TV classes, wired TV linking separate schools, new ideas about teaching personnel (e.g., school aides), new conceptions of inter-school cooperation (e.g., transporting teachers and equipment rather than students), new conceptions of the contributions of the community to educational objectives, and new materials and standards for school construction are freeing schools from past molds.

These new developments, taken with the findings reported here, provoke the question: How large should a school be?

The present research, in itself, cannot answer this question. Some of the crucial variables such as academic learning were not investigated. Furthermore, "should" in this query implies purpose, and educational purposes differ.

Common-sense theories about schools are not adequate bases for policy decisions. An example of this is the common-sense assumption that there is a direct coupling between the facilities or properties of schools and the behavior and experiences of students. This simple view of reality, so common in education, has been long passed in physical and biological sciences. No one would seriously argue that because one bridge is stronger than another the individual beams of which it is constructed must also be stronger. Good facilities provide good experiences only if they are used.

The educational process is a subtle and delicate one about which we know little, but it surely thrives on participation, enthusiasm, and responsibility. Our findings and our theory posit a negative relationship between school size and individual student participation. What seems to happen is that as schools get larger and settings inevitably become more heavily populated, more of the students are less needed; they become superfluous, redundant.

What size should a school be?

The data of this research and our own educational values tell us that a school should be sufficiently small that all of its students are needed for its enterprises. A school should be small enough that students are not redundant.

References

ALLPORT, F. H.   *Theories of perception and the concept of structure.* New York: Wiley, 1955.

ASCH, S. E.   *Social psychology.* New York: Prentice-Hall, 1952.

BARKER, R. G.   Ecology and motivation. In M. Jones, (Ed.), *Nebraska symposium on motivation.* Lincoln: University of Nebraska Press, 1960, Pp. 1-49.

BARKER, R. G. (Ed.).   *The stream of behavior.* New York: Appleton-Century-Crofts, 1963.

BARKER, R. G. *Ecological psychology.* Stanford, Calif.: Stanford University Press, 1968.

BARKER, R. G. and BARKER, LOUISE S.   Behavior units for the comparative study of cultures. In B. Kaplan, (Ed.), *Studying personality cross-culturally.* New York: Harper & Row, 1961. Pp. 457-476.

BARKER, R. G., WRIGHT, H. F., BARKER, L. S. and SCHOGGEN, M.   *Specimen records of American and English children.* Lawrence: University of Kansas Press, 1961.

BARKER, R. G. and GUMP, P. V.   *Big school, small school.* Stanford, Calif.: Stanford University Press, 1964.

BARKER, R. G. and WRIGHT, H. F.   *Midwest and its children.* New York: Harper & Row, 1955.

LEWIN, K.   The conceptual representation and measurement of psychological forces. *Contributions to Psychological Theory,* 1938, 1, (4).

LEWIN, K.   *Field theory in social science.* New York: Harper, 1951.

SCHOGGEN, P.   A study in psychological ecology: a description of the behavior objects which entered the psychological habitat of an eight-year-old girl during the course of one day. Unpublished Master's thesis, University of Kansas, 1951.

WILLEMS, E. P.   Forces toward participation in behavior settings of large and small institutions: a field experiment. Unpublished Master's thesis, University of Kansas, 1963.

WRIGHT, H. F.   *Recording and analyzing child behavior.* New York: Harper and Row, 1967.

❊ ❊ ❊ ❊ ❊

Much of educational practice is not derived from, or even informed by, any systematic set of ideas. Much of what we do in the classroom from day to day represents institutional holdovers, folklore, even impulse.

This article by Pilnick and his colleagues illustrates with considerable clarity what an educational environment would look like if it were designed around some clear theoretical principles. It can thus be seen as a model of "development"—the process which occurs when someone tries to design a solution to a problem, using available knowledge.

Substantively, the authors reject the "disease" model of juvenile delinquency, and begin designing their educative environment around the the idea of *normative influence*. The "pro-social" freedom-expanding norms they successfully developed in opposition to the norms of the street are analytically similar to the "creative individualism" norms Newcomb (in the present volume) found at Bennington College.

Though the article is weak on data, its primary usefulness lies in illustrating how—in a "non-school" but essentially educative setting—it is possible to apply the architectural dictum that "form follows function." The interested reader may wish to try his hand at redesigning a classroom environment, using Pilnick's ideas.

The Essexfields Concept:

A New Approach to the Social Treatment
of Juvenile Delinquents*

Saul Pilnick,
Albert Elias, Neale W. Clapp

Individual behavior is only partly determined by one's personal history. Except for the extraordinary person, people do not usually surpass the limitations of the culture into which they are born. By and large the societies in which we live are mediated for us through units called primary groups, which are characterized by a high degree of informality. The family is the best example of such a primary group found in every culture.

Primary groups have considerable face-to-face interaction and a considerable degree of ingroup cohesion. These small groups are often more crucial in shaping individual standards than the school or the institution in which they are embedded. Mannheim (1955) writes:

> Where pilfering is practiced by an influential section of the workers, those who do not take part will be not only unpopular as nonconformists but even suspect as traitors, with all the unpleasant consequences which this entails [p. 24].

The individual finds his niche and commits himself to a set of values in primary groups (familial, occupational, ethnic, peer, and neighborhood). His identity is largely shaped by these emotionally charged relationships.

Much of what is termed "delinquency" consists of behavior patterns which are socially proscribed and which have evolved out of experiences in peer groups and in the community. The group character of delinquency has attracted increasing attention from various research and action programs both in the community and in correctional facilities. In social work, Breckenridge and Abbott (1912) many years ago called attention to the group nature of delinquency. In psychology, Aichhorn (1935), Healy and Bronner (1936), and Redl and Wineman (1951), among others, have recognized that effective preventive work with delinquents must take into account the empirical evidence that many delinquent acts have a distinct social character. Slavson's (1954) emphasis upon the education of the delinquent through a corrective experience in democratic community living

* From *Journal of Applied Behavioral Science*, 1966, 2(1), 109-125. Used by permission of the authors and publisher.

recognized the group nature of much antisocial behavior. The research efforts of sociologists, particularly Shaw and McKay (1931) in their classic studies of urban delinquency, have highlighted the crucial role of the group factor as the context for a considerable amount of delinquent behavior. The work done by McCorkle and Korn (1954) and Ohlin and Lawrence (1959) has been instrumental in focusing attention upon the role of the inmate social system in neutralizing the treatment programs in our correctional institutions. It has been suggested that current treatment programs be reorganized and oriented toward group objectives rather than predominantly toward individual needs, as is now generally practiced in clinical therapy groups. This suggestion is based upon the assumption that the delinquent's behavior is due in large part to the internalization of a set of norms and values which are obtained from a "subcultural" life which is in conflict and is deviant from our major cultural values.

The delinquent's meaningfully real world is extended beyond the family constellation. Contemporary knowledge of the psychological forces impinging upon the adolescent enables us to begin to understand the full meaning and impact of peer group affiliations for the adolescent. The need of adolescents to conform to peer group norms and values has often been witnessed by youth workers as well as parents. When one refers to the "tyranny of adolescents," one is expressing an awesome appreciation of the powerful energies and pressures generated by this strange social configuration called the peer group. A careful examination of the life of a "gang" or the life of delinquent "crowds" often reveals certain norms and values which are desperately upheld by each peer group member. Norms and values are not necessarily a part of the deep psychological equipment of the individual delinquent, but often—and this is crucial—these norms and values are adopted as modes of behavior primarily because through the dynamic process of the group interaction (involving coercion and conformity) these values have been so designated to each member. In delinquent groups, conformity to "street" norms contains the opportunity for status as well as masculine identification. Cloward and Ohlin (1960, pp. 108-109) have pointed out the significance of opportunity structures as related to delinquent behavior.

> Since discrepancies between aspiration and opportunity are likely to be experienced more intensely at some social positions than at others, persons in status locations where the discrepancy is most acute may develop a common perception and sense of indignation about their disadvantages as contrasted with the advantages of others. Interaction among those sharing the same problem may provide encouragement for the withdrawal of sentiments in support of the established system of norms. Once freed of allegiance to the existing set of rules, such persons may devise or adopt delinquent means of achieving success.

A treatment approach founded upon these assumptions would attempt to reduce conformity to delinquent peer-determined norms and would encourage the development of new behavior patterns which are "prosocial" in nature. This can be accomplished within the context of a treatment environment which provides the *opportunity* for delinquent adolescents to make responsible choices among a variety of possible alternatives and which makes it possible for the adolescent to transfer his peer group allegiances to a more prosocial group whose values are nondelinquently oriented.

The Essexfields Program

In 1961, under a grant from The Ford Foundation, the Department of Institutions and Agencies in the State of New Jersey established a group rehabilitation center in the heart of Newark. This program is designed to rehabilitate sixteen- and seventeen-year-old delinquent boys who are referred by the Essex County Juvenile Court. The criteria for admission to the program are that the boys not be severely disturbed, not be homosexual, and not have had a previous institutional experience. The type of boy Essexfields seeks is the individual whose participation in delinquent activities is usually accompanied by peer group affiliations. The "lone wolf" type of boy is excluded from the program. The average stay in the program is approximately four months, although this varies from boy to boy. A boy is released from the program when his Essexfields peers feel he is ready to resume his place in the community.

This program design was patterned after the Highfields Residential Group Center in Hopewell, New Jersey. For the past 15 years, the Highfields program has been notably successful in working with a similar group of boys in a residential setting (McCorkle, Elias, and Bixby, 1958). The Essexfields program differs from this design in that the boys return to their homes every evening and are at home during the weekend.

The program is housed in an old three-story building located in an area of high delinquency in Newark. Twenty boys participate at any one time and thereby maintain the necessary intimacy of interpersonal relationships. The boys meet in the building each weekday morning at 7:30 a.m. Under the supervision of a (nonprofessional) work supervisor, they are transported by bus to the grounds of a nearby county mental hospital. At 8:30 a.m., they begin their workday, for which they are paid $1.00 per day. They are assigned to various duties such as chopping wood, weeding, cutting hedges, trimming and edging grass, and snow removal in the wintertime. The boys eat their lunch and supper at the hospital with hospital employees in the employees' cafeteria. At 5:30 p.m., they are transported back to the facility in Newark.

The Essexfields work situation is an essential ingredient in the program, since it provides a primary opportunity for the boys to get to know one another intimately. Almost all boys who come to Essexfields initially express a dislike for work. Nevertheless, there is something about work which tends to reveal a boy's behavior for all to see. As a result, Essexfields boys, while at work, deal with one another in an atmosphere filled with tension, gratification, success, and failure. In addition, the boys travel on the Essexfields bus together for 1½ hours a day, eat two meals together for 1½ hours a day, have recreation together for 2½ hours a day, and work as a group for 6½ hours a day. After returning to the building in Newark, the boys relax, play cards or ping-pong until 7.00 p.m., at which time the guided group interaction sessions begin, under the direction of two professional group therapists. Two group meetings are held, each lasting 1½ hours and each consisting of ten boys. At 10:00 p.m., the boys return to their homes, to report back again the following morning. This procedure is followed five days per week.

The Essexfields Social System

Essexfields is basically a self-contained social system with its own subculture. Norms, traditions, language, and conceptions of deviancy have developed which are indigenous to the system. Since only about five boys are admitted to the program each month and the same number released, it is possible for the program always to have "old" boys and "new" boys interacting concurrently, which enables the peculiarities of the culture to be transmitted at all times. It is believed that through exposure to this experience the adolescent offender can assume "conventional" or "law-abiding" norms as he discards delinquent norms. The same pressure to conform which afflicts delinquents in the community through a delinquent peer group is applied at Essexfields by a peer group ascribing to conventional norms.

However, intrinsic to the "new" norms built into Essexfields experience is an emphasis upon a freedom of choice. Delinquents, not unlike other adolescents, present a pattern of rigidity of behavior. Alternative forms of reacting to life situations are rarely considered by the delinquent adolescent. Consequently, the effort at Essexfields is to create a social system which, through the utilization of group pressures, results in a greater freedom of behavioral choices. It might be stated that Essexfields establishes a process of interaction which creates a "conformity to freedom."

The social system at Essexfields was initiated by transferring boys from the already-existing Highfields project in Hopewell, New Jersey. Ten boys, transferred over a period of two months, provided the norms necessary for the establishment of the Essexfields "culture." This system of "seeding" has since been utilized in establishing the Collegefields project and other youth-serving programs in the New Jersey area. However, it is obvious that a method depending upon this form of seeding cannot have wide application. Other methods have therefore been developed. Getting a culture started is largely dependent upon the skill of the "therapist" or group leader. He must be "culture" conscious and highly aware of the subtlety and nature of the existing norms which each delinquent brings into the new group experience. His role initially is that of the "gatekeeper" of the norms. All prodelinquent norms need to be commented upon as being dysfunctional; otherwise the group would interpret the leader's passivity as implying support of the "old" norms. At the same time the leader must be cautious not to allow himself to do battle with the total group's delinquent norms. Allies need to be gathered and group support developed for the prosocial norms. The initial phase of developing a culture can be time-consuming, but is obviously crucial. The establishment of a prosocial culture enables the marshaling of powerful group pressures toward a group evaluation of deviant behavior.

Representative of the pressure which the peer group can apply to a deviant member is this excerpt from a recent group meeting:

> Carl took on a very sorrowful expression and then started to explain why he found it necessary to defend people. He started out, "I just can't help it. I feel sorry for people. I want to help them."
>
> Fred: Help them? You defend against help. Why can't you see it?
>
> Allen: You ain't trying to help. You're just sponging and you know it. That's why the hell you don't bust cliques. (reveal other boy's deviances)
>
> Fred: You're messing up our lives.
>
> Carl: I didn't want to see people get busted. (arrested)
>
> Allen: You realize you messed up our lives. Why did you continue?
>
> At this point even the boys that don't usually say much started getting on Carl. Carl cringed before this onslaught and then confessed. "Now I realize. Now I'm scared for the boys. I didn't take things in before. I still saw it my way. This program was a lot of bull to me."
>
> The circle closed in and the entire meeting fired questions from all directions.
>
> Carl: When the pressure is on me I had to bust cliques. I wasn't involved before.
>
> Gary: You're supposed to be involved with everything that goes on at Essexfields. You just wanted to sponge.
>
> Carl: I accept that now. I see it now.
>
> Allen: Admit it, Carl. You don't give a damn for this program, do you?
>
> Carl: Yes I do. Why would I bust my cliques if I didn't care about the program?
>
> The meeting replies in unison, as if it has been rehearsed: "To save your own skin."
>
> Allen, Frank, and Fred continued on Carl. Frank was very good—strong and perceptive. Allen supported him admirably.
>
> Gary: Tell us the real reason you busted those cliques.
>
> Carl pretended he didn't know at first, but Fred pointed out that Carl feared going to jail and had only busted his and other cliques to impress rather than help.
>
> Frank: You are helping yourself and you didn't care about us. Who do you care about? Tell the truth. Who in the hell do you really care about?
>
> Carl: Myself! Myself! Myself! I cared about me. I see it all now. I realize now.
>
> Allen: When did you realize? Right now? Right this moment?
>
> Carl: Yes. Now. Tonight.

The entire meeting was on Carl now.

Frank: Do you mean to tell us you played a role until right now?

Not only does the group apply pressure but in so doing enables the deviant to re-examine his behavior and find suitable alternatives.

> Ed began his meeting by explaining how when he first came to Essexfields he would take the bus to East Orange with Roger and then turn around and take it back to Newark. When he was caught doing this he gave it up and began to stay at his aunt's house. He admitted that he had been sneaky and had tried every possible excuse to remain in Newark. He did not tell of this past weekend incident until I reminded him, and then he admitted that he had left East Orange after his aunt had squabbled with him, had come to Newark, and called Dr. P. When Dr. P. had advised him to return to East Orange to sleep, Ed had agreed but then had remained in Newark anyway. The meeting began to show Ed several alternative procedures which he might have followed. They asked him if he had requested his father to give his aunt some money for his weekend meals and also asked if he could not use part of his pay for subsistence in East Orange. They suggested that he do his own laundry as long as his aunt seemed to object to his using her soap and water and in general showed good sense of purpose for an immature meeting. Most active in this respect were Bob and Roger, with Sam and Dan making occasional contributions. The boy grew more sincere as the meeting continued. The boys drew parallels to Ed's behavior in this situation with his behavior at Essexfields, and Ed listened carefully. On one occasion Roger said, "How come you could only stand listening to your aunt for two hours on Saturday night, yet you can take the boys' getting on you from 7:30 in the morning until 10:00 at night, six days a week?" Ed gave the "right" response by saying that he could take the boys' criticism because they were trying to help him, but his aunt obviously was not.

Hopefully, the loyalty of the delinquent will be transferred from his peer group in the community to the peer group at Essexfields. If this can be accomplished, alternatives to delinquent behavior can be evaluated by each boy and utilized, and the adolescent can find satisfaction in conforming to law-abiding values. Through the Essexfields process, the culture becomes so ingrained, yet dynamic, that the individual involvement and commitment to this new peer group creates an untenable anxiety which seems to result in a gradual shift in loyalties. Initially, a "new" boy is unable to accept Essexfields as a legitimate alternative to his delinquent associates and often continues to involve himself in delinquent behavior. However, his deviancy when visible is condemned by his new peer group. Hoping to achieve status among this new group, the individual begins a process of examining the validity of his previous behavior patterns as well as the new "norms" he is exposed to. When the process of emotional commitment to the new group begins to occur, delinquent behavior seems to diminish. Simultaneously, ties to neighborhood peer groups also tend to diminish. This process seems to occur quite unconsciously and often to the surprise of the boy himself.

Formal Structure

Some of the aspects of the culture as perceived by Essexfields boys are
most vividly described in their terms. For the new boy, Essexfields becomes
a *task* which he must solve. He is expected by his peers first to tell his "story."
This consists of relating to the other boys the details concerning all of
the "trouble" he has ever been in. The "how" and the "what" of his behavior
are stressed. He then "gets his problems." Usually, these problems consist of
those deviancies easily recognized by the conventional community,
supplemented by those attitudinal deviancies as perceived by other
Essexfields boys. In other words, while a boy might receive a "light finger"
problem for stealing, he may also receive a "cold-hearted" problem or an
"easily influenced" problem. While these characteristics as such would not
result in an appearance before juvenile authorities, they are related to the
underlying causes for the boy's delinquencies and constitute possible sources
of delinquency for the boy in the future. Thereafter, in order to achieve
acceptance, the new Essexfields boy devotes himself to overcoming these
"problems" by utilizing the aid, the suggestions, and insight of his peers
and the Essexfields staff. The ability to perceive the underlying causes
of a boy's problems at Essexfields is known as "going deep" and being able
to ask "why" questions. This trait is well esteemed in the hierarchy of
Essexfields values.

Informal Structure

Although occasionally many of the informal norms of the program achieved
the status of formal norms, at Essexfields this process has been accomplished
by the boys rather than through the direction or intent of the staff. The
jargon, or language, of Essexfields is accepted by all boys, and as it becomes
part of the pattern, the definition of terms occasionally becomes more rigid.

Most of the jargon reflects deviancies as perceived by Essexfields boys.
The alliance of two or more boys to conceal a deviancy from the group
is termed "cliquing." A boy may also be accused of "cliquing with himself"
if he fails to reveal his own misdemeanors. "Playing a role" is considered
a major deviancy, as it conceals a boy's "true feelings." Without the
revelation of these "true feelings," a boy cannot be "helped." Of course,
both of these techniques are used by almost all Essexfields boys in an effort
to sustain themselves within the program during the early stages. These
"adaptive" mechanisms are similar to the ones utilized by Essexfields boys
at school and at home prior to their involvement with the Essexfields
"treatment community." Nevertheless, there is a blanket condemnation of
this procedure, and gradually a boy will learn to adapt himself to the
program without the use of these defenses. Frequently, this is done through
assuming responsibility and status within the program, which allows a

boy to become respected by the peer group in such a manner that it is not necessary for him to protect himself from their criticism. Frequently, the so-called "stronger," more "sophisticated" boys master the group techniques in such a manner that they become virtually unassailable. This method of coping with the Essexfields system must also result in failure, as the boy is reminded that unless he allows himself to be criticized and have his deviancies exposed he cannot be "helped."

Through the three years of operation of this program, certain traditions have been established by the boys. Some of the boys have carved their names and the dates of their attendance on an old plank of wood which they found in the basement of the building. Others take pride in "changing their pin" on a map in the office which shows the location of all Essexfields boys past and present, with a color key. Among the less obvious traditions are the responsibilities which an older boy is expected to assume, such as "checking up" on other younger boys on weekends and delegating "hours" to be worked off. Boys will "check" themselves if they suddenly become aware of their own deviant behavior or they will admonish other boys to "check" themselves.

The function and purpose of social control at Essexfields is flexible, nonpunitive, and essentially nonpredictable and noninstitutional. Basically, those measures employed are intended to arouse individual and group responses, create certain anxieties, and cause the individual and the group to reflect upon the nature of the deviancy and the need to alter behavior.

Among those sanctions which are present at Essexfields are the following:

1. *Hours:* A boy is given hours by the staff or the group as a result of those infractions which endanger his status in the program. Normally, it would include such actions as arriving at the program late, purposeful or accidental avoidance of responsibility, stealing, fighting, or difficulty in adjusting to the program.

2. *On Report:* A boy is put on report, which means a loss of a day's pay, as the result of behavior problems at the work situation or while at the facility.

3. *Keeping a Boy Back:* Occasionally a boy is not allowed to accompany the group to the work situation. Kept at the center, he is expected to ponder his deviancies. This is done less frequently and implies a more serious problem of adjustment to the program.

4. *Bringing a Boy Back:* Much in the manner that a boy is kept at the house, a boy may be picked up at the work situation by the staff and returned to the center. The purpose of this action is similar in nature and severity to the aforementioned policy.

5. *Extra Duty:* Extra duty is imposed by the work supervisor at the work situation for minor deviancies there. "Extra duty" results in the loss of certain privileges enjoyed by the boys at work, such as a short break for smoking.

6. *Returning a Boy to Court:* The ultimate sanction imposed at Essexfields is to return a boy to court. This measure is utilized only when a boy is regarded as being unsuitable for the program. Occasionally, the members of the group themselves urge this action and, in the

meetings, may give opinions as to whether they feel a boy can be
"helped" or not. This final sanction is known as "giving up on a boy."
Frequently, one or two boys will attempt to "save" the individual.
Sometimes this is accomplished by "taking responsibility" for the boy.
(In this case, all efforts are exerted to "help" the boy in question.)

In essence, a variety of strains have gone into the development of the
conceptual framework of Essexfields. The offender must be made aware
of the fact that (a) he has been defined as a delinquent by conventional
society and (b) he must take account of this conception of himself if he is
to change. Frequently, offenders—particularly those of middle-class origin—
do not see themselves as delinquents but rather as unfortunate victims of
an irrational system of social justice. To paraphrase Tannenbaum, their evil
has not been dramatized sufficiently to permit the development of a
delinquent self-conception (1938, p. 16).

Opportunities must be provided for the delinquent to experiment with
a fairly wide range and variety of social roles and relationships. The social
world of the delinquent does not allow for exploration of too many
interactions outside the prescribed ones, especially those with a conventional
tinge, without imposing severe sanctions.

The peer group must be seen as a medium of change and a source of
influence over its members. In this way, plans and efforts to change can be
accepted and supported by the group. In other words, change, as an end in
itself, must be legitimized by the group conduct for its members.

A setting must be provided for the peer group to develop a system for assigning status to its members on the basis of prosocial patterns of interaction
that is independent of the system for allocating status within the delinquent
social world. All too frequently delinquents are evaluated in terms of surface conformity to institutional norms. This procedure serves only to encourage the emergence and maintenance of therapeutic parasites.

Alumni

Essexfields graduates frequently return on visits. In some instances specific
help is requested, such as information re obtaining a driver's license or en-
listment in the Armed Services. In other instances, personal problems at
home or at school result in a visit. Little of the "street" culture's reluctance
to admit "weakness" or the need for help is visible in the Essexfields graduate. On occasion, a graduate will obtain a job for an Essexfields boy or aid
in the resolution of a family problem. "Alumni" meetings are held every
Saturday morning to provide assistance for boys currently· in the program
who are having difficulty adjusting to the conventional norms.

Family Contact

Experience has indicated that severe pressures at home can impede a boy's
attempt at accepting and adjusting to the peer group's new expectations of

him. Parents who do not have a full understanding of the purposes of the program tend to subvert its efforts. Many parents distrust governmental agencies. Consequently, parental interviews take place with the parents of all boys shortly after their admission to the program. For the most part, experience has revealed a desire on the part of the parents to support the prosocial norms of the peer group culture, although continued contact through home visits is often necessary.

Transition to the Community

Presumably, when an Essexfields boy leaves the program his interpersonal sensitivity and his self-insight have increased and his motivation to engage in new behavior patterns in the community has been heightened. Near the end of his stay at Essexfields, a boy concerns himself in his discussions with his peers and with the staff about his future plans. The following summary written by a boy upon leaving Essexfields gives some indication of the degree of insight gained in Essexfields and also reveals the way in which a boy approaches the transition to the community:

> When I first came to Essexfields I thought it was a nut house. I figured I would survive four or five months and that was it. When I went downtown when I wasn't supposed to, I figured it would be best not to say anything. When I confessed, I did so only because I was tricked into it by one of the boys. I still cliqued after that because I was afraid to have the boys get on me.
>
> After my second month I started to take the program as a place to help me and not to hurt me. I started understanding some of my problems, and then the program became interesting and I wanted to understand more about myself.
>
> All through the program I had a hard time getting along with the boys because of the way I carried myself and the manner in which I impressed to get in good with the boys, which I tried to do all my life. I didn't know how to deal with boys. Then one helped meeting brought this out, but at first I thought they just said that because they didn't like me. I kept it on my mind all that weekend and then I saw it in myself. Then my real self came to light and my role was left behind. Also it was seen that I didn't have enough self-confidence in myself as a person and seemed to belittle myself and impressed to bring up my own standings to myself. I still have not gained all my self-confidence in myself, but I can see myself, and I looked back on myself to see my good points. It wasn't hard to look at my good points, but it was hard to gain self-confidence. The way I have to do this is by completing goals and accomplishing things.

Occasionally an "early release" is recommended by the peer group. This enables a boy to look for a job or return to school while still in the program. In this manner, a boy with severe problems focusing around work and school can utilize the evening group meetings to develop further insight regarding his behavior. An employment opportunity committee has been established with the aid of a number of employers in the area. The primary purpose of this committee is to develop job contacts for Essexfields graduates. In addition, Essexfields alumni have provided "job leads" for boys who are leaving the program. In some instances, the transition to the community has been facilitated by a referral to a child guidance clinic or to a family agency, if the need arose. Nevertheless, it has been our experience that a job market that is unable to absorb the unskilled, poorly educated "ex-delinquent" tends to create severe problems even for the highly motivated youngster.

Modifications and Program Implications
of the Essexfields Approach

The utilization of the peer group as an effective treatment agent for the adolescent has many implications beyond the field of correction. Recently, through a grant from the President's Committee on Juvenile Delinquency, Department of Health, Education, and Welfare, a modification of the Essexfields program was initiated in the New Jersey area. Collegefields is a nonresidential treatment center for fourteen- and fifteen-year-old boys. As in the case of the Essexfields program, Collegefields provides a daily experience in guided group interaction. However, instead of the work experience which exists in the Essexfields situation, Collegefields provides an intensive educational experience which is designed to assist potential school dropouts in developing sufficient skills and motivations to want to remain in school after release from the Collegefields program. Consequently, an attempt is being made through this new program to deal with educational limitations as well as delinquent patterns.

More recently, the Kilmer Job Corps Training Center in Edison, New Jersey, has adopted a modification of the Highfields-Essexfields approach in their work with culturally disadvantaged youngsters, ages 16 through 21. At this writing, the plan is to develop approximately 200 peer groups within the total Kilmer setting. Using the guided group interaction approach, it is hoped that norms can be developed within these groups which will make it possible to redirect and reorient the culturally disadvantaged children who will arrive from all sections of the United States.

Other illustrations are beginning to abound in work with adolescents. Child guidance clinics and family service agencies are beginning to re-examine their more traditional approaches to the treatment of the adolescent. It would appear that the potentiality of peer group approaches has hardly been tapped. With a little creativity and imagination, one can easily begin to envision the implications of this approach within school systems themselves. Educators have neglected for many years the group implications of the experience of children in school systems. Hopefully, the Highfields-Essexfields experience may point toward these new directions.

Research Design

An important part of the Essexfields experiment is an evaluation of the project extending over a period of several years. The evaluation includes three aspects: (1) the recidivism study; (2) analysis of the treatment process in the program; and (3) an examination of the experiences and problems encountered by the administration in the course of its brief history.

Research is still under way and data are presently being collected for analysis. These findings will be presented in a later article.[1] However, the results have been encouraging. During the four years of the operation of the Essexfields program, 246 boys were admitted. Fifty boys, or approximately 20 per cent, were found to be unsuitable while in the program and were returned to the Juvenile Court for further disposition. In many of these instances, the boys involved refused to participate in the program, leaving the Essexfields staff no alternative. In some instances, severe psychiatric problems prevented participation, and in only a few instances were boys apprehended while in the program for committing a new offense in the community. Of the remaining 196 boys who successfully completed the program, only 24 boys, or 12 per cent, were commmitted to a correctional institution after their release from Essexfields. This is a remarkable figure as compared with reported recidivist statistics ranging anywhere from 50 to 75 per cent elsewhere. Figures have not as yet been gathered regarding arrest statistics. Additional Essexfields releases have been apprehended for new offenses, but have not been committed to a correctional institution. An analysis of these data will be forthcoming; but present indications seem to imply that even when Essexfields releases do get into trouble again, the nature of their offense is less severe than was their original offense. The above findings will, of course, be compared with the control groups so as to ascertain the true effectiveness of the Essexfields approach.

1. See Stephenson and Scarpitti (1967) for data. In general, the Essexfields program was more effective in terms of recidivism rates than the program at the state reformatory, but less effective than full-residential group treatment centers, and less effective than weekly probation meetings. The latter difference is somewhat tempered by the fact that high-risk boys tended not to complete the probation program.

References

AICHHORN, A.   *Wayward youth.* New York: Viking, 1935.

BRECKENRIDGE, S. P. and ABBOTT, E.   *The delinquent child and the home.* New York: Russell Sage Foundation, 1912.

CLOWARD, R. A. and OHLIN, L. E.   *Delinquency and opportunity.* Glencoe, Ill.: Free Press, 1960.

HEALY, W. and BRONNER, A.   *New light on delinquency and its treatment.* New Haven: Yale University Press, 1936.

McCORKLE, L. W., ELIAS, A. and BIXBY, F. L.   *The Highfields story.* New York: Holt, Rinehart and Winston, 1958.

McCORKLE, L. W. and KORN, R.   Resocialization within walls. *Annals,* 1954, 293, 88-89.

MANNHEIM, H.   *Group problems in crime and punishment.* New York: Humanities Press, 1955.

OHLIN, L. E. and LAWRENCE, W.   Social interaction among clients as a treatment problem. *Social Work,* 1959, 4, 3-13.

REDL, F. and WINEMAN, D.   *Children who hate.* Glencoe, Ill.: Free Press, 1951.

SHAW, C. R. and McKAY, H. D.   *Social factors in juvenile delinquency.* Washington, D.C.: Government Printing Office, 1931.

SLAVSON, S.   *Re-educating the delinquent.* New York: Collier (Macmillan), 1954.

STEPHENSON, R. M. and SCARPITTI, F. H.   *The rehabilitation of delinquent boys.* New Brunswick, N.J.: Rutgers—The State University, 1967.

TANNENBAUM, F.   *Crime and the community.* Boston: Ginn, 1938.

❊ ❊ ❊ ❊ ❊

It was always asserted that the British empire took its far-flung course because the British "public" schools, keeping their upper-class students away from their parents in an intensive residential environment, produced traits of independence, fair-mindedness, and resourcefulness in the young men who became colonial administrators.

This class of assertion has rarely been tested empirically; Winter and his colleagues do so for the case of an American private school, "St. Grottlesex," examining carefully, yet holistically, the impact of the school on public high school students who attended summer sessions there.

That an impact—not wholly the one predicted—does occur on students' "associative network," or imagery produced in response to semi-structured projective materials, is well-documented here. The reader might want to add his speculations to the authors' as to why other standardized measures show no change—and should also take a look at a recent review of studies which have measured motives via projective means (E. Klinger, "Fantasy Need Achievement as a Motivational Construct," *Psychological Bulletin*, 1966, 66 (4), 291-308). The issue of how to predict changes in imagery is by no means straightforward: should a boy who has learned more self-control write stories with that theme in them, or (as the authors suggest) stories about lazy, greedy boys?

Would the study's findings hold up with students of lower ability, drawn from lower-class backgrounds? The pioneer work at the North Carolina Advancement School suggests that residential schools may be worth developing further as an approach to the learning problems of disadvantaged youth. If so, what sort of "personal style" ought to be emphasized?

In passing, the North Carolina experiment came under political attack from its environment [see *Southern Education Report*, 1968, 3 (8)] while St. Grottlesex enjoyed not only immunity but high prestige. What are the implications here?

The Classic Personal Style*

David G. Winter,
Richard Alpert, David C. McClelland

Traditionally, in the United States private schools and colleges lay claim to having a strong influence on character—on the values of their students. Catalogs stress that the purpose of the educational institution is not just to "teach facts," but to develop a capacity for disciplined thought, a lively intellectual curiosity, a concern for service, or a passion for beauty, for goodness, or for truth.

The unfortunate fact is that few carefully controlled research studies have been able to demonstrate any such effects of higher education. As Jacob (1957) has pointed out in his review of these studies, variations in teaching style, in subjects studied, or even in the personalities of the teachers—all seem to make very little difference so far as the values of the students exposed to them are concerned. Is it really true that the educators are all deceived in thinking they influence the lifelong habits of thought and beliefs of their students, or here, as elsewhere, is it the psychologists who are at fault for not having invented sensitive enough measuring instruments to detect the changes that do occur?

The present study was undertaken largely to get some kind of an answer to this question. It grew out of an opportunity provided by a foundation grant to an elite boys' boarding school—here called St. Grottlesex[1]—for a summer advanced study program for bright high school boys from all over the New England state in which the school was located. The purpose of the grant was quite simply to provide a better education for the able boys than they would be likely to get at home, since many of them attended small rural high schools. Yet it also brought into being a miniature social "experiment" in which some but not all boys in the state of high ability were exposed to a dramatically different educational experience for 6 weeks in the

* From *Journal of Abnormal and Social Psychology*, 1963, 67 (3), 254-265. Used by permission of the authors and publisher.

The research reported in this paper was made possible by a grant from the National Institute of Mental Health (M2980) to David C. McClelland, and by the kind cooperation of many staff members at the school and in Department of Education of the state where it was carried out. We also gratefully acknowledge the assistance of Graham Stellwagon and Elliott Gershon in administering the tests.

1. St. Grottlesex is of course a fictitious name, borrowed from McArthur (1955) who used it as others have before him to refer collectively to six prominent New England boarding schools for boys, including the one involved in the present study.

summer. Such an enriched study program would undoubtedy contribute to their factual knowledge, but would it also "change" them as people? Would their values and attitudes be different after this experience as compared to a similar group of boys not exposed to the St. Grottlesex educational atmosphere?

The opportunity seemed a particularly favorable one for demonstrating the effects, if any, of an educational experience on values because St. Grottlesex is a school with the kind of "peculiar potency" which Jacob found is most likely to exert such an influence. It is wealthy, religious, of the highest prestige, attended by children of the best families from cities on the Eastern seaboard, traditional in its approach to education and character building—in short different in almost every respect from the small town public high schools most of these boys were used to. To assess the effects of exposure to such an atmosphere, the psychologist must understand some-what the nature of the educational influence, design tests that will sensi-tively detect its effects, if any, and administer the tests before and after the summer school to boys who attended it and to comparable boys who did not. Finally, he should repeat the whole procedure a second time to make sure the results for the first summer were not an accident. This procedure was followed in the present study and will be described in the order outlined.

Nature of the Educational Experience

What was the nature of the educational influence? Of primary importance is the fact that the summer program was held at St. Grottlesex, directed and staffed largely by regular masters from the school, and supplied with teach-ing interns, many of whom came from such private school backgrounds or at least were currently in attendance at Ivy League colleges. Social rules and living arrangements were largely the same as they were during the regular winter term at St. Grottlesex. In short the summer program was managed according to the social and educational philosophy that guides the school at all times. This philosophy in turn is shaped by the model of the English "public" school, as understood in America in the nineteenth century, and contains elements of Greek thinking about character in the late Classical period. In fact the Greek model was so consciously in the minds of the New England educators that shaped such private schools that we may sensibly refer to their ideal as the "classic personal style." Around the turn of the century Irving Babbitt (1908) of Harvard speaks eloquently for this point of view when he describes ancient Greece as the ideal, as "perhaps the most humane of countries, because it not only formulated clearly the law of measure (nothing too much), but also perceived the avenging Nemesis that overtakes every form of insolent excess or violation of this law [p. 24]." The person who understands this law will naturally tend to stress measure, balance, and wholeness. Education then should develop these qualities. Its end product should be a seasoned, moderate, mature individual with taste, discrimination, and good judgment. Babbitt contrasts such a person with what he calls the typical American "humanitarian" who is indiscriminate in his sympathies for mankind "in the lump" and specialized in his knowledge, "who feels free to burrow ever more and more deeply into his own specialty, like the traditional rat in the Holland cheese. What does it matter, he would seem to argue, if a man himself is but a poor lopsided fragment if only this fragment is serviceable, if only it can be built into the very walls of the Temple of Progress [p. 44]." In short the classic personal style contrasts at almost every point with the typical American style as it would be developed in the public schools (see McClelland, Sturr, Knapp, and Wendt, 1958): it stresses not freedom and self-actualization of the individual, but discipline and respect for tradition; not enthusiastic, "lopsided" action, but reflection and the realization of life's complexities; not achievement and success, but moderation, balance, and selective sympathy; not other-directedness or humanitarian concern but polished wholeness of the individual.

But how much of this educational philosophy really touched the lives of the summer school boys in any significant way? To find out, one of us (DGW) attended the summer session as a participant observer having the status of an intern. That is, he lived in one of the houses and served as an assistant in the educational and social program like the other interns whom he resembled in background, though it was recognized by all that he was there in part to study what was going on. He kept a daily record of what happened and interviewed the participants, often recording what was said for future analysis (cf. Winter, 1960).

Out of the enormous mass of data collected by participant observation, several major "themes" or value emphases of the summer school culture emerged. In many cases they coincided quite closely to the elements in the classic personal style as outlined by Babbitt. A brief description of each will serve to summarize the type of educational influence to which the boys were exposed during the summer.

Themes in the St. Grottlesex Summer School Culture

INTELLECTUAL PRESSURE.   The explicit goal of the summer study program was to provide advanced course work for bright high school sophomores and juniors to prepare them for entry and even advanced placement in good colleges, and thus to set them on their way to high-level careers, thereby checking talent loss throughout the state. This theme was emphasized constantly by the administrative staff, by the masters, by the interns, by the demanding daily schedule, and even eventually by the boys themselves. Entry into a "good" college became a prominent goal for all, as the students questioned the interns, who came from such colleges, as to what life and study was like at college, how one got in, etc.

But the main pressure to increase what the boys expected of themselves came from the course work itself. The academic program was very intensive. Classes of about 10 students met 4–6 hours daily, 6 days each week, for 6 weeks. The goal was to cover a year's work in 6 weeks. Most of the courses were in the science area (chemistry, physics, biology, and mathematics), though all students were required to take 3 hours of English weekly (involving study of both literature and composition) and courses were also in Latin, Greek, Russian, and Modern European history. The courses were taught at a high level, under constant reminders that they had only so many days left to complete the work, and most of the boys soon realized that they had to study harder and at a deeper level than they had ever studied before. As one of them put it, "Up here you find out what real work is, what college work is." Students started getting up before 7 A.M. to study, keeping graphs showing their progressive records on tests and quizzes in mathematics, and complaining that the psychological tests given for this research project "took up homework time."

Obviously, such high pressure is not consonant with the classic ideal of moderation and contemplative browsing in many different intellectual fields. As a matter of fact, there was evidence that it was too career oriented and too demanding to be completely accepted by St. Grottlesex. One faculty wife wondered, "Do they really learn things in this concentrated a period, in this dosage with no break?" A St. Grottlesex master referred to one instructor (from a public high school) as "the mad scientist," and explained, "I couldn't take it, this four straight hours of classes a day, every day, for more than six weeks." Another master expressed wistful admiration for the low energy, low pressure, B− students. He worried about the number of students who were sensitive and nervous under the summer pace, and suggested that imagination and accomplishment under pressure was not always the same thing. The greater respect at St. Grottlesex for the leisurely, non-career oriented, intellectual life showed up more clearly in the Wednesday night programs. They included lectures on *Hamlet* as a symbol of human problems and human life, the contributions of the classic age to contemporary life, probability theory and its applications, and a concert of violin and harpsichord music.

So while the dominant theme was certainly one of pressure for intellectual achievement for immediate practical ends like getting into college and pursuing a high-level career, the school could not help giving some minor clues to the boys that its own idea was cast more in the classical mold of a relaxed enjoyment of the life of the mind.

SELF-CONTROL. Certainly the pressures toward accomplishment and academic effort required sublimation or subordination of desires to "hack around," waste time, or enjoy life as teenagers normally do. But the philosophy of the school went far beyond this in demanding discipline and self-control. The catalog stated, "Students will be expected to use common sense and intelligence in their behavior, and to live amicably, respecting the rights and interests of others." Furthermore, each student accepted into the program was sent information on school regulations, printed in red on a white 3 × 5 card, stating that there was to be no smoking, no drinking, no firearms or possession of explosive materials, and no use of automobiles except to get to and from the school. On arrival at the school each student was assigned an individual room in one of the four dormitories of the "Middle School" (ninth and tenth grades) which form a quadrangle. Each dormitory or "house" was administered by a "housemaster" (who served as such during the winter school also), assisted by the interns. At the opening of school the housemaster explained the rules to the boys thoroughly and justified them as being based on over 100 years of experience of what was good for boys and their life together. They were also told that in town they were not to wear old clothes, to obey the same rules as applied at the school, and stay out of movies, bowling alleys, and poolrooms. Subsequently, there was no hesitation about enforcing any of these rules or those having to do with the daily schedule—rising at 7 A.M., prompt attendance at classes, meals, and chapel, and turning lights out at night at 10:30 P.M.

The tone of disciplinary action was also important. During the opening days, a group of second-year students attempted an initiation of first-year boys, involving wrestling and "roughing around" in the squash court. The director immediately told them that "he liked tradition, but did not approve of this sort of tradition." The disapproval was in calm, yet firm and strong tones. He emphasized that while this behavior might have occurred at high schools, it was not "expected" here. Later at a Saturday night movie, a group of students began to hiss the villain, exclaim at the sight of an appealing woman, etc. The director immediately made a disciplinary remark at the movie, and then at a house meeting following, the housemaster said that the director "wanted me to tell you that this sort of conduct, this hissing and talking and laughing so that others couldn't hear lines, was not looked upon with favor. It was not mature." In short, any display of noisy or boisterous behavior was immediately labeled as "ungentlemanly," "cheap," "immature," or simply "not done" at the school.

The discipline served not only to cut out emotional display, it also was frequently phrased in positive terms that contributed to the formation of a new identity, namely, that of a mature, self-controlled member of an elite. The new self-image was strengthened by the fact that the boys were away from home and could not be visited regularly by their parents, by the fact that they were constantly reminded that they were the "brightest students in the state," and by the fact that they realized that they were attending a "prestige" school with a distinctive social style. They quickly picked up local terminology used in the winter school—e.g., "master," "Tuck shop" (room with beverage machines), "cooler" (infirmary), etc. They were required to wear coats and ties on Sunday mornings and at the Wednesday night supper following the lecture. On the day parents visited, punch was served with a white linen tablecloth and silver ashtrays inscribed with the name of the school. The meals were served in a large dining hall, with each table presided over by a master. Unfamiliar formal manners were taught on the first day: at meals, standing until the director has given a brief prayer, passing food first to the master at the head of the table, holding chairs for ladies, and waiting on formal permission to leave after a meal. Seating charts and attendance slips added to the formality of the meals. The plates were inscribed with the initials and colors of the school, while portraits of past rectors lined the wall. Names of the alumni who had been elected to Phi Beta Kappa were cut into the wooden walls of the Common Room just outside the dining hall. As one student put it, "Everything up here looks so damned aristocratic. It is just the feeling of the place." In short, St. Grottlesex by precept and example tried to develop individuals who realized that the mark of being mature and a member of a privileged minority was good manners or the control of one's tendencies to childish excess— a central part of the classic personal style.

AUTHORITY: IMPERSONAL, STRONG, AND GOOD. One of the almost unique characteristics of St. Grottlesex was its "old-fashioned" respect for authority and tradition. Most American institutions are ambivalent about authority. They realize it is necessary, but are afraid of exercising it too strongly. Certainly the high schools are, since they must share authority with the family. At a boarding school like St. Grottlesex, the parents are told politely but firmly that they must not interfere, that the boy is the school's responsibility while he is in attendance. For example, when one boy was homesick, the Director suggested that the father was not to assist his son unless summoned by the St. Grottlesex authorities expressly. When parents were to visit during "College day," it was stated that, "When the bell rings, shut your mother up, because there will be other mothers there just as eager, and then move them on," and "today you will be encumbered by parents." In place of this personal parental authority, the school was pictured as presenting an impersonal, institutional type of authority, commonly expressed in such phrases as "it is expected that . . . " or "you will report to . . . ," or "it is not done that way here." The authority is impersonal in the sense that it applies equally to everyone. It represents what is right and proper for all. It is also both strong and friendly. The masters and the director who enforced it were sympathetic, yet they kept their distance. The ideal attitude of a student toward a master should be one of friendly respect. As one student remarked, at the school "you get to know the teacher as a person, while at high school you know him as a teacher, an iron hand who gives us the homework, and that is about all you know about him." In other words, the master is not seen as a policeman imposing his will arbitrarily, but as a respected and well-known adult who is interested in the boy's welfare. For it is constantly stressed that the exercise of authority is for the boy's own welfare. Authority is required, but autonomy is the reward; it is exercised for their own good. Here again, the St. Grottlesex practice is very close to the classic ideal. Authority is good; it is based on tradition, or the accumulated wisdom of the past; it does not need to be exercised personally, since its essential correctness can be recognized in its own right; and above all, it is exercised to contribute to the perfection of the individual.

CYNICISM, "SOPHISTICATION." The themes of the summer school culture so far mentioned all represent a high degree of pressure to work hard and be good, for a group of teenage boys accustomed to noisy play, rock-and-roll music, dating, driving around in cars, and going to the beaches in the summertime. The school realized this and arranged for a compulsory athletic program "to let off steam." Some of the boys were surprised that they were required to participate, because they were not particularly gifted athletically. However, the school realized that, in order to maintain the stress on its other values, it must provide some means for encouraging every boy to "let loose" his normal frustrations, aggressions, and emotional impulses. So great stress was put on the athletic program, particularly by the interns who were there to promote it. Eventually nearly all the boys entered into it enthusiastically and it served its purpose. As one student put it, "When I came here I don't think I could say I was looking forward to the athletics; since I've been here, it has been a life saver. You become a nervous wreck unless you have some time to let off steam that was building up in the classroom.

The students soon invented another way of letting off steam, however. Pressured by the demands to do well in their course work, to exercise self-control at all times, and to knuckle under to a friendly yet firm authority, they retaliated with a brand of humorous, yet cynical, mockery. Greek students discussed how the *Iliad* might be phrased in rock-and-roll style; they put signs above their rooms saying, "Welcome to Hades," "Mount Olympus," "Apollo." Another student made a sign recommending that one "Flunk now, avoid the rush," to which someone added, "Why hurry?"

In short, the boys developed a brand of "sophistication" that "prep school boys" are commonly accused of. Since the humor is aggressive and cynical, it allows them to aim some of their hostility directly at the source of their many frustrations, namely, the school and the masters. It also has a certain "superior" or "aloof" tone to it that at one and the same time serves to mimic the way the masters control emotionalism ("we don't do it that way here") and emphasizes the boys' apartness, alienation, or detachment from normal life. The following statement posted in one of the dormitories serves to illustrate not only this theme but several of the others in the summer culture:

A PRAYER FOR DELIVERANCE

We, the people, hereby proclaim that St. Grottlesex School has robbed us of our integrity, our free will, our spare time, our home, our friends and their vices, i.e., smoking, drinking, and marijuana. Shall we tolerate this for an inexorable length of time? Are we to continue to subject ourselves to the torments of this Hades, or shall we like the great priest of Apollo, Chryses, call upon the wrath of Achilles to resolve the unforgivable privations that our dictatorial overseers have thrust upon us. We do not wish to become Spartans. May the great God-man Achilles render unto us the spirit to cast off this yoke of suppression that we might emerge victorious over these haughty and arrogant Trojans, e.g., interns, housemasters, teachers, and the rest of the blimey ilk. Unto thee, great god Achilles, we send this humble supplication by the God messenger Isis. Out of the depths we have cried to thee. Despise not us, great God-man Achilles. Hear our prayer!

The prayer nicely sums up the four themes mentioned so far—the intellectualism (as represented in the classical format of the prayer), impulse control ("robbed us of our vices"), authority ("dictatorial overseers"), and the cynical, sophisticated mocking of the whole situation.

Cynicism is certainly not an explicit goal of the classical ideal, yet humorous detachment certainly is, because humor above all reflects a man's ability to stand apart and see things in balance. Yet even Babbitt (1908) recognized that the sense of superiority that comes from stressing perfection of the individual tends all too easily to slide over into disdain, or contempt for the masses (p. 12). If cynical sophistication is not an explicit ideal of the classic personal style, it is a frequent implicit accompaniment of it.

ANTIHUMANITARIANISM. The final theme in the summer culture was the absence of any particular stress on the dominant American value pattern, called humanitarianism by Babbitt (1908). There was simply not much idealistic talk about what Babbit calls "mankind in the lump, faith in its future progress, and desire to serve the great cause of this progress [p. 7]." In fact, several of the values stressed were directly opposed to the dominant American value creed: the emphasis was on self-control, not self-expression and self-fulfillment; on the authority of tradition, not on what others more or less your own age and status want you to do; on a humorous and somewhat cynical detachment, not on idealism. To make the point even clearer, the Wednesday night lectures dealt with *Hamlet*, probability theory, and harpsichord music, not with racial discrimination, what to do about juvenile delinquency, or how to make the United Nations more effective. For the sake of simplicity, we have labeled this theme "antihumanitarianism," although the school was certainly not so much against humanitarian values as it was simply concerned with other things.

Testing Procedure

Such were the value themes of the St. Grottlesex advanced study program in the summer of 1959, as analyzed by the participant observer. Did they change the attitudes or values of the boys who attended that session? To answer the question the boys were tested in their local high schools in groups May 20-26, 1959, at the start and end of the summer session (June 20 and July 27), and again about 6 months later back in their high schools (January 7-13, 1960). In other words, an attempt was made to follow the course of any changes that occurred by testing before, during, and after the experience. To make certain any changes that might occur were not just due to repeated testing or growing older, matched groups of boys were included in the testing sessions in May and the following January who did not attend the St. Grottlesex summer session.

Every attempt was made to sample a wide variety of attitudes and values in the tests chosen for administration to the boys. The initial selection of tests had to be made without direct knowledge of the themes of the summer culture, but it was based on two general guidelines: that standardized, objective tests, preferably factor analyzed, should be included to assess changes in "established" dimensions of personality and that open-ended or fantasy tests should be included to pick up changes that might not be measured by the more standard procedures. Therefore, Winter (1960) administered a 65-item questionnaire in the May and January sessions, which permitted him to get factor scores on Idealism, Interest in Science, Theoretical Interest, Antireligious sentiments (from Brogden's, 1952, factor analysis of the Allport-Vernon Study of Values), and also scores on Fatalism, Loyalty to the Family, Homework Policy, Willingness to Delay Gratification, etc., after Strodtbeck's (1958) questionnaire for teenagers. To the summer school boys he also gave several other such tests, e.g., the Stern Activities Index, the Semantic Differential (Osgood, Suci, and Tannenbaum, 1957) covering "college," "myself," "my high school," etc., both at the beginning and end of the session (see Winter, 1960).

By and large he found no significant changes in scores on these tests, either immediately following the summer session or in the following January, thus confirming the findings reported by Jacob (1957) in many similar studies. But the results for the tests of imagination or associative processes were more promising. Here the usual procedure was followed of presenting some pictures to the boys in test booklets and asking them to write imaginative stories suggested by the pictures in the 5 minutes allotted for each one. The initial pictures used were from the standard list published by Atkinson (1958, Appendix III, Numbers 88, 8, 1, 52, and 103 in that order), but it was discovered that they did not suggest enough material related to the educational experience. So five new pictures were chosen for the retesting in January that were related to the themes observed in the summer culture. They included pictures of two boys talking at lunch, with a girl in the background; a boy loafing on a bed, reading; boys and a teacher in a classroom; "parents" meeting "master" (in a black tie); man at crossroads (Number 20 in Atkinson's list). Most of these pictures produced the kind of associations about parents, teachers, discipline, and life that were relevant to the educational experience except for the last one which was supposed to elicit material about making choices at the "crossroad of life" but actually produced pretty stereotyped stories. It was replaced by a picture of a boy and a girl seated on a bench by a river in the cross-validating study that was carried out the following summer.

For it was decided that while the changes in associative processes that occurred after the summer experience were interesting and significant, it was essential to duplicate the whole procedure for a variety of reasons. It was desirable to know first of all if the results were peculiar to this particular group of boys, this particular summer session, the presence of the participant observer at the time of retesting or perhaps even the particular time of year at which the retesting was done. In other words we wanted to know how generalizable the results were that had been obtained. Furthermore, in the retest it was possible to eliminate some flaws in the initial design by using improved TAT for initial and final testing and by matching the two groups of boys to be compared better for IQ and educational level of parents. Specifically each group of 34 boys in the 1960 testing averaged about 118.5 in IQ and had fathers whose occupational level averaged between clerical or small business and minor professionals and medium business (4.25 on the Edwards scale where 1 = unskilled labor and 6 = major professionals or business executives; see Strodtbeck, 1958). Parents of both groups averaged about 1 − 1.5 years beyond high school graduation.

One further step was taken to see whether the changes discovered in the tests of imagination were "real" or theoretically meaningful. In February 1960, 23 bright boys from the regular St. Grottlesex winter school were given the test of imagination to see whether they wrote stories more like those that had attended the summer school than those who had not.

Results and Discussion

The results of this rather elaborate testing schedule for 2 successive years may be rather briefly summarized. So far as the objective tests were concerned, there were none of any importance. That is, very few significant changes of any kind appeared in the responses of either group of boys to the objective tests from one administration to another (Winter, 1960). The tests were "reliable" in the sense that the boys gave more or less the same replies when asked the same questions on repeated occasions. Several conclusions are possible from this finding:

1. The summer experience had effects but the tests were not relevant to the effects it had and therefore did not pick them up. The wide variety of tests used does not support this inference.
2. The summer school, despite its apparent potency as a value shaping experience, did not have any lasting effects on the boys' values or attitudes. This is the conclusion that similar studies have reached over and over again, as summarized by Jacob (1957).

3. The summer school had an effect but the objective tests were not sensitive enough to pick it up because many of them were designed to be stable measures of individual differences across variations in the person's life situation.

Support is given this third conclusion by the fact that the projective measuring instrument, the picture-story test, yielded some quite interesting

Table 1

MAIN THEMES IN SUMMER SCHOOL CULTURE AND CATEGORIES
DESIGNED TO DETECT THEIR INFLUENCE IN THE THINKING
OF THE BOYS WHO ATTENDED

THEMES	RELATED CODING CATEGORIES FOR CONTENT OF IMAGINATIVE STORIES[a]
A. Intellectualism, college preparation	+1: Discussion of an intellectual problem +2: Mention of college with a modifying adjective +3: Teacher as intellectual advisor or as the main character in the story
B. Self-control, restraint	+4: Mild impulses, evaluated as bad, e.g., laziness, commercialism, greed, deception (unless a crime), wild behavior, negligence, disorder, etc. 05: Serious bad actions, planned or carried out, e.g., in contrast to 4, murder, rape, fire, war, punishable crimes (not just the result of carelessness or "wildness")
C. Authority: good, strong, impersonal	+6: An influence attempt for a person's "own good" (not out of ill-will), that is competent (not weak or self-doubting), by an "impersonal" agency (either an institution or an unrelated person, e.g., not a parent) 07: An influence attempt that fails on the above counts, e.g., is bad, weak, or personal
D. Cynicism, "sophistication"	+8: Flip or cynical attitude toward the story; "sophisticated" attitude that "things are seldom what they seem," that evil exists in high places, romantic pretensions hide lecherous motives, etc.
E. Antihumanitarianism	−9: Earnest idealism: general social problems, (crime, scientific discoveries, community service, getting ahead, getting married and settling down), that are earnestly and idealistically treated

Note: + = Expected increase after St. Grottlesex Summer School (SGS); − = Expected decrease after SGS; 0 = no expectations after SGS.

[a] Categories have been simplified slightly over Winter's (1960) original list. He also gives a detailed scoring manual and reports coding reliability coefficients varying between .75 and 1.00 for most categories.

results that were consistent across both summer sessions. The thinking of the boys who attended St. Grottlesex summer school underwent some significant changes not shown by their matched controls. Table 1 presents the scoring system that was developed for the stories which was designed to detect the value themes present in the St. Grottlesex atmosphere. The categories are described briefly on the right-hand side of the table opposite the values they are related to, and in most cases the nature of the relationship is so obvious as not to require further explanation. For example, it was suspected that if the high pressure, intellectual atmosphere of the summer school had a permanent effect on a boy's thinking, then when he was presented with a picture suggesting a discussion between two boys some 6 or 8 months later, his thoughts should turn more readily to a discussion centering on an intellectual problem than on some other adolescent interest like girls or cars. Or if this same high pressure had made the boys more aware of colleges or differences among colleges, then they should write more stories in which a particular college was mentioned or characterized in some special way. If self-control had become more dominant as an issue in their lives, then they should tell more stories about boys who were having difficulty with impulses to be lazy, greedy, negligent, or disorderly. If the normal American value emphasis on self-expression for the good of society was underemphasized, then there should be a decrease in the number of vaguely idealistic stories having to do with scientific progress, bringing about world peace, reducing juvenile delinquency, etc. The scoring categories were derived partly a priori and partly by comparing in detail 10 protocols from the January 1960 testing written by boys who had attended St. Grottlesex with 10 others written by boys who had not been there. More details on the scoring system are given by Winter (1960), who reports scoring reliability coefficients varying between .75 and 1.00 for most categories. Differences obtained from comparing the initial two sets of 10 protocols were subsequently cross-checked on the remaining protocols for the 1959 session and also for the 1960 session without the knowledge of which protocols were produced by which group of boys. Since the 1960 results provide an adequate cross-check of the 1959 findings, the data from the 1959 sample presented in Table 2 include those subjects whose protocols were used to set up the scoring system.

The main results of the study, as brought together in summary form in Table 2, prove to be quite interesting in the sense that they confirm our expectation that the St. Grottlesex value atmosphere had a lasting effect on the boys who attended summer school there, though not always exactly as expected. In the 1959 session, each of the themes of the summer culture affected the boys' thinking significantly in some way as contrasted with the thinking of matched boys who had not been there. But the effect of the intellectual high pressure was not very strong or lasting, at least as it was picked up by our measuring instrument. Significantly more of the summer school boys wrote stories dealing with intellectual discussion in January, but

Table 2

CHANGES IN CONTENT OF STORIES WRITTEN BY BOYS ATTENDING AND NOT ATTENDING SUMMER SCHOOL IN 1959 AND 1960

	SUMMER OF 1959 GROUP TESTING IN HIGH SCHOOLS					SUMMER OF 1960 GROUP TESTING IN HIGH SCHOOLS				
	BEFORE (MAY 1959) N	%[a]	AFTER (JAN. 1960) N	%[a]	DIFF. (A−B)	BEFORE (MAY 1960) N	%[a]	AFTER (MARCH 1961) N	%[a]	DIFF. (A−B)
A. Intellectual discussion (1)										
Winter school (W)			23	48				30	33	
Summer school (S)	32	9	32	69		32	9	30	33	
No summer school (NS)	30	10	30	33		31	13	28	39	
Difference (S−NS)				36					−8	
p diff.				<.01					*ns*	
	BEFORE N	M	AFTER N	M	DIFF. (A−B)	BEFORE N	M	AFTER N	M	DIFF. (A−B)
B. Mild bad impulses (4)										
W				1.61					.73	
S		.53		1.16	+.63		.13		.73	+.60
NS		.33		.30	−.03		.10		.25	+.15
Difference (S−NS)					.66					.45
p diff.					<.05					<.02[b]
C. Authority (6)										
W				.52					.13	
S (good, strong)		.28		1.03	+.75		.19		.13	−.06
NS (impersonal)		.67		.40	−.27		.13		.18	+.05
Difference (S−NS)					1.02					−.11
p diff.					<.001					*ns*

Table 2 (CONTINUED)

CHANGES IN CONTEXT OF STORIES WRITTEN BY BOYS ATTENDING AND NOT ATTENDING SUMMER SCHOOL IN 1959 AND 1960

	SUMMER OF 1959					SUMMER OF 1960				
	GROUP TESTING IN HIGH SCHOOLS					GROUP TESTING IN HIGH SCHOOLS				
	BEFORE (MAY 1959)		AFTER (JAN. 1960)		DIFF. (A−B)	BEFORE (MAY 1960)		AFTER (MARCH 1961)		DIFF. (A−B)
	N	%[a]	N	%[a]		N	%[a]	N	%[a]	
		M		M			M		M	
D. Cynicism (8)										
W				1.22					1.23	
S		.84		1.75	.91		.38		1.23	.85
NS		.70		.60	−.10		.29		.71	.42
Difference (S−NS)					1.01					.43
p diff.					<.05					<.10[b]
E. Earnest (9)										
W				.48						
S (idealism)		2.50		.84	−1.66		2.56		1.67	−.89
NS		2.27		2.10	−.17		2.19		2.07	−.12
Difference (S−NS)					1.49					.77
p diff.					<.01					<.05[b]

Note: Letters refer to themes, numbers to scoring categories in Table 1.

[a] Percentage of boys who mention an intellectual discussion in at least one story.

[b] p values are in the predicted direction and based on t tests for paired differences, using only those subjects on whom both a Before and After measure were available. The means are based on the full number of cases.

there was no difference in the other two categories to tap the same influence, and the difference did not appear at all in the comparison of the two groups of boys following the summer of 1960. Furthermore, the winter school boys also showed no significantly greater concern with intellectual matters than boys who had never left their high schools. This brings up an interesting point, noted earlier: the intellectual high pressure of the summer session was in many ways at variance with the St. Grottlesex ideal and also the ideal of the classic personal style. Such intensive concentration, such concern with academic and career achievement, such specialization, was really foreign to the normal value climate of the school. Perhaps this idea was conveyed to the boys by the "aristocratic feel" of the place or by subtle attitudes of the masters. At any rate, the effect of the intellectual high pressure was not marked after the 1959 session and not detectable at all after the 1960 session.

The other effect found in 1959 and not in 1960 deals with the way boys represented authority in their stories. As expected, the boys who attended the 1959 session wrote more stories which depicted authority as good, strong, and impersonal. They seem to have interiorized the stress the school placed on viewing authority in a positive light which was acting impersonally for the welfare of others. However, it is again interesting to note that the boys attending the winter school where this influence, if anything, should have been even stronger, also did not show much evidence of its making a significant impression on the way they wrote about authority. And so far as the 1960 session is concerned, no results or trends of any kind are observable, although, since the frequency of this story theme is so much lower than for the 1959 protocols, one might suspect that the scorer had lost some feeling for the category. On the whole, however, one must conclude that the view of authority presented by the school does not get through to the boys very effectively, at least in the sense of modifying their conception of authority. One might argue that the prevailing American conception of authority as often arbitrary and ineffective or weak (see Wolfenstein and Leites, 1950) is simply too strong to be significantly altered by experience at the school.

The remaining effects are marked: they occurred following both summer sessions and in the thinking of the winter school boys. In the protocols of the boys who came under the influence of St. Grottlesex School, shiftlessness, impulsiveness, and emotionality are mentioned more often and in negative terms; a sophisticated, cynical approach to life is more frequent; and few stories are written dealing with vague idealistic or humanitarian goals. The stress the school consciously or unconsciously puts on self-control, on selective sympathy (or alienation from the masses), and on perfection of the individual rather than "mankind in the lump" gets through to the boys and significantly alters their thinking about these matters. The classic personal style is not only promoted at St. Grottlesex, it is apparently effective in influencing the thinking of boys who have been exposed to it for only 6 weeks.

Two questions might be raised about this conclusion—one methodological the other substantive. The methodological problem arises from the fact that as in all natural experiments, the boys who underwent the educational "treatment" were not randomly selected. Does not the very fact that they chose to go and study hard all summer make them really different from the otherwise comparable boys who stayed home? And if they are really different, may that not mean that the subsequent differences in their thinking are not due to the St. Grottlesex experience but to different maturing patterns in, say, serious and "not-so-serious" boys? Perhaps, but such skepticism can be challenged fairly effectively on two grounds: a number of the boys in the control groups would have liked to go to St. Grottlesex and were even chosen for entry but could not because they had to work. Even more importantly, it is hard to imagine how results so specifically related to the educational experience could have occurred in the natural course of growing up for one type of boy rather than another.

The substantive query about the findings boils down to this: what importance do they have? After all, we have only shown that the boys' fantasies have changed a little. Is that of real significance so far as their future behavior is concerned? To consider the question a little more vividly, let us compare some stories written by a boy before and after the summer school experience which typify the average trends shown in Table 2. The italicized phrases are coded according to the category numbers shown which refer back to Table 1.

[Before, May testing] This is a student working on a *chemical research*
[9]
project. Here he is staying up until the wee hours of the morning trying to make his computations balance. He asks himself, "What could I have done wrong?" "I checked this experiment twenty-five times and it still won't work." Rather than take a breather, he keeps pondering over his problem—checking and rechecking his procedure. Seeing no solution to the problem as yet, his attitude is something like "Well, it's going to be a long night."

[After, January testing] Here is a college sophomore *who believes in*
[4]
not killing himself. Unfortunately, this idea carries over into his school work too! He is more interested in the daily scratch sheet than his history
[8]
homework! *"Too much concentration ruins the mind."* After all, his father is rich enough to send him to college, so he should be entitled to a little fun. *He doesn't have to work off his head like those scholarship*
[8]
boys, anyhow! His idea of college life is *football games, rallies, fast cars,*
[8]
girls, and high living. And when he graduates, he will be a man of the world.

These stories were written by the same boy. *Before* he writes an *earnest, idealistic story* (Category 9, Table 1) about a student staying up late to work hard on a chemical research project. This is typical of the "romantic" high school culture before it is eroded away by the sophistication of the "prep school" climate. *Afterwards* he writes cynically of a wild college sophomore who *unfortunately* is not doing his school work either. In other words he describes the laziness and high living (mild bad impulses) but evaluates then negatively (Category 4, Table 1). Furthermore his cynical or "flip" attitude is repeatedly evident: "too much concentration ruins the mind," "doesn't have to work like those scholarship boys," and "fast cars, girls, and high living" equals "man of the world" (Category 8, Table 1). Both quantitatively and qualitatively the second story illustrates concretely three of the characteristics of what we have called the classic personal style: absence of earnest idealism, presence of many wild impulses that are negatively evaluated (that need controlling), and presence of a cynical, "flip," sophisticated, or superior attitude toward life or the masses (represented by the "scholarship boys").

Now to return to our earlier question, is this an important change? What has happened to the boy and others like him? In the most literal sense, their "associative network" has been changed. When a certain issue comes up like studying, it reminds them of different things. For example, in this boy's mind "bad impulses" are much more prominent as alternatives to studying. He does not evaluate the impulse life differently afterwards, so far as we can tell from his answers to items on objective tests dealing with the issue. But the *salience* of the issue has changed. When he is asked to produce his own ideas, rather than choose among equally salient alternatives as in a questionnaire, impulse control emerges as a more prominent issue after the summer experience than it was before.

How extensively has the associative network changed in these boys? Are the new associative chains cued off only by circumstances very similar to the St. Grottlesex experience or are they now the boys' normal pattern of thought about life? Our testing conditions—particularly in 1960—were removed sufficiently from the St. Grottlesex setting to indicate some generality and importance for the associative changes. They were detected 8 months after the summer experience in 1960, in the high school in the presence of strange test administrators not connected with St. Grottlesex, after the boys had readapted to their normal home and school environments. One has good reason to expect that these thoughts will continue recurring and shaping the behavior of the St. Grottlesex boys for some time to come.

However, it is equally obvious that these thoughts will not be elicited under all social conditions. Some of our own results illustrate the point. We made an attempt in the 1960 study to get a larger sample by sending the tests by mail to rural high schools to be filled out by matched and control boys both for the before and after testing. None of the results shown in

Table 2 was obtained for the groups tested by mail.[2] The simplest explanation of this failure appears to be that the changes observed in the associative network will not show up under all social conditions. Enough extraneous cues were introduced in the individual testing by mail to cancel out any general effects produced by the summer school. Or the social cues of a rural high school or a rural setting are so different from the St. Grottlesex social cues that the associations connected with St. Grottlesex are simply not aroused. In short, the new associations learned in the school appear under *some* other social conditions, but not all. Nevertheless, the very fact that we are dealing with fantasy, or changes in the associative network, practically insures a greater degree of generality of the change than if an overt response was involved. Consider learning to type, for example. One can show the response only when a typewriter is available and when one is not doing other things, e.g., reading, walking, listening to a teacher, but one can *think* about typing (or about impulse control) at any time or place.

2. The "earnest idealism" variable is a possible exception. While only about 4% of the 45 subjects in each group wrote *no* stories containing earnest idealism before the summer, 26% of the boys who attended St. Grottlesex wrote no such stories the following March as contrasted with 8% of the boys not attending St. Grottlesex ($\chi^2 = 4.29$, $p < .05$). While the difference in the mean number of such stories written by the two groups was not significant, apparently there were a few boys who were so markedly affected by the summer school experience that they showed its impact even under these uncontrolled testing conditions.

References

ATKINSON, J. W. *Motives in fantasy, action, and society*. Princeton: Van Nostrand, 1958.

BABBITT, I. *Literature and the American college*. Boston: Houghton Mifflin, 1908.

BROGDEN, H. E. The primary personal values measured by the Allport-Vernon test, "A Study of Values." *Psychological Monographs*, 1952, 66 (16, Whole No. 348).

JACOB, P.E. *Changing values in college*. New York: Harper, 1957.

McARTHUR, C. C. Personality differences between middle and upper classes. *Journal of Abnormal and Social Psychology*, 1955, 50, 247-256.

McCLELLAND D. C., STURR, J., KNAPP, R. H. and WENDT, H. W. Obligation to self and society. *Journal of Abnormal and Social Psychology*, 1958, 56, 245-255.

OSGOOD, C. E., SUCI, G. J. and TANNENBAUM, P. H. *The measurement of meaning*. Urbana: University of Illinois Press, 1957.

STRODTBECK, F. L. Family interaction, values and achievement. In D. C. McClelland, A. L. Baldwin, U. Bronfenbrenner, and F. L. Strodtbeck (Eds.), *Talent and society*. Princeton: Van Nostrand, 1958.

WINTER, D. G. Personality effects of a summer advanced studies program. Unpublished bachelor's thesis, Harvard University, 1960.

WOLFENSTEIN, M. and LEITES, N. *Movies: A psychological study*. Glencoe, Ill.: Free Press, 1950.

✻ ✻ ✻ ✻ ✻

Like Barker and his colleagues, whose work is represented in the opening selection of this volume, Robert Pace has devoted much of his career
to the systematic measurement of environments, college environments in
particular. He and his associate, George Stern, drew their inspiration for
the College Characteristics Index (CCI) from the noted Harvard psychologist, Henry Murray, and they put into operational terms Murray's theoretical concept of *environmental press*. One of the features of the Pace-
Stern measure of "college press" is the potential it offers in pairing press
with parallel measures of psychological needs. This potentiality, contained
in Murray's elaboration of his theoretical system, was not lost on the investigators, and a parallel measure was, indeed, constructed. Thus, the old
question of the relative influence of persons and their surrounding environment on important variables can be assessed. In subsequent years the CCI
has been thoroughly revised and now is published as CUES (College and
University Environment Scales).

It is noteworthy, we believe, that this significant methodological contribution to social psychology has taken place wholly inside of education,
and in response to educational issues. It illustrates the fact that advances
in science often come through the struggle to illuminate immediate problems of practice, such as counseling students with respect to college attendance, and not through "pure research" alone.

The Pace article is retained from the first edition of the *Readings*. To
review the large amount of research that has gone into the CCI and CUES
since 1960, the date of the original selection, the editors asked Professor
Pace to furnish an Epilogue. This he has done, borrowing from the introductory section of a report on one of his most recent investigations.

Differences in Campus Atmosphere*

C. Robert Pace

What are the experiences and conditions for student learning and living which a college provides? Whatever they may be, they define the environment, the college culture, the campus atmosphere. To some extent, of course, the character of a college is determined by the character of the students it admits. Other information about a college however is much more commonly available. How large is it, is it coeducational or not, where is it located, when was it founded, what degrees does it offer, is it public or private, religious or non-sectarian, what does it cost? Having learned the answer to all these questions, one knows little that is important about a college. Suppose one asked the same kind of questions about a prospective college student. What is his height and weight, sex, residence, age, vocational goal, religious affiliation, and family income? Knowing all these things, one is still left in ignorance about what kind of a person the prospective student really is. The important knowledge concerns his aptitudes and interests, his motivations, and emotional and social maturity. In short, the crucial knowledge concerns his personality. So too with the college. The crucial knowledge concerns its over-all atmosphere or characteristics, the kinds of things that are rewarded, encouraged, emphasized, the style of life which is valued in the community and is most visibly expressed and felt.

The concept of environmental press was described in 1938 by the psychologist Henry Murray. Individuals were seen as having characteristic needs, and the strength and relationships of these needs was what characterized the personality. In corollary fashion, the environment was seen as having potentials for satisfying or frustrating these needs. The model for studying behavior was thus the interaction between personality needs and environmental press. Stern, Stein, and Bloom (1956) elaborated this need-press concept by applying it to assessment studies and showing that the prediction of performance was improved as one defined the psychological demands of the situation in which the performance was to occur. The psychological demands of the situation are the environmental press. Pace and Stern (1957) constructed the first version of a test, called the College

* From W. W. Charters and N. L. Gage (Eds.) *Readings in the social psychology of education.* Boston: Allyn and Bacon, 1963. Pp. 73-79. "Epilogue" adapted from C. R. Pace, *Analyses of a national sample of college environments.* Washington: U. S. Office of Education, Bureau of Research, 1967. Final Report, Project No. 5-0764, Contract No. OE 5-1-321. Used by permission of the author and publisher.

Characteristics Index (CCI), applying the concept of environmental press to the study of college atmospheres. The instrument was constructed as a parallel to the Activities Index (AI), which is an inventory of personality needs that had been previously constructed by Stern (1956). Thus, a pattern of personality needs scales was paralleled by a corresponding pattern of environmental press scales. For example, a personality need for Order would be suggested by liking such activities as: "keeping an accurate record of the money I spend," "arranging my clothes neatly before going to bed," etc. An environmental press for Order would be suggested by such features of the college as: "professors usually take attendance in class," "in many classes students have an assigned seat," etc.

Each instrument, the AI and the CCI, consists of 30 scales of 10 items, or a total of 300 items. In answering the CCI, students act as reporters, saying what they believe is generally true or not true of their college. The items refer to a wide range of topics—rules and regulations, facilities, student-faculty relationships, classroom methods, extra-curricular activities, etc. The argument is that all these characteristics and events and practices, added together, constitute an educational press upon the students. The aggregate awareness of students about their college environment constitutes a press in the sense of exerting a directive influence on their behavior. Preliminary results were reported by Pace and Stern (1958).

In the late 1950's, groups of students in approximately 100 different colleges filled out the CCI.[1] In the Spring of 1959 a norm group of 32 colleges, representing a wide assortment of sizes and locations and shapes, was selected to develop standard scores for the scales. Much is now known about college environments from this testing activity and from various studies that have been made of the data. Some of the major results are described below.

Some things are true about all colleges. Students everywhere agree that certain things are true about their college. By agree is meant that at least 4 out of 5 students across the total norm group of 32 colleges, and at least 3 out of 4 in each sub-category of the norm group (private liberal arts, denominational liberal arts, universities, education, engineering, and business) describe press identically.

Thus, it is generally reported as true everywhere that—

> There are many opportunities for students to get together in extra-curricular activities.
>
> There is a lot of excitement and restlessness just before holidays.
>
> Student papers and reports must be neat.
>
> Classrooms are kept clean and tidy.
>
> Most courses are very well organized and progress systematically from week to week.
>
> Most of the professors are dedicated scholars in their fields.

1. Support for parts of this research program has come from the College Entrance Examination Board, the Carnegie Corporation, the Social Science Research Council, and the Cooperative Research Branch of the U.S. Office of Education.

Similarly, it is generally reported as false everywhere that —

> If a student wants help he usually has to answer a lot of embarrassing questions.
>
> Students don't argue with the professors; they just admit that they are wrong.
>
> When students dislike a faculty member they make it evident to him.
>
> Students pay little attention to rules and regulations.
>
> The student leaders here have lots of special privileges.
>
> There are practically no student organizations actively involved in campus or community reforms.
>
> Spontaneous student rallies and demonstrations occur frequently.
>
> The campus and buildings always look a little unkempt.
>
> "Alma mater" seems to be more important than "subject matter" at this school.
>
> Students who work hard for high grades are likely to be regarded as odd.

In short, one might say that college campuses and classrooms are generally well manicured, the students are not especially belligerent or demontrative[2] but neither are they uninterested in reforms, faculty members are scholarly, and there is no stigma attached to hard work and honest inquiry.

Beyond these few common characteristics, however, colleges are vastly different from one another. By comparing the rank order of mean scores on the 30 scales one gets a general index of the degree of similarity between one environment and another. For the 32 institutions these rank order correlations ranged from $+.93$ to $-.87$ (Pace, 1960). Among some colleges the relative environmental pressures are nearly identical; among others the relative pressures are almost totally opposite. Between Swarthmore and Hamline, for example, there were 70 items characteristic of both schools, with characteristic being defined as agreement by 3 out of 4 students, or more. Sixteen items, however, were answered in exactly the opposite ways at the two schools, meaning that more than 3 out of 4 students at one school said "yes" and more than 3 out of 4 students at the other school said "no." Here are some of these opposite characteristics:

> Most courses require a lot of library work.
>
> The professors really push the students' capacities to the limit.
>
> Concerts and art exhibits always draw big crowds of students.
>
> Students address faculty members as professor or doctor.
>
> Professors usually take attendance in class.
>
> There is a recognized group of student leaders.
>
> Pep rallies, parades, dances, carnivals, or demonstrations occur very rarely.
>
> Education here tends to make students more realistic and practical.

2. The reader is reminded that these data were collected in the late 1950's. *Ed.*

Moreover, the familiar structural classifications of schools—as liberal arts or professional, college or university, non-sectarian or denominational—are not very good indicators of environmental press similarity. Among schools in any one of these structural categories the rank order correlation of the press scales range from high to zero and sometimes negative.

The differences between college environments, across a wide assortment of schools, fall into several fairly clear patterns. There are certain kinds of pressures or characteristics which tend to go together in college environments generally. Five such clusters were described in Pace (1960). The first two are both strongly intellectual, with one more strongly oriented toward humanism, sentience, and reflectiveness, and the other more strongly oriented toward scientism, uncertainty, and competition. The third cluster emphasizes the practical and applied rather than the abstract or theoretical, and is heavily concerned with establishing status in relation to peers and accepting status in relation to authority. The fourth cluster exhibits a strong press toward group welfare, human relations, and social responsibility. And the fifth cluster suggests a rebellion against the well managed, group welfare oriented community.

These clusters form a pattern of interrelationships. The humanistic and scientific clusters are positively related, owing to their common intellectual component, and both are negatively related to the practical, status-oriented cluster. The humanistic cluster, however, is unrelated to either the social welfare or the rebellion clusters. The scientific cluster, on the other hand, is negatively related to social welfare and positively related to rebellion. The practical, status-oriented cluster has a positive but low relationship to social welfare, and a somewhat higher positive relationship to rebellion.

This same pattern which is true nationally is also true within the environments of individual colleges. The profiles of Vassar and Antioch illustrate this point. (See Figure 1.) These profiles show the complete range of standard score means for all of the scales included in each cluster. In both colleges the intellectual-humanistic-scientific clusters emerge as the strongest emphasis in the environment, with the practical, status-oriented cluster being correspondingly low. At Vassar the rebellion emphasis is about average. At Antioch the social welfare emphasis is about average. Rebellion is somewhat higher at Antioch and social welfare is somewhat lower at Vassar. Comparing the two schools, one finds Antioch having the stronger scientific press, and also being higher in rebellion and in social welfare.

Syracuse, as its profile shows, emerges as a high practical, status-oriented environment, with correspondingly lower press toward humanism and scientism. It is average in its emphasis on social welfare, and high on the rebellion cluster. Some schools have a relatively flat profile, as seen in the example of San Jose State College. Its strongest press is in the practical, status-oriented direction, but it is neither very high nor very low on any of the press clusters

For the most part, as the examples indicate, the variables fall into distinctive patterns within individual colleges. There is a dominant character which emerges.

Distinctive patterns of college environments have predictable and demonstrable consequences. A number of validity studies have been made which lend support to this statement. For many of the colleges that have been studied, a variety of additional data from educational directories and other sources has been correlated with the environmental press data. For example, the intellectuality of the college environments, as measured, should have a positive relationship with intellectually motivated behavior of students and with other features of a college commonly supposed to contribute to the intellectuality of the college. The per cent of students who go on to graduate school would be an example of intellectually motivated behavior; the adequacy of library resources would be an example of a

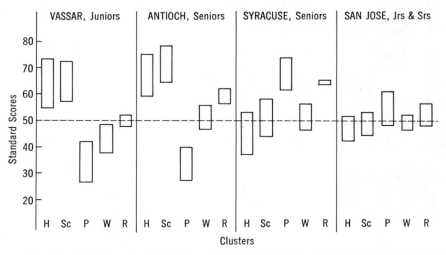

H = Humanistic (Humanism, Reflectiveness, Sentience, Understanding, Achievement, Energy, Objectivity)
Sc = Scientific (Scientism, Change, Fantasied Achievement, Low Supervision, Low Order)
P = Practical (Practicality, Abasement, Dominance, Play, Sex)
W = Welfare (Affiliation, Nurturance, Succorance, Conjunctivity)
R = Rebellion (Aggression, Impulsion)

The standard score scale has a mean of 50, and a sigma of 20. The bars in the chart show the range of mean standard scores for the variables included in each cluster.

Figure 1. Four College Profiles on the CCI.

condition or feature which presumably contributes to intellectuality. Similar logical or expected relationships with other patterns or clusters of environmental press were also studied. The results of these correlational studies are shown in Table 1.[3] The correlations are Pearson r's except when labeled otherwise. For the CCI clusters, the mean of the scales comprising the cluster was used to characterize the college.

3. The correlation data were assembled by Sheila Best as part of a master's thesis at Syracuse University.

Table 1

CORRELATIONS BETWEEN CCI DATA AND OTHER
INFORMATION ABOUT COLLEGES

| | | CCI CLUSTERS | |
NUMBER OF COLLEGES	OTHER INFORMATION OR VARIABLES	INTELLECTUAL-HUMANISTIC	INTELLECTUAL-SCIENTIFIC
10	Per cent men who go to graduate school	.80	.79
10	Per cent women who go to graduate school	.84	.93
33	Productivity index AHSS (See note below)	.47	
33	Productivity index NS (See note below)		.25
17	Attainment index (See note below)	.48	*
11	SAT verbal score of applicants	.89	
12	SAT math score of applicants		.50
36	National Merit Scholarship Corporation test score of students	.55	.49
41	Ratio library volumes to enrollment	.61	.66
41	Ratio library periodicals to enrollment	.51	.51
41	Ratio money spent on library to enrollment	.51	.59
15	Per cent Ph.D.s on total faculty	.53	.59
38	Per cent Ph.D.s on full time faculty	.33	*
17	Honors program	*	.45
17	Per cent seniors in Liberal Arts	.62	*
36	Percent majoring in "intellectual" subjects	.31	.38

		PRACTICAL-STATUS	
17	Per cent seniors in applied fields		.36
8	Per cent students from same state		.63
17	Having fraternities or sororities	C†	.52
50	State supported	C	.40

		GROUP WELFARE	
17	Index of student involvement (See note below)		.48
17	Per cent full-time students		*
39	Per cent full-time faculty		*
16	Per cent faculty in American Association of University Professors		.73
13	Per cent alumni contributing to alumni fund		*
50	Church-related	C	.39

		SPECIFIC CCI SCALES		
50	Church-related	Abasement		*
50	Church-related	Closeness of Supervision	C	.33
50	Church-related	Deference	C	.32
50	Church-related	Order	C	.31
50	Church-related	Nurturance	C	.55
50	Church-related	Succorance	C	.40

* Not significant.

† *C* designates contingency coefficient.

Note: Productivity index "Arts, Humanities, and Social Sciences" and "Natural Sciences." For a description of these, see Thistlethwaite, 1959 (b).

Attainment index and Index of Student Involvement. For a description of these see Rogoff, 1957.

The table shows 28 correlations with the intellectual-humanistic and the intellectual-scientific press of the environment. Twenty-four of these are significant in the expected direction. Four other correlations are with the practical-status press of the environment. All are significant. Six relationships are reported with the group welfare press. Three of the six are significant. Six relationships are shown between specific CCI scales and the religious orientation of the college. Five of the six are significant. In other words, many features or conditions or types of behavior which one would expect to find associated with different patterns of environmental press are, in fact, associated with them.

The best evidence that different environments have a differential influence on the behavior of students comes from studies made by Thistlethwaite (1959a):

> One type of college environment is associated with achievement in the natural sciences, while a different kind of environment is related to accomplishment in the arts, humanities, and social sciences. Productivity in the humanities is positively related to Humanism, Reflectiveness, Sentience, Harm-avoidance, and Understanding. It is negatively related to Pragmatism, Deference, and Abasement. Productivity in the natural sciences is positively related to Scientism, Aggression, and Impulsion, and negatively related to Order, Deference, and Sentience.

He went on to point out that there was some ambiguity in these results owing to the fact that most of the CCI scales contained items which referred to students as well as to faculty or other non-student aspects of the environment. He proceeded, therefore, to revise the scales into two categories, one referring only to the student press, and the other referring only to the faculty press. With these revised scales he found that

> . . . student cultures characterized by Humanism, Breadth of Interest, and Reflectiveness are associated with scholarly productivity (humanistic), whereas cultures characterized by Participation and Aggression are negatively related. . . . Motivation to seek the Ph.D. in the natural sciences, on the other hand, seems to be stimulated by student cultures which are high in Scientism and Aggression and inhibited by those which stress Social Conformity.

Then, considering only the faculty press scales, he found that ". . . colleges outstandingly successful in encouraging undergraduates to get the doctorate in humanistic fields are characterized by excellent social science faculty and resources, a flexible, or somewhat unstructured curriculum, energy and controversiality of instruction, and informality and warmth of student-faculty contacts . . ."

Colleges high in natural science productivity are characterized, also, by informality and warmth of student-faculty contacts, but, beyond this, they are characterized by relatively non-directive or non-predictable teaching methods and the lack of close supervision. In a study in 1960 Thistlethwaite predicted that motivation to seek graduate education would be associated with certain characteristics of faculty and student press in the undergraduate college environment. He found that all his predictions about faculty press were confirmed, but that there was no evidence that student press influenced the aspirations of the National Merit students he studied. It seems quite clear from these studies that different college environments do have demonstrable consequences on student behavior, over and above the student culture which is part of the total college culture.

To the question, "Do students make the college?," the answer is both yes and no. There are results from the AI and CCI, administered to students in 43 colleges, which show clearly that students with strong needs in certain directions tend to be found at colleges which exert a strong press in those same directions. The public image which a college has makes it especially attractive to students who sense that they would find such an environment congenial to them.

A correlation matrix was developed, based on the mean AI scores, and the mean CCI scores, for this group of 43 schools.[4] This shows the extent to which students with certain kinds of needs are found in institutions with corresponding kinds of press. For three selected and most important scales in the humanistic press cluster—humanism, reflectiveness, and sentience— the median correlation with the three corresponding personality needs scales is .55. For the three most important scales in the science cluster— scientism, change, and negative order—the correlation with the corresponding three personality needs scales is .54. For the three most diagnostic scales in the practical-status cluster—practicality, dominance, and play—the correlation with the three corresponding personality needs scales is .23. For the four scales in the social welfare cluster, the correlation with the parallel personality scales is .60. And for the two scales in the rebellion cluster, the correlation with the parallel personality scales is .54. The median correlation between all thirty parallel need-press scales is .35. For the special scales noted above, it appears that the similarity between student bodies and college environments is indicated by a correlation of about .55. Translating this relationship into other statistical language, and projecting its meaning onto a broader plane, one might suggest that about 30 per cent of the distinctive environment of a school is accounted for by the distinctive character of the students it admits. This leaves much of the potential impact of a college squarely up to the decisions of its faculty, administration, and trustees. Environmental press is clearly more than the student culture alone.

Summarizing, and turning to implications, one can say that it now seems possible and certainly fruitful to think about the college environment as a whole. Many apparently disparate pieces of the environment fit together in a pattern of relationships, and these pieces cut across the familiar parts

---

4. This matrix was prepared by George Stern, as part of an Office of Education-sponsored research project, directed jointly by Pace and Stern.

into which environments have usually been divided. Across the national scene the patterns of college culture illustrate the diversity of higher education. With variations in emphasis, the same patterns are revealed in the environments of individual colleges and illustrate the uniqueness of certain institutions. There are predictable and demonstrable consequences which follow from different major patterns of emphasis in college environments. These consequences cannot be fully explained by the selective distribution of students to environments which are already congruent with their needs. Nor can they be explained fully by the influence of student characteristics or student life within the total culture of the college.

The most important implication for evaluation studies lies in the new awareness of relationship between many different parts of the college environment. Whether a college class is taught by lectures or by discussions, whether the class size is large or small, whether the professor is permissive or strict, whether counseling is directive or non-directive, whether teaching machines or audio-visual aids are used liberally or not at all, whether general education courses are required or are selected from alternative offerings, all these, and many others, are relatively small phenomena in the total college culture. They are separately important, of course. But their real significance, and the clue to their influence, lies in the relationships between them. Do they "add up" to some dominant direction? Or is their possible influence dissipated through isolation and lack of reinforcement from the rest of the college environment? To the extent that a college environment is an unrelated assortment of policies and practices and events and features, its influence upon the student is probably small. To the extent that a college environment is a culture, in the anthropologist's sense of the word, its influence on the student is probably large.

Epilogue

CUES: a New Measure of College Environments

Differences between college students, and between the student bodies at different campuses, have long been familiar to psychologists and educators; but the systematic study of college environments is a much more recent enterprise. College & University Environment Scales (CUES) was published by Educational Testing Service in the spring of 1963, and its availability has resulted in considerable use by researchers and college administrators. CUES was an outgrowth of the College Characteristics Index (CCI), developed jointly by the present writer and George Stern in 1957, and discussed in the preceding article.

In 1958-59, the CCI had been used by some 50 or 60 institutions, and from these reports a tentative norm group of 32 colleges and universities had been selected. When the data were analyzed to show the major dimensions along which institutions differed, using the mean score of institutions as the unit of analysis rather than scores of individual students, four factors, or directions of environmental press, seemed to emerge: an intellectual, humanistic, esthetic press; a friendly, group welfare press; a scientific, independent press; and a practical, status-oriented press (Pace, 1960). During the years 1960-62, as CCI data from more institutions became available, it became possible to base analyses on a better cross-section of institutions and thus to see more clearly the ways in which institutions differed. These analyses led to the development of CUES, replacing the CCI.

CUES consists of half of the items in the 1958 version of the CCI, but its structure and rationale are fundamentally different. Like the CCI, it consists of statements about conditions, events, and practices which might occur in, or be true of, college campuses; but unlike the CCI, the measures provided by CUES are along five dimensions which emerged from factor-analytic studies of differences between environments, and the rationale is based on the concept of collective perception about what is characteristic of the campus.

The basic dimensions are labeled Practicality, Community, Awareness, Propriety, and Scholarship. Each of these scales consists of 30 items. The score on a scale is the number of items that are characteristic of the particular campus, with "characteristic" defined as a high level consensus, two to one or greater, among the reporters. The development of this instrument, together with tentative norms for its interpretation, was described in a Preliminary Technical Manual (Pace, 1963).

It seems reasonable to say that CUES has further stimulated the curiosity of researchers and educators. It has apparently tapped concepts and variables which social scientists have wanted to deal with, but have heretofore lacked the instrumentation for doing so. Moreover, the initial promise of the CCI, and its subsequent realization in the clearer structure of CUES, stimulated other social scientists to explore other ways of characterizing college environments. Over the past ten years a substantial literature has developed around concepts and measures of the college environment (Pace and McFee, 1960; Pace, 1963; Michaels, 1965). In the fall of 1966, the present writer prepared an article on the college environment for inclusion in the Fourth Edition of the Encyclopedia of Educational Research, published in 1969. This is a new topic for the Encyclopedia, and its appearance testifies to the salience this line of research has attained in the past decade.

Measuring College Environments

Basically, one can identify four systematic approaches to the description and measurement of college environments. The initial concept, illustrated by the work of Pace and Stern (1958), Pace (1963), Thistlethwaite (1959a, b), and Kirk (1965) can be described as the *collective perception* or *image* approach. What do people perceive as characteristic of the environment? A second approach, illustrated by the work of McConnell and Heist (1959), Astin and Holland (1961), and Trow (1960), asks a different question: What kind of *people* live in the environment? The assumption here is that students make the college, and that by knowing the characteristics of students one can infer the characteristics of the environment. A third approach is a *demographic* one. What demographic features are characteristic of the environment? Features such as size, money, library resources, proportion of men and women, faculty-student ratio, etc. are examples. Astin (1962) and Richards (1959) have used this approach. A fourth kind of question has been: How do people *behave* in the environment? The most recent studies of Astin (1965), and the earlier participant-observer methods of Becker (1961) illustrate this approach.

As alternative approaches have been used, the investigators have compared their results with those obtained from the CCI or CUES, using such comparisons as partial evidence for the validity of their methods. To some extent, then, the CCI and CUES have served as a central reference for much of the research over the past decade. Although each approach produces some unique results, the similarities in conclusions obtained by various methods are quite apparent. All of the investigators find dimensions or scales which have some similarity to one or more of the five scales in CUES—the magnitude of these similarities being expressed by correlations in the .40s to .60s.

Regardless of the method of inquiry, the accumulated results show very clearly that college environments differ greatly from one another. In educational and psychological research there is ample evidence that different treatments produce different results, that different stimuli produce different responses. Rather commonly, when significant differences are not obtained, the treatments have not been substantially different in the first place, or the outcome measures have been only partially relevant to the differential treatments. It is not surprising that large significance is rarely found in small phenomena. College environments, however, are large phenomena; and the differences between them are also demonstrably large. Theoretically, the effects of such different environments should be easily documented by empirical studies.

In a study of nine colleges, Pace (1964) demonstrated that students' attainment of relevant objectives was definitely related to the environmental press of the college and, to a lesser extent, to the press of subcultures within the college. Two recent dissertations at UCLA (Dean, 1966; Fisher, 1966) showed that the magnitude of entering students' misperceptions about the environment was clearly related to how well they subsequently liked the environment, and to the frequency with which they experienced some difficulty in adapting to it. A similar finding was reported by Pervin (in press). In the NORC studies, students' career plans were influenced by certain aspects of the college environment (Davis, 1961). Similar college effects were also shown by Thistlethwaite (1965).

Most of these studies have used limited criteria—such as students' plans to enter graduate school—or have used self-report data, such as students' estimated progress toward various objectives, or estimated satisfaction with college. Until there are large-scale studies, using criterion measures relevant to a variety of educational objectives, the full impact of different environments on different students cannot be adequately demonstrated.

One might add, too, that measures of the environment which are based upon projections from the characteristics of students cannot really be used to sort out the relative influence of personality *vs.* environment upon subsequent outcomes. CUES, as a measuring instrument, is relatively free of this kind of contamination. What students collectively perceive to be characteristic of their college environment has little or no relationship to the personal characteristics of the students themselves (Pace, 1966; McFee, 1961).

A New Study of American College Environments

Because the whole notion of measuring the characteristics of environments is an intriguing one, opening up the possibility for new and more rigorous research on the effects of higher education and providing new knowledge about the diversity of educational environments across the country, the quality of an instrument used for such purposes is of particular importance. A new study (Pace, 1967) was made in recognition of this importance. Its objectives were to provide a broader baseline of data from which to examine and improve the psychometric adequacy of the measuring instrument, to obtain a wider network of information bearing on the validity of the test and its relationships with other measures in current use, and to document more fully the range and patterns of diversity and similarity that are descriptive of American college and university environments.

SAMPLE. In the spring of 1965, when the study began, CUES data were available from approximately 100 institutions. Invitations were issued to 193 colleges and universities to administer CUES to a representative sample of their students. These colleges were ones which had previously been included in studies of students' career plans made in 1961 and 1964 by the National Opinion Research Center. Their inclusion in the present study enabled us to relate a good deal of recent information about the schools and the students to the characteristics of the school environment measured by CUES; and through a data sharing agreement with NORC, we provided NORC with information for their subsequent use in making further analyses of environmental factors influencing students' educational and career plans. Of the 193 institutions invited to use CUES, 124 did so. The total number of student reporters from these 124 schools was 15,286. By adding these data to the CUES reports already on hand, and other reports received during the first part of 1966, we had information from 237 colleges and universities. Since the preliminary CUES manual was developed from a base of only 50 schools, the new base of 237 represented a major improvement.

From this pool we selected 100 institutions to serve as a national reference group for the subsequent psychometric studies. Various cluster analysis computer programs, designed to identify similarities between institutions in the profiles of their five CUES scores, produced information which led us to identify eight "types" of environments: (1) highly selective liberal arts colleges, (2) highly selective universities—public and private, (3) general liberal arts colleges, (4) general universities—public and private, (5) state colleges and other universities, (6) teachers colleges and others with major emphasis in teacher education, (7) strongly denominational liberal arts colleges—Catholic and Protestant, (8) institutions with a predominant emphasis in engineering and sciences.

To assure maximum diversity and representation, we selected ten institutions of each type, except general liberal arts colleges and general universities, which were represented by 20 institutions each. These 100 institutions were further selected so that their resulting distribution was nationally appropriate with respect to level of program, geographic region, and public and private control—with "nationally appropriate" defined as the number of institutions one should have by level, region, and form of control in a sample midway between being representative of *institutions* and being representative of *enrollments*.

PSYCHOMETRIC FINDINGS. The psychometric properties of the current edition of CUES were found to be generally adequate but capable of improvement. All items correlated positively with the score on the scale in which they were located, but some items correlated higher with other scale scores. No definable factors other than the ones represented by the present scales were revealed, thus confirming the basic structure of the test, but nearly a third of the items were not as factorially clear as they ought to be. As a result of these studies it was decided to adopt a new scoring system and to try to improve the test, psychometrically, by eliminating the least satisfactory items.

THE REVISED CUES INSTRUMENT. 1ne revised test consists of five 20-item scales. Studies of this test, using the modified scoring system, revealed that significant improvements were produced. All items correlated .40 or higher with the score on the scale in which they were located; scale independence increased; and factor analyses revealed a much higher clarity in each of the five factors. The reliabilities of the revised scales, based on the distribution of responses across the national reference group of 100 institutions, and using Kuder-Richardson Formula No. 20, were as follows: Practicality, .94; Community, .95; Awareness, .96; Propriety, .93; and Scholarship, .95.

RESULTS. Based on these shorter and better scales, the scores of the 100 institutions were plotted and grouped into the eight types of institutions previously described. The diversity of educational environments across the country is striking. On all five of the scales, one finds that nearly everything characteristic of some institutions is equally uncharacteristic of others. Moreover, there are large differences between many of the institutional types. The highest mean scores of the institutions within a given type are from two and one-fourth to four times higher than the mean score of institutions within another type. In many cases there is no overlap in the scores of institutions of different types. In most of the types, the range of scores between the highest and lowest case is less than half the range of scores across the total group of 100 schools.

An indication of the validity of the typology is the fact that there were only five per cent deviant cases, that is, cases in which a score was noticeably different from other scores within the type.

Profiles based on the mean scores for institutions within each type showed that each type of school had a distinctly different pattern of environmental press. Thus, within the great diversity of college environments across the country there are patterns of similarity, a fact which has definite practical utility for aiding parents, counselors, and prospective students in the process of college choice.

Correlations between measures of the college environment from CUES and other relevant measures—such as the characteristics of students, the behavior and attitudes of students, the curricular emphasis in the college program, and various institutional features such as size, selectivity, financial resources, etc.—are supportive of associations one might reasonably expect.

Whether the environment is characterized directly by the collective perceptions of the students who live in it, or whether it is inferred from student behavior, student characteristics, the emphasis in the college curriculum, or other features such as size, selectivity, financial resources, the results are generally congruent. Different approaches and different questions produce somewhat different answers; but no approach produces answers which are opposite or contrary to those produced by other methods.

In general, scores on CUES correlate with other relevant variables to about the same degree as scores on the Scholastic Aptitude Test correlate with college grades—namely, from the low .30s to the high .60s. The conclusion from such associations is that campus atmosphere, as measured by CUES, is a concept buttressed by substantial evidence of both concurrent and construct validity.

The end results of the present study are a more reliable and psychometrically adequate instrument; an improved scoring system; a new type of national baseline for studying college environments; a richer documentation of the facts of institutional diversity; a new typology of institutions which has practical value for college admissions decisions; and an expanded network of correlations between various measures of college environments and student characteristics and behavior. Different methods of describing environments do produce broadly congruent results.

References

ASTIN, A. W.   An empirical characterization of higher educational institutions. *Journal of Educational Psychology,* 1962, 53, 224-235.

ASTIN, A.W.   Classroom environments in different fields of study. *Journal of Educational Psychology,* 1965, 56, 275-282.

ASTIN, A. W. and HOLLAND, J. L.   The environmental assessment technique: a way to measure college environments. *Journal of Educational Psychology,* 1961, 52, 308-316.

BECKER, H. S. and others.   *Boys in white: student culture in medical schools.* Chicago: University of Chicago Press, 1961.

DAVIS, J. A. and others.   *Great aspirations: career plans of America's June 1961 college graduates.* Chicago: University of Chicago Press, National Opinion Research Center, 1961.

DEAN, G. S.   *High school seniors' preferences and expectations for college environment in relationship to high school scholastic achievement and intellectual satisfaction.* Ph.D. dissertation, University of California at Los Angeles, 1966.

FISHER, M. S.   *Environment, expectations, and the significance of disparity between actual and expected environment at the University of Utah.* Ph.D. dissertation, University of California at Los Angeles, 1966.

KIRK, J.   *Cultural diversity and character change at Carnegie Tech.* Pittsburgh: Carnegie Institute of Technology, 1965.

McCONNELL, T. R. and HEIST, P.   Do students make the college? *College and University,* 1959, 34, 442-452.

McFEE, A.   The relation of students' needs to their perceptions of a college environment. *Journal of Educational Psychology,* 1961, 52, 25-29.

MICHAELS, W. B.   Campus environment. *Review of Educational Research,* 1965, 35, 264-276.

MURRAY, H. A.   *Explorations in personality,* New York: Oxford University Press, 1938.

PACE, C. R.   Five college environments. *College Board Review,* 1960, 41, 2-28.

PACE, C. R.   *College and University Environment Scales: Technical Manual.* Princeton: Educational Testing Service, 1963.

PACE, C. R.   *The influence of academic and student subcultures in college and university environments.* Final report, Cooperative Research Project No. 1083, Office of Education, U.S. Department of Health, Education, and Welfare, 1964.

PACE, C. R.   *Comparisons of CUES results from different groups of reporters.* College Entrance Examination Board, Report No. 1. Los Angeles: University of California, July, 1966.

PACE, C. R.   *Analyses of a national sample of college environments.* Final Report, Project No. 5-0764, Contract No. OE 5-1-321. Washington: U. S. Office of Education, Bureau of Research, 1967.

PACE, C. R. and McFEE, A.   The college environment. *Review of Educational Research,* 1960, 30, 311-320.

PACE, C. R. and STERN, G. G.   *College Characteristics Index, Form 457.* Syracuse University Psychological Research Center, 1957.

PACE, C. R. and STERN, G. G.   An approach to the measurement of psychological characteristics of college environments. *Journal of Educational Psychology,* 1958, 49, 269-277.

PERVIN, L. A.   A twenty-college study of student-college interaction using TAPE (Transactional Analysis of Personality and Environment): rationale, reliability, and validity. (In press.)

RICHARDS, J. M., Jr., and others.   Description of junior colleges. *Journal of Educational Psychology,* 1959, 50, 207-214.

ROGOFF, N.   *College board members: a comparative analysis.* New York: Bureau of Applied Social Research, Columbia University, 1957.

STERN, G. G.   *Activities Index, Form 156.* Syracuse: Syracuse University Psychological Research Center, 1956.

STERN, G. G., STEIN, M. I., and BLOOM, B. S.   *Methods in personality assessment.* Glencoe: The Free Press, 1956.

THISTLETHWAITE, D. L.   College environments and the development of talent. *Science,* 1959, 130, 71-76. a.

THISTLETHWAITE, D. L.   College press and student achievement. *Journal of Educational Psychology,* 1959, 50, 183-191. b.

THISTLETHWAITE, D. L.   College press and changes in study plans of talented students. *Journal of Educational Psychology,* 1960, 51, 222-234.

THISTLETHWAITE, D. L.   *Effects of college upon student aspirations.* Cooperative Research Project No. D-098, Office of Education, U.S. Department of Health, Education, and Welfare, 1965.

TROW, M.   The campus viewed as a culture. In *Research on college students.* Boulder, Colorado: Western Interstate Commission for Higher Education. 1960. Pp. 105-123.

2. *INSIDE THE CLASSROOM*

Social psychologists do not often enter classrooms just to look around and observe the group phenomena occurring naturally there. Why they do not is a little puzzling, because classrooms are among the most common, certainly the most accessible, havens of group behavior in all society. Louis M. Smith, in his recent book, *Complexities of an Urban Classroom* (Holt, Rinehart and Winston, 1968), makes a compelling case for the "micro-ethnography of the classroom," as he calls it. Perhaps more scholars will begin to appear at the teacher's door.

Jackson and Lahaderne are two who have poked around classrooms with their social-psychological eyes and ears attuned to the commonplace events of life. Their report is suggestive of what simple observation can reveal. As social psychologists, they are especially interested in the interaction between people, in this case the talk that goes on. They find classrooms full of it. Narrowing in somewhat more systematically on the talk between teachers and students, they note some interesting variations in rates from one classroom to the next, and differences in the kinds of talk to students within the classrooms. What they make of what they see and hear is an important part of the story.

A number of researchers, such as Ned A. Flanders (in Biddle and Ellena, *Contemporary Research on Teacher Effectiveness*, Holt, Rinehart and Winston, 1964), have studied teacher-student interaction, too, but using systematic observation schedules. Theirs is a more rigorous, more formal approach. The reader may wish to compare the two styles of research. What are the weaknesses, the strengths of each?

Inequalities of Teacher-Pupil Contacts*

Philip W. Jackson,
Henriette M. Lahaderne

Elementary school classrooms are busy places, as every teacher who works in one knows. Activities stop and start, conversations wax and wane, minor crises come and go. The teacher moves about the room, from blackboard to desk, to supply closet, now talking to a group in front of the map, now pausing to quell a disturbance at the science table, now examining the work of a girl in the corner, now shaking his head at a boy on his way to the pencil sharpener. Bells ring, chalk breaks, books drop, and a small boy enters with an announcement that today there will be an indoor recess. Anyone witnessing such events for a considerable length of time is inevitably impressed, if not overwhelmed, by the variety of things going on in these densely populated hives of educational activity.

The purpose of this report is to describe and discuss one aspect of this busyness as it was observed in four sixth-grade classrooms. The observations focussed on the flow of communication between the teacher and individual students. Certain features of that flow are evident to even the most casual observer. For example, the teacher's communicative energies are spread about and, sooner or later, they touch all of his students. For a time he talks to Billy, then he turns to Sam, then to Sarah, then back to Billy, then on to Elaine, and so forth. Only slightly less obvious is the uneven distribution of these energies throughout the class. Over a long period of time Billy may get more than his share of personal attention from the teacher, and Sarah less than her share. Another salient feature of these communications is that either the teacher or the student may initiate them. Moreover, some students speak to the teacher only when called on; others are incessant hand-wavers. Finally the careful observer may note that students differ not only in the total amount of attention, or communicative "bits," they receive from their teacher but also in the over-all content of these interchanges. Some students talk about instructional matters more than do others; some receive more disciplinary messages than do most of their classmates. The aim of this

---

* Expanded version of a paper read as part of a symposium entitled, "Observing in Schools: Studies of Classroom Life" at the American Psychological Association meetings, 1966. From *Psychology in the Schools*, 1967, 4 (3), 201-211. Used by permission of the authors and publisher.

The research reported herein was performed pursuant to a contract with the United States Department of Health, Education and Welfare, Office of Education, under the provisions of the Cooperative Research Program.

study was to describe these apparent inequalities with greater precision than is possible through casual observation.

Method

The data were collected in four sixth-grade classrooms located in a predominantly white, working-class suburb. Two of the classrooms, each containing 34 pupils, were in one school; the other two, each containing 29 pupils, were in another school. Two of the four teachers were men and two were women. Pupil placement in the two schools was based solely on the student's place of residence. So far as could be determined by test results and observation, the pupil composition of each room was heterogeneous.

Visits to the classrooms began in late September and continued for two months. The length of the visits ranged from a half hour to a full day. During each visit periodic tallies of teacher-pupil communications were made along with other observations whose content is not relevant to this paper. When the visit lasted for an hour or longer, the communication tallies were spaced throughout that time in units of approximately twenty minutes each.

Cumulatively, the periods during which communication counts were taken averaged about nine-and-a-half hours in each room. The exact totals for the four classrooms were 9.0, 9.4, 9.7, and 10.2 hours. These totals comprised approximately 36 periods of tallying in each room. The observations were distributed over the entire school week and sampled all the activities of each room.

The observation schedule required an entry to be made on a tally sheet each time there was an intentional transmission of information between the teacher and an individual student. Messages directed to more than one student were ignored. The tally sheet was designed so that each entry designated (a) which student was involved in the communication; (b) whether the initiator of the message was the teacher or the student; and (c) whether the content of the message was primarily instructional, managerial, or prohibitory. Instructional messages were defined as those in which some reference was made to curriculum content or to the attainment of educational objectives. Managerial messages dealt with the interpretation of classroom rules and the definition of permissible behavior. Prohibitory messages dealt with keeping order and punishing misbehavior.

A major advantage of the observational technique, from the standpoint of the person using it, is its simplicity. The number of content categories are relatively few and fairly clear-cut. A second advantage is that it can be employed even when the precise content of the teacher's or student's remarks cannot be heard or when the communication is non-verbal. When a student approaches the teacher with an open workbook in his hand or when the teacher leans over the desk of a student to examine his seatwork, the observer is usually safe in classifying the interchange as instructional, even though the remarks are inaudible. Similarly, when a teacher snaps his fingers and points to a student across the room, the observer can be fairly certain that he is witnessing a prohibitory message even though no words are spoken. The ability to categorize messages that are only partially overheard or that do not entail words is particularly important in elementary classrooms where teachers and students are very mobile and where the occasion for certain messages recurs so frequently that their transmission becomes highly stylized and abbreviated.

Although the simplicity of the observational scheme is one of its chief advantages, it is also its major weakness. When the buzz of classroom talk is reduced to a set of hash marks clustered under three broad headings, the resultant picture reveals only the palest outline of the complex reality from which it was extracted. Instructional talk can be clear or confused, managerial messages can be consistent or inconsistent, disciplinary commands can be shouted or whispered. Under the present scheme all of this richness, which includes much of the information on which teacher evaluations are commonly based, is lost. It is true that all observational procedures succeed in capturing only a small fraction of the events to which they are applied, but the device employed here is perhaps a more ruthless filter than most.

Results

The choice of four classrooms at the same grade level and in the same community was designed to reduce the effect of grade level and social class variation. An eleven-year-old child in this community might have been assigned, by chance, to any one of the four rooms. What difference would the assignment make to the individual teacher-pupil contacts he would witness and participate in? A partial answer to that question is provided by the data in Table 1.

Table 1

HOURLY RATES OF TEACHER-PUPIL INTERACTION

CONTENT OF INTERACTION	CLASSROOM*			
	A	B	C	D
Instructional	73	76	82	88
Managerial	24	9	8	12
Prohibitory	24	8	13	10
Total	121	93	103	110

* A and B are male teachers; C and D are female.

The most obvious conclusion to be derived from Table 1 is that no matter in which room a student found himself he would discover his teacher to be busy talking to individual students. The number of hourly interchanges described in that table becomes even more impressive when it is recalled that communications with groups of students or with the entire class are not included in this summary. Here, incidentally, is one more scrap of evidence, if any more is needed, to explain why teachers are fatigued at the end of a working day.

Only slightly less obvious than the rapid rate of interaction is the fact that most of the four teachers' time is taken up in instructional interchanges. In other words, the teachers spend much energy communicating with individual students and most of that energy is spent talking about or listening to academic matters. Moreover, so far as the sheer frequency of instructional interchanges is concerned, it still does not seem to matter too much in which of the four classrooms an eleven-year-old lands. No matter where he goes he is apt to see his teacher talking with an individual student about an instructional matter slightly more often than once a minute.

The four rooms, however, no longer look alike when compared on hourly rates of managerial and prohibitory interchanges. Classroom A is noticeably different from the other three. Presumably a student in that room would witness or be involved in almost three times as many managerial interchanges as would, say, a student in Classroom C. He might also perceive three times as many disciplinary commands as might a student in Classroom B—the room directly across the hall.

Although they usually can be clearly differentiated by the observer, managerial and prohibitory messages have something in common. They both deal with the institutional workings of the classroom. They entail the expectations defining the rights and privileges of students and governing the flow of people and material in the room. In these terms, the teacher in Classroom A seemed to be much more involved in institutional matters than were his colleagues. This is not to say that such a difference in involvement is good or bad, only that it exists and seems pronounced enough to be noticed by a student moving from Classroom A to one of the other rooms.

Finally, in order to appreciate the size of the differences revealed in Table 1 it is necessary to recall that the numbers depicted there are hourly rates based on observations spanning a period of two months. If each of those rates were multiplied by the number of hours in a school year (approximately 1000), the absolute differences among the four classrooms would become quite striking. Thus, over the year a student in Classroom A might witness as many as 16,000 more disciplinary messages than might a student in Classroom B. In Room A, when the teacher turns to a misbehaving student and says, "If I've told you once, I've told you a thousand times . . ." he probably means it. Admittedly, this kind of comparison is questionable because it assumes that the hourly rates hold throughout the year. None the less, the projected yearly totals call attention to the cumulative significance of events that otherwise might pass unnoticed during a brief observation.

The data in Table 2 reveal who initiates the interchanges. The line showing the totals reveals that the flow of communication in these four classrooms is much more under the control of the teacher than of the students. Moreover, the hourly rate of initiated messages is fairly uniform for the four teachers. In each room the teacher sets into motion about 80 individual interchanges every hour.

Although the initiation rates are roughly equal for the four teachers, the rates for the students are not. In two of the classrooms, A and D, students

Table 2

HOURLY INTERACTIONS INITIATED BY TEACHERS AND PUPILS

CONTENT OF INTERACTION	CLASSROOM							
	A		B		C		D	
	TEACHER	PUPIL	TEACHER	PUPIL	TEACHER	PUPIL	TEACHER	PUPIL
Instructional	49.0	24.0	67.0	8.0	67.0	15.0	56.0	32.0
Managerial	9.0	15.0	3.0	6.0	6.0	2.0	6.0	6.0
Prohibitory	23.7	0.3*	7.9	0.1	13.0	0.0	9.5	0.5
Total	81.7	39.3	77.9	14.1	86.0	17.0	71.5	38.5

* A pupil occasionally requested a teacher to discipline one of his classmates. This was the only way in which a pupil could initiate a prohibitory message.

are much more active in initiating messages than they are in the other two. Also, in Classrooms A and D the students directed unsolicited communications to their teacher two or three times as often as they did in Classrooms B and C. One gets the feeling that the teachers in rooms with high student initiation are kept more on the go, in the sense of being called on to respond to students' queries.

The subdivision of the interactions into the three categories—instructional, managerial, and prohibitory—reveals further differences in the patterns of initiating messages. The rooms having high student initiation rates differ in the way students divide their energies between instructional and managerial matters. When students initiate contacts with the teacher in Classroom D they are more likely to deal with instructional affairs than is true in Classroom A. In the latter classroom, student queries more frequently have an institutional focus. Thus, although the teachers in both rooms seemingly deal with about the same number of students' requests every hour, the professional demands represented by those requests are noticeably different in the two settings.

The classroom differences revealed by this crude analysis are blurry, to be sure, but they are sufficiently clear to confirm what every school boy knows: the quality of school life depends partially on the particular room in which fate deposits him. In addition, the differences call attention to the institutional character of school life, a feature so pervasive that it is often overlooked. Classrooms may be designed for instructional ends, but much that goes on there has little to do with instruction per se. Furthermore, there seem to be real differences from room to room in the extent to which the institutional aspects of school are salient. In some rooms, if our data are to be believed, students seem to bang against the bars more than in others.

So far as total classroom experience is concerned it matters not only in which room a pupil is but also whether the pupil is a boy or a girl. Even with observational categories as broad as those employed in this study, there emerges a marked sex difference in teacher-pupil interaction. This difference is summarized in Table 3.

Table 3

PERCENTAGES OF TEACHER-PUPIL INTERACTIONS INVOLVING BOYS

CLASSROOM	PERCENTAGE OF MALE PUPILS	PERCENTAGE OF INTERACTIONS		
		INSTRUCTIONAL	MANAGERIAL	PROHIBITORY
A	50.0	60.9**	61.6**	89.6**
B	58.8	61.2	75.0*	85.5**
C	44.8	36.4**	42.0	69.6**
D	44.8	61.0**	58.9**	90.1**

** $p < .01$; * $p < .02$.

The percentages in Table 3 almost speak for themselves. They show, first, that though sex makes a difference in every classroom it does not always make the same difference. Second, they dramatically confirm the popular notion that boys are the major source of classroom misbehavior. Each of these findings deserves comment.

The least clear pattern of sex differences is seen in the findings on instructional messages. In Classrooms A and D, boys receive more than their share of such messages and in Classroom C, they receive less than their share. The boys in Classroom B participate in a proportion of instructional interchanges commensurate with the size of their sub-group. Thus, at least with respect to this observational category there seems to be no sex difference that holds across all four classes. Yet the fact that three of the four percentages differ significantly from what might be expected by chance suggests that the sex of students is an important variable even though it may function differently from room to room.

The percentages of managerial interchanges involving boys are somewhat more consistent than are those dealing with instructional matters. In three of the four classrooms boys are involved in noticeably more than their share of these interactions. Even in Classroom C, where they received proportionately fewer instructional interchanges than did girls, boys seem to hold their own when it comes to talking with the teacher about managerial affairs. Remembering what was said earlier about the institutional character of managerial communications, we might consider these percentages to mean that boys, more often than girls, are actively engaged in coping with the network of rules, regulations, and routines in which they are embedded as students.

The final set of differences in Table 3, involving the percentages of prohibitory messages, is clearest of all and leaves no doubt about this one aspect of classroom life. When these four teachers responded to instances of classroom misbehavior they were almost always reacting to a boy. This fact comes as no surprise but although the direction of the difference might have been easily predicted, the actual percentages are impressively large. The psychological significance of these differences becomes more evident when the percentages are transformed into the absolute number of prohibitory messages observed in the various rooms. In Classroom A, for example, the teacher delivers approximately 24 prohibitory messages every hour, or roughly 120 messages each day. About 108 of those daily messages are received by one or another of the 17 boys in that room.

Another aspect of the sex differences in teacher-pupil interaction is revealed in relationships observed among the three different message categories. These relationships are summarized in the form of correlation coefficients in Table 4. The correlations in that table show the communicative behavior of boys to be more of a piece, as it were, than is true for girls. Boys who are active in instructional interchanges tend also to be active in managerial interchanges and those same boys, it would seem, tend to have more than their share of disciplinary messages from the teacher. A similar phenomenon is not apparent for girls, and though it does seem to appear in the relationship between managerial and prohibitory messages, it is much less pronounced than is true for boys.

Table 4

INTERCORRELATIONS AMONG THREE TYPES OF TEACHER-
PUPIL INTERACTION

Classroom	INSTRUCTIONAL				MANAGERIAL				PROHIBITORY			
	A	B	C	D	A	B	C	D	A	B	C	D
Instructional					.54*	.47*	.70*	.60*	.39	.33	.60*	.82**
Managerial	.49*	−.35	.53*	.19					.66**	.14	.69**	.56*
Prohibitory	−.02	−.10	.20	−.09	.32	.51	.42	.03				
	Correlations for girls below the diagonal								Correlations for boys above the diagonal			

* $p < .05$;   ** $p < .01$.

The greater cohesiveness of the three types of interaction for boys was not predicted and, therefore, the reaction to it can only be speculative. If boys have as many brushes with teachers as the data indicate, the teachers may find it advantageous to sidestep as many open clashes as possible. Thus, they sometimes might use instructional or managerial messages as preventive measures for averting harsher and more disruptive interchanges. When a teacher calls on a boy whom she suspects of daydreaming or when she refuses to give a pupil permission to go to the pencil sharpener because of what she believes will happen on the way, she is using non-prohibitory messages for control purposes. Anyone who has ever watched teachers at work can doubtlessly offer many more examples of these somewhat devious strategies. If these techniques were used frequently enough, they would result in heightened correlations among the three interaction categories, such as those appearing for the boys in Table 4.[1]

In the final analysis, the quality of school life is determined not only by a pupil's sex or by what room he is in but also by what he is like as a person. Within each room and within each sex group there remain wide differences in the pattern of teacher-pupil interactions. Such differences only become discernible when the descriptive unit is the individual student and his experience.

In each of the four classrooms one or two students have fewer than one interchange per hour with their teacher. At the other extreme a few students in each room have so many communications that, if the interactions were distributed equally throughout the day, these students would be in contact with their teacher every five or ten minutes. Unexpectedly, the totals for the least active students are strikingly similar for the four classrooms, whereas the totals for the most active students are markedly different from room to room. A plausible explanation for the differences between these two extremes is that some minimal level of interaction with the teacher is demanded by the mere fact of membership in the class whereas the maximal number possible is more a function of the idiosyncratic matching of teachers and students.

The educational significance of these differences emerges when we imagine a classroom composed exclusively of either low-interacting or high-interacting students. If it were necessary for a teacher to interact with each student only once an hour, and if he maintained a "moderate" rate of interaction, that is, engaging in a hundred or so individual interactions each hour, he possibly could manage a class of a hundred or so students. Conversely, if a teacher had to interact with each student ten or twelve times an hour and he maintained the same rate of interaction, he could barely accommodate a dozen students in his class.

These extreme situations are no more than fanciful speculations, but they do lead to further thoughts about what life must be like in a regular classroom. For at least a few students, individual contact with the teacher is as rare as if they were seated in a class of a hundred or more pupils, even though there are actually only 30 or so classmates present. For others, the teacher's presence is the same as it might be if there were but a handful

1. The reader will recall that A and B are male teachers, C and D female. Sex of teacher does not seem to have a consistent effect, except for two sets of correlations: those between instructional and prohibitory interactions for boys; and (less strongly) those between instructional and managerial interaction for boys. In both cases the relationship is somewhat higher in classes taught by women. This result was not predicted, but suggests that the explanation above needs qualifying, depending on the sex of the teacher.

of classmates in the room. What does it mean, therefore, when we describe a child as being in a classroom of thirty pupils? Such a description does tell us how many people are present, but it tells very little about the social density of the child's psychological world and the relative saliency of his teacher in that world.

Discussion

The view of classroom activity provided by the observations is exceedingly narrow, but it was sufficient to direct attention to several important educational issues. These issues have been discussed partly in the presentation of results and now are briefly reviewed to bring them into sharper focus.

First, the data have shown how classrooms can be very different from one another even when described in ways that were not meant to underscore the differences. Moreover, the differences revealed by the findings are not easily placed on a continuum whose poles represent pedagogical vice and virtue. It is difficult to say, for example, whether a great number of managerial interchanges is a good or a bad thing, or whether it is better to have students or teachers initiate instructional interchanges. This ambiguity is tolerable so long as the differences described hold the promise of being related to the total quality of the student's experience in school—so long, in other words, as the differences cannot be brushed aside as psychologically trivial.

Second, the data have called attention to the institutional character of classroom life. Schools are places where large groups of people congregate and work together. Inevitably, a significant portion of the total energy required to operate a classroom is spent in the mundane business of managing the movement of social traffic and of responding to violations of institutional expectations. Perhaps these matters are incidental to the main business of teaching and learning, but psychologists in particular need no reminder that school has a greater impact on a student's total personality than an examination of textbooks and curriculum guides would have us believe. In addition to learning their ABC's children must learn to make their way in the social labyrinth of the school. The high frequency of managerial and control messages in the observations suggests how important, and possibly how tough, that learning can be.

Third, the findings support the commonly held belief that boys have a more difficult time in school than do girls. If control messages are treated as crude measures of that difficulty, these sixth-grade boys, as a group, have eight or ten times more trouble than do their female classmates. Although it is wrong to leap to the conclusion that the boys are miserable in school and girls wild about it, the experience of going to school is clearly very different for boys than for girls. Perhaps this fact is too well known to require further scrutiny, but the frequency with which sex is ignored in educational research would lead one to suspect otherwise.

Fourth, and finally, the findings reveal a range of individual differences in each classroom broad enough to weaken any hopes of making facile generalizations about what goes on there. In each classroom there are a few students who are almost out of the teacher's range of vision, so to speak, and a few others who are almost always underfoot. What this difference means and how it comes about is anybody's guess, but it is fair to conclude that by the end of the year some students likely will be more familiar to the teacher than will others, even though they have all lived together in the same room for about the same number of days. This observation calls into question the conventional view of looking upon each classroom as a unit whose participants have shared a common educational experience. In a sense, each classroom contains as many environments as it does pairs of eyes through which to view them.

※ ※ ※ ※ ※

There is a growing literature in the domain called "social reinforcement," growing out of Skinner's work on operant conditioning (*The Behavior of Organisms*, Appleton-Century-Crofts, 1938). This work eschews the idea that motivational or other "internal" states need be evoked in understanding (or controlling) behavior, and explores ramifications of the basic idea that behaviors followed by rewards will be repeated.

Thomas and his colleagues present a particularly fruitful study in this tradition. It is done in a naturalistic setting rather than a laboratory; it gathers data from many children rather than a single subject; it specifies a series of meaningful teacher and child behavior variables, rather than focusing on a single one, such as "attending" or "talking," and it employs an own-control design to assess the effects of varied teacher style over time.

As reinforcement theorists (but not teachers) would predict, punishing children for disruption tends to *increase* disruption. (Why?) The reader should examine the data presented closely to see if the claimed converse (that approval of relevant classroom behavior leads to more relevant behavior) is supported.

From a social-psychological viewpoint, the crucial issue in this study is: *what was learned?* Have the children in this classroom (a) simply complied with the short-run influence efforts of the teacher; (b) accommodated to, formed a working relationship with, this particular teacher; (c) developed a working group norm about how things should go in this classroom; or (d) learned more clearly what the student role is, and how to carry it out? The theoretical and practical consequences of these four answers vary considerably.

P.S. Notice the interesting "substitute teacher" data in Figure 2.

Production and Elimination of Disruptive Classroom Behavior By Systematically Varying Teacher's Behavior*

Don R. Thomas,
Wesley C. Becker, Marianne Armstrong

Teachers are sometimes unaware of the effects of their actions on the behavior of their students. Many teachers assume that if a child performs disruptive acts in the classroom then the child must have a problem at home, or at the very least, must not have reached a stage of sufficient maturity to function adequately in the school situation. However, an increasing body of evidence indicates that many of the behaviors which teachers find disruptive are actually within their control. A teacher can modify and control the behavior of her students by controlling her own responses.

Contingent use of social reinforcement has been shown to control such motor behaviors as walking, standing, and running (Bijou and Baer, 1963), talking and crying (Kerr, Meyerson, and Michael, 1965; Hart, Allen, Buell, Harris, and Wolf, 1964), and classroom conduct (Becker, Madsen, Arnold, and Thomas, 1967; Zimmerman and Zimmerman, 1962).

Becker *et al.* (1967) worked in public schools with teachers who had problem children in their classes. Behaviors exhibited by the students were observed and the frequency of these behaviors was estimated for each child. Each teacher was taught to use praise, smile, etc. to reinforce good behavior. The rate of appropriate classroom behaviors increased in most cases as soon as teacher approval and recognition were made contingent on such behavior.

The present study evolved from prior research showing the importance of social reinforcement, and Becker's work, which suggests that specific procedures, or definable classes of teacher behaviors can be used by the teacher to increase appropriate classroom behaviors. In order to provide more convincing data on the role of different teacher behaviors, the present study was designed to produce and remove problem behavior in students

* From *Journal of Applied Behavior Analysis*, 1968, 1, 35-45. Used by permission of the authors and publisher. Copyright 1968 by The Society for the Experimental Analysis of Behavior, Inc.

The authors wish to thank Urbana School District #116 and the principal of Thomas Paine School, Mr. Richard Sturgeon, for their cooperation. The observers (Loretta Nielson, Barbara Goldberg, Marilyn Goldberg, and Darlene Zientarski) deserve thanks for their conscientious work. This research was supported, in part, by National Institute of Child Health and Human Development Grant HD-00881-05. Reprints may be obtained from Wesley C. Becker, Bureau of Educational Research, University of Illinois, Urbana, Illinois.

by systematically varying teacher behaviors in an initially well-behaved class.

Method

Subjects

STUDENTS.   A class of 28 elementary students at the middle-primary level was selected. According to the teacher her class was "a good class, with an above-average distribution of ability and no 'bad' kids." Most of the children were from upper-middle- and middle-income-range families. Ages at the beginning of the study ranged from 6 yr., 11 months to 7 yr., 11 months; I.Q. range (group test) was from 99 to 134.

TEACHER.   The teacher, age 23, obtained her student teaching experience with a class of "maladjusted" children. In addition, she had 1-yr. experience with a class of "slow learners." Preliminary observations indicated that she rarely attended in an approving manner to children who behaved inappropriately, and rarely reprimanded children who were performing their assigned tasks. She volunteered to participate in the study because of its potential contribution to teacher training in the future.

Observation Procedures

The basic data for the study consisted of the relative frequency of occurrence of classes of child behaviors in relation to classes of teacher behaviors utilizing rating schedules to be described. One to three observers were placed in the classroom each morning from approximately 9:15 to 10:00 a.m. while the students were completing reading and reading workbook assignments. To insure obtaining a daily sample of both child and teacher behaviors during this 45-minute work period, a 20-minute observation time was decided on for both child and teacher observations. Thus, even if only one observer was present, the relevant information could be obtained. This time restriction limited the number of children who could be observed each day. Ten children were selected for observation each morning by drawing numbers from a hat. During Baseline$_1$ and the first No Praise condition a no-replacement procedure was used so that all children had to be observed before a child's number could be drawn a second time. At the start of Baseline$_2$ this restriction was removed. Through the use of a numbered seating chart, the observers recorded the behaviors of selected children in the order in which they were chosen. Five extra numbers were drawn each day to provide observation targets in case one or more of the first 10 subjects drawn were not available for observation. Target children were observed for 2 minutes each. Each minute was divided into six 10-second intervals. Observers were trained to record classes of behavior which occurred in a given interval.

Recordings were made during the first five intervals of each minute. During the sixth 10-second interval the observers made notes, checked for synchronization, and/or prepared to switch to a new child. Thus, the daily child observation sample consisted of ten 10-second observation intervals on each of 10 children.

Teacher behaviors were recorded on a similar schedule, the only difference being that for teacher behaviors each occurrence of a response in a specified class was recorded (frequency measure), whereas for child behaviors a given class of behavior could be rated only once in a 10-second interval. This difference in procedure was necessitated by the greater difficulty in separating child behaviors into discrete response units. Observers used a clipboard, stopwatch, and a recording sheet which had spaces for 100 observation intervals, guides for computing reliability, and a place for comments.

Undergraduate university students were hired and trained to collect the data. Each observer memorized the definitions of classes of child and teacher behaviors. Pre-baseline training in recording of behavior was carried out in the experimental classroom to allow the children to become accustomed to the presence of the observers. The children were already well adapted to the classroom before observer training was started. Observers were instructed to avoid all interactions with the students and teacher while in the class or on the school grounds. At the scheduled time they would enter the class, walk directly to chairs provided for them, sit down, and begin the observations. A hand signal was used to insure synchronization of observation times. Initially two observers were scheduled to observe on Monday, Wednesday, and Friday, and two on Tuesday and Thursday. When a systematic difference developed between the two sets of observers, one of the Tuesday-Thursday observers was placed on a three-day-a-week schedule to tie the two sets of observations together with reliability checks. Thus, on some days there were as many as three observers in the classroom. The number of observers in the classroom varied from one to three. Due to illness or the need to obtain observations in other classrooms, there were times when only one observer was available. Observers were not informed of changes in experimental conditions.

Classes of Teacher Behaviors: The Independent Variable

The behaviors emitted by the teacher were defined as belonging to three general classes: (1) Disapproving Behavior, (2) Approving Behavior, and (3) Instructional Behavior. Disapproving and Approving Behaviors were rated only when they immediately followed discriminable child behaviors falling into inappropriate or appropriate classes (see below).[1] Listings were made of the teacher behaviors that could occur within each class.

---

1. As it turned out, approval following inappropriate behavior occurred only three times and disapproval following appropriate behavior did not occur. Also, this teacher did not make non-response-contingent approval or disapproval comments. Thus, we were dealing essentially with two response-contingent classes of teacher behavior.

The general class of Disapproving Behaviors included Physical Contact, Verbal, and Facial subclasses. The subclasses of Physical behaviors included forcibly holding a child, grabbing, hitting, spanking, shaking, slapping, or pushing a child into position. The Verbal subclass of Disapproving Behaviors included yelling, scolding, raising voice, belittling, or making fun of the child, and threats. Threats included "if-then" statements of loss of privilege or punishment at some future time. For example, the teacher might say to the class, "If you don't remain quiet, you will have to stay in from recess." The Facial subclass of Disapproving Behaviors included frowning, grimacing, side-to-side head shaking, gesturing, etc.

The general class of Approving Behaviors also included Physical Contact, Verbal, and Facial subclasses. Approving Physical Contacts included embracing, kissing, patting, holding hand or arm of child, or holding the child in the teacher's lap. Approving Verbal comments included statements of affection, approval, or praise. Approving Facial response was rated whenever the teacher smiled, winked, or nodded at one or more of the children.

The general class of Instructional Behavior included any response from teacher to children which involved giving instructions, information, or indicating correct responses.

In addition to recording the above classes of teacher behavior, note was taken of those times when the teacher terminated social interaction by turning out lights and saying nothing, turning her back on the class and waiting for silence, or stopping talking and waiting for quiet.

As noted earlier, the observers recorded every teacher response falling in a given class. Thus, the measures of teacher behaviors are frequency counts.

Child Behaviors: The Dependent Variable

The classes of child behaviors were developed by categorization of behaviors occuring with some frequency in the repertoire of problem children (Becker *et al.*, 1967). It was assumed that certain behaviors, because of their common topography, could be grouped together. Five classes of Disruptive Behavior (Gross Motor, Noise Making, Orienting, Verbalizations, and Aggression) and one class of Appropriate Behavior (Relevant) were defined. Behaviors not specifically defined were rated in a separate category (Other Task). Disruptive Behaviors were essentially behaviors apparently incompatible with good classroom learning conditions.

Included in the category of behaviors labeled as Gross Motor activities were: getting out of seat, standing up, walking around, running, hopping, skipping, jumping, rocking chair, moving chair, sitting with chair in aisle, kneeling in chair, arm flailing, and rocking body without moving chair.

The category of Noise Making was rated with the stipulation that the observers must hear the noise as well as see the noise-making action, and included tapping feet, clapping, rattling papers, tearing papers, throwing books or other objects onto desks, slamming desk top, tapping objects on desk, kicking desk or chair, and scooting desk or chair.

The Verbalization category was rated only when the observer could hear the response. Lip movements alone were not rated. Carrying on conversations with other children, calling out teacher's name to get her attention, crying, screaming, singing, whistling, laughing, and coughing were included in the category.

The Orienting class of behaviors required that the child be seated. Turning of head or head and body toward another person, showing objects to another child, and looking at another child were rated. Looking behaviors of less than 4-second duration were not rated except for any turn of more than 90 degrees from the desk. When an Orienting response overlapped two rating intervals, and could not be rated in the first interval, because it began too late in the interval to meet the 4-second criterion, it was rated in the second interval.

Aggression was defined as hitting, pushing, shoving, pinching, slapping, striking with objects, poking with objects, grabbing objects or work belonging to another, knocking neighbor's property off desk, destroying another's property, throwing objects. No judgments of intent were made.

Appropriate behaviors were labeled Relevant and were made more easily identifiable by restricting the observations to a period in the morning when all of the children were preparing reading and workbook assignments. Specific Relevant Behaviors were: looking at the teacher when she was speaking to the entire class or to the child being observed, answering questions of the teacher, raising hand and waiting for teacher to respond, writing answers to workbook questions, looking at pages of text in which reading was assigned. It was required that the entire 10-second interval be filled with on-task behavior before the Relevant rating was made.

When a child being observed performed a response not defined by one of the categories of Disruptive Behaviors or by Relevant Behavior, a rating of Other Task was made. The Other Task rating was incompatible with Relevant, but could be recorded in the same interval as any or all of the categories of Disruptive Behavior.

When rating the children, the observers were instructed to record each class of behaviors which appeared in an interval regardless of how many other classes had already been recorded in that interval. All five categories of Disruptive Behaviors and the Other Task category were compatible with each other. Relevant Behavior was incompatible with the other categories. No category of behavior was rated more than once in an interval. If a child was conversing with his neighbor, and he made two verbal responses in one interval, this class of behaviors was recorded only once. Thus, each child-behavior measure was a record of intervals in which the response occurred, rather than a count of the number of discrete responses as in the recording of teacher's behavior.

The over-all level of Disruptive Behaviors was defined as the percentage of intervals in which one or more Disruptive Behaviors occurred.

Reliability

Two types of reliability were calculated. Reliability I reflects simply the degree to which two observers obtained the same score for each category of behavior during a 20-minute observation period. The smaller score is divided by the larger. Reliability I most appropriately applies to the data as reported in Figure 1, since these are averages for an observation period. Random errors tend to cancel each other out when a score is based on a series of observations and a reliability measure should reflect the gain in accuracy obtained by averaging. For training purposes, and for greater confidence in the accuracy of the observation procedure, a second type of reliability was also calculated (Reliability II). Reliability II required that the same behavior category be recorded in the same interval by each observer to define an agreement. Reliability II was calculated by dividing the number of agreements by the number of agreements plus disagreements.

During the pre-baseline observer training, reliability checks were required for every observation. Before baseline observations were started, consistent reliabilities (Type II) above 80% were required. Reliability I data based on a weighted average of the reliabilities of the child-behavior codes are reported in Figure 1, as are the average reliabilities by conditions for teacher behaviors. Comparable Reliability II data averaged 82.6% for child behaviors and 83.2% for teaching behaviors. Reliabilities for individual categories are well represented by these averages.

Sequence of Conditions

The first phase of the study (Baseline$_1$) consisted of measuring both teacher and child behaviors. No attempt was made to manipulate teacher behavior.

The second phase (No Approval$_1$) was defined by the absence of Approval Behaviors. The teacher discontinued the use of praise statements and used only contingent Disapproving Behaviors to control the children.

These phases were then repeated (Baseline$_2$, No Approval$_2$). At the beginning of No Approval$_2$ and throughout the rest of the study, the teacher carried a small "supermarket" adding machine with her to count the frequency of Disapproval Behaviors so that she could better monitor her behavior.

The fifth phase of the study, Frequent Disapproval, involved increasing the level of Disapproving Behaviors to approximately three times that given during Baseline$_1$ while continuing to withhold Approving Behaviors.

Phase 6 returned to the lower level of Disapproval (No Approval$_3$) and Phase 7 again returned to the baseline conditions (Baseline$_3$).

The teacher was instructed to maintain experimental conditions throughout the day, not just during the observation period. During the periods when praise was withheld beginning with No Approval$_2$, checks of the daily counts of Disapproving Responses obtained by the teacher with her counter corresponded closely to those which would have been predicted by extrapolation from the observation periods.

Results

The relationships of greatest interest are the effects of presence and absence of Approval Behaviors on Relevant Behaviors and the effects of levels of Disapproval Behaviors on Disruptive Behaviors. Because of a systematic rater bias which entered into the data for Other Task Behavior (discussed later), and therefore also affected Relevant Behaviors incompatible with Other Task, greater emphasis is given to the analysis of Disruptive Behaviors in presenting the results.

Average Level of Disruptive Behavior

In Baseline$_1$ Disruptive Behaviors occurred in an average of 8.7% of the intervals observed. When Approving Behaviors were discontinued (No Approval$_1$) Disruptive Behavior increased to an average of 25.5% (Figure 1). Approving Behaviors were again provided (Baseline$_2$) and Disruptive Behavior dropped to an average of 12.9%. In order to show more conclusively that the changes in Disruptive Behavior were related to the changes in teacher behavior, Approving Behaviors were again discontinued (No Approval$_2$) and the level of Disruptive Behaviors stabilized near the same level as in No Approval$_1$ condition (average 19.4%). When the Disapproving Behaviors (critical comments) were tripled (Frequent Disapproval), while Approving Behaviors were still withheld, Disruptive Behavior increased to an average of 31.2% with high points far above any observed before. The behavior stabilized, however, near the level at which the two previous No Approval phases had stabilized. When the rate of disapproval was lowered (No Approval$_3$), no great reduction in Disruptive Behavior occurred. The average level of Disruptive Behaviors over No Approval$_2$, Frequent Disapproval, and No Approval$_3$ was 25.9%. At the end of No Approval$_3$, Approval was again added to the low level of Disapproving Behaviors, and Disruptive Behavior dropped to an average of 13.2%, with the trend indicating a level far below this average.[2]

2. Conservative statistical analysis was performed (F test) to compare those three conditions where approval responses were available with those two conditions where approval responses were withdrawn. For this test the Frequent Disapproval and No Approval$_{2+3}$ conditions were collapsed into one condition. In order to insure independence of observations, the average values within each condition were used, thus providing four degrees of freedom. Significant differences were found for Relevant Behavior ($p < 0.01$), Noise Making ($p < 0.05$), Gross Motor ($p < 0.025$), and for the overall level of Disruptive Behavior ($p < 0.01$).

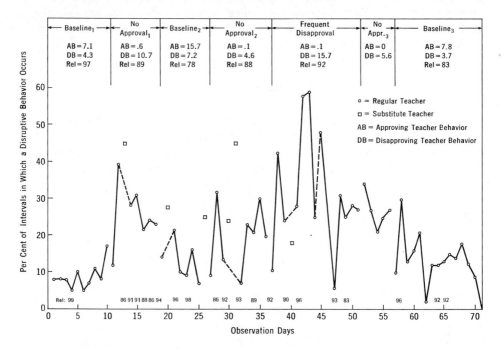

Figure 1. Disruptive Classroom Behaviors as a Function of Nature of Teacher Behavior. Data points represent 2-minute samples on 10 children each day. Dotted lines cross observations where the regular teacher was absent due to a recurrent illness, including a 10-day hospitalization between Days 39 and 41. The dotted line connecting days 44 and 45 represents the Easter vacation break. The data for Day 26 were taken with the teacher out of the room.

Analysis of Classes of Behavior

Discontinuation of approving behaviors. In reviewing the changes in the individual categories of behavior through the first two withdrawals of Approving Behavior, the majority of the increase in Disruptive Behaviors could be attributed to changes in Verbalization and Orienting categories (Table 1). The mean of verbalization in No Approval₁ was 22.6% due to one extremely high observation on the second day of the condition; however, these behaviors stabilized between 9% and 17% (Figure 2). Orienting showed a slight decrease across No Approval₁ (Figure 2). The second time Approval was discontinued, Orienting increased across the condition while Verbalization remained relatively stable except for two high observations. Gross Motor behaviors followed the same pattern as Orienting and Verbalization through No Approval (1 and 2), increasing each time Approving Behavior was discontinued and decreasing when Approving Behaviors were present (Figure 2).

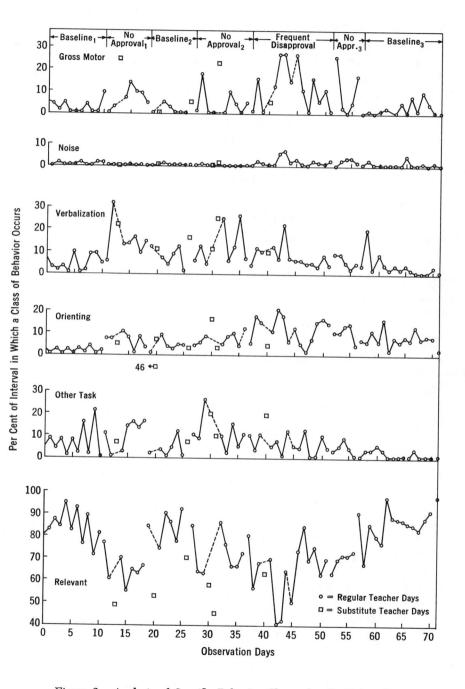

Figure 2. Analysis of Specific Behavior Classes by Condition. Data points represent 2-minute samples on 10 children each day. See notes under Figure 1.

Noise Making and Aggression followed a pattern through No Approval$_1$ and $_2$ which was distinctly different from the other categories of disruptive behavior. Both of these categories of behavior were already occurring at a low frequency in the Baseline condition (Table 1), but they occurred even less often when only Disapproving Behavior was given.

INCREASE OF DISAPPROVING BEHAVIORS.   In the Frequent Disapproval condition, Noise Making, Gross Motor, and Orienting all increased (Table 1). Verbalizations showed a decline over this condition and continued to decline through the rest of the study.

Table 1

AVERAGE PERCENTAGES FOR SPECIFIC BEHAVIOR CLASSES FOR
EACH EXPERIMENTAL PHASE

BEHAVIOR CLASSES	BASE-LINE$_1$	NO APPROVAL$_1$	BASE-LINE$_2$	NO APPROVAL$_2$	FREQUENT DIS-APPROVAL	NO APPROVAL$_3$	BASE-LINE$_3$
Disruptive Behaviors[a]	8.7	25.5	12.9	19.4	31.2	26.8	13.2
Gross Motor	2.7	6.7	2.0	4.8	12.3	10.4	2.4
Noise	0.9	0.1	0.7	0.09	4.1	4.4	0.9
Verbalization	4.6	22.6	7.7	9.6	7.9	6.0	3.9
Orienting	1.4	6.5	4.1	7.1	11.5	10.2	7.6
Aggression	0.25	0.01	0.2	0.01	0.04	0.04	0.1
Other Task	7.0	10.4	5.9	10.7	5.9	4.2	1.2
Relevant	84.1	65.3	83.9	72.1	64.3	69.4	85.6

[a] The addition of percentages for the five classes of Disruptive Behaviors will usually lead to a sum higher than that reported as percentage of Disruptive Behaviors, since the latter does not reflect the occurrence of more than one subclass of Disruptive Behaviors in a given 10-second interval.

Changing from a high level of Disapproving Behaviors to a lower level did not markedly change the frequency of the various categories of Disruptive Behaviors relative to their terminal level under the Frequent Disapproval condition.

When Approving Behaviors were again used by the teacher (Baseline$_3$), the frequency of Gross Motor, Noise Making, and Orienting behaviors decreased noticeably (Figure 2). Verbalization continued to show the steady decrease in frequency which had started in the Frequent Disapproval condition. In Baseline$_3$ Aggression again occurred, but rarely. All Disruptive Behaviors except Orienting dropped to the level of the initial Baseline (or below) during the final Baseline.

RELEVANT BEHAVIOR.   Appropriate behaviors were initially high in the classroom (Figure 2). Behaviors such as getting out of seat to move to a reading group or to check a completed workbook assignment were rated in the Gross Motor category. The requirements for such behaviors, however, remained constant through all conditions so changes in the level of Relevant Behaviors cannot be attributed to changes in classroom requirements. Relevant Behavior decreased each time Approving Behavior was discontinued and increased each time the Approval was reinstated. Relevant Behavior was at a slightly higher level during the final Baseline than during the initial Baseline.

OTHER TASK BEHAVIOR NOT SPECIFICALLY DEFINED. As indicated earlier, a systematic rater difference was encountered early in the study in rating Other Task behaviors. In Figure 2 this bias can be seen by contrasting data collected on Days 2, 4, 6, 8, and 10 from one set of observers with that collected on Days 1, 3, 5, 7, and 9 by another set of observers. While an attempt was made to correct this bias by interlocking reliability checks, it is apparent that the bias continued to some extent throughout the study. Since Other Task is by definition incompatible with Relevant Behavior, Relevant Behavior shows the same bias. By looking at Disruptive Behavior, defined so as to exclude Other Task behaviors, the systematic bias was largely eliminated from the data presented in Figure 1.

Teacher Behaviors

The behavior of the teacher remained under good control throughout the study. Averages by conditions for Approving and Disapproving Behaviors are given in the upper part of Figure 1. As the conditions were changed, little difficulty was found in withholding behaviors in the Approving category. Some difficulty was reported by the teacher in regulating the frequency of Disapproving Behaviors while withholding Approving Behaviors, but a partial solution to this problem was found. The teacher found that by carrying a small hand-counter (mentioned earlier) she could more accurately judge the frequency of her critical comments. In the Frequent Disapproval Phase there were days when the children were not emitting enough Disruptive Behaviors for critical comments to be appropriate at the programmed frequency. Rather than make inappropriate comments, the rate of Disapproving comments was adjusted to the frequency of the Disruptive Behaviors. When enough Disruptive Behaviors were available, Disapproving Behaviors were dispensed at a maximum rate of one per minute throughout the day; thus, many of the responses of the children were reprimanded very quickly.

General frequency of instructional comments did not change appreciably across conditions. However, the teacher did increase the frequency with which she would say in a neutral tone whether responses were correct or incorrect in the phases where Approval was not given.

The behaviors characterized as Terminating Social Interaction occurred only twice during the study and were, therefore, not subject to further analysis.

SUBSTITUTE TEACHERS.   Observations taken on the days when a substitute teacher was in charge of the classroom appear in four conditions of the study. The frequency of Disruptive Behaviors increased in the presence of a temporary teacher as long as the regular teacher was in either Baseline or No Approving Behavior phases. When the Disapproving Behavior was being dispensed at a high rate, however, the level of Disruptive Behaviors decreased in the presence of a temporary teacher (Figure 1).

DAY 26.   The data for this day were taken while the teacher was out of the room. Since the experimental conditions were not operative, this point should have been omitted altogether.

Discussion

The results indicate that some aspects of the behaviors included in the category of Approving Behaviors were reinforcing for task-appropriate behaviors. The frequency of Relevant Behaviors was high whenever Approving Behaviors followed Relevant child Behavior, and decreased whenever Approving Behaviors were discontinued.

In each change of conditions that involved discontinuation of Approving Behaviors, there appeared a reliable transition effect (observation Days 11 and 27). This effect may be an example of the typical increase in rate found when a positive reinforcer is removed. In support of this explanation, the teacher reported, "When I stop praising the children, and make only negative comments, they behave very nicely for three or four hours. However, by the middle of the afternoon the whole classroom is chaotic." Since observations were taken during a study period in the morning, the periods of good behavior show up in the data each time a condition was changed. A similar low deviant behavior point occurred at the transition to Frequent Disapproving Behaviors (day 37), but it is not clearly explained. "The children seemed stunned."

Reviewing the individual classes of Disruptive Behaviors brings out certain similarities and differences among the classes. During the first alternations of Baseline with discontinuation of Approving Behaviors, Gross Motor, Orienting, and Verbalization Behaviors increased with discontinuation of Approval, while Noise Making and Aggressive Behaviors remained at their already low frequency. The increases are interpreted as suggesting that some responses in the disruptive classes may be reinforced by peer attention or other environmental circumstances when control through approving teacher responses to incompatible behaviors is withdrawn. For example, Orienting behaviors, such as looking around the room or out the window may be reinforced by seeing other children playing, by observing a custodian cleaning up the schoolyard, or by seeing any of numerous events which have no relationship to the classroom. Observational evidence for this inference was clearest in the Frequent Disapproval phase (below). It is also possible to attribute the increases in Disruptive Behaviors during No Approval₁ to the increase in use of Disapproval. However, the data for No Approval₂, where Disapproval was held to the Baseline level, would argue that the effect was primarily related to the withdrawal of approval.

Increasing Disapproving Behaviors to a high level produced four days where Disruptive Behaviors were above 40%. Several individual categories of behavior also showed marked changes. The increase in Gross Motor Behaviors was related to an increase in interactions with other students. During the Frequent Disapproval condition, two or three children would make alternate trips to check their workbooks at a table provided for that purpose. Only one child was permitted at the table at a time. During Baseline and No Approval phases, it was rare to see a child make more than one trip to the table; in the Frequent Disapproval phase, some of the children would check their papers several times. Others responded by pushing their papers off of their desks and then getting up to get them. There was a noticeable "pairing off" with two or more children exhibiting the same behaviors.

Another consequence of the Frequent Disapproval phase was a marked increase in the noise level in the room. A majority of the noises during this period were created by children scooting their desks and chairs. One observer reported, "I waited for a few minutes after the regular observation period was over and counted the noises. During one 40-second period, I counted 17 separate chair scraping noises. They came in bursts of two or three at a time. It looked as though the kids were trying to irritate the teacher." The noises in "bursts of two or three" seemed similar to the "pairing off" of children noted with the Gross Motor behaviors, and strengthens an hypothesis that reinforcement from peers is one of the elements which accounts for the increase in Disruptive Behaviors during this time. Peer attention cannot be the only element affecting the behavior of the children, however, because the Verbalization category of behaviors showed a constant decrease throughout the Frequent Disapproval condition. The inhibition of Verbalization could be due to interfering emotional responses being elicited by the high level of critical comments by the teacher. More probable, however, is that the children simply talked more quietly to avoid being caught by the teacher. Observers' reports indicate that a substantial number of verbalizations would have been recorded during the Frequent Disapproving Behaviors condition if there had been no requirement that the responses be heard by the observers. The children could be seen to turn their heads, and lip movements could be seen frequently, but the verbalizations could not be heard.

Work by Lövaas, Freitag, Kinder, Rubenstein, Schaeffer, and Simmons (1964) suggests that for some children any adult attention may be reinforcing. Some of the present findings under the Disapproval conditions could also be interpreted as indicating that teacher behavior of the Disapproving variety was positively reinforcing. The level of Disruptive Behaviors during each of the conditions when only Disapproving and Instructional attentions were available does appear to vary with the level of Disapproving Behaviors dispensed by the teacher. Unfortunately, the illness-caused absences and Easter break make the results less clear than hoped. It should be apparent that the effect of Frequent Disapproval on the behavior of the children is not subject to a simple interpretation. Some criticized behaviors decreased, some increased, and several possible controlling stimuli could have been operating with contradictory effects on behavior. It is obviously difficult in a field-experimental study of this complexity to maintain control of all the possibly relevant variables at once.

Another limitation of the present design should be noted. Because of a shortage of observation time under the desired classroom conditions, a sample of 10 children was observed daily. A procedure which included all children each day would have provided a stronger basis for analysis of effects on individuals. A rough analysis of individuals with the present data confirms, however, that an average of 76% of the students made changes in the same direction as the group changes. From Baseline, to No Approval, 81% of the students showed increases in Disruptive Behavior. When Approving Behavior became available, 75% of the students improved within two weeks. Discontinuing Approving Behavior a second time resulted in 78% of the students being more disruptive, while the final addition of Approving Behavior showed an increase in appropriate behavior for 71% of the children. Across condition changes, 5% of the children showed no change on the average, and 19% showed change (usually minor) in an opposite direction. Procedures which permitted specifications of which children were praised or criticized for which behaviors would be needed to clarify fully individual effects. It is quite possible that the children who changed opposite to the group trend were being responded to differently. Of course, there are many ways one can speculate here. In an as yet unpublished study we have shown that praising some children but not others leads to changes in the behavior only for the children who are praised. Results of this sort emphasize the importance of looking at individual contingencies.

Brief mention should be made of the possible ethical considerations involved in producing disruptive behaviors. One needs to weigh the potential gains in knowledge against the short-term or long-term deleterious effects on the children or teacher. On the basis of prior research and the return to baseline after the first No Approving Behaviors condition, the teacher and the experimenters were confident that appropriate behaviors could be readily reinstated at any time it was felt necessary. It may also be reassuring to know that this accelerated middle primary class did achieve well academically during the year. The children completed all second and third grade work and were all performing on a fourth grade level by the end of the year.

Implications

This further demonstration of the importance of specific teacher behaviors in influencing classroom behavior has a double implication. First, the teacher who uses her Approving Behaviors as immediate consequences for good behavior should find that the frequency and duration of appropriate behaviors increase in her classroom (at least for most children). On the other hand, the teacher who cuddles the miscreant, tries pleasantly to get a child to stop behaving disruptively, talks with a child so that he "understands" what he was doing wrong, or who pleasantly suggests an alternative activity to a child who has been performing inappropriately, is likely to find an increase in the very behaviors she had hoped to reduce. This view of the functional importance of teacher's behavior in creating, maintaining, or reducing classroom behavior problems contrasts sharply with that generated by psychodynamic models of problem behaviors and what to do about them. Work of this sort also suggests a need to re-evaluate the popular cliché about the importance of the interaction of the "personality" of the teacher with that of the child in looking at classroom management procedures.

The suggestive evidence that peer reinforcement (among other stimuli) takes over when social reinforcement is not provided by teacher is given support by the recent work of Wahler (1967). Wahler has shown how preschool children can systematically control the behavior of their peers by differential use of social reinforcement. The more general implication for the teacher is this: unless an effort is made to support desirable classroom behaviors with appropriate consequences, the children's behavior will be controlled by others in ways likely to interfere with the teacher's objectives.

Finally, the possibility that critical comments may actually function to increase some behaviors upon which they are contingent cannot be overlooked. A recent study (Madsen, Becker, Thomas, Koser, and Plager, 1967), gives clear evidence that some forms of critical comment do function to strengthen behavior. The more often a teacher told first graders to "sit down," the more often they stood up. Only praising sitting seemed to increase sitting behavior.

References

BECKER, W. C., MADSEN, C. H., JR., ARNOLD, CAROLE, R. and THOMAS, D. R. The contingent use of teacher attention and praise in reducing classroom behavior problems. *Journal of Special Education*, 1967, 1, 287-307.

BIJOU, S. W. and BAER, D. M. Some methodological contributions from a functional analysis of child development. In L. P. Lipsitt and C. S. Spiker (Eds.), *Advances in child development and behavior*. New York: Academic Press, 1963. Pp. 197-231.

HART, BETTY M., ALLEN, K. EILEEN, BUELL, JOAN S., HARRIS, FLORENCE R. and WOLF, M. M. Effects of social reinforcement on operant crying. *Journal of Experimental Child Psychology* 1964, 1, 145-153.

KERR, NANCY, MEYERSON, L. and MICHAEL, J.   A procedure for shaping vocalizations in a mute child. In L. P. Ullman and L Krasner (Eds.), *Case studies in behavior modification*. New York: Holt, Rinehart and Winston, Inc., 1965. Pp. 366-370.

LÖVAAS, O. I., FREITAG, G., KINDER, M. I., RUBENSTEIN, D. B., SCHAEFFER, B. and SIMMONS, J. B.   Experimental studies in childhood schizophrenia—Establishment of social reinforcers. Paper delivered at Western Psychological Association, Portland, April, 1964.

MADSEN, C. H., JR., BECKER, W. C., THOMAS, D. R., KOSER, LINDA and PLAGER, ELAINE.   An analysis of the reinforcing function of "sit down" commands. In R. K. Parker (Ed.), *Readings in educational psychology*. Boston: Allyn and Bacon, 1968.

WAHLER, R. G.   Child-child interactions in free field settings: Some experimental analyses. *Journal of Experimental Child Psychology*, 1967, 5, 278-293.

ZIMMERMAN, ELAINE H. and ZIMMERMAN, J.   The alteration of behavior in a special classroom situation. *Journal of the Experimental Analysis of Behavior*, 1962, 5, 59-60.

※ ※ ※ ※ ※

Cognitive theory is one of the more important underpinnings of social psychology. O. J. Harvey has been a prime contributor to it through his theoretical and empirical work on concrete-abstract modes of conceptual functioning, which is described more fully in Harvey, Hunt and Schroder (1961). Briefly put: if all goes well, the child develops through four stages from concrete (absolutistic, dependent) ways of thinking to abstract (open-minded, task-oriented, independent) ones. Development can, of course, be arrested at various stages along the way (i.e., some adults think very much like young children).

It is fitting that this line of work be represented in this book in connection with a classical problem of education, the effects of teacher attributes on the classroom performance of pupils.

In this study, Harvey and his co-authors make a two-step linkage. First they show a connection between the measured concreteness–abstractness of kindergarten and first-grade teachers' belief systems and the teachers' observed behavior in the classroom. This was an effort to replicate findings from some of their earlier research. Secondly, they demonstrate an association between the overt behavior of teachers (and their measured concreteness–abstractness) and observed performance variables of the young pupils in their classes. The authors are careful to warn against premature conclusions regarding the direction of causation in their correlational study, but it is clear what inference they would prefer to draw.

Studies of "teacher effectiveness" have a forty-year history of inconclusive and contradictory results. Harvey and his colleagues use a "weak" measure of pupil effects—ratings by observers of entire classes. It remains to be seen whether subsequent investigation will bear out their findings, especially as attempts are made to establish the next link to a "strong" measure of cognitive learning among individual pupils. If we take seriously the results of other similar studies, we might well expect that teachers will be found to have differential effects on students, depending upon the students' own conceptual styles. To check this, though, will require a study design different from Harvey's.

Teachers' Beliefs, Classroom Atmosphere, and Student Behavior*

O. J. Harvey, Misha Prather,
B. Jack White, James K. Hoffmeister

Harvey, White, Prather, Alter and Hoffmeister (1966) found recently that preschool teachers of concrete and abstract belief systems differed markedly in the class room environments they created for their students. Teachers representing System 4, the most abstract belief system treated by Harvey, Hunt and Schroder (1961) differed from representatives of System 1, the most concrete mode of functioning characterized by Harvey and others (1961), in what was presumed to be an educationally desirable direction on all 26 dimensions of classroom behavior on which they were rated.

The difference was statistically significant on 14 dimensions: System 4 teachers expressed greater warmth toward children, showed greater perceptiveness of the children's wishes and needs, were more flexible in meeting the interests and needs of the children, were more encouraging of individual responsibility, gave greater encouragement to free expression of feelings, were more encouraging of creativity, displayed greater ingenuity in improvising teaching and play materials, invoked unexplained rules less frequently, were less rule oriented, were less determining of classroom and playground procedure, manifested less need for structure, were less punitive, and were less anxious about being observed.

A cluster analysis of these 14 dimensions (Tryon and Bailey, 1965, 1966) yielded three factors of resourcefulness, dictatorialness and punitiveness. System 4 teachers were more resourceful, less dictatorial and less punitive than System 1 teachers.

While consistent both with our theoretical stance and a wide range of other differences found between the more concretely and the more abstractly functioning individuals (Adams, Harvey, and Heslin, 1966; Harvey, 1963; 1966; Harvey and Ware, 1967; Ware and Harvey, 1967; White and Harvey, 1965), the finding that teachers' belief systems affect their

* From *American Educational Research Journal*, 1968, 5, 151-166. Used by permission of the authors and publisher.

The collection of these data and part of their analyses were supported by the Office of Economic Opportunity, Contract OEO-1274 with the Extension Division of the University of Colorado.

Harvey's participation in the data collection part of this study occurred while he was a Fellow at the Center for Advanced Study in the Behavioral Sciences. His subsequent participation has been supported by a Career Development Award from the National Institute of Mental Health, No. K03 MH28117.

overt behavior in the classroom does not bear directly upon the more educationally significant question of the influence of teachers' beliefs and behavior upon the learning and performance of their students. It is with this latter question that the present study is concerned.

More specifically, the main aim of this study was to assess the relationship between students' performance and teachers' resourcefulness, dictatorialness and punitiveness. In addition, the study provided a test of the replicability of the earlier findings that concrete and abstract teachers differ in the kinds of classroom behavior they manifest.

The general expectancies were that teachers of more concrete belief systems would display less resourcefulness, more dictatorialness and more punitiveness in the classroom than the more abstract teachers, as found in the previous study (Harvey and others, 1966); and that greater abstractness, greater resourcefulness, less dictatorialness and less punitiveness on the part of the teacher would be associated with more educationally perferable performances of the children.

Method

Concrete and abstract[1] teachers of kindergarten and first grade were rated on the 14 dimensions found by Harvey and others (1966) to discriminate significantly between concrete and abstract teachers. Their students were rated, as a class, on a specially constructed 31-item rating scale.

TEACHER RATING SCALE. This instrument, while providing the necessary information for a test of the replicability of the earlier results (Harvey and others, 1966), was intended primarily as a measure of teachers' overt resourcefulness, dictatorialness and punitiveness. It consisted of the 14 items from which these three factors were derived: (1) warmth toward the children, (2) perceptiveness of the children's needs and wishes, (3) flexibility in meeting the needs and interests of the children, (4) maintenance of relaxed relationships with the children, (5) encouragement of individual responsibility, (6) encouragement of free expression of feelings, (7) encouragement of creativity, (8) ingenuity in improvising teaching and play materials, (9) use of unexplained rules, (10) rule orientation, (11) determination of classroom procedures, (12) need for structure, (13) punitiveness and (14) anxiety induced by the observers' presence.

STUDENT RATING SCALE. This measure of student behavior, which provided the major dependent variables of this study, consisted of the following items: (1) over-all adherence to the teacher's rules, (2) immediacy of response to the rules, (3) adherence to the spirit (vs. the letter) of the rules, (4) information seeking, (5) independence, (6) cooperativeness with the teacher, (7) task attentiveness, (8) enthusiasm, (9) voice in

1. As measured by two pencil-and-paper instruments (see below).

classroom activities, (10) voluntary participation in classroom activities, (11) free expression of feelings, (12) diversity of goal relevant activities, (13) student-initiated activity, (14) amount of activity, (15) considerateness toward classmates, (16) reciprocal affection between classmates, (17) cooperation with classmates, (18) taking turns with classmates, (19) amount of interaction with classmates, (20) novelty of response to problem or teacher's question, (21) appropriateness of response, (22) accuracy of facts, (23) integration of facts, (24) orientation toward specificity of facts (vs. more general principles), (25) roteness of answers or solutions, (26) active hostility toward the teacher, (27) passive hostility toward the teacher, (28) fear attentiveness (anxiety), (29) aggression toward classmates, (30) guidance seeking, and (31) approval seeking.

Each of the dimensions in both the teacher and student rating scale was rated on a six-point scale: 3, 2, and 1 for "far," "considerably" and "slightly," above average respectively; and -1, -2, and -3 for "slightly," "considerably" and "far" below average respectively. The "average" category was omitted with the aim (by creating a forced choice condition) of avoiding the common tendency of observers (Os) to assign a wide variety of discriminably different behaviors to this category. Through a training program described later, an attempt was made to establish equivalent "averages" for all Os.

Subjects

Since the present study was part of a larger investigation concerned with the effects of prior participation in Head Start, classrooms were selected for observation if they contained at least one kindergarten or first grade student who had gone to Head Start nine months earlier (i.e., during the summer of 1965) and who was attending public school for the first time. These criteria yielded 118 classes, 92 kindergarten and 26 first grade, in 18 rural and urban Colorado school districts. The 92 kindergarten classes were taught by 64 teachers while the 26 first grade classes were taught by 26 teachers. Each of the 118 classes, with an average of 26 students, was observed and rated *as a class,* not as individual students, on the student rating scale.

Of the 90 teachers, 67 completed the "This I Believe" (TIB) Test and 66 completed the Conceptual Systems Test (CST). Both the TIB and CST are tests of concreteness-abstractness of belief systems, the former being based upon sentence completions and the latter upon responses to objective items.

THE "THIS I BELIEVE" (TIB) TEST.   This test, developed specifically as a measure of concreteness-abstractness of conceptual or belief systems (e.g., Harvey, 1964, 1966; Harvey and others, 1966; Ware and Harvey, 1967; White and Harvey, 1965), requires S to indicate his beliefs about a number of socially and personally relevant concept referents by completing in two or three sentences the phrase "This I believe about————," the blank being replaced successively by one of the referents. The referents employed in the present study were "religion," "friendship," "the American way of life," "sin," "education," "the family," "people on welfare," "punishment," "teaching" and "sex."

From the relativism, tautologicalness, novelty and connotative implications or richness of the completions, together with criteria implied below, respondents may be classified into one of the four principal systems posited by Harvey and others (1961) or into some mixture of two or more systems.

More specifically, Ss are classified as representing predominantly System 1, the most concrete mode of dimensionalizing and construing the world, if their completions denote such characteristics as high absolutism, high tautologicalness, high frequency of platitudes and normative statements, high ethnocentrism, high religiosity, assertion of the superiority of American morality and expression of highly positive attitudes toward institutional referents.

Subjects are categorized as representing System 2, the next to the lowest level of abstractness, if, in addition to being highly evaluative and absolute, they express strong negative attitudes toward such referents as marriage, religion, the American way of life—the same referents toward which System 1 representatives manifest highly positive attitudes.

Responses to the TIB are scored as representing System 3 functioning, the next to the highest level of abstractness posited by Harvey and others (1961), if they indicate more relativism and less evaluativeness than System 1 and 2 and at the same time express strongly positive beliefs about friendship, people and interpersonal relations.

System 4 functioning, the highest of the four levels of abstractness, is indicated by TIB responses that imply a high degree of novelty and appropriateness, independence without negativism, high relativism and contingency of thought, and the general usage of multidimensional rather than unidimensional interpretive schemata.

Of the 67 teachers who completed the TIB, 50 were classified as System 1, none was categorized as System 2, four were scored as System 3, eight were classified as weak instances of System 4, and five were scored as admixtures of Systems 1 and 3. In the analysis involving the TIB the admixtures were omitted; Systems 3 and 4 were combined into the *more abstract group;* and System 1 teachers were treated as the *more concrete group.* Of the 50 concrete teachers, 30 taught 44 classes of kindergarteners and 20 taught 20 classes of first-graders. Seven of the 12 abstract teachers taught 11 kindergarten classes while the other five abstract teachers taught five first-grade classes. Thus it should be noted that while both concrete and abstract first grade teachers each taught only one class, kindergarten teachers, both concrete and abstract, each taught an approximate average of 1½ classes.

THE CONCEPTUAL SYSTEMS TEST. All but one of the 67 teachers who completed the TIB Test also completed the objective measure of belief systems, the CST. From a pool of several hundred items and numerous runs through Tryon's program of cluster analysis (Tryon and Bailey, 1965, 1966) seven factors have been extracted and replicated which are theoretically consistent with the major characteristics of the four principal belief systems posited by Harvey and others (1961). These factors as we have tentatively labeled them (Harvey, 1967) are (1) Divine Fate Control, (2) Need for Simplicity-Certainty, (3) Need for Structure Order, (4) Distrust of Social Authority, (5) Friendship Absolutism, (6) Moral Absolutism, and (7) General Pessimism.

While the CST was administered in its entirety, for purposes of this study scores were derived for only the three clusters of Divine Fate Control, Need for Simplicity-Certainty and Need for Structure-Order. The combined scores from these three factors were treated as our second measure of a teacher's concreteness-abstractness. Representative items comprising each of the three of these component factors include:

1. Divine Fate Control (DFC) is assessed by such items as "There are some things which God will never permit man to know," "In the final analysis, events in the world will be in line with the master plan of God," and "I believe that to attain my goals it is only necessary for me to live as God would have me live."

2. Need for Simplicity-Certainty (NS-C) is inferred from response to such statements as "I dislike having to change my plans in the middle of a task," "It is annoying to listen to a lecturer who cannot seem to make up his mind as to what he really believes," and "A group which tolerates extreme differences of opinion among its own members cannot exist for long."

3. Need for Structure-Order (NS-O) is derived from such items as "I don't like to work on a problem unless these is a possibility of coming out with a clear-cut, definite answer," "I don't like for things to be uncertain and unpredictable," and "I like to have a place for everything and everything in its place."

TRAINING OF OBSERVERS AND ASSESSMENT OF INTER-OBSERVER RELIABILITY.   Each of the nine *O*s, all females, participated in six training sessions during which six teachers and their classes were observed and independently rated. Each observation session was followed by a lengthy group discussion among the *O*s and other staff members aimed at increasing the reliability of the ratings through improving observation techniques and clarifying and standardizing meaning and usage of the rating categories.

Inter-judge reliability for the nine *O*s was assessed for both the teacher and student rating scales at three points: immediately following the last training session, one week after field observations began, and immediately preceding completion of the experimental observations, two weeks later. The mean correlation between every pair of judges for the teacher scale was .78, .76 and .70 for the three periods respectively; the corresponding reliability values for the student scale were .84, .75 and .77.

PROCEDURE.   Each teacher and her students were observed in the class-room on a single occasion by a single O for approximately two hours. All teachers had been advised earlier by their principals of the dates on which they were to be observed.

Observation occurred during normal classroom activities on a day free of special events in order to render the conditions of observation as comparable as possible across classrooms. The O arrived before class, introduced herself, explained (with the aim of allaying the teacher's apprehension and fostering her cooperation) that the purpose of the visit was to gather examples of good teaching procedure that could be utilized as bases for future teacher training programs, and requested that she be allowed to observe while remaining as inconspicuous as possible in order to minimize the effects of her presence upon the children. To further O's unobtrusiveness and simultaneously to increase the likelihood of both the teacher and her students behaving in their usual fashion, each teacher was asked not to converse with O during the observation period.

The teacher and her class were rated by the same O, the students being observed and rated first as independently as possible of the teacher's behavior. This procedure was aimed at minimizing the contamination between the dependent and independent variables likely to result from the students and teacher being rated by the same O. Extensive pretesting indicated that this procedure, of having the O first concentrate on and rate the behavior of the students as a class before focusing on the teacher, yielded a relationship between student and teacher ratings that was no higher than that between separate ratings of the teacher and her students by different judges. In fact, the evidence indicated clearly that, while the use of a single O for both the teacher and her students may have produced contamination, at the same time it produced seemingly more valid ratings than those yielded by the practice of one judge observing only the teacher while the other O noted only the responses of the children. Thus, the degree of contamination inherent in the method of observation we employed appears to be preferable to the loss of validity that results from attempts of Os to rate the behavior of the teacher and her students without the use of the other as a referent.

In rating the children, care was exercised to rate the class as a whole and not to give inordinate weight to a small minority by concentrating on the behavior of a single child or a few children.

Results

Tests of Assumptions

Before analyzing the effects of teachers' overt behavior upon students' performance, it was necessary to test two basic assumptions: (1) that the 14 items of the teacher rating scale would yield the three factors of resourcefulness, dictatorialness and punitiveness, as they had in the earlier study (Harvey and others, 1966); and (2) that variations in the concreteness-abstractness of the teachers' beliefs would lead them to score differently on these three behavioral factors.

The validity of the first assumption was demonstrated by the results of a factor analysis of the teacher rating scale by Tryon's method of cluster analysis (Tryon and Bailey, 1965; 1966) which yielded the three anticipated clusters.

Resourcefulness was comprised of four behavioral items. They, together with their factor loadings (represented by the values in the parentheses) were: utilization of physical resources (.77), diversity of simultaneous activities (.77), encouragement of creativity (.72) and ingenuity in improvising teaching and play materials (.71).

Dictatorialness contained seven items: need for structure (.90), flexibility (−.90), rule orientation (.86), encouragement of free expression of feelings (−.84), teacher determination of classroom procedures (.81) and the use of unexplained rules (.70).

Punitiveness was based on three items: warmth toward the children (−.86), perceptiveness of the children's needs and wishes (−.85) and punitiveness (.77).

The second assumption also proved to be warranted. Teachers classified on the basis of the TIB as being concrete were significantly less resourceful ($t = 4.03$, $p < .001$), significantly more dictatorial ($t = 1.67$, $p < .05$), and were more punitive, although not significantly more, ($t = 1.05$, $p > .10$) than the teachers classified as abstract. Moreover, the abstractness measures from the CST correlated significantly positively with teacher resourcefulness ($r = .37$, $p < .005$), and significantly negatively with both teacher dictatorialness ($r = −.19$, $p < .05$) and punitiveness ($r = −.19$, $p < .05$). These results, through replicating the more essential findings of our earlier study (Harvey and others, 1966), make it clear that variation in the concreteness-abstractness of teachers' beliefs generates theoretically consistent and predictable parallels in the overt behavior of these individuals. Thus an examination of the effects of teachers' beliefs and behavior upon their students, the major concern of this study, becomes appropriate.

Concreteness-Abstractness of Teachers' Beliefs and Student Performance

FACTOR ANALYSIS OF THE STUDENT RATING SCALE. In order to extricate the more generic dimensions encompassed within the 31-item student rating scale and thus enhance the coherency of the presentation of results, the student rating scale was factorized by Tryon's method of cluster analysis (Tryon and Bailey, 1965; 1966) and the resulting factors related to variation in teachers' beliefs and overt behavior.

Seven factors were derived from the student rating scale. The first cluster, termed *cooperation,* was comprised of five items, which with their factor loadings were: immediacy of response to rules (.91), over-all adherence to teachers' rules (.86), child-sustained activity (.68), cooperativeness with teacher (.57) and adherence to the spirit of the rules (.55). The second factor, which centered around *student involvement,* consisted of eight items: enthusiasm (.89), voluntary participation in classroom activity (.82), free expression of feelings (.78), voice of students in classroom activity (.78), independence (.76), information seeking (.72), insecurity ($-.66$) and task attentiveness (.63). The third factor, labeled *activity level,* was derived from two items: amount of activity (.81) and diversity of goal-relevant activity (.81). The fourth factor, *nurturance seeking,* contained two items: guidance seeking (.68) and approval seeking (.59). The fifth factor, termed *achievement* level, included three items: accuracy of facts (.81), appropriateness of solution (.80) and integration of facts (.71). The sixth factor, *helpfulness,* was comprised of four items: considerateness toward classmates (.79), cooperativeness with classmates. (.71), taking turns (.56) and aggression ($-.49$). The seventh cluster, referred to as *concreteness of response,* contained three items: roteness of answers or solutions (.88), orientation toward specificity of facts (.71) and novelty of answer or solution ($-.56$). Factor scores were obtained by computing the mean score on the items constituting the factor.

Four of the items from the student rating scale were not included in any of the seven clusters: amount of interaction, reciprocal affection, passive and active hostility. Results relating to these four items will not be reported.

TIB CLASSIFICATION AND STUDENT PERFORMANCE. Comparisons were made between the 64 classes taught by the 50 teachers classified by the TIB as being concrete and the 16 classes taught by the 12 abstract teachers on each of the seven factors derived from the student rating scale.

As indicated in Table 1, students of more abstract teachers, in comparison to their counterparts, were significantly more involved in classroom activities, more active, higher in achievement and less concrete in their responses. They were also less nurturant seeking, more cooperative and more helpful, but not significantly so, than students of concrete teachers.

CST FACTORS AND STUDENT PERFORMANCE. Teachers' scores on the abstractness measure from the ÇST and on each of the three factors going into this measure were correlated with each of the seven factors from the student rating scale. These relationships are presented in Table 2.

The CST measure of abstractness related significantly to every one of the student performance factors. Greater abstractness of the teacher was accompanied by greater involvement, greater cooperation, more activity, less nurturance seeking, higher achievement, greater helpfulness and less concreteness on the part of the students.

Table 1

PERFORMANCES OF STUDENTS OF CONCRETE AND ABSTRACT
TEACHERS (AS CLASSIFIED BY THE TIB)

STUDENT RATING SCALE FACTORS	CONCRETE TEACHERS		ABSTRACT TEACHERS		
	MEAN	SD	MEAN	SD	*t*
Cooperation	4.05	0.82	4.34	0.75	1.26
Involvement	3.60	0.87	4.09	0.90	1.96*
Activity	3.29	1.01	4.22	1.02	3.29**
Nurturance seeking	2.91	0.99	2.56	0.95	−1.27
Achievement	3.90	0.71	4.25	0.56	1.81*
Helpfulness	4.03	0.65	4.20	0.63	0.97
Concreteness	3.78	0.88	3.27	0.80	−2.12*

Note: *df* for all tests = 78
  * one-tailed $p < .05$
 ** one-tailed $p < .01$

Table 2

CORRELATIONS BETWEEN CLUSTERS FROM THE CONCEPTUAL
SYSTEMS TEST AND THE STUDENT RATING SCALE

STUDENT RATING SCALE FACTORS	TEACHER VARIABLES: CST CLUSTERS			
	1. DIVINE FATE CONTROL	2. SIMPLICITY-CERTAINTY	3. STRUCTURE-ORDER	4. ABSTRACT-NESS (Σ 1-2-3)
Cooperation	−.14	−.21*	−.22*	.21*
Involvement	−.10	−.18*	−.21*	.18*
Activity	−.12	−.13	−.34**	.19*
Nurturance Seeking	.14	.12	.24*	−.18*
Achievement	−.22*	−.21*	−.30**	.27**
Helpfulness	−.17	−.17	−.15	.19*
Concreteness	.06	.23*	.29**	−.19*

Note: *df* for all significance tests = 84
  * one-tailed $p < .05$
 ** one-tailed $p < .01$

While all three of the factors constituting the measure of teacher abstractness correlated in the predicted direction with performance of the children,
the teachers' need for structure-order correlated the highest and most consistently. In fact, the teachers' need for structure-order had greater influence on the performance of the children than her belief in divine fate control, need for simplicity-certainty and over-all abstractness.

TEACHERS' OVERT BEHAVIOR AND STUDENT PERFORMANCE.   Teachers' scores on the behavioral factors of resourcefulness, dictatorialness
and punitiveness were correlated with the seven student performance clusters. These results are included in Table 3.

Table 3

CORRELATIONS OF TEACHER DICTATORIALNESS, PUNITIVENESS, AND RESOURCEFULNESS WITH STUDENT PERFORMANCE FACTORS

| | TEACHER BEHAVIOR | | |
STUDENT BEHAVIOR	RESOURCEFULNESS	DICTATORIALNESS	PUNITIVENESS
Cooperativeness	.23**	−.18*	−.34**
Involvement	.69**	−.84**	−.73**
Activity	.76**	−.33**	−.29**
Nurturance Seeking	−.12	−.05	−.01
Achievement	.28**	−.28**	−.32**
Helpfulness	.02	−.23**	−.32**
Concreteness	−.60**	.67**	.56**

Note: *df* for all tests of significance = 116

  * one-tailed $p < .05$

** one-tailed $p < .01$

The resourcefulness of the teacher correlated significantly positively with student cooperation, involvement, activity and achievement and significantly negatively with the concreteness of students' responses.

The teachers' dictatorialness correlated significantly negatively with the students' cooperation, involvement, activity, achievement and helpfulness and significantly positively with students' concreteness of responses.

Teachers, punitiveness correlated significantly negatively with student cooperation, involvement, activity, achievement and helpfulness and significantly positively with the concreteness of the students' responses.

Nurturance seeking was the only one of the seven student performance clusters that did not relate significantly to any one of the teacher behaviors.

Discussion

By replicating the findings of our earlier study (Harvey and others, 1966), these results make it clear that the concreteness-abstractness of teachers' belief systems affect their overt resourcefulness, dictatorialness and punitiveness in the classroom. In addition, the results show that the classroom behavior of the teacher and the behavior of the students are significantly related. Clearly, this relationship does not tell us the nature of the causality. Theoretically, the teacher's behavior could determine the children's behavior, the reverse could be true, both could be determined by a third factor (such as the organizational climate), or the effects could be produced by the interaction among all of these factors. The possibility that the relationship between teachers' and students' behavior is a result of organizational climate is minimized by the fact that the concrete and abstract teachers, while selected from the same organizational climates, nevertheless differed markedly in their classroom behaviors, as did their students. Further, while students no doubt affect the behavior of their teachers, it appears more likely that, because of her socially prescribed power, her influence is greater and more direct than theirs.

The obtained differences between concrete and abstract teachers probably would have been accentuated had the group of more abstract teachers been comprised only of clear instances of System 4. Instead unclear instances, together with cases of System 3, were combined with clear instances of System 4 to constitute the abstract group in this study. Yet, if our experiences from the earlier (Harvey and others, 1966) and the present study are typical, a large sample of teachers would be necessary to yield an adequate number of clear cases of System 4. Of the 292 teachers to whom we have administered the TIB, only 18, or six percent, have been classified as System 4, not all of which were ideal cases. While strongly suggesting that in terms of absolute numbers few teachers operate at the System 4 level, it should be noted that this percentage is almost identical to the seven percent of System 4 individuals we have found from among approximately 3000 undergraduates administered the TIB. In fact, this percentage appears to be so constant across a large sample of subjects that some special factor(s) may be necessary to account for it.

Indeed the whole question of the determinants of the different belief systems is far from being answered, having been resolved only partially at the theoretical level and even less empirically. One of the more theoretically viable determinants seems to be the freedom the individual had as a child to explore the world of values and to evolve and internalize rules on the basis of direct experience and pragmatic outcomes (Adams *et al.*, 1966; Harvey, 1967). Although this freedom and the differential evolution of systems should be expected to relate to a host of sociological factors, the only significant demographic variable we have found, from the study of two large samples of subjects made up of college students and school teachers, centers around religion. Thus, while representatives of the belief systems did not differ in such background factors as socio-economic status, educational level of themselves or their parents, or even in intelligence, they did differ in such religion-related behavior as frequency of church attendance. This kind of evidence, together with background information on the present teachers, which showed that the representatives of the different systems did not differ in level of education, kind of degrees, or years of teaching, indicate that the results obtained in this study can more parsimoniously and directly be attributed to differences in teachers' belief systems than to possible sociological correlates.

References

ADAMS, D. K., HARVEY, O. J. and HESLIN, R. E.   Variation in flexibility and creativity as a function of hypnotically induced past histories. In O. J. Harvey (Ed.) *Experience, structure, and adaptability.* New York: Springer, 1966. Pp. 217-234.

HARVEY, O. J.   Cognitive determinants of role playing. Technical Report No. 3, Contract Nonr 1147(07), University of Colorado, 1963. 22 pp.

HARVEY, O. J.   Some cognitive determinants of influencibility. *Sociometry,* 1964, 27, 208-221.

HARVEY, O. J.   System structure, flexibility and creativity. In O. J. Harvey (Ed.) *Experience, structure, and adaptability.* New York: Springer, 1966. Pp. 242-262.

HARVEY, O. J.   Conceptual systems and attitude change. In C. W. Sherif and M. Sherif (Eds.) *Attitude, ego-involvement and attitude change.* New York: Wiley, 1967. Pp. 201-226.

HARVEY, O. J., HUNT, D. E. and SCHRODER, H. M.   *Conceptual systems and personality organization.* New York: Wiley, 1961. Pp. 85-112; 158-203.

HARVEY, O. J., and WARE, R.   Personality differences in dissonance resolution. *Journal of Personality and Social Psychology,* 1967, 7, 227-230.

HARVEY, O. J., WHITE, B. J., PRATHER, M., ALTER, R. D. and HOFFMEISTER, J. K.   Teachers' belief systems and preschool atmospheres. *Journal of Educational Psychology,* 1966, 57, 373-381.

TRYON, R. C. and BAILEY, D. E.   *Try user's manual.* Boulder: University of Colorado Computing Center, 1965. 186 pp.

TRYON, R. C. and BAILEY, D. E.   *The B.C. Try system of cluster analysis.* Boulder: University of Colorado Computing Center, 1966. Pp. 3-35.

WARE, R. and HARVEY, O. J.   A cognitive determinant of impression formation. *Journal of Personality and Social Psychology,* 1967, 5, 38-44.

WHITE, B. J. and HARVEY, O. J.   Effects of personality and own stand on judgment and production of statements about a central issue. *Journal of Experimental Social Psychology,* 1965, 1, 334-347.

✻ ✻ ✻ ✻ ✻

The classical hypothetico-deductive method in science stresses the building
of conceptual frameworks, the rigorous derivation of hypotheses therefrom,
and their operational testing, leading to revisions in the framework to
make it more powerful (i.e., more accurately predictive). Better *theory* is
the output.

Kounin and his colleagues began in a direction 180 degrees away from
this: with a recurring educational problem ("discipline"). They aimed to be
holistic, to *avoid* building frameworks first, to examine nature closely to
see what lawfulness could be discerned, with the background intent of
helping educational practitioners know exactly *what* the maintenance
of order in a classroom depends on—not that "it depends on many factors,
most of which were not examined in this experiment." They were particularly successful in Part I of this article (reprinted as a "classic" from the
1963 edition) in isolating novel and useful variables, such as "clarity," "firmness" and "roughness" in "desist techniques."

Yet plausibility is not all. As examination of Parts II and III will show,
subsequent efforts to replicate the earlier work showed that the generalizations made there did not hold up when longer-term classroom situations
were examined. (Replication failures are common in the hypothetico-
deductive method too.) Kounin's efforts to make sense of the earlier and
later findings are instructive. To know that you may have been deceiving
yourself, as Kounin acknowledges, is painful but useful.

Explorations in Classroom Management*

Jacob S. Kounin,
Paul V. Gump, James J. Ryan, III

The origins of the research to be summarized here lay in the authors' feelings of inadequacy in trying to help teachers, especially beginning ones, with problems of importance to them. Discipline is one problem frequently verbalized by teachers. Teachers' questions about "what to do when Johnny disturbs" have been shrugged off with impatience, or have been answered with slogans or "principles." Scientific research about the technology and theory of controlling misbehavior in a classroom is either lacking or inadequate.

Consequently, we turned our attention to a study of the practical problem of classroom management, from the standpoint of technology. We wanted to see whether there is not some lawfulness about discipline in classrooms or, on the other hand, whether the variety of variables involved is so great as to preclude the possibility of predicting pupils' reactions from the qualities of disciplinary techniques employed.

Since the teacher must work with groups or, at least, "aggregates" of pupils, we shifted the focus from the effects of disciplinary measures upon an individual child to that of the audience reactions, or the "ripple effects."

Specifically, how does a teacher's method of handling the misbehavior of one child (henceforth to be referred to as a *desist-technique*) influence *other* children who are audiences to the event but not themselves targets?

The factors to be discussed can be grouped into two major classifications: (1) variables operating at the time of the desist-technique (e.g., the qualities of the desist-technique, the social position of the target) and (2) prevailing variables (e.g., the audience-pupils' intensity of motivation to learn and their liking for the teacher).

* From *The Journal of Teacher Education*, 1961, 12, 235-246. Abridged. Used by permission of the authors and publisher. The studies discussed in this paper have been supported by Grant M-1066 from the National Institute of Mental Health, United States Public Health Service. Parts II and III were written especially by J. S. Kounin for the present volume.

I. Variables Operating at the Time of the Desist-Technique

Threatening vs. Supportive Desist-Techniques

In a fashion characteristic of psychologists, we started with an experiment using college students (these are "captive subjects" who do not require administrative clearances and parental approvals). Four classes of students in a college of education were used as subjects. Two classes were taught by a young instructor of educational methods; two classes were taught by an older professor of psychology.

The experiment was conducted as follows:

1. At the second meeting of the class a researcher, posing as a graduate student, obtained questionnaire data on the attitudes of students regarding their instructors, the degree of seriousness of classroom misbehaviors (including "coming late to class"), and causes of racial prejudice. The student reports were anonymous.
2. The two instructors of each of the four classes began the third class period with a lecture which gave "his own evidence" that the single most important cause of racial prejudice was repressed hostility toward punitive parents that is displaced upon minority groups.
3. A male student, previously informed about the experiment, arrived late to class—toward the end of the instructor's lecture.
4. The instructor directed either a threatening or a supportive desist-technique at the late-comer. Both desist-techniques stated that coming late interfered with the instructor's presentation and should cease. The supportive desist-technique went on to offer the late-comer help in acquiring the lecture material he had missed. The threatening one stated coldly that "this cannot help but affect my evaluation of you and your grade."
5. The "graduate student" readministered his attitude questionnaire.

Two conclusions emerged from this preliminary experiment:

1. Students who are not themselves targets of a desist-technique *are* affected by it.
2. The *two methods* of handling misbehavior in a classroom *produce* statistically significant *different results*. That is, there is a degree of predictability from some dimensions of desist-techniques to some effects upon audience students.

Threatening desist-techniques, for both instructors, resulted in significantly lowered judgments of the instructors' helpfulness, likability, freedom from authoritarianism, and fairness; threatening techniques also raised ratings of the amount of classroom tension.

For the young instructor—but not for the professor—differences between the two desist-techniques produced significant changes in ratings of the instructor's competence in his subject-area and in the freedom of the students to communicate with the instructor.

Students in none of the groups changed their attitudes about the seriousness of the deviancy (coming late), and all groups shifted significantly towards the position of the instructors about the causes of racial prejudice.

It would seem, then, that differences in the effects of certain qualities of desist-techniques are more marked in some areas than in others; that the prestige of the emitter of the desist-technique makes some difference; and that some norms of classroom behavior are so well established in colleges as to be rather resistant to change by an instructor's stand on the issue. Influence attempts of instructors that are directly related to course content are not readily changed in relation to a single example of their desist-technique style.

However, another finding may well serve to limit the generalizability of the above results. Although 97 per cent of the students reported that they did *not* perceive that the event was contrived, the students who witnessed either technique were surprised that a college instructor would take time out to correct a student for coming late, even though they rated coming late as a serious misbehavior. Most of them, especially those who witnessed the threatening desist-technique, felt that the behavior was *not* typical for the instructor. There were frequent comments on a post-incident questionnaire such as: "He must have had an argument with his wife," or "He probably got caught in a traffic jam." This reaction to an unexpected behavior of an instructor, in a sense "excusing it away," may actually function to reduce the changes produced by differences in desist-techniques. From the viewpoint of research methodology and strategy these findings also point to the advisability of using teacher-style variables that are within expectations and that have some ecological prevalence.

Punishing vs. Reprimanding vs. Ignoring

In an experiment with eighth and ninth graders (for whom teachers' use of desist-orders is not unexpected) Ryan, Gump, and Kounin[1] investigated whether qualities of a desist-technique make any difference in audience-pupils' reactions.[2] Volunteer paid subjects were recruited from three metropolitan junior high schools during the summer months to come to a university campus for the purpose of participating in a research project studying different methods of teaching. Volunteers were randomly assigned to

1. Ryan, J. J., Gump, P. V. and Kounin, J. S. An experiment on the effect of motivation to learn upon students' reactions to teachers' desist techniques. Reported more fully in Kounin (1969).

2. This experiment was actually started at a later time in the sequence of explorations in order to study the effects of pupil-motivation. (It will be referred to later as the "high school experiment.") We are referring to it here because it does show that qualities of the desist technique make some predictable differences in audience-pupils' reactions.

groups of about twenty-five each where they were asked to consider themselves as being in a regular classroom.

After each group assembled it experienced the following sequence of events: the experimenter introduced the activities of the day; a female teacher (the same for each group) introduced herself to the class; the subjects filled out a questionnaire containing mostly ratings of their first impression of the teacher; the teacher taught a lesson, using slides, about Turkey; a pretrained pupil (also the same person for all groups) misbehaved (got up and sharpened a pencil while the slides were being shown); the teacher issued a desist-technique; the subjects filled out another questionnaire about the activities, the teacher, and the deviancy-event.

Three desist-techniques were used: (1) punitive and intense (walked toward him, saying "Hey you, who do you think you are?" in a firm, irritated voice, put her arm on his shoulders in a gesture of pushing him into his seat, saying, "Now sit down! If you ever do that again, I'll really make trouble for you."); (2) simple reprimand (saying in a matter-of-fact tone: "Don't do that again. Please sit down in your seat now,"); and (3) ignoring (indicated awareness of the behavior, but did nothing).

The "take" of the experimental manipulation was evidenced by the existence of a significant difference between all groups in the predicted direction regarding the subjects' ratings of the teacher's meanness, anger, and degree of determination to stop the misbehavior.

Compared to the others, the punitive technique resulted in the subjects' rating the *deviancy* as "most serious," the degree of *interference* with attention to the task as "greatest," the *teacher* as "making too much of an issue" over the event, the experience "most discomforting," and the *teacher* "best able to maintain order in a class of 'tough kids.'"

The simple reprimand produced the highest ratings for teacher fairness and also resulted in the subjects' reporting their paying more attention to the lesson following the event and to the teacher being judged as best able to maintain order in "most classes."

Subjects witnessing "ignoring" as the desist-technique thought the misbehavior most likely would recur, but rated the teacher highest in her degree of liking her pupils.

There were no differences between the groups in subjects' ratings of how much the teacher knew about the subject or how well she could explain it. When equivalent effects are considered (likability, fairness, felt discomfort) it should be noted that the results of punitiveness in this experiment are quite similar to the results obtained from the threatening desist-technique in the college experiment.

Clarity, Firmness, and Roughness

In one study by Kounin and Gump (1958) fifty observers were trained to record critical incidents in Barker and Wright's (1954, p. 532) specimen-record style. These were incidents in which an audience-child was aware of a teacher directing a desist-technique at another child. Twenty-six kindergarten classes were selected to represent the range of socio-economic and ethnic neighborhoods in a large city. All observations were made during the first four days of beginning kindergarten. The observers were instructed to record: (1) what the deviant and the audience-child were doing immediately before the teacher intervened, (2) the full content and manner of the desist-technique and the deviant's immediate reaction, and (3) the behavior of the audience-child during and for two minutes following the desist-technique.

When the resulting 406 incidents were analyzed, it was possible to reliably characterize both the teachers' desist-techniques and the behavior of the audience-children.

The qualities of the desist-technique were rated along dimensions of: (1) clarity (defining the deviancy and stating what to do to stop it); (2) firmness (this included items conveying an "I mean it" quality—walking closer to the deviant, or continuing to look at the deviant until he stopped); and (3) roughness (angry remarks and looks, or punishment).

The reactions of the audience-child were classified as (1) no reaction (no overt behavior which the coder could interpret as related to the desist-technique incident); (2) behavior disruption (overt signs of negative emotionality such as fear, anxiety, and restlessness or a shift away from an originally constructive direction); (3) conformance (stops a deviancy of his own or behaves even better, i.e., sitting more "correctly" himself); (4) nonconformance (engages in a misbehavior of his own); and (5) ambivalence (both conforms and misbehaves).

Statistically significant differences were obtained in the overt behavior of the audience-children as related to the desist-technique used by the teacher. Techniques of increasing "clarity" resulted in increased "conformance," but had no effect upon "behavior disruption." Techniques of increasing "roughness," on the other hand, had no effect on "conformance or nonconformance," but did increase "behavior disruption." The effects of "firmness" differed from both.

Some of the conclusions of this study are as follows:

1. What teachers *do* makes a difference. There is some lawfulness about the effects of techniques. It was not necessary to obtain personality ratings or IQ tests of the teachers as persons; it was only necessary to find out what they do and how they do it. (Whether teachers with personality factor-*x* can or cannot *do* things certain ways is another issue.)

2. There are contextual or prevailing variables that also affect how an audience-child will react to an event. Two such contextual variables stand out from the kindergarten study. One refers to the degree of familiarity the pupil has with the teacher and the situation. (Such familiarity, of course, relates to the amount of time one has spent in a particular experience. For example, there were more "no reactions"

on the *last* three days than on the first day.) The other contextual
variable is the audience-child's orientation at the time of the incident. Techniques high in "firmness," for example, produced increased "conformance," but *only* for audience-children who were
themselves oriented toward, or interested in deviancy at the time of
the event.

3. "Roughness" is not an increased degree of "firmness." In terms of
their effects, it is evidence that these are different dimensions.

Although it does not deal specifically with the ripple effect, we would
like to summarize another study on the effects of "punitiveness" since it is
closely related to the dimension of "roughness." In a study by Kounin and
Gump (1961) we attempted to determine the influence of teachers judged
to be punitive upon children's attitudes toward misconduct. Three pairs of
first-grader teachers, each pair from the same school, were *selected*. One of
a pair was rated as "punitive" (anti-child, ready to threaten and inflict
harm) by principals, assistant principals, the two investigators, and a supervisor of student teachers; the other member of the pair was rated as
"non-punitive." All teachers were rated as having good organization and as
achieving the learning objectives for their grade. Children from these classes
were interviewed individually during the third month of attendance at
school. The interview consisted of the question: "What is the worst thing a
child can do at school?" and, following the reply, "Why is that so bad?"
The misconducts talked about were coded for content and for certain qualities. The following was found:

1. Children with teachers judged to be punitive showed more preoccupation with aggression—their misconducts were more serious, their
targets suffered more harm; they more frequently cited physical
assaults on others as misconduct, and their replies contained more
gory—or "blood and guts"—phrases.

2. Children with punitive-rated teachers had more conflicts and were
more unsettled about misbehavior in school. They selected misconducts to talk about for which they expressed abhorrence and yet
which required premeditation, or "malice aforethought."

3. The children with nonpunitive teachers gave more "reflexive justi-
fications" as explanations for why given misconducts were bad. This
was coded when a child gave no consequence for either himself or
others in his explanation of why the misconduct was bad—the reason
given being "because it's not nice" or "because it's bad." We suggested two interpretations for this finding: (a) that children with
nonpunitive teachers have less conflicts about misconduct than have
children with punitive teachers—to say "you don't do *x* because it's
not nice" reflects a settled issue; and (b) a sort of naive faith and
trust in the teacher is reflected by children with nonpunitive teachers
—a reflexive justification for a school misconduct is like, say, "*x* is
bad because teacher says so."

4. Punitiveness of teachers detracts from children's concern with school-
unique values and results in less internalized socialization. Children
with punitive teachers talked more about physical attacks on peers

—misconduct by no means unique to the classroom setting. Children with nonpunitive teachers talked more about learning, achievement losses, and violations of school-unique values and rules.

Task-Focus vs. Appraisal-Focus

Since discipline is centrally related to problems of power and influence and methods of exerting power and influence, another study was undertaken in which Alden (1959, p. 158) dealt with some variables pertaining to these factors. Following French (1956), she hypothesized the following bases for teacher power and influence: the coercive role (the teacher as one who can punish); the "legitimate" role (the teacher as an official leader); reward; pupils' liking for a teacher, and teacher expertness.

The base of a new teacher's power (specifically, "expertness" and "liking") was manipulated by varying the experimenter's introduction of the teacher. All classes were given a lesson in secret writing. A "high expert" was introduced as knowing all about codes and as having a high position in the military intelligence for coding and decoding secret codes; the "low expert" was introduced not as an expert but simply as a teacher who had agreed to teach the lesson. The "high liking" new teacher was introduced as being very fond of children and the "low liking" as not caring about children one way or another.

The desist-techniques used by the teacher were related to these concepts. Some desist-techniques focused upon liking and teacher approval ("I see a boy playing with some paper clips. I just don't like a boy who plays with things when he should be paying attention."). Other desist-techniques related to expertness and focused upon the task ("I see a boy playing with some paper clips. Because secret writing demands concentration, I don't see how he can learn much about it when he plays with things instead of paying attention.").

Fifth graders were divided randomly into eight classes in which a new teacher taught a lesson (in a pedantic, "academic" manner) about secret writing. In this manner, both "high" and "low expert" and "high" and "low liking" teachers used both approval-focused and task-focused desist-techniques. In each group three desist-orders were directed at three children who had been trained to act the role of misbehaving pupils. In four of the groups, the desist-technique focused upon teacher liking and approval and in four groups the desist-technique focused upon the task.

One of Alden's most impressive findings was the following: in all cases, desist-techniques focusing upon the task were more effective in eliciting desirable student reactions than desist-techniques focusing upon the teacher's approval. (With the exception of scores on a test of how much was learned from the lesson, measurements of results were all based upon differences between measures given before the lesson and measures given after the lesson.) For some effects, the superiority of the task-focused desist-techniques held, regardless of whether the introduction of the teacher focused upon her expertness or her liking for children. Thus, in all groups, task-focused desist-techniques increased audience-children's ratings of the teachers' skill in handling children and increased their rated degree of interest in secret writing.

For some effects, the use of a task-focused desist-technique combined with the teacher's expertness to effect the pupils' reactions. Thus, when an expert teacher used a task-focused technique it increased the children's judgment of how much she liked pupils and would be inclined to reward pupils; it resulted in the pupils considering the deviancies she corrected as being more serious and feeling less inclined to misbehave themselves; and it led to a greater amount of information recalled by the pupils from the lecture itself. The influence of being introduced as having high liking for children made a significant difference on one measurement: a teacher with high liking for children *and* high expertness using task-focused desist-techniques resulted in pupils feeling more inclined toward discussing personal matters with her.

The Deviant's Reaction and Prestige

An experiment by Gnagey (1960) was directed at two questions: (1) What is the effect of the deviant's reaction to a teacher's desist-technique upon audience-pupils? (Specifically, does whether the deviant submits to or defies the teacher's desist-order make any difference on how audience-children react to the event?) (2) Does the prestige of the deviant among his classmates influence audience-pupils' reactions to a desist-order event?

In this study, four intact classes of fifth graders were shown a science film during which a male classmate "misbehaved" (saying aloud, "Hey, is this film about over?"). This deviant boy then became the target of a desist-order exerted by the teacher. This teacher, who was new to the class, directed the deviant to leave the room and report to the principal. The deviants were pre-selected on the basis of sociometric scores. (Of course, their classmates didn't know that the deviancies were part of an act.) Two male deviants had high attributed influence among their classmates and two had low influence. Two (one high-influence and one low-influence) were trained to behave in a *submissive* manner (saying, "Yes ma'am, I'm sorry," on leaving the room) and two were trained to react in a *defiant* manner (saying belligerently, "I'll leave the room, but I won't go to the principal's office. The heck with you!").

Gnagey found that the target's reaction did make a predictable difference in audience-pupils' reactions. Compared to pupils who saw the deviant defy the teacher, pupils who witnessed the deviant submit to the teacher rated the teacher as "more capable of handling kids" and as more expert in showing films; they rated the desist-technique as fairer; and they recalled more facts from the film. The magnitude of the differences between the effects of the two kinds of deviant reactions was greater for boys than for girls and was greater for boys who were audience to a high-influence deviant than boys who were audience to a low-influence deviant.

The Gnagey study also points up one reason for an audience-person to be affected by a desist-order directed at someone else, namely, some sort of linkage with the deviant. In this case it is a sociometric linkage—the linkage of an audience-pupils' motivation to identify with a same-sexed person in a high prestige position. Hence, the finding, for boys only, of a greater effect of a high-influence male's reaction than that of a low-influence male's reaction. Another sort of linkage—to the deviancy event—was illustrated by the previously mentioned kindergarten study. Here, when the audience-child was either deviant himself or was watching the deviancy, he was more likely to react to the desist-technique than if he had no such relationship to the deviancy. In both the Gnagey study and the kindergarten study, then, linkages are shown to be important: linkages to the defiant person, and linkages to the deviancy event.

II. The Influence of Prevailing Variables

An interview study was conducted with 125 students who were just entering high school. They were interviewed between the fourth and tenth day of their attendance at high school and again three months later. The interview centered around their description of a most recent incident when another student engaged in a misbehavior which the teacher did something about. As complete as possible a description of the deviancy, and of the teacher's method and manner of handling it, was obtained. Both open-ended and forced-choice items were utilized to obtain information about the event and the student's reactions to, and evaluation of it.

Reports of two such incidents were obtained from each student: one based on the academic class in which he was "most determined to learn" and one relating to the academic class in which he was least determined to learn the subject matter. These two classes were used for each student to test the hypothesis that a student with a goal of learning the subject would react differently to a deviancy event than a student without such a goal. Specifically, a misbehaving student would be a barrier to an audience student with the goal of learning, and a teacher effort to remove this barrier would be reacted to favorably.

The results relating qualities of a desist technique to students' reactions showed only one dimension of a desist technique that made any difference in how students reacted. The presence of teacher anger was associated with more reported discomfort.

Motivation to learn *was* associated with student reactions to desist events. When talking about a desist event in high motivation-to-learn classes, students rated the deviancies as more disturbing and serious and the desist-technique as more fair, tended to take the teacher's side as opposed to the deviant, reported more inclinations to behave even better and to pay more attention to the subject, and tended to approve of how the teacher handled the deviancy. In low motivation classes, students tended to report more teacher punitiveness and anger, and to judge more of the teachers as "making too much of an issue" of the incident. In open-ended evaluations of the event, more of those in the high motivation group evaluated it on the basis of its effectiveness in stopping the misbehavior, whereas more in the low motivation group used teacher manner (anger, fairness) as a basis for evaluating the incident.

It would appear, then, that the motivation-to-learn theory was supported by the data. However, we happened to ask the students to rate their degree of liking for the teacher, and whether they would recommend the teacher to a friend. These latter were highly correlated and both gave the same results. The differences between the high liking and low liking groups were in the same direction and approximate magnitude as the differences between the high motivation and low motivation groups. Moreover, motivation to learn and liking (or recommending) the teacher were highly correlated. So far, it looked like one global "halo," in which motivation to learn, liking for the teacher, and favorable reactions to a desist event go hand in hand.

In order to unravel this global halo, we categorized the reactions and proposed a theory of *commitment*. We assumed that motivation to learn a subject and liking for the teacher are prevailing variables extending over time—that is, commitments. When a student says that he is highly motivated to learn geometry we assume that he is talking about more than a specific theorem that he wants to learn between one o'clock and one-fifteen on the day of the interview. Similarly, we assume that the degree of liking for the teacher is a molar attitude lasting for more than one class period, whatever the source of this liking might be. Four types of commitment groups were then compared: high motivation to learn and high liking, high motivation to learn and low liking, low motivation and high liking, and low motivation and low liking.

The students' reactions were categorized as follows: 1) *Task related* reactions having to do with the students' orientation to the official classroom requirements at the time. These are inclination to pay more or less attention or to behave better or worse following a desist incident. 2) *Teacher evaluations* having to do with favorable or unfavorable evaluations of the teacher's behavior in the desist event. These are: whether the teacher is judged as making too much of an issue of the deviancy or not, whether she is fair or not, and whether the student tended to take the teacher's or the deviant's side in the event. 3) *Deviancy judgments* in which an evaluation of the teacher is not involved. This dealt with the students' ratings of the seriousness of the deviancy.

The results show that *students' reactions to desist events are determined by the nature of their commitment and its related effect.* Task related effects (attention to official activity and inclination to behave better) are determined by motivation to learn the subject, independently of liking for the teacher or the qualities of the desist technique. Reactions having to do with positive or negative evaluations of the teacher (such as fairness) are determined by liking for the teacher, independently of motivation to learn or the qualities of the desist-technique. These latter results are in line with Heider's (1958) theory of balance: a liked person tends to be perceived as doing "good" things and a disliked person as doing "bad" things, so that the perceiver maintains balanced perceptions.

The quality of a desist technique made a difference in only *one* very specific set of circumstances, namely those involving: 1) a judgment having no clear task or teacher evaluation properties (such as judgments of the seriousness of deviancy); 2) low motivation to learn (where student is not already inclined to see a deviancy as intruding); 3) high liking for the teacher (is inclined to receive a teacher's non-task messages); and, 4) teacher's emission of strong message that she regards the deviancy as bad (by punishment, anger, or strong firmness). In this circumstances the presence of punishment, anger, and firmness in a desist lead to students judging deviancies as more serious than when these desist qualities are absent.

This interview study was replicated in a questionnaire study with other groups of entering high school students. Again, commitment to learning predicted to task related effects, and liking for the teacher predicted to teacher evaluation judgments. Qualities of the desist-technique had no relationship to either of the above effects, except (as in the interview) that the presence of anger was associated with felt discomfort.

Since liking for the teacher stands out as an important variable influencing a student's evaluation of a desist event, it should be pointed out that the role of teacher probably carries its unique properties in terms of what is associated with being liked. Osborne's (1962) coding of the open-ended descriptions of both liked and disliked teachers in the interview study found that task property descriptions were predominant, e.g., "explains well," "assigns the right amount of homework." This is in contrast to a study by Polansky and Kounin (1956) of descriptions by clients of professional helpers (social workers, physicians, counselors); there relationship-centered descriptions (friendly, understanding) were much more prevalent. Liking for the teacher correlated with ratings of both task proficiency (ability to "get subject across") and managerial proficiency. These descriptions of teachers also differed from descriptions given by campers of camp counselors where "gratuitous supplier" ("brings in watermelons," etc.) was the most prevalent dimension talked about. We suspect that these saliencies in perceptions of teachers are also different (we hope) from what is salient in liked girl-friends and boy-friends.

At this point, we should mention that in the second experiment summarized in Section I of this article we also assessed motivation to learn as an independent variable. In the experiment, this prevailing variable did *not* make a difference. Gump and Kounin (1959) also attempted to replicate the kindergarten study (Section I) in a boys camp, where desist events were observed for two weeks in eight different cabin groups. Unlike the kindergarten study, the camp study showed that variations in desist-techniques, including clarity, roughness, and firmness, made *no* difference in how campers reacted to a counselor desisting another's misbehavior. (One might also note that the differences obtaining in kindergarten were obtained predominantly on the first day.)

III. Epilogue—The Videotape Study

At this point we were left with what appeared to be conflicting findings. All the desist technique studies involving first-contact experiments or conducted on the first day of kindergarten showed that variations in desist-techniques produced statistically significant differences in pupil's reactions. The studies conducted during the first two weeks in camp and high schools showed that desist-techniques, as such, did *not* make a difference, but that other dimensions of classroom management, as yet undefined (but probably related to the antecedents of motivation to learn and to liking for the teacher) *do* make a difference, The experiment (in Section I, as described above) on the other hand, did *not* show a difference in the motivation to learn variable. Which findings correspond to the realities of classrooms?

By this time our grant had expired. Our next step was to obtain another United States Public Health grant for studying the management of emotionally disturbed children in regular classrooms. We had hoped to secure data for desist-techniques as well as for other variables of classroom management. (This work is reported more fully in Kounin, Friesen, and Norton, 1966; and Kounin and Obradovic, 1968).

We decided to use television to study actual classrooms. This method would not only provide a means of measuring preselected events (i.e., desist techniques), and of checking existing hypotheses and ideas, but would provide a nonselective, complete, and objective record of most events in a classroom which could be viewed an endless number of times, and thus provide data or variables not thought of at the time of data gathering.

A total of 80 elementary school classrooms were videotaped by remote control—30 for one-half day each and 50 for a full day each. We were concerned with teachers' management of overt behavior. Consequently, children's behaviors were scored for deviancy, deviancy-contagion, and work involvement in academic subsettings. Our first look was at desist-techniques —at direct behavior management efforts. The dimensions of desist-techniques scored were: clarity, firmness, punitiveness, intensity, length, and focus.

For only one of 30 teachers was there any correlation between any aspect of her desist-technique and the immediate success of the effort in getting the target child to stop his deviancy or to take up the prescribed task. Teachers were also ranked by their mean desist style scores for the above dimensions. These rankings did *not* correlate with the rankings on deviancy, work involvement or deviancy contagion, for any subsetting, or for either the disturbed or nondisturbed children.

These findings disagree with the findings of the experiments, and with the findings from the kindergarten study. They do agree with the findings obtained from the high school interview and questionnaire studies. In some respects, they also agree with the findings from the kindergarten study where we found significantly more "no observable effects" during the second through fourth day than on the first day.

Looking back at the negative findings from the field studies and the experiments, we are now inclined to feel that the experimenters were deceived more than the subjects by the reasons we gave them for conducting the studies. Our disguise that we were studying first impressions is probably nearer to the truth than our hidden purpose of studying control techniques. As a matter of fact, we might conjecture that we were actually studying opinions, rather than first impressions of teachers. When our high school subjects rated the experimental teacher that used rough techniques as being able to better "control a bunch of tough students" but *not* as being able to better "control students like myself" we may have been studying that *opinion*.

In the videotape study, we did, however, find other measurable dimensions of teacher behavior that predicted to children's deviancy and work involvement. Some teacher style variables[3] that do not correlate with children's behaviors are: With-it-ness (selecting correct child target, on time); Overlappingness (attending to two issues simultaneously); Programming for learning variety and cognitive challenge (especially in seatwork); Smoothness (absence of dangling, thrusting,[4] stimulus-boundedness); Maintaining Movement (absence of slowdowns and drags, target fragmentation,[5] and teacher overtalk); Group Alerting (maintaining focus on a group or subgroup rather than immersing energy in a single child); Accountability (communicating knowledge of non-reciters' performances during recitations). Correlations between a teacher style and children's behaviors varied between seatwork or recitation subsettings; single correlations were as high as .69, and multiple correlations were as high as .81.

The videotape studies demonstrate that it is possible to delineate concrete aspects of teacher behavior that lead to managerial success, and that apply to both emotionally disturbed and non-disturbed children, to boys and to girls. These are *not* techniques of directly controlling misbehavior; that is, of desist style as such. Rather, they are techniques that create an effective classroom ecology, which apply to the group, and not merely to individual children. It is not a simple matter of admonishing teachers to "create rapport" or "make it interesting." Nor do these techniques entail preoccupation with classical personality attributes as such. Nor is it a matter of extrapolating from other adult-child relationships, whether with parents,

---

3. Details of these dimensions may be obtained in Kounin (1967), Kounin and Obradovic (1968), and Kounin (1969).

4. "Dangling" refers to initiation of an activity without follow-through; "thrusting" involves initiating a new activity without assessing the target group's readiness to receive the induction.

5. "Slowdowns and drags" refer to teacher techniques which slow classroom activity flow. "Target fragmentation" involves having individual members move when the group as a whole is to move into a new activity.

psychotherapists, or even tutors. Rather, the business of running a classroom is based upon a complicated set of techniques directed towards multiple ends: developing a non-satiating learning program with some cognitive challenge; initiating and maintaining group and individual movement in classroom tasks with smoothness and without drag; observing and eliciting feedback for many different events; coping with more than one event simultaneously; directing actions at correct targets and on time (and doubtless still others yet to be measured).

In conclusion, we would like to point out the value of naturalistic, ecological researches in which many coexisting events are studied in real settings. This is asserted for purely empirical reasons, and not from any Gestalt, organismic, or existential principles. More simple-mindedly, such research is necessary to make sure that important prevailing variables are not overlooked for less important ones, no matter how testable and statistically significant the latter might be. In the current stage of behavioral sciences, there is room for researches conducted in the spirit of inquiry, to see what can be learned—rather than in the spirit of debate, to see what hypothesis or theory can be tested.

References

ALDEN, E.   The effects on non-target classmates of the teacher's use of expert power and liking power in controlling deviant behavior. Unpublished doctoral dissertation, Wayne State University, 1959.

BARKER, R. G. and WRIGHT, H. F.   *Midwest and its children.* New York: Harper & Row, 1954.

FRENCH, J. R. P.   A formal theory of social power. *Psychological Review*, 1956, 63, 181-195.

GNAGEY, W. J.   Effects on classmates of a deviant student's power and response to a teacher-exerted control technique. *Journal of Educational Psychology*, 1960, 51, 1-9.

GUMP, P. V. and KOUNIN, J. S.   Issues raised by ecological and "classical" research efforts. *Merrill-Palmer Quarterly of Behavior and Development*, 1959, 6, 145-153.

HEIDER, F.   *The psychology of interpersonal relations.* New York: Wiley, 1958.

KOUNIN, J. S.   An analysis of teachers' managerial techniques. *Psychology in the Schools*, 1967, 4 (3), 221-227.

KOUNIN, J. S.   *Discipline and group management in classrooms.* New York: Holt, Rinehart & Winston, 1969.

KOUNIN, J. S., FRIESEN, W. V. and NORTON, A. E.   Managing emotionally disturbed children in regular classrooms. *Journal of Educational Psychology*, 1966, 57 (1), 1-13.

KOUNIN, J. S. and GUMP, P. V.   The ripple effect in discipline. *Elementary School Journal*, 1958, 62, 158-162.

KOUNIN, J. S. and GUMP, P. V.   The comparative influence of punitive and non-punitive teachers upon children's concepts of school misconduct. *Journal of Educational Psychology*, 1961, 52, 44-49.

KOUNIN, J. S. and OBRADOVIC, S.   Managing emotionally disturbed children in regular classrooms: a replication and extension. *Journal of Special Education*, 1968, 2 (2), 129-135.

OSBORNE, K.   Saliencies in students' perceptions of teachers. Unpublished doctoral dissertation, Wayne State University, 1962.

POLANSKY, N. and KOUNIN, J. S.   Clients' reactions to initial interviews. *Human Relations*, 1956, 9, 237-264.

꙾ ꙾ ꙾ ꙾ ꙾

As we have suggested in the introduction to Bronfenbrenner's article in this book, few efforts seem to have been made to interpret the body of knowledge available on the functioning of small groups to educational practitioners. (One exception is Bany and Johnson's *Classroom Group Behavior*, Macmillan, 1964.) Likewise, few small-group researchers seem to have made a serious effort to explore the classroom group.

Schmuck's study aims to fill this gap. In it, he examines closely what the consequences of "centralized" and "diffuse" liking structures in the classroom peer group are. Looking at it from the learner's point of view, it turns out that if your classroom has a few heroes and a few scapegoats, as contrasted with feeling more like a large happy family, *and* if you feel yourself to be on the lower end of the pecking order, you will like yourself less, be less satisfied, and do less well in school work. "Diffuse" liking structures, especially when the student is actively involved in the group, appear to be associated with more satisfaction and learning.

The study is marred by the measurement of the basic dependent variable, "utilization of abilities," which simply boils down to teacher ratings of achievement. Had Schmuck used achievement tests, and/or dealt only with high-IQ children who were under-performing, and low-IQ children who were "over-performing," the study would be even stronger.

The analysis of "deviant cases" (students who didn't perform as predicted) is useful, as are the suggestions for additional research. We do need many more studies in this area.

Some Relationships of Peer Liking Patterns in the Classroom to Pupil Attitudes and Achievements*

Richard A. Schmuck

Since the important research contributions of Whyte (1943), Newcomb (1943), Lewin, Lippitt and White (1939), Riesman (1950), Coleman (1961) and others, laymen, youth workers, and social scientists have been interested in understanding the mechanisms by which peer groups influence their members. Some explorations of juvenile delinquents (see notes, Lippitt and Withey, 1959) and of industrial work groups (March and Simon, 1958) have focused systematically on these mechanisms. Also some current research concerning peer-group influences is being undertaken in the context of educational inquiry, especially in studies on school and classroom milieu. Along these lines, several theoretical analyses (Gronlund, 1962) and empirical studies (see Sewell, Haller and Straus, 1959, and Wilson, 1959) directly relate peer-group processes to the academic motivations and successes of individual pupils. These contributions leave little doubt concerning the interrelatedness of youth friendship patterns and norms on the one hand; and the school-related attitudes, self-concepts, and performances of individual pupils on the other. However, even with this current interest in school peer culture, few studies present in detail empirical associations between interpersonal processes of school peer groups, the psychological processes of individual pupils, and pupil behavior in the classroom.

In reviewing studies on classroom peer groups we have been able to derive social psychological organization and continuity among the results of research only by integrating findings from studies using various concepts and methods. Of course, when a number of different pieces of research are

* Reprinted from *School Review*, 1963, 71 (3), 337-359. Used by permission of the author and the publisher, The University of Chicago Press. Copyright 1963 by the University of Chicago.

This article is based on Schmuck (1962). It is also a revised and extended version of a paper presented at meetings of the Society for Research in Child Development in 1963. The work reported here was part of the Inter-Center Program of Research at the University of Michigan. It was supported by grants from the National Institute of Mental Health (Grant OM-376) and the U.S. Office of Education (Cooperative Research Project No. 1167). Principal investigators were Ronald Lippitt and Robert Fox. Richard Schmuck was study director. Special thanks are due to the doctoral committee, Ronald Lippitt, Robert Fox, Martin Gold, Wilbert McKeachie, and Theodore Newcomb for their guidance of this work; and to Alvin Zander and Mark Chesler for their helpful comments about this paper.

described side by side, they do tend to exhibit a conceptual thread. One problem in seeking continuity in this fashion, however, is that diverse populations of children might be construed as one. Nevertheless, we will integrate and summarize briefly some findings of several classroom studies to give the research presented below some initial perspective.

Studies completed by Echelberger (1959), Lippitt and Gold (1959), Van Egmond (1960), and Sears (1959) on elementary-school groups, as well as studies by Elkins (1959) and Keislar (1955) on high-school youth, indicate that peer liking relations are associated with a pupil's classroom behavior, that over time these liking relations achieve stability, and that having low liking status in the peer group is associated both with negative manifestations of mental health and low utilization of academic abilities. Two of the studies cited above on elementary classroom groups are especially relevant for the analyses developed in this paper. In the first, Lippitt and Gold (1959), assuming that one indicator of mental health is the facility for positive affect toward others, had pupils specify how much they liked each of their classmates. The results indicate that pupils low in peer-group liking status express less positive affect toward others than those high in liking status. In the second study, Van Egmond (1960) sought to link a pupil's sociometric status with his utilization of abilities (defined as how much each pupil was achieving in relation to his intelligence). He found that girls with high liking status utilize their abilities more highly than girls with low, and that boys with high influence status utilize their abilities more highly than boys with low.

Neither of these two studies focuses on the intervening cognitive processes connecting actual liking status with classroom performance; nor has either of them treated peer groups qua groups as units for analysis. Indeed, few studies analyze systematically the entire conceptual span connecting peer groups as social systems, through relevant perceptual-cognitive processes of peer-group members, to the members' overt behaviors or performances. We attempted to do this conceptually and only partially empirically in an earlier paper (1962). In that paper, the social-psychological bonds between classroom informal peer processes and pupil performance were designated by specifying several assumptions connecting so-called "social space" factors, through life-space factors, to individual performance. The term, "social space," was employed to refer to group properties that are pre-perceptual for any given individual, while the term "life-space," was employed to refer to psychological events that are post-perceptual and pre-behavioral. Performance was used to designate overt behavioral events.

The several assumptions outlined in that paper were viewed as setting the stage for a program of research. The initial step in that program was the consideration of the differential effects of one important variable in the social space—peer-group sociometric structure. Two types of sociometric structures were conceptualized and examined. These were (1) centrally structured groups, characterized by a narrow focus of interpersonal acceptance and rejection, and (2) diffusely structured groups, characterized by a wide range of positive and negative choices—that is, little or no focus of inter-personal acceptance and rejection upon a few members. In other words, a large number of pupils agree in selecting a small cluster of their classmates as highly accepted or rejected in centrally structured groups. Diffusely structured groups, on the other hand, are not typified by small clusters of highly accepted and highly rejected pupils, that is, there are no distinct subgroups whose members receive most of the sociometric choices.

In a preliminary analysis of eight upper elementary-school classrooms we found that (1) pupils are more accurate in estimating their status positions in centrally structured groups than in diffusely structured groups, and (2) pupils who are accurate and have low status in the peer group are lower utilizers of their academic abilities than pupils who are accurate and have high status. The purpose of our presentation here is to report conceptualizations and empirical results that considerably refine and extend these preliminary findings.

Theory and Variables

Pupils in a classroom can be viewed either as a group adjusting through patterns of informal relations to the formal organizational demands of the school or as a collection of parallel and co-operatively or competitively acting individuals engaged in intellectual and emotional change. We assume that informal relations among peers, in particular peer liking relations, have some effect on the way individual youngsters conceive of and carry out the more formal role requirements of being a pupil. This assumption holds especially when these peer likability patterns become intensely intimate and affective. Indeed, the more peer liking relations acquire importance for the individual pupil, the more they affect his definition and evaluation of self and the more psychologically threatening or supportive it is possible for them to become. Furthermore, the more threatening or supportive these relation-ships become, the more probability they have of effecting individual pupil's adjustments to the formalized learning and behavioral demands of the school.

In short, a pupil's academic performance is conditioned by emotional con-tents associated with his self-concepts as peer and pupil, and these self-concepts are formed, in part, by that pupil's liking relations with his peers. As was noted before, we assume from Van Egmond's (1960) study that a pupil's actual sociometric status and his utilization of abilities are associated. We want to go beyond that finding here, looking for peer-group conditions that either enhance or mitigate that relationship, as well as some inter-vening psychological processes that link sociometric status to classroom performance.

In approaching a more refined analysis than those presented in previous studies concerning peer influences, several theoretical questions arise. The answers to each of these questions involve variables for empirical study. For instance, we ask: What peer-group conditions, beyond a pupil's liking status in the group, have impact on the ways he perceives himself in the classroom? Our tentative answer to this query involves two variables: the structure of peer-group liking choices, and a pupil's potency of involvement in the peer group. Further, we ask: What psychological processes intervene between these peer-group conditions and subsequent classroom behaviors? Here our answer involves three variables: cognized liking status in the peer group, attitude toward self, and attitude toward school. Finally, we ask: What performance factor makes sense conceptually as an outcome of these social psychological processes? We answer by making use of the variable, utilization of academic abilities. Each of these variables is elaborated on briefly below.

PEER-GROUP LIKING STRUCTURE.   Peer liking structure involves the way pupils of a classroom group distribute their interpersonal preferences. We already have made reference to two types of sociometric structure—central and diffuse. Centrally structured peer groups are characterized by a large number of pupils who agree in selecting only a small cluster of their classmates as pupils they like. Along with this narrow focus on a small number of pupils, many other pupils are neglected entirely. Diffusely structured peer groups, on the other hand, are distinguished by a more equal distribution of liking choices; by no distinct subgroups whose members receive a large proportion of preferences; and by fewer entirely neglected pupils.

The theoretical basis for these two varieties of sociometric structure emanates from two diverse perspectives in social science, Gestalt perceptual theory (Kohler, 1947) and group dynamics (Cartwright and Zander, 1960). From the former, for instance, an important assumption is that at least one significant determinant of perceptual veridicality lies in the structure of the distal stimulus object, that is, its "good form," clarity, symmetry, distinctiveness, etc. Here we argue that the centrally structured sociometric situation represents a clearer and more distinct distal stimulus for individual pupils than the diffusely structured situation. From group dynamics, studies on communication nets and group structure (see Leavitt, 1951) indicate that task leadership is recognized more quickly and easily in centrally structured groups. It can be argued from this work that social-emotional status might also be more easily recognized in groups with centrally structured sociometric dimensions. In any case, both of these perspectives represent the theoretical and empirical bases for our thinking on group sociometric structuring and individual cognition of the classroom environment.

PUPIL POTENCY OF INVOLVEMENT IN THE PEER GROUP.   The amount of psychological investment a pupil has in his peer relations represents his potency of involvement in the classroom peer group. More specifically, we define potency of involvement in the classroom peer group as the degree that a pupil is limited to his classmates for like-age friendship ties.

ACTUAL LIKING STATUS IN THE PEER GROUP. Actual liking status refers to the preferential position that an individual pupil actually holds within his classroom peer group.

COGNIZED LIKING STATUS IN THE PEER GROUP. Cognized liking status is defined as the preferential position that an individual pupil conceives of himself as holding within his classroom peer group.

ATTITUDE TOWARD SELF. Attitude toward self is defined as those general cognitions and associated feelings a pupil has regarding himself.

ATTITUDE TOWARD SCHOOL. Attitude toward school is defined simply as an individual pupil's cognitions and associated feelings, both positive and negative, concerning aspects of the school environment.

UTILIZATION OF ABILITIES. Utilization of abilities is the degree a pupil's performance is congruent with his academic abilities, or how well he fulfils the formal learning demands of the classroom, taking his intelligence level into consideration.

Ten hypotheses involving these variables arise out of our theoretical scheme. These are stated formally, along with relevant data, in the "Hypotheses and Results" section below.

Methods

The data reported in this study were derived from public school classrooms, in rural, industrial, suburban, and university communities. The data about each classroom were obtained from three sources: (1) questionnaires and group interviews with pupils, (2) questionnaires and interviews with teachers, and (3) a brief period of classroom observation. Pupil and teacher responses to selected items on these questionnaires are used as data in this study.

A sample of twenty-seven teachers was selected from those who volunteered to participate in the research. The final selections were made with the objective of sampling diverse types of communities and grade levels. As a result, a subject pool comprising 727 children was available from the classrooms of these teachers. These twenty-seven classrooms included eighteen elementary-school and four junior high and five senior high school groups. Our analyses here involve the elementary-school classrooms primarily. The fathers' occupations for the pupils in the sample differ significantly from classroom to classroom. For instance, in one classroom 90 per cent of the fathers are professional, while in another 97 per cent are classified as unskilled. The racial composition ranges from predominantly Negro in one class to all white in others.

All the questionnaires were administered by members of the research staff in the spring of 1961. The only exceptions to this general procedure were a short family-background information form and a sentence-completion test that were administered by the classroom teacher. Each teacher was instructed carefully in the standard administration procedure.

Nearly all the pupils had filled out a shorter but similar pilot questionnaire in the fall of the school year. Children who did not have adequate reading skills to follow the questionnaire (which was read to all pupils by the examiner) were eliminated from the sample. Approximately 2 per cent of the original sample did not complete their questionnaires. The generalizations made in this study, therefore, must be restricted to those chilldren without severe academic disabilities.

The following operational definitions of our variables are used in this study.

PEER-GROUP LIKING STRUCTURE. Every pupil nominates four class-mates he likes most and four he likes least. Each pupil is awarded one "choice-status" score whenever he is nominated by another pupil as highly liked and one "rejection-status" score whenever he receives a low liking nomination. Since each pupil chooses four pupils as high in liking and four others as low, the mean "choice" and "rejection" scores for each class are both equal to four. Centrality of the peer-group liking structure increases, and diffuseness decreases, as the variability of the "choice" and "rejection" score distributions increase. Three types of peer group structures are studied here. Peer groups referred to as having *bimodal centrality* have high variability (above median of all classrooms studied) in both the "choice" and "rejection" distributions. Peer groups of *monomodal centrality* have one score distribution of high variability and one of low. Finally, groups characterized by *diffuseness* have low variability in both score distributions.

PUPIL POTENCY OF INVOLVEMENT IN THE PEER GROUP. Each pupil designates how many peers outside the classroom he likes the same or better than his classmates. A classroom median is used to distinguish high involvement from low involvement for each pupil.

ACTUAL LIKING STATUS IN THE PEER GROUP. The pupils in each class are rank-ordered according to their liking "choice-status" scores. This distribution is split at the median in deriving high- and low-status pupils.

COGNIZED LIKING STATUS IN THE PEER GROUP. Each pupil is asked to estimate whether he is in the first, second, third, or fourth quarter of his class in liking. Each pupil is then designated as holding either high (first and second quarter) or low (third and fourth quarter) cognized liking status.

ATTITUDE TOWARD SELF. The measurement of attitude toward self is obtained from a sentence completion test. The test as a whole consists of forty-six sentence stems, three of which relate to feelings about the self, as, for example, "When I look in the mirror I ——," "Sometimes I think I am ——," or "When I look at other boys and girls and then look at myself I feel ——." The completed sentences are rated on a seven-point scale and combined into an index concerning attitude toward self.

This technique yields rich and interesting personal data. For instance, a sixth-grade boy, scored as having a very positive attitude toward self by our scoring system, answered in the following ways:

> When I look in the mirror I *see a nice face.*
> Sometimes I think I am *a great man in sports.*
> When I look at other boys and girls and then look at myself I feel *I'm glad I am myself.*

A much different psychological picture is exhibited by a tenth-grade boy. His protocol is scored low for attitude toward self:

> When I look in the mirror I *look like Mike—ugly.*
> Sometimes I think I am *Bob M. and Dick S. who are no good farmers and wastes.*
> When I look at other boys and girls and then look at myself, I feel *very different.*

An internal consistency check for this measure indicates that each single item contributes about the same to the over-all index. For instance, the item, "When I look in the mirror I ——" is in agreement with the index 77 per cent of the time, for high and low designations. The other two items both agree with the total measure 72 per cent of the time. These moderately high and consistent percentages indicate a fair amount of internal consistency and imply that each item is contributing in its own right to the total index. An analysis of the inter-item associations also supports this latter point. Each of the items is moderately and positively correlated with every other item at levels ranging from $+.36$ to $+.58$.

ATTITUDE TOWARD SCHOOL. Five items from the sentence completion test, "Studying is ——," "This school ——," "My schoolwork ——," "Homework is ——," and "Learning out of books is ——," are used to obtain an index of attitude toward school by rating each completed sentence on a seven-point scale and computing the mean of the five.

A fifth-grade girl, scored as having a positive attitude toward school, wrote the following:

> Studying is *good for me because it helps me learn things.*
> This school is a *very very pretty place.*
> My schoolwork *is more important than playing around and wasting time.*
> Homework is *better than playing around.*
> Learning out of books is *about as much fun as learning from the teacher.*

On the other hand, another fifth-grade girl, scored as low in school adjustment, wrote the following contrasting material:

> Studying is *awful*.
> This school *is awful, I don't like it*.
> My schoolwork *is good enough*.
> Homework is *terrible*.
> Learning out of books is *lousy—you don't learn much*.

Analyses of both internal consistency and inter-item associations for the index of attitude toward school are quite similar to those for the index of attitude toward self. Single-item per cent agreement with the total index ranges from 68 per cent to 77 per cent, while inter-item correlations range from $+.36$ to $+.54$.

Preliminary analyses of rater reliability for both the attitude toward self and the attitude toward school indexes indicated 95 per cent agreement for high-low scoring. Thus, it appears that our scoring procedure affords very high reliability especially for high-low estimates.

UTILIZATION OF ABILITIES.   Each class is split at the median into a high-intelligence group and low-intelligence group by scores from standard intelligence tests. The teacher then divides each of these groups into high-achieving and low-achieving subgroups. Thus, the class is divided into four ability-achievement groups; high ability-high achievement, high ability-low achievement, low ability-high achievement, and low ability-low achievement. The two high-achieving groups are considered to be utilizing their abilities more completely and are designated as the "high utilizers" while the two low-achieving groups are considered to be "low utilizers."

A comparison of the mean I.Q. scores yielded no difference for these two groups of utilizers. I.Q. mean for the "high utilizers" is 109.38, while that of the "low utilizers" is 109.00.

GROUP AFFECT.   Our one remaining variable, group affect, is measured by each pupil designating on a nine-point scale how much he values every pupil in the class. Peer groups with higher mean scores on this measure have more positive group affect than those with lower scores.

Hypotheses and Results

All data reported below, except those concerning hypotheses one and ten, are derived from upper elementary-school classrooms (Grades 3-6). When appropriate, however, the generalizability of these findings to other developmental levels will be mentioned. Hypothesis 1 (which involves the proposed association between two group variables) and hypothesis 10 (which involves one added control variable) require a population larger than that afforded by our eighteen elementary classrooms for statistical analysis. In light of this, the full sample of twenty-seven classrooms is used for testing these two hypotheses.

Hypothesis 1 states:

1. Classroom peer groups distinguished by more liking diffuseness exhibit more positive group affect than groups with more centrality.

This hypothesis involves the general assumption that as interpersonal support increases its scope in a group, the effects tend to be circular in nature. That is, the more affective support, personal esteem, and personal well-being become evident in a peer group, the more easily a diffuse distribution of interpersonal attraction is perpetuated.

A rank-order correlation of $\rho = -.33$ $(p < .05)$ indicates a negative association between the centrality of liking "choice" scores and group affect. As predicted, group affect decreases as a narrow focus of liking choices increases. Further, a correlation of $\rho = -.26$ $(p < .10)$ indicates a probable negative association between the centrality of liking "rejection" scores and group affect. These correlations, though small, indicate at least a tendency for peer groups with diffuse liking structures to have more supportive socialemotional atmospheres.

Hypothesis 2 is:

2. The more liking choices are centrally structured in the peer group, the more accurate pupils are when estimating their actual liking status in the group.

In other words, pupils should more accurately judge where they stand in relation to their peers as the relationships among pupils approach a clear status hierarchy. Peer-group situations like this, in which interpersonal choices tend to be narrowly and distinctly focused, make shared awareness of this situation more probable. As we noted above, this proposition of "accuracy" received empirical support in a previous study (Schmuck, 1962).

Table 1 delineates the results relevant to this hypothesis. These data indicate a positive association between structural centrality and accuracy of

Table 1

LIKING STRUCTURAL TYPES AND PUPILS' ACCURACY IN
ESTIMATING STATUS[*]

	ESTIMATE OF STATUS			
	ACCURATE PUPILS		INACCURATE PUPILS	
LIKING STRUCTURAL TYPE	NO.	PER CENT	NO.	PER CENT
Bimodal centrality	97	66	51	34
Monomodal centrality†	83	64	46	36
Diffuseness	75	51	72	49

[*] $\chi^2 = 7.85, p < .02$.

† Includes either "choice" or "rejection" centrality.

personal status in the peer group. The results show, moreover, that as the liking dimension approaches a more narrowly focused distribution, bimodal centrality, more pupils accurately estimate their status in the peer group. These results were also substantiated for high-school classrooms ($\chi^2 = 15.51$, $df = 2$, $p < .001$).

A more refined analysis further supports Hypothesis 2. Table 2 indicates that pupils who have low actual liking status in elementary-school peer groups tend to cognize their low status more accurately in the centrally structured situations. In the diffusely structured classrooms about 60 per cent of those pupils with low actual status cognize themselves as being highly liked in the group. We contend that the profusion of emotional support for individuals in the diffusely structured peer group accounts for this condition. Similar results were obtained for a combined analysis of the junior and senior high age levels, ($\chi^2 = 9.95$, $df = 2$, $p < .01$).

Table 2

PUPIL ACCURACY IN COGNIZING LOW STATUS IN THREE
LIKING STRUCTURES*

	COGNITION OF LOW STATUS			
	ACCURATE PUPILS		INACCURATE PUPILS	
LIKING STRUCTURAL TYPE	NO.	PER CENT	NO.	PER CENT
Bimodal centrality	44	58	32	42
Monomodal centrality	29	45	35	55
Diffuseness	29	40	44	60

* $\chi^2 = 14.65, p < .001$.

Table 3*

ACTUAL LIKING STATUS, COGNIZED LIKING STATUS, AND UTILIZATION
OF ABILITIES†

ACTUAL LIKING STATUS	COGNIZED LIKING STATUS	HIGH UTILIZERS (N = 210)		LOW UTILIZERS (N = 214)		TOTAL COGNIZED STATUS	TOTAL ACTUAL STATUS
		NO.	PER CENT	NO.	PER CENT		
High	High	100	65	53	35	153⎱	211
	Low	25	43	33	57	58⎰	
Low	High	53	48	58	52	111⎱	213
	Low	32	31	70	69	102⎰	

* The χ^2 partitioning statistic used in Tables 3-5 is explained by Hays (1955, pp. 24-33).

† χ^2 (actual status-cognized status) $= 18.77$, $p < .001$; χ^2 (actual status-utilization) $= 15.85$, $p < .001$; χ^2 (cognized status-utilization) $= 19.87$, $p < .001$; χ^2 (interaction) $= .02$, N.S.; χ^2 (actual status-cognized status-utilization) $= 54.51$, $p < .001$.

Some ramifications of having low liking status and knowing it become evident in analysis of the results for Hypotheses 3 and 4. Hypothesis 3 states:

> 3. Pupils with low actual liking status are lower utilizers of their abilities than pupils with higher actual liking status.

Hypothesis 4 is:

> 4. Pupils who cognize themselves as holding low liking status are lower utilizers of their abilities than pupils with higher cognized status.

The data shown in Table 3 strongly support both hypotheses. Furthermore, an inspection of the percentages in Table 3 shows that pupils who cognize themselves as being liked, though they have low actual liking status, are utilizing their abilities more highly than those who have low status and know it. Results for older pupils are essentially the same. These results emphasize the importance of introducing cognized status into studies relating sociometric status to performance.

The data for hypotheses 5 and 6 emphasize again the importance of considering cognized liking status along with actual status in studies of classroom peer groups. Hypotheses 5 and 6 state:

> 5. Pupils who cognize themselves as holding low liking status have more negative attitudes toward self than pupils with higher cognized status.
> 6. Pupils who cognize themselves as holding low liking status have more negative attitudes toward school than pupils with higher cognized status.

The results in Tables 4 and 5 show that cognized liking status is related positively and significantly to both attitude toward self and attitude toward

Table 4

ACTUAL LIKING STATUS, COGNIZED LIKING STATUS, AND
ATTITUDE TOWARD SELF[*]

		ATTITUDE TOWARD SELF					
		POSITIVE ($N = 212$)		NEGATIVE ($N = 209$)		TOTAL	TOTAL
ACTUAL LIKING STATUS	COGNIZED LIKING STATUS	NO.	PER CENT	NO.	PER CENT	COGNIZED STATUS	ACTUAL STATUS
High	{ High	90	60	61	40	151 }	211
	{ Low	24	40	36	60	60 }	
Low	{ High	63	58	46	42	109 }	210
	{ Low	35	35	66	65	101 }	

* χ^2 (actual status-cognized status) $= 17.22$, $p < .001$; χ^2 (actual status-attitude toward self) $= 2.28$, N.S.; χ^2 (cognized status-attitude toward self) $= 19.60$, $p < .001$; χ^2 (interaction) $= .57$, N.S.; χ^2 (actual status-cognized status-attitude toward self) $= 39.67$, $p < .001$.

Table 5
ACTUAL LIKING STATUS, COGNIZED LIKING STATUS, AND
ATTITUDE TOWARD SCHOOL*

ACTUAL LIKING STATUS	COGNIZED LIKING STATUS	POSITIVE (N = 206)		NEGATIVE (N = 216)		TOTAL COGNIZED STATUS	TOTAL ACTUAL STATUS
		NO.	PER CENT	NO.	PER CENT		
High	High	82	54	69	46	151 }	211
	Low	24	40	36	60	60 }	
Low	High	62	56	48	44	110 }	211
	Low	38	38	63	62	101 }	

* χ^2 (actual status-cognized status) = 16.88, $p < .001$; χ^2 (actual status-attitude toward school) = .34, N.S.; χ^2 (cognized status-attitude toward school) = 11.06, $p < .001$; χ^2 (interaction) = .56, N.S.; χ^2 (actual status-cognized status-attitude toward school) = 28.84, $p < .001$.

school, while actual liking status shows no such relation to these variables.

Thus, one could be misled if he were to conclude from previous studies that peer-group sociometric relations are not related to pupil attitudes toward self and school on the basis of an analysis of actual liking status alone. Cognized liking status as well as actual liking status should be analyzed together when making a complete social psychological analysis of the classroom peer group. Indeed our data indicate that one important conditioner of attitudes toward self and school is the liking status a child cognizes himself as holding in relation to his peers. Presumably, the group-structured properties that were highlighted in our results for hypothesis 2 represent at least one dynamic aspect of this.

The data for the first six hypotheses support the notion that peer-group sociometric diffuseness, extensity of interpersonal support for the individual pupil, attitudes toward self and school, and academic productivity vary together in a systematic fashion. The remaining hypotheses involve another significant variable in analyzing the impact of peer-group liking patterns on individual pupils: pupil potency of involvement in the peer group.

Hypotheses 7-9 deal with the predicted differential effects on the individual pupil of high or low involvement in his classroom peer group. The general proposition underlying each of these hypotheses is that peer-group status should have a greater impact on those pupils who are highly involved in classroom life (those with few additional alternatives for interpersonal gratifications) than on those pupils lacking such involvement. The results for hypotheses 7 and 8 are quite clear, while those for hypothesis 9 are less so.

Hypothesis 7 states:

7. Associations exist between actual liking status and one's utilization of abilities, only for pupils with high potency of involvement in the peer group.

A comparison of the χ^2 analyses in Table 6 supports this hypothesis. For pupils with high potency of involvement condition, there is a positive association between actual liking status in the peer group and the utilization of academic abilities. However, this association does not hold for those pupils with low potency of involvement. Thus, it appears that the ability utilization of those pupils most involved in the classroom peer group is more

Table 6

ACTUAL LIKING STATUS AND UTILIZATION WITH POTENCY
OF INVOLVEMENT

LIKING STATUS	HIGH UTILIZERS		LOW UTILIZERS	
	NO.	PER CENT	NO.	PER CENT
*HIGH POTENCY OF INVOLVEMENT**				
High	73	65	47	45
Low	39	35	58	55
LOW POTENCY OF INVOLVEMENT†				
High	48	49	44	40
Low	50	51	67	60

* $\chi^2 = 9.14, p < .005.$
† $\chi^2 = 1.84,$ N.S.

Table 7

ACTUAL LIKING STATUS AND ATTITUDE TOWARD SELF WITH
POTENCY OF INVOLVEMENT

LIKING STATUS	POSITIVE ATTITUDE		NEGATIVE ATTITUDE	
	NO.	PER CENT	NO.	PER CENT
*HIGH POTENCY OF INVOLVEMENT**				
High	65	61	53	46
Low	42	39	62	54
LOW POTENCY OF INVOLVEMENT†				
High	46	44	46	45
Low	59	56	57	55

* $\chi^2 = 4.78, p < .05.$
† $\chi^2 = .02,$ N.S.

highly associated with actual liking status than is true for those pupils less involved.

Hypotheses 8 and 9 state:

8. Associations exist between actual liking status and one's attitude toward self only for pupils with high potency of involvement in the peer group.

9. Associations exist between actual liking status and one's attitude toward school only for pupils with high potency of involvement in the peer group.

Hypothesis 8, concerning attitude toward self, is supported by our data, while Hypothesis 9 is not. A comparison of the χ^2 analyses in Table 7 does confirm the proposition that actual liking status is associated more highly with attitude toward self for pupils highly involved in the peer group than for those with less involvement. The results for Hypothesis 9 concerning potency of involvement, actual liking status, and attitude toward school are not significant.

Finally, combining the variables of structure and involvement, hypothesis 10 states:

> 10. Attitude toward self of pupils with high potency of involvement in the peer group is more positive as peer group structure increases in diffuseness.

Hypothesis 10, analyzed with the entire sample, is supported by our data. Table 8 shows that the attitude toward self of pupils with high potency of involvement in the classroom group is higher as group structure increases in diffuseness.

Table 8

ATTITUDE TOWARD SELF OF PUPILS HIGHLY INVOLVED IN THE
PEER GROUP FOR THREE LIKING STRUCTURES[*]

LIKING STRUCTURAL TYPE	POSITIVE ATTITUDE		NEGATIVE ATTITUDE	
	NO.	PER CENT	NO.	PER CENT
Bimodal centrality	56	41	82	59
Monomodal centrality	67	46	79	54
Diffuseness	50	58	36	42

[*] $\chi^2 = 6.63, p < .05.$

Briefly, then, the bulk of the empirical data reported here concerning relations among peer-group, attitudinal, and academic-performance variables support our hypotheses. These data point out, among other things, that peer groups characterized by a wide spread of liking relations among members have more positive emotional climates; that peer-group liking structure and pupil involvement in the group help to fashion a pupil's cognition of himself in relation to the peer group; that this cognition of self in relation to others is associated with a pupil's attitudes toward self and school; and that a pupil's personal conception of his place in the peer group is related also to his utilization of abilities.

Implications for Further Research

In most systematic studies in social science, data are considered to support hypotheses when legitimate statistical devices indicate that little possibility exists that the results occurred by chance. Of course, many negative cases always are present in tables of data, even though we formally consider a hypothesis as generally confirmed. Certainly one reason that these negative cases occur is that most complex social psychological phenomena are multidetermined, and in studies such as this one, one is not always able to conceptualize and measure all of the significant variables while making a prediction. This means, then, that negative cases in the tables should give impetus to ideas for future research.

For example, consider pupils who are highly liked in the classroom peer group and who view themselves as being liked. Our data indicate that fifty-three pupils in this category in the elementary grades are low utilizers of their academic abilities. How might one begin to explain the occurrence of the negative cases? One explanation is that the crude measures of socioeconomic status, cognized status, and utilization were invalid for some individual cases. This is undoubtedly true to some extent. Another explanation is that these pupils are receiving so much satisfaction in their social relations and using so much energy in that area of life that they have little left for classroom learning. On the other hand, what about the thirty-two high-utilizing pupils who are not liked and who know it? It could be that these pupils are not much concerned with social relations; perhaps classroom learning presents them with the most satisfying school condition and all of their energies are exerted here. In any case, we should point out that our theoretical framework is quite simple and that many variables must be introduced into it before it reflects completely the realities of classroom peer-group life.

Consider the pupil who has a high affiliation motive; will not being disliked by his peers affect his academic work more than a pupil who has little desire for affiliation? Consider the pupil who has a much stronger achievement than affiliation motive; perhaps for him social relations can be disregarded except with relevant authorities such as the teacher. Consider the pupil with little power motive; will it matter much to him if he is not influential with his peers? Probably many other psychosocial motives, attitudinal clusters, and personal values could be presented here to show the need for more elaboration on the framework presented in this report. One impetus for future study comes from a systematic investigation of negative cases and some speculating on the reasons for these.

Some other relevant areas for future research concerning classroom peer groups include:

1. A statistical partitioning of the relative impact of several social psychological variables on the utilization of abilities, attitude toward self, and attitude toward school. Variables could include social class, sex, cognized peer liking status, attitudes toward the teacher, and cognized home support for school.
2. An investigation of the determinants of different sociometric structures. We might ask, for instance: Can one predict to types of sociometric structures by knowing some relevant personality characteristics of children, by knowing something about the social back-

grounds of the children, by analyzing teacher values and behavior, or by analyzing some other set of variables?

3. A laboratory experiment, testing whether peer-group rejection leads to a decrement in intellectual performance and attitude toward self under controlled conditions. Also important would be experimentation indicating the conditions under which learning and attitude toward self decrements do not occur even when peer rejection is present.

4. Research on alternative ways of conceptualizing and measuring the utilization of abilities. The utilization of academic abilities has been central throughout this study, yet, just as there are varous kinds of ability, there may also be different forms of utilization. Extended conceptualization and empirical work is needed here for a more complete delineation of this concept.

Summary

This study was undertaken in an attempt to fill some social psychological gaps left by recent studies on peer relations, learning, and mental health in the classroom. Indeed, most research on classroom groups does not deal systematically with the interrelationships between interpersonal peer-group variables and intrapersonal individual variables. Our research professes to delineate some of these relations both conceptually and empirically.

The framework of conceptual linkages considered in this analysis ranged from peer-group conditions through intervening psychological processes to individual performance. Specific empirical variables studied under the rubric of *peer-group conditions* include liking sociometric structure, group affect, potency of involvement in the classroom group, and actual liking status in the peer group. The *intervening psychological processes* include cognized liking status, attitude toward self, and attitude toward school, while the *performance* indicator is the pupil's utilization of his abilities. The central problems for this study involved how social-situational factors shape emotional-personal factors; and how these latter factors related to a pupil's utilization of his academic abilities.

A sample of 727 pupils representing Grades 3–12 was drawn from twenty-seven classrooms. Our analyses here centered on the elementary classrooms primarily—Grades 3–6. The sample included classrooms from rural, suburban, industrial, and university communities in southeastern Michigan. The occupational categories of the father of each pupil were quite diverse, ranging from professional to unskilled. The pupils and teachers were administered questionnaires and interviews by the research staff and data were drawn also from school files. The data were collected as part of a broader study concerning classroom group dynamics, teacher in-service training, and educational innovation.

Our theoretical framework proposed that an individual's academic performance is conditioned to some extent by the emotional and cognitive contents associated with his self-concepts as peer and pupil. Furthermore, we argued that these self-concepts are formed, at least in part, by one's social relations in the classroom peer group; and that they have some effect on the way in which a pupil carries out the more formal learning requirements of the classroom. Ten hypotheses were delineated systematically using this general framework.

In general, our empirical findings supported the major hypothesized associations between peer-group conditions, intervening psychological processes, and individual performance in the classroom. Among the important findings confirming our hypotheses were the following:

1. Classroom peer groups with a wide range of liking choices (diffuse liking structures) tend to have more positive group affect than classrooms with narrowly focused liking distributions (central liking structures).

2. Pupils are more accurate in estimating their actual liking statuses in peer groups characterized by bimodal centrality (both positive and negative dimensions of liking area narrowly focused) than in groups characterized by diffuseness (both positive and negative dimensions widely focused). Specifically, pupils who have low liking status in elementary classrooms tend to cognize their low position more accurately in the centrally structured situation than in the diffusely structured one.

3. Pupils who are accurate when estimating their position in a liking structure and who are negatively placed in that structure are lower utilizers of academic abilities and have less positive attitudes toward self and school than pupils who are accurate and positively placed. Furthermore, pupils who cognize themselves as being liked, though they have low actual liking status, are utilizing their abilities more highly and have more positive attitudes toward self and school than those pupils who have low status and know it.

4. For elementary-school pupils who are highly involved in the classroom peer group (high potency of involvement), significant relationships exist between actual liking status on the one hand and utilization of abilities, attitude toward self, and attitude toward school on the other hand. These same associations do not exist under conditions of low potency of involvement in the classroom peer group.

5. The attitude toward self of pupils with high potency of involvement in the peer group is more positive as peer-group liking structure increases in diffuseness.

References

CARTWRIGHT, D. and ZANDER, A.   *Group dynamics.* Evanston: Row, Peterson, 1960.

COLEMAN, J.   *The adolescent society.* New York: Free Press, 1961.

ECHELBERGER, E.   Relationships between personality traits and peer status. Ph.D. dissertation, University of Michigan, 1959.

ELKINS, D.   Some factors related to the choice-status of ninety eighth-grade children in a school society. *Genetic Psychology Monographs,* 1959, 42, 207-272.

GRONLUND, N.   *Sociometry in the classroom.* New York: Harper, 1959.

HAYS, W.   *Analysis of qualitative data.* Ann Arbor: University of Michigan, 1955.

HUDGINS, B. and SMITH, L. (Eds.)   The classroom as a social system. Unpublished conference paper, Washington University, 1962.

KEISLAR, E.   Peer group rating of high school pupils with high and low marks. *Journal of Experimental Education,* 1955, 23, 369-373.

KOHLER, W.   *Gestalt Psychology.* New York: Liveright, 1947.

LEAVITT, H.   Some effects of certain communication patterns on group performance. *Journal of Abnormal and Social Psychology,* 1951, 46, 38-50.

LEWIN, K., LIPPITT, R. and WHITE, R.   Patterns of aggressive behavior in experimentally created "social climates." *Journal of Social Psychology,* 1939, 10, 271-299.

LIPPITT, R. and GOLD, M.   Classroom social structure as a mental health problem. *Journal of Social Issues,* 1959, 15, 40-49.

MARCH, J. and SIMON, H.   *Organizations.* New York: Wiley, 1958.

MOLES, O., LIPPITT, R. and WITHEY, S.   *A selective review of research and theory on delinquency.* Document Series No. 2, Inter-Center Program of Research on Children, Youth and Family Life. Ann Arbor: Institute for Social Research, 1959.

NEWCOMB, T.   *Personality and social change.* New York: Dryden, 1943.

RIESMAN, D.   *The lonely crowd.* New Haven: Yale University Press, 1950.

SCHMUCK, R. A.   Social-emotional characteristics of classroom peer groups. Ph.D. dissertation, University of Michigan, 1962.

SCHMUCK, R. A.   Sociometric status and utilization of academic abilities. *Merrill-Palmer Quarterly,* 1962, 8, 165-172.

SEARS, P.   A look at measures of achievement motivation. Paper presented at APA symposium on Achievement Motivation and Achievement Anxiety in Children, 1959.

SEWELL, W., HALLER, A. and STRAUS, M.   Social status and educational and occupational aspiration. *American Sociological Review,* 1959, 22, 67-76.

SMITH, E.   *American youth culture.* New York: Free Press, 1962.

VAN EGMOND, E.   Social interrelationship skills and effective utilization of intelligence in the classroom. Ph.D. dissertation, University of Michigan, 1960.

WILSON, A.   Residential segregation of social classes and aspirations of high school boys. *American Sociological Review,* 1959, 24, 836-845.

WHYTE, W.   *Street corner society.* Chicago: University of Chicago Press, 1943.

3. THE RACE PROBLEM

We tend to forget that mothers are teachers. This study shows clearly that the way a mother communicates with—teaches—her child as he works on specific tasks varies considerably, depending on the mother's socio-economic status, and that the child's performance (and presumably net learning) suffers or prospers accordingly.

Hess and Shipman's introduction places their work in context; here it should only be stressed that the study is important because it goes beyond socio-economic status as an "explanation" of why "disadvantaged" children get that way, to analyze the actual interaction between mother and child.

As Backman and Secord (in *A Social Psychological View of Education*, Harcourt, Brace and World, 1968) have pointed out, we need longitudinal data, rather than only cross-sectional studies to know whether a mother's way of talking to her child has the long-term effects we suspect it does. And, we do not really know, either, whether a mother whose communications are "status-oriented" does in fact ill-fit her child to function well in school. Schools are rather "status-oriented" institutions, as Hoy's article in the present volume reminds us.

Readers who are especially interested in maternal teaching behavior should also examine the extended treatment by Hess and Shipman in Hill's *Minnesota Symposium on Child Psychology* (University of Minnesota Press, 1967). And for a charming and very relevant study, Feshbach and Devor's work in the present volume. Do four-year-olds teach the way their mothers taught them? It seems so.

Early Experience and the Socialization of Cognitive Modes in Children[*]

Robert D. Hess, Virginia C. Shipman

The Problem

One of the questions arising from the contemporary concern with the education of culturally disadvantaged children is how we should conceptualize the effects of such deprivation upon the cognitive faculties of the child. The outcome is well known: children from deprived backgrounds score well below middle-class children on standard individual and group measures of intelligence (a gap that increases with age); they come to school without the skills necessary for coping with first grade curricula; their language development, both written and spoken, is relatively poor; auditory and visual discrimination skills are not well developed; in scholastic achievement they are retarded an average of 2 years by grade 6 and almost 3 years by grade 8; they are more likely to drop out of school before completing a secondary education; and even when they have adequate ability are less likely to go to college (Deutsch, 1963; Deutsch and Brown, 1964; Eells, Davis, Havighurst, Herriels, and Tyler 1951; John, 1963; Kennedy, Van de Riet, and White, 1963; Lesser, 1964).

For many years the central theoretical issues in this field dealt with the origin of these effects, argued in terms of the relative contribution of genetic as compared with environmental factors. Current interest in the effects of cultural deprivation ignores this classic debate; the more basic problem is to understand how cultural experience is translated into cognitive behavior and academic achievement (Bernstein, 1961; Hess, 1964).

The focus of concern is no longer upon the question of whether social and cultural disadvantage depress academic ability, but has shifted to a study of the mechanisms of exchange that mediate between the individual and his environment. The thrust of research and theory is toward conceptualizing social class as a discrete array of experiences and patterns of ex-

* Reprinted from *Child Development*, 1965, 36, 869-886. Used by permission of the authors and publisher, The University of Chicago Press. Copyright 1965 by The Society for Research in Child Development, Inc.

This research was supported by the Research Division of the Children's Bureau, Social Security Administration; Department of Health, Education, and Welfare; Ford Foundation for the Advancement of Learning; and grants-in-aid from the Social Science Research Committee of the Division of Social Sciences, University of Chicago. Project staff members who made specific contributions to the analysis of data are Jere Brophy, Dina Feitelson, Roberta Meyer, and Ellis Olim.

perience that can be examined in relation to the effects they have upon the emerging cognitive equipment of the young child. In short, the question this paper presents is this: what *is* cultural deprivation, and how does it act to shape and depress the resources of the human mind?

The arguments we wish to present here are these: first, that the behavior which leads to social, educational, and economic poverty is socialized in early childhood—that is, it is learned; second, that the central quality involved in the effects of cultural deprivation is a lack of cognitive meaning in the mother-child communication system; and, third, that the growth of cognitive processes is fostered in family control systems which offer and permit a wide range of alternatives of action and thought and that such growth is constricted by systems of control which offer predetermined solutions and few alternatives for consideration and choice.

In this paper we will argue that the structure of the social system and the structure of the family shape communication and language and that language shapes thought and cognitive styles of problem-solving. In the deprived-family context this means that the nature of the control system which relates parent to child restricts the number and kind of alternatives for action and thought that are opened to the child; such constriction precludes a tendency for the child to reflect, to consider and choose among alternatives for speech and action. It develops modes for dealing with stimuli and with problems which are impulsive rather than reflective, which deal with the immediate rather than the future, and which are disconnected rather than sequential.

This position draws from the work of Basil Bernstein (1961) of the University of London. In his view, language structures and conditions what the child learns and how he learns, setting limits within which future learning may take place. He identifies two forms of communication codes or styles of verbal behavior: *restricted* and *elaborated*. Restricted codes are stereotyped, limited, and condensed, lacking in specificity and the exactness needed for precise conceptualization and differentiation. Sentences are short, simple, often unfinished; there is little use of subordinate clauses for elaborating the content of the sentence; it is a language of implicit meaning, easily understood and commonly shared. It is the language form often used in impersonal situations when the intent is to promote solidarity or reduce tension. Restricted codes are nonspecific clichés, statements, or observations about events made in general terms that will be readily understood. The basic quality of this mode is to limit the range and detail of concept and information involved.

Elaborated codes, however, are those in which communication is individualized and the message is specific to a particular situation, topic, and person. It is more particular, more differentiated, and more precise. It permits expression of a wider and more complex range of thought, tending toward discrimination among cognitive and affective content.

The effects of early experience with these codes are not only upon the communication modes and cognitive structure—they also establish potential

patterns of relation with the external world. It is one of the dynamic features of Bernstein's work that he views language as social behavior. As such,
language is used by participants of a social network to elaborate and express social and other interpersonal relations and, in turn, is shaped and
determined by these relations.

The interlacing of social interaction and language is illustrated by the
distinction between two types of family control. One is oriented toward
control by *status* appeal or ascribed role norms. The second is oriented
toward *persons*. Families differ in the degree to which they utilize each
of these types of regulatory appeal. In status- (position-) oriented families,
behavior tends to be regulated in terms of role expectations. There is little
opportunity for the unique characteristics of the child to influence the
decision-making process or the interaction between parent and child. In
these families, the internal or personal states of the children are not influential as a basis for decision. Norms of behavior are stressed with such
imperatives as, "You must do this because I say so," or "Girls don't act
like that," or other statements which rely on the status of the participants
or a behavior norm for justification (Bernstein, 1964).

In the family, as in other social structures, control is exercised in part
through status appeals. The feature that distinguishes among families is the
extent to which the status-based control maneuvers are modified by orientation toward persons. In a person-oriented appeal system, the unique
characteristics of the child modify status demands and are taken into account in interaction. The decisions of this type of family are individualized
and less frequently related to status or role ascriptions. Behavior is justified
in terms of feelings, preference, personal and unique reactions, and subjective states. This philosophy not only permits but demands an elaborated
linguistic code and a wide range of linguistic and behavioral alternatives
in interpersonal interaction. Status-oriented families may be regulated by
less individuated commands, messages, and responses. Indeed, by its
nature, the status-oriented family will rely more heavily on a restricted
code. The verbal exchange is inherent in the structure—regulates it and
is regulated by it.

These distinctions may be clarified by two examples of mother-child
communication using these two types of codes. Assume that the emotional
climate of two homes is approximately the same; the significant difference
between them is in style of communication employed. A child is playing
noisily in the kitchen with an assortment of pots and pans when the telephone rings. In one home the mother says, "Be quiet," or "Shut up," or
issues any one of several other short, peremptory commands. In the other
home the mother says, "Would you keep quiet a minute? I want to talk
on the phone." The question our study poses is this: what inner response is
elicited in the child, what is the effect upon his developing cognitive network of concepts and meaning in each of these two situations? In one instance the child is asked for a simple mental response. He is asked to
attend to an uncomplicated message and to make a conditioned response

(to comply); he is not called upon to reflect or to make mental discriminations. In the other example the child is required to follow two or three ideas. He is asked to relate his behavior to a time dimension; he must think of his behavior in relation to its effect upon another person. He must perform a more complicated task to follow the communication of his mother in that his relationship to her is mediated in part through concepts and shared ideas; his mind is stimulated or exercised (in an elementary fashion) by a more elaborate and complex verbal communication initiated by the mother. As objects of these two divergent communication styles, repeated in various ways, in similar situations and circumstances during the preschool years, these two imaginary children would be expected to develop significantly different verbal facility and cognitive equipment by the time they enter the public-school system.

A person-oriented family allows the child to achieve the behavior rules (role requirements) by presenting them in a specific context for the child and by emphasizing the consequences of alternative actions. Status-oriented families present the rules in an assigned manner, where compliance is the *only* rule-following possibility. In these situations the role of power in the interaction is more obvious, and, indeed, coercion and defiance are likely interactional possibilities. From another perspective, status-oriented families use a more rigid learning and teaching model in which compliance, rather than rationale, is stressed.

A central dimension through which we look at maternal behavior is to inquire what responses are elicited and permitted by styles of communication and interaction. There are two axes of the child's behavior in which we have a particular interest. One of these is represented by an *assertive, initiatory* approach to learning, as contrasted with a *passive, compliant* mode of engagement; the other deals with the tendency to reach solutions impulsively or hastily as distinguished from a tendency to *reflect*, to compare alternatives, and to choose among available options.

These styles of cognitive behavior are related, in our hypotheses, to the dimensions of maternal linguistic codes and types of family control systems. A status-oriented statement, for example, tends to offer a set of regulations and rules for conduct and interaction that is based on arbitrary decisions rather than upon logical consequences which result from selection of one or another alternatives. Elaborated and person-oriented statements lend themselves more easily to styles of cognitive approach that involve reflection and reflective comparison. Status-oriented statements tend to be restrictive of thought. Take our simple example of the two children and the telephone. The verbal categoric command to "Be quiet" cuts off thought and offers little opportunity to relate the information conveyed in the command to the context in which it occurred. The more elaborated message, "Would you be quiet a minute? I want to talk on the phone," gives the child a rationale for relating his behavior to a wider set of considerations. In effect, he has been given a *why* for his mother's request and, by this example, possibly becomes more likely to *ask* why in another situation. It may be through this type of verbal interaction that the child learns to look for action sequences in his own and others' behavior. Perhaps through these more intent-oriented statements the child comes to see the world as others see it and learns to take the role of others in viewing himself and his actions. The child comes to see the world as a set of possibilities from which he can make a personal selection. He learns to role play with an element of personal flexibility, not by role-conforming rigidity.

Research Plan

For our project a research group of 163 Negro mothers and their 4-year-old children was selected from four different social status levels: Group A came from college-educated professional, executive, and managerial occupational levels; Group B came from skilled blue-collar occupational levels, with not more than high-school education; Group C came from unskilled or semiskilled occupational levels, with predominantly elementary-school education; Group D from unskilled or semiskilled occupational levels, with fathers absent and families supported by public assistance.

These mothers were interviewed twice in their homes and brought to the university for testing and for an interaction session between mother and child in which the mother was taught three simple tasks by the staff member and then asked to teach these tasks to the child.

One of these tasks was to sort or group a number of plastic toys by color and by function; a second task was to sort eight blocks by two characteristics simultaneously; the third task required the mother and child to work together to copy five designs on a toy called an Etch-a-Sketch. A description of various aspects of the project and some preliminary results have been presented in several papers (Brophy, Hess, and Shipman, 1965; Jackson, Hess, and Shipman, 1965; Meyer, Shipman, and Hess, 1964; Olim, Hess, and Shipman, 1965; Shipman and Hess, 1965).

Results

The data in this paper are organized to show social-status differences among the four groups in the dimensions of behavior described above to indicate something of the maternal teaching styles that are emerging and to offer examples of relations between maternal and child behavior that are congruent with the general lines of argument we have laid out.

Social-Status Differences

VERBAL CODES: RESTRICTED VERSUS ELABORATED.   One of the most striking and obvious differences between the environments provided by the mothers of the research group was in their patterns of language use. In our testing sessions, the most obvious social-class variations were in the total amount of verbal output in response to questions and tasks asking for verbal response. For example, as Table 1 shows, mothers from the middle-class gave protocols that were consistently longer in language productivity than did mothers from the other three groups.

Taking three different types of questions that called for free response

Table 1

MEAN NUMBER OF TYPED LINES IN THREE DATA-
GATHERING SITUATIONS

	UPPER MIDDLE N = 40	UPPER LOWER N = 40	LOWER LOWER N = 36	ADC N = 36
School situations	34.68	22.80	18.86	18.64
Mastery situations	28.45	18.70	15.94	17.75
CAT Card	18.72	9.62	12.39	12.24
Total	81.85	51.12	47.19	48.63

on the part of the mothers and counting the number of lines of typescript of the protocols, the tally for middle-class mothers was approximately 82 contrasted with an average of roughly 49 for mothers from the three other groups.

These differences in verbal products indicate the extent to which the maternal environments of children in different social-class groups tend to be mediated by verbal cue and thus offer (or fail to offer) opportunities for labeling, for identifying objects and feelings and adult models who can demonstrate the usefulness of language as a tool for dealing with interpersonal interaction and for ordering stimuli in the environment.

In addition to this gross disparity in verbal output there were differences in the quality of language used by mothers in the various status groups. One approach to the analysis of language used by these mothers was an examination of their responses to the following task: They were shown the Lion Card of the Children's Apperception Test and asked to tell their child a story relating to the card. This card is a picture of a lion sitting on a chair holding a pipe in his hand. Beside him is a cane. In the corner is a mouse peering out of a hole. The lion appears to be deep in thought. These protocols were the source of language samples which were summarized in nine scales (Table 2), two of which we wish to describe here.

The first scale dealt with the mother's tendency to use abstract words. The index derived was a proportion of abstract noun and verb types to total number of noun and verb types. Words were defined as abstract when the name of the object is thought of apart from the cases in which it is actually realized. For example, in the sentence, "The lion is an *animal*," "animal" is an abstract word. However, in the sentence, "This animal in the picture is sitting on his throne," "animal" is not an abstract noun.

Table 2

SOCIAL STATUS DIFFERENCES IN LANGUAGE USAGE
(SCORES ARE THE MEANS FOR EACH GROUP)

	SOCIAL STATUS			
SCALE	UPPER MIDDLE N = 40	UPPER LOWER N = 42	LOWER LOWER N = 40	ADC N = 41
Mean sentence length[a]	11.39	8.74	9.66	8.23
Adjective range[b]	31.99	28.32	28.37	30.49
Adverb range[c]	11.14	9.40	8.70	8.20
Verb elaboration[d]	.59	.52	.47	.44
Complex verb preference[e]	63.25	59.12	50.85	51.73
Syntactic structure elaboration[f]	8.89	6.90	8.07	6.46
Stimulus utilization	5.82	4.81	4.87	5.36
Introduced content	3.75	2.62	2.45	2.34
Abstraction[g]	5.60	4.89	3.71	1.75

[a] Average number of words per sentence.

[b] Proportion of uncommon adjective types to total nouns, expressed as a percentage.

[c] Proportion of uncommon adverb types to total verbs, adjectives, and adverbs, expressed as a percentage.

[d] Average number of complex verb types per sentence.

[e] Proportion of complex verb types to all verb types, simple and complex.

[f] Average number of weighted complex syntactic structures per 100 words.

[g] Proportion of abstract nouns and verbs (excluding repetitions) to total nouns and verbs (excluding repetitions), expressed as a percentage.

In our research group, middle-class mothers achieved an abstraction score of 5.6; the score for skilled work levels was 4.9; the score for the unskilled group was 3.7; for recipients of Aid to Dependent Children (ADC), 1.8.

The second scale dealt with the mother's tendency to use complex syntactic structures such as coordinate and subordinate clauses, unusual infinitive phrases (e.g., "To drive well, you must be alert"), infinitive clauses (e.g., "What to do next was the lion's problem"), and participial phrases (e.g., "Continuing the story, the lion . . ."). The index of structural elaboration derived was a proportion of these complex syntactic structures, weighted in accordance with their complexity and with the degree to which they are strung together to form still more complicated structures (e.g., clauses within clauses), to the total number of sentences.

In the research group, mothers from the middle class had a structure elaboration index of 8.89; the score for ADC mothers was 6.46. The use of complex grammatical forms and elaboration of these forms into complex clauses and sentences provides a highly elaborated code with which to manipulate the environment symbolically. This type of code encourages the child to recognize the possibilities and subtleties inherent in language not only for communication but also for carrying on high-level cognitive procedures.

CONTROL SYSTEMS: PERSON VERSUS STATUS ORIENTATION. Our data on the mothers' use of status- as contrasted with person-oriented statements comes from maternal responses to questions inquiring what the mother would do in order to deal with several different hypothetical situations at school in which the child had broken the rules of the school, had failed to achieve, or had been wronged by a teacher or classmate. The results of this tally are shown in Table 3.

As is clear from these means, the greatest differences between status groups is in the tendency to utilize person-oriented statements. These differences are even greater if seen as a ratio of person-to-status type responses.

The orientation of the mothers to these different types of control is seen not only in prohibitive or reparative situations but in their instructions to their children in preparing them for new experiences. The data on this point come from answers to the question: "Suppose your child were starting to school tomorrow for the first time. What would you tell him? How would you prepare him for school?"

Table 3

PERSON-ORIENTED AND STATUS-ORIENTED UNITS

ON SCHOOL SITUATION PROTOCOLS (MOTHERS)

A. MEAN NUMBER

SOCIAL CLASS	PERSON-ORIENTED		STATUS-ORIENTED		P/S RATIO	N
Upper middle	9.52	(1-19)	7.50	(0-19)	1.27	40
Upper lower	6.20	(0-20)	7.32	(2-17)	0.85	40
Lower lower	4.66	(0-15)	7.34	(2-17)	0.63	35
ADC	3.59	(0-16)	8.15	(3-29)	0.44	34

B. MEAN PER CENT

SOCIAL CLASS	PERSON-ORIENTED	STATUS-ORIENTED	N
Upper middle	36.92	27.78	40
Upper lower	31.65	36.92	40
Lower lower	26.43	40.69	35
ADC	20.85	51.09	34

One mother, who was person-oriented and used elaborated verbal codes, replied as follows:

"First of all, I would remind her that she was going to school to learn, that her teacher would take my place, and that she would be expected to follow instructions. Also that her time was to be spent mostly in the classroom with other children, and that any questions or any problems that she might have she could consult with her teacher for assistance."

"Anything else?"

"No, anything else would probably be confusing for her at her particular age."

In terms of promoting educability, what did this mother do in her response? First, she was informative; she presented the school situation as comparable to one already familiar to the child; second, she offered reassurance and support to help the child deal with anxiety; third, she described the school situation as one that involves a personal relationship between the child and the teacher; and, fourth, she presented the classroom situation as one in which the child was to learn.

A second mother responded as follows to this question:

"Well, John, it's time to go to school now. You must know how to behave. The first day at school you should be a good boy and should do just what the teacher tells you to do."

In contrast to the first mother, what did this mother do? First, she defined the role of the child as passive and compliant; second, the central issues she presented were those dealing with authority and the institution, rather than with learning; third, the relationship and roles she portrayed were sketched in terms of status and role expectations rather than in personal terms; and, fourth, her message was general, restricted, and vague, lacking information about how to deal with the problems of school except by passive compliance.

A more detailed analysis of the mothers' responses to this question grouped their statements as *imperative* or *instructive* (Table 4). An imperative statement was defined as an unqualified injunction or command,

Table 4

INFORMATION MOTHERS WOULD GIVE TO CHILD ON HIS FIRST
DAY AT SCHOOL

SOCIAL STATUS	IMPERATIVE	INSTRUCTIVE	SUPPORT	PREPARATION	OTHER	N
			% OF TOTAL STATEMENTS			
Upper middle ..	14.9	8.7	30.2	8.6	37.6	39
Upper lower ...	48.2	4.6	13.8	3.8	29.6	41
Lower lower ...	44.4	1.7	13.1	1.2	39.6	36
ADC	46.6	3.2	17.1	1.3	31.8	37
			% OF MOTHERS USING CATEGORY			
Upper middle ..	48.7	38.5	76.9	33.3	87.2	...
Upper lower ...	85.4	17.1	39.0	19.5	70.7	...
Lower lower ...	75.0	5.6	36.1	8.3	77.8	...
ADC	86.5	16.2	43.2	8.1	86.5	...

such as, "Mind the teacher and do what she tells you to do," or "The first thing you have to do is be on time," or "Be nice and do not fight." An instructive statement offers information or commands which carry a rationale or justification for the rule to be observed. Examples: "If you are tardy or if you stay away from school, your marks will go down"; or "I would tell him about the importance of minding the teacher. The teacher needs his full cooperation. She will have so many children that she won't be able to pamper any youngster."

STATUS DIFFERENCES IN CONCEPT UTILIZATION.   One of the measures of cognitive style used with both mothers and children in the research
group was the S's mode of classificatory behavior. For the adult version,
(Kagan, Moss and Sigel, 1963) S is required to make 12 consecutive
sorts of MAPS figures placed in a prearranged random order on a large
cardboard. After each sort she was asked to give her reason for putting certain figures together. This task was intended to reveal her typical or preferred manner of grouping stimuli and the level of abstraction that she
uses in perceiving and ordering objects in the environment. Responses fell
into four categories: descriptive part-whole, descriptive global, relational-
contextual, and categorical-inferential. A descriptive response is a direct
reference to physical attributes present in the stimuli, such as size, shape,
or posture. Examples: "They're all children," or "They are all lying down,"
or "They are all men." The subject may also choose to use only a part of
the figure—"They both have hats on." In a relational-contextual response,
any one stimulus gets its meaning from a relation with other stimuli.
Examples: "Doctor and nurse," or "Wife is cooking dinner for her husband,"
or "This guy looks like he shot this other guy." In categorical-inferential
responses, sorts are based on nonobservable characteristics of the stimulus
for which each stimulus is an independent representative of the total class.
Examples: "All of these people work for a living" or "These are all handi-
capped people."
As may be seen in Table 5, relational responses were most frequently

Table 5

MEAN RESPONSES TO ADULT SIGEL SORTING TASK (MAPS)

	SOCIAL STATUS			
CATEGORY	UPPER MIDDLE N = 40	UPPER LOWER N = 42	LOWER LOWER N = 39	ADC N = 41
Total descriptive................	3.18	2.19	2.18	2.59
Descriptive part-whole	1.65	1.33	1.31	1.49
Descriptive global	1.52	0.86	0.87	1.10
Relational-contextual	5.52	6.79	7.38	6.73
Categorical-inferential	3.30	3.00	2.23	2.66

offered; categorical-inferential were next most common, and descriptive
most infrequent. The distribution of responses of our status groups showed
that the middle-class group was higher on descriptive and categorical; low-
status groups were higher on relational. The greater use of relational categories by the working-class mothers is especially significant. Response times
for relational sorts are usually shorter, indicating less reflection and evaluating of alternative hypotheses. Such responses also indicate relatively low
attention to external stimuli details (Kagan, 1964). Relational responses are
often subjective, reflecting a tendency to relate objects to personal concerns

in contrast with the descriptive and categorical responses which tend to be objective and detached, more general, and more abstract. Categorical responses, in particular, represent thought processes that are more orderly and complex in organizing stimuli, suggesting more efficient strategies of information processing.

The most striking finding from the data obtained from the children's Sigel Sorting Task was the decreasing use of the cognitive style dimensions and increasing nonverbal responses with decrease in social-status levels. As may be seen in the tables showing children's performance on the Sigel Sorting Task (Tables 6 and 7), although most upper middle-class children and a majority of the upper lower-class children use relational and descriptive global responses, there is no extensive use of any of the other cognitive style dimensions by the two lower lower-class groups. In looking at particular categories one may note the relative absence of descriptive part-whole responses for other than the middle-class group and the large rise in non-

Table 6

CHILDREN'S RESPONSES TO SIGEL SORTING TASK (MEANS)

	SOCIAL STATUS			
	UPPER MIDDLE	UPPER LOWER	LOWER LOWER	ADC
CATEGORY	N = 40	N = 42	N = 39	N = 41
Descriptive part-whole	2.25	0.71	0.20	0.34
Descriptive global	2.80	2.29	1.51	0.98
Relational-contextual	3.18	2.31	1.18	1.02
Categorical-inferential	2.02	1.36	1.18	0.61
Nonscorable verbal responses	5.75	6.31	6.64	7.24
Nonverbal	3.00	6.41	7.08	8.76
No sort	1.00	0.62	2.21	1.05

Table 7

PERCENTAGE OF FOUR-YEAR-OLD CHILDREN
RESPONDING IN EACH OF THE CATEGORIES

	SOCIAL STATUS			
	UPPER MIDDLE	UPPER LOWER	LOWER LOWER	ADC
CATEGORY	N = 40	N = 42	N = 39	N = 41
Descriptive part-whole	40.0	28.6	18.0	14.6
Descriptive global	70.0	54.8	53.8	31.7
Total descriptive	80.0	66.7	59.0	39.0
Relational-contextual	77.5	66.7	41.0	43.9
Categorical-inferential	52.5	45.2	30.8	24.4
Nonscorable verbal	85.0	88.1	92.3	85.4
Nonverbal	52.5	66.7	82.0	87.8
No sort	12.5	7.1	25.6	19.5

verbal responses below the middle-class level. These results would seem to reflect the relatively undeveloped verbal and conceptual ability of children from homes with restricted range of verbal and conceptual content.

Relational and descriptive global responses have been considered the most immature and would be hypothesized to occur most frequently in pre-school children. Relational responses are often subjective, using idiosyncratic and irrelevant cues; descriptive global responses, often referring to sex and occupational roles, are somewhat more dependent upon experience. On the other hand, descriptive part-whole responses have been shown to increase with age and would be expected to be used less frequently. However, these descriptive part-whole responses, which are correlated with favorable prognostic signs for educability (such as attentiveness, control and learning ability), were almost totally absent from all but the upper middle-class group. Kagan (1964) has described two fundamental cognitive dispositions involved in producing such analytic concepts: the tendency to reflect over alternative solutions that are simultaneously available and the tendency to analyze a visual stimulus into component parts. Both behaviors require a delayed discrimination response. One may describe the impairment noted for culturally disadvantaged children as arising from differences in opportunities for developing these reflective attitudes.

The mothers' use of relational responses was significantly correlated with their children's use of nonscorable and nonverbal responses on the Sigel task and with poor performance on the 8-Block and Etch-a-Sketch tasks. The mothers' inability or disinclination to take an abstract attitude on the Sigel task was correlated with ineffectual teaching on the 8-Block task and inability to plan and control the Etch-a-Sketch situation. Since relational responses have been found (Kagan, Moss, and Sigel, 1963) to be correlated with impulsivity, tendencies for nonverbal rather than verbal teaching, mother-domination, and limited sequencing and discrimination might be expected and would be predicted to result in limited categorizing ability and impaired verbal skills in the child.

Analysis of Maternal Teaching Styles

These differences among the status groups and among mothers within the groups appear in slightly different form in the teaching sessions in which the mothers and children engaged. There were large differences among the status groups in the ability of the mothers to teach and the children to learn. This is illustrated by the performance scores on the sorting tasks.

Let us describe the interaction between the mother and child in one of the structured teaching situations. The wide range of individual differences in linguistic and interactional styles of these mothers may be illustrated by excerpts from recordings. The task of the mother is to teach the child how to group or sort a small number of toys.

The first mother outlines the task for the child, gives sufficient help and explanation to permit the child to proceed on her own. She says:

"All right, Susan, this board is the place where we put the little toys; first of all you're supposed to learn how to place them according to color. Can you do that? The things that are all the same color you put in one section; in the second section you put another group of colors, and in the third section you put the last group of colors. Can you do that? Or would you like to see me do it first?"

Child: "I want to do it."

This mother has given explicit information about the task and what is expected of the child; she has offered support and help of various kinds; and she has made it clear that she impelled the child to perform.

A second mother's style offers less clarity and precision. She says in introducing the same task:

"Now, I'll take them all off the board; now you put them all back on the board. What are these?"

Child: "A truck."

"All right, just put them right here; put the other one right here; all right put the other one there."

This mother must rely more on nonverbal communication in her commands; she does not define the task for the child; the child is not provided with ideas or information that she can grasp in attempting to solve the problem; neither is she told what to expect or what the task is, even in general terms.

A third mother is even less explicit. She introduces the task as follows:

"I've got some chairs and cars, do you want to play the game?" Child does not respond. Mother continues: "O.K. What's this?"

Child: "A wagon?"

Mother: "Hm?"

Child: "A wagon?"

Mother: "This is not a wagon. What's this?"

The conversation continues with this sort of exchange for several pages. Here again, the child is not provided with the essential information he needs to solve or to understand the problem. There is clearly some impelling on the part of the mother for the child to perform, but the child has not been told what he is to do. There were marked social-class differences in the ability of the children to learn from their mothers in the teaching sessions.

Each teaching session was concluded with an assessment by a staff member of the extent to which the child had learned the concepts taught by the mother. His achievement was scored in two ways: first, the ability to correctly place or sort the objects and, second, the ability to verbalize the principle on which the sorting or grouping was made.

Children from middle-class homes were well above children from working-class homes in performance on these sorting tasks, particularly in offering verbal explanations as to the basis for making the sort (Tables 8 and 9). Over 60 per cent of middle-class children placed the objects correctly on all tasks; the performance of working-class children ranged as low as 29 per cent correct. Approximately 40 per cent of these middle-class children who were successful were able to verbalize the sorting principle;

Table 8

DIFFERENCES AMONG STATUS GROUPS IN CHILDREN'S PERFORMANCE
IN TEACHING SITUATIONS (TOY SORT TASK)

SOCIAL STATUS	PLACED CORRECTLY (%)	VERBALIZED CORRECTLY (%)		N
A. Identity sort (cars, spoons, chairs):				
Upper middle	61.5	28.2	45.8[a]	39
Upper lower	65.0	20.0	30.8	40
Lower lower	68.4	29.0	42.3	38
ADC	66.7	30.8	46.2	39
B. Color sort (red, green, yellow):				
Upper middle	69.2	28.2	40.7[a]	39
Upper lower	67.5	15.0	22.2	40
Lower lower	57.9	13.2	22.7	38
ADC	33.3	5.1	15.4	39

[a] Per cent of those who placed object correctly.

Table 9

DIFFERENCES AMONG STATUS GROUPS IN CHILDREN'S PERFORMANCE
IN TEACHING SITUATIONS (8-BLOCK TASK)

SOCIAL STATUS	PLACED CORRECTLY (%)	ONE-DIMENSION VERBALIZED (%)		BOTH VERBALIZED (%)		N
A. Short O:						
Upper middle ...	75.0	57.5	57.5[a]	25.0	33.3[a]	40
Upper lower	51.2	39.0	43.2	2.4	4.8	41
Lower lower	50.0	29.0	33.3	15.8	31.6	38
ADC	43.6	20.5	22.2	2.6	5.9	39
B. Tall X:						
Upper middle ...	60.0	62.5	64.1[a]	27.5	45.8[a]	40
Upper lower	48.8	39.0	42.1	17.1	35.0	41
Lower lower	34.2	23.7	26.5	7.9	23.1	38
ADC	28.2	18.0	20.0	0.0	0.0	39

[a] Per cent of those who placed object correctly.

working-class children were less able to explain the sorting principle, ranging downward from the middle-class level to one task on which no child was able to verbalize correctly the basis of his sorting behavior. These differences clearly paralleled the relative abilities and teaching skills of the mothers from differing social-status groups.

The difference among the four status levels was apparent not only on these sorting and verbal skills but also in the mother's ability to regulate her own behavior and her child's in performing tasks which require planning or care rather than verbal or conceptual skill. These differences were revealed by the mother-child performance on the Etch-a-Sketch task. An Etch-a-Sketch toy is a small, flat box with a screen on which lines can be drawn by a device within the box. The marker is controlled by two knobs: one for horizontal movement, one for vertical. The mother is assigned one knob, the child the other. The mother is shown several designs which are to be reproduced. Together they attempt to copy the design models. The mother decides when their product is a satisfactory copy of the original. The products are scored by measuring deviations from the original designs.

These sessions were recorded, and the nonverbal interaction was described by an observer. Some of the most relevant results were these: middle-class mothers and children performed better on the task (14.6 points) than mothers and children from the other groups (9.2; 8.3; 9.5 [Table 10]). Mothers of the three lower-status groups were relatively persistent, rejecting more complete figures than the middle-class mothers; mothers from the middle class praised the child's efforts more than did other mothers but gave just as much criticism; the child's cooperation as rated by the observer was as good or better in low-status groups as in middle-class pairs (Table 11), there was little difference between the groups in affect expressed to the child by the mother (Brophy et al., 1965).

Table 10

PERFORMANCE ON ETCH-A-SKETCH TASK (MEANS)

	SOCIAL STATUS			
	UPPER MIDDLE N = 40	UPPER LOWER N = 42	LOWER LOWER N = 40	ADC N = 41
Total score (range 0-40)	14.6	9.2	8.3	9.5
Average number of attempts	12.7	17.2	12.2	15.1
Complete figures rejected	2.3	3.6	3.5	3.4
Child's total score	5.9	4.0	3.4	4.0
Child's contribution to total score (per cent)	40.4	43.5	41.0	42.1

In these data, as in others not presented here, the mothers of the four status groups differed relatively little, on the average, in the affective elements of their interaction with their children. The gross differences appeared in the verbal and cognitive environments that they presented.

Against this background I would like to return for a moment to the problem of the meaning, or, perhaps more correctly, the lack of meaning in cultural deprivation. One of the features of the behavior of the working-

Table 11

MOTHER-CHILD INTERACTION ON ETCH-A-SKETCH TASK (MEANS)[a]

	SOCIAL STATUS			
	UPPER MIDDLE N = 40	UPPER LOWER N = 41	LOWER LOWER N = 39	ADC N = 39
Praises child	4.6	6.9	7.2	7.5
Criticizes child	6.4	5.5	6.4	5.9
Overall acceptance of child	2.2	3.2	3.4	3.6
Child's cooperation	5.6	5.3	4.5	5.1
Level of affection shown to child ...	4.8	5.4	5.2	5.8

[a] Ratings made by observer; low number indicates more of the quality rated.

class mothers and children is a tendency to act without taking sufficient time for reflection and planning. In a sense one might call this impulsive behavior—not by acting out unconscious or forbidden impulses, but in a type of activity in which a particular act seems not to be related to the act that preceded it or to its consequences. In this sense it lacks meaning; it is not sufficiently related to the context in which it occurs, to the motivations of the participants, or to the goals of the task. This behavior may be verbal or motor; it shows itself in several ways. On the Etch-a-Sketch task, for example, the mother may silently watch a child make an error and then punish him. Another mother will anticipate the error, will warn the child that he is about to reach a decision point; she will prepare him by verbal and nonverbal cues to be careful, to look ahead, and to avoid the mistake. He is encouraged to reflect, to anticipate the consequences of his action, and in this way to avoid error. A problem-solving approach requires reflection and the ability to weigh decisions, to choose among alternatives. The effect of restricted speech and of status orientation is to foreclose the need for reflective weighing of alternatives and consequences; the use of an elaborated code, with its orientation to persons and to consequences (including future), tends to produce cognitive styles more easily adapted to problem-solving and reflection.

The objective of our study is to discover how teaching styles of the mothers induce and shape learning styles and information-processing strategies in the children. The picture that is beginning to emerge is that the meaning of deprivation is a deprivation of meaning—a cognitive environment in which behavior is controlled by status rules rather than by attention to the individual characteristics of a specific situation and one in which behavior is not mediated by verbal cues or by teaching that relates events to one another and the present to the future. This environment produces a child who relates to authority rather than to rationale, who, although often compliant, is not reflective in his behavior, and for whom the consequences of an act are largely considered in terms of immediate punishment or reward rather than future effects and long-range goals.

When the data are more complete, a more detailed analysis of the findings will enable us to examine the effect of maternal cognitive environments in terms of individual mother-child transactions, rather than in the gross categories of social class. This analysis will not only help us to understand how social-class environment is mediated through the interaction between mother and child but will give more precise information about the effects of individual maternal environments on the cognitive growth of the young child.

References

BERNSTEIN, B.   Social class and linguistic development: a theory of social learning. In A. H. Halsey, J. Floud and C. A. Anderson (Eds.), *Education, economy, and society.* Glencoe, Ill.: Free Press, 1961.

BERNSTEIN, B.   Family role systems, communication, and socialization. Paper presented at Conference on Development of Cross-National Research on the Education of Children and Adolescents, University of Chicago, February, 1964.

BROPHY, J., HESS, R. D. and SHIPMAN, V.   Effects of social class and level of aspiration on performance in a structured mother-child interaction. Paper presented at Biennial Meeting of Society for Research in Child Development, Minneapolis, Minn., March, 1965.

DEUTSCH, M.   The disadvantaged child and the learning process. In A. H. Passow (Ed.), *Education in depressed areas.* New York: Teachers College Press, 1963. Pp. 163-180.

DEUTSCH, M. and BROWN, B.   Social influences in Negro-white intelligence differences. *Journal of Social Issues,* 1964, 20 (2), 24-35.

EELLS, K., DAVIS, A., HAVIGHURST, R. J., HERRICK, V. E. and TYLER, R. W. *Intelligence and cultural differences.* Chicago: University of Chicago Press, 1951.

HESS, R. D.   Educability and rehabilitation: the future of the welfare class. *Marriage and Family Living,* 1964, 26, 422-429.

JACKSON, J. D., HESS, R. D. and SHIPMAN, V.   Communication styles in teachers: an experiment. Paper presented at American Educational Research Association meetings, Chicago, February, 1965.

JOHN, V.   The intellectual development of slum children: some preliminary findings. *American Journal of Orthopsychiatry,* 1963, 33, 813-822.

KAGAN, J., MOSS, H. A. and SIGEL, I. E.   Psychological significance of styles of conceptualization. *Monographs of Society for Research in Child Development,* 1963, 28, No. 6.

KAGAN, J.   Information processing in the child: significance of analytic and reflective attitudes. *Psychological Monographs,* 1964, 78, No. 1 (Whole No. 578).

KENNEDY, W. A., VAN DE RIET, V. and WHITE, J. C., JR.   A normative sample of intelligence and achievement of Negro elementary school children in the southeastern United States. *Monographs of Society for Research in Child Development,* 1963, 28, No. 6.

LESSER, G.   *Mental abilities of children in different social and cultural groups.* New York: Cooperative Research Project No. 1635, 1964.

MEYER, R., SHIPMAN, V. and HESS, R. D.   Family structure and social class in the socialization of curiosity in urban preschool children. Paper presented at American Psychological Association meetings, Los Angeles, September, 1964.

OLIM, E. G., HESS, R. D. and SHIPMAN, V.   Relationship between mothers' language styles and cognitive styles of urban preschool children. Paper presented at Biennial Meeting of Society for Research in Child Development, Minneapolis, Minn., March, 1965.

SHIPMAN, V. and HESS, R. D.   Social class and sex differences in the utilization of language and the consequences for cognitive development. Paper presented at Midwestern Psychological Association meetings, Chicago, April, 1965.

The dependence of national policy on the findings of the social sciences (exclusive of economics) is a recent event in our country's history. Even more recent is the initiative on the part of the Federal government, especially the legislative branch, in directing that social research be carried out to aid in policy planning. Educational policy is one of the domains in which the bearing of the fruits of sociological and social-psychological research has been most clearly seen.

A section of the landmark Civil Rights Act of 1964 commissioned a large-scale investigation of the disparities in educational opportunity in school systems across the country, North to South, slum to suburban, and farm to city. The research was conducted on a crash basis by a team of eminent social scientists, led by James S. Coleman. Mountains of data were collected and processed by the most sophisticated statistical techniques available and the so-called Coleman Report, running to over 700 pages, was issued in 1966 (*Equality of Educational Opportunity*. Washington: U.S. Government Printing Office). It was a major research study of a major social issue.

Even as the report was being released it attracted extensive commentary directed toward its findings, its policy implications, and its methodology. The tide of events set in motion by it is still flowing full as this book goes to press. Coleman's data are being reworked by people under less severe time pressures; more balanced and carefully documented criticism is just now reaching journal publication. The editors wished to capture the vigor of the Report and the commentary it has generated, even at the risk of foregoing the distilled perspective that time will bring. This and the next selection try to do that.

Dentler's article is a non-critical, non-technical review of those features of the Coleman Report that relate to issues of school desegregation in Northern cities. Thus it is a partial summary. The wide range of issues on which the study touches can only be appreciated by reading the Report itself.

Equality of Educational Opportunity—
A Special Review*

Robert A. Dentler

Science is more than a method and body of knowledge. It is also a way of asking questions, and the hallmark of good scientific inquiry is a substantial contribution to the economy of further research. *Equality of Educational Opportunity,* by James S. Coleman and associates (1966), when judged by this standard, makes a contribution to the study of American intergroup relations second only to Myrdal's *American Dilemma* (1944). More than this, though, when its full implications have been mined, *Equality of Educational Opportunity* will very likely become the single best empirical work in the American sociology of education.

Social scientists and educators who are heavily invested in the study and designing of school desegregation in Northern cities should be especially delighted with the *reductive* power of this monumental survey analysis. Certain important questions which are expensive to answer, in terms of ingenuity as well as money or time, have been answered here authoritatively. And among the essential researchable questions that remain, this study has reduced their scope considerably.

Several aspects of the Coleman Report seem to have obfuscated rapid reception of its message. The survey team's early difficulties in securing a representative sample were over-advertised among researchers: the fact that 30 per cent of the schools selected for the survey did not participate became widely known. Somewhat neglected, however, was the fact that all district superintendents, principals, teachers and third, sixth, ninth, and twelfth-grade pupils in 4,000 schools, along with first graders in about 2,000 schools, did take part, and the fact that the estimates of both sampling and measurement reliability were extremely impressive. Then, too, the little summary of the analysis, which was separately printed as well as included in the chief publication, has been much more widely distributed and read, yet it contains only a handful of the essential implications to be found in the full monograph.

More crucially, many of the findings run contrary to the favorite assumptions of three of the most concerned audiences: militant school integrationists, militant school segregationists (along with their camp-following, the militant proponents of the neighborhool school), and the many professional educators who focus their efforts too exclusively upon school facilities, curriculum reform, and teacher training.

* From *The Urban Review,* 1966, 1 (5), 27-29. Used by permission of the author and publisher.

Many schoolmen and elective as well as appointed local, state, and federal officials have said that the statistical density of the report has prevented their understanding the findings. This will be remedied partly by time, as various reviewers and education writers translate the results, and partly by the discovery of readers who take the trouble to look between the tables and figures to discover that the verbal exposition is plain and stripped of educational or sociological jargon.

The aim of this review is to identify some of the questions I believe have been answered well enough to be set aside, and to suggest the lines of inquiry that ought to be emphasized strongly in all future research and planning on Northern urban school desegregation issues. I would emphasize, however, that this is not a *technical* review of the significant innovations, or the difficulties, in the techniques of analysis used in the Coleman Report. Here, instead, let us accept the over-all reliability and validity of the research in a willing suspension of disbelief. Further, this discussion shall concentrate on findings concerning the metropolitan North.

The basic findings of the Coleman Report in this regard are these: in the metropolitan North, Negro and Puerto Rican pupils, as compared to white pupils, attend school in older, larger, more crowded buildings. They have access to fewer laboratories and library books, auditoriums and gymnasiums. Their elementary teachers show a slightly lower score on a short vocabulary test. Even their cafeterias and athletic playing fields are in shorter supply.

Accelerated programs for rapid learners are typically more available to white than to Negro or Puerto Rican pupils, as are course opportunities for 12th graders to obtain advanced placement or college credit. Negro pupils on the average enjoy a greater advantage in but three respects: more of their teachers are Negroes, and more remedial and correctional programs and services are available in their schools.

What awaits the Northern metropolitan Negro or Puerto Rican learner, of course, complements what he brings with him to school as a burden of background disadvantages. When this burden is joined with those of his peers, he

> *attends a school where his fellow students generally come from economically poorer, less stable homes, which are more poorly equipped to give stimulation to the educational pursuits of the children. The families are larger, and less frequently have both real parents living at home; the parents' level of education is lower, and the homes more frequently lack modern conveniences and reading materials such as daily newspapers, encyclopedias and home libraries.* Of all the characteristics of schools which distinguish the education being provided the average white and Negro students, it is the environment provided by the fellow students where the differences are most dramatic [emphasis mine].

These findings confirm authoritatively dozens of much smaller studies conducted during the late nineteen fifties and early sixties in dozens of individual cities and suburbs throughout the Northeast. Here, however, the

Coleman Report clears the deck and allows the research to get on with what is less obvious. The Coleman data are comprehensive enough and the findings distinct enough to release us from endless cycling on questions of equality of public educational services. *Facilities, staffs, and services are distributed unequally.* Without exception, on the factors catalogued, the pattern of the inequality uniformly reinforces handicaps brought to the school by the low-income, minority-group learner. If further studies must be carried out on these surface factors, let them be done against norms struck in the Coleman Report: how much, and in what particulars, does a school district depart from the unequal distribution common to the northeastern metropolitan region as a whole? How much better are the facilities and services provided for the whites within a given city or suburban district, when contrasted with those of the region as a whole? The basis for settling this general question or for enlarging its meaning through comparison is now at hand.

The same economy of future efforts is made possible by the definitiveness of the Coleman Report on the over-all differences in achievement between white, Puerto Rican, and Negro students in the metropolitan Northeast. The mean grade levels on three tests of each of these groups can be summarized as follows:

TEST	GROUP	6TH GRADE	9TH GRADE	12TH GRADE
Verbal Ability	White	6	9	12
	Puerto Rican*	3.3	6.1	8.4
	Negro	4.4	6.6	8.7
Reading Comprehension	White	6	9	12
	Puerto Rican	2.9	5.7	8.3
	Negro	4.2	6.4	9.1
Mathematics	White	6	9	12
	Puerto Rican	3.2	5.6	7.2
	Negro	4	6.2	6.8

* Puerto Rican means are for entire sample, which includes other regions. But the sample, like the population itself, is heavily concentrated in the metropolitan Northeast.

Obviously, the achievement differences between whites, on the one hand, and Negroes and Puerto Ricans, on the other, are very great. At grade 6, the average Negro in this region is more than 1¾ years behind the average white in reading comprehension. At grade 9, he is more than 2½ years behind that of the average white. And, at grade 12, he is nearly 3 years behind. The record of Puerto Rican performance is even poorer than that of Negroes, except at one point: 12th grade mathematics.

Obviously, too, something happens over the school years that widens the gap in achievement between whites and the two minority groups. In no instance is the initial gap narrowed rather than widened as a result of intervening educational experiences. Thus, the disadvantage with which Negro and Puerto Rican students begin school remains with them when they finish high school. No doubt, certain students manage to overcome initial handicaps, but their gains are swamped statistically by the cumulative retardation of the great majority.

Similarities and differences between the three groups in the Northeast metropolitan region on attitudes, aspirations, and future plans are also portrayed in the Coleman Report. Below is a summary of the principal findings:

	12TH-GRADE PERCENTAGE DISTRIBUTION		
QUESTION AND RESPONSE	WHITE	NEGRO	PUERTO RICAN*
If something happened and you had to stop school now, how would you feel? *"Would do almost anything to stay."*	47	47	35
How good a student do you want to be? *"One of the best students."*	36	48	36
How much time do you spend on an average school day studying outside of school? *(Sum of 2 hour & 3 hour replies.)*	44	45	32
About how many days did you stay away from school last year just because you did not want to come? *"None."*	61	68	53
How many books did you read during the Summer of 1965? *"One to five books."*	50	47	39
How far do you want to go in school? *All responses for beyond high school.*	86	86	67
Do you plan to go to college next year? *"Definitely yes."*	46	31	26
Have you ever read a college catalog? *"Yes."*	73	59	45
Have you ever written to or talked to a college official about going to college? *"Yes."*	46	32	25
What type of job do you think you will have when you finish your education? *"Professional or technical."*	53	39	28

* Puerto Ricans not restricted to Northeast.

On attitudes toward school and academic work generally, differences between whites and Negroes in this region are negligible. Only when it comes to matters of firm steps toward college do the proportions of Negro students fall notably below the characteristics common to whites. Puerto Rican students, in contrast, present differences in all areas. They display lower aspirations, do less reading, and are much less likely to be taking steps to continue their schooling beyond high school.

Both minority groups, however, depart substantially from the favored white group on Coleman's three indicators of the student's sense of control over his environment. This is a central point.

	NORTHEASTERN METROPOLITAN		
PER CENT WHO AGREE THAT:	WHITE	NEGRO	PUERTO RICAN*
Good luck is more important than hard work for success.	4	9	19
Every time I try to get ahead, something or somebody stops me.	13	21	30
People like me don't have much of a chance to be successful in life.	5	12	19

* Puerto Ricans not restricted to Northeast.

There is an objective basis for these differences, Coleman asserts: "Minority children have less chance to control their environment than do the majority whites." Coleman goes on to demonstrate the relation between feelings of control and individual achievement, when other background differences have been held constant and concludes: "Of all the variables measured in the survey, including all measures of family background and all school variables, these attitudes showed the strongest relation to achievement, at all three grade levels (6th, 9th, and 12th). . . . These attitudinal variables account for more of the variation in achievement than any other set of variables (all family background variables together, or all school variables together). When added to any other set of variables, they increase the accounted for variation more than does any other set of variables." Further, among the attitude items used in the correlation analyses, none was more firmly associated with achievement than the three indicators of a sense of control over one's environment.

This association is *not*, at least for minority groups, a by-product of the natural relation between achievement and a student's subjective assessment of his school abilities, or his feelings about his life chances. It is rather that "for children from disadvantaged groups, achievement . . . appears closely related to what they believe about their environment: whether they believe the environment will respond to reasonable efforts, or whether they believe it is instead merely random or immovable."

Very little educational research and development work is currently aimed specifically at these student attitudes, although they are generally well understood by teachers. But, when one considers the range of factors that matter *very little* by comparison, and on which most of our efforts at reconstruction in the research and development tradition are based, the ironies are noteworthy.

For instance, the Coleman Report documents a long-respected generalization in the sociology of education as it has never been so solidly documented before: "School to school variations in achievement, from whatever source (community differences, variations in the average home background of the student body, or variations in school factors), are much smaller than individual variations within the school, at all grade levels, for all racial and ethnic groups. . . . Over 70 per cent of the variation in achievement . . . is variation within the same student body." Indeed, when the analysis is restricted to differences in achievement between Negroes and whites, "Only about 10 to 20 per cent of the total variation in achievement for the groups that are numerically most important lies between different schools."

In case the point is not as clear as it ought to be: "Our schools have great uniformity insofar as their effect on the learning of pupils is concerned. . . . Variations in school quality are not highly related to variations in achievement of pupils."

This principle is counterbalanced solely by the qualification that Negro and Puerto Rican students in the North are more sensitive (that is, more responsive) to differences in quality from school to school than are whites. The percentage of the difference in individual verbal achievement scores that can be accounted for by differences between schools is summarized below as evidence of this qualification:

VERBAL ACHIEVEMENTS: GROUP	PER CENT OF TOTAL VARIANCE BY GRADE LEVEL				
	1ST	3RD	6TH	9TH	12TH
Whites, North	11.1	11.4	10.3	8.7	7.8
Negroes, North	10.6	19.5	13.9	12.7	10.9
Puerto Ricans	16.7	26.6	31.3	21.0	22.3

Let us explore in more detail what factors *do* affect achievement before summarizing what Coleman reveals as being of little or no significance. We have emphasized the importance of student attitudes, particularly the part played by the learner's sense of control over his environment. Two other rather classic sociological variables—family socioeconomic status and aggregate socioeconomic status of the student's classroom peers—are also shown to be critically related to academic ability.

The Coleman Report, it should be said, nowhere discusses social status with the forthrightness that it uses in the analysis of ethnic groups. But its indicators of "family background" are impressively comprehensive. Objective items include urbanism of background, migration, parents' educational attainment, structural integrity of the home, size of family, the presence of selected items in the home (e.g., TV, telephone, record player, refrigerator, automobile, vacuum cleaner), and reading material in the home. Subjective items include parents' interest in the child's schooling and parents' educational desires for their children.

When between-school and within-school differences are considered together, the family background and attitudes account for 35.7 per cent of these differences among sixth grade Northern whites, 26.4 per cent among sixth grade Northern Negroes, and 40.3 per cent among sixth grade Puerto Ricans. Because the accounted for differences decline from the sixth to 12th grade, Coleman concludes that "the family's impact on the child has its greatest effect in earliest years, so that family-to-family differences in achievement . . . decline after the beginning of school." The impact of

differences in the socioeconomic status of the family on the school performance of children is, if anything, *understated* in the Coleman Report.
For the influence of this variable is exceeded only by students' own attitudes
toward their life chances, attitudes which are themselves highly associated
with background differences. In other words, the degree to which a learner
believes himself to be in control of his fate is very likely to be a function of
his understanding—conscious or unconscious, realistic or unrealistic—of his
socioeconomic place in life.

The backgrounds and attitudes of peers also strongly affect school
achievement. Coleman notes: "Attributes of other students account for far
more variation in the achievement of minority group children than do any
attributes of school facilities and slightly more than do attributes of staff."
Individual achievement is facilitated when a student attends school with
peers who are socioeconomically advantaged, whose parents are more interested in school success, and whose mobility is low. Achievement is
dampened for students whose classmates are relatively more disadvantaged,
whose parents are less interested, and whose movement from school to
school or community to community is high. Moreover, Negro and Puerto
Rican students are more affected than Northern whites by this peer
influence.

Of equal interest are factors that contribute only negligibly to explaining
achievement differences. For example: "Contrary to much that has been written, the structural integrity of the home (principally the father's presence or
absence) shows very little relation to achievement for Negroes." In grades
one and three, neither school characteristics nor student body composition
contributes much to explaining variations in achievement. Also intriguing is
the fact that Coleman dropped class size or pupil-teacher ratio from the
multivariate analysis because "it showed a consistent lack of relation to
achievement among all groups under all conditions." Thus, while class size is
important to the well-being of the teacher, its direct significance for student
achievement remains questionable.

But then questions which rage most enduringly among schoolmen and
women fare rather poorly at all points in the Coleman Report. The following
table summarizes the differences in verbal achievement accounted for by
teacher characteristics, as against school variables and student environment
or peer composition:

GROUP	GRADE 12			GRADE 6		
	TEACHER	SCHOOL	STUDENTS	TEACHER	SCHOOL	STUDENTS
Whites, North	1.9	3.2	3.8	1.7	2.0	4.8
Negroes, North	4.3	6.7	8.9	2.2	2.7	4.9
Puerto Ricans	18.4	20.0	26.4	8.1	10.8	13.9

The school factor includes per-pupil expenditures on staff, volumes per
student in library, science laboratory facilities, extracurricular activities,

size, school location, and several indicators of quality of curriculum. The relative *unimportance* of these factors can be shown when the total variance accounted for by facilities and curricular measures for 12th grade Northern Negroes is shown as 3.1 per cent, if student background is held constant. For sixth grade Northern Negroes, it is .77 per cent, and for sixth grade Northern whites, .32 per cent.

Teacher characteristics were more influential in explaining variations in verbal achievement than were factors of facilities and curriculum. But when considered alone they were discouragingly limited in effect. Even when background factors were controlled (as in the summary table above), teacher characteristics were second in strength of influence to student peer characteristics. Teacher differences made about a 2 per cent contribution for sixth grade Northern whites and Negroes, but contributed more for Puerto Ricans (8.1 per cent).

Among the teacher characteristics that showed most marked association with pupil verbal achievement, and which became part of the Coleman index, were educational attainment of the teacher's mother (and her socioeconomic status), years of teaching experience, localism of the teacher, educational attainment of the teachers themselves, vocabulary test scores, teacher's preference for teaching middle class and white collar students, and proportion of teachers who were white. The index is an aggregate and so does not allow for analysis below the level of school-to-school differences.

Teachers, then, do influence achievement, but slightly. Moreover, "Good teachers matter more for children from minority groups." For children who enter school with background advantages or who attend schools filled with advantaged peers, teacher quality is of much less importance in predicting pupil achievement. And limited as is the over-all influence of teacher characteristics, the influence is cumulative in effect over the years in school. It appears to be very small initially and then expands notably between ninth and 12th grade.

One of the central implications for Northern urban school desegregation that arises from the Coleman Report may now be understood in its full complexity: What the child brings with him to school as strengths or weaknesses determined by his social class is the prime correlate of school achievement. It is influenced—offset or reinforced—most substantially not by facilities, curriculum, or teachers but by what other pupils bring with *them* as class-shaped interests and abilities. In practical terms, as the proportion of white pupils increases in a school, achievement among Negroes and Puerto Ricans increases because of the association between white ethnicity and socioeconomic advantage.

It should be said that while the peer influence *may* increase the minority child's sense of control over his environment, it *may* also decrease his self-concept. There likely are probable costs as well as benefits for achievement involved in desegregation. But the Coleman Report makes crystal clear that *desegregation does affect factors of immediate relevance to stu-*

dent achievement. These factors are: individual academic motivation and peer environment.

Further implications may include the suggestion that changes in student composition have little direct bearing upon the achievement of Northern urban *white* students (save that through intergroup contact, if properly treated by the school and community, they may become better citizens, matters that are not dealt with in the Coleman Report). These majority group students achieve more or less well because of what they bring with them to school from their homes. Negro and Puerto Rican students, however, can gain from positive changes at nearly all points: improved peer environment, improved levels of interest that spring from peer influences, better teaching, facilities, and curricula. As the case studies in the Coleman Report suggest, minority group children can gain in achievement to the extent that the desegregation plan is deliberately executed to accomplish that objective.

What are we left with, then, as important unanswered questions? We are more certain than ever that the peer environment, including racial mix, is a social determinant of school achievement, but we know very little about the particulars of this environment in the elementary or junior high school. What blend of social heterogeneity is optimal under what conditions of age, past school experience, and so forth? If we can answer this through field research, how can the results be translated into school districting, zoning, and grouping practices? Schoolmen have long given detailed attention to arranging peer environments. When some of their traditional practices, e.g., in segregating pupils racially or economically, are called sharply into question through research, what feasible alternatives can we suggest? Desegregation procedures can prove as indiscriminate and thus unhelpful for learners as segregation has proved to be harmful for learning. Mere gross ethnic balancing will hardly speak to this question, vital as it may be as a start.

We need to know much more, as well, about the nature of changes in achievement on the one hand and attitudes and peer relations on the other *over time.* What handful of pupils exhibit achievement gains somewhat independent of social context? At what strategic points in the process of cumulative retardation among urban Negro and Puerto Rican learners would intervention or school reform prove truly influential? Panel surveys and longitudinal studies of whole school districts and communities are among the inquiries that are needed most if processes of change are to be identified.

In connection with both peer environments and changes in school achievement over time, we need to confront the fact that the greatest variance in school learning occurs under what Coleman calls "within-school" conditions. His survey, however, offers little illumination of the internal reward structure of the neighborhood school which helps to produce student differentiation. What is the nature of the "within-school" stratification system? How do principals and teachers sustain it and thus reinforce selectively the achievement of some students, perhaps at the expense of the retardation of others? Could one redesign this reward structure? How far can one depart from the stratification system of the larger community and still operate a neighborhood public school?

Finally, professional leadership is so important a factor, I believe, that the Coleman Report needs supplementing through analysis of the relation between the quality of school administration and the variations in student achievement between school districts and within them. Superintendents and principals were questioned but by and large they were not questioned about themselves or their professional behavior. Rather, they reported upon the schools, staffs, and students for whom they have legal responsibility.

My own hypothesis is that differences in the quality of school administrations—holding pupil backgrounds constant—should account for as much of the difference in student achievement as does peer environment. The validity of the argument hinges strongly, of course, upon measures of leadership.

This review has ignored not only the technical aspects of the Coleman Report, but it has also neglected its contributions to the survey analysis of future teachers, to higher education, school withdrawal, case studies of integration planning, pre-school education, and vocational education. By mentioning these oversights, it is hoped to stimulate even wider reading than this appreciation of the heart of the report may accomplish.

References

COLEMAN, J. S.   *Equality of educational opportunity.* Washington: U.S. Government Printing Office. Catalogue Number FS 5.238:38001, 1966. Correlations separately bound.

MYRDAL, G.   *An American dilemma.* New York: Harper and Row, 1944.

※ ※ ※ ※ ※

The Coleman Report (see preceding selection) did not emerge from an empirical vacuum. One of the study's great merits is that Coleman and his colleagues addressed themselves to questions which many years of educational and social research had already helped define. Its location in a continuous stream of investigation on disparities in educational opportunity means that its findings and conclusions do not rest exclusively on the adequacy of the study's methods. Critics of the Coleman Report—or any major research undertaking—who are unable to see it in the context of related empirical knowledge will applaud or condemn it on too narrow, perhaps irrelevant grounds. Social research which enters the realm of public policy and debate must inevitably run this danger

Dyer's article, which we have chosen in an effort to sample the critical commentaries directed to the Coleman Report, does not fall prey to the danger. Focusing on one of the several substantive problems tackled by the report, the effects of various school characteristics (like student body composition and per-pupil expenditure) on pupil achievement, Dyer reviews the data and methods in the context of findings from earlier research. Detailed inspection points up some anomalies and contradictions, but it also suggests hypotheses as to how the anomalies might have come about.

Dyer takes another step that sets his review apart from run-of-the-mill criticism. He examines the data in the Report, not just to raise questions about Coleman's conclusions, but to search for new information and additional conclusions. As he says, ". . . the data in the Coleman Report can be a rich source of educational ideas to be tried out—of hypotheses to be tested." In illustrating how the data can be exploited, he demonstrates how criticism can be made constructive.

School Factors and Equal Educational Opportunity*

Henry S. Dyer

During the years when the separate-but-equal doctrine was in full force, the method of trying to prove or disprove that schools were giving Negroes and whites equal treatment consisted mainly of counting those school characteristics that are easiest to count. Testimony before the courts was full of such matters as the age, size, and location of school buildings; the number of hours in the school day, days in the school year, courses in the curriculum; and the ratios of pupils to basketball courts, drinking fountains, toilets, textbooks, and teachers. In order to make some sense out of these miscellaneous data, the courts translated them into fiscal terms, with the result that assessing the quality of educational opportunity finally boiled down to counting dollars and cents (Ashmore, 1954, pp. 109-110). It was assumed, on the basis of intuition uninhibited by data, that if the schools in a given district were spending as much per pupil for Negroes as for whites, the quality of education for both groups must be equal. The same assumption still has a strong hold on educational thought.

A major contribution of the Coleman *et al.* (1966) survey—possibly *the* major contribution—is its massive challenge to the simplistic notion that counting educational dollars, or the things dollars buy, is a sufficient measure of the equality of educational opportunity. There is no question that the survey has some faults, many of which the authors themselves have conceded: the sample of schools leaves something to be desired; a longitudinal design rather than a cross-sectional design would have made for sounder inferences; there are weaknesses in the measures derived from questionnaire data which make one wonder whether the noise in the information system may not be drowning out some variables that are struggling to be heard; there is too much dependence on a single measure of verbal learning as comprehending the whole of what is meant by academic achievement; and the analysis neglects to show the possible impact of schools on the development of pupil attitudes and outlook.

Despite these flaws, the effect of the Report is to bring us closer to a true national assessment of educational opportunity than we have ever been before. It looks across school district lines and concerns itself with the educational development of minority group children whoever and wherever

* From Henry Dyer, "School Factors and Equal Educational Opportunity," *Harvard Educational Review*, 1968, 38, Winter (1), 38-56. Used by permission of the author and publisher. Copyright © 1968 by President and Fellows of Harvard College.

they may be. In broad terms, it says that the quality of education a school offers is to be measured by reference to those characteristics of a school that bear a known, empirically determined relationship to what pupils learn presumably as a consequence of having gone to school. Basketball courts, teachers' salaries, classroom footage per pupil, and the like may legitimately enter into the assessment of educational opportunity only to the extent that they can be shown to be associated with the intellectual, emotional, and social development of pupils. In the absence of information about such relationships, any attempts to equalize education will of necessity be blind.

I

Following this logic, the Coleman survey, by means of a series of regression analyses, investigates the relationships of pupil achievement with various aspects of pupil background and some forty-five measures that describe the schools the pupils attend.[1] These measures fall into three main categories: characteristics of the student body, characteristics of the instructional staff, and characteristics of plant, programs, and finances. Thus, these forty-five measures attempt to characterize the schools as social institutions as well as physical and economic entities.

The logic of the analysis is of course not ironclad. There is no guarantee that the school characteristics that turn up with the largest correlation coefficients or regression weights are the factors that have actually produced the differences among schools in pupil performance, regardless of how elaborate the statistical procedures may be. Even were the analysis to give the teacher salary variable, for instance, a relatively large regression weight in the prediction of pupil achievement, the simple act of a salary increase in the low-achieving schools would be more likely to depress the regression weight than to elevate pupil performance. This line of reasoning is in strict accord with the classical doctrine that correlation does not necessarily imply causation. The doctrine, however, is oversimple. If indeed the data were to yield a relatively large regression weight for teachers' salaries, such a phenomenon *could* be translated into the not unreasonable working hypothesis that if salaries in low-achieving schools are made competitive with salaries in high-achieving schools, then *over the long haul* there is at least a chance that pupil performance in the low-achieving schools will approach that in the high-achieving schools *because* of improved instruction.[2]

1. The regression analyses are given in section 3.2 of the report itself, pp. 290-330; the correlation tables are presented in the *Supplemental Appendix to the Survey on Equality of Educational Opportunity* (1966). For a convenient listing of the variables, see the introduction to the *Supplemental Appendix*, pp. iii-vii.

2. As far back as 1912, Bertrand Russell (1954, pp. 171-196) was questioning whether the notion of cause had any validity whatever. "In any advanced science," he said, "there is nothing that can be called a cause, and nothing that can be called an effect; there is merely a formula." He conceded, however, that "in daily life and in the infancy of a science," the notion of cause as probable sequence might be useful. Presumably education as a science is still sufficiently infantile and close to daily life to find some uses for the notion of cause.

As a basis for the appraisal of school characteristics in terms of their relative importance for pupil achievement, the Coleman analyses employ a refinement on the regression model which, though theoretically interesting, may actually be concealing some important factors. The authors of the survey assumed, quite reasonably, that the pattern of relationships between pupil achievement and school characteristics would vary from region to region and, perhaps more importantly, from one ethnic group to another. Some pupils not only need more help than other pupils, but the kinds of help they need, and consequently the means by which to provide it, will depend on the kinds of pupils they are. (See Coleman *et al.*, 1966, pp. 310-311). On this assumption separate regression analyses were performed on each of ten groups: Mexican-Americans, Puerto Ricans, Indian-Americans, Oriental-Americans, Northern Negroes, Southern Negroes, Northern whites, Southern whites, all Negroes, and all whites. The effect of this grouping is to partial out in some degree the factor of ethnicity and, in the case of Negroes and whites, the factor of geography. From one point of view, the partialling out does not go far enough with respect to ethnicity, region, or other characteristics (social class and religion for instance), and therefore does not take into account the innumerable qualitative differences in the developmental needs of different kinds of pupils, e.g., those in the hard-core poverty areas of the big cities as against those in the rural backwaters. On the other hand, one can also suppose that the subdividing of the sample has gone so far that it has produced groups so homogeneous in respect to schooling and achievement as to conceal many instructive relationships that may in fact exist between the two sets of variables. It would have been illuminating to see what the regression analyses would have produced if all the subsamples had been merged. A re-analysis of some of the Coleman data reported recently by George W. Mayeske (1967) takes this tack and provides some useful new insights on what it is about schools that makes a difference in pupils.

II

Some of the problems encountered by the Coleman survey have turned up in at least three earlier studies. The first such study was one carried out by Mollenkopf and Melville (1956) in 1953. It took essentially the same approach as the Coleman study, that is, it regressed measures of cognitive development, as measured by tests, on a variety of school, parent, and community characteristics, as measured by questionnaire data. The study involved one hundred high schools that differed with respect to size, region, staff training, percentage of graduates going to college, and financial support. Unlike the Coleman study, which sought a representative cross-section of the nation's schools, the Mollenkopf-Melville study assembled a sample of schools that was as diverse as possible so that those characteristics of schools that are in fact related to pupil achievement would have the best possible chance of emerging from the data. Achievement and aptitude tests were given to some ninety-six hundred pupils at grade 9 and eighty-four hundred pupils at grade 12. The school averages on each of these sets of tests were correlated with thirty-four different school characteristics derived from questionnaire data supplied by the school principals. Four characteristics that showed relatively high relationships with the test scores were geographical location (whether or not the school was in the South), cost of instructional support per pupil, urbanism (whether the school was in an urban, suburban, or rural community), and the number of specialists on the school staff (psychologists, guidance counselors, etc.).

A problem that beclouds this and all later studies of school factors in pupil achievement is the role of socioeconomic variables and family background. The correlation of socioeconomic status with pupil achievement generally runs high—so high indeed that it is difficult to tease out with certainty how much impact the schools *per se* are having on pupils. This first study is no exception. Mollenkopf and Melville caution the reader at length about drawing causal conclusions from correlational data, about illusory distinctions between measures of aptitude and measures of achievement, and especially about the difficulty, if not the impossibility, of disentangling home and community variables from those that might be attributed strictly to the operations of the schools. They nevertheless suggest—almost as it were grudgingly—"that the results support the conclusion that certain characteristics descriptive of the school situation do have a distinct influence on the achievement of students" [p. 37].

The Mollenkopf-Melville study was followed by one undertaken by the New York State Education Department in 1957-58. It was carried out by Samuel M. Goodman (1959) and is known as the Quality Measurement Project. Goodman accumulated IQ and achievement test data on some seventy thousand pupils in grades 4, 7, and 10 in 103 school systems which were chosen to be approximately representative of the school systems in the state at large. His report does not explore all the possibilities of his data: correlational results, for instance, focus mostly on grade 7 performance. For this and other reasons—differences in the sample, in the tests, in the school characteristics observed, and in the methods used to observe them— the results of the Goodman study cannot be directly compared with those of the Mollenkopf-Melville study. Even so, the two studies, taken together, begin to give us some notion of how far we can and cannot go in generalizing about school characteristics. Both studies found that per-pupil expenditure and amount of special staffing were associated significantly with achievement. On the other hand, the two differ sharply on how much importance is to be attached to teacher experience. Goodman found this to be the school characteristic most strongly associated with pupil performance; Mollenkopf and Melville found its importance negligible.

Goodman's study gives a fairly clear-cut indication of the effect of socioeconomic status on the relationship of four school characteristics with achievement. Table 1 summarizes some of his relevant findings. The table

Table 1

CORRELATIONS OF CERTAIN SCHOOL FACTORS WITH
PUPIL ACHIEVEMENT AND SOCIOECONOMIC STATUS[a]

VARIABLE	CORRELATION WITH COMPOSITE ACHIEVEMENT SCORE AT GRADE 7	
	RAW CORRELATION	PARTIAL CORRELATION (SES PARTIALLED OUT)
Teacher experience	.56	.37
Per-pupil expenditure	.51	.31
Special staff per 1000 pupils	.24	.12
Classroom atmosphere[b]	.24	.23
Socioeconomic status of parents	.61	—

[a] Adapted from Goodman (1959), Tables 9 and 10.

[b] "Classroom atmosphere" is a measure of the degree to which a school is rated "subject-centered" vs. "child-centered," the ratings being based on an instrument known as *The Growing Edge* by P. R. Mort, *et al.*, (1957).

contains two bits of information that are of particular interest. First, even though the correlation of socioeconomic status and achievement is of the usual rather high magnitude (.61), partialling out socioeconomic status leaves apparently enough variance in the pertinent variables to suggest that there is still room for the hypothesis that teacher experience and per-pupil expenditure have something to do with how much children learn in school. Secondly, although the ratings on "classroom atmosphere" are only very modestly related to pupil performance, they nevertheless seem to be essentially independent of the socioeconomic factor. The fact that the variable "classroom atmosphere" is based on *direct* observations of what goes on in classrooms may have something to do with this result. While such *indirect* measures as the number of credentials a teacher has accumulated, or the number of years she has been teaching, or the sizes of the classes she teaches have their uses in describing schools, they are likely to be contaminated with so many irrelevancies that the interpretation of any statistics in which they are involved leaves an uncomfortable amount of room for confusion.

The Goodman study, like the Mollenkopf-Melville (1956) study before it and the Coleman (1966) study after it, was forced by circumstances to rely on cross-sectional rather than longitudinal data. As the authors of the Coleman Report suggest, and as most educational evaluators have been saying for years, the best way to find out what schools are doing to pupils is to observe the pupils before and after the schools have had a chance to influence the way they think, feel, and act. A true definition of achievement must rest ultimately on measures of change. It is not unlikely, therefore, that the school characteristics that are associated with students' *gains* in performance over a particular period could conceivably be quite different from those associated with students' achievement *status* at a given point in time (Coleman *et al.*, 1966, p. 292).

A study of cognitive growth in the high school years by Marion F. Shaycoft (1967) provides some information on this point. She analyzed data on 6583 students who were tested in Project TALENT in 1960, when they were in grade 9, and were retested in 1963, when they were in grade 12. During the interim they attended 101 nonvocational and 17 vocational high schools. The schools were approximately representative of all such schools; the sample of students, however, consisted only of those who had continued in the same schools throughout their high school years. Another feature that distinguishes the Shaycoft study from the other three is that many of the achievement tests used concentrate on knowledge specific to school subjects. Tests in the other three studies were focused mainly, though not exclusively, on general conceptual development.

The Shaycoft study is concerned, first of all, with a question that seems so obvious that no one has ever before attempted to answer it adequately: Is there indeed a substantial amount of cognitive development in students between grades 9 and 12, and if so, is there any reason to believe that their schooling has anything to do with it? Miss Shaycoft's answer on both counts is strongly in the affirmative. After investigating student gains on the forty-two Project TALENT tests ranging from abstract reasoning and arithmetic to knowledge of such matters as literature, advanced mathematics, mechanics, art, accounting, and electricity, she finds that the gains "are uniformly in the right direction . . . and in the more important areas they are quite substantial in magnitude" (ch. 7, p. 8). By "quite substantial" she means that the average gain on certain measures is as much as a full standard deviation in terms of the grade 9 distribution. She notes further that the larger gains are usually associated with subjects actually taught in school—"curriculum-related" areas of knowledge like literature, mathematics, social studies, and many of the vocational fields like mechanics and accounting (ch. 7, p. 8).

As to the question whether schools are *differentially* effective, Miss Shaycoft finds statistically significant variation among schools in all but two of the forty-two gains scores (Tables 7-2a, 7-2b, 7-2c, and 7-2d), and takes this to mean that "students in some schools learn more, or improve their ability more, than in other schools" (ch. 7, p. 11). In other words, it is reasonably safe to conclude that quality of schooling makes a genuine difference in pupil growth, but the Shaycoft data do not tell us how pronounced the differential effects actually are or how far one may go in attributing differences in school effectiveness to variations in the qualities of the schools *per se* (the teaching, the curriculum, the facilities, the general atmosphere) as contrasted to the variation in the quality and character of the communities of people who support the schools and whose children the schools serve. Since, however, many of the most pronounced differences from school to school are in precisely those areas of student growth that are associated with "curriculum-related" content (literature, accounting, etc.), the hypothesis is rather compelling that qualitative differences in the schools themselves account for much, if not all, of the variation in academic and vocational achievement between one school and another. Miss Shaycoft concludes on the cautionary note that "since the sources of these differences among schools resist ready identification, there would appear to be no easy panacea for the problems of education" (ch. 7, pp. 25-26).

III

None of the three studies preceding the Coleman survey was addressed specifically to the problem of equality of opportunity of minority groups. The main thrust of their results, however, tends to run counter to a salient finding of the Coleman Report, that the differential effects of schools on pupil achievement "appear to arise not principally from factors that the school system controls, but from factors outside the school proper" (Coleman *et al.*, 1966, p. 312). The Shaycoft study in particular throws doubt on this conclusion by suggesting that it may hold for some kinds of cognitive development but not for others. A serious weakness in the Coleman analysis is at just this point: its criterion of academic achievement is almost exclusively a measure of verbal ability which has long been known to be a slow developing function that for obvious reasons is likely to be far more the product of the child's home than of his school experience.[3] The Coleman study pays scant attention to the kinds of achievement on which the schools have traditionally focused. By contrast many of the criteria of achievement used in the Shaycoft study relate specifically to the subjects pupils actually study in school (literature, mathematics, business subjects, etc.), and it is precisely in these subjects that there appear to be substantial differential effects among schools *even when differences in socioeconomic levels have been accounted for.* The other two earlier studies tend to reinforce this finding. In short, the nearly exclusive use of verbal ability as the measure of pupil achievement in the Coleman analysis probably makes for an underestimate of the importance of factors that school systems do in fact control. As suggested above, this underestimate is further exacerbated by the confining of the analysis to ethnic subsamples in which the schools, pupils, and pupil achievement are likely to be so homogeneous as to prevent important relationships from appearing. *On both counts, then, the Coleman results have the unfortunate, though perhaps inadvertent, effect of giving school systems the false impression that there is not much they can do to improve the achievement of their pupils.*

In light of this situation, it may be useful to consider some other measures, in addition to verbal ability, that are available in the Coleman data as criteria for checking out the importance of school characteristics. These measures include tests in reading and mathematics in grades 3, 6, 9, and 12, and, additionally, a test of general information in grades 9 and 12. The latter encompasses the practical arts, natural science, literature, music, art,

---

3. See Coleman, *et al.* (1966, pp. 292-295) for the authors' explanation of why they relied so heavily on the measure of verbal ability.

history, and public affairs.[4] Generally speaking, the zero-order correlations between each of these three measures and measures of the forty-five school characteristics run low. An inspection of the correlation tables in the *Supplemental Appendix* shows that in no case are the correlations over 0.5, and the vast majority are under 0.2. At first glance, this swarm of low correlations would seem to reinforce the Coleman hypothesis that the characteristics of schools *per se* have little or nothing to do with the achievement of pupils. But this interpretation needs a closer look.

In both the Mollenkopf-Melville study and the Goodman study, the relation between per-pupil expenditure and various measures of cognitive achievement was modest but significant. In the Mollenkopf-Melville study, the median of the correlations between instructional cost and seven measures of cognitive performance was .36 at grade 9 and .41 at grade 12. Goodman reported that in his sample of New York State schools the zero-order correlation between instructional cost and composite achievement was .34 at grade 4 and .51 at grade 7. The data from the Coleman survey are in sharp

Table 2

MEDIAN CORRELATIONS BETWEEN PER-PUPIL EXPENDITURE
AND VARIOUS MEASURES OF COGNITIVE PERFORMANCE
IN THE COLEMAN DATA

GROUP	GRADE					
	1[a]	3[b]	6[b]	9[c]	12[c]	MEDIAN
Mexican-American	.09	.00	.08	.07	.09	.08
Puerto Rican	−.24	−.02	.15	.09	−.05	−.02
American Indian	.07	.04	.07	.00	−.10	.04
Oriental-American	.03	.30	.36	.03	.04	.04
Negro North	−.08	−.07	.04	.00	−.01	−.01
Negro South	.07	.01	.19	.11	.20	.11
White North	−.03	.02	.04	.05	.05	.04
White South	.04	.03	.03	.02	.01	.03

[a] Correlation with scores on picture vocabulary test only.

[b] Medians based on correlations with scores on verbal ability, reading, and mathematics tests.

[c] Medians based on correlations with verbal ability, reading, mathematics, and general information tests.

contrast to these earlier findings. In this case, the medians of the correlations between instructional cost per pupil and various measures of achievement for each of the eight subgroups at each of the five grade levels are, for the most part, scarcely different from zero. (See Table 2.)

The contradiction between the Coleman results and the earlier ones is puzzling, since there is every reason to expect that the amounts of money

---

4. These measures are described with examples on pp. 576-587 of Coleman, *et al.* (1966).

school systems spend on their pupils *should* bear some positive relationship to the cognitive performance of the pupils in those systems. Even if one is unwilling to grant the not unlikely possibility of a causal connection between the amount of money a school spends on instruction and the amount of learning that takes place in pupils, the relationship should nevertheless be positive if only because the money a community spends on its schools should be a partial reflection at least of the socioeconomic factors normally associated with the pupils' intellectual performance. The data in two of the pre-Coleman studies suggest that there is indeed such an association.[5] But in the Coleman study, the median correlations between per-pupil expense and socioeconomic level are essentially zero at each of the grade levels examined (Coleman, 1966, Supplemental Appendix). This result, again, may be explained in part by the homogeneity of the subsample, but it also raises doubts about the credibility of some of the basic data in the Coleman survey. For example, the magnitude of the nonresponse rate for some of the crucial items in the questionnaires, particularly those having to do with socioeconomic status, may be seriously affecting the validity of the measures derived from them. The manner of computing per-pupil expense is also less than adequate since it is based on district-wide figures that may be quite inapplicable to particular schools, especially in slum areas. Regression analyses, no matter how sophisticated they may be, can hardly compensate for, and indeed may inadvertently gloss over, inadequacies in the basic numbers on which they rely. A somewhat cruder approach to the Coleman data may therefore be useful in giving an idea of what is going on behind the numbers.

IV

This cruder approach consists of sorting the forty-five school characteristic variables into correlates and noncorrelates of pupil achievement by simply inspecting the zero-order correlations in the tables of the *Supplemental Appendix*. For this purpose, a correlate is loosely defined as any school characteristic that correlates 0.2 or better with any one or more of the three achievement measures—reading, mathematics, and general information—in any one of the eight ethnic groups at either grade 6 or grade 9. This may seem like an excessively lenient acceptance criterion, but in view of the probable amount of noise in the basic data, a considerable amount of leniency is needed if one is to identify any school variables at all that might be worth speculating about.

The application of this acceptance test to all forty-five school characteristic items turns up nineteen that pass the test and twenty-six that fail it. The nineteen correlates are shown in Table 3a, and the twenty-six noncorrelates in Table 3b.

---

5.   See Mollenkopf-Melville (1966), Tables 11 and 12 and Goodman, (1959), Table 9.

Table 3a

CORRELATES OF PUPIL ACHIEVEMENT[a]
(GRADES 6 AND 9)

SCHOOL CHARACTERISTICS[b]	GROUPS OF PUPILS								TOTAL
	MEXICAN-AMERICANS	PUERTO RICANS	INDIAN-AMERICANS	ORIENTAL-AMERICANS	NEGROES NORTH	NEGROES SOUTH	WHITES NORTH	WHITES SOUTH	
Student Body Characteristics									
Proportion of pupils with encyclopedia in the home	X	X	X	X		X			5
Proportion of school's graduates in college		X							1
Proportion in college prep curriculum	X	X	X	X		X		X	6
Average attendance as percentage of enrollment	X		X						2
Proportion of pupils who are white	X	X	X						3
Average number of white pupils in preceding year	X	X	X						3
Mean nonverbal test score	X	X	X	X	X	X	X	X	8
Mean verbal test score	X	X	X	X	X	X	X	X	8
Proportion of pupils who think teacher expects their best work	X	X							2
Proportion of pupils whose mothers went to college			X					X	2
Characteristics of Instructional Personnel									
Teacher's estimate of quality of own college	X	X		X					3
Teacher's verbal score	X	X	X	X		X			5
Teacher's race	X	X	X	X					4
Teacher's preference for teaching middle class	X	X							2
Teacher's attitude toward integration	X	X	X						3
Teacher's salary		X		X		X			3
Finances and Program									
Per-pupil expenditure				X					1
Comprehensiveness of curriculum				X	X				2
Mathematics offering	X		X						2
Totals	14	14	12	10	3	6	2	4	

[a] Based on data in Coleman, *Supplemental Appendix* (1966).

[b] An X in any column indicates that the school characteristic in question correlates 0.2 or higher with one or more achievement test variables at either grade 6 or grade 9 or both.

Table 3b

NONCORRELATES OF PUPIL ACHIEVEMENT (GRADES 6 AND 9)

Student Body Characteristics
    Number of twelfth-grade pupils
    Pupil mobility (transfers in and out)
    Average hours pupils spend on homework
    Proportion of pupils who read over 16 books the preceding summer
    Teacher's perception of quality of student body
    Proportion of students whose mothers expect their best work

Characteristics of Instructional Personnel
    Teacher's socioeconomic status
    Teacher's experience
    Teacher's localism
    Teacher's highest degree received
    Teacher's absences
    Amount of teacher turnover
    Availability of guidance counselors
    Pupil-teacher ratio

Program, Facilities, Other
    Extracurricular offerings
    Tracking
    Movement between tracks
    Accelerated curriculum
    Policy on promotion of slow learners
    Foreign language offering
    Number of days in session
    Length of school day
    Number of science labs
    Volumes per pupil in school library
    School location (urban-rural)
    Teacher's perception of quality of school

Probably the most striking thing about Table 3a is the relatively large number of correlates in some of the minority groups as compared with the small number in the white majority. Fourteen of the functioning items, for instance, are found in the Puerto Rican group; only two in the Northern white group. These differences between groups in the number of functioning school items are, from one point of view, a source of encouragement. For although they can scarcely be regarded as pinpointing the remedies needed to close the educational gaps between the minority and majority groups, some of them may at least provide useful clues about where to begin to look for the remedies.

Another striking feature of Table 3a is that the great majority of the functioning items have to do with characteristics of the *people* who make up the schools—the pupils and their teachers. The proportion of pupils headed for college, the race of the teachers, the racial mix of the student body, the level of verbal ability in both pupils and teachers, the teachers' attitudes toward integration—these are the kinds of school characteristics that appear to be primarily involved with differences in academic achievement.

A comparison of these functional items with the nonfunctional items in Table 3b suggests that closing the educational gap between the white majority and the colored minorities is going to require more social and educational imagination and sustained effort than has hitherto been typical of most school systems. It is fairly obvious that the school characteristics that turn out to be functional are for the most part the *hard-to-change* characteristics, while those that turn out to be nonfunctional are the *easy-to-change* characteristics. As a consequence, over the next decade or two, educators will no doubt be having to fight off pressures from without and temptations from within to try to achieve instant improvement by pouring money and effort into the easy-to-change nonfunctioning features of school systems (the paper credentials, the readily purchasable gimmicks) at the expense of the hard-to-change features that in the long run are more likely to make a real difference in what children become.

Among the easy-to-change items are the things that can be readily bought by spending a little more money here or there or by making a change in administrative or program policy. They include such things as pupil-teacher ratio, the length of the school day, extracurricular activities, and, interestingly enough, such agonizing policy matters as whether slow learners shall receive automatic promotions and whether students shall be assigned to "tracks." These matters, which are much in the minds of educators, are, according to the crude analyses here being applied to the Coleman data, *non*functional school characteristics: their zero-order correlations with academic achievement *never* get as high as 0.2 for any group at grades 6 or 9. Furthermore, they are characteristics that show no appreciable variability across the several regional and ethnic groups, but do show considerable variability within the groups.

By contrast, the school characteristics that tend to be associated with differential levels of academic performance are not the sort that are readily affected by on-the-spot administrative decisions or by the spending of a little more money here or there. Many of them tend to be linked to the socioeconomic level of the pupils' parents and classmates; they tend to be the kind that are deeply rooted in the economic, social, and cultural level of the communities, and no important educational improvements in these schools are likely to take place until changes have occurred in the total community complex in which the schools are embedded.

V

A consideration of the nature of the variables in both Tables 3a and 3b may throw some light on strategies for upgrading schools.

As suggested above, most of the school correlates of pupil achievement are fairly obviously linked to the socioeconomic level of the communities where the schools operate. Clearly, "proportion of graduates in college" is just such an item: students whose families are in the higher income brackets go to college far more frequently than those whose families are in the bottom brackets. There is some tendency among school authorities to stand helpless before this sort of fact, to argue in effect that their schools are either the victims or the beneficiaries of the social environment, and that any efforts to change their fundamental characteristics are almost certain to be exercises in futility.

There is a more hopeful way of looking at the matter. The fact that the student-body characteristics of schools may be strongly linked to socio-economic factors does not necessarily mean that explicit attention to the more manipulable of such factors may not bear fruit in upgrading pupil performance. No doubt the item "proportion of pupils with encyclopedia in the home" is an item so linked: rich families tend to buy encyclopedias; poor families don't. Nevertheless the item raises a couple of intriguing and presumably researchable questions. First, what would in fact happen to a group of low-achieving pupils if they were actually moved from a school where none of their fellow pupils had encyclopedias at home to a school where all of them had one available? And second, what would happen to achievement levels if, in a district where there are no encyclopedias in the homes, the school authorities supplied one free, or almost free, to every family in the district—accompanied, of course, by the kind of high-powered sales pitch that goes with a normal purchase?

This suggestion that the student-body correlates can be useful in generating hopeful hypotheses to be tested is not to be taken as in any way supportive of the flat assertion in the summary of the Coleman Report that "if a minority pupil from a home without much educational strength is put with schoolmates with strong educational backgrounds, his achievement is likely to increase" (Coleman *et al.*, 1966, p. 22). Quite the contrary. There is nothing whatever in the Coleman analysis that can justify such an inference. The Coleman study contains no data at all on the effects that might accrue from "putting" minority pupils with different kinds of schoolmates. It is one thing to suppose that a pupil's attitudes and behavior reflect those of the peer group in which, because of innumerable circumstances, including possibly his own predilections, he happens to be; it is quite another thing to infer that if he is moved from one group to another, his attitudes and behavior will change in predictable ways. This is not to say that changing the mix of children in a school will not change the children in the mix; it is merely to call attention to the fact that the Coleman data, by their very nature, are incapable of providing any information at all on what changes will occur or the likelihood of their occurrence.

In a word, the data in the Coleman Report can be a rich source of educational ideas to be tried out—of hypotheses to be tested—but always with the reservation that actual outcomes may be the reverse of expectation. The same data, however, cannot and should not be regarded as sure determiners of educational policy and practice. This is no doubt a hard saying for those who insist that only certainties are acceptable in the conduct of the schools. But until educators and the makers of educational policy can get used to the idea that the management of instruction in all its aspects is of necessity a perpetual trial-and-error process, there is little likelihood that the educational enterprise will ever be liberated from the routines in which it seems now to be frozen.

Some of the "nonfunctioning" items are also instructive, in a negative way, about the kinds of thinking that must go into the development of strategies for change. The item on "tracking" is a case in point. The information on this item at grades 9 and 12 was supplied by the school principals. The questions used to elicit the information asked first whether the school carried out "grouping or tracking according to ability or achievement" for all or some of its pupils and then asked whether the grouping system, if any, put pupils in a particular group for all their classes or used differing groups for differing subjects (Coleman *et al.*, 1966, p. 667). The Report does not make clear how the question was scored, but the mean and standard deviation for each of the eight subsamples in both grades 9 and 12 vary scarcely at all from 2.1 and .6, respectively. The correlations with reading and mathematics scores range from $-.07$ to $+.08$ with the median almost exactly at 0. It is as though the responses had been perfectly random.

Such results forcibly raise the question whether it is the item in the questionnaire or the policy concept of tracking itself that is nonfunctional. This is not a trivial matter; it goes to the heart of what may be getting in the way of constructive change in education. The idea of ability grouping or tracking, like many other educational concepts, is not a simple notion; it can mean any number of things in actual practice. There are innumerable ways of placing pupils in tracks and of organizing the activities that go on between teachers and pupils after they have been so placed. All research on the subject has been quite inconclusive for the very reason that the researchers have failed to observe, in any systematic fashion, how teachers actually organize instruction and how pupils actually learn under various conditions of grouping and nongrouping.[6] In short, the negative findings of the Coleman Report with respect to tracking were predictable from past experience and the nature of the question asked. The outcome is hardly surprising inasmuch as tracking and similar concepts, whether used in questionnaires or in the formulation of educational policy, are too semantically soft to penetrate the complexities of the teaching-learning process as it actually operates in classrooms. The same consideration applies with equal if not greater force to more familiar but even less differentiated educational concepts: for instance, reading or writing or arithmetic. The cliché is still good: we are not likely to get meaningful answers until we can figure out how to ask meaningful questions.

6. For recent reviews of research supporting this point see Ekstrom (1961); Borg (1966); and Marklund (1963).

VI

So the question remains: What school factors should be considered of primary importance in any effort to equalize educational opportunity for pupils of all kinds and conditions in all parts of the United States? The Coleman study and the three that preceded it have helped to illuminate the question, but they have hardly supplied definitive answers. We strongly suspect that the amount of money spent on instruction can make a considerable difference in the quality of pupil performance, but how the funds are deployed and used probably makes even more of a difference. It seems reasonably clear that the effectiveness of schools is very largely a function of the characteristics of the people in them—the pupils and their teachers—but we are still a long way from knowing in useful detail what specific changes in the people or in the educational mix will produce what specific benefits for what specific kinds of children. Even were the information on this point more firm than it is, there is still much to be learned about how the changes can be brought about. The only thing that is reasonably certain is that they will not be easy to manage, that they will take years rather than months to effect, and that they will require attention to factors in the total environment of the school as well as to those in the school itself. The weaknesses of American education are less likely to be corrected by the rhetoric of educational administration and curriculum development than by closer attention to the realities of the teaching-learning process as they actually are and as they might be.

One of the great unsolved problems of American education, or of education anywhere in the world, is that of providing a continuous flow of dependable information on how well the schools are meeting the developmental needs of children and in what respects they are failing to do so. The Coleman study and its three predecessors are beginnings toward this end; but massive though they seem, they are only beginnings. All four of them have weaknesses that are attributable, in part at least, to the fact that they have had to deal with a vast number of technical, theoretical, and logistical problems that are new and difficult. A weakness common to all of them is their exclusive focus on the purely cognitive outcomes of education. The Coleman study touches on three noncognitive variables—self-concept, interest in learning, and sense of control of the environment—but these are treated as conditions of learning rather than as its goals.[7]

The very great importance of the Coleman Report is that it has highlighted the problems, the possibilities, and the need for an evaluation sys-

7. Mayeske's (1967) re-analysis of the Coleman data, however, shows a multiple correlation of .59 between sense of control (which he re-labels "attitude toward life") and an optimum combination of 31 school variables, which does not include characteristics of the student body. When the latter are added to the independent variables, the R increases to .64. The result gives some credence to the idea that the characteristics of a school may indeed have an influence for good or ill on how children see their world.

tem that will be capable of informing educational practitioners and policy makers about what is actually going on out there in their schools and what might be tried to improve the situation. Until such information is forthcoming at regular intervals and in large quantities, it is reasonably certain that in spite of large infusions of money and the frenzied innovations that money may bring, the schools will become increasingly inconsequential in helping us toward a viable society.

References

ASHMORE, H. S.   *The Negroes and the schools.* Chapel Hill: University of North Carolina Press, 1954.

BORG, W. R.   *Ability grouping in the public schools.* Madison, Wis.: Dembar Educational Services, 1966.

COLEMAN, J. S. *et al.*   *Equality of educational opportunity.* Washington: United States Government Printing Office, 1966.

COLEMAN, J. S.   *Supplemental appendix to the survey on equality of educational opportunity.* Washington: National Center for Educational Statistics; United States Government Printing Office, 1966.

EKSTROM, R. B.   Experimental studies of homogeneous grouping: a critical review. *School Review,* 1961, 60, 217-226.

GOODMAN, S. M.   *The assessment of school quality.* Albany: New York State Education Department, 1959.

MARKLUND, S.   Scholastic attainments as related to size and homogeneity of classes. *Educational Research,* 1963, 6, 63-67.

MAYESKE, G. W.   A model for school achievement. Paper delivered at United States Office of Education Symposium: Operations Analysis in Education, Washington, 1967.

MOLLENKOPF, W. G. and MELVILLE, S. D.   A study of secondary school characteristics as related to test scores. Research Bulletin 56-6. Princeton, N.J.: Educational Testing Service, 1956.

MORT, P. R.   *The growing edge.* New York: Metropolitan School Study Council, 1957.

RUSSELL, B.   On the notion of cause. Reprinted in *Mysticism and logic.* Hammondsworth, England: Penguin Books, 1954. Pp. 171-196.

SHAYCOFT, M. F.   *The high school years: growth in cognitive skills.* Pittsburgh: American Institutes for Research and School of Education, University of Pittsburgh, 1967.

※ ※ ※ ※ ※

In the late 1950's, as the New Morality regarding racial integration was gaining ground, small groups of school people around the country were busy "integrating" the curriculum materials they set before students. Commercial publishers, resisting at first, gradually began bringing out textbooks and readers that might well have borne the imprint, Color Added. What earthly difference, you might have asked, could darkening the skins of some of the Dicks, Janes, and Sallys make in the entrenched prejudices of the white society?

This simply-executed study by Litcher and Johnson says that it does make a difference, at least it did among second graders in a nearly all-white Midwestern city.

Their study makes the reduction of racist prejudice look easy—perhaps too easy. If attitudes can be so readily swayed one way, then they can also be swayed the other way. What the study does not tell us is *why* the change. It offers little information about the particular circumstances that enabled the effects to appear—or the conditions under which we could expect no change. As a matter of fact, social psychologists know a good deal about the whys and conditions of prejudice reduction. The student might read the chapter by Harding *et al.*, in the newly-revised *Handbook of Social Psychology* (Addison-Wesley, 1969), then try to suggest some reasons for the change himself. He might even try to replicate Litcher and Johnson's study; given its clarity and directness, this would not be difficult to do.

Changes in Attitudes Toward Negroes of White Elementary School Students After Use of Multi-Ethnic Readers*

John H. Litcher, David W. Johnson

Problem

Changing racial attitudes on a wide-scale basis is one of the most important social psychological problems of our society. It is evident that from a very early age white children are prejudiced against Negroes (Horowitz, 1936, 1939; Katz and Braly, 1933; Blake and Dennis, 1943; Radke, Trager, and Hadassah, 1949; Goodman, 1948; Radke and Trager, 1950; Landreth and Johnson, 1953; Gregor and McPherson, 1966). There is some empirical evidence which indicates that under certain conditions (which have not been adequately researched) the attitudes of whites toward Negroes may be changed through direct experience. Singer (1967), for example, in a recent study of the effects of integrated classrooms upon the racial attitudes of fifth-grade children, found that white children in integrated schools, compared with white children in segregated schools, are more accepting of Negroes and more familiar with Negro celebrities. The more intelligent the white child in the integrated school, the more favorable are his attitudes toward Negroes.

It is not possible, however, to provide every white child with direct experiences with Negroes. In Minnesota and North Dakota, for example, the Negro population is so small that such direct experiences are impossible. One alternative to direct experience with Negroes is exposure to materials which portray Negroes in a positive way, contradicting prevailing prejudices and stereotypes. Research in social perception (Bartlett, 1932; Allport and Postman, 1945) and in the learning of controversial material (Edwards, 1941; Levine and Murphy, 1943; Jones and Aneshansel, 1956) suggests that materials portraying Negroes positively would be either distorted in various ways to support the prevailing stereotypes and prejudices or ignored and quickly forgotten. Research in counter-conditioning (Bandura and Walters, 1963), however, would predict that such an approach would be effective. If, for example, the stimulus "Negro" (which elicits a negative response) is repeatedly paired with the cluster of stimuli characteristic of "middle class"

* From *Journal of Educational Psychology*, 1969, 60, 148-152. Used by permission of the authors and publisher.

(which elicits a positive response), the stimulus "Negro" will elicit the positive response associated with "middle class"—if the stimulus "Negro" does not elicit a more powerful response than the response elicited by the stimuli characteristic of "middle class."

An exploratory study was conducted contrasting the social perception, social learning and the counter-conditioning hypotheses by investigating the effect of multi-ethnic readers upon the racial attitudes of white elementary students. Multi-ethnic readers are readers which contain characters from several different racial and ethnic groups. In the readers used, Negroes are portrayed as having middle-class characteristics (works hard, dresses nicely, is clean, etc.) in integrated situations.

Method

This study employed a pretest-posttest control group design. Experimental groups used a multi-ethnic reader for four months while control groups used the traditional reader. Both groups were interviewed before and after the experimental treatment. The study was conducted from February, 1967 through May of the same year. Sixty-eight white, middle-class children were studied, thirty-four classified by their teachers as upper group readers and thirty-four classified as middle group readers. Both the multi-ethnic and the regular second-grade readers were used by each teacher in each classroom. Eight reading groups in four second-grade classrooms in two public elementary schools participated in the study. Through random assignment, two classrooms (one in each school) used the multi-ethnic reader in their upper reading group and the regular reader in their middle reading group. The other two classrooms (one in each school) used the regular reader in their upper reading group and the multi-ethnic reader in their middle reading group.

The four teachers who participated in the study were randomly selected from volunteers within the school system. The teachers' interest in this study was prompted by the opportunity it offered them to participate in research. They were generally informed as to the nature of the study and asked to teach the experimental and control groups as similarly as possible. Since the basal approach to reading instruction was followed, the teaching included the development of word recognition skills, comprehension skills, reading skills in other content areas, oral and silent reading, and emphasis on a personal reading program. A record of any discussion relating to race relations was requested. According to their reports, the teachers did not at any time initiate a discussion of the fact that many of the characters in the multi-ethnic reader were non-white. Neither did they encourage student discussion of the racial differences of the characters in the reader while the study was in progress. The students commented very little on the differences in race of the characters about whom they were reading. The multi-ethnic readers were the only multi-ethnic materials in the classroom.

The Scott-Foresman multi-ethnic (Robinson, Monroe, and Artley, 1965) and regular (Robinson, Monroe, and Artley, 1963) second-grade readers were used in the study. These readers are identical except for the pictures (some of the characters in the pictures in the multi-ethnic reader are non-white) and the names used to represent the characters of the racial and ethnic groups found in the readers.

For both the pretest and the posttest each child was interviewed individually. Four tests were presented in random order and all were given in one sitting. On the average it took nine minutes to administer the tests. All questions were asked of each child, but answers were not made compulsory.

During the four months of the experimental treatment three children, all in the experimental group, moved out of the school district. They were, therefore, not available for the posttest.

The study was conducted in a Midwestern city of 50,000 inhabitants. The total Negro population in this city is less than 100. Of the 6,181 children attending the city's elementary schools, 10 are Negroes. No Negro children attended the two elementary schools studied.

The instruments used in this study were a variation of the Clark Doll Test (Gregor and McPherson, 1966), the Horowitz and Horowitz (1938) "Show Me" and Categories test, and a Direct Comparison test (Blake and Dennis, 1943). In the Clark Doll Test the children were presented with two dolls which differed only in skin color (one white, one dark brown). The children were asked to point to one doll as a response to the following questions: Show me the doll that (1) you would like to play with, (2) you like best, (3) is a nice doll, (4) has a nice color, (5) looks bad, (6) looks like a white child, (7) looks like a colored child, (8) looks like a Negro child, and (9) looks like you.

The "Show Me" test developed by Horowitz and Horowitz (1938) consists of 12 portraits (3 white boys, 3 white girls, 3 Negro boys, and 3 Negro girls) placed randomly on a large sheet of paper. The following questions were asked of the children: Please show me the one that (1) you'd like to sit next to at school, (2) you'd want to play with, (3) comes from a poor home, (4) you do not want in your school, (5) you'd like to have as your cousin, (6) doesn't look very smart, (7) you would want to come to your house for a long visit, and (8) you do not like.

In the categories test (Horowitz and Horowitz, 1938) five pictures mounted on a page were presented to each child. The children were asked to reject one picture as not belonging to the group. Categories of race versus sex and race versus age were used. For example, one page might contain five pictures, 3 white boys, 1 white girl, and 1 Negro boy. If the Negro boy was selected as not belonging, race is a more salient category than sex for that child. If the white girl was selected, sex could be considered as the more salient category. The test was designed to analyze the strength of race, sex, and age categories for the children.

The Direct Comparison Test (Blake and Dennis, 1943) required the children to make direct comparisons between Negroes and whites in regard to

18 traits. The children were asked to indicate whether the trait was more characteristic of whites or Negroes or to respond "no difference" or "don't know." Examples of the traits used are: cheerful, honest, lazy, forgetful, neat, clean, lies.

Results

Table 1

FREQUENCY OF RESPONSES OF WHITE SECOND-GRADE CHILDREN TO
ITEMS OF RACE IDENTIFICATION ON THE CLARK DOLL TEST

PRETEST

WHICH DOLL:	MULTI-ETHNIC READER GROUP		REGULAR READER GROUP	
	N = 31		N = 34	
	N. DOLL	W. DOLL	N. DOLL	W. DOLL
Looks like a white child	1	30	—	34
Looks like a colored child	31	—	34	—
Looks like a Negro child	31	—	34	—
Looks like you	1	30	—	34

As part of the pretest each child was asked to respond to several questions dealing with racial identification. From Table 1 it may be seen that with the exception of one child, all the children correctly identified the dolls used in the Clark Doll Test with their appropriate racial group. From these data it may be concluded that with one possible exception, all the children studied were able to respond to questions dealing with racial membership.

Each child studied responded to four tests of racial attitudes. Since the investigators were interested only in general changes in racial attitudes resulting from the use of multi-ethnic readers and not in responses to the specific questions of each test a general score of favorableness of attitudes toward Negroes was derived for each child for each test. A child was given one point for each response which indicated favorable attitudes toward Negroes. For the Clark Doll Test the range of possible scores was 0 to 5, for the "Show Me" test the range of possible scores was 0 to 8, and for the Categories test, 0 to 6. For the Direct Comparison test the proportion of responses favorable to Negroes was used, the possible range of scores being from 0 to 100%.

In order to see if the tests were independent of each other the responses of the children to the four tests were correlated. From Table 2 it may be seen that the tests were only slightly correlated and, therefore, the data for each were analyzed separately.

On all tests there were no significant differences between the experimental and control group on the pretests. In order to control for slight differ-

Table 2

CORRELATIONS BETWEEN TESTS OF RACIAL ATTITUDES
PRETEST AND POSTTEST

N = 65

RACIAL ATTITUDE TESTS CORRELATED	PRETEST	POSTTEST
Clark Doll and Show Me Test	.19	.25
Clark Doll and Categories Test	.13	.08
Clark Doll and Direct Comparison Test	.12	.35
Show Me and Categories Test	−.08	.22
Show Me and Direct Comparison Test	.22	.26
Categories and Direct Comparison Test	.17	.18

Table 3

COMPARISON OF ATTITUDES TOWARD NEGROES
OF WHITE SECOND-GRADE CHILDREN

POSTTEST

TESTS	MULTI-ETHNIC READER GROUP N = 31	REGULAR READER GROUP N = 34	SIGNIFICANCE
Clark Doll Test .... (Range: 0-5)	1.39	0.44	$F = 15.90; p < .0002$
Show Me Test .... (Range: 0-8)	2.58	1.47	$F = 8.71; p < .005$
Categories Test .... (Range: 0-6)	4.42	3.44	$F = 4.38; p < .04$
Direct Comparison Test ..	51%	24%	$F = 14.94; p < .0003$

Note: (1) The higher the score the more favorable the attitudes toward Negroes.
     (2) An analysis of covariance was used in analyzing the data.

ences between the groups, however, an analysis of covariance was used in analyzing the results of the posttest. The data in Table 3 indicate that on all four tests the children using the multi-ethnic readers responded significantly more favorably toward Negroes than the children using the regular readers.

Discussion

The results of this study dramatically indicate that the use of multi-ethnic readers in an elementary school will result in more favorable attitudes toward Negroes. The data from the Clark Doll Test indicate that the use of the multi-ethnic reader decreased the preference for one's own racial group over the other. While the control group expressed marked preferences for the white rather than the Negro doll, the experimental group members were far less unanimous about their preferences.

In a recent study on the Clark Doll Test, Greenwald and Oppenheim (1967) report that 19% of the white children they interviewed (taking their more conservative figure) identified the Negro doll in response to the question, "Show me the doll that looks like you." In an earlier study Morland (1963) found that 14% of the white children interviewed responded similarly. Greenwald and Oppenheim (1967) concluded on the basis of these findings that the amount of Negro misidentification found in the Clark and Clark (1940) and other similar studies is misleading as they did not have a control group of white children. The present study (1.5% white misidentification) and the study of Gregor and McPherson (1966) (0% white misidentification) give no support to their findings or their conclusion.

On the "Show Me" test, the use of the multi-ethnic reader resulted in a reduction of the amount of social distance placed between the white and Negro racial groups. On the Categories test, the children in the experimental group were less likely to exclude a child on the basis of race than were the controls. The data for the Direct Comparisons test, furthermore, indicate that the experimental subjects were less likely to attribute negative traits to Negroes and positive traits to whites than were the control subjects. Examination of the individual items revealed that the experimental group basically became equalitarian in their response. Johnson (1967) found that Negro children who were taught Negro history in a Freedom School became much more convinced that Negroes and whites are equal. Thus, the use of the multi-ethnic reader had much the same effect on white children as learning Negro history had upon Negro children.

The evidence is quite clear. Through the use of a multi-ethnic reader white children developed markedly more favorable attitudes toward Negroes. Under the conditions of this experiment, this finding supports the counter-conditioning hypothesis and does not support the social perception and social learning hypothesis. The implications of this finding hardly need elaboration. While it is not possible, due to lack of material resources and the distribution of the Negro population in the United States, for every white child to have direct experiences with Negroes (although the investigators believe it is desirable), it is possible to increase the visibility of the Negro in the curriculum materials of the schools. Such an action should, through the reduction of prejudice, increase racial harmony.

A limitation on the generalization of the results of this study should be noted. The Negro population in the city in which this study was conducted is quite small (Negroes make up less than 0.2% of the total population of the city). The probability is very high that the children participating in the study had no direct experience with Negroes and that the Negro community does not represent an economic or social threat to the white community. The racial attitudes of the children studied, therefore, are probably not firmly rooted in direct experiences or reference group norms.

References

ALLPORT, G. W. and POSTMAN, L. J.   The basic psychology of rumor. *Transactions of the New York Academy of Sciences,* Series II, 1945, 8, 61-81.

BANDURA, A. and WALTERS, H.   *Social learning and personality development.* New York: Holt, Rinehart, and Winston, Inc., 1963.

BARTLETT, F. C.   *Remembering.* Cambridge, England: Cambridge University Press, 1932.

BLAKE, R. and DENNIS, W.   The development of stereotypes concerning the Negro. *Journal of Abnormal and Social Psychology,* 1943, 38, 525-531.

CLARK, H. B. and CLARK, M. K.   Skin color as a factor in racial identification of Negro preschool children. *Journal of Social Psychology,* 1940, 11, 160.

EDWARDS, A. L.   Political frames of reference as a factor influencing recognition. *Journal of Abnormal and Social Psychology,* 1941, 36, 34-50.

GREENWALD, H. J. and OPPENHEIM, D. B.   Reported magnitude of self-misidentification among Negro children—artifact? *Journal of Personality and Social Psychology,* 1968, 8, 49-52.

GREGOR, A. J. and McPHERSON, D. A.   Racial attitudes among white and Negro children in a deep-South standard metropolitan area. *The Journal of Social Psychology,* 1966, 68, 95-106.

GOODMAN, M. E.   Evidence concerning the genesis of interracial attitudes. *American Anthropologist,* 1948, 48, 624-630.

HOROWITZ, R. E.   The development of attitude toward the Negro. *Archives of Psychology,* 1936, 194, 5-47.

HOROWITZ, R. E.   Racial aspects of self identification in nursery school children. *Journal of Psychology,* 1939, 7, 91-99.

HOROWITZ, L. and HOROWITZ, R. E.   Development of social attitudes in children. *Sociometry,* 1938, 1, 301-339.

JOHNSON, D. W.   The effects of a freedom school on its students. In R. Dentler, B. Mackler, and M.E. Warshauer (Eds.). *The urban R's: race relations as the problem in urban education.* New York: Praeger, 1967. Pp. 226-245.

JONES, E. E. and ANESHANSEL, J.   The learning and utilization of contravaluant material. *Journal of Abnormal and Social Psychology,* 1956, 53, 27-33.

KATZ, D. and BRALY, K. W.   Racial stereotypes of one hundred college students. *Journal of Abnormal and Social Psychology,* 1939, 28, 280-290.

LANDRETH, C. and JOHNSON, B. C.   Young children's responses to a picture and insert test designed to reveal reactions to persons of different skin color. *Child Development,* 1953, 24, 63-80.

LEVINE, J. M. and MURPHY, G.   The learning and forgetting of controversial material. *Journal of Abnormal and Social Psychology,* 1943, 38, 507-517.

MORLAND, J. K.   Racial self-identification: a study of nursery school children. *American Catholic Sociological Review,* 1963, 24, 231-242.

RADKE, M. J., TRAGER, H. G. and HADASSAH, D.   Social perceptions and attitudes of children. *Genetic Psychology Monographs,* 1949, 40, 327-447.

RADKE, M. J. and TRAGER, H. G.   Children's perception of the social roles of Negroes. *Journal of Psychology,* 1950, 29, 3-33.

ROBINSON, H. M., MONROE, M. and ARTLEY, A. S.   *More new friends and neighbors 2-2* and *New friends and neighbors 2-1.* Chicago: Scott, Foresman and Company, 1963.

ROBINSON, H. M., MONROE, M. and ARTLEY, A. S.   *More friends old and new 2-2* and *Friends old and new 2-1,* Chicago: Scott, Foresman and Company, 1965.

SINGER, D.   The influence of intelligence and an interracial classroom on social attitudes. In R. Dentler, B. Mackler, and M. E. Warshauer (Eds.). *The urban R's: race relations as the problem in urban education.* New York: Praeger, 1967. Pp. 99-117.

꙰ ꙰ ꙰ ꙰ ꙰

Consider young Negroes who now sit with their white peers in school and college classrooms around the country. It has been a long, hard struggle for many of them to get there, and in all too many places one would still look in vain to find blacks among the whites. But for those who have made it, is their battle for an excellent (or at least an equal) education over? Some would say yes: now it is up to the student to profit from what is offered him. Others take a less sanguine view, emphasizing the need for special compensatory programs of instruction. The author of this selection would also say no: problems of learning are severe for the Negro in racially mixed classes, and the battle is only half over. The reasons are intimate, social-psychological ones.

In classrooms, people worry about succeeding and failing, about meeting standards they set for themselves, about doing poorly in the eyes of their peers—or outshining them and invoking their hostility. In one way or another, self-evaluation is at stake. Anxieties associated with these matters can seriously affect both the effort to perform and performance itself. Self-esteem is an especially delicate issue among blacks, when their performance is open to invidious comparison with whites', or white standards. The experiments by Katz and his associates on Negro performance in racially mixed settings dramatically illustrate the difficulties which black members of integrated classrooms still face in managing scholastic achievements equal to those of their white companions. The other half of the battle will be won with the elimination of white racism and its dignity-destroying consequences.

Experiments on Negro Performance in Bi-Racial Situations*

Irwin Katz

In recent years this author and his associates have been engaged in a series of experiments on the intellectual productivity of Negro male college students in situations involving white peers and/or white authority figures. The general aim of the research is the identification of underlying psychological factors that have either favorable or detrimental effects on Negro efficiency. In connection with the interpretation of the results that are now to be presented there evolved a set of postulated situational determinants of performance, as follows. The determinants were developed to apply equally to school and college situations, so the words "children," "pupils," and "students" are used interchangeably to refer to learners.

Postulated Situational Determinants of Negro Performance in Desegregation

SOCIAL THREAT.   Social threat refers to a class of social stimulus events that tend to elicit anxious expectations that others will inflict harm or pain. One may assume that novel types of contact with white strangers possess a social-threat component for members of a subordinated minority group. The degree of threat should be a direct function of (a) the amount of evidence of white hostility (or the extent to which evidence of white friendliness is lacking) and (b) the amount of power possessed by whites in the contact situation, as shown by their numerical predominance, control of authority positions, etc. It seems likely that Negro children would be under some degree of social threat in a newly integrated classroom. Mere indifference on the part of white peers may frustrate their needs for companionship and approval, resulting in lowered self-esteem and the arousal of impulses to escape or aggress. In more extreme instances, verbal harassment and even

* Excerpted from *American Psychologist*, 1964, 19, 381-383, 390-396. Used by permission of the author and publisher. The article from which the excerpt was drawn was prepared at the request of the Society for the Psychological Study of Social Issues because of the social importance of the problem. The author wishes to express his gratitude to John R. P. French for his warm encouragement and helpful suggestions during the preparation of this paper. Thanks are due also to my many colleagues who read and commented on an earlier draft. The research by the author and his associates reviewed in this paper was conducted under Contract Nonr 285 (24) between the Office of Naval Research and New York University.

physical hazing may elicit strong fear responses. These external threats are likely to distract the minority child from the task at hand, to the detriment of performance.

In addition, psychological theory suggests that the Negro's own covert reactions to social threat would constitute an important source of intellectual impairment. In discussing the effect of psychological stress on the learning of skills, Deese (1962) mentions distraction by the internal stimuli of autonomic activation, as well as disruption of task responses by neuromuscular and other components of the stress reaction. Mandler and Sarason (1962) and others call attention to the disruptive role of task-irrelevant defensive responses against anxiety. Spence (1958) and Taylor (1963) propose that anxiety, conceptualized as drive, increases intratask response competition. And according to Easterbrook (1959), emotion lowers efficiency on complex tasks by narrowing the range of cue utilization. Also relevant is Bovard's (1959) hypothesis of a specific physiological mechanism to account for the apparent lowering of the stress threshold under conditions of social isolation.

Another way in which social threat may impair performance is by causing Negro children to abandon efforts to excel in order not to arouse further resentment and hostility in white competitors. That is, the latter may possess what French and Raven (1960) refer to as "coercive power." When academic success is expected to instigate white reprisals, then any stimulus which arouses the motive to achieve should also generate anxiety, and defensive avoidance of such stimuli should be learned. This response pattern would not be wholly non-adaptive in a situation where a small number of Negro students stood relatively powerless against a prejudiced white majority—if one assumes that evidence of Negro intellectual competence might have an ego-deflating effect on these white students. The Group for the Advancement of Psychiatry (1957) has put the matter this way:

> A feeling of superior worth may be gained merely from the existence of a downgraded group. This leads to an unrealistic and unadaptive kind of self-appraisal based on invidious comparison rather than on solid personal growth and achievement . . . (**p. 10**).

Finally with regard to possible social threat emanating from a white teacher—given the prestige of the adult authority, any expression by a white teacher of dislike or devaluation, whether through harsh, indifferent, or patronizing behavior, should tend to have unfavorable effects on Negro performance similar to those just described, and perhaps of even greater intensity.

SOCIAL FACILITATION. When the minority newcomer in a desegregated school is accepted socially by his white classmates, his scholastic motivation should be influenced favorably. It was noted earlier that achievement standards tend to be higher in previously all-white schools than in

Negro schools. From studies based on white subjects, it is apparent that individuals are responsive to the standards of those with whom they desire to associate (reviewed by Bass, 1961; French and Raven, 1960; Thibaut and Kelly, 1959). That Negro children want friendship with white age mates was shown by Horowitz (1936), Radke, Sutherland, and Rosenberg (1950), and Yarrow (1958). Another study, by Criswell (1939), suggests that Negro children in racially mixed classrooms accept white prestige but increasingly withdraw into their own group as a response to white rejection. Thus, if their desire for acceptance is not inhibited or destroyed by sustained un-friendliness from white children, Negro pupils should tend to adopt the scholastic norms of the high-status majority group. Experimental support for this supposition comes from Dittes and Kelley (1956), who found with white college students that private as well as public adherence to the atti-tudinal standards of a group were highest among persons who had experi-enced a fairly high degree of acceptance from the group, with a possibility of gaining even fuller acceptance, while those who received a low degree of acceptance showed little genuine adherence to group norms.

Friendliness and approval on the part of white teachers should be benefi-cial to Negro motivation by increasing the incentive strength of scholastic success. Assuming that white teachers have more prestige for the minority child than do Negro teachers, the prospect of winning their approval should be more attractive. Hence, when such approval can be expected as a reward for good performance, motivation should be favorably influenced.

PROBABILITY OF SUCCESS.   When the minority child is placed in a school that has substantially higher scholastic standards than he knew previ-ously, he may become discouraged and not try to succeed. This common sense proposition is derivable from Atkinson's (1958a) theory of the moti-vational determinants of risk taking and performance. For individuals in whom the tendency to approach success is stronger than the tendency to avoid failure, task motivation is assumed to be a joint function of the sub-jective probability of achieving success and the incentive value of success. From a postulated inverse relationship between the latter two variables (assuming external influences on incentive strength are held constant) he derives a hypothesis that the strength of motivation is at a maximum when the probability of success is .50, and diminishes as this probability approaches zero or unity. The hypothesis is supported by findings on arithmetic performance of white college students (Atkinson, 1958b), and white elementary-school children (Murstein and Collier, 1962), as well as on digit-symbol performance of white high-school students (Rosen, 1961). (In these studies, the effect occurred regardless of whether subjects had scored relatively high or low on a projective personality measure of the motive to approach success.) It follows that if the Negro newcomer per-ceives the standards of excellence in a desegregated school as being sub-stantially higher than those he encountered previously, so that the likelihood of his attaining them seems low, his scholastic motivation will decline.

FAILURE THREAT.   Failure threat is a class of stimulus events in an achievement situation which tend to elicit anxious expectations of harm or pain as a consequence of failure. High probability of failure does not by itself constitute failure threat—it is necessary also that the failure have a social meaning. Thus in Atkinson's formulation, the negative incentive strength of failure varies inversely with the subjective probability of failure, so that fear of failure is most strongly aroused when the probability of failure is at an intermediate level. This leads to the paradoxical prediction that as the probability of failure increases beyond .50, fear of failure declines. The paradox is resolved when one recognizes that Atkinson's model deals only with that component of incentive strength that is determined by the apparent difficulty of the task. Sarason, Davidson, Lighthall, Waite, and Ruebush (1960) call attention to the important influence of anticipated disapproval by parents and teachers on the negative valence of failure. (While their primary interest is in test anxiety as a personality variable, their discussion seems applicable to the present problem of identifying situational determinants of fear of failure.) Presumably, the child's belief that his failure to meet prevailing standards of achievement will bring adult disapproval is relatively unaffected by his own perception of the difficulty of a given task. Hence, fear of disapproval should increase as it becomes more probable—i.e., as the subjective probability of failure increases. Sarason and his associates suggest that a high expectancy of failure arouses strong unconscious hostility against the adults from whom negative evaluation is foreseen. The hostility is turned inward against the self in the form of self-derogatory attitudes, which strengthen the expectation of failure and the desire to escape the situation. Distraction by these and other components of emotional conflict may cause a decrement in the child's performance.

Experimental Evidence

The author and his associates conducted a series of experiments testing some of the determinants postulated above.

Bi-racial Teams

In two exploratory studies, conducted at a Northern university (Katz and Benjamin, 1960; Katz, Goldston, and Benjamin, 1958), various cognitive and motor tasks were assigned to groups composed of two Negro students and two white students. Initially the men were total strangers. They worked together in several sessions for a total of 12½ hours. In general, it was found that Negroes displayed marked social inhibition and subordination to white partners. When teams were engaged in cooperative problem solving, Negro subjects made fewer proposals than did whites and tended to accept the latter's contributions uncritically. On all tasks combined, Negroes made fewer remarks than did whites and spoke more to whites, proportionately, than to one another. White men, on the other hand, spoke more to one another, proportionately, than to the Negroes. These behaviors occurred even when group members could expect a monetary bonus for good team-work and were informed that their abilities were higher than those of sub-jects in other teams. Moreover, in the second experiment, Negro and white partners were matched on intelligence and were even made to display equal ability on certain group tasks (by means of secret manipulation of tasks). Yet on a terminal questionnaire Negroes ranked whites higher on intellectual performance, preferred one another as future work companions, and ex-pressed less satisfaction with the group experience than did whites.

The findings on Negro behavior may have been a result of (*a*) social threat (i.e., Negroes were fearful of instigating white hostility through greater assertiveness), (*b*) low task motivation in confrontation with white achievement standards (as derived earlier from Atkinson's model), or (*c*) failure threat (high expectancy of failure combined with anxious anticipa-tion of disapproval and rejection by white peers and the white experi-menter). The experimental data provide no basis on which to reject any of these factors as irrelevant.

In the next experiment, Katz and Cohen (1962) attempted to modify Negro behavior toward white partners in the direction of greater assertive-ness and autonomy. It was predicted that (*a*) when Negroes were com-pelled to achieve on a task that was performed cooperatively with a white peer, they would subsequently display an increased amount of achieving behavior on another shared task of different content, and (*b*) Negro sub-jects who were not compelled to achieve on the first task would show an opposite tendency. Negro-white student dyads at a Northern university engaged in cooperative solving of problems adapted from the Raven Pro-gressive Matrices. Some of the problems were made easy, to insure that both participants would perceive the correct answer. On other problems the sub-jects unknowingly received different information, so that one person had an insoluble version. Each subject had the easy version half the time. On every problem partners had to agree on a single team answer, after which the experimenter announced the correct solution. Before and after the problem-solving experience a disguised measure of social influence between the two men was obtained on a task which required group estimates of certain quantitative characteristics of briefly exposed photographs (e.g., the number of paratroopers in the sky).

In a control condition, the rules of the problem-solving situation did not require that each person openly propose an answer to every problem. It was found that Negroes tended to accept passively the suggestions of their white companions *even when they held the easy version and the teammate had to be in error*. Regarding intellectual efficiency, the private responses of Negroes, which they wrote down before each discussion began, showed *more errors than were made on the same problems at an earlier, individual testing session*. White subjects, on the other hand, made *fewer* private errors than they had made previously. As a consequence of the problem-solving experience in the control condition, Negroes showed increased social compliance on the picture estimations.

In an "assertion-training" condition the men were given their answer sheets from the previous session when they had worked alone. On every problem the two partners were required to read aloud their previous answers before negotiating a team reply. Thus, Negro subjects had the experience of openly announcing correct solutions in about half of all instances of disagreement (both men read off approximately the same number of correct answers). In the subsequent interactions over picture estimation there was an *increase* in the amount of influence Negroes had over the white partner. Further, Negro subjects were now inclined to accept the other person's influence only to the extent that he had displayed superior accuracy on previous pictures.

Thus, unless *forced* to express opinions at variance with those of a white peer, Negro students tended to suppress their own ideas in deference to the other person and to show increased compliance on another task. But when they were *forced* to act independently on one task, they achieved greater autonomy in the second situation. The responses of white subjects on a postexperimental questionnaire indicate there may have been some hostility aroused against Negro partners who displayed intellectual competence. After working in the assertion-training condition whites tended to downgrade the Negro's performance and to accept him less as a future co-worker. However, since there were no all-white control groups, it is not known whether these reactions of white subjects were specifically interracial.

The results suggest that Negro submissiveness with the white companion was an effect primarily of social threat and that probability of success was a relatively unimportant factor. As already mentioned, in both the assertion-training and control conditions disagreement was experimentally arranged on almost all problems, with random alternation between partners in the assignment of easy and insoluble versions (on a few items *both* men had either easy or hard versions). Also, after each team decision the experimenter announced the correct answer (fictitious when both men had hard items) so that subjects could check the accuracy of their own private response and of the solution the partner had openly proposed. While there was a stable tendency in control teams for whites to make slightly fewer private errors than Negroes (all partners had been matched on pre-test scores), it is doubtful that the average race difference of about two private errors on 49 items could have been discriminated by the average Negro subject. Hence the relative accuracy of own and partner's solutions was much the same for Negro subjects in the two experimental conditions, and the only difference between conditions was that in assertion training the Negro subject was forced to *disagree openly* with the partner. The disinhibiting effect of this experience on the Negro subject's behavior on another task seems attributable to a reduction in anxiety about instigating white hostility.

The Effect of Induced Threat in
Different Racial Environments

In the next experiment, Katz and Greenbaum (1963) examined more directly the influence of threat on Negro verbal performance by systematically varying the level of threat in different racial environments. Individual Negro students at a predominantly Negro college in the South were given a digit-symbol substitution task in the presence of two strangers who were both either white or Negro—an adult administrator and a confederate who pretended to be another student working on the same task. In order to minimize the amount of uncontrolled threat implicit in the white condition, there was no social interaction between the Negro subject and his white peer, and the task was described as a research instrument of no evaluative significance.

In addition to the variation of racial environment, the students were exposed to a condition of either high or low threat. Since the purpose of the threat variation was to determine whether individual Negroes were more vulnerable to debilitative effects of stress when they were alone with whites than when they were with other Negroes, it seemed desirable to use a threat stimulus that would not lead to intentional suppression of responses, by changing the social meaning of the task situation. The experimenters used an announcement that severe electric shock (high-threat condition) or mild electric shock (low-threat condition) would be administered to the subject and the co-worker at random times during the task. No shocks were actually delivered.

The results indicated that Negro students' scores on the digit-symbol task depended upon the particular combination of stress and racial-environment conditions under which they worked. When only mild shock was threatened they performed better in the presence of whites than of other Negroes. But when told to expect strong shock their efficiency in the Negro condition improved, while in the white condition it went down. Apparently, the prospect of successful competition against a white peer, and of approval from a white authority figure, had greater incentive strength than the corresponding prospect in the all-Negro situation. This is reasonable on the assumption that the whites (particularly the experimenter) had higher prestige for the subject than their Negro counterparts. Since in all experimental conditions the instructions for the task played down its intellectual significance, Negro subjects in the white-environment—low-shock threat condition would not have experienced strong failure threat. Hence, they could respond to the stronger incentive strength of success in the white condition.

There are a number of ways of looking at the effects of shock threat. First, if Negro subjects cared more about performing well in the white condition they would have been more fearful lest the strong shock disrupt their task responses (failure threat). The expected stimulus would thus become more salient and distracting. An upward spiral of debilitation could then be set in motion as distraction and fear made the task seem more difficult, and this in turn aroused further emotion. Subjects in the Negro environment, on the other hand, had a relatively relaxed attitude toward the task in the low-threat condition (*too* relaxed for good performance). Hence they would not have been fearful of possible decrements due to shock but perhaps just enough concerned to work harder than before. Also relevant to these data is Bovard's (1959) notion that the ability to withstand stress is strengthened by the presence of familiar social stimuli that have nurturant associations (in this case other Negroes).

The Hullian conception of the energizing effect of drive is also applicable: efficiency declined in the white condition because the subject's initial stimulation in this racial environment, in combination with the additional stimulation of the strong shock threat, produced a total drive strength that exceeded the optimum for the assigned task. In the Negro condition, initial stimulation was relatively low, so that the increment in arousal due to strong threat brought the total drive level closer to the optimum than it had been under mild threat.

Effects of IQ versus Non-IQ Instructions

In a follow-up on the preceding experiment, Katz, Roberts, and Robinson (in press) investigated the effects of three factors on Negro students' efficiency; the race of the task administrator, the difficulty of the task, and the evaluative significance of the task. All subjects were students at a Southern Negro college. Half of them were tested individually by a Negro adult and the other half were tested by a white adult. In addition, one-third of the total sample worked on a relatively easy digit-symbol code, one-third were given a code of medium difficulty, and one-third had to do a relatively hard code. In order to attach a relatively nonthreatening significance to the situation, the task was described as a research instrument for studying eye-hand coordination, a nonintellectual characteristic. Unlike the Katz and Greenbaum experiment, there was no experimental confederate who posed as a second subject. The findings were consistent with results obtained in the low-threat condition of the earlier study—Negro subjects worked more efficiently when tested by a white adult than when tested by a Negro adult. However, the favorable influence of the white administrator was apparent only on the most difficult of the three tasks. On the two easier codes there were no statistically reliable differences in achievement associated with the skin color of the experimenters. Apparently the easier tasks were too simple to reflect the differences in motivation.

Then two additional groups of Negro students were tested by the same Negro and white administrators on the most difficult task only. But instead of being told that the task measured eye-hand coordination, it was presented to these subjects as a test of intelligence. Now the subjects did not attain higher scores in the presence of a white experimenter; rather, the effect of the IQ instructions was to slightly elevate performance with a

Negro tester and to lower scores markedly in the white-tester group, so that the means for both testers were at about the same level. Thus, in this experiment, making the most difficult task relevant to intellectual ability had effects not unlike those of strong threat in the previous study by Katz and Greenbaum (1963). On the assumption that intellectual instructions were more highly motivating than the motor-test instructions, one can again apply the Hullian interpretation that motivation in the IQ-test—white-administrator treatment was excessive.

More directly relevant is Atkinson's (1958a) conception of motivation as a joint function of the subjective probability and incentive value of success, which was discussed earlier. Assuming again that a white experimenter has higher prestige for the Negro student than does a Negro experimenter, the prospect of eliciting the white person's approval would be more attractive. It follows that when the likelihood of winning approval by scoring well is equally high whether the tester is Negro or white, the subject will work harder for the white person. Thus, in this experiment Negro students performed better with a white adult than with a Negro adult when the task was supposed to assess an ability which Negroes are not stereotyped as lacking (eye-hand coordination). Presenting the task as an intelligence test ought to have raised the incentive value of achievement in both racial conditions, with perhaps an even greater increment occurring when the experimenter was white (since *intellectual* approval by a white adult might be uniquely gratifying to the Negro students' self-esteem.)

But suppose that on the intellectual task the Negro subject saw very little likelihood of meeting the white experimenter's standard of excellence. Unless the incentive strength of success increased enough to counterbalance the drop in subjective probability, Atkinson's model would predict a reduction in task motivation. As an additional source of impairment in this situation, low expectancy of success could have aroused fear of earning the white tester's *dis*approval (failure threat).

Turning now to the situation where the tester is Negro, there is no reason to assume that the subject's expectation of success would be markedly lower when the task was described as intellectual than when it was presented as a motor test. In both instances the racial identity of the tester would tend to suggest to the subject that he was to be compared with other Negroes. Accordingly, performance with the Negro tester ought to go up under IQ instructions. The fact that it rose only slightly in our experiment may be ascribed to the subject's unclarity about the tester's frame of reference for evaluating his score. That is, he was not actually informed whether he would be compared with norms for Negro students only, or with norms for *all* college students. The next study deals directly with this issue.

Effects of Variations in Anticipated Comparison

Katz, Epps, and Axelson (1964) investigated the effects on Negro students' digit-symbol performance of being told that they would be compared intellectually with other Negro students or with white students. Hard and easy versions of the digit-symbol task were administered to different groups of students at a Southern Negro college under three different instructions: no test, scholastic aptitude test with own college norms, and scholastic aptitude test with national (i.e., predominantly white) college norms. Scores in all three conditions were reliably different from one another, with highest achievement occurring in the Negro-norms condition, intermediate achievement in the white-norms condition, and lowest achievement when no comparison was expected. These differences tended to be larger on the hard task than on the easy one.

Again referring to Atkinson's model, Negro performance was lowest in the no-test condition because of low incentive, while the difference between the two test conditions was due to higher subjective probability of success (closer to .50) when Negro subjects believed they were competing with members of their own race than when they expected to be compared with whites.

White students from a nearby state university were tested under comparable instructions on the hard task only. It was found that scores of the two norms groups—i.e., own college and national—did not differ, and *both* groups were more efficient than subjects in the no-comparison condition.

Future research[1] can determine the usefulness of this application of Atkinson's theory for understanding Negro behavior in integrated schools. For example, the present formulation predicts that if the subjective probability of success were held constant, Negro subjects would perform *better* on certain types of intellectual test when the administrator was white than when he was Negro or when they were competing with white peers rather than with Negro peers.

A Pilot Experiment on the Effect of Probability Feedback

In a recent pilot study (unpublished), done in preparation for a larger experiment, students at a Southern Negro college were individually given a digit-symbol task by a white administrator under two conditions of probability of success. All subjects performed an initial trial under instructions that the task measured intelligence. Upon completing the first trial, every subject was informed that his final score would be compared with racially integrated norms. Half of all the subjects were told, in addition, that on the basis of their first-trial scores there was a statistical probability of about 60% that their final scores would exceed the mean for their age group. Then a second trial was administered to everyone. It was found that subjects who

---

1. Research carried out subsequent to the preparation of this article is reviewed in Katz (1967). It suggests, among other things, that bi-racial peer comparison is facilitating of Negro performance because it provides useful *information* for self-evaluation by Negroes. This is distinct from the effect of bi-racial peer comparison on *incentives*.

were given the probability information performed better on the second trial than those who were not. This preliminary investigation gives further weight to the suggestion that the perceived probability of success is an important determinant of Negro reactions to competition with whites.

Emotional Reactions to Test Situations

Another line of investigation has to do with the appraisal of Negro subjects' emotional reactions to various test situations. In connection with the earlier discussion of failure threat, reference was made to the research of Sarason and his associates (Sarason, 1960; Sarason *et al.*, 1960) on emotional factors in the test-taking behavior of white school children. In their view, the child who chronically experiences anxiety when tested is reacting with strong unconscious hostility to the adult tester, who he believes will in some way pass judgment on his adequacy. The hostility is not openly expressed, but instead is turned inward against the self in the form of self-derogatory attitudes, which strengthen the child's expectation of failure and his desire to escape the situation. Thus, he is distracted from the task before him by his fear of failure and his impulse to escape.

Sarason has not as yet presented direct evidence that situations of adult evaluation arouse hostility in highly test-anxious children. However, in clinical studies by Lit (1956), Kimball (1952), and Harris (1961), difficulty in expressing aggression openly was found to be associated with scholastic underachievement. Rosenwald (1961) found that students who were relatively unwilling to give aggressive responses on a projective test showed greater impairment in solving anagrams after a hostility induction than did students who showed less inhibition of aggression on the projective test. Goldman, Horwitz, and Lee (1954) demonstrated an association between the degree to which strong hostility against an instigator was denied expression and the amount of disruption of intellectual functioning.[2]

These studies are pertinent to the problem of Negro children's learning efficiency in integrated classrooms, because these children often have to suppress strong hostility. It was seen that Yarrow (1958) found a much higher incidence of covert symptoms of emotional disturbance in Negro children than in white children at a desegregated summer camp. White children, it will be recalled, aggressed openly against their Negro cabin mates, but the latter did not respond in kind. Rather, they tended to deny aggressive impulses in themselves and to show heightened alertness to aggressive behavior in other Negro children. Another investigator who has reported stronger trends toward denial of hostile impulses in Negro children than in white children is Karon (1958), who examined individual personality by means of a projective technique, the Picture Arrangement Test.

It was suggested earlier that when the administrator of an intellectual test is white, or when comparison with white peers is anticipated, Negro

2. Reported more fully in Horwitz (1963).

subjects tend to become fearful of failure. Anticipation of failure would tend to generate feelings of victimization and covert hostility against the white tester. Since hostility against white authorities is dangerous, the hostile impulse would be strongly inhibited. Katz, Robinson, Epps, and Waly (in press) undertook to find out whether suppression of hostile responses occurs when a white adult makes Negro students take an intelligence test. Negro male students at a segregated high school in the South were given a test of aggression disguised as a concept-formation test. It consisted of 58 four-word items, with instructions to "circle the word that does not belong with the others." In half of the items one word had aggressive meaning, one word was nonaggressive, and two words were ambiguous. Hence the subject could choose either a hostile or a neutral concept. Two equivalent forms of the test were administered on successive days. On the first day it was given informally to all subjects by a Negro teacher. The following day the entire sample was divided into four groups, each of which was tested by either a white or a Negro adult stranger, with instructions that described the task as either an intelligence test or a research instrument.

The results show that when neutral instructions were used on the second day, average scores in both the white-tester and Negro-tester groups were the same as on the pretest. But in the intelligence-test condition, hostility scores *increased* over the previous day when the experimenter was a Negro, and they *decreased* when the experimenter was white. The authors' interpretation is that both administrators instigated hostile impulses in the subjects when they announced that the task would be used to evaluate intelligence; when the adult authority was a Negro person, students revealed their annoyance by responding to the aggressive connotations of ambiguous words, but when the adult was a white person, the need to deny hostile feelings resulted in avoidance of aggressive word meanings. (The "denial" interpretation is of course inferential, since the results merely show that hostility scores in the white-adult–IQ-test condition went down; there was no *direct* evidence of increased emotional conflict in this condition.)

Assuming that these findings actually reflect variations in ability to express hostile impulses under different testing conditions, they furnish an interesting clue as to the nature of emotional processes attendant upon the disruption of Negro students' performance in the white-adult–IQ-test condition of an earlier experiment (Katz, Roberts, and Robinson, in press).

Summary

Experiments on Negro male college students by the author and his associates have shown that in work teams composed of Negro and white students of similar intellectual ability, Negroes are passively compliant, rate their own performance as inferior even when it is not, and express less satisfaction with the team experience than do their white companions. These results are seen as due to social threat and/or failure threat. Later studies have sought to identify specific situational determinants of Negro behavior in bi-racial settings.

Forcing Negro subjects into attempts to influence nonhostile white partners in problem solving had the effect of increasing their ascendancy on another task with the same white partner, apparently mainly through reduction of their fear of instigating hostility.

Experimentally creating a verbal-task situation that was low in both social threat and failure threat resulted in better performance by Negroes in the presence of whites than in the presence of other Negroes, suggesting that the incentive value of success was greater in the white environment. But when threat of strong electric shock was introduced, the white setting became less favorable to performance than the Negro one. Thus *vulnerability* to stress was greater in the white condition, even though it was not apparent until a strong explicit threat was introduced.

The evaluative significance of a verbal task (e.g., whether it was described as a perceptual-motor test or an intellectual test) interacted with race of the tester in determining Negro performance in a manner consistent with the notions that (*a*) the incentive value of success was higher with a white tester than with a Negro tester, and (*b*) the probability of success was lower with a white tester than with a Negro tester only when the task was defined intellectually.

Anticipated intellectual comparison with Negro peers was found to produce a higher level of verbal performance than anticipated comparison with white peers, in accordance with the assumption that the subjective probability of success was lower when the expected comparison was with whites. Also, performance was facilitated when a white tester raised the subject's expectancy of attaining a white standard of performance by giving him suitable "information" about his score on a previous trial.

Finally, suppression of hostile impulses appeared to occur in Negro students who were tested by a white adult, but not in those who were tested by a Negro adult.

References

ATKINSON, J. W.   Motivational determinants of risk taking behavior. In J. W. Atkinson (Ed.), *Motives in fantasy, action, and society.* New York: Van Nostrand, 1958. Pp. 322-340. (a)

ATKINSON, J. W.   Towards experimental analysis of human motives in terms of motives, expectancies, and incentives. In J. W. Atkinson (Ed.), *Motives in fantasy, action, and society.* New York: Van Nostrand, 1958. Pp. 288-305. (b)

BASS, B. M.   Conformity, deviation, and a general theory of interpersonal behavior. In I. A. Berg and B. M. Bass (Eds.), *Conformity and deviation.* New York: Harper, 1961. Pp. 38-100.

BOVARD, E. W.   The effects of social stimuli on the response to stress. *Psychological Review,* 1959, 66, 267-277.

CRISWELL, J. H.   A sociometric study of race cleavage in the classroom. *Archives of Psychology*, 1939, No. 235.

DEESE, J.   Skilled performance and conditions of stress. In R. Glaser (Ed.), *Training research and education*. Pittsburgh: Univer. Pittsburgh Press, 1962. Pp. 199-222.

DITTES, J. E. and KELLEY, H. H.   Effects of different conditions of acceptance upon conformity to group norms. *Journal of Abnormal and Social Psychology*, 1956, 53, 100-107.

EASTERBROOK, J. A.   The effect of emotion on cue utilization and the organization of behavior. *Psychological Review*, 1959, 66, 183-201.

FRENCH, J. R. P., JR. and RAVEN, B.   The bases of social power. In D. Cartwright and A. Zander (Eds.), *Group dynamics*. (2nd ed.) Evanston, Ill.: Row, Peterson, 1960. Pp. 607-623.

GOLDMAN, M., HORWITZ, M. and LEE, F. J.   Alternative classroom standards concerning management of hostility and effects on student learning. *Office of Naval Research Technical Report*, 1954.

GROUP FOR THE ADVANCEMENT OF PSYCHIATRY.   *Psychiatric aspects of school desegregation*. New York: GAP, 1957.

HARRIS, I.   *Emotional blocks to learning*. Glencoe, Ill.: Free Press, 1961.

HOROWITZ, E.   The development of attitudes toward the Negro. *Archives of Psychology*, 1936, No. 194.

HORWITZ, M.   Hostility and its management in classroom groups. In W. W. Charters and N. L. Gage (Eds.), *Readings in the social psychology of education*. Boston: Allyn & Bacon, 1963. Pp. 196-212.

KARON, B. P.   *The Negro personality: a rigorous investigation of the effects of culture*. New York: Springer, 1958.

KATZ, I.   Desegregation or integration in public schools? The policy implications of research. Paper prepared for National Conference on Equal Educational Opportunity in America's Cities, U.S. Commission on Civil Rights, Washington, D.C., Nov. 16-18, 1967.

KATZ, I. and BENJAMIN, L.   Effects of white authoritarianism in biracial work groups. *Journal of Abnormal and Social Psychology*, 1960, 61, 448-456.

KATZ, I. and COHEN, M.   The effects of training Negroes upon cooperative problem solving in biracial teams. *Journal of Abnormal and Social Psychology*, 1962, 64, 319-325.

KATZ, I., EPPS, E. G. and AXELSON, L. J.   Effect upon Negro digit-symbol performance of anticipated comparison with whites and with other Negroes. *Journal of Abnormal and Social Psychology*, 1964, 69, in press.

KATZ, I., GOLDSTON, J. and BENJAMIN, L.   Behavior and productivity in biracial work groups. *Human Relations*, 1958, 11, 123-141.

KATZ, I. and GREENBAUM, C.   Effects of anxiety, threat, and racial environment on task performance of Negro college students. *Journal of Abnormal and Social Psychology*, 1963, 66, 562-567.

KATZ, I., ROBERTS, S. O. and ROBINSON, J. M.   Effects of difficulty, race of administrator, and instructions on Negro digit-symbol performance, *Journal of Abnormal and Social Psychology*, in press.

KATZ, I., ROBINSON, J. M., EPPS, E. G. and WALY, P.   Effects of race of experimenter and test vs. neutral instructions on expression of hostility in Negro boys. *Journal of Social Issues*, in press.

KIMBALL, B.   Sentence-completion technique in a study of scholastic underachievement. *Journal of Consulting Psychology*, 1952, 16, 353-358.

LIT, J.   Formal and content factors of projective tests in relation to academic achievement. *Dissertation Abstracts*, 1956, 16, 1505-1506.

MANDLER, G. and SARASON, S. B.   A study of anxiety and learning. *Journal of Abnormal and Social Psychology*, 1952, 47, 166-173.

MURSTEIN, B. I. and COLLIER, H. L.   The role of the TAT in the measurement of achievement as a function of expectancy. *Journal of Projective Techniques*, 1962, 26, 96-101.

RADKE, M., SUTHERLAND, J. and ROSENBERG, P.   Racial attitudes of children. *Sociometry,* 1950, 13, 154-171.

ROSEN, M.   Valence, expectancy, and dissonance reduction in the prediction of goal striving. *Dissertation Abstracts,* 1961, 21, 3846.

ROSENWALD, G.   The assessment of anxiety in psychological experiments. *Journal of Abnormal and Social Psychology,* 1961, 63, 666-673.

SARASON, I. G.   Empirical findings and theoretical problems in the use of anxiety scales. *Psychological Bulletin,* 1960, 57, 403-415.

SARASON, S. B., DAVIDSON, K. S., LIGHTHALL, F. F., WAITE, R. R. and RUE-BUSH, B. K.   *Anxiety in elementary school children.* New York: Wiley, 1960.

SPENCE, K. W.   A theory of emotionally based drive (D) and its relation to performance in simple learning situations. *American Psychologist,* 1958, 13, 131-141.

TAYLOR, J. A.   Drive theory and manifest anxiety. In Martha T. Mednick and S. A. Mednick (Eds.), *Research in personality.* New York: Holt, Rinehart and Winston, 1963. Pp. 205-222.

THIBAUT, J. and KELLEY, H. H.   *The social psychology of groups.* New York: Wiley, 1959.

YARROW, M. R.   (Issue Ed.), Interpersonal dynamics in a desegregation process. *Journal of Social Issues,* 1958, 14(1, entire issue).

This chapter from Crain's recent book synthesizes his case studies of school desegregation in eight Northern cities of the United States. The reader might wonder how *any* general hypotheses can be adduced from eight cases covering so complex a matter as the politics of desegregation. Surely the investigators must have been overwhelmed by the utter uniqueness of each case and the infinite variety of the whole. But Crain does adduce general hypotheses. He conducts statistical analyses to support them, like correlations where $N=8$, and he even has the temerity to draw inferences about the direction of causality underlying the correlations. He says, for example, that the level of civil rights activity in Northern cities (boycotts, demonstrations, and the like) did not determine the acquiescence of school board decision makers to such pressures. Just the reverse. School board acquiescence, or the lack of it, determined the level of civil rights activities. Strikes and demonstrations had no bearing on the final outcome.

What is Crain's secret? The student should make a determined effort to fathom it, for it is instructive. For one thing, he did not study everything there was to study about desegregation in each city, but focused on one narrow event, the desegregation decision itself. This helped to make the problem manageable. Crain also used a carefully conceived analytical framework—stages in the desegregation controversy—and superimposed it on the eight cases. The overlay revealed strands of similarity in the variety. And the framework (or "accounting scheme," as Lazarsfeld and Rosenberg call it in *The Language of Social Research*, Free Press, 1955) had a time dimension in it so that antecedent events could be distinguished from consequent events and the direction of causation could be unravelled. The student can take it from here.

School System Acquiescence to Pressures for Desegregation*

Robert L. Crain

This is an analysis of the way in which eight northern American city school systems,[1] faced with demands for the elimination of *de facto* segregation, made decisions regarding school integration.

Politics, however it is defined, is mainly concerned with the process by which groups of people make decisions that are binding on the members of the group. Studies like this one, which focus on a single decision as it is made in different cities, are one way to approach the study of urban politics. Of course, no theory can be derived from studying a single issue, and therefore this sort of study will need to be repeated for other types of decisions. But this disadvantage is more than compensated for by the fact that concentrating on a single decision permits us to examine simultaneously a number of cities and to determine not only how the decision is made in each city, but also what factors cause cities to differ.

School integration is an interesting issue for our purposes because it is a new issue. Rigid decision-making techniques have not yet been developed, and the range of possible outcomes is large. Furthermore, decisions are made in highly ambiguous situations where there are no simple formulas to follow. Thus, the decision will vary from one place to another, and we can expect this variation to be caused not by trivial differences in administrative structure, but by differences in basic political style. Our analysis suggests that this is indeed the case. Cities that resemble each other in their handling of school integration have fundamental political similarities. For example, the most important factor determining the behavior of the school boards we studied seems to be the amount of influence in the hands of the civic elite—the businessmen and others who participate in city decision making from outside the government and the political parties.

In addition, the study serves a quite different function. It describes one aspect of one of the most important social movements in recent American history. Some writers have seen the 1954 Supreme Court decision as the

* Reprinted from Robert L. Crain, *The politics of school desegregation.* (with the assistance of M. Inger, G. A. McWorter and J. J. Vanecko) Chicago: Aldine Publishing Company, 1968, chs. 1, 11. Copyright © 1968 by National Opinion Research Center. Used by permission of the author and publisher.

1. St. Louis, Mo.; Lawndale (pseudonym for a medium-sized Western city); Bay City (pseudonym for a large New England city); Newark, N. J.; Buffalo, N.Y.; Baltimore, Md.; San Francisco, Calif.; Pittsburgh, Pa.

most important single cause of the "Negro revolution," and in the northern cities we studied, school integration has frequently been the leading edge of the civil rights movement. A good look at this issue, and the way it has been handled, may help us to understand and anticipate the future course of race relations in America.

In the past, most of our information about school integration has come from newspapers and news magazines, and they have presented a highly distorted picture. The national press usually portrays the school system and the civil rights movement as two uncompromising opponents. Newspapers report the conflicts in detail—the picketing, the boycotts, the resignations of superintendents, and the role of race in school board election campaigns. Conflict is news. Peace is not. The newspapers have not given the public a systematic picture—a census of where the news is good as well as where it is bad. This is also a goal of our study.

But in this study we try to be more than systematic journalists. We also want to spell out more precisely the nature of the school desegregation issue. The prevailing myths—that civil rights leaders want total integration immediately and that they would rather demonstrate than negotiate, that school superintendents are narrow-minded autocrats, that school boards are representatives of a segregationist power structure, that white voters will rise up in arms at the first sign of a school bus—are, we think, simply not true. One of our main concerns is to estimate precisely what civil rights leaders expect from the schools and what they are willing to accept and how school boards, school administrators, and voters feel about the issue. Perhaps we only reflect the social scientist's faith that things look simpler when we understand them, but we think that the school integration issue is less complicated and less irrational than it has been made to look.

Another goal of the study is to explain differences between cities. Why was there so much controversy in San Francisco and so little in Baltimore? Since school desegregation decisions are made by groups of people (school boards) which are influenced by other groups of people (the civil rights movements), it therefore follows that differences in the kinds of decisions made will depend upon differences in the composition and interests of these groups. From this common-sense perspective, school integration is merely one of the many issues handled by local government. This study can then add to our general knowledge of the community and, conversely, the recent renaissance in the study of local governments and community structure can provide some conceptual tools to look at civil rights and the schools. This returns to the first goal of the study—by understanding the way in which many cities handled a common issue we can develop some general ideas about how American public schools and American cities are governed.

Research Design

Our method was essentially that of the case study. The great advantage of the case study is that it makes minimal restrictions on the research. The observer can feel free to pursue a particular hypothesis as far as his imagination and the cooperation of his respondents will permit. In each city, we tried to answer seven very general questions:

1. What is the issue? Who wants integration, and what do they mean? Who is opposed? Why? (Can we distinguish between the demands publicly made by the civil rights leaders and the philosophy which lies behind the demands? Similarly, can we find fundamental attitudes behind the position held by the other actors?)

2. Who are the actors? How many persons participate in developing a demand for integration? Who are the actors who decide how to reply to the demand? (Was the decision made by the school board, the superintendent, the power elite, the mayor?)

3. What are the channels of communication and influence that connect the actors to each other and to the holders of various kinds of power? (Is poor communication an important factor in the creation of controversy? Does the school board tend to go to influential persons for help?)

4. What resources did the various actors have at their disposal (votes, prestige, money, etc.)?

5. What are the factors that placed the particular men in decision-making positions? (Does an appointed school board differ from an elected one? Under what conditions do militants take over leadership of a civil rights organization?)

6. Is there a relationship between the behavior of the actors in the school integration issue and the general structure of politics in the city?

7. What is the relationship between the behavior of elites and that of the masses? To what extent do the masses depend upon the leadership for cues concerning when a "spontaneous" protest for or against desegregation should occur?

We also tried to trace the causes of variation in school integration decisions back to fundamental characteristics of the city: its population composition, its economy, and its political structure. This would have been impossible if we had restricted ourselves to highly specific data. But instead, we tried to collect as much related, miscellaneous information as possible about each city.

The great disadvantage of the case study is that it is time consuming, and in the past this has meant that one social scientist studied only one city.[2] The single case study has some serious drawbacks, since it is impossible to know whether the conditions reported are unique or whether they are representative.

Empirical research on the community is fundamentally no different from empirical research in any other area; it simply aims to establish relationships that exist between variables. To note that both competitive politics

2. Some recent valuable exceptions to this statement in the area of community decision-making are the studies by Banfield and Wilson (1963), Williams and Adrian (1963), and Agger, Goldrich and Swanson (1964); all were based on comparisons between a number of cities.

and large public expenditures for projects such as urban renewal are present in New Haven is not very helpful. We need to know whether these two variables are systematically linked in most cities.

Our research budget would have permitted a complete case study of one or two cities; but two cities would not be sufficient for this purpose. There would be a great risk of selecting a biased sample. We could have studied one hundred cities, if we had limited ourselves to the study of two or three variables. But we could not take chances on our ability to guess which were the crucial variables. Our solution to the dilemma was a rather novel research design. We selected fifteen cities, eight in the North and seven in the South, by modified random sampling scheme (Crain, 1968, Appendix I), based on size, geographical location, and percentage of the Negro population.

In each city we made a case study. We then selected what we thought were the key variables and assigned each city scores on each variable, so that survey-style statistical analysis could be used. This design gave us the advantage of the case study, since we could search for the most important factors in each case, and also permitted at least a tentative demonstration that these factors were important in all our cities. We were able to stay within a research budget by taking the smallest number of cities that would permit comparative analysis and then economizing on data collection techniques.

The data were collected by a team of two or three interviewers who usually spent one week in each city. During that time they interviewed most of the members of the school board, the leaders of the civil rights movement, local informants such as newspapermen or social scientists who were familiar with the local situation, and, where possible, key elites such as the mayor or the most influential businessmen. We collected, on the average, twenty-two interviews per city, ranging from thirty minutes to eight hours in length. The interviews focused upon determining what was demanded by the civil rights movement, what the school system did in response, and what actions (demonstrations, suits, countersuits, etc.) took place or were threatened. In the process of collecting these data, we found out who the most important actors were. We interviewed these men to determine the pattern of communication and the channels of influence that connected them and to determine their personal characteristics—in particular their social origins and their political ideology. We then began tracing the reasons why these particular men were in decision-making positions by trying to find out how persons are recruited to these roles and obtaining information about the community's general political and civic structure. Finally, in each city the interviewers gathered several pounds of printed documents—school board minutes, reports, complete sets of newspaper clippings, and even copies of private correspondence.

Our fears that a week of interviewing in each city would not be enough time proved to be unfounded. We had no difficulty in learning the detailed story of the decision; there may be some well-kept secrets that we did not uncover, but we think that in almost every city we have a story complete enough for analysis. In addition, we found, as other researchers have noted, that a clear impression of the particular "tone" or "style" of a city is immediately apparent, although sometimes we were not successful in identifying all the factors that make up a city's "style" of action.

It would be pleasant to pretend that we had conducted a total analysis—one that considered every possible factor and then developed the relationship of each variable to the outcome of the integration controversy. Of course, one cannot design research that will do this. However, by the use of open-ended interviewing, a flexible data collection schedule, and a willingness to rewrite the questionnaires repeatedly, we were able to keep in mind many possible hypotheses. In addition, we often found that when a hypothesis developed from our study of one city, we could search the files and our memories for the necessary data to make at least a rough test of the hypothesis in the cities we had visited earlier.

Selected Results

In this article we shall use a comparative analysis of the eight cities to demonstrate two facts: first, that the behavior of the school board is largely independent of the extent of civil rights activity; second, that the outcome of the school integration issue is very largely dependent upon the character of the school board.

The Stages of the Decision Process

Following our case analysis (Crain, 1968, chs. 2-9, 10), we are in a position to construct the profile of the typical northern school integration controversy. The issue seems to divide itself into six stages. We can describe the controversies in all eight cities in terms of these stages.

STAGE 1: APPEARANCE OF THE ISSUE. The desegregation issue does not arise in a vacuum. In each of our cities civil rights groups had previously made occasional statements, and in some cases there was a full-scale discussion of some issue. Usually these events were of minor importance or were far enough in the past to have little effect on the present negotiations. Some time after 1961, the issue was raised again. This time, however, the groups who presented the request were armed with the tactics developed by the southern civil rights movement and the legal precedent of the *New Rochelle* case. The demands may vary from concrete (opposing a proposed boundary line for a new school) to procedural (demanding the preparation of a report on *de facto* segregation) to highly symbolic (demanding the adoption of a policy statement).

STAGE 2: THE REJECTION OF THE DEMANDS. In most cases this initial complaint was rejected, and in several cases the civil rights movement interpreted this as an insult. In St. Louis and Baltimore, the board appointed committees to prepare reports on the question; in both cases the school administration released a report first which denied every charge made. In Bay City the board refused to make the requested policy statement. In Lawndale and San Francisco the superintendent issued statements rejecting the demands. In Newark the board refused to reconsider the Vailsburg school situation. Only in Buffalo and Pittsburgh did the board take a particularly sympathetic position to these first demands, and only the Pittsburgh board actually did anything—they adopted an open enrollment plan at the next meeting.

These initial rejections of demands can be seen as the result of three different factors: the delegation of authority to the superintendents, who are opposed to expanding the school's value system to include integration as a goal; the reluctance of the school board to deal with an issue which has not yet become very salient, and the school board's distrust or disapproval of the civil rights movement.

STAGE 3: THE FIRST CIVIL RIGHTS ACTION. The civil rights leadership next proceeds to call the issue to the board's attention more forcibly. In most cases this means threatening demonstrations. In Baltimore, it meant preparing the report, threatening to release it to the press, and then threatening to bring suit. In Bay City the first school boycott was held. In Newark suit was filed. The effect of these first demonstrations was to make it clear that the issue would not be a transient one, and that the board would soon be forced to take a clear public position on the issue.

STAGE 4: THE KEY RESPONSE. At this point, the school board makes a response, which we call the key response, simply because it sets the tone for almost all the later actions. In most cases, the body which makes this decision (except in Newark, the school board) makes all later ones as well. The actions taken at this point tended to be more favorable to the civil rights movement than anything the board did previously. In St. Louis the Maher report was more favorable than the earlier administration report; similarly, the Baltimore board began to look as if it would not support Superintendent Brain's position. Newark adopted open enrollment in order to settle the suit out of court. In San Francisco the board agreed to close the proposed Central Junior High School. In Buffalo and Lawndale, however, the board rejected the demands of the civil rights movement.

STAGE 5: ESCALATION AND RESOLUTION. By its action, the board has taken a position, and in the eyes of the civil rights movement "has shown its true colors." If the board has begun to acquiesce to the demands made of it, continued demonstrations will be accompanied by negotiations until additional concessions are made. Three things can happen: the civil rights leadership will be satisfied and drop the issue; the school board can publicize certain concessions that will tend to satisfy the general Negro community leaders or the Negro community as a whole, thus cutting off the movement's grass roots support; or the civil rights movement will remain dissatisfied, but will be unable to find a particular issue to focus on. In this last case, the issue will remain dormant for a period of time, only to spring up again later. Baltimore is the best example of the first case; St. Louis is a good example of the second case; and San Francisco and Newark are cases where the issue was resolved, but only temporarily.

In the remaining cities the issue was not resolved. Here demonstrations in protest of the board's position increased in intensity. In some cases they were not directed so much to bringing about negotiations, but were efforts to embarrass and therefore punish the board for its failure. Since the position of the civil rights leadership tends to be directed toward bringing the board members to a position supporting racial equality, it defines those board members who do not respond as immoral; since they are immoral, they should be punished. The board may reply in similar language, attempting to define the protesters as themselves lacking in moral qualities; they may, for example, emphasize that the movement is made up of beatniks, Communists, or just "troublemakers." At this point the issue has escalated beyond a point of resolution, and in principle this state of affairs could continue indefinitely.

It is interesting to note that the comparison of the case studies suggests that demonstrations, once they have succeeded in raising the issue, have little effect on the board's behavior. The board has committed itself in what we have called the "key" response and continues on this line thereafter. If the key response was favorable to the movement, then continued low-pressure demonstrations will be sufficient to extract the additional concessions which the movement wants. But if the initial response was not favorable, more intensified demonstrations will do little to change the public attitude of the board. Additional concessions will be given grudgingly if at all. However, the increased pressure may have the important effect of bringing other actors onto the scene. The second boycott in Bay City resulted in state intervention, for example. Similarly, it was rumored that large-scale demonstrations in Buffalo would have caused State Commissioner of Education James Allen to intervene. (The demonstrations flopped, but the commissioner did take action when the Buffalo NAACP petitioned his office formally.)

STAGE 6: INTRODUCTION OF NEW ACTORS. If the state commissioner or some other new actor enters the picture, the issue is drastically redefined. The board is no longer negotiating with the civil rights movement, but with a figure of authority. Thus, the board is provided with a new frame of reference. If integration is necessary in order to conform to state law, then few school boards will oppose integration. The entry of the state (or federal) authority is also gratifying to the civil rights movement. The school board has taken an immoral stand; the state has therefore rebuked them. Higher authority has recognized the principle of racial equality. Because it clarifies the issue so well, it may be to the school board's advantage to encourage state or federal intervention. The school board will sacrifice some freedom, but it is not obvious that they will regret the loss.

Acquiescence

In order to capture the element of "tone" in the response of school boards, we will define a special variable called acquiescence. Acquiescence can be thought of as the extent to which the school board acted to bring the civil rights movement closer to its goals, both welfare and symbolic. Thus, acquiescence must consist of two elements—actions taken to further integration or upgrade education for Negroes, and actions that recognize the value of racial equality and the legitimacy of the civil rights movement. Acquiescence can be defined for any particular period of time, but throughout most of the study we will define it for the entire period from the first raising of the issue to the time of our interviewing.[3] This rank ordering, like most of those to be presented in this report, is subjective. In this case it was developed by first having the interviewers fill out a questionnaire summarizing the actions taken by the school system. Armed with these questionnaires, the staff met several times to clarify the definition of acquiescence and agree upon a rank ordering. We cannot demonstrate with "hard" numerical data that this is the correct rank ordering; instead, we will describe in detail the basis for this ranking of the cities.[4]

First, let us consider our ranking of cities based only upon the specific actions taken. We were unable to arrive at a complete rank ordering and were forced to permit some ties. In particular, is was difficult to distinguish between the two cities which seemed to have done the most to meet the specific demands of the civil rights movement, and the two cities which have done the least. Our ranking is as follows; for each city we have listed the factors that seem most important in locating the city on the scale.

3.   This time period does not include the 1965 controversy in Pittsburgh, nor the integration plan adopted by Buffalo that year.

4.   Since this use of "subjective" ratings of the cities on variables may properly be considered suspect, we should perhaps point out how it differs from more conventional techniques of analysis. In any analysis we are concerned with the correlation between two variables, which we shall call A and B. Ordinarily, we measure A and B with "indicators." Indicators are usually measures taken from a questionnaire or from some other "hard" source of data, so that there is little opportunity for bias to enter the analysis. However, the indicator is very frequently not an exact measure of the variable with which we are concerned. Furthermore, it is usually impossible to know what the true relationship between the indicator and the variable is. And bias does enter, in an important way, in the choice of indicator. Once the indicators which connect the two variables are agreed upon, routine statistical analysis can be used from this point on. Schematically, the result is shown in the accompanying figure.

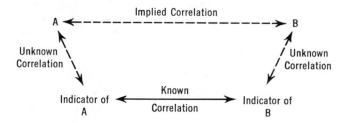

The existence of a correlation between *A* and *B* can be assumed only if there is a correlation between the two indicators, there is a high correlation between the two indicators and the two variables which they are assumed to measure and if *A* and *B* are unbiased indicators. There is relatively little opportunity for the investigator's bias to enter, but there is a good deal of opportunity for unknown bias and error. The result is that it is usually very difficult to make any statement about the size of the true correlation between *A* and *B*; even if the correlation between *A* and *B* is high, we can expect the use of the two indicators to give us a much lower measured correlation; on the other hand, a low measured correlation could be the result of bias or some other error, without a real correlation between *A* and *B*.

We have chosen to approach this problem in a different way. We have not used indicators, but have instead measured subjectively the magnitude of the real variables and performed our analysis with these subjective measures. This procedure should increase the amount of bias but decrease the other kinds of errors. In our judgment the technique we have used is preferable for this particular problem, but of course we cannot prove that this is a better procedure.

1-2 *Baltimore and St. Louis* are tied for most acquiescent. Baltimore's large-scale increases in bussing, its total elimination of double shift, and its expansion of open enrollment qualify it for first place; St. Louis' integration of the bussing program greatly increased the amount of integration. In addition St. Louis increased teacher integration, adopted open enrollment, and has a widely publicized and apparently successful compensatory education project.

3 *Pittsburgh*, which began limited bussing, adopted open enrollment and has a highly regarded compensatory education program. We rank Pittsburgh below Baltimore and St. Louis because the number of students affected by desegregation is not as large as in the other two cities.

4 *San Francisco* met the specific demands of the movement by closing Central Junior High School and building schools as requested. However, it did not adopt any general program which increased integration as the first three cities did.

5 *Newark*, which adopted open enrollment and met the specified demands to reassign the students from the Hawthorne school, has done little else to further integration. Like San Francisco, its program of bussing to relieve overcrowding has not figured directly in the integration issue. It also has not met various criticisms of the education in Negro schools.

6,7,8 It is difficult to distinguish among the last three cities, all of which have refused some demands made but have also made other concessions. *Buffalo* refused to integrate the Woodlawn school, but did integrate other elementary and high schools. (It adopted open enrollment after our interviewing was completed.) *Lawndale* refused to adjust the boundaries of Woodside or permit transfers into it, but it did adopt an open enrollment plan. *Bay City* publicly refused all demands, but in fact was bussing Negroes into integrated schools to relieve overcrowding. Of the three, we rank Buffalo highest, leaving Lawndale and Bay City tied for seventh place.

We next attempted to rank the cities according to the tone of the board's behavior. Tone is mostly dependent upon the public and private statements of the board members or other decision makers to the civil rights leadership.

1-2 Both *Pittsburgh* and *Baltimore* reacted to the movement in highly positive ways. However, we considered that Pittsburgh took some action without being prodded, and that Baltimore's administration was hostile during the first days of the negotiations. Therefore, we placed Pittsburgh ahead of Baltimore.

3-4 We found it difficult to distinguish between *St. Louis* and *San Francisco*, both of whom took a generally pro-integration stance, but were also publicly critical of the civil rights movement. However, we felt that San Francisco's refusal to oppose Proposition 14 was sufficient to place it below St. Louis.

5,6,7 *Newark's* board was generally unfriendly to the civil rights movement, but not in a very aggressive way. It remained graciously silent most of the time. *Buffalo,* on the other hand, alternated between some strong anti-civil rights statements from some of the board members and strong pro-integration statements from the superintendent. *Lawndale* took a firm anti-civil rights position, but was not critical of the civil rights leadership. We found it impossible to distinguish among the three cities and left them tied.

8 A review of the case study indicated clearly that *Bay City* qualified for this position.

Our final ranking of acquiescence is simply the average of these two rankings. There is a strong correlation between the two. Whether this was caused by our inability to separate the two factors or by the natural correlation between public attitude and public behavior is difficult to say. The most acquiescent cities are simply those with the lowest ranking on both scales as shown in Table 1. After considerable discussion, we were unable to agree upon the ranking of the first two cities, and left them tied in the ranking.

Civil Rights Activity and the Key Response

Now let us look at some of the relationships among the stages of the decision process as we have described it. First, let us define the key response in each city and look at the effect of civil rights action on the key response and on final acquiescence. The key response is defined as the first response made by the school board after civil rights has been defined as an issue of importance. In keeping with this, we chose the following incidents; they are listed from most to least acquiescent.

1. *Pittsburgh:* adoption of open enrollment after hearing parents' testimony
2. *Baltimore:* decision by ad hoc committee to eliminate districting (June, 1963)

Table 1

RANKING OF CITIES ON ACQUIESCENCE SCALE*

RANKING	NAME OF CITY
1-2	Pittsburgh, Baltimore
3	St. Louis
4	San Francisco
5	Newark
6	Buffalo
7	Lawndale
8	Bay City

* Ranking is from 1 (most acquiescent) to 8 (least acquiescent).

3. *San Francisco:* decision to close Central Junior High School (August, 1962)
4. *Newark:* adoption of open enrollment to settle suit (January, 1962)
5. *St. Louis:* receipt and adoption in general terms of Maher committee report (June, 1963)
6. *Lawndale:* refusal to change Woodside boundaries (January, 1961)
7. *Bay City:* fruitless discussion of *de facto* segregation prior to the first boycott (June, 1963)
8. *Buffalo:* designation of Woodlawn School boundaries (March, 1963)

It should be noted that in most cases the action taken in the key response plays only a partial role in determining the final level of acquiescence for the city.

We noted earlier that the key reponse seems to depend upon the civil rights movement's acting forcefully enough to make it clear that the issue will have to be resolved, but that otherwise the response is relatively independent of the level of civil rights demonstrations. We ranked the eight cities on the level of civil rights activity preceding the key response.[5]

When we compare this ranking to the key response, we see that there is virtually no correlation between the two rankings. Spearman's rank-order correlation coefficient is −.15, indicating a negligible tendency for cities

5. The ranking is as follows, from highest to lowest:

1 *St. Louis:* street demonstrations, partial boycott
2 *Newark:* suit filed
3 *San Francisco:* threats of suits and boycotts
4-5 *Bay City* and *Buffalo:* threat of boycotts
6 *Baltimore:* threat of public release of *Seven Years* report
7 *Lawndale:* testimony of NAACP
8 *Pittsburgh:* testimony of parents' group

with less civil rights activity to be more acquiescent in their key response; the coefficient is far below statistical significance, however. One reason why there is no significant relationship is evident if we contrast Pittsburgh and Newark. Both adopted open enrollment. In the one case the action was criticized; in the other it was accepted. In Newark it seemed clear that open enrollment was accomplished only because of the court suit. The fact that it took a suit to get it left a bitter taste in the mouths of some of the NAACP leadership. On the other hand, the decision in Pittsburgh was unanticipated, and therefore doubly pleasant. Given our definition of the symbolic goals of the movement, this is as it should be. That demonstrations are required is evidence of the school board's unwillingness to endorse integration. Therefore, the more one demonstrates, the more likely it is that the school board will capitulate, but the less value their capitulation will have in paying homage to racial equality as a community value. Demonstrations both encourage and prevent acquiescence. Actually, this is only a minor part of the story. In general there is simply no correlation between the level of civil rights activity and action taken by the board. San Francisco agreed to close Central Junior High School under considerable public pressure; under much less pressure the Baltimore board did more. Presumably neither of these cities would have acted without some pressure from the movement, but how much pressure seems irrelevant.

Let us now move to the next phase, which we have called the period of escalation and resolution. What effect does the key response have on this period? In Figure 1 we have plotted the acquiescence of the key response against the level of the civil rights activity following the response.[6] The

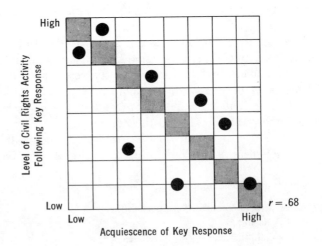

Figure 1.   Influence of Board's Key Response on Subsequent Civil
Rights Activity.

correlation, as one might expect, is negative and of considerable magnitude. The cities that were acquiescent thereby earned themselves a period of grace; those that refused to take action were punished accordingly. Two cities are deviant cases in that there was considerably less civil rights activity than one would expect, so that they are located below the diagonal in Figure 1. They are Lawndale and Newark.

On the basis of this finding, we might expect the school desegregation issue to behave in a cyclic manner in these cities. The cities that initially acquiesce avoid further demonstrations and hence can avoid further concessions, while the initially unresponsive cities are subjected to more demonstrations. Later these cities respond to the demonstrations by becoming more acquiescent, and the demonstrations shift back to the cities which have rested on their laurels. In the long run, all cities become targets for demonstrations, and all cities acquiesce. This is in part true, in the sense that there is not quite as wide a divergence between the most and least acquiescent cities at this time as there once was. But this is a minor part of the story; in general, cities which are acquiescent at the beginning remain most acquiescent.

In Figure 2 we have plotted the acquiescence of the key response against the final acquiescence scale developed in detail earlier. The correlation between the two ratings is very high. Two deviant cases lie above the diagonal (meaning that their later actions were more acquiescent than one would guess from the key response), while the rest are very near it. The deviant cities are St. Louis and Buffalo. St. Louis lies above the line because at the time of the key response, it was still unclear whether the board intended to take action or not. In retrospect, it seems likely that action would have been taken under almost any condition; that Trafford Maher—a man with impeccable credentials as an integrationist—had been asked to head the citizens' committee should have been a tip-off to this. The other case, Buffalo, is simply unstable because of the delicate balance of power between the liberal superintendent and the more conservative school board, and because of changes in the composition of the board.

Thus, we see that the acquiescence of the school board is determined almost at the very beginning of the decision process. It follows as a corollary that the extent of civil rights activity has relatively little influence on the degree to which the school system meets the demands made. Rather, the

6. Our ranking of level of civil rights activity in the period immediately following the key response is as follows, from highest to lowest:

1   *Bay City:* two boycotts, sit-ins, etc.
2   *Buffalo:* demonstrations, a boycott, and a petition to the state department of education
3   *St. Louis:* some picketing, threat of boycott
4   *San Francisco:* testimony, threat of pursuing suit
5   *Baltimore:* threaten suit
6   *Lawndale:* testimony
7-8 *Pittsburgh* and *Newark:* no action

extent of acquiescence determines the level of activity, as we have seen. In Table 2 we have summarized the total civil rights activity over the entire period of the decision,[7] and in Figure 3 we have plotted this against the level of acquiescence. Civil rights activity includes various types of demonstrations, testimony, and threats of demonstrations, and court suits and petitions to other authorities.

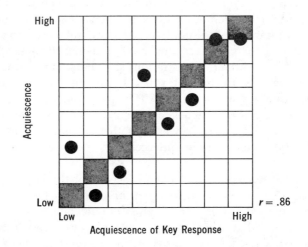

Figure 2.   Relationship of Board's Key Response to Its Final Level of
Acquiescence.

We see that the general negative correlation persists; non-acquiescent cities are faced with the most activity. The correlation is not especially high. More important, there is no single deviant case that can be singled out as lowering the correlation. Throughout the middle range of the figure, there is considerable free variation. Apparently the civil rights activity is not wholly determined by the behavior of the board.

That civil rights activity tends to be caused by level of acquiescence, rather than the other way around supports our thesis that the civil rights movement is concerned with symbols of interracial morality; we might think of the demonstrations as attempts to punish the board for its "sinful" behavior. This may in part explain why the later stages of the decision process in some non-acquiescent cities take on the character of a war, in which punishing the enemy becomes more important than anything else.

Of course, we are neglecting the effect of demonstrations in one city on the national climate of opinion, which in turn affects other cities. Certainly, cities like Pittsburgh seem to have been affected by their desire to avoid the rancorous situations in Chicago, Cleveland, and a dozen other places.

7.   It is difficult to arrive at this ranking of cities in total level of civil rights activity, simply because we must necessarily compare apples and oranges in the process. (How many boycotts are equal to a court suit?)

Table 2

RANKING OF CITIES ON TOTAL AMOUNT OF CIVIL RIGHTS ACTIVITY*

RANKING	NAME OF CITY	AMOUNT OF CIVIL RIGHTS ACTIVITY
1	Bay City	Sit-ins, vigils, street marches, two boycotts, election activity
2	San Francisco	Two suits (one settled, one dropped), intense but sporadic demonstrations
3	Buffalo	No suit, but petition to state commissioner of education, one boycott and one threat of a boycott, limited other demonstrations
4-5	St. Louis and Lawndale	St. Louis threatened a suit, held a limited boycott, threatened a general boycott, and held a street demonstration
		Lawndale did not engage in very much direct action but did file a suit and conducted a well-organized election campaign
6	Newark	Settled suit out of court, and in one neighborhood boycotted a school
7	Baltimore	Threatened a suit, prepared reports
8	Pittsburgh	Prepared reports, testified

* Ranking is from 1 (most activity) to 8 (least activity).

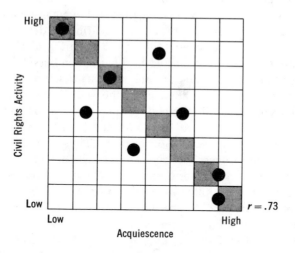

Figure 3.   Relationship between Acquiescence and Amount of Civil Rights Activity.

We can summarize the data shown thus far in two statements:

1. The acquiescence of the school system is determined to a large extent at the beginning of the decision process. It is not greatly affected by the amount of civil rights activity that takes place.

2. The amount of civil rights activity is, however, partly caused by the board response—the less the school system acquiesces, the greater the civil rights activity in retaliation.

The Aquiescent School Board

We are now ready to begin tracing out the causes of the differences between our cities. We shall approach this problem with a conceptual scheme that can be summarized as follows: In the final analysis, a decision is made by the group of men who have the legal authority to make it. They make the decision in the way they do because of the kind of men they are and the kind of pressures operating on them.

In this case the final authority for the decision lies with the school board. They must determine what the issue is, assemble needed information, decide upon their range of alternatives, evaluate the pressures operating on them, and make a decision. Our task is to sort out those factors influencing their decision and decide which ones make important differences. All this is conceptually a simple process. The problems arise from the large number of components, all interacting simultaneously. We have sketched the main components in Figure 4.

The solid lines in the figure represent communication between the incumbents in the various positions and also perceptions of attitudes between actors who are unable to communicate. The dashed lines represent the recruitment of actors to fill the positions. For example, in the top of the figure, we admit to the possibility that the local economic elite can influence the decision two ways—by directly communicating its desires and by having its unspoken desires anticipated (this is the meaning of the solid line); or by participating in the selection of the board members (the dashed line). Let us look first at the solid lines, which represent channels of possible influence. The most important influence on the school board comes from the civil rights movement. While the civil rights movement is trying to influence the board to acquiesce to their demands, the board is also trying to influence the movement to cease demonstrations. Thus, we should have a continuous negotiation process between these two actors. But the board is limited in its possible range of action by influences from the political and economic leaders, by the influence of the superintendent of schools, and by its perception of what the Negro and white voters in the community will accept. The kinds of influence which these actors will exert on the board depend upon a host of factors: the importance to the community of racial peace, the history of previous racial negotiations in other areas of the community, and the balance of political power, to cite three. We can then trace the chain of causation back one more step, by observing that the kinds of pressure exerted (the solid lines) will depend upon the kinds of economic elites, politicians, and voters who are present in the city. This is presumably a function of the background characteristics of the city—the kind of industry, the character of the population, and the formal rules for electing political leaders.

Given this conception of the political process, the background characteristics of the city—its industrial structure, population composition, and its

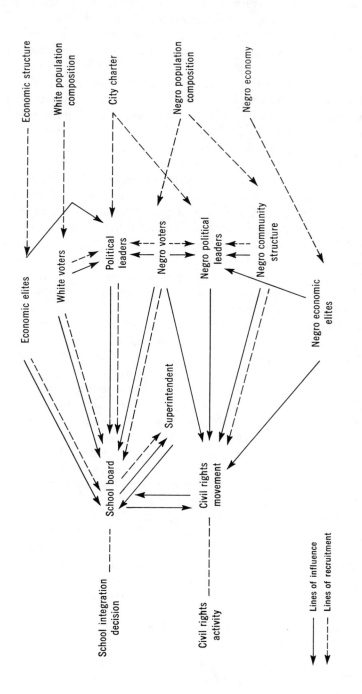

Figure 4. Flow Chart of Recruitment of Decision Makers in School Integration Decision and Channels of Influence Operating on Them.

formal rules for electing city officials—affect the behavior of the school board in three different ways. First, they determine the types of economic elites, voters, and politicians the city will have, and hence the way in which these groups will attempt to influence the school board. Second, by influencing the types of actors in these roles, they in turn influence the recruitment process for the school board, and hence the kind of board members the city has. Third, these background factors influence the relationship between the economic elites, voters, and politicians and hence set a pattern for the amount of influence exerted by each group on both the recruitment process for the school board and the actual school integration decision. For example, a city with a high status population will presumably be more liberal in racial matters, but in addition, a high status city will have a public opinion which will not permit political appointments to the school board. Or, to cite a different causal factor, a city with nonpartisan elections and a strong civil service might have weaker political parties; hence the school board might be more susceptible to influence by the mass of voters.

If we attempt to trace out the ways in which the character of the city might affect the behavior of the civil rights movement, we complete the flow chart of Figure 4. Ultimately, the behavior of the civil rights movement and the school board can be traced to a final cause (for our purposes) in the economy, population, and governmental charter of the city. But the flow chart, with its thirty-five lines of direct influence and indirect influence through recruitment, indicates that there may be as many as one hundred ways in which these factors affect the behavior of the school board. And of course the chart is not complete. There are other structural relationships. For example, the influence of the white economic elites on their Negro counterparts is not shown. There are also factors that cannot easily be represented in the flow chart, such as the influence of recent history on the actors. The model pictured is that of an influence system in equilibrium, where the influences balance each other out in such a way that there is no change. If there were change, we would have to allow for actors who are being influenced by the way things used to be.

We have painted a picture of a hopelessly complex process. Fortunately, the bulk of these possible chains of causation are of no importance. In the first part of this chapter we discussed the goals of the civil rights movement, and from this discussion developed a definition of the key variable—acquiescence. We then found that the tactics of the civil rights movement had relatively little effect on the rank ordering of the cities by acquiescence, and in particular the amount of civil rights activity had no discernible effect. We also accumulated some evidence to show that usually the superintendent had little effect on the final acquiescence score and observed that we could find little evidence of any direct and effective influence on the school board from the political or economic elites. If we are right, the solid lines in Figure 4 can be largely dropped from consideration. Most important, we can avoid any complex analysis of the school board-civil rights movement negotiation process and partition the flow chart into two separate figures—

one showing the factors that influence the board and the other showing the factors that influence the civil rights movement.

We shall next attempt to demonstrate that such a partitioning can be made. First, we shall show that some of the factors which could be expected to correlate with acquiescence if certain influences were operating do not in fact correlate, or do not correlate well. Then we will show that a factor which is not directly related to the kinds of influence the board is subjected to does explain most of the variation.

If the school board were directly influenced by the power of the civil rights movement, then we would assume that the ultimate currency in political influence—the vote—would play a role. Presumably the school board will be most strongly influenced if the civil rights movement is backed by a large bloc of Negro votes. In Figure 5 we have correlated acquiescence with a ranking of the cities by percentage of Negroes living in each city. There is a correlation: the cities with the largest Negro populations are most likely to have acquiescent school boards. The correlation is not very good, however. Four of the cities lie on the main diagonal, but four lie some distance away from it. The correlation is actually a little worse than it looks, for the only sharp break in the percentage Negro comes between the cities which rank fourth and fifth in percentage Negro—Pittsburgh (17 per cent Negro) and Lawndale (28 per cent Negro). But Pittsburgh is very high on the acquiescence scale, and Lawndale very low. (It may be that Lawndale is in a state of political instability, and the present non-acquiescent board will be replaced by a more acquiescent one in the future.) The size of the Negro population does have an effect, but it is not a very large one.

Possibly one reason why percentage Negro does not correlate so well is that the cities with the largest Negro populations have more anti-Negro sentiment among whites. We cannot test this hypothesis directly, but we can look at it indirectly in two ways. The hypothesis is that the pressure from a large Negro population is offset by the stronger anti-Negro sentiment among whites which results from having a larger Negro population. We have no direct measure of the attitudes of whites in each city, but the indirect evidence indicates that the school system is not affected by the attitudes of the white population. Suppose, for example, that we consider the region of the country that each city is located in, in hopes that cities in the far West will be most acquiescent, while those in the border states, with more conservative white voters, will be least so. But when we do this, the result makes no sense. School systems in the liberal West and Northeast are least acquiescent; those in the border states are most acquiescent.

We can also look at the socioeconomic level of the cities. High status persons are less prejudiced, so that boards in high status cities should be most acquiescent. The data do not support this, either. Figure 6, which plots the percentage of the white population who are high school graduates against acquiescence, shows a weak correlation in the opposite direction; high status cities are least acquiescent.

So apparently we are correct in arguing that the board operated inde-

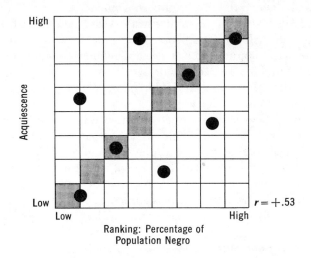

Figure 5.   Percentage of Population Negro and Acquiescence.

pendently of the attitudes of the white population. This is reasonable, of course, since they have no easy way to determine what those attitudes are.

Civil Rights Liberalism

On the basis of these three figures, this approach of searching for community factors which might influence the board does not seem very efficient. Let us instead work backwards, beginning with the characteristics of the board and exploring their cause. The most obvious characteristic is the liberalism of the board members on racial issues: their attitudes toward Negroes, civil rights, and the civil rights movement. We administered a questionnaire containing five agree-disagree questions dealing with attitudes toward race relations and other issues, and found that the questions (listed in Table 3) produced a useful scale. Of the five questions, only the first deals with a simple question of civil rights. Obviously, these school board members believe that whites do not have a "right" to segregated neighborhoods. They also reveal themselves to be much more liberal than the population at large. When a similar question was addressed to a national sample in 1963, only 43 per cent gave the liberal response. Questions 18, 26, and 27 all measure perceptions of the civil rights movement. The respondent is asked, in effect, whether the civil rights movement asks too much, demonstrates too often, or is uncompromising. Of course, there is no obviously right or wrong answer to these questions, but that does not concern us. We only want to know whether one person respects the civil rights movement more than another.

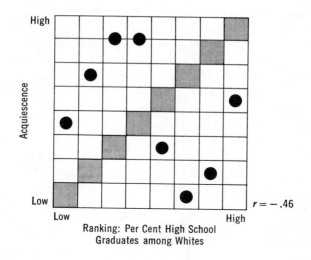

Figure 6. Education of White Population and Acquiescence.

The five questions do seem to measure the same basic factor. People who give liberal responses to the "hard" questions—such as whether Negro leaders are willing to make reasonable compromises—are almost certain to give liberal responses to the other, "easier" questions as well. This is indicated in Table 4, where the association between each pair of questions is indicated

Table 3

QUESTIONS USED TO MEASURE ATTITUDES TOWARD CIVIL RIGHTS

QUESTION	PER CENT SAYING "DISAGREE" OR "TEND TO DISAGREE"	N
7. White people have a right to keep Negroes out of their neighborhoods if they want to, and Negroes should respect that right	91	(45)
18. There is a problem with the civil rights movement because many Negroes are demanding privileges which whites do not have	68	(44)
17. There is no reason to think Negroes will learn more in integrated schools (not used in scale)	61	(44)
26. Most demonstrations have hurt the Negroes' cause more than they have helped	57	(42)
27. In many cases, Negro leaders have not been willing to make reasonable compromises on civil rights issues	43	(21)

by a matrix of Yule's Q's.[8] The fact that all the Q's are high indicates that all the questions tend to tap the same basic attitude.

One might also criticize the questions by arguing that civil rights movements vary from city to city. A school board member in a city with a militant civil rights movement might give a different answer from one in a more peaceful town, without necessarily being more conservative. However, this does not seem to be the case. Most of the questions are worded so vaguely as to be nearly meaningless, and consequently it is very difficult to give an objective answer. In any case, this would not explain the fact that there is a high correlation between the answer to these three questions and the other two, which presumably have nothing to do with local conditions. In constructing the final liberalism scale, we dropped Question 17, which deals specifically with schools, in order to avoid contaminating the data with the actual experience a board member has had. (If he has helped to integrate schools, we might expect him to justify his action by saying that this is educationally beneficial.) This question also has the lowest correlations with the others. The remaining four questions, which have nothing to do

Table 4

ASSOCIATION BETWEEN ITEMS OF CIVIL RIGHTS LIBERALISM SCALE (YULE'S Q)

	ITEM				
ITEM	7	18	17	26	27
7	—	1.00	.72	1.00	1.00*
18		—	.76	.82	.87*
17			—	.57	1.00*
26				—	.95*
27					—

Note: Item 17 was deleted from the final scale.

* These Q's are based on nineteen or twenty cases. All other cells have forty-one or forty-two cases.

with education directly, were then combined into a simple score for each respondent. He was given three points for each "disagree" response, two points each time he said "tend to disagree," one point if he only "tended to agree," and zero if he "agreed." With four questions, this gave us a scale ranging from 0 to 12, 12 being the most liberal response possible. (If a person did not answer one question, his score was developed by extrapolating from the other persons who answered the other three questions the same way he did.) We shall simply refer to the scale as "civil rights liberalism."

8. Q is a measure of the association which ranges from -1 to $+1$. It will be 0 if there is no relationship between the answers to one question and the answers to another. If it is $+1$, as it is in four places in the table, this means that everyone who gave a conservative response to the question numbered in the row (the "easy" question) gave a conservative response to the one numbered in the column (the "hard" question) and everyone who gave a liberal response to the "hard" question gave a liberal response to the "easy" one.

We intend to examine the relationship between the average "civil rights liberalism" of the board and its level of acquiescence. To do this, however, we must first take into consideration the twenty-eight board members who for one reason or another did not fill out this questionnaire. We were able to solve this problem by independently estimating the scale score of everyone in the entire sample, without looking at the data. We found that we could do this rather easily, from other interview data and the person's voting record. The agreement between our estimate and the actual score for the forty-three board members who did respond is shown in Table 5.

The amount of agreement is extremely high ($Q = +.93$), which means that we can estimate with considerable accuracy the position of other board members relative to those who filled out the questionnaire. We then used our estimated scores to locate the median person on each board—the person who fell in the center of the board and hence could be considered the swing vote to make up a liberal or a conservative majority. On the scale from 0 to 12, the medians varied from 9.0 for the most liberal board down to a low of 5.5.

Table 5

ACTUAL CIVIL RIGHTS LIBERALISM SCORES AND INTERVIEWER
ESTIMATES OF LIBERALISM

INTERVIEWER ESTIMATE	ACTUAL SCORE			
	12-15	9-11	5-8	0-4
Liberal	8	11	3	0
Conservative	0	4	10	7

In Figure 7 we have plotted median civil rights liberalism against the acquiescence of the school board. At first glance, the correlation (.65) is disappointingly low. However, a second glance reveals an intriguing pattern. The three cities which fall below the line, being less acquiescent than we would expect from the liberalism score, are all elected boards; the other five are all appointed. The correlation of liberalism with acquiescence is perfect among the three elected boards and the five appointed boards taken separately.

With only eight cases, we must proceed cautiously in our analysis. If we can assume that the elected boards are, because they are elected, less acquiescent, then we can conclude that the median liberalism score of the board explains most if not all of the variations in acquiescence. Can we make this assumption about the effect of elections? It has a certain amount of plausibility. Certainly, if our analysis of Bay City is correct, the refusal of the board members to acquiesce was largely due to the fact that they were in a competition for the votes mobilized by Mrs. Smith, a school board member well known for her anti-integrationist attitudes. And in Lawndale, race was very much an issue in the school board elections.

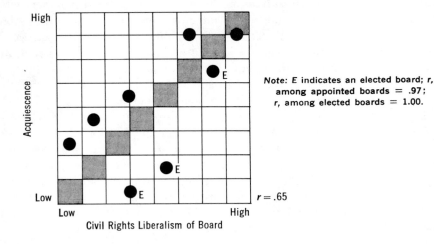

Figure 7.   Civil Rights Liberalism of Board and Acquiescence.

In all three elected boards there was considerable internal friction—even in the elite-controlled St. Louis board. In our analysis of Lawndale we suggested that this conflict within the board seriously hampered the negotiation process. In St. Louis the wide differences in opinion, and the slightly different political bases of different board members, may have slowed the decision process so that the liberal actions taken did not have the tremendous impact on the civil rights movement that they did in Baltimore or Pittsburgh. And in all three cities we believe that there was more thorough newspaper coverage, and hence a higher level of community interest. This also should have the effect of immobilizing the board, at least until an election like Bay City's could clarify the vote-getting appeal of the participants.

When we add to this picture the fact that the boards that were acquiescent—Baltimore and Pittsburgh—seem to be least concerned with representing the community, or with public opinion, we see that we have reason to believe that the same school board will take more acquiescent action if it is freed from having to participate in general elections. In the next section of this chapter we shall present more evidence for this point of view.

If we accept the premise that the correlation between election of the board and acquiescence is a true and causal relationship, then we can conclude that the civil rights liberalism of the board is by far the dominant factor in explaining acquiescence. This may seem altogether reasonable, but this finding does raise some disturbing questions. We would like to believe that the school board is somehow more than the sum of its parts, that the interaction of board members in the solution of school problems should cause a group consensus to develop which would play down the importance of the subjective attitudes of the board members. We would also like to believe that the negotiation process itself affects what the board does—that there are some ways of influencing the board which are more effective than others. Instead we are continuing to find the school integration outcomes virtually predetermined before the negotiation process begins.

Cohesion

We can support our argument that the correlation between board appointment (rather than election) and acquiescence is real in another way. We suggested two possible reasons: first, that the elected board is more conservative because it must face an election campaign. There is nothing we can do to prove or disprove this with our data. However, we also suggested that the elected board has more difficulty in taking innovative action because of the higher level of internal disagreement. If this is true, then appointed boards which have high internal disagreement should also have difficulty taking acquiescent action. Certainly, there seems to be considerable difference between boards in their decision-making style. Some seem to handle an issue quietly and smoothly; others seem to be constantly involved in some difficult or tense situation. Several efforts were made to define a variable which would capture this difference. The final choice was "cohesion."

Cohesion (as used by Festinger, Schachter, and Back, 1950, for example) refers to the average level of positive feelings between the members of the group. It might be operationalized by asking each board member to give a numerical score to every other board member according to the extent of agreement (or friendliness) between them, and then averaging these values across every pair of board members. Thus, a board would be lowest in cohesion if every board member disagreed with or disliked every other; it would be higher if the board were divided into two factions, with members on each side who support each other, but argue with the members of the other faction; it would be fairly high if the board members agreed with each other with the exception of a single deviant whom all others disliked; it would, of course, be highest if all the board members were friendly with one another. With this criterion in mind, we were able to arrive at a rank ordering. There is a great deal of variation on this variable. At one extreme, we estimated that if two members were selected at random from one particular board, the chances would be two to one that they would disapprove of each other! Several boards are divided into a majority and minority faction, and three boards seem to have very little internal dissension.

The cities were ranked on cohesion using several pieces of data. School board members had been asked to name the board members they agreed with and disagreed with. They were also asked to evaluate the level of agreement. In addition, for each board we collected many public statements, some private statements of opinion about other board members, and records of votes on various issues.

There is a definite correlation between cohesion and acquiescence, as indicated by Figure 8. The least acquiescent elected board, Bay City, is the least cohesive; and the least acquiescent appointed board, Buffalo, is the least cohesive of its group. Conversely, the boards which are most acquiescent seem to have the least internal conflict. Thus, this figure supports our argument that elected boards are less acquiescent because they are less cohesive.

Are there any grounds for supposing that there is in fact a causal relationship between cohesion and acquiescence? There are only two obvious incidents which were the result of dissension and clearly prevented acquiescence. One was Buffalo's handling of the Woodlawn junior high school redistricting situation, where the board members prepared four different plans and submitted them to the public, rather than agreeing privately on a single plan. The result was the building of sentiment for a board member's proposal that the school be all-Negro. The other case was the inability of the Bay City board to vote for a policy statement on *de facto* segregation drafted by a board member to avert a school boycott, despite the fact that

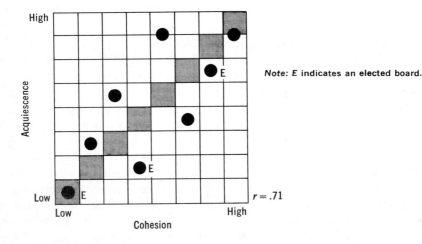

Figure 8.   Cohesion and Acquiescence.

three of the five board members favored it. Both these incidents were important, and they came in the two boards with the lowest level of consensus. There is also a suggestion in San Francisco that the relatively low level of consensus there kept the board from acting decisively. In San Francisco a board which frequently had difficulty taking action dragged its feet in responding to the civil rights movement. It seems plausible that this inability to act is partly a consequence of lack of consensus.

From these first three cities, we can present three hypotheses:

1. The uncohesive board will be less acquiescent because it will be unable to prevent the issue from becoming a matter of public controversy. Each board member will attempt to win public support of his point of view; but the public statements will invite public reaction. Under conditions of controversy, the most extreme positions in the community will be articulated first. The liberals are already organized in the civil rights movements; hence public discussion will next lead to organization of the segregationist extreme. In the ensuing controversy the board will be unable to evaluate public opinion, yet hesitant to act in the face of public opposition; further, it will be unable to determine the extent of opposition. The result parallels a finding from a study of fluoridation controversies. Public debate tends to prevent adoption of fluoridation even though repeated surveys have indicated that it has public support (see Crain, Katz, and Rosenthal, in press).

2. Whereas the cohesive board may be able to put up a "united front," each dissenting board member will air his public position. This means that the most conservative board member will become a symbolic leader for the segregationists, whose position will gain legitimacy from the support of a public official. Thus, the segregationists not only have more opportunity to organize, they also have a more legitimate position to organize around.

3. Even if the board does not have to contend with segregationist public opinion, the demands of the civil rights movement require change on the part of the school board. There is an inertia in any public body which tends to maintain the status quo, and any innovative action requires discussion and agreement on the part of the board members. However, discussion will be inhibited in the non-cohesive board, and the remnants of previous arguments will plague efforts to obtain agreement on any new issue.

These seem to be plausible arguments for assuming that the correlation between cohesion and acquiescence is a causal relationship. This means that we have three variables—civil rights liberalism, election versus appointment, and cohesion—which are sufficient to predict level of acquiescence. If we combine the variables by adding each city's ranks on each variable, we can (depending upon the amount of weight we assign to each variable) arrive at correlations with acquiescence which range as high as $+.96$. Of course, with only eight cities, such techniques are not very helpful, and we have almost no grounds for drawing any conclusions about the relative importance of each variable.

Summary

The main task of this article has been to demonstrate that the principal dimension of the outcome of the school integration issue—the extent to which the board acquiesced to the demands of the civil rights movement—

can be largely explained by differences in the structure and composition of the school board. We have attempted to demonstrate this in three ways. First, by separating the decision process into stages, we have shown that the behavior of the school board can be predicted from the action it takes early in the campaign, before the negotiations with the civil rights groups have reached their peak, and that rather than higher levels of civil rights activity causing the board to take action, the board's actions determine the extent of demonstrations.

Second, we considered such factors as the region in which the board is located, the socioeconomic status of the white population (which should indicate the extent of white opposition to integration), and the size of the Negro population (which should reflect the power of the civil rights movement) and found that these factors were not very helpful. (Only the size of the Negro population correlated with acquiescence; $R = +.53$.) Apparently a line of analysis based on these factors is unpromising.

Third, when we turned to examine the characteristics of the school board, we found three factors which do explain acquiescence—the liberalism of the attitudes of individual board members, the cohesiveness of the board, and whether it is an elected or appointed body. The correlation of race liberalism with acquiescence is only $+.65$, but the correlation is perfect among the elected or appointed boards considered separately. The correlation of cohesion with acquiescence is $+.71$.

School board structure and functioning, we conclude, are major factors in the outcome of school desegregation issues.

References

AGGER, R. E., GOLDRICH, D. and SWANSON, B. E.   *The rulers and the ruled: political power and impotence in American communities.* New York: John Wiley, 1964.

BANFIELD, E. C. and WILSON, J. Q.   *City politics.* Cambridge, Mass.: Harvard University Press, 1963.

CRAIN, R., KATZ, E. and ROSENTHAL, D.   *The politics of community conflict.* Indianapolis: Bobbs-Merrill, in press.

CRAIN, R. L.   *The politics of school desegregation.* Chicago: Aldine, 1968.

FESTINGER, L., SCHACHTER, S. and BACK, K.   *Social pressures in informal groups.* New York: Harper, 1950.

WILLIAMS, O. P. and ADRIAN, C. R.   *Four cities.* Philadelphia: University of Pennsylvania Press, 1963.

4. ASPIRATIONS AND THE SCHOOL

What makes a research study important, a classic? Coleman's study, retained here from the first edition, certainly qualifies as a modern classic, and it may furnish some clues in answering the question. The investigator's competence in conducting the study, and the coherence and style in which it is reported, both so obvious in Coleman's case, are not sufficient (and may not even be necessary) conditions for the making of a classic. Some additional features:

Coleman's study challenged prevailing thought. It had been well known for nearly twenty years that a student's academic performance in high school (and all other levels of schooling) was intimately associated with the standing of the student's family in the social class structure. The establishment of this fact was the sociologists' most important contribution to education. Coleman, however, proposed with evidence to support him that social class differences can be overridden by the levelling effect of the adolescent peer culture in the high school.

It was a germinal study. It has spawned scores of additional studies, some designed to refute Coleman's thesis, but many more to extend the proposition to its limits. The following selections in this section are illustrative.

Coleman's study held social significance, and its timing was fortuitous. The study appeared just after Sputnik was launched and national attention had turned to the neglect of excellence in our schools. Coleman had a diagnosis, and the diagnosis suggested a treatment. So long as the problem of academic achievement was seen to rest in the stratification system of American society, treatment was not readily at hand, but Coleman's diagnosis put the problem in the educational institution, within arm's reach of people who could do something about it.

One cannot discount the importance of wide distribution in the making of a classic. The study was reported in several major journal articles, one of which is reprinted here, in a monograph published by the U. S. Office of Education, the funding agency, and in a full-length book.

The Adolescent Subculture and Academic Achievement*

James S. Coleman

Industrial society has spawned a peculiar phenomenon, most evident in America but emerging also in other Western societies: adolescent subcultures, with values and activities quite distinct from those of the adult society —subcultures whose members have most of their important associations within and few with adult society. Industrialization, and the rapidity of change itself, has taken out of the hands of the parent the task of training his child, made the parent's skills obsolescent, and put him out of touch with the times—unable to understand, much less inculcate, the standards of a social order which has changed since he was young.

By extending the period of training necessary for a child and by encompassing nearly the whole population, industrial society has made of high school a social system of adolescents. It includes, in the United States, almost all adolescents and more and more of the activities of the adolescent himself. A typical example is provided by an excerpt from a high-school newspaper in an upper-middle-class suburban school:

SOPHOMORE DANCING

FEATURES CHA CHA

Sophomores, this is your chance to learn how to dance! The first day of sophomore dancing is Nov. 14 and it will begin at 8:30 A.M. in the Boys' Gym. . . .

No one is required to take dancing but it is highly recommended for both boys and girls. . . .

If you don't attend at this time except in case of absence from school, you may not attend at any other time. Absence excuses should be shown to Miss ——————— or Mr. ———————.

In effect, then, what our society has done is to set apart, in an institution of their own, adolescents for whom home is little more than a dormitory and

---

* Reprinted from *American Journal of Sociology*, 1960, 65, 337-347. Used by permission of the author and the publisher, The University of Chicago Press. Copyright © 1960 by the University of Chicago.

The research discussed in this paper was carried out under a grant from the United States Office of Education; a full report is contained in "Social Climates and Social Structures in High Schools," a report to the Office of Education; see also J. Coleman, *The adolescent society*. New York: Free Press, 1961. The paper was presented at the Fourth World Congress of Sociology, Milan, Italy, September, 1959.

whose world is made up of activities peculiar to their fellows. They have been given as well many of the instruments which can make them a functioning community: cars, freedom in dating, continual contact with the opposite sex, money, and entertainment, like popular music and movies, designed especially for them. The international spread of "rock-and-roll" and of so-called American patterns of adolescent behavior is a consequence, I would suggest, of these economic changes which have set adolescents off in a world of their own.

Yet the fact that such a subsystem has sprung up in society has not been systematically recognized in the organization of secondary education. The theory and practice of education remains focused on *individuals;* teachers exhort individuals to concentrate their energies in scholarly directions, while the community of adolescents diverts these energies into other channels. The premise of the present research is that, if educational goals are to be realized in modern society, a fundamentally different approach to secondary education is necessary. Adults are in control of the institutions they have established for secondary education; traditionally, these institutions have been used to mold children as individuals toward ends which adults dictate. The fundamental change which must occur is to shift the focus: to mold social communities as communities, so that the norms of the communities themselves reinforce educational goals rather than inhibit them, as is at present the case.

The research being reported is an attempt to examine the status systems of the adolescent communities in ten high schools and to see the effects of these status systems upon the individuals within them. The ten high schools are all in the Midwest. They include five schools in small towns (labeled 0-4 in the figures which follow), one in a working-class suburb (6), one in a well-to-do suburb (9), and three schools in cities of varying sizes (5, 7, and 8). All but No. 5, a Catholic boys' school, are coeducational, and all but it are public schools.

The intention was to study schools which had quite different status systems, but the similarities were far more striking than the differences. In a questionnaire all boys were asked: "How would you most like to be remembered in school: as an athletic star, a brilliant student, or most popular?" The results of the responses for each school are shown in Figure 1 where the left corner of the triangle represents 100 per cent saying "star athlete"; the top corner represents 100 per cent saying "brilliant student"; and the right corner represents 100 per cent saying "most popular." Each school is represented by a point whose location relative to the three corners shows the proportion giving each response.[1]

The schools are remarkably grouped somewhat off-center, showing a greater tendency to say "star athlete" than either of the other choices. From each school's point is a broken arrow connecting the school as a whole with

1. I am grateful to James A. Davis and Jacob Feldman, of the University of Chicago, for suggesting such graphs for presenting responses to trichotomous items in a population.

its members who were named by their fellows as being "members of the leading crowd." In almost every case, the leading crowd tends in the direction of the athlete—in all cases *away* from the ideal of the brilliant student. Again, for the leading crowds as well as for the students as a whole, the uniformity is remarkably great; not so great in the absolute positions of the leading crowds but in the direction they deviate from the student bodies.

This trend toward the ideal of the athletic star on the part of the leading crowds is due in part to the fact that the leading crowds include a great number of athletes. Boys were asked in a questionnaire to name the best athlete in their grade, the best student, and the boy most popular with girls. In every school, without exception, the boys named as best athletes were named more often—on the average over twice as often—as members of the leading crowd than were those named as best students. Similarly, the boy most popular with girls was named as belonging to the leading crowd more often than the best student, though in all schools but the well-to-do suburb and the smallest rural town schools (9 and 0 on Figure 1) less often than the best athlete.

These and other data indicate the importance of athletic achievement as an avenue for gaining status in the schools. Indeed, in the predominantly middle-class schools, it is by far the most effective achievement for gaining a working-class boy entrée into the leading crowd.

Similarly, each girl was asked how she would like to be remembered: as a brilliant student, a leader in extracurricular activities, or most popular. The various schools are located on Figure 2, together with arrows connecting them to their leading crowd. The girls tend slightly less, on the average, than the boys to want to be remembered as brilliant students. Although the alternatives are different, and thus cannot be directly compared, a great deal of other evidence indicates that the girls—although better students in every school—do not want to be considered "brilliant students." They have good reason not to, for the girl in each grade in each of the schools who was most often named as best student has fewer friends and is less often in the leading crowd than is the boy most often named as best student.

There is, however, diversity among the schools in the attractiveness of the images of "activities leader" and "popular girl" (Figure 2). In five (9, 0, 3, 8, and 1), the leader in activities is more often chosen as an ideal than is the popular girl; in four (7, 6, 2, and 4) the most popular girl is the more attractive of the two. These differences correspond somewhat to class background differences among the schools: 2, 4, 6, and 7, where the activities leader is least attractive, have the highest proportion of students with working-class backgrounds. School 9 is by far the most upper-middle-class one and by far the most activities-oriented.

The differences among the schools correspond as well to differences among the leading crowds: in schools 2, 4, and 6, where the girls as a whole are most oriented to being popular, the leading crowds are even more so; in the school where the girls are most oriented to the ideal of the activities leader, No. 9, the leading crowd goes even further in that direction.[2] In other words, it is as if a pull is exerted by the leading crowd, bringing the rest of the students toward one or the other of the polar extremes. In all cases, the leading crowd pulls away from the brilliant-student ideal.

Although these schools vary far less than one might wish when examining the effects of status systems, there are differences. All students were asked in a questionnaire: "What does it take to get into the leading crowd?" On the basis of the answers, the relative importance of various activities can be determined. Consider only a single activity, academic achievement. Its importance for status among the adolescents in each school can be measured simply by the proportion of responses which specify "good grades," or "brains" as adolescents often put it, as a means of entrée into the leading crowd. In all the schools, academic achievement was of less importance than other matters, such as being an athletic star among the boys, being a cheerleader or being good-looking among the girls, or other attributes. Other measures which were obtained of the importance of academic achievement in the adolescent status system correlate highly with this one.[3]

If, then, it is true that the status system of adolescents *does* affect educational goals, those schools which differ in the importance of academic achievement in the adolescent status system should differ in numerous other ways which are directly related to educational goals. Only one of those, which illustrates well the differing pressures upon students in the various schools, will be reported here.

In every social context certain activities are highly rewarded, while others are not. Those activities which are rewarded are the activities for which there is strong competition—activities in which everyone with some ability will compete. In such activities the persons who achieve most should be those with most potential ability. In contrast, in unrewarded activities, those who have most ability may not be motivated to compete; consequently, the persons who achieve most will be persons of lesser ability. Thus, in a high school where basketball is important, nearly every boy who might be a good basketball player will go out for the sport, and, as a result, basketball stars are likely to be the boys with the most ability. If in the same school volleyball does not bring the same status, few boys will go out for it, and those who end up as members of the team will not be the boys with most potential ability.

2. This result could logically be a statistical artifact because the leaders were included among students as a whole and thus would boost the result in the direction they tend. However, it is not a statistical artifact, for the leading crowds are a small part of the total student body. When they are taken out for computing the position of the rest of the girls in each school, schools 2, 4, 6, and 7 are still the most popularity-oriented, and school 9 the most activities-oriented.

3. Parenthetically, it might be noted that these measures correlate only imperfectly with the proportion of boys or girls who want to be remembered as brilliant students. These responses depend on the relative attractiveness of other ideals, which varies from school to school, and upon other factors unrelated to the status system.

Similarly, with academic achievement: in a school where such achievement brings few social rewards, those who "go out" for scholarly achievement will be few. The high performers, those who receive good grades,
will not be the boys whose ability is greatest but a more mediocre few.
Thus, the "intellectuals" of such a society, those defined by themselves and
others as the best students, will not in fact be those with most intellectual
ability. The latter, knowing where the social rewards lie, will be off culti-
vating other fields which bring social rewards.

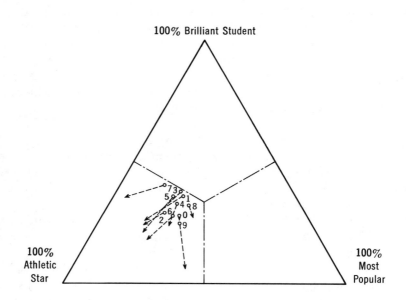

Figure 1. Positions of Schools and Leading Crowds in Boys'
Relative Choice of Brilliant Student, Athletic Star, and Most Popular.

To examine the effect of varying social pressures in the schools, academic
achievement, as measured by grades in school, was related to IQ. Since the
IQ tests differ from school to school, and since each school had its own
mean IQ and its own variation around it, the ability of high performers
(boys who made A or A− average[4] was measured by the number of standard deviations of their average IQ's above the mean. In this way, it is

4.   In each school but 3 and 8, those making A and A− constituted from 6 to 8 per
cent of the student body. In order to provide a correct test of the hypothesis, it is necessary
to have the same fraction of the student body in each case (since IQ's of this group are
being measured in terms of number of standard deviations above the student body). To
adjust these groups, enough 6's were added (each being assigned the average IQ of the
total group of 6's) to bring the proportion up to 6 per cent (from 3 per cent in school 3,
from 4 per cent in school 8).

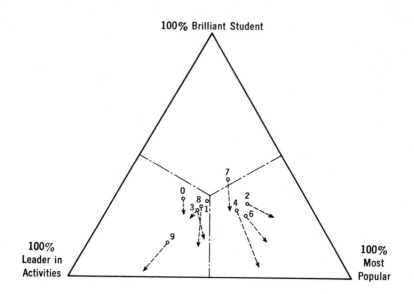

Figure 2. Positions of Schools and Leading Crowds in Girls' Relative Choice of Brilliant Student, Activities Leader, and Most Popular.

possible to see where the high performers' ability lay, relative to the distribution of abilities in their school.[5]

The variations were great: in a small-town school, No. *1*, the boys who made an A or A− average had IQ's 1.53 standard deviations above the school average; in another small-town school, No. *0*, their IQ's were only about a third this distance above the mean, .59. Given this variation, the question can be asked: Do these variations in ability of the high performers correspond to variations in the social rewards for, or constraints against, being a good student?

Figure 3 shows the relation for the boys between the social rewards for academic excellence (i.e., the frequency with which "good grades" was mentioned as a means for getting into the leading crowd) and the ability of the high performers, measured by the number of standard deviations their average IQ's exceed that of the rest of the boys in the school. The relation is extremely strong. Only one school, a parochial boys' school in the city's slums, deviates. This is a school in which many boys had their most important associations outside the school rather than in it, so that its student

5. The IQ tests used in the different schools were: (0) California Mental Maturity (taken seventh, eighth, or ninth grade); (1) California Mental Maturity (taken eighth grade); (2) SRA Primary Mental Abilities (taken tenth grade); (3) California Mental Maturity (taken ninth grade; seniors took SRA PMA, which was tabulated as a percentile, and they have been omitted from analysis reported above); (4) Otis (ninth and tenth grades; taken eighth grade); Kuhlman Finch (eleventh and twelfth grades, taken eighth grade); (5) Otis (taken ninth grade); (6) California Mental Maturity (taken eighth grade); (7) California Mental Maturity (taken eighth grade); (8) Otis (taken ninth or tenth grade); and (9) Otis (taken eighth grade).

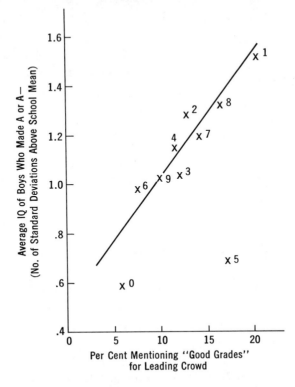

Figure 3. IQ's of High Achieving Boys by Importance of Good
Grades Among Other Boys.

body constituted far less of a social system, less able to dispense social
rewards and punishments, than was true of the other schools.

Similarly, Figure 4 shows for the girls the IQ's of the high performers.[6]
Unfortunately, most of the schools are closely bunched in the degree to
which good grades are important among the girls, so that there is too little
variation among them to examine this effect as fully as would be desirable.
School 2 is the one school whose girls deviate from the general relationship.

The effect of these value systems on the freedom for academic ability to
express itself in high achievement is evident among the girls as it is among
the boys. This is not merely due to the school facilities, social composition
of the school, or other variables: the two schools highest in the importance

6.   For the girls, only girls with a straight-A average were included. Since girls get
better grades than boys, this device is necessary in order to make the sizes of the "high-
performer" group roughly comparable for boys and for girls. Schools differed somewhat
in the proportion of A's, constituting about 6 per cent of the students in the small schools,
only about 3 per cent in schools 6 and 7, 1 per cent in 8, and 2 per cent in 9. In 8 and 9,
enough girls were added and assigned the average grade of the 7 (A−) group to bring
the proportion to 3 per cent, comparable with the other large schools. The difference,
however, between the large and small schools was left.

of scholastic achievement for both boys and girls are *1* and *3*, the first a small-town school of 350 students and the second a city school of 2,000 students. In both there are fewer students with white-collar backgrounds than in schools *9* or *3*, which are somewhere in the middle as to value placed on academic achievement, but are more white-collar than in schools *7* or *4*, which are also somewhere in the middle. The highest expenditure per student was $695 per year in school *9*, and the lowest was little more than half that, in school *4*. These schools are close together on the graphs of Figures 3 and 4.

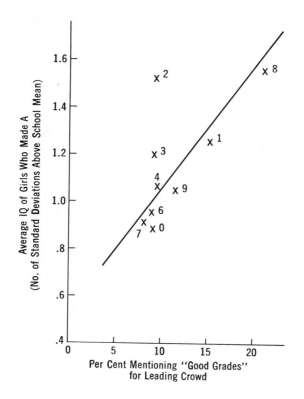

Figure 4. IQ's of High Achieving Girls by Importance of Good Grades Among Other Girls.

It should be mentioned in passing that an extensive unpublished study throughout Connecticut, using standard tests of achievement and ability, yielded consistent results. The study found no correlation between per pupil expenditure in a school and the achievement of its students relative to their ability. The effects shown in Figures 3 and 4 suggest why: that students with ability are led to achieve only when there are social rewards, primarily from their peers, for doing so—and these social rewards seem little correlated with per pupil expenditure.

So much for the effects as shown by the variation among schools. As mentioned earlier, the variation among schools was not nearly so striking in this research as the fact that, in all of them, academic achievement did not count for as much as other activities. In every school the boy named as best athlete and the boy named as most popular with girls was far more often mentioned as a member of the leading crowd and as someone to "be like," than was the boy named as the best student. And the girl named as best dressed, and the one named as most popular with boys, was in every school far more often mentioned as being in the leading crowd and as someone "to be like," than was the girl named as the best student.

The relative unimportance of academic achievement, together with the effect shown earlier, suggests that these adolescent subcultures are generally deterrents to academic achievement. In other words, in these societies of adolescents those who come to be seen as the "intellectuals" and who come to think so of themselves are not really those of highest intelligence but are only the ones who are willing to work hard at a relatively unrewarded activity.

The implications for American society as a whole are clear. Because high schools allow the adolescent subcultures to divert energies into athletics, social activities, and the like, they recruit into adult intellectual activities people with a rather mediocre level of ability. In fact, the high school seems to do more than allow these subcultures to discourage academic achievement; it aids them in doing so. To indicate how it does and to indicate how it might do differently is another story, to be examined below.

Figures 1 and 2, which show the way boys and girls would like to be remembered in their high school, demonstrate a curious difference between the boys and the girls. Despite great variation in social background, in size of school (from 180 to 2,000), in size of town (from less than a thousand to over a million), and in style of life of their parents, the proportion of boys choosing each of the three images by which he wants to be remembered is very nearly the same in all schools. And in every school the leading crowd "pulls" in similar directions: at least partly toward the ideal of the star athlete. Yet the ideals of the girls in these schools are far more dispersed, and the leading crowds "pull" in varying directions, far less uniformly than among the boys. Why such a diversity in the same schools?

The question can best be answered by indirection. In two schools apart from those in research, the questionnaire was administered primarily to answer a puzzling question: Why was academic achievement of so little importance among the adolescents in school 9? Their parents were professionals and business executives, about 80 per cent were going to college (over twice as high a proportion as in any of the other schools), and yet academic excellence counted for little among them. In the two additional schools parental background was largely held constant, for they were private, coeducational day schools whose students had upper-middle-class backgrounds quite similar to those of school 9. One (No. 10) was in the city; the other (No. 11), in a suburban setting almost identical to that of No. 9. Although the two schools were added to the study to answer the question about school 9, they will be used to help answer the puzzle set earlier; that of the clustering of schools for the boys and their greater spread for the girls. When we look at the responses of adolescents in these two schools to the question as to how they would like to be remembered, the picture becomes even more puzzling (Figures 5 and 6). For the boys, they

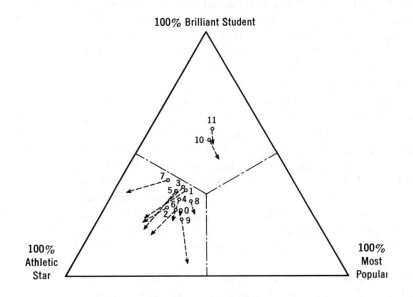

Figure 5. Positions of Schools and Leading Crowds in Boys' Relative Choice of Brilliant Student, Athletic Star, and Most Popular (Two Private Schools [10, 11] Included).

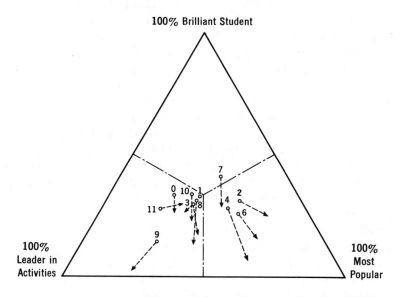

Figure 6. Positions of Schools and Leading Crowds in Girls' Relative Choice of Brilliant Student, Activities Leader, and Most Popular (Two Private Schools [10, 11] Included).

are extremely far from the cluster of the other schools; for the girls, they are intermingled with the other schools. Thus, though it was for the boys that the other schools clustered so closely, these two deviate sharply from the cluster; and for the girls, where the schools already varied, these two are not distinguishable. Furthermore, the leading crowds of boys in these schools do not pull the ideal toward the star-athlete ideal as do those in almost all the other schools. To be sure, they pull away from the ideal of the brilliant student, but the pull is primarily toward a social image, the most popular. Among the girls, the leading crowds pull in different directions and are nearly indistinguishable from the other schools.

The answer to both puzzles, that is, first, the great cluster of the boys and now, in these two additional schools, the greater deviation, seems to lie in one fact: the boys' interscholastic athletics. The nine public schools are all engaged in interscholastic leagues which themselves are knit together in state tournaments. The other school of the first ten, the Catholic school, is in a parochial league, where games are just as hotly contested as in the public leagues and is also knit together with them in tournaments.

Schools 10 and 11 are athletically in a world apart from this. Although boys in both schools may go in for sports, and both schools have interscholastic games, the opponents are scattered private schools, constituting a league in name only. They take no part in state or city tournaments and have almost no publicity.

There is nothing for the girls comparable to the boys' interscholastic athletics. There are school activities of one sort or another, in which most girls take part, but no interscholastic games involving them. Their absence and the lack of leagues which knit all schools together in systematic competition means that the status system can "wander" freely, depending on local conditions in the school. In athletics, however, a school, and the community surrounding it, cannot hold its head up if it continues to lose games. It *must* devote roughly the same attention to athletics as do the schools surrounding it, for athletic games are the only games in which it engages other schools and, by representation, other communities. These games are almost the only means a school has of generating internal cohesion and identification, for they constitute the only activity in which the school participates *as* a school. (This is well indicated by the fact that a number of students in school 10, the private school which engages in no interscholastic games, has been concerned by a "lack of school spirit.") It is as a consequence of this that the athlete gains so much status: he is doing something for the school and the community, not only for himself, in leading his team to victory, for it is a school victory.

The outstanding student, in contrast, has little or no way to bring glory to his school. His victories are always purely personal, often at the expense of his classmates, who are forced to work harder to keep up with him. It is no wonder that his accomplishments gain little reward and are often met by ridiculing remarks, such as "curve-raiser" or "grind," terms or disapprobation which have no analogues in athletics.

These results are particularly intriguing, for they suggest ways in which rather straightforward social theory could be used in organizing the activities of high schools in such a way that their adolescent subcultures would encourage, rather than discourage, the channeling of energies into directions of learning. One might speculate on the possible effects of city-wide or state-wide "scholastic fairs" composed of academic games and tournaments between schools and school exhibits to be judged. It could be that the mere institution of such games would, just as do the state basketball tournaments in the midwestern United States, have a profound effect upon the educational climate in the participating schools. In fact, by an extension of this analysis, one would predict that an international fair of this sort, a "Scholastic Olympics," would generate interscholastic games and tournaments within the participating countries.

※ ※ ※ ※ ※

True or false? Peer influences are the major factor in adolescents' decisions, far outweighing what their parents want.

False. This study by Kandel and Lesser, beginning with a thorough and thoughtful literature review, shows us decisively that the "hydraulic" model (if peer influence increases, parent influence decreases) is not adequate. Parent and peer influences are much more mutually supportive than otherwise, as in Flacks' analysis of student protesters in this book.

The study is done with great care. The use of Danish and American samples, across social classes, provides us with more confidence in the findings, as does the authors' effort to remove possible spurious or artifactual reasons for their findings.

It is interesting to note here (as in the Gottlieb study of graduate student socialization in this book) that the formal properties of a socializing relationship (its closeness, equalitarianism, etc.) are not helpful to us in predicting its results: the *content* of what goes on between professor and student, or mother and child, is what makes the difference.

And in passing, the differences between Danes and Americans as far as the meaning of friendship goes might well be examined further; they parallel a famous discussion by Kurt Lewin (*Resolving Social Conflicts*, Harper, 1948) of the differences between German and American character structure.

Relative Influences of Parents and Peers on the Educational Plans of Adolescents in the United States and Denmark*

Denise Kandel, Gerald S. Lesser

Adolescents are said to belong to a distinct adolescent subculture and to be influenced more by their peers than by their parents. In *The Adolescent Society*, Coleman (1961) develops the thesis that adolescents form their own culture, which stands in isolation from the adult culture in the society at large. He argues that the goals and values of adolescents are at odds with those of adults. Most studies of adolescence similarly are based on an implicit "hydraulic" model, which assumes that strong commitment to peer standards is accompanied uniformly by weak commitment to parents, and *vice versa*.

However, the extent to which the values and goals of adolescents and adults differ, and the degree to which significant adults and peers actually influence the development of adolescents have not been adequately tested and specified (Berger, 1963; Jahoda and Warren, 1965). For example, most research on parental and peer influences on the educational plans of adolescents has looked at one influence or the other but not at both simultaneously. Furthermore, the matched samples of adolescents, their mothers and their peers, which are required for an adequate assessment are lacking in existing studies, even those concerned with relative influences.

Results from the rare studies that have been concerned with the relative influences of parents and peers on the educational plans of adolescents are contradictory: McDill and Coleman (1965) and Herriott (1963) conclude that peer influences exceed parental influences; Simpson (1962), on the other hand, concludes that parents are more influential than peers.

McDill and Coleman's (1965) panel sample included students from six public high schools who were questioned in their first and last years of high school. Father's education was the principal indicator of parental educa-

* Adapted from paper read at the American Sociological Association meetings, 1968. Used by permission of the authors. This research has been supported through the Cooperative Research Program of the Office of Education, DHEW (Project #2139, OE-4-10-069); and by the Harvard Center for Research and Development in Educational Differences (Office of Education Contract OE-5-10-239). An abbreviated version of this paper, including only the American data, was published in *American Sociological Review* (Kandel and Lesser, 1969a).

The authors would like to thank the Bureau of Applied Social Research, Columbia University, for providing technical assistance with the processing of the data.

tional aspirations. The measure of peer influence consisted of the respondent's status in the high school social structure as indicated by the number of mentions as member of the leading crowd. The use of this variable was based upon the finding reported in *The Adolescent Society* (Coleman, 1961) that members of the leading crowd have higher college aspirations than non-members. McDill and Coleman conclude that:

> by the end of the senior year of high school, the prestige of the adolescents in the school social system contributes more to variations in their stated college plans than does their father's or mother's education (McDill and Coleman, 1965, p. 125).

However, data on the parents' actual desires for their children also presented by McDill and Coleman (1965), show that even in the senior year the influence of parental desires (.282) on adolescents' plans is greater than school status (.237).[1]

Herriott (1963) used adolescents' perceptions of the educational expectations held by eleven different types of persons as sources of data on parental and peer influences. His sample consisted of 1489 students in a Massachusetts high school. The highest correlation was obtained between adolescents' educational aspirations and perceived expectations of a same age friend.

On the other hand, in a study of occupational aspirations of high school students, Simpson (1962) found that for both middle-class and lower-class boys, "parental influence was more strongly related to aspirations than peer influences" (p. 521). Parental influence was measured by the child's report of his parents' pressure to enter a profession. High peer influence was defined by two criteria: belonging to two or more school clubs, and mentioning at least one middle-class friend.

In their use of indirect indicators for parental or peer goals, these studies of relative influences follow the same procedures as single-influence studies. The majority of studies on parental influences have used parental social class or parental education as indicators of parental educational aspirations for their children. (For review of existing studies see Haller and Butterworth, 1960; McDill and Coleman, 1965; Sewell and Shah, 1967.) However, while social class is strongly related to educational goals, parental aspirations or parental encouragement of higher education can override a lower-class background (Bordua, 1960; Cohen, 1965; Ellis and Lane, 1963; Floud, Halsey and Martin, 1956; Kahl, 1953; Lipset and Bendix, 1959; Rehberg and Westby, 1967; Sewell and Shah, 1968; Strodtbeck, 1958).

Similarly, the studies of peer influences on academic achievement and aspirations have been concerned with the influence of the value climate of

1. The measure of influence is Coleman's effect parameter, which has also been used in the present study. It is designed to measure the effect of one or more independent variables on a dependent variable (Coleman, 1964). The underlying model is analogous to a factorial design in analysis of variance for quantitative data. The statistics require that the dependent variable be dichotomized. Weighting procedures can be carried out to weigh each difference according to the size of the sample on which it is based.

schools on the adolescents within them, and rarely with the specific plans and attitudes of the adolescent's friends (Boyle, 1966; Coleman, 1961; *et al.*, 1966; Herriott, 1963; McDill and Coleman, 1965; McDill, Meyers, and Rigsby, 1966; Michael, 1961; Ramsøy, 1962; Turner, 1964; Wallace, 1966; Wilson, 1959). The greater the proportion of middle-class students in a school, the greater the tendency for students to plan on college, irrespective of social class background.

However, the consensus between matched pairs of adolescents in the school has been investigated in two studies. Alexander and Campbell (1964) studied the college plans of 1,410 male seniors in 30 high schools in North Carolina when matched to their best-school-friend and concluded that "a student and his best friend tend to be similar in college plans and that the extent of similarity is greater when the choice is reciprocated" (p. 571). Haller and Butterworth (1960), on the other hand, found low intra-class correlations on levels of occupational and, particularly, educational aspirations between pairs of high school boys and their best-school-friend. The sample included 245 peer-pairs among 17-year-old high school boys in Michigan. (For a recent reanalysis of these data in the light of a model to estimate the magnitude of peer influences, see Duncan, Haller and Portes, 1968.)

Our own work stems from the attempt to investigate the relative influences of parents and peers under differing cultural conditions. To overcome in part the difficulties of previous studies, we have used a sample of triads in which the adolescent has been matched with his mother and his best friend in school. The indicators of educational goals are direct rather than indirect. Furthermore, in order to establish that concordance on goals reflects the influence of mothers or of best friends upon the adolescent, we have studied concordance while holding certain characteristics of the social environment constant, such as social class or program in school, and under different types of interaction with mother and friend. Indeed, agreement between any two individuals does not necessarily reflect influence from one person to the other, since agreement by itself can result from the common social situation in which the interacting members are located and not from the interaction itself (Furstenberg, 1967; Hyman, 1959; Newcomb and Svehla, 1937).[2]

---

2. Only through a longitudinal design is it possible definitely to establish the source, nature and direction of influences. Such longitudinal data were not collected in the present study. In the absence of such data, there are problems of interpretation, involving in particular reciprocity and interrelationship of influences, which no statistical manipulation of data can resolve. For example, we cannot ascertain the extent to which adolescents influence their parents by demonstrating or arguing that they are qualified for a specific level of educational attainment, which the parents then come to accept and encourage. In dealing with friends' influence, we cannot establish the extent to which parents influence the eligible range of friends from which adolescents have a choice. Nor can we estimate the extent to which similarity of values and attitudes between friends is the basis for friendship, rather than an outcome of friendship. An attempt is made to deal with some of these points in the analysis of the data, but we would like to stress the limitations inherent in the concept of influence as it is used throughout this paper.

The data are taken from a larger cross-cultural study of adolescents and their families in the United States and Denmark (Kandel and Lesser, 1969b). In this paper, we consider three interrelated questions:

1. What is the relative agreement, or concordance, on educational goals between the adolescent and his mother, and between the adolescent and his best-school-friend?
2. What is the influence of common social factors, for example, social class membership, on concordance on educational goals within dyads?
3. What is the influence of patterns of interaction within dyads on concordance on educational plans?

Method

Sample

In the Spring and Summer of 1965, data were collected from all students in 3 high schools in the United States (N = 2327) and 12 secondary schools in Denmark[3] (N = 1552) through use of structured questionnaires. Each student was asked to name his three closest same-sex friends in school. In addition, the students' mothers were mailed self-administered structured questionnaires containing many questions identical to those included in the student's instrument: 68% of the mothers in the United States and 75% in Denmark returned completed questionnaires.[4]

The samples were not selected to be representative of the total adolescent population in each country, but rather to include schools in different ecological settings, such as urban and rural. The 3 American schools are located in the Eastern United States. They include a large lower-class urban school,

---

3.   A short description of the unfamiliar Danish educational system (for a more detailed description, see Dixon, 1965) is presented here in order to provide a background for the subsequent discussions of the sample and of the results.

Danish children are not required to begin school until they are seven years old. They are permitted to leave after seven years of schooling at age 14, but most of them (70%-80%) remain beyond this age. Most schools begin to divide the children after fifth grade according to their interests and abilities, as judged by teachers and parents; some schools postpone the separation until the end of the seventh grade. Beginning with the 8th grade, one part of the student body will attend *almen line,* stressing basic training and preparation for later vocational and community life. Another part will attend *real line,* stressing academic studies and preparing for *real eksamen.* This examination admits the students to many kinds of office or business jobs, or to *gymnasium,* where they prepare for university study or for other schools on that academic level. The *gymnasium* is the advanced part of the secondary school and is roughly equivalent to our junior college. The university in Denmark is roughly equivalent to the last two years of college and graduate or professional schools. Vocational training which culminates in the passing of an examination is much more prominent in Denmark than in the United States.

4.   The comparison of answers from students whose mothers replied with those of students whose mothers did not reply reveals no differences between the two groups of adolescents in socio-demographic characteristics. There is a slight tendency for responding mothers to be more interested in educational matters.

a small rural school and a regional school which draws its student body from several small adjacent communities. The Danish schools are distributed throughout Denmark and include 7 rural schools, 1 regional school in a rural setting and 4 schools in an urban setting.

While an attempt was made to match Danish and American schools, differences do appear in the occupational distribution of the American and Danish samples. The Danish sample contains a larger proportion of farmers (24%), managers and officials (28%), and a smaller proportion of skilled 15%) and unskilled workers (20%) than the American sample, where these groups amount to 2%, 11%, 36% and 34%, respectively. These differences reflect occupational differences between the two countries.

Subsamples of dyads and triads were identified:

    a. Adolescent/mother dyads consisting of matched adolescent/mother pairs from intact families; there are 1141 such dyads in the American sample and 977 in the Danish. The intact families represent 83% and 90%, respectively, of the total American and Danish samples of matched adolescent/mother pairs.

    b. Adolescent/best-school-friend dyads consisting of all identified adolescent/best-school-friend pairs, regardless of whether or not there was a mother match. A best-school-friend could be identified for over 90% of the adolescents in both the American and the Danish samples. There are 2157 such dyads in the U.S. and 1423 in Denmark.

    c. Adolescent/mother/best-school-friend triads consisting of all adolescents from intact families who could be matched to both their mother and their best-school-friend. There are 1065 basic triads in the United States and 905 in Denmark.

The analyses are based alternatively on pairs drawn from the triads or the dyads. To compare simultaneously concordance with mother and concordance with best friend, the samples are restricted to pairs drawn from the triads. To investigate factors related to concordance, all the dyads are included in order to maximize the number of cases. This procedure is justified by the fact that levels of concordance are almost identical among pairs from dyads and from triads (data not presented).

Measurement of Educational Plans

Students and mothers were asked parallel questions about the adolescent's educational plans. Students and their best friends were asked to indicate the highest level of education they expected to complete; mothers were asked: "What is the highest level of education you would like your child to complete?" An "undecided" alternative was provided the students, but not their parents. Thus, the measures used for parental and peer influences are not identical, since mothers' expectations are specifically for their child, while peers' expectations are for themselves. This point is discussed in the interpretation of the findings.

Because of differences in the educational systems in the United States and Denmark, different levels of education have been considered in each country. The United States alternatives are: high school, two-year college, four-year college and graduate education. The Danish alternatives are: secondary school, vocational training, gymnasium or teachers college, and university. Respondents who did not answer the educational question, and adolescents who checked the alternative "undecided" were not included in the analysis. Concordance within dyads was measured by Kendall's tau-beta[5] (Kendall, 1962).

Results

1. Concordance on Educational Plans with Mothers and Peers

To assess the relative influence of parents and peers on educational plans, we have examined the degree of concordance on plans among matched adolescent/mother pairs and adolescent/best-school-friend pairs in the sample of triads.

The results are striking and follow identical trends in both the United States and Denmark (see Table 1).

Table 1

CONCORDANCE[*] ON EDUCATIONAL PLANS BETWEEN ADOLESCENT
AND MOTHER AND ADOLESCENT AND BEST-SCHOOL-FRIEND BY SEX,
IN THE UNITED STATES AND DENMARK (TRIADS)

CONCORDANCE ON EDUCATIONAL PLANS	UNITED STATES CONCORDANCE WITH		DENMARK CONCORDANCE WITH	
	MOTHER	BEST-SCHOOL-FRIEND	MOTHER	BEST-SCHOOL-FRIEND
Total sample	.504	.389	.475	.268
Total N	(740)	(531)	(532)	(378)
Boys	.427	.308	.452	.294
Total N	(357)	(245)	(273)	(210)
Girls	.532	.423	.482	.217
Total N	(383)	(286)	(259)	(168)

* As measured by tau-beta. All associations significant at .001 level.

5.   No existing statistics are truly satisfactory to measure concordance, since none gives a measure that takes into account simultaneously the absolute amount of observed agreement within pairs and the relative amount of agreement given the marginal distributions of answers.

a. In both countries, concordance on educational goals is highly significant both for mother and best-school-friend.

b. In both countries, concordance is higher for mother than for best-school-friend. Thus, concordance is .504 for mother and .389 for best-school-friend in the United States and .475 and .268, respectively, in Denmark.[6] This holds for both boys and girls (see Table 1). By using parental educational or occupational background as an indirect indicator of parental influence previous investigators have underestimated the actual degree of parental influence on the child's educational aspirations. In our own study, the associations between mothers' education and adolescents' educational aspirations (.199 in the United States and .195 in Denmark)[7] are much lower than the associations between mothers' actual plans for their children and adolescents' educational aspirations.

c. In both countries, girls have higher levels of agreement with their mothers than boys. Thus, we are able to replicate with respect to educational goals the oft-reported finding of greater consensus among mother-daughter than mother-son pairs (Furstenberg, 1967).

It must be noted that the measures of mother's and friend's influence which we are using have somewhat different meanings. In the case of the mother, we are measuring her aspirations for her child and assume that they are communicated to the child in the form of influencing attempts. In the case of the friend, we are measuring his aspirations for himself and assume that he influences the adolescent as an example and role model. While we do not know friends' educational aspirations for each other, we do have data on peers' encouragement for college plans. Adolescents were asked: "How would your close friends here at school react if you decided to attend college?" The response alternatives included: "they would encourage me," "they would discourage me," "they wouldn't care." The answers to that question indicate the adolescent's perception of his friends' educational aspirations for him. The association (as measured by tau-beta) between this question and the adolescent's educational goals is .259 in the United States and .176 in Denmark. These tau-beta values are lower than the measures of concordance on actual educational goals within friendship pairs. (Compare with data presented in Table 1.) Thus, we believe that the use of friends' self-aspirations does not artificially lower the measured effect of friends' educational influence. The variables we use reflect in our opinion the actual processes of influence, since we assume that peers influence each other by imitation of each other's behaviors.

That parents influence adolescents' educational plans more than peers is illustrated further when one examines simultaneously the adolescent's aspirations, his mother's aspirations for him, and the plans of his best-school-friend. In order to simplify the analysis, educational plans in both countries

6. Parental influence is in all likelihood even greater than is indicated by our data, since we restrict ourselves to maternal desires and do not also take into account the father's educational aspirations for his child.

7. The correlation with father's education is .177 in the U.S. and .241 in Denmark.

have been dichotomized. In the United States, the categories are high school and two-year college and over; in Denmark, vocational training has been included in the secondary school category. The results in Table 2, particularly for the triads in which mother and best friend hold divergent plans, show that in both countries the influence of the mother is greater than that

Table 2

PER CENT OF ADOLESCENTS PLANNING TO CONTINUE THEIR ACADEMIC
EDUCATION BY BEST-SCHOOL-FRIEND'S EDUCATIONAL PLANS AND
MOTHER'S EDUCATIONAL ASPIRATIONS FOR ADOLESCENT, IN THE
UNITED STATES AND DENMARK (TRIADS)

	PER CENT OF ADOLESCENTS PLANNING TO CONTINUE ACADEMIC EDUCATION							
	UNITED STATES MOTHER'S ASPIRATIONS				DENMARK MOTHER'S ASPIRATIONS			
BEST-SCHOOL-FRIEND'S PLANS	HIGH SCHOOL %	N	COLLEGE† %	N	SECONDARY VOCATIONAL %	N	UNIVERSITY† %	N
High school .... (secondary, vocational)	8	(88)	49	(134)	8	(166)	66	(64)
College .... (university[1])	21	(38)	83	(267)	26	(47)	84	(77)

† In United States: two year college and over
  In Denmark: gymnasium, teachers college and university

Weighted effect parameter of:	United States	Denmark
Mother's aspirations	.492**	.578**
Best-school-friend's plans	.288**	.179**

** $p < .01$

of the friend. In the United States, 49% of adolescents want to continue beyond high school when their mothers have college plans for them and their best-school-friends intend to stop at the high school level. By contrast, only 21% of adolescents plan on college when their mothers have no college aspirations, even though their best-school-friends intend to go on to college. That friends have influence beyond that of the mother is shown by the increase in college plans when both mother and best-school-friend have college plans: in the United States, the proportion of adolescents with college plans increases to 83% when both their best-school-friend and their mother have college aspirations. Similar trends are observed in Denmark with respect to plans for further academic education. As measured by Coleman's weighted effect parameter, the influence of the mother in the United States is approximately twice as high as that of best-school-friend; in Denmark three times as high. The effect of the mother is relatively stronger in Denmark (.578 in Denmark versus .492 in the United States) while that of the best friend is smaller (.179 versus .288) (see Table 2).

The greater influence of the mother as compared to the best-school-friend in both countries can also be observed in relation to future occupational goals. Adolescents were asked what jobs they would like to have 15 years hence if their desires could be realized, and what job they actually expected to hold at that time. Mothers were asked parallel questions about the occupational aspirations and occupational expectations they held for their children. As shown by Table 3, concordance with mother on occupational goals is consistently higher than concordance with best-school-friend in both countries, and for both boys and girls.

Table 3

CONCORDANCE[†] ON OCCUPATIONAL GOALS BETWEEN ADOLESCENT
AND MOTHER AND ADOLESCENT AND BEST-SCHOOL-FRIEND, IN THE
UNITED STATES AND DENMARK (TRIADS)

	UNITED STATES CONCORDANCE WITH		DENMARK CONCORDANCE WITH	
CONCORDANCE ON	MOTHER	BEST-SCHOOL-FRIEND	MOTHER	BEST-SCHOOL-FRIEND
OCCUPATIONAL ASPIRATIONS[‡]				
Total sample	.358***	.209***	.560***	.129**
Total N	(619)	(769)	(565)	(710)
Boys	.254*	.159*	.525***	.092
Total N	(374)	(431)	(302)	(380)
Girls	.485***	.240***	.620***	.188**
Total N	(245)	(338)	(263)	(330)
OCCUPATIONAL EXPECTATIONS[‡]				
Total sample	.600***	.189***	.660***	.222***
Total N	(367)	(430)	(301)	(456)
Boys	.528***	.211***	.623***	.164**
Total N	(249)	(281)	(209)	(323)
Girls	.835***	.114	.751***	.356***
Total N	(118)	(149)	(92)	(133)

† As measured by tau-beta. $*p < .05$, $**p < .01$, $***p < .001$.

‡ Includes only boys and girls and their mothers who made a specific occupational choice; excludes girls and mothers who chose housewife. Occupational categories include: blue collar, white collar, and professional.

Far from supporting the notion that adolescents belong to adolescent subcultures completely separate from parents and are influenced by their peers more than by their parents, these data suggest the opposite: namely that parents are *more* influential than peers as regards future life goals.[8]

8. The adolescent's best-school-friend, of course, does not represent all possible peer influences, nor does it necessarily represent the influence of the adolescent's very best friend, who may not be in the same school with him. Data presented later on in this paper indicate that even among adolescents for whom the school friend is the very best friend over-all, concordance on educational plans is lower with friend than with mother.

Furthermore, far from acting at odds with parents' goals, peers seem to reinforce these goals. In both countries, the majority of adolescents hold plans which are in agreement with those of their mothers *and* their friends. Adolescents who agree with their parents are also more likely to be in agreements with their peers than those who disagree; correlatively, adolescents who disagree with their parents are also less likely than those who agree to be in agreement with their peers. Thus, 76% of American adolescents have congruent plans with their best-school-friend when they agree with their mother; the percentage drops to 59% when they are in disagreement with her; the percentages for Danish adolescents are 74% and 57%. Our data suggest that, in the area of future life goals, there is no polarization of adolescents toward either parental or peer groups.

That peer influences are compatible with, and supportive of, parental influences is illustrated further by the positive association that exists between the mother's and the best friend's plans (Table 4). While this association is much lower than that which exists between the mother and her own child,

Table 4

CONCORDANCE† BETWEEN MOTHER AND BEST-SCHOOL-FRIEND
ON EDUCATIONAL PLANS BY SEX, IN THE UNITED STATES
AND DENMARK

| | UNITED STATES | | DENMARK | |
	TAU-BETA	N	TAU-BETA	N
Total sample	.262***	(740)	.171***	(538)
Boys	.167***	(360)	.121*	(276)
Girls	.290***	(380)	.220***	(262)

† As measured by tau-beta.   * $p < .05$,   *** $p < .001$.

it is positive and highly significant. It is also higher for girls than for boys, paralleling the greater adolescent-peer concordance that is observed among girls than among boys in both countries.

Perhaps friends reinforce parental aspirations because adolescents associate with peers whose goals are congruent with parental goals. When parents have college aspirations for their children, the overwhelming majority of their children's friends also have college plans; when parents have high school plans, the majority of their children's friends have high school plans. Thus, 65% of the friends of American adolescents whose parents have college aspirations for them have college plans; the proportion of friends with college plans drops to 34% when the adolescents' parents have only high school aspirations. The comparable Danish percentages are 49% and 26%. These trends hold true within each social class (data not presented).

Our data indicate not only that parental influence on future life goals is stronger than peer influence, but also that it remains strong throughout the entire adolescent period (Table 5). The decreasing influence of parents throughout adolescence has been accepted as fact by many sociologists

(Parsons, 1942; McDill and Coleman, 1965; Douvan and Adelson, 1966). Our data, however, do not support this conclusion. Table 5 shows that, in both countries, concordance levels vary irregularly from year to year between the ages of 14 to 18. While at age 14, concordance with mother in both countries is higher than at any other age, from ages 15 through 18 it does not show any consistent decrease, nor does concordance with friend

Table 5

CONCORDANCE† ON EDUCATIONAL PLANS BETWEEN ADOLESCENT AND MOTHER AND ADOLESCENT AND BEST-SCHOOL-FRIEND BY AGE, IN THE UNITED STATES AND DENMARK (DYADS)

CONCORDANCE WITH	AGE				
	14	15	16	17	18
UNITED STATES					
Mother	.613*	.561*	.418*	.542*	.432*
Total N	(23)	(112)	(229)	(261)	(159)
Best-school-friend	.394*	.436*	.341*	.315*	.406*
Total N	(47)	(178)	(291)	(333)	(199)
DENMARK					
Mother	.822*	.483*	.540*	.416*	.582*
Total N	(10)	(174)	(178)	(163)	(55)
Best-school-friend	.000	.172*	.296*	.320*	.188
Total N	(4)	(188)	(197)	(148)	(51)

† As measured by tau-beta. *$p < .01$.

show a consistent increase. These trends are not altered when sex of the child is taken into account (data not presented).

2. Concordance: Influence or Convergence

The levels of concordance on educational plans are high. However, the existence of a positive correlation between members of a dyad does not necessarily reflect the influence of one individual by the other, since both could be subject to the same external social influence. For instance, concordance on values between mother-children pairs has been found not to differ from levels of concordance with non-related adults living in the same household (Furstenberg, 1967) or members of artificial families (Basset, 1949; Dentler and Hutchinson, 1961). In order to demonstrate transmission of values, or influence, from one member of the pair upon another, one must be able to show (1) that agreement between the two is not explained by a common external factor which both experience, and (2) that agreement is modified by characteristics of the interaction between the two individuals. If agreement results from the direct influence of one individual over the other, different patterns of interaction should affect the degree of influence observed.

Thus, the very high concordance on educational plans between adolescent and mother observed in our samples could very well result from the fact that adolescents and their mothers belong to the same social class and are independently affected by it.

Similarly, concordance between the adolescent and his best-school-friend could result from common experiences (either outside or inside the school) that lead to identical educational plans, rather than from the specific influence of one friend upon the other. In this sample of dyads, social and economic background are relatively unimportant criteria for personal choice of friends (Kandel, *et al.*, 1968). In both countries, criteria such as age or program in school are much more important.[9] The common school experience of American and Danish adolescents could account for the observed agreement on educational plans between in-school friendship pairs, since school program is highly related to educational plans. In the United States, the proportion of adolescents planning to go to college varies from 92% among students in the college preparatory course to 30% in the general program. In Denmark, 51% of the students in the *real line* are planning to go on at least to gymnasium, as compared to only 10% in the *almen line*.

When social class[10] is held constant (see Table 6), concordance remains at a high and significant level, suggesting that agreement with mother or best-school-friend within a particular social class is not spurious and does not result from its independent association with social class. The data for the mothers are particularly striking.[11] The measures of concordance within

Table 6

CONCORDANCE[*] ON EDUCATIONAL PLANS BETWEEN ADOLESCENT
AND MOTHER AND ADOLESCENT AND BEST-SCHOOL-FRIEND, CONTROLLED
BY SOCIAL CLASS IN THE UNITED STATES AND DENMARK (DYADS)

| | UNITED STATES | | DENMARK | | |
| | MIDDLE | LOWER | MIDDLE | LOWER | |
CONCORDANCE WITH	CLASS	CLASS	CLASS	CLASS	FARMER
Mother	.542	.495	.507	.431	.436
Total *N*	(215)	(493)	(252)	(198)	(125)
Best-school-friend	.418	.325	.199	.345	.231
Total *N*	(261)	(612)	(259)	(210)	(111)

* As measured by tau-beta. All significant at .01 level.

9.   Among the American adolescent-peer dyads, the similarity (measured by tau-beta) in father's occupation of the two friends is remarkably low: .085, as compared to .539 for age or .598 for program in school. The comparable tau-beta coefficients for Danish dyads are: .147, .641 and .818. All the tau-betas are statistically significant.

10.   The social class variable is based upon father's occupation.
Middle class includes: professionals, technical, managers, officials, white collar, and sales; Lower class includes: foremen, skilled and unskilled workers, and laborers.

11.   Other indicators of social status, such as family income, father's and mother's education, give rise to similar results (data not shown). Although concordance with mother varies irregularly when these social factors are controlled, it remains consistently high.

each social class are very similar to what they were for the sample as a whole. They certainly have not disappeared, nor have they even been appreciably reduced, as would have been the case had social class explained the initially high association between adolescent's and mother's plans. The cross-tabulations of mother's and adolescent's plans which correspond to the correlations in Table 6 are most striking. In the United States, when mothers have college aspirations for their children, 80% of middle-class and 67% of lower-class adolescents plan to go on to college; when mothers have no college aspirations for their children, the proportion of adolescents with college plans drops to 20% and 16%, respectively, in the middle and lower class. Similar trends are observed in Denmark: the proportion of adolescents planning for higher academic education are, respectively, 78%, 72%, 15%, and 7%. The weighted effect parameters reflect these trends very strongly. In the United States, the effect of mother's plans on adolescent aspiration is .530 as compared to .108 for social class; in Denmark, .637 for mother's plans and .077 for social class.

These data provide strong evidence for Kahl's (1953) original observation that parental aspiration is a more important determinant of children's educational aspirations than is social class membership per se. (See also Sewell and Shah, 1968.) This is not to deny the importance of social class as a determining factor in educational aspirations—but our data can be interpreted to show that the impact of social class on the adolescent, to the extent that there is one, is absorbed in the nature of the maternal influence. We would conclude that social class is a major determinant of parental aspirations, which in turn is a determinant of adolescent aspirations. Social class itself has only a slight independent influence on the *adolescent's* aspirations.

It can be noted (Table 6) that while the coefficients of concordance remain highly significant within each social class, there are variations among them, especially as regards friends. In the United States, there is higher concordance with mother and in particular with best friend in the middle class than in the lower class. In Denmark, concordance with mother is also higher in the middle class; on the other hand, concordance with best friend is higher in the lower than in the middle class. The somewhat weaker exposure to congruent social influences of the lower-class American adolescent and of the middle-class Dane is illustrated even more convincingly by the degree of inter-triad agreement in each class. The proportion of adolescents who agree with both their mothers and their friends is higher in the middle than in the lower class in the United States; the opposite is observed in Denmark (see Table 7). These social class differences can be explained in part by the distribution of educational plans in each country and the relation that these plans bear to social class. The most inter-triad agreement is observed among adolescents who choose the modal educational aspiration in each country (college in the United States, and secondary school level in Denmark). In the United States, 73% of adolescents who plan to go on to college are in agreement both with their mother and their friends as con-

Table 7

AGREEMENT ON EDUCATIONAL PLANS WITHIN TRIADS BY SOCIAL CLASS
AND TYPE OF EDUCATIONAL PLANS, IN THE UNITED STATES
AND DENMARK

PROPORTION OF ADOLESCENTS WHO AGREE BOTH WITH MOTHER AND FRIEND	UNITED STATES		DENMARK	
	MIDDLE CLASS	LOWER CLASS	MIDDLE CLASS	LOWER CLASS
Total sample	66	54	55	70
Total N	(146)	(327)	(160)	(116)
When plan to stop at high school level	41	36	60	76
Total N	(44)	(160)	(82)	(88)
When plan to go to college*	77	71	50	50
Total N	(102)	(167)	(78)	(28)

* In United States: two year college and over
In Denmark: gymnasium, teachers college and university

trasted to 36% among those who plan to stop at the high school level; in Denmark, the comparable percentages are 49% and 69%. When we control both for social class and type of plans held, we find, especially in the United States, that type of plan is a much stronger correlate of inter-triad agreement than social class (Table 7). Regardless of social class, American adolescents are in greater agreement with both parents and peers when they wish to go to college than when they wish to stop their education at the high school level. In Denmark, they are most in agreement when they do not want to continue their education.

We also examined concordance with peer, with school program held constant (Table 8). As expected, school program explains more of the

Table 8

CONCORDANCE[†] ON EDUCATIONAL PLANS BETWEEN ADOLESCENT
AND BEST-SCHOOL-FRIEND, CONTROLLED BY ADOLESCENT'S SCHOOL
PROGRAM, IN THE UNITED STATES AND DENMARK (DYADS)

CONCORDANCE WITH BEST-SCHOOL-FRIEND	UNITED STATES				
	COMMERCIAL	GENERAL	COLLEGE PREPARATORY	VOCATIONAL	TOTAL
Concordance ..	.293***	.156**	.153***	.084	.367***
Total N	(430)	(216)	(346)	(33)	(1060)

	DENMARK		
	ALMEN	REAL	TOTAL
Concordance ..	.192**	.230***	.279***
Total N	(240)	(348)	(588)

† As measured by tau-beta.   * $p < .05$,   ** $p < .01$,   *** $p < .001$.

concordance on educational plans between friends than does social class. Within each school program, concordance is lower than for the sample as a whole, but is still highly significant statistically, except in the vocational program in the United States. Within each program, adolescents' plans are influenced to some extent by the plans of their school friends. For example, the proportion of American students with college plans in the commercial programs increases from 25% when their best friend intends to stop at the high school level to 56% when their best friend plans to go on to college.

These results provide evidence that concordance between adolescent and mother, and adolescent and best-school-friend represents direct influence on the adolescent, rather than the independent influence of the common social situation in which both dyad members are situated, as represented by social class. This is especially true for parental influence. The parent stands as the link between social class and the adolescent. Peer influence can be understood in part in terms of the fact that friendships form among adolescents enrolled in the same school program.

If concordance between adolescent and mother, and adolescent and best-school-friend is independent in great part of the external social conditions in which the pairs are located, factors which increase or decrease that influence must be sought in the characteristics of the relationship itself. Therefore, the effects of interactional patterns which could increase or decrease concordance within dyads are examined next.

3. Concordance and Mother's Influence

A. PATTERNS OF FAMILY INTERACTION. Family variables are of particular interest in the study of parental influence because socialization theory assumes that the structure of parent-child interaction affects the degree to which parents are able to transmit their values and goals to their children.

> The form and quality of interaction between parent and child . . . affect the learning of normative behavior patterns, values and other aspects of culture that parents regard as appropriate and desirable for the child (Rosen, 1964, p. 59).

A number of family variables, such as type of parental power, amount of communication, degree of closeness between parent and child and reliance on parental advice have been suggested as facilitating transmission of values from parent to child. (For a review of relevant studies see Furstenberg, 1967; Kandel, *et al.*, 1968.) Data on these patterns of adolescent-parent interaction were available for the families in our study. We expected these interactional variables to affect concordance on educational plans between mother and adolescent. We had found (Kandel, *et al.*, 1968) that these family variables were positively associated with the adolescents' *subjective* reports of parental influence, such as feeling that their opinions were close to those of their parents and with preferring the opinions of parents to those of peers.

However, these subjective perceptions of parental influence are *not* supported by the analyses of *actual* influence. No consistent effect of family patterns on the degree of agreement between mother and child on educational goals could be identified. The results are inconsistent from country to country and mostly negative. The family patterns examined included the mother's authority pattern, the extent to which she explains her decisions, the adolescent's feeling of closeness to his mother, his reliance on his mother for advice, his score on an index of peer orientation, his preference for the opinions of friends or mother, whether he feels that his opinions are similar to or different from those of his mother, and whether he experiences enough freedom from his mother. Selected findings are presented in Table 9. The

Table 9

CONCORDANCE[†] ON EDUCATIONAL PLANS BETWEEN ADOLESCENT
AND MOTHER BY SELECTED PATTERNS OF FAMILY INTERACTION, IN THE
UNITED STATES AND DENMARK (DYADS)

| | UNITED STATES | | DENMARK | |
FAMILY PATTERNS[‡]	TAU-BETA	N	TAU-BETA	N
Maternal authority				
Authoritarian	.476	(298)	.419	(81)
Democratic	.499	(272)	.501	(343)
Permissive	.450	(115)	.527	(147)
Mother explains decisions				
Always	.443	(206)	.444	(252)
Usually	.525	(206)	.559	(203)
Sometimes	.482	(268)	.484	(110)
Closeness to mother				
Extremely	.488	(216)	.659	(128)
Quite	.537	(202)	.404	(201)
Moderately	.447	(174)	.491	(166)
Not at all	.439	(85)	.451	(70)
Reliance on mother's advice				
High	.530	(254)	.523	(164)
Medium	.461	(364)	.458	(332)
Low	.455	(123)	.538	(82)

* As measured by tau-beta. All significant at .001 level.

‡ Adolescent's perceptions.

only positive results are obtained in the United States, where concordance varies according to the adolescent's reliance on his mother and where democratic maternal authority leads to slightly greater concordance than either the authoritarian or permissive pattern. But these trends are weak and most other results inconclusive.[12] These findings were completely unexpected,

12. The same lack of effect is observed when the child's academic ability is controlled for in the analysis.

when we consider our finding that the strength of concordance between mother and child is independent of the family's social class background, and the strong statements in the socialization literature.[13]

These findings are difficult to interpret if they mean indeed that parental influence takes place irrespective of the nature of the parent-child relationship. It is possible that our measures of these variables are inadequate or that the variables are attributes of family life too general to reveal the differential influence of parents on children on a particular issue, such as educational plans. As we will now see, more specific variables do indeed show some effect.

B. COMMUNICATION ABOUT EDUCATIONAL PLANS.   The influence of the mother on the adolescent's educational plans is strongly revealed when we examine the actual content of her interactions with the adolescent about these plans. Parents were not only asked their educational aspirations for the adolescent, but also how strongly they had encouraged him (or her) to pursue his education after secondary school.

The mother's encouragement of higher education has a noticeable effect on the educational aspirations of her child. In the United States, 82% of adolescents plan to continue their education beyond high school if the mother strongly encourages the pursuit of higher education, but the percentage drops to 14% when the mother reports she has advised against college attendance. Similarly, in Denmark, increased maternal encouragement toward higher education substantially increases the proportions of students who aspire to academic higher education (the gymnasium, the university, and teachers college). This proportion decreases from 69% when mothers provide strong encouragement to 10% when they are actually against higher education. These findings are in agreement with studies which have examined the effect of parental encouragement on educational occupational aspirations. (See for instance, Bell, 1963; Bordua, 1960; Cohen, 1965; Hollingshead, 1949; Kahl, 1953; Mannino, 1962; Morrow and Wilson, 1961; Sewell and Shah, 1968.)

The mother's choice of educational level and her degree of encouragement are very highly related, but they are not identical. A few mothers encourage higher education but actually hold only a low educational goal, while a few state that they discourage higher education, but nevertheless, hold a high educational goal. We analyzed simultaneously the effects of mother's encouragement and specific educational aspirations upon the adolescent's plans (Table 10). Specific maternal aspirations and general maternal encouragement affect the child's level of aspiration independently, but the effect of the specific plans is the stronger of the two. The greater

13. In an empirical investigation based on matched parent-adolescent pairs Furstenberg (1967) similarly was unable to isolate any effect of family variables on concordance between parent and child in 6 out of 7 values he considered. He did find effects on mobility orientation, a composite index that included several items, including educational aspirations.

Table 10

ADOLESCENT'S EDUCATIONAL PLANS BY MOTHER'S PLANS AND
STRENGTH OF ENCOURAGEMENT FOR CHILD TO CONTINUE HIS
EDUCATION, IN THE UNITED STATES AND DENMARK

	MOTHER'S EDUCATIONAL PLANS AND STRENGTH OF ENCOURAGEMENT‡							
	UNITED STATES				DENMARK			
	HIGH SCHOOL		COLLEGE†		SECOND; VOC.		UNIVERSITY†	
		MEDIUM		MEDIUM	STRONG		STRONG	
	STRONG	AGAINST	STRONG	AGAINST	MEDIUM	AGAINST	MEDIUM	AGAINST
PER CENT OF ADOLESCENTS PLANNING TO CONTINUE ACADEMIC EDUCATION[1]	35	17	85	53	13	7	78	50
Total N	(17)	(149)	(361)	(219)	(176)	(125)	(206)	(10)

† In United States: two year college and over
In Denmark: gymnasium, teachers college and university
‡ Mother's perception. Different groupings of categories of encouragement to continue education have been used in the two countries because of great differences in the distributions of answers.

	United States	Denmark
Weighted Effect of:		
Mother's plans	.382**	.621**
Mother's encouragement	.302**	.089*

    * $p < .05$,   ** $p < .01$.

the mother's encouragement, the greater the concordance on educational plans in those families in which the mother has college aspirations. Thus, among mothers with college aspirations for their children, 85% of American adolescents plan to continue their education when their mother also provides strong encouragement, as compared to only 53% when the mother has college aspirations but her encouragement is not as high. Comparable differences are observed in Denmark (Table 10). Similarly, the proportion of adolescents who agree with their mother when she does not have college plans for them is higher in those families in which the mother is consistent in her attitudes and *does not* provide strong encouragement to go on to college.

Parents of different social classes vary not only in the kinds of educational goals they have for their children, but also in the encouragement they give their children to continue their education. Middle-class mothers provide more encouragement than lower-class mothers. When the mother's educational plans and strength of encouragement are controlled simultaneously, the social-class effects on the child's own plans have almost completely disappeared in both countries (Table 11). Thus, the social class differences in adolescents' educational plans can be explained mostly by the fact that parents have different levels of aspiration and provide differential encouragement for their children to pursue their education. The parents' attitudes

Table 11

PER CENT OF ADOLESCENTS PLANNING TO CONTINUE ACADEMIC
EDUCATION, WHEN MOTHER HAS COLLEGE ASPIRATIONS, BY MATERNAL
ENCOURAGEMENT‡ AND SOCIAL CLASS, IN THE UNITED STATES
AND DENMARK (DYADS)

	MOTHERS WITH COLLEGE ASPIRATIONS							
	UNITED STATES				DENMARK			
	STRONG ENCOURAGEMENT		MEDIUM, AGAINST		STRONG, MEDIUM		AGAINST	
PER CENT OF ADOLESCENTS	MIDDLE CLASS	LOWER CLASS	MIDDLE CLASS	LOWER CLASS	MIDDLE CLASS	LOWER CLASS	MIDDLE CLASS	LOWER CLASS
PLANNING TO CONTINUE ACADEMIC EDUCATION†	89%	82%	56%	50%	78%	72%	(2)	(2)
Total N	(122)	(196)	(48)	(153)	(124)	(50)	(4)	(3)

† In United States: two year college and over
  In Denmark: gymnasium, teachers college and university

‡ Mother's perception. Different groupings of categories of encouragement have been used in the two countries because of great differences in the distributions of answers.

and plans, in turn, are associated with their class position. But for the child, the parent is clearly the link between social class position and future life goals.

The student was also asked to whom he had talked about his educational plans. The mother is unanimously mentioned in both countries as the one person most often consulted, by 85% of adolescents in the United States and 89% in Denmark. There is a slight tendency for adolescents who discuss their plans with their mother to be in greater agreement with her than when they do not communicate to her about this. Concordance is .471 among American adolescents who talk to their mother as compared to .400 when they do not talk about college plans; Danish tau-betas are .510 and .483.

4. Concordance and the Influence of Best Friend

In contrast to the findings for mother, we find that the influence of the best-school-friend on the adolescent varies according to the intensity of the interaction with the friend. We have several indicators of the intensity of interaction between members of friendship pairs. We know (1) whether or not the friendship choice is reciprocated, (2) how frequently the adolescent see his friend out of school, and (3) whether the best-school-friend is also the best friend over-all. We expected that friendship pairs characterized by greater intimacy and greater frequency of contact would show greater concordance. Alexander and Campbell (1964) had found that reciprocity of choice increased the similarity in college plans of high school seniors.

The results confirm these expectations. As shown by the relative size of the tau-betas in Table 12, friends whose choice is reciprocated have more influence upon each other than friends involved in unreciprocated choices. Similarly, friends whom the adolescent sees frequently out of school are more influential than those he sees more rarely (Table 12). And school

Table 12

CONCORDANCE† ON EDUCATIONAL PLANS BETWEEN ADOLESCENT
AND BEST-SCHOOL-FRIEND BY STRENGTH OF FRIENDSHIP, IN THE
UNITED STATES AND DENMARK (DYADS)

| | UNITED STATES | | DENMARK | |
STRENGTH OF FRIENDSHIP	TAU-BETA	N	TAU-BETA	N
Reciprocity of Choice				
Reciprocated	.390*	(438)	.355*	(326)
Not reciprocated	.346*	(622)	.197*	(262)
Frequency of Contact out of School				
More than once a week	.369*	(732)	.337*	(345)
Once a week-month	.350*	(213)	.229*	(179)
Never	.316*	(114)	.085	(54)
School Friend is Best Friend Over-all				
Yes	.406*	(710)	.300*	(357)
No	.291*	(338)	.250*	(221)

† As measured by tau-beta. * $p < .001$.

friends who are also the adolescent's very best friend over-all, outside school as well as in school, are more influential than those school friends who are not the adolescent's best over-all friend (Table 12).

The degree of friendship was refined further by taking into account simultaneously whether the choice was reciprocated *and* whether the friend in school was the best friend over-all. The "very best friend" in terms of this classification, is the best friend over-all whose choice is reciprocated. Concordance on educational plans with reciprocated best friends over-all is higher than for any other category of friendships. However, concordance with the very best friend over-all is still not as high as with the mother. In the United States, concordance with reciprocated very best friend is .423 as compared to .504 for the mother; in Denmark, concordance is .391 and .475, respectively.

While objective indicators of the intensity of friendship interactions among peers influence the degree of concordance on educational goals among adolescents, items indicative of the adolescent's *subjective* orientation to peers show no such effect. The adolescent's report of whether he respects more his mother's or his best friend's opinions has no effect on concordance with best-school-friend (data not presented).

The data in Table 12 also indicate that the Americans' receptivity to their friends' influence is not as sensitive as is the Danes' to the degree of intimacy of the friendship (whether or not the friendship choice is reciprocated, or how often the adolescent sees his friend out of school). These findings, together with other findings of our study, suggest important differences in the meaning of adolescent friendships in the United States and Denmark. The Danes appear to have one very good friend, while the Americans appear to move within a large circle of friends, without any one of them being especially more significant. When asked how frequently they see their three best-school-friends out of school, Danes show a greater disparity than the Americans in the frequency with which second and third friends are seen as compared to the one listed as first in closeness. Similarly, in Denmark, reciprocity of friendship choice increases the similarity between friends not only on educational and occupational goals but also in background characteristics, leisure-time activities, and interests to a greater extent than in the United States. By a number of criteria, Americans appear to have a larger circle of significant friends than the Danes.

Summary and Conclusion

The findings reported in this paper have relevance for several current controversies about sources of influences on adolescents' educational plans, about the separateness of adolescents and adults, and about the process of family socialization. The design of the study provides an unusual opportunity to deal with these issues since the sample includes triads of adolescents matched with their mothers and their best-school-friends and since the data include direct indicators of the educational aspirations of each of these three statuses, and information on patterns of parent-adolescent and friend-adolescent interactions.

The same general processes of influence are observed in the United States and in Denmark. The data show most strikingly that in both countries, concordance with mother is much higher than concordance with best-school-friend, even when that friend is the adolescent's very best friend over-all, outside or in school.[14]

Controlling for external social factors such as social class or program in school suggests that the influence of mother and friend, especially that of the mother, is intrinsic to the interaction itself. In both the United States and Denmark, parental desires for their children are more important direct determinants of the child's educational plans than is socioeconomic status.[15] This is not to deny the fact that the parents' aspirations are determined in great part by the parents' position in society.

14. Of course, we cannot ascertain the extent to which these aspirations will be translated into reality, and the extent of the influence of the mother on actual college attendance. Results from American studies which have correlated educational plans with actual college attendance suggest that the correlation between the two is high (Haller and Butterworth, 1960; Sewell and Shah, 1967). There is strong reason to believe that the mother's influence would thus also extend to actual college attendance.

15. This supports a thesis which has been developed with increasing frequency since Kahl's original paper (Kahl, 1953; McDill and Coleman, 1965).

While the influence of peers increases with the intimacy of the friendship, the influence of the mother appears to be remarkably independent of family structure and of the closeness of the adolescent to his mother. There is thus a beginning body of empirical data (Furstenberg, 1967) which fail to confirm empirically most assumptions about the role of family structure in socialization.

The notion of a separate adolescent subculture isolated from the parental culture is similarly not supported by our findings. To the contrary, in both countries there is a good deal of agreement both with parents and with peers. Furthermore, agreement on educational goals with parents goes together with agreement with friends, and adolescents who disagree with their parents are also likely to disagree with their friends.

The assumption is commonly made that peers provide a deterrent to intellectual development and educational aspirations during adolescence (Coleman, 1961; Gordon, 1957; Braham, 1965). Our own data confirm that the climate of American high schools does not appear to reward intellectual achievement (Kandel, *et al.*, 1968). But peers have much less influence on adolescents than parents with regard to future educational goals.

On this last point, the findings of a rarely quoted study by Riley, *et al.*, (1961) are quite relevant. These investigators found that the self-expectations which adolescents had for themselves as adults were very close to the adolescents' perceptions of their parents' current expectations. These authors believe that adolescents distinguish between values which are relevant to their current peer relationship and those which are relevant to the roles they will have to play in the future as adults. The present results suggest that one cannot speak of separate adolescent cultures or of general peer versus parental influences. One must specify the particular content area under discussion. For certain values or certain areas, peers may be more influential than parents; for other issues, the reverse may be true (Brittain, 1963). We have shown that parents are more important than peers for future life goals.

Thus, we take exception to what we have called the "hydraulic" view taken by many investigators regarding the relative influence of adults and peers, especially parents, which assumes that the greater the influence of the one, the less the influence of the other. Our data lead to another view: that, in critical areas, interactions with peers support the values of parents for the peer context.

References

ALEXANDER, C. N. and CAMPBELL, E. Q.   Peer influences on adolescent educational aspirations and attainments. *American Sociological Review*, 1964, 29, 568-575.

BASSET, R.   Opinion differences within the family. *Public Opinion Quarterly*, 1949, 13, 118-120.

BELL, G. D.   Process in the formation of adolescents' aspirations. *Social Forces*, 1963, 42, 179-186.

BERGER, B.   Adolescence and beyond: an essay review of three books on the problems of growing up. *Social Forces*, 1963, 10, 394-408.

BORDUA, D. J.   Educational aspirations and parental stress on college. *Social Forces*, 1960, 38, 262-269.

BOYLE, R. P.   The effect of the high school on students' aspirations. *American Journal of Sociology*, 1966, 71, 628-639.

BRAHAM, M.   Peer group deterrents to intellectual development during adolescence. *Educational Theory*, 1965, 15, 248-258.

BRITTAIN, C. V.   Adolescent choices and parent-peer cross-pressures. *American Sociological Review*, 1963, 28, 385-390.

COHEN, E. G.   Parental factors in educational mobility. *Sociology of Education*, 1965, 38, 405-425.

COLEMAN, J. S.   *The adolescent society.* New York: Free Press, 1961.

COLEMAN, J. S.   *Introduction to mathematical sociology.* New York: Free Press, 1964.

COLEMAN, J. S. *et al.*   *Equality of educational opportunity.* Washington: U.S. Government Printing Office, 1966.

DENTLER, R. A. and HUTCHINSON, J. G.   Socioeconomic versus family status as sources of family attitude consensus. *Child Development*, 1961, 32, 249-254.

DIXON, C. W.   *Society, schools and progress in Scandinavia.* London: Permagon Press, 1965.

DOUVAN, E. and ADELSON, J.   *The adolescent experience.* New York: Wiley, 1966.

DUNCAN, O. D., HALLER, A. O. and PORTES, A.   Peer influences on aspirations: a reinterpretation. *American Journal of Sociology*, 1968, 74, 119-137.

ELLIS, R. A. and LANE, C.   Structural supports for upward mobility. *American Sociological Review*, 1963, 28, 743-756.

FURSTENBERG, F. F., JR.   Transmission of attitudes in the family. Unpublished Ph.D. dissertation, Columbia University, 1967.

GORDON, C. W.   *The social system of the high school.* Glencoe: Free Press, 1957.

HALLER, A. O. and BUTTERWORTH, C. E.   Peer influences on levels of occupational and educational aspirations. *Social Forces*, 1960, 38, 289-295.

HALSEY, A. H. *et al.*   *Education, economy and society.* New York: The Free Press, 1961.

HERRIOTT, R. E.   Some social determinants of educational aspiration. *Harvard Educational Review*, 1962, 33, 157-177.

HOLLINGSHEAD, A. B.   *Elmtown's youth.* New York: Wiley, 1949.

HYMAN, H. H.   *Political socialization.* Glencoe, Ill.: Free Press, 1959.

JAHODA, M. and WARREN, N.   The myths of youth. *Sociology of Education*, 1965, 38, 138-149.

KAHL, J. A.   Educational and occupational aspirations of "common man" boys. *Harvard Educational Review*, 1953, 23, 186-203.

KANDEL, D. B. *et al.*   *Adolescents in two societies: peers, school, and family in the United States and Denmark.* Final Report, Project No. 2139, Contract No. OE-4-10-069. Bureau of Research, Office of Education, U.S. Department of Health, Education, and Welfare, 1968.

KANDEL, D. and LESSER, G. S.   Parental and peer influences on adolescent educational plans. *American Sociological Review*, 1969, 34, 212-223. (a)

KANDEL, D. and LESSER, G. S.   Parent-adolescent relationships and adolescent independence in the United States and Denmark. *Journal of Marriage and the Family*, 1969, 31, 348-359. (b)

KENDALL, M. G.   *Rank correlation methods.* New York: Hafner, 1962.

LIPSET, S. M. and BENDIX, R.   *Social mobility in industrial society.* Berkeley: University of California Press, 1959.

MANNINO, F. V.   Family factors related to school persistence. *Journal of Educational Sociology*, 1962, 35, 193-202.

McDILL, E. L. and COLEMAN, J. S.   Family and peer influence in college plans of high school students. *Sociology of Education*, 1965, 38, 112-126.

McDILL, E. L. *et al.*   *Sources of educational climates in high schools.* Final Report. The Johns Hopkins University, Contract No. OE-3-10-080, U.S. Department of Health, Education, and Welfare, 1966.

MICHAEL, J. A.   On neighborhood context and college plans. *American Sociological Review*, 1966, 31, 706-707.

MORROW, W. R. and Wilson, R. C.   Family relations of bright high-achieving and under-achieving high school boys. *Child Development*, 1961, 32, 501-510.

NEWCOMB, T. and SVEHLA, G.   Intra-family relationships in attitude. *Sociometry*, 1937, 1, 180-205.

PARSONS, T.   Age and sex in the social structure of the United States. *American Sociological Review*, 1942, 7, 604-616.

RAMSØY, N. R.   *Social structure and college recruitment.* New York: Bureau of Applied Social Research, Columbia University, 1962.

REHBERG, R. A. and WESTBY, D. L.   Parental encouragement, occupation, education and family size: artifactual or independent determinants of adolescent educational expectation? *Social Forces*, 1967, 45, 362-374.

RILEY, M. W. *et al.*   Adolescent values and the Riesman typology: an empirical analysis. In Lipset, S. and Lowenthal, L. (Eds.), *Culture and social character.* New York: Free Press, 1961. Pp. 370-386.

ROSEN, B. C.   Family structure and value transmission. *Merrill-Palmer Quarterly*, 1964, 10, 59-76.

SEWELL, W. H. *et al.*   Social status and educational and occupational aspiration. *American Sociological Review*, 1967, 22, 67-73.

SEWELL, W. H. and SHAH, V. P.   Socioeconomic status, intelligence and the attainment of higher education. *Sociology of Education*, 1967, 40, 1-23.

SEWELL, W. H. and SHAH, V. P.   Social class, parental encouragement, and educational aspirations. *American Journal of Sociology*, 1968, 73, 559-572.

SIMPSON, R. L.   Parental influence, anticipatory socialization, and social mobility. *American Sociological Review*, 1962, 27, 517-522.

STRODTBECK, F. L.   Family interaction, values, and achievement. In McClelland, D. C. *et al., Talent and society.* New York: Van Nostrand, 1958. Pp. 135-194.

TURNER, R. H.   *The social context of ambition.* San Francisco: Chandler, 1964.

WALLACE, W. L.   *Student culture.* Chicago: Aldine, 1964.

WILSON, A. B.   Residential segregation of social classes and aspirations of high school boys. *American Sociological Review*, 1959, 24, 836-845.

※ ※ ※ ※ ※

Much current social research concentrates on educationally disadvantaged youth—Negroes, children of the slums, the unmotivated, the unprepared, the drop-outs. Today's mission is to find the forces—in school and out—that depress their levels of school achievement so far below that of more fortunate children. All will be well and good, the researchers seem to be saying, when these youngsters can be brought to share the school experiences of the high-aspiring, high-achieving children of the upper-middle classes.

Rhea breaks with the fashion of the times and turns his gaze on these more fortunate students and their presumably desirable educational experiences. What he sees in some of the leading high schools he studied should give us pause. These schools too bear down on their students, he believes, with a pressure that warps and distorts the educative process into a form quite different from what educators expect or intend. One even gains a sense of admiration for the rationality and skill with which students learn to "work the system" and for their refusal to let it get them down (though Rhea sounds a warning note about the latter).

Rhea's views are only hypotheses and must not be taken for more than that until they are tested. With his remarkable insight, he has made a great deal out of his questionnaires and interviews. Possibly there is more of Rhea in the report than his respondents. But from where else do fruitful hypotheses come, if not through the interaction of an imaginative, order-seeking intelligence with the facts of the phenomenal world?

The interested reader might like to play Rhea's ideas against the remarkable documentary film *High School*, produced by Frederick Wiseman (OSTI: Cambridge, Mass., 1969).

Institutional Paternalism in High School*

Buford Rhea

Prominent in the literature of contemporary educational criticism is the charge that schools stifle learning, that they are basically self-defeating. This criticism takes several forms, e.g., that the school extinguishes vital adolescence (Friedenberg, 1959), that it perpetuates student inadequacies (Riessman, 1962), that it destroys creativity and the desire to learn (Henry, 1963, ch. 8) or that it positively brutalizes (Kozol, 1967); but a common theme is that the "system" itself, the bureaucratic system, is largely at fault.

This is no new criticism, nor is it indigenous to education; in most respects it is merely the traditional complaint against bureaucracy in general applied to the school in particular. There, however, it acquires a special urgency. When a Harvey Swados (or an Adam Smith) (Swados, 1957; Smith, 1789, Book I, ch. 2) suggests that factory workers are lessened by their work, we are inclined to feel sorry for the worker, but, after all, a factory is intended to produce automobiles, or pins, not happy workers. Yet when a Paul Goodman (or a Robert Owen)[1] makes the same charge about the school, we are inclined to be indignant: schools *are* supposed to improve their student members, that is their reason for existing in the first place.

Is it really true, though, that the bureaucratic structure of the school subverts education? In spite of the obvious importance of the question, and in spite of a great deal of discussion, the fact of the matter is that we simply do not know, and one of the reasons we do not know is that we do not have enough information about how students react to their schools. In early 1965, therefore, my colleagues and I began to gather information about just how this educational version of the organization-individual encounter is actually experienced by students. The present paper is a first report of some of our findings.

* From *Urban Review*, 1968, 2 (4), 13-15, 34. Used by permission of the author and publisher.

This is a revision of a paper read at the 1967 meetings of the American Sociological Association. The research reported herein was supported by a grant from the Office of Education, U.S. Department of Health, Education, and Welfare (Project No. S-383). The "we" used in this paper is not editorial; my associates on this study, Robert G. Williams, Richard A. Minisce, and Delene D. Rhea, made substantial contributions to all phases of the work.

1. Cf. Goodman (1964), and Owen (1817), especially those comments on the Bell-Lancaster system, an early form of bureaucratized education.

Are Students Alienated?

Most of the undesirable human consequences of bureaucratization are summarized by the term "alienation,"[2] and certainly the condition of the American high school student seems to exhibit most of the organizational features which are said to alienate: they are virtually powerless, their work seldom has relevance to their immediate concerns, they are segregated from the larger community, etc.[3] So our research question was: Does the bureaucratic organization of the school alienate students?

To explore this topic we gave questionnaires to the entire student bodies of two leading high schools in the Boston area, one ("West High") a public school, the other ("Parochial High") a Roman Catholic school. The questionnaires were supplemented by verbatim transcripts of interviews with 46 students at "East High," another leading public school.[4] Selecting only superior schools made optimum such otherwise influential factors as quality of staff, administration, facilities, and student background, thus allowing us to concentrate on the purely organizational aspects of the schools. Similarly, interview topics and questionnaire items emphasized organizational matters, and many of the questions were taken directly from studies of alienation in other settings.[5]

If bureaucratic structure alone alienates, then students in these schools might be expected to speak poorly of them, and to take no pride in being

2. The term is an ancient one, taken from Roman law, and thus has a number of accreted meanings; that is why so many social and psychological events can be designated by it. Karl Marx is usually credited with first presenting the term as a researchable variable, though there is great confusion about just what he meant by it, and its most orthodox employment still seems to be to describe the psychological consequences of routinized work. That at any rate is the sense in which it is used in this paper, though the final report of our project (Rhea *et al*, 1966) discusses other meanings. A good overview of contemporary studies in alienation is provided by Josephson and Josephson (1962); for industrial applications, see Blauner (1964), and for the Marxist tradition see Drachkovitch (1966), especially the essays by Sidney Hook and Lewis S. Feuer.

3. The most influential discussion of alienation for purposes of empirical research in sociology is Seeman (1959). Seeman concludes from a survey of the literature that alienation is used in five ways: to describe feelings of powerlessness, meaninglessness, anomie, isolation, and self-estrangement. With the exception of the latter, all of these terms refer to some environmental characteristic, to situations in which the individual has no power, where purpose is not apparent, where means are ambiguous, or where the individual is isolated from the larger community—these presumably lead to alienation. The classic description of student powerlessness is still Waller (1932). For meaninglessness and anomie in school see Mallery (1962). The segregation of the school from the rest of society is a common theme whose surrealism is nicely captured by Kaufman (1965). For a more methodical listing of relevant organizational characteristics, see Turner and Lawrence (1965), and for additional discussion of the school as a bureaucracy, see Corwin (1965).

4. East and West High are almost identical, and are neighbors, so interview materials from the former can be applied with some assurance to the latter. West and Parochial Highs differed primarily in the reactions of their students to authority, but the differences were not great.

5. In addition to the works by Blauner (1964) and Mallery (1962), the most useful sources were Stinchcombe (1964); Clark (1959); Dean (1961); Coser (1963); Pearlin (1962); Pearlin and Rosenberg (1962); and Middleton (1963).

members of them, despite the adequacy of the components. This, however, was emphatically not the case: large majorities agreed that "Compared to other schools, this school provides a first-rate education" (55 out of 2,329 disagreed), and all but one hundred agreed that "I'm proud to be a student here" (another 144 were neutral).

An "aggrandizement effect"[6] is doubtless operative here, but it apparently only magnifies the genuine satisfaction felt by these students. When, for example, we asked about specifics, our respondents also expressed satisfaction with the teachers, the curriculum, the marking system, and indeed *every* organizational feature of the school that was mentioned. In sum, and to make a long story short, the great majority of our students simply did not exhibit the usual symptoms of alienation, so these highly bureaucratized schools cannot be said to alienate their student bodies.

On the other hand, we quickly discovered that the students, though involved, were involved in relatively uninspiring things:

> *Have your courses been helpful?* Just to get into college. I need them to get into college. I do like History, though, and English.
>
> My main purpose is to get the diploma. College is a help, but if you don't get that diploma, well, that's pretty bad. It's getting pretty tough to get a good job, you know. The main purpose for me and to other students who are not going on to further education is to get that diploma.
>
> I think in high school the goal you are trying to reach is college, and in college the goal you are trying to reach is knowledge and social maturity as well as intellectual maturity.

There are some things of intrinsic worth in high school, but the experience is generally viewed as an instrumental one, as a means to college admission or to a better job. Among the most unequivocal responses to our questionnaire was a 91 per cent agreement with the statement: "What we do in high school is essentially preparation for what will come later; the payoff will be in college or on the job."

And our respondents were utterly realistic about what was required: A good record.

> Well, in East High you work for good grades so you can go to college. It's just—you know—everybody is obsessed with the fact and I know even I [am].
>
> Your parents don't know what you know, and people don't know what you know, and the colleges don't know what you know, so if you're going to try for anything you're going for the grade. I mean the payoff. I mean, you may have the knowledge, but it's not going to do you any good. If you want to go someplace and you want to go to college or anyplace, you have to have the grades, anyway at least to graduate from high school.

6. "...an upward distortion of an organization's prestige by its own members" (Caplow, 1964, p. 213).

> In high school kids go out for clubs and athletics and things of that nature to build up their all-aroundness so that they can get into college. *Extracurricular activities help you get into college?* Yes, they are very important. Colleges like students of varied interests. *What if you just like to sit and think?* Well, I suppose you could put this down on your application.
>
> I think if you're popular in this school you've got half the battle licked, because so many kids go home and, I think, they worry just because they're not known, and that eats away at them so much that their grades go down. . . .

Everything, it would seem, from class work to extracurricular activities to social life, comes to be related to the maximization of the record, to the building of a favorable "paper shadow" in the files of the front office.[7]

With "looking good" thus defined as the matter of highest priority, it is not surprising that some 40 per cent of our students would rather cheat than flunk, and that most would hypocritically give the teacher a wrong answer if the teacher thought it to be a right one. Over-emphasis on this sort of success breeds concentration on what Argyris (1957, pp. 59-60 *et passim*) calls the "skin-surface" performance aspects of work,[8] and this too is reflected in various student responses: most felt that "personality, pull, and bluff" get students through many courses, that performance is more important than character, and that ability to express oneself is more important than knowledge.

Our students are involved, then, but they are clearly involved in the *task* of getting through school, or maximizing the record, not in the *experiences* which educators postulate as the essence of curriculum.[9] The resulting

7. On paper shadows, see Goffman, 1961, p. 75. The paper image is so important because it is an "actionable entity," and the actions taken on the basis of it, as our students fully recognized, have a major effect on one's life.

8. Parochial High differs somewhat from West High on this, for although Parochial High students begin as freshman by generally denying that they would cheat or give a hypocritical Right Answer, by the time they are seniors a majority would do both. Proportions saying that they would rather cheat than flunk, for instance, are: Freshmen (33.7 per cent), Sophomores (34.7), Juniors (48.0), Seniors (59.2). West High responses do not change appreciably over time, though interview respondents noted that they had become "savvy" in junior high, i.e., earlier than the relatively unsophisticated Catholic students. Incidentally, these figures should not be interpreted as reflecting moral decay caused by attending Parochial High; rather they seem to measure the greater pressure to succeed found there.

9. The distinction between performing and experiencing has been central to educational theory since Rousseau's *Emile*. A child, or a horse, can be trained to *do* almost anything; all that is needed is a big stick and proper supervision. But education in the best sense is a process whereby the child comes to *be* something better than he was, and this requires that he experience educational events in a personal way. Cf. Dewey (1963). Of course one experiences the doing of a task, but the experience need not be an educational one: factory workers, for example, frequently experience nothing but boredom. Similarly, when students are forced to act as if they are educated, the act of looking good need not itself be educational. See Holt (1964). There is in fact some reason to believe that performing a task and becoming educated involve *opposite* processes: cf. Parsons, Bales, and Shils (1953), esp. Chap. 5, and later works of Parsons and his associates contrasting task-performance sequences and socialization or re-socialization. One of the most seminal articles in the recent educational literature makes a similar point: Washburne (1958).

student attitudes may be disturbing to the educator, but they should come as no surprise to the sociologist: given the prime fact of task-orientation, the students' attitudes could be predicted from the literature of industrial sociology.

But there is still a problem here. Organizational theory indicates that trivial work alienates, and that a condition of powerlessness alienates. Our students recognize that "making out" in high school is not true education, but they are also proud of making out; they take a sort of pride of workmanship in accumulating good marks and looking good. Our students also recognize their virtual powerlessness, but this too does not lead to feelings of alienation.

If students can most profitably be viewed as task-oriented workers, and this seems to be the case, how is involvement in trivial work possible? And how does near-total powerlessness fail to result in alienation? These are the questions to be discussed in the remainder of this paper. It will be our general contention that a special set of definitions, which we call "the myth of institutional paternalism," intervenes between the perceived situation and the student's reaction to it, converting the situation from one conducive to alienation into one characterized by a high level of involvement.

Meaning in School

One of the most popular sociological explanations for poor performance in school—often referred to as the "articulation hypothesis"—argues that the academic curriculum is meaningless to students who do not expect to go to college.[10] This is a plausible hypothesis, but our research indicates that it needs more consideration.

First, as we have seen, there is little or no intrinsic motivation exhibited by students in our elite high schools: Grades, not substantive achievement are the important thing. Presumably these students would be just as workmanlike in the performance of *any* task, regardless of its content, so long as it resulted in an entry for the dossier. The importance of class work for college-bound students, therefore, stems primarily from the importance of *marks*, not from any supposed relationship between high school and college subject matter.

In point of fact, and this is our second observation, student goals are very poorly defined by students:

> You know, ever since I came up here they've been testing me and one of the tests was in mathematics and another in business stuff. I guess business is just what I'm headed for.
> I didn't know what I wanted to do until maybe a couple of weeks ago, and I don't think any of the other kids do either (laughs); and, I don't know if that's what I'll be, so these are just general courses that you've got to take to fill the quota.

10.   For a good discussion of this hypothesis see Stinchcombe (1964).

Most of our respondents intended to go to college, but just what going to college means is another question. Of course students recognize that going to college is the best way to become successful, but it is also interesting to note that college is an alternative to making the sort of *commitment* that would give meaning to present activities:

> I'd rather go to college than work. Like going to college for four years I can also gain learning that will help me and also postpone my having to go to work.
>
> I'm not sure what I'm going to do and I don't want to limit myself. I don't want to sit back and say I'm going into business. I'm afraid I wouldn't be happy at this point if I decided to go into a four year business school like (School). I'd come out and, O.K., I could go into business; but if I said I wanted to do anything else, I wouldn't be able to. I want to go to a liberal arts school.

This hesitancy about making a commitment ran through all of our interviews, and it appears in our questionnaire returns as a willingness to let others, i.e., the school staff, make the major decisions for the student.[11]

Of course students *are* young, and this means that they cannot be sure of their "real" desires. Our interview respondents frequently pointed this out to us, and it would in fact be unrealistic to expect them to have clear-cut notions about adult roles; they have never been adults.

In such a situation, students behave quite rationally, i.e., they pursue a policy of noncommitment, delaying it for as long as possible. Commitment means abandoning alternatives, and premature commitment can mean abandoning opportunities which might later prove more desirable. (Cf. Becker, 1960.) But noncommitment also means not having criteria to assess the meaning of current experiences.

High school work is thus viewed as a generalized preparation, a "making ready" (*praeparare*) for future commitments. And so, paradoxically, the very absence of specific purpose allows the student to impute a sort of generalized worth, or "preparation value," to all of his school activities. Conversely, to know one's specific goal in life might reveal many of these activities to be irrelevant.

To elaborate on the articulation hypothesis, then, we might first suggest that it is the critical relevance of marks, not the academic nature of the typical high school curriculum, that makes college-bound students work harder than others. Second we would suggest that plans for further education do not necessarily reveal the long-range significance of high school studies; rather such plans allow the student to avoid or postpone the entire issue of relevance, and thus allow him to impute a vague preparation-value

---

11. For example, 61 per cent of our students disagree with the statement: "Students have too little responsibility for their own education here," with another 10 per cent having no opinion, while 66 per cent agree that: "Students should be sufficiently supervised so that their mistakes have no serious consequences." Students in fact have very little authority, but that is apparently not "too little."

to his current activities. Students not destined for college and the white-collar world may accurately perceive the lack of articulation between school work and adult role, but this need not mean that college-bound students perceive a congruence; they do see the relevance of good marks, though, and that is sufficient to account for their dedication to the task of accumulating them.

Powerlessness and Paternalism

The most common cause of (or synonym for) alienation mentioned in the research literature is powerlessness, and high school students are among the most powerless members of our society. By and large, though, our respondents said that they had *enough* power, and our interviews indicate why:

> I think the student has freedom to take more or less what he wants. [This is wrong] because a kid can take very easy courses the rest of the year and maybe, maybe he's got the potential to do something with himself instead of being lazy. I don't know how they could fix it or prearrange it, but I think the student is given too much freedom to choose what he wants.
>
> *Do you think students have enough say about who runs this place and the policy of the school?* Yes, I think if it wasn't run by the administrative part of the school system then things would get out of hand. I think there has to be somebody to lay down the law and say it's going to be this way. . . . I don't think students at this age know everything, and I think they need somebody to guide them and tell them what's right. They might think something is right now, but twenty years from now it might not be, in their opinion.

These students do not *want* power, in part because, as implied, they would not know what to do with it even if they had it. Their educations are too important to be left in inexperienced hands, and they are quite realistic about their own inexperience.

Satisfaction with powerlessness, though, must reflect satisfaction with the way power is wielded by those who possess it, and indeed our students thought highly of their superiors, especially their teachers.[12] They liked their teachers because they thought them competent, but what they think teachers are competent *at* is not entirely clear. It seems that teachers make school work more pleasant, by being entertaining, informed, clear, in control of the classroom, enthusiastic about the subject, and fair. In addition, teachers are apparently expected to make the student want to do the work; teachers motivate. In any event, the teacher is seen as the major determiner of the educational process, he rather literally "makes" education happen.

The student, on the other hand, sees himself as relatively passive; he learns, to be sure, but it is the teacher who causes the learning to occur.

---

12. Students were asked to "grade" (A, B, C, D, F) various aspects of the school. Teachers wound up second—and a close second—to peers as a source of satisfaction.

Accordingly, teachers are often evaluated by the critical standards of an audience, as actors are, with performance being judged by the relatively nonvolitional responses of the student-critics. A better analogy would be the doctor-patient relationship: The patient is expected to follow orders, and to that extent he participates in his own cure, but the prime responsibility for a successful outcome rests with the physician. It is the student's job to do what the teacher tells him to do; it is the teacher's job to know what to tell the student to do, and it is therefore the teacher's responsibility to know *why* the student should do it.

As in the doctor-patient relationship, so in the teacher-pupil one: confidence in the professional is a necessary ingredient. This is not only confidence in technical ability, it also includes the belief that the professional is working for the client's benefit. From the student's point of view, then, the teacher is both competent and benevolent, and the relationship is a professional one, or, as we have phrased it (in order to avoid unnecessary implications), a *paternalistic* one.

But competence and benevolence are not personal qualities of teachers, they are attributes of the teaching role. Thus, students do not express gratitude for adequate teaching services, though they may be warm in their critical applause for an exceptional performance, and they tend to be morally indignant about uninspiring teaching: teachers are *supposed* to be capable and concerned, that is the nature of their job. We have therefore referred to this set of attitudes as faith in "institutional" paternalism.

It should be emphasized that these are student beliefs, not necessarily school policy or actuality; but if students define the situation to be paternalistic, then for them it is. So institutional paternalism may be thought of as a "useful myth," a myth because its reality-content has little to do with its efficacy, and useful because it intervenes between the potentially alienating conditions of student powerlessness and curricular meaninglessness to produce a *faith* that one is in good hands and that there is meaning in what one does. Indeed, belief in institutional paternalism may appear precisely because there is a *need* for a faith of this sort, a need for some sort of redefinition of what might otherwise be an intolerable situation.

Our evidence is only impressionistic on this point, but many interview respondents described how they "willed" a good opinion of their teachers. To think poorly of a teacher means to do poorly in the course, so in order to make a good mark (and to enjoy, or at least make tolerable, the work) these students go into new classes with a determination to like them, i.e., to think the teacher able and the subject somehow worthy of serious effort. Need therefore seems to precede experience, and it is not at all hard to see why students need to believe in institutional paternalism: to be at the mercy of unconcerned incompetents, in school or in surgery or wherever, is hardly a pleasant prospect, and to be forced to spend the first part of one's life doing pointless exercises would be no better. Unable to withdraw or rebel (this route leads to failure), these ambitious students seem eager to detect, and perhaps even to fantasize, competence and concern among the staff.

Whether faith in institutional paternalism stems from the genuine ability of the personnel of these privileged schools, though, or from the ambition and single-mindedness of these middle-class students, or from some combination of the two, remains an open question.

Conclusions

Our initial research question was, "Does the formal organization of the school alienate students?" and we may now answer, "No, not necessarily," at least not if the myth of institutional paternalism intervenes. On the other hand, bureaucratization does apparently lead to a massive and near-total conversion of organizational means into proximate student goals, so that what the student is involved *in* is something much less than what either educators or students think of as true education. Students give meaning to these activities by defining them as preparation for the real education that will come later, in college, or as contributions so some distant good known to teachers and other adults. In the meantime they may take pride in their skill at obtaining marks and building a presentable dossier.

During the course of our research we had occasion to amend some educational sociology, e.g., the "articulation hypothesis" was seen to be incomplete, and we raised questions about current formulations of the concept of alienation, e.g., it is obvious that powerlessness *per se* does not cause alienation, nor can it be equated with it. There are also numerous practical implications that might be drawn from this study. For example, if the present findings are correct, it is obvious that a good deal of our national effort to erase class and ethnic differentials in educational achievement may be misguided: to succeed in school and to become truly educated are quite separable goals, and the means to one need not at all be suitable for the other (Rhea, 1967).

But there is a more important question which has not been dealt with here, a question which probably cannot even be answered yet, but one whose eventual answer will determine the larger significance of what we have discussed: Although the myth of institutional paternalism allows students to become involved in their work, *is that what we want?* If involvement in work shapes character, and if the work of the student is as shallow as the task-performance model suggests, then might we not be guilty of shaping trivial personalities in our schools? This is the *moral* charge behind the alienation issue, and our present findings lend themselves more to its support than to its refutation.

If the charge is correct, and it may or may not be, then alienation is vastly preferable to involvement, for under these conditions alienation is a positive response of the healthy personality insulating itself against the effects of an unhealthy situation. The myth of institutional paternalism, that is to say, may not be so useful after all.

References

ARGYRIS, C. *Personality and organization*. New York: Harper, 1957.

BECKER, H. S. Notes on the concept of commitment. *American Journal of Sociology,* 1960, 66, 32-40.

BLAUNER, R. *Alienation and freedom.* Chicago: University of Chicago Press, 1964.

CAPLOW, T. *Principles of organization.* New York: Harcourt, Brace and World, 1964.

CLARK, J. P. Measuring alienation within a social system. *American Sociological Review,* 1959, 24, 849-852.

CORWIN, R. C. *A sociology of education.* New York: Appleton-Century-Crofts, 1965.

COSER, R. L. Alienation and the social structure. In E. Freidson (Ed.), *The hospital in modern society.* New York: Free Press, 1963. Pp. 231-265.

DEAN, D. G. Alienation: its meaning and measurement. *American Sociological Review,* 1961, 26, 753-758.

DEWEY, J. *Experience and education.* New York: Collier Books, 1963.

DRACHKOVITCH, M. M. (Ed.). *Marxist ideology in the contemporary world.* New York: Praeger, 1966.

FRIEDENBERG, E. Z. *The vanishing adolescent.* Boston: Beacon Press, 1959.

GOFFMAN, E. *Asylums.* Garden City, N.Y.: Doubleday Anchor Books, 1961.

GOODMAN, P. *Compulsory mis-education.* New York: Horizon Press, 1964.

HENRY, J. *Culture against man.* New York: Random House, 1963.

HOLT, J. *How children fail.* New York: Pitman, 1964.

JOSEPHSON, E. and JOSEPHSON, M. (Eds.). *Man alone.* New York: Dell, 1962.

KAUFMAN, B. *Up the down staircase.* Englewood Cliffs, N.J.: Prentice-Hall, 1965.

KOZOL, J. *Death at an early age.* Boston: Houghton Mifflin, 1967.

MALLERY, D. *High school students speak out.* New York: Harper, 1962.

OWEN, R. *A new view of society.* Glencoe, Ill.: The Free Press, m.d. Facsimile reproduction of the third edition of 1817.

PARSONS, T., BALES, R. F. and SHILS, E. A. *Working papers in the theory of action.* Glencoe, Ill.: The Free Press, 1953.

PEARLIN, L. I. Alienation from work: a study of nursing personnel. *American Sociological Review,* 1962, 27, 314-326.

PEARLIN, L. I. and ROSENBERG, R. Nurse-patient social distance and the structural context of a mental hospital. *American Sociological Review,* 1962, 27, 56-65.

RHEA, B. *et al. Measures of child involvement and alienation from the school program.* Washington: U.S. Office of Education, 1966.

RHEA, B. School organization and differential achievement in education. Paper read at Missouri Society for Sociology and Anthropology meetings, 1967.

RIESSMAN, F. *The culturally deprived child.* New York: Harper and Row, 1962.

SEEMAN, M. On the meaning of alienation. *American Sociological Review,* 1959, 24, 849-852.

SMITH, A. *An inquiry into the nature and causes of the wealth of nations.* New York: Modern Library, 1937; from the fifth edition of 1789.

STINCHCOMBE, A. *Rebellion in a high school.* Chicago: Quadrangle Books, 1964.

SWADOS, H. *On the line.* New York: Bantam Books, 1957.

TURNER, A. N. and LAWRENCE, P. R. *Industrial jobs and the worker.* Boston: Division of Research, Harvard University Graduate School of Business Administration, 1965.

WALLER, W.   *The sociology of teaching.* New York: Wiley, 1965. First published in
    1932.
WASHBURNE, C.   Conflicts between educational theory and structure. *Educational
    Theory,* 1958, 8, 87-94.
MIDDLETON, R.   Alienation, race, and education. *American Sociological Review,*
    1963, 28, 973-977.

5. EDUCATIONAL PROCEDURES

In thinking about educational procedures, perhaps we should start rather fundamentally. Teaching can be construed as person X helping person Y to understand something (or to accomplish something, with the presumption that Y has understood it in the process). Given this definition, we know that learners can be very young (i.e., neonate). But how young can "teachers" be?

This study shows us that people can teach at the age of 4 (and that teaching styles differ according to socio-economic class and race); these findings are not only delightful, but potentially useful in understanding why white middle-class children do better in school than lower-class black ones.

The reader who would like to explore the literature referred to in this article should try Bronfenbrenner's "Socialization and Social Class Through Time and Space" in Maccoby, Newcomb and Hartley, *Readings in Social Psychology* (Holt, 1958), as well as the material discussed by Hess and Shipman in the present book.

There are some methodological problems in Feshbach and Devor's work: we do not know how the experimenter "helped" the 4-year-old teacher in Trial 1; nor what the instructions to the teacher were before he or she taught the 3-year-old; nor the race, class or sex of the experimenter. As Beez' study (just following) shows, these matters could have made some important differences. Finally, the measures of 3-year-olds' learning were simply time taken and errors made during the teaching/learning experience. We do not know what the 3-year-olds learned "durably."

Still, the study remains a fascinating and simply done piece of research; there should be more like it.

Teaching Styles in Four-Year-Olds*

Norma D. Feshbach, Geraldine Devor

This investigation deals with the relationship between social class factors and patterns of reinforcement used by preschool children when instructing younger peers. Research on child rearing has reflected consistent differences between working- and middle-class groups in the modes of discipline employed in socializing children. In general, the working-class parent tends to make greater use of physical punishment and related negative, external reinforcements such as ridicule or shouting while middle-class parents are more permissive, resort more often to reasoning and make greater use of guilt arousing appeals. It can be assumed that these parental behaviors will have multiple effects on the child, one of which is providing a model for the child to imitate.

If a child duplicates, in his social transactions with peers, modal patterns of reinforcement observed at home, then peer group interactions and influences may vary with social class. Although there have been studies of the effects of reinforcements provided by peers, the exploration of the child's use of particular classes of reinforcement as an individual difference variable has not previously been undertaken.

The purpose of this study was to investigate the relationship of social class and ethnic factors to the child's spontaneous use of positive and negative reinforcement, a response dimension which is likely to be a reflection of the child's imitation of the parents. In view of the literature documenting the differences in socialization techniques of different socio-economic groups, it was predicted that children from middle-class Caucasian homes would make greater use of positive reinforcement, while children from more deprived backgrounds would manifest greater instances of negative reinforcement. In an effort to distinguish the effects of social class from race, the relationship between social class and mode of reinforcement was investigated in lower- and middle-class Negro and Caucasian children.

Subjects

The subjects were 204 three- and four-year-old boys and girls selected from nine private nursery schools and children's centers. The four-year-olds acted

* Paper read at the American Educational Research Association meetings, Chicago, February, 1968. Used by permission of the authors.

This research was supported in part by Contract 4-6-061646-1909, from the Office of Education, HEW, to the Research and Development Center, School of Education, University of California, Los Angeles.

as "teachers" while the three-year-old group acted as "pupils." The subjects were divided into four groups on the basis of social class and race: Middle-Class Caucasian, Lower-Class Caucasian, Middle-Class Negro and Lower-Class Negro.

Procedure

The four-year-old "teacher-child" was taken to an adjoining room by the experimenter. After the experimenter carefully described the details of a simple wooden puzzle, the child was then given three trials to assemble it. During the first trial, the experimenter actively helped the child. For the second trial the experimenter made one positive verbal remark ("that's very good") and one critical remark ("that's not right") concerning the child's performance. For the third trial the four-year-old completed the puzzle by himself while the experimenter left to get the three-year-old.

Experimental Situation

After being provided appropriate instructions, the four-year-old proceeded to teach the puzzle to the younger child. In each case the social class and race of the four-year-old "teacher-child" was the same as that of the three-year-old "pupil-child." However, the sexes of the two children were systematically varied so that within each social class-race grouping, the roles of the "teacher" and the "pupil" were represented by either sex in approximately 50% of the cases. With the exception of this restriction, assignment of a "pupil" to a "teacher" was random.

Dependent Measures

All comments made by the "teacher-child" pertaining to the "pupil's" performance were recorded verbatim and subsequently categorized as either positive or negative reinforcements. The positive category included statements of praise, encouragement and affirmation such as "See, she can put it together," "She did it," "That's a girl," while the negative category included criticism, negations and derogatory comments such as "Wrong way," "Not that way," "You stupid." To determine the reliability of this dichotomous classification, 80 randomly selected statements of reinforcement were scored by two independent raters. There was only one instance in which the raters disagreed.

The total number of positive and total number of negative statements was determined for each child and constituted the basic dependent measures. In addition, the number of errors and time taken to complete the puzzle were obtained for one-third of the younger children.

Table 1

MEAN FREQUENCIES OF POSITIVE REINFORCEMENTS USED BY
FOUR-YEAR-OLD BOYS AND GIRLS AS A FUNCTION OF SOCIAL
CLASS, RACE, SEX OF THE TEACHER-CHILD AND SEX OF THE PUPIL-CHILD

	MIDDLE-CLASS CAUCASIAN		MIDDLE-CLASS NEGRO		LOWER-CLASS CAUCASIAN		LOWER-CLASS NEGRO	
	BOY TEACHER	GIRL TEACHER	BOY TEACHER	GIRL TEACHER	BOY TEACHER	GIRL TEACHER	BOY TEACHER	GIRL TEACHER
Boy Pupil	1.83	1.17	0.17	0.50	0.17	0.83	0.71	0.29
Girl Pupil	3.17	2.80	0.17	0.00	0.67	1.67	1.29	0.37
Total	2.50	2.08	0.17	0.25	0.42	1.25	1.00	0.33
Social Group	2.28		0.21		0.83		0.66	

Table 2

A COMPARISON OF RACE AND SOCIAL CLASS
DIFFERENCES IN THE USE OF POSITIVE REINFORCEMENT

GROUPS		U	z
MCC versus MCN			
($N = 25$)	($N = 24$)	120.0	4.05*
MCC versus LCC		183.0	2.48**
($N = 25$)	($N = 29$)		
MCC versus LCN		210.0	2.82**
($N = 25$)	($N = 29$)		
MCN versus LCC		212.5	2.05***
($N = 24$)	($N = 24$)		
MCN versus LCN		259.0	2.06***
($N = 24$)	($N = 29$)		
LCC versus LCN		339.0	0.19
($N = 24$)	($N = 29$)		

   * $p < .001$ (2-tailed)
  ** $p < .01$ (2-tailed)
 *** $p < .05$ (2-tailed)

Positive Reinforcement

The mean frequencies of positive reinforcements for each of the experimental sub-groups are presented in Table 1. The Mann-Whitney U Test was used to compare the effects of social class and race. The results of this analysis, presented in Table 2, indicate that the middle-class Caucasian children used a significantly greater number of positive reinforcements than each of the other three groups. In contrast, the middle-class Negro children used significantly less positive reinforcement than either of the two lower-class groups. The findings for the middle-class Caucasian children are consistent with the experimental hypothesis. The data for the middle-class Negroes present an interesting deviation from the hypothesized relationship between social class and use of reinforcement.

The over-all pattern of social class and race differences in the use of positive reinforcement was reflected by both sexes. As Table 3 indicates, however, the size and statistical significance of the differences vary for each sex.

Negative Reinforcement

The mean frequencies of negative reinforcements used by the four groups are presented in Table 4. In comparison to the positive reinforcement means, which ranged from 2.28 to 0.21, the variations in the negative reinforcement means are relatively small, ranging from 2.07 to 1.25. The middle-class Negro children again had the least number of responses,

Table 3

COMPARISONS OF RACE AND SOCIAL CLASS
DIFFERENCES AMONG BOYS AND AMONG
GIRLS IN USE OF POSITIVE REINFORCEMENTS

| GIRL TEACHERS | | GROUPS | BOY TEACHERS | |
U	z		U	z
31.0	2.89*	MCC versus MCN	30	2.72*
58.5	1.10	MCC versus LCC	35	2.34**
44.5	2.67*	MCC versus LCN	59	1.35
42.5	2.12**	MCN versus LCC	65	0.57
75.5	1.04	MCN versus LCN	52	1.95***
62.5	1.56	LCC versus LCN	61.55	1.33

 * $p < .01$
 ** $p < .05$
*** $p < .10$

followed by the middle-class Caucasians, the lower-class Caucasians, and the lower-class Negroes in ascending order. None of these differences, including comparisons across social class and race and separate analyses by sex, was statistically significant. However, it is interesting that 21 of the 49 combined middle-class children and only 10 of the 46 combined lower-class children did *not* use negative reinforcements in instructing a younger child (Chi square = 3.9, $p < .05$).

Other Behavioral Comparisons

An analysis was made of the number of words in positive and negative reinforcing statements to determine the possible contributions of verbal facility to the type of reinforcement used. It was found that the number of words used by all groups in making negative and positive responses was comparable. The mean number of words for the positive reinforcing comments was 2.3, and for the negative comments, 3.5. It does not appear that positive reinforcing statements require greater verbal facility than negative ones.

The relationship between the "pupil's" performance and his "teacher's" use of reinforcement was ascertained to determine whether differences in pupil performance could have contributed to the type of reinforcement administered by the "teacher." The time taken by the "pupil" to complete the puzzle and the number of errors made were correlated with the number of positive and number of negative reinforcements administered by his "teacher." None of the correlations was significantly greater than zero. These results indicate that the frequency of positive and negative reinforcements was independent of the "pupil's" performance.

Table 4

MEAN FREQUENCIES OF NEGATIVE REINFORCEMENTS USED BY
FOUR-YEAR-OLD BOYS AND GIRLS AS A FUNCTION OF SOCIAL
CLASS, RACE, SEX OF THE TEACHER-CHILD AND SEX OF THE PUPIL-CHILD

	MIDDLE-CLASS CAUCASIAN		MIDDLE-CLASS NEGRO		LOWER-CLASS CAUCASIAN		LOWER-CLASS NEGRO	
	BOY TEACHER	GIRL TEACHER	BOY TEACHER	GIRL TEACHER	BOY TEACHER	GIRL TEACHER	BOY TEACHER	GIRL TEACHER
Boy Pupil	0.50	1.50	0.67	0.83	0.50	1.17	2.57	1.00
Girl Pupil	2.67	1.57	2.17	1.33	2.83	2.17	2.57	2.12
Total	1.58	1.54	1.42	1.08	1.67	1.67	2.57	1.60
Social Group	1.56		1.25		1.67		2.07	

Discussion

The hypothesis bearing on the use of positive reinforcement was strongly supported by the data, while little support was obtained for the prediction concerning the use of negative reinforcement. The behavior that differentiated these groups was the greater use of positive reinforcement by the middle-class Caucasian children. Thus, middle-class Caucasian children in this sample employed both types of reinforcement, while lower-class children relied predominantly on one mode of reinforcement. The middle-class Negro group made the least use of positive reinforcements and of negative reinforcements as well.

The patterns of reinforcement which the children displayed are of interest because of their possible reflection of different child-rearing practices and also because of their informational and motivational consequences. Since reinforcement is a significant parameter of learning, one important factor which appears to differentiate the learning environment of children from different social groups is the manner in which members of the peer group reinforce each other. The middle-class Caucasian child in this study, by using both classes of reinforcement, provided more information to his younger peer. Children from all of the social groups were provided feedback when they made errors, but only the middle-class Caucasian youngster got sufficient feedback when making correct responses. In addition, the middle-class Caucasian child, by being provided more positive reinforcement, received greater encouragement and had more experiences of success and accomplishment.

Research on social class differences in learning has emphasized the differential responsiveness of lower- and middle-class children to various types of positive reinforcement and some attention has also been given to comparisons of the effects of praise and reproof on children varying in social class, race and other individual characteristics. The results of the present study suggest that a fuller understanding of social class and race differences in learning requires an assessment of the typical reinforcement contingencies present in the child's peer and home environments.

Further research is needed directly linking specific parental behaviors to the child's use of, and differential responsiveness to, different classes of reinforcement. The present data suggest that, as early as age four, children display very different reinforcement patterns as a function of their race and social class background. These behavioral differences could well exert a significant influence upon subsequent cognitive and social development.

The results further indicate that generalizations concerning social class differences must also take into account the ethnic composition of the group. The difference in reinforcement pattern between the middle-class Negro and the middle-class Caucasian child was particularly striking, and it is conceivable that this difference may partially account for the differences in intellectual functioning and school achievement that have been reported between these two populations.

※ ※ ※ ※ ※

In recent years, a good deal of interest has developed in the idea that "self-fulfilling prophecies" may be an important aspect of interpersonal relationships. What a person expects to be true of another seems to condition his own behavioral output in such a way that the expected behavior of the other is somehow "pulled," produced by the prior fact of the expectancy. The work of Robert Rosenthal (see article) in this area has received wide attention, and Beez' study is a well-designed effort to assess the expectancy effect as it occurs during teacher-pupil interaction in a tutorial setting.

Rosenthal's widely-cited finding that teacher expectancies can apparently alter IQ scores in young children has severe methodological faults (see, for example, the critical discussions by Thorndike in *American Educational Research Journal*, 1968, 5(4), 708-711, and by Gumpert and Gumpert in the *Urban Review*, 1968, 3(1), 21-25). Thus it has *not* been shown to date that teacher expectancies have durable long-term effects on children's IQ's or academic performance. However, short-term effects like those documented here by Beez are clearly achievable—whether or not the teacher intends them. It remains to be seen whether these effects occur over longer periods of time, in ordinary classrooms. That they do is plausible—but not yet demonstrated. Researchers and practitioners: beware of over-eager expectancies in regard to expectancy effects!

Influence of Biased Psychological Reports on Teacher Behavior and Pupil Performance*

W. Victor Beez

Experimental research in the area of effects of expectancies (Rosenthal, 1964a, 1964b, 1966) indicates that the experimenter's orientation and expectation can influence the data. As Rosenthal (1964a) has demonstrated, expectancies of this sort can be communicated in very subtle ways. A variety of cues, so-called *demand characteristics,* unintentionally communicate to the subject something of what the experimenter is after (Orne, 1962). Communication can be subtle, unintentional, and differential depending upon the subjects or the expectations the experimenter holds for them. Even in highly standardized situations, a subject can be influenced by another person's expectations (Rosenthal, 1966).

That expectancies also influence behavior outside the laboratory has in recent years been demonstrated in educational research (Cahen, 1965; Rosenthal and Jacobson, 1966, 1967, 1968). The findings of these investigators raise serious questions as to present practices in our educational system, and make further investigation imperative. It appears that teacher-pupil interaction operates similarly to laboratory interaction between experimenter and subject.

While Rosenthal and Jacobson investigated changes in IQ due to differential information given to teachers, the present study was mainly concerned with changes in teaching behavior and performance by pupils. It also attempted to investigate the question raised by Rosenthal's work as to how a teacher's expectation becomes translated into behavior in such a way as to elicit the expected pupil behavior (Rosenthal and Jacobson, 1966).

* Adapted from a paper read at the American Psychological Association meetings, San Francisco, 1968. Used by permission of the author.

This study is based upon a dissertation submitted by the author as a partial requirement for the Ph.D. degree at Indiana University. The author is grateful to S. Guskin, thesis director, for his generous guidance, and the members of his committee, D. Beier, D. Gliesman, W. Hodges (chairman). The author is presently at the Pupil Services, San Francisco Unified School District.

Method

Subjects

Sixty children from the summer Head Start program in Bloomington, Indiana participated in this study. They ranged in age from 5 years, 7 months to 6 years, 6 months, and had IQs on the Peabody Picture Vocabulary Test from 55 to 127, with a mean of 91. IQ assessment was made *after* completion of the experimental study, so that at the time of experimentation the actual IQ was not known. Children were randomly assigned to either a "low ability" or a "high ability" group. With the exception of name and age nothing was known about a particular child prior to assignment to one of the groups. The names of the children were taken from the list of children attending the Head Start program and none of the children was discussed with either the principal or the regular teacher. Each of the two groups consisted of 15 boys and 15 girls. None of the children in the study had previously attended regular classes.

Sixty "teachers" served as the actual subjects of this study. Ss were graduate students in the School of Education of Indiana University during the summer of 1967. Ss ranged in age from 19 to 51 years ($M = 28$-9) and had from 0 to 22 years teaching experience ($M = 4$-6). Ss were assigned at random to one of the two groups.

Experimenters

Two graduate students in English served as experimenters. Although Es were not given details of the study they did guess the general idea. However, throughout the study they did not know what group a particular child was in nor what Ss had been told about the child's intellectual prospects. Instructions were given in writing to Es.

Procedure

Experimentation took place in separate rooms in the elementary school which was used for the Head Start program. Of the school personnel, the principal alone was aware of the purpose of the study. Each S worked individually with one child. S was told that the purpose of the study was to see how well Head Start children would perform on a number of experimental tasks. Prior to seeing the child, S was given a folder containing a faked "psychological evaluation" of the child (see Figures 1 and 2).

All reports were identical for the children belonging to the same groups, with the exception of name and age of child. Reports included "background information," "testing behavior and clinical observation," and "recommendations." The fake IQ data described all children as falling within the average

Figure 1.   Psychological Evaluation.

Name: James Carpenter   Date: June 27, 1967
Sex: Male
Birthdate: 8-3-61
Age: 5-11   C o n f i d e n t i a l
Examiner: R. L. Simons

REASON FOR TESTING:

Intelligence Testing for Special Project in Educational Research, summer 1967.

BACKGROUND:

James lives with his parents in Bloomington, Ind. Mr. Carpenter is employed at a local department store as a stock clerk and has completed the eighth grade. Mrs. Carpenter is a housewife and completed nine years of school. There are two younger siblings in the family.

TEST BEHAVIOR AND CLINICAL OBSERVATION:

James was an open and friendly boy who related well to the examiner. He smiled readily and seemed to enjoy adult attention. He frequently initiated conversation and reported at length about things he liked, his home, his play activities, etc.

The boy responded freely to the questions asked him and seemed to be interested in most all the tasks. He responded well to encouragement, was quite attentive and seemed to be well motivated.

Both the Peabody Picture Vocabulary Test, Form A, and the Stanford-Binet, Form L-M, were administered to James. On the PPVT he obtained an IQ of 102, and he received an IQ of 105 on the Stanford-Binet. The two IQ scores are quite similar, and one can classify James as falling within the normal range of intelligence in comparison to children his age.

RECOMMENDATIONS:

Although James comes from a culturally disadvantaged home he has, nevertheless, very good potential for school related tasks and activities. He seems highly motivated and well adjusted to learning situations. It is expected that he will experience little or no difficulty in his school work and should do quite well on the proposed project tasks.

---

range of intelligence. The reports for the "low ability" children, however, (Figure 2) called the IQ score "low average," and interpreted the results negatively, stressing negative aspects of cultural deprivation, and predicted that school adjustment would be difficult. The reports for the "high ability" group children (Figure 1) interpreted the IQ information positively, terming it "normal," stressed positive aspects in the child's fictional behavior, and suggested that despite cultural deprivation the child should do well in school. These reports were given in closed folders to Ss so that Es would not know what they contained. Ss were also told not to discuss the "case" with Es.

After S had read the report, the child was brought into the room and given the first task. This task (symbol learning) consisted of a series of 20

Figure 2. Psychological Evaluation.

Name: Richard Walters   Date: June 27, 1967
Sex: Male
Birthdate: 10-28-61
Age: 5-8   C o n f i d e n t i a l
Examiner: R. L. Simons

REASON FOR TESTING:

Intelligence Testing in connection with Special Project in Educational Research, summer 1967.

BACKGROUND:

Richard is a member of a family of 7, living in a two room house. The owner of the house is currently adding one room which will be used as a bedroom. His father is employed in Martinsville as a truck driver, and his mother is a full time housewife. Both parents were born in Gary, Ind., and moved to Bloomington eight years ago. Both parents have an eighth grade education.

When Richard appeared for testing he was somewhat carelessly dressed. He was sulky, appeared unresponsive, and it was difficult to engage him in any lengthy conversation. It is the feeling of the examiner that the boy disliked the testing situation and, in general, feels uncomfortable in adult company.

TEST BEHAVIOR AND CLINICAL OBSERVATION:

Despite the examiner's attempts to establish good rapport with Richard the boy did not appear to feel comfortable. It was often difficult to elicit a response from him, or at times he even remarked that he did not like the test and it was "dumb." It was necessary to ask him repeatedly to sit up and to pay attention. He was quite fidgety, asking how much longer it was to last, yawned and put his head on the table. It would appear from this that motivation for school related tasks is lacking in Richard.

Richard was first administered the Peabody Picture Vocabulary Test, Form A, on which he obtained an IQ of 95. On the Stanford-Binet Intelligence Scale, Form L-M, he obtained an IQ of 94. The results of the two tests are quite similar and it is suggested that they can be taken as a fairly good estimate of Richard's intellectual abilities. This would place the boy in the "low average" range of intelligence in comparison to children his age. Richard, coming from a culturally disadvantaged home, lacks many of the experiences of normal children his age, and shows a lack of motivation toward learning tasks.

RECOMMENDATION:

Richard's present level of intellectual functioning would suggest that school adjustment will be difficult for him, and there are serious doubts that he will profit from average learning tasks. This might be due in part to a lack of motivation but mainly also because of a lack of previous experience. It is doubtful that he will be able to perform satisfactorily on the proposed learning tasks of the project.

---

signs printed on individual cards (e.g. "STOP," "WALK," "GO," "BOYS," "GIRLS," "DANGER," etc.). S was told to teach as many signs as he could in a standard order within a 10-minute period, using whatever technique or strategy he wanted to use. *E* unobtrusively recorded the time spent on each sign, the number of signs covered, and tallied *S*'s responses, such as the number of times: a word was read to the child, the child was asked to say the word, the child was asked to identify the word from the card, the meaning of the word was explained or demonstrated, etc.

After the 10-minute teaching period, the signs were removed and *S* was asked to present a series of 5 jigsaw puzzles to the child for a 5-minute period, in a standard order. Each puzzle had to be successfully completed before the next could be given. *S* was told to present it any way he wished and that he could interact with the child. *E* again recorded the time spent on each puzzle and number of times *S* gave clues to the child. After this task the child was moved to a different room, where he was retested by *E* for recall of the signs covered in the first task.[1]

Finally, after *E* returned to record *Ss*' estimates of their children's intelligence test performance level, *S* was asked to complete a questionnaire, rating the child as to expected achievement level, social competency, and intellectual ability, as compared with children in the regular classroom. *S* also had to indicate on a rating scale how difficult he thought the sign task was for the child.[2]

Results and Discussion

1. Teachers who had been given favorable expectations about a pupil tried to teach more symbols than did the teachers given unfavorable expectations ($p < .001$). The mean for the "high ability" group was 10.43 words, the mean for the "low ability" group was 5.66 words attempted. The difference in teaching effort was dramatic. Eight or more symbols were taught by 87% of the teachers expecting better performance, but only 13% of the teachers expecting poorer performance tried to teach that many words ($p < .0000001$).

2. The two groups differed significantly ($p < .001$) in the number of symbols learned by the children. While the mean for the "high ability" group was 5.9, the "low ability" group had a mean of only 3.1 symbols. Most (77% of the children alleged to have better intellectual prospects learned five or more symbols but only 13% of the children alleged to have poorer intellectual prospects learned five or more symbols ($p < .000002$).

---

1.   During this time, *S* made an estimate of the level of performance the child would achieve on the French Pictorial Test of Intelligence (one of 4 levels of difficulty into which the French cards had been sorted). In the "low ability" group, only 4 children were judged by *Ss* to be able to master the test above the 2nd level of difficulty; in the "high ability" group, 22 children were judged as performing above the 2nd level.

2.   *Ss* also indicated whether they liked or disliked working with the child (all reported liking it); rated the helpfulness of the psychological report (all but 3 subjects felt they were "very" or "somewhat" helpful, with no differences across treatments); and rated how comfortable they had felt with the tasks (the majority of the *Ss* felt comfortable, with no significant differences across treatments).

3. Ss' ratings of achievement, social competency, and intellectual ability were made on 5-point scales. On achievement, the "low ability" group received a mean of 1.93 as compared with 3.50 for the "high ability" group ($p<.001$). The difference for social competency is smaller, but still significant beyond the .01 level. The "low ability" group had a mean of 2.57 and the "high ability" group a mean of 3.33. Ratings of intellectual ability gave the "low ability" group a mean of 1.93 and the "high ability" group a mean of 3.43 ($p<.001$).

4. There was also a difference between the groups in the number of times the meanings of the symbols were explained and, of course, the time spent on each symbol. Ss in the "low ability" teaching group explained the meaning of a word significantly more often, gave more examples, and spent more time on non-teaching activities than did Ss in the "high ability" teaching group ($p<.01$).

5. All children, except one, completed the puzzles within the permitted time. No significant difference was found between the groups in the number of clues given by Ss.

6. Only one S evaluated the symbol-learning task as too difficult for the pupil in the "high ability" group (3.3%) whereas 63% of Ss felt that it was too difficult for children in the "low ability" group.

The results strongly support findings by others (e.g. Rosenthal and Jacobson, 1966) that pupils are influenced by their teachers' expectations and have a tendency to behave accordingly. Teachers also act differently depending upon their expectations for the child. When they expect the child to do poorly they attempt to teach less, spend more time on each task, give more examples of meaning, are more likely to engage in non-teaching activities, and repeat the task more often than when they expect better performance from the child. It needs to be pointed out that in this study S had practically no time to get acquainted with the child prior to the start of the teaching task and, therefore, relied heavily on the faked "psychological report." However, the data of the evaluation and rating of the child by S would support the hypothesis that even in the face of successful performance on the puzzle tasks, S's expectation is not changed.

Some anecdotal material is of interest. One child in the "high ability" group whose actual IQ was 71 (measured *after* the experiment) was taught 14 signs and learned 7; another child in the "low ability" group with a tested IQ of 127 was taught only 5 signs and learned 3.

After the total experiment was over, the author reported to the groups of Ss on the actual intent of the experiment. While the "high ability" teachers were rather pleased, the "low ability" teachers seemed more inclined to argue ("but my child *really* was retarded"). Two teachers, in fact, believed that the report had given the IQ as falling within the retarded range.

Mismatches between the report and the events of the teaching situation occurred, but did not seem to affect S expectations. One child did not speak, though the report had described him as "frequently initiating conversation." S nevertheless rated the report as "most helpful." In another case, a boy was mis-identified as a girl in the report; S found the report "most helpful" and proceeded with "high ability" expectations.

Conclusions

Results of this sort have serious implications for present practices in educational settings. Even if we consider that this was a somewhat artificial situation and that normally the teacher has a much better knowledge of the child, we are, nevertheless, overwhelmed by the data suggesting drastic effects of expectancies. School children are frequently evaluated throughout their school years in terms of IQ tests, psychological reports, labeling through special classes, etc. For example, a child who is labeled a "slow learner" or "mentally retarded" is automatically expected to do less well than a "normal" child. This expectation might, in fact, retard the performance of the child even more than is necessary. The findings would suggest that one should be very careful as to what information a teacher should receive about a child. On the other hand, the findings may be applied in a constructive way; that is, positive aspects in a child's behavior or ability should be stressed.

References

CAHEN, L. S.   An experimental manipulation of the "halo effect": A study of teacher bias. Unpublished manuscript, Stanford University, 1965.

ORNE, M. T.   On the social psychology of the psychological experiment: With particular reference to demand characteristics and their implications. *American Psychologist,* 1962, 17, 776-783.

ROSENTHAL, R.   The effect of the experimenter on the results of psychological research. In N. A. Maher (Ed.), *Progress in experimental personality research.* Vol. I, New York: Academic Press, 1964. Pp. 79-114. (a)

ROSENTHAL, R.   Experimenter outcome-orientation and the results of the psychological experiment. *Psychological Bulletin,* 1964: 61, 405-412. (b)

ROSENTHAL, R.   *Experimenter effects in behavioral research.* New York: Appleton-Century-Crofts, 1966.

ROSENTHAL, R. and JACOBSON, L.   Teacher expectancies: determinants of pupils' IQ gains. *Psychological Reports,* 1966, 19, 115-118.

ROSENTHAL, R. and JACOBSON, L.   Self-fulfilling prophecies in the classroom: teachers' expectations as unintended determinants of pupils' intellectual competence. Paper read at the American Psychological Association meetings, Washington, D.C., 1967.

ROSENTHAL, R. and JACOBSON, L.   *Pygmalion in the classroom: teacher expectation and pupils' intellectual development.* New York: Holt, Rinehart and Winston, 1968.

※ ※ ※ ※ ※

Games are an ancient and interesting part of man's life. Scientific interest in them, stimulated by Huizinga's classic *Homo Ludens* (1938) and von Neumann and Morgenstern's *Theory of Games and Economic Behavior* (1947) has developed rapidly. Game situations have proved to be a primary tool for studying interpersonal relationships in the social-psychological laboratory. Yet until recently little effort has been made to examine the potential of games as educative experiences.

Boocock and Coleman, in effect, ask the reader to up-end his ideas as to what teaching and learning procedures are like. They suggest that in conventional schooling the reward system, the teacher's role definition, and the learner's goals and time perspective may all be operative in reducing net learning. In a sense, the host of "no-difference" findings obtained when familiar educational procedures are studied (cf. Stephens' *The Process of Schooling*, Holt, 1967) may well mean that social psychologists have not taken hold of the prepotent variables in classroom learning.

Like games themselves, the analysis in this article has a fresh, heuristic quality. However, the data do not provide direct support of the assertions made. Other data on game consequences (see Boocock and Schild, *Simulation Games in Learning*, Sage Publications, 1968) are not substantially more assuring. Boocock and Coleman's comments in this article under the heading "What is Learned" are thoughtful, and need continued experimentation and research. Otherwise the supposed potential of games as a new educational technology may not materialize.

Games With Simulated Environments in Learning*

Sarane S. Boocock, James S. Coleman

The general approach to be outlined here takes as its starting point the observation that the structure of education for adolescents may be as important as its content. The present structure of education in American high schools—courses with prescribed content, delivered by teachers who lecture, make assignments, and guide classes through a textbook—was established at a time which differed in two ways from our own. First, only a small proportion of adolescents continued academic training into secondary school. At the turn of the century, only about half of the fifteen-year-olds and less than a third of the seventeen-year-olds were attending school, as compared with 93 and 76 per cent, respectively, in 1960 (See U.S. Bureau of the Census, 1963, p. 117; Drucker, 1961, pp. 15-21; Clark, 1962, ch. 2). Those who did stay in school were principally from professional classes and destined for professional occupations, and for them school fit well with the future they or their parents were planning. Second, methods of child rearing were more rigid and strict, with less reliance on "persuasion," more on "coercion" than our present patterns.[1] The great egalitarian drift of the past century had not yet reached down to adolescents, and their position was clearly subordinate to and dependent upon adults. Under such conditions, it was not inconsistent for high school students to be attentive and respectful of a teacher's authority, and strongly directed by the demands and rewards of adult society generally.

Today, neither of these conditions holds for some adolescents, and one or the other is absent for most. In schools where few students are college bound, there is little motivation, and the teen-age culture encourages its members to defy discipline and to hold down effort in scholastic directions, and diverts energies into exciting and autonomous activities that interfere

* From *Sociology of Education*, 1966, 59 (3), 215-236. Used by permission of the authors and publisher, The American Sociological Association.

This is a revised version of a paper read at the annual meetings of the American Sociological Association, September, 1965. The research reported herein was carried out under a grant from the Carnegie Corporation. In addition to the grantor we wish to thank Mr. Edgar Reeves, of the U.S. Department of Agriculture, for stimulation in development of the games, and for providing opportunities to test them with large numbers of adolescents. The games described in this paper were developed by the authors and by Michael Inbar, who is responsible for the disaster game.

1. Bronfenbrenner (1961). For a review of literature on the developing status of the adolescent, see Matza (1964), esp. pp. 192-200.

with the school's task. In schools where most students are college bound, on the other hand, there are most likely to be found those adolescents raised by permissive standards emphasizing free expression and self-reliance, who are least willing to consider themselves as "children" and subordinates. In such schools, although the students as individuals are highly motivated, they are no more willing to accede to the authority of adults, and instead turn to one another for their direction and their rewards. Among such sophisticated adolescents, hard work in scholastic directions and visible devotion to getting good grades may be scorned and disdained as childish. In short, the structure of secondary education is no more appropriate in these schools than in the schools populated by unmotivated students who will at most finish high school.

Three Structural Defects in Secondary Education

Perhaps the most fundamental defect in secondary education is the fact that it teaches for a long-distance future. All children, even unintelligent ones, learn to speak a language well at a very early age. Immigrants forced into a new linguistic environment learn to speak a second language well. Yet few persons, even among the brightest, learn in school to speak a second language, even after spending years of classwork on it. This is only a single example of a remarkable disparity that occurs in general between the effectiveness of a young child's learning to get along in his environment, and the ineffectiveness of an older child's learning in school.

It seems likely that the major reason is this: in learning to talk, a young child is learning those skills that enable him to get along in his present environment, an environment of primary, face-to-face relations. An older child, however, is being taught in school those skills that will enable him to get along in a *future* environment of secondary relations. He still lives in a world of primary, face-to-face relations, with little necessity in his daily life to calculate, or to write, or even to read, and no necessity whatsoever to speak a foreign language. He will, of course, need many of these skills later, but this later need provides no motivation for the present. This is true among students of all economic levels for the more advanced subjects, but it is true among students of lower economic levels even for such a basic skill as reading, since the lives of their family and friends include little reading.

The greatest problem, then, appears to be due to a mismatching of time. The child is being taught for a future whose needs have not yet impressed themselves upon him; hence, he sees little need to focus his energies upon learning. He is, moreover, being taught for a future different from the one that his familiar adults are presently experiencing. The rapidity of social change induces an uncertainty about what skills will be relevant to it.

A second structural defect in high schools lies in the enforced, involuntary character of the curriculum. In contrast to scholarship in graduate schools, where a student is rewarded for spectacular achievement, in high school a curriculum has both a floor and a ceiling, and students are expected to perform within the range. The structure of education provides little support for inner motivation to carry on in a direction as far as one can, but instead fixes standards or limits that make a high school education consist of completing "assignments." Furthermore, this comes at a time when children are looking less to adults, more to one another for rewards. Consequently, one response to these superimposed activities is to substitute for them activities that adolescents can call their own, activities that allow more positive voluntary action with high rewards for spectacular achievement, such as athletics and other extracurricular activities.

The dual role of the teacher as both teacher and judge is a third structural defect of the school. A teacher has not only the task of teaching students, but also the task of giving them grades, grades that can greatly affect the students' futures. As a result, students develop attitudes toward the teacher that can interfere greatly with learning: hostility, servility, alienation, and other reactions to an authority figure.

One might at first argue that this is inevitable. Yet there are situations in which the role of teacher is divorced from that of judge. Athletic coaches, debate coaches, and coaches in other sorts of games are much less in the role of judge, since the game itself decides the winner. The teacher of a student preparing for a national scholarship examination is in a similar role, for the standardized examination is the judge, and the teacher is only the aide. Yet such situations occur seldom in high schools; the usual task of the teacher includes a large component of the unpleasant task of giving punishments and rewards to students in the form of grades.

Games with Simulated Environments

Although no educational tools can fully overcome these structural defects, there seem to be possibilities for altering the structure of secondary education in ways that go some distance to meet these problems. One way derives from the conjunction of a very old form of activity, games, with a very new one, simulated environments. Such games have been devised in several areas, and are now being used in one area, management training, by several business schools and corporations. In games of this type, certain features of the socio-economic environment—principally the market—are simulated, and players, taking the role of business firms, make decisions about product development, investment, marketing and other areas. At various points in the game, players receive "feedback" on the consequences of their actions. In some of these games feedback is calculated by the game administrators; in others a computer is programmed to act as the socio-economic environment.

The values of such games for children's learning arise from several sources. First, and perhaps most important, they bring the future into the present, allowing the child to play roles in a large differentiated society of which he otherwise gets hardly a glimpse. Thus, they surround a child with an environment which is artificial for the present, but realistic for the future. His academic task is not to carry out assignments, but to "survive" in this complex environment. In playing a management game, a child is forced to turn to economic texts not to get a grade, but for economic survival in this complex environment. In a consumer game (involving allocation of income in the face of credit financing, advertising pressures, and unpredictable events), a boy or girl must learn both economics and mathematics, as well as the necessity to defer gratifications. More generally, a boy or girl will be able to play at those roles that he must play in earnest once he becomes an adult, and enters the complex modern society of adults. In so doing, he learns both the intellectual skills relevant for those roles, and the moral traits—that is, the traits which schools presently attempt to inculcate under the general label of "citizenship education."

The manipulation of time through the use of games with simulated environments is even more general than this, for games can simulate the past just as they can the future. Thus, games to simulate historical events have been successfully developed, both as commercial parlor games (e.g., "Gettysburg," "Diplomacy"), and as games for use in schools (e.g., the Empire, Hunting, Slave Trade, Steam, and other historical games developed by Clark Abt and his associates).

A second important value of such games arises from the very fact that they are games. The virtues of games as motivating devices have long been noted. As one economist put it (Knight, 1921, p. 53):

> Most human motives tend on scrutiny to assimilate themselves to the game spirit. It is little matter, if any, what we set ourselves to do; it is imperative to have some objective in view, and we seize upon and set up for ourselves objectives more or less at random—getting an education, acquiring skill at some art, making money, or whatnot. But once having set ourselves to achieve some goal it becomes an absolute value, weaving itself into and absorbing life itself. It is just as in a game where the concrete objective—capturing our opponents' pieces, carrying a ball across a mark, or whatever it may be—is a matter of accident, but to achieve it is for the moment the end and aim of being.

Thus, games have a peculiarly valuable motivating ability. They also are far more self-disciplining than most other forms of learning. In games, the discipline arises internally, from the necessity to obey the rules if the game is to continue. Thus, children who have never been socialized into the need to obey rules can become socialized when the rules are not arbitrarily imposed, but arise from the game itself. Students of socialization often see the ability to play a game with other children as an important stage in the process of socialization.

Finally, games are self-judging; the outcome decides the winner, and a player knows that he has won or lost by his own actions. Thus, in large part, the teacher can escape from the role of judge, and return to his original function, that of teacher, or helper for the student.

With this as a general orientation, research in the development of games with simulated environments was begun three and a half years ago at Johns Hopkins University. In a few other centers, work has developed along similar lines.[2] This work has now developed to the point at which some of the values that arise in the use of such games as well as some of the pitfalls which can arise have become evident. Three games have been developed, with extensive testing, in the work at Johns Hopkins, and the points below will be based on some of the results with these games.

These three games are:

—*A career game*, to be played by any number of teams, each consisting of two to four players. Each team works with a profile or case history of a fictitious person (usually a student about the age of the players).

The game is organized into rounds or decision periods, each of which represents one year in the life of this person. During each decision period, players plan their person's schedule of activities for a typical week, allocating his time among school, studying, a job, family responsibilities, and leisure time activities. Most activities require certain investments, of time, training, money and so on (for example, a full-time job takes a certain amount of time and often has some educational or experience prerequisites as well; similarly having a child requires a considerable expenditure of time, in addition to financial expenses), and a person clearly cannot engage in all the available activities. Thus, the players' problem is to choose the combination of activities which they think will maximize their person's present satisfaction and his chances for a good life in the future. In addition, for certain activities—a job, or higher education—a person must make a formal application and be accepted. (An integral feature of the Life Career Game is that in the normal course of playing, students acquire such skills as filling out college or job application forms correctly.)

When players have made their decisions for a given year, scores are computed in four areas—education, occupation, family life, and leisure. Calculators use a set of tables and spinners—based upon U.S. Census and other national survey data—which indicate the probabilities of certain things happening in a person's life, given his personal characteristics, past experiences, and present efforts. A chance or "luck" factor is built into the game by the use of spinners and dice (so students can also gain an understanding of some of the principles of probability theory through seeing how it operated in a concrete social situation).

A game runs for a designated number of rounds (usually 10-12), and the team with the highest total score at the end of the game is the winner.

2.   Some of the centers where such work is proceeding are Northwestern University, under the direction of Harold Guetzkow, in the development of inter-nation games; Abt Associates in Cambridge, Mass.; University of North Carolina, under Andrew Scott, in the development of political games; Northern Westchester Board of Cooperative Educational Services, under Richard Wing, in the development of economic games; and the Western Behavioral Sciences Institute at La Jolla, California, in the testing of a variety of simulation games and the training of teachers to administer such games.

—*A legislative game,* to be played by a set of six to ten players, each acting as a legislator, and collectively acting as a legislative body deciding upon a series of public issues. Each player is dealt a set of cards which indicate his constituents' attitudes about various issues. For example, one such card reads: Federal aid to education—70 persons against, 30 persons for. Another reads: Retaining military base in your constituency—250 persons for, 50 persons against. By studying his whole set of cards, a player can tell how his "district" feels about the various issues, and which issues are most important to them.

After an initial round of short speeches, the game alternates between (a) informal "bargaining" sessions of two or three minutes, when players may contact any other legislators and try to gain their support on issues of the greatest importance to them and (b) formal sessions of the legislature, during which players bring issues to the floor, discuss them according to rules of parliamentary procedure, and vote. A legislator's success—i.e., whether or not he is re-elected at the end of the game—is determined by his success in getting passed or defeated those measures his constituents most want passed or defeated.

—*A community disaster game,* to be played by six to nine players. Players sit around a schematic "map" which gives the location of police station, fire department, industrial and residential areas, and other areas of a medium sized town, with the network of roads connecting them. When the game starts, players are informed that a catastrophe has occurred in an unspecified part of the town and that people may have been injured and property destroyed. Each player is given a role in the simulated community, including his location at the start of the game, the relatives and friends he has in the community, his job, and any special obligations or interests such as property owned. Everyone is therefore anxious about the fate of persons and things he cares for.

To alleviate their anxiety, players may try to find out what has happened by listening to radio broadcasts, telephoning relatives, friends, or agencies, or by moving around the community (each such activity requires expenditure of a given number of "energy units"). In the course of their activity, players will see how much of what subsequently happens in the community (e.g., telephone or road jams, the operation or non-operation of key public agencies) are the direct consequence of their own decisions and actions.

When players learn where the disaster area is and the extent of the damages, community organization becomes imperative. To evacuate relatives in the disaster area requires entering that area, and this requires the intervention of the department of public works to clear the roads, of the fire department to control any blazes, of the police station to control road jams, etc. If the community cannot organize itself quickly or efficiently enough, the disaster can spread, possibly causing damage beyond repair (in such a case everyone "loses").

At the end of the game, the players elect from among the three with the lowest total "anxiety" score the one who did most for the community. The winner is then the player who was both most efficient in committing his own energies and most visibly cooperative in helping his neighbors overcome the disaster.

Experimental Design for Testing Effects of the Games

The games described above have been tested in a variety of settings: in several high schools, located in both high and low status neighborhoods or communities, and testing at more than one grade level within a school; in various young people's groups outside the classroom, from small extracurricular clubs to large conferences of several hundred students. A few tests have been done with junior high and younger students. Modified forms of the games are being developed for testing with the least literate, least motivated types of adolescents.

Besides providing experience upon which to base revisions of game materials, the purpose of testing has been to discover what students gain from playing. To this end, questionnaire and interview data have been gathered from players and from control groups of students who have not had the experience of a particular game. The remainder of this paper will discuss findings from the largest experiments carried out with each game.

Data to be reported on the career and legislative games (except for Table 3) were gathered at a conference of California 4-H Club members at Berkeley, California, in September, 1964. As indicated in Figure A, 1,200 young people (ranging in age from 13 to 21) were randomly assigned to one or the other of two simulation games. All participants filled out identical questionnaires before and after the game session, with some additional questions after the session related to the particular game a subject

Figure 1.

DESIGN OF DATA COLLECTION FOR LEGISLATIVE AND CAREER GAMES

	Experimental Group (for legislature game)—600 boys and girls[a]	*Control Group* (for legislature game)—600 boys and girls[a]
	Control Group (for career game)	*Experimental Group* (for career game)
time 0	Questionnaire a	Questionnaire a
	Legislature game	Career game
time 1	Questionnaire b, + questions about legislature game	Questionnaire b, + questions about career game

[a] Individuals assigned randomly to legislature or career games.

had played. The majority of questions were of the structured, closed-answer type, based upon responses we had obtained in previous interviewing and open-ended questionnaires.

Each group acts as a control for the other, since each had the experience of one of the games but not the other. The special virtue of this design— besides the large sample and the random assignment on an individual basis —is its control of the Hawthorne effect, in that everyone was subjected to the "novelty" of a game (and to the experience of the Berkeley conference as a whole). Thus, differences between the changes found in the question- naire responses of the experimental and control groups can be described as effects of that particular game with little fear of spuriousness.

Two important factors are not assessed in this design. One is the compara- tive effects of alternative methods of teaching the same materials. This raises a particularly thorny problem in educational research. The most con- sistent finding in studies comparing the relative effectiveness of different teaching methods is no significant difference—or when there is a difference it is not consistent with other studies comparing the same teaching methods. Besides the "criterion" problem—the problem of designating exactly what results should be obtained from a given method and then designing test items to measure this accurately—there is the virtual impossibility of match- ing any two teaching devices on material covered, difficulty, clarity of in- structions, and so on. The difficulty is compounded in that minor changes within a set of teaching materials can change its effects. For example, it has been found in research on programmed instruction that simply shifting the *order* of a set of frames can produce different results with stu- dents. In other words, comparative testing of different teaching methods is an extremely complex problem in itself, and it will not be treated here. Perhaps the best solution to this problem is not to meet it head on, but to develop a variety of learning techniques separately, and then assess their efficiency in terms of a whole set of criteria: the learning per unit of time invested, the regenerative effects in subsequent independent learning, the amount of teacher preparation and ability required, and other costs.

The other factor not studied in the California sample is the type of stu- dent who participated in the conference. These players were clearly not a representative sample of American or even California students (e.g., over 80 per cent claimed to be in the top half of their high school class academically).[3]

Data on the disaster game were gathered at a national 4-H conference at Washington, D.C., in April, 1965, at which 256 boys and girls played this game. Participants completed questionnaires before and after the game. There was no control group for this test.

---

3. Data not reported here from an earlier experiment in two high schools with students from lower socio-economic backgrounds showed that most students felt that academically poorer students would profit *more* from the games, relative to usual classroom activities, than better students. See Boocock (1963). Thus, the positive results to be shown here, with this above-average group, would seem to hold for below-average students as well.

Results

The first and most pervasive result in all experiments concerns the *motivating and self-sustaining qualities* of the activity. The level of involvement and activation of the adolescents who have played is remarkable. A flavor of this is provided by the statements players make after playing. A sample of the statements after the disaster game runs as follows:

> This game should be played by every citizen in the world. It gave us an opportunity to relive a situation which we may be faced with every day or someday in the near future.
>
> Terrifically stimulating: And useful—you are forced to evaluate yourself.
>
> This is a novel and refreshing approach to disaster preparedness. When I first saw a 3 and ½ hour assembly scheduled, I anticipated a lecture and, well, sweet dreams. I really dreaded a long civil defense lecture. This, however, was not only a memorable lesson but a pleasurable experience as well. I am extremely glad to have a chance to figure out the entire game by myself. If someone had told me at the beginning that "community spirit counts," the lesson would not have had any impact and the afternoon would have been wasted. This is one of the few Conference programs which was truly "beyond expectation."

A girl who played the career game wrote:

> The game was delightful and interesting and offered an extremely new way to plan for the future. It was extremely thrilling to plan this girl's life and make the most of her future.

While it is always difficult to quantify something like enthusiasm, a clue is provided in responses to an open-ended question asking students who had played the disaster game whether they had learned anything from it. Even though this question did not ask them directly whether or not they *liked* the game, almost twenty per cent of the 256 players spontaneously wrote in something to the effect that the game was wonderful or that they would like to play it again.

Similar responses have occurred in our experiments with each game. The great majority of players thoroughly enjoy the games and will play them as long as they are allowed to.[4] The positive reaction and extreme involvement of players may well be the most important kind of result such games could have. For the essence of a good tool for learning is its self-

---

4. It should be noted that there typically is a small proportion of players—less than ten per cent in the groups we have tested—who are very negative to the games, who say they disliked a game or would not want to play it again. We have not yet studied a group of these players in detail, to determine whether it is a particular game, games in general, or simply learning itself to which they are responding negatively.

Table 1

MEAN NUMBER OF CORRECT ITEMS LISTED RELATING TO JOB OPPORTUNITIES AND
MARITAL SATISFACTIONS, BEFORE AND AFTER THE GAMES

MEAN # OF CORRECT ITEMS ON LIST OF:	BOYS				GIRLS			
	EXPERIMENTAL		CONTROL		EXPERIMENTAL		CONTROL	
	BEFORE	AFTER	BEFORE	AFTER	BEFORE	AFTER	BEFORE	AFTER
—Jobs open to non-high school graduates	2.8	2.8	3.0	2.5	4.0	4.1	4.3	3.4*
—Jobs open to college graduates	3.0	3.1	2.9	1.8*	4.5	4.4	5.0	3.5*
—Resources I might use in planning for future	2.8	3.1	2.9	3.0	3.3	3.7	3.1	3.1
—Occupations I have thought of for myself	2.6	3.0	3.0	2.7	3.1	3.3	3.2	3.2
—Factors related to marital satisfaction	2.1	2.2	2.1	1.7*	2.8	2.8	2.9	2.4
Total respondents	(238)	(238)	(225)	(225)	(371)	(371)	(376)	(376)

* Difference between change in experimental (career game) group and change in control (legislature game) group significant at .05 level, two-tailed test.

motivating quality, its ability to capture attention and induce the learner
to seek to learn more. And probably the key factor in the failure of so many
adolescents to learn effectively in our schools is lack of motivation.

What is Learned?

Once the major element of motivation is achieved, the question arises: what
is or can be learned in such games? The findings in this area will be divided into two parts: (1) the kinds of specific things that players learn in
each of the three games; and (2) some effects that seem to be common to
all three.

1. *Specific effects of the career, legislative, and disaster games.*

The career game is designed to give familiarity with the job market,
with educational choices, and with some of the major family decisions. The
results of the Berkeley conference indicated that players did acquire some
of the information. When asked to list the kinds of occupations available
to persons with varying educational levels, the kinds of factors related to
marital stability and satisfaction (both of which were manifest in the game)
or the kinds of resources they could think of to use in making their own
career plans, the delegates who played the career game did better on the
average than those who played the legislative game (Table 1).[5] The mean

scores of respondents who played the career game (experimental group)
is higher than the mean score for respondents in the control group for each
of the five listing items, for both boys and girls. And while the mean remains the same or goes up slightly in every case but one in the experimental
groups, the tendency is toward lower scores after the game for the control
groups. (The "after" questionnaire was administered at the end of the playing session, when respondents were quite pressed for time, which probably
explains the apparent loss of knowledge in the control groups. That the
respondents in the experimental groups were able to retain their scores,
and improve them in many cases, supports the claim that this kind of information was communicated to them during the career game.)

5. A note about the form of the tables: In Table 1, and all those based upon data
from the Berkeley conference, the groups to be compared will be identified as "experimental" or "control." Note that the experimental group will sometimes be the students
who played the career game, as in Table 1, and sometimes the students who played the
legislative game, as in Table 4.

An asterisk (*) following a *pair* of before-after comparisons indicates that the difference
between the *change* in the experimental group and the *change* in the control group is
significant at the .05 level, in a two-tailed test. That is, the test used indicates not whether
the before per cent is significantly different from the after per cent in the same group, but
whether the before-after *difference* in one group is significantly different from the before-
after difference in the other group of the same sex. This test is used in Tables 1, 2, 4, 6,
7, and 8.

It should also be noted that while these tables show only marginal data (for purposes
of clarity), the estimate of variance in the significance test is based upon *individual turn-
over data* and thus takes into account the total amount of change within a group.

Table 2

RESPONSES TO QUIZ QUESTIONS, BEFORE AND AFTER THE GAMES

PER CENT OF RESPONDENTS WHO AGREE THAT:	BOYS				GIRLS			
	EXPERIMENTAL		CONTROL		EXPERIMENTAL		CONTROL	
	BEFORE	AFTER	BEFORE	AFTER	BEFORE	AFTER	BEFORE	AFTER
	%	%	%	%	%	%	%	%
The amount of education a person has affects his satisfaction with his marriage and family	60	66	50	50	60	60	57	58
Among colleges, the greatest course variety is usually at state universities	53	63	51	55	45	61	48	55*
A person's income is related to how much education he has	95	93	93	86	91	96	92	92*
Total respondents	(238)	(238)	(225)	(225)	(371)	(371)	(376)	(376)

* Difference between change in experimental (career game) and control (legislature game) groups significant at .05 level, two-tailed test.

Table 2 shows further evidence of the learning of specific information in the career game. The table shows a tendency for the players of this game to do better on some "quiz" type questions relating to material covered in the game (and built into the game model), such as identifying the relationship between education and income, or the range of course offerings at different types of colleges.

Table 3

WHAT PLAYERS LIST AS THE MOST EFFECTIVE STRATEGY IN THE
LEGISLATURE GAME

	BOYS	GIRLS
	%	%
Exchanging votes or support with others in return for their support	43	41
Cooperating with others in the legislature	27	43
Not revealing one's position or strategies fully	13	6
Being good at persuading others; giving good speeches	14	14
Knowing how other players feel about all the issues	8	8
Being very well informed about the issues	9	6
Using elusive or dishonest tactics	11	1
Making one's own positions very clear	2	5
Total respondents	(84)	(86)

The legislative game is designed to teach the basic processes of negotiation through which collective decisions are reached on issues in which different segments of society have differing interests. This is similar to the kind of bargaining and exchange they have engaged in throughout their lives, but they see them as an essential element—some for the first time—in the legislative process. Following a session of the legislature game with a group of students in Washington, D.C., players were asked to describe what they thought were the most effective strategies in the game. Results are shown in Table 3. Seventy per cent of the boys and 84 per cent of the girls mentioned either exchanging support or cooperating with others, indicating that the players had learned the major principle of the game model, i.e., the need to build up exchange relationships with other legislators.[6]

In a number of tests of the legislature game, players were asked about various types of political processes or strategies. The responses of the students at the Berkeley conference to three of these items are shown in Table 4. Boys and girls in the experimental groups were more likely than those in the control group to move toward agreeing that pressure groups are a useful feature of representative government; girls were more likely to move away from agreeing that legislators should always vote according to their

6. There are no "before game" responses from these players nor any control group data in Table 3. Since the respondents were asked to discuss the strategies for the legislative game, they must, of course, have played that game. Note also that these data are not from the Berkeley conference, as this question was not included in the Berkeley questionnaire.

Table 4

RESPONDENTS' ORIENTATIONS TOWARD POLITICAL PROCESSES BEFORE AND AFTER THE GAME

PER CENT OF RESPONDENTS WHO:	BOYS				GIRLS			
	EXPERIMENTAL		CONTROL		EXPERIMENTAL		CONTROL	
	BEFORE	AFTER	BEFORE	AFTER	BEFORE	AFTER	BEFORE	AFTER
	%	%	%	%	%	%	%	%
agree that pressure groups are useful ..	23	34	23	25	17	24	13	17*
disagree that legislators should always vote convictions	24	23	17	17	23	28	25	23*
disagree that letters etc. to legislators a waste of time	44	43	48	39*	47	48	39	40
Total respondents	(225)	(225)	(238)	(238)	(376)	(376)	(371)	(371)

* Difference between changes in experimental (legislature game) and control (career game) groups significant at .05 level, two-tailed test.

own convictions, even when they do not reflect the interests of their constituents. In other words, what some players seem to get is a more realistic
understanding of how things are actually done in political institutions.

One unanticipated effect of the legislative game concerns players' attitudes toward the content of the issues. Although the changes were slight,
on each issue respondents in the experimental group took stronger attitude
positions, pro or con, after playing the game than before the game. In
addition, there is some indication that they changed their attitudes toward
the position they worked for in the game. (Data not shown. A parallel finding in the career game is that players working on the career of a particular
type of boy or girl appear to see such a person more sympathetically after
the game. While analysis of data on this point is not complete, there appears
to be a general effect in these games that depends on the *role* one plays.)

Table 5

PLAYERS' OPINIONS ABOUT THE BEST WAY TO BE HELPFUL IN A DISASTER,
BEFORE AND AFTER THE GAME

PER CENT OF PLAYERS WHO SAY ONE SHOULD—	BEFORE GAME	AFTER GAME
	%	%
—get to the headquarters of an agency (such as police or fire department) to see what help is needed	48	61
—stay put in order not to jam the roads	39	27
—get to the disaster area to help with rescue work	5	5
Total respondents	(256)	(256)

The community disaster game is designed to give familiarity with the
kinds of reactions a person undergoes in a crisis situation and the kinds
of strategies that are most effective in solving a crisis. Table 5 suggests
that players have learned the importance of cooperating in order to operate
the key community agencies which can enable a community to overcome
the after-effects of a disaster. Note that players also tend to espouse a more
active role in certain situations (active participation in a community agency
gains at the expense of passively "staying put"), a finding which we shall
return to again later in the paper.

2. *General learning in the games.* Three kinds of effects seem to have occurred in some form in all of the games described in this paper. First, students can acquire a *very real feeling* for the processes simulated, including
an appreciation of the *complexity of the real-life situation.* The following
comments were written after the disaster game:

> The pressures, anxieties, frustrations, seemed very real. The realism of
> people not cooperating or not knowing what to do seemed very much
> present.
>
> Many times a catastrophe has happened and has been televised. The
> people and their remarks were very much like ourselves and ours.

On a minor scale each of us did experience the tension and confusion which might arise.

I have learned that everything is a mess and you don't know what to do. I actually felt panicked.

In response to a structured question asking, "Do you think that the game you just played is realistic?" fifty-eight per cent of the players checked one of the two most extreme positive responses on a seven-point scale.[7]

Similar opinions have been expressed in connection with the career game. As one girl put it: "All the possibilities that popped up in the game made me realize how difficult decisions will be when I get older." Another said:

Most students would have had impractical views of their future lives before they played this game, just as I did. After playing the games they would learn that a twenty-four hour day is not long enough to allow a girl to hold a job, be a wife, raise a family and get an education. Something must be left out.

That the game makes some players more conscious of the complexities of the future is indicated by comparing responses of those who played the career game with the control group to a question asking them whether they agreed that: "It's awfully hard to plan your life in advance, because there are so many things to take into account."

Table 6

PER CENT OF RESPONDENTS WHO AGREE THAT IT IS HARD TO
PLAN YOUR LIFE IN ADVANCE

BOYS				GIRLS			
EXPERIMENTAL		CONTROL		EXPERIMENTAL		CONTROL	
BEFORE GAME	AFTER GAME	BEFORE GAME	AFTER GAME	BEFORE GAME	AFTER GAME	BEFORE GAME	AFTER GAME
24% (238)	34% (238)	27% (225)	30%* (225)	19% (371)	30% (371)	22% (376)	21%* (376)

* Difference between change in experimental (career game) and control (legislature game) groups significant at .05 level, two-tailed test.

Table 6 shows that change among both boys and girls who played the career game (experimental group) is greater than change among those who did not play this game, in the direction of agreeing that it is difficult to plan for the future because of its complexity.

7. The disaster game enabled us to evaluate the realism of the game more than most games, in that a number of the players had actually experienced a flood, tornado, or some other kind of natural disaster. These students were much more likely to say that the game was very realistic. (The difference between those who had experienced a real-life disaster and those who had not was significant at the .01 level, two-tailed test).

Second, while many players become aware of the amount of information they must assimilate and the amount of planning necessary to make decisions in certain real life situations, they also gain confidence in their own ability to do something or to act effectively in such situations. For example, one reaction of girls to the career game has been a realization that they could do more with their own lives than they had previously thought possible.

Table 7

PER CENT OF GIRLS WHO THINK A GIRL SHOULD DO MORE
THAN MARRY AND RAISE A FAMILY, BEFORE AND AFTER THE GAME

EXPERIMENTAL		CONTROL	
BEFORE GAME	AFTER GAME	BEFORE GAME	AFTER GAME
42%	50%	55%	46%*
(371)	(371)	(376)	(376)

* Difference between change in experimental (career game) and control (legislature game) groups is signficant at .05 level, two-tailed test.

A girl who played the game in a Florida high school wrote:

> I think many girls would be happy to learn of all the things they can do besides being wives and mothers. Many girls who might have been resigned to being a housewife could see that if a girl in the game could get a successful job, so could they.

This kind of broader vision is suggested in Table 7. While the control group at the Berkeley conference moved away from agreement with the statement: "An intelligent girl with a good education really should do more with it than just get married and raise a family," girls who played the career game were more likely to endorse the expanded feminine role after the game.[8]

> A woman can have a successful life without going to college and the same goes for a man. As long as I can remember, it has been drilled into me that anyone who doesn't go to college is a moron.

This feeling of greater control of one's environment is a result found in both the other games as well. After playing the legislature game, students

8. Table 7 does point to a possible danger of a game like the career game—i.e., that it may influence students' values in an unrealistic direction. For example, one might fear that all girls who play will be led to believe that they should have careers. Of course, the purpose of the game is not this, but rather to lead students toward planning lives that are congruent with their particular interests. While we do not have any quantitative data on this, players' comments such as the following suggest that the game gives a broader rather than a narrower view of the alternatives in a successful life:

were more likely to disagree with the statement that "People like me don't have any say about what the government does," while this was not true of the control group who played another game (Table 8).

Table 8

PER CENT OF RESPONDENTS WHO DISAGREE THAT PEOPLE HAVE NO
SAY IN GOVERNMENT

BOYS				GIRLS			
EXPERIMENTAL		CONTROL		EXPERIMENTAL		CONTROL	
BEFORE GAME	AFTER GAME	BEFORE GAME	AFTER GAME	BEFORE GAME	AFTER GAME	BEFORE GAME	AFTER GAME
41%	51%	40%	42%*	44%	48%	45%	41%*
(225)	(225)	(238)	(238)	(376)	(376)	(371)	(371)

* Difference between change in experimental (legislature game) and control (career game) groups is significant at .05 level, two-tailed test.

And after playing the disaster game, players tend to express greater confidence both in the efficacy of community preparedness and in their own ability to cope with a real-life disaster situation, as shown in Table 9.

Table 9

PLAYERS' FEELINGS ABOUT COMMUNITY PREPAREDNESS AND THEIR
OWN ABILITY TO COPE, BEFORE AND AFTER PLAYING THE
DISASTER GAME

PER CENT OF RESPONDENTS WHO THINK—	BEFORE GAME	AFTER GAME
	%	%
—community preparedness can really improve the chances of limiting the damages caused by a catastrophe	41	62*
—they themselves would know just what to do if there was a catastrophe in their community	31	42*
Total respondents	(256)	(256)

* Difference of proportions (test for matched pairs) significant at .05 level, two-tailed test.

This general indication that games increase players' confidence in their own capacities for coping with complicated situations suggests a possible long-run consequence of games. While a major goal of American schools is the production of adults trained and motivated to participate in community affairs, few classroom activities are really designed to do this. One variable that has been found to be related to participation is confidence that one's efforts will be effective. Sociological studies of political behavior, for example, have shown that the people most likely to take an active part in politics are those with relatively strong feelings of political "potency" or "efficacy." (Cf. Campbell, Gurin, and Miller, 1954, 187-194; Knupfer, 1953.) Applying this finding to the games, one might predict that players who acquire greater self-confidence from the game experience will in turn be more willing to participate in the real-life activities simulated in the game. The finding in Table 5 reported earlier—that players were more likely to endorse a plan of active involvement in community agencies after playing the game—would support such a prediction. We are now designing some simple measures, to be used in follow-up studies, to determine students' level of participation in areas related to the games they have played.

A third kind of change that occurs for many students is an increased sense of the interconnections between various aspects of a situation, or *interdependence in the environment.* This may occur either through seeing more dimensions of the total situations than they had been aware of before, or through grasping some general principle which enables them to organize their thinking. Although data on this effect are still largely impressionistic, they are presented here because aiding students to see complex processes as a whole seems an important potential contribution of games.

This effect is most evident in students' own evaluation of games. The following quotations, two from the career game questionnaires and two from the disaster game, are examples:

> This game makes one realize what your life must consist of, that is, it is more than education or marriage or children or money. It is all of these, and one's life must be planned in relation to all aspects of life, not just one.
>
> I became familiar with some of the experiences a woman has during her whole life. I got an idea of what things are important and need to be taken into consideration when planning any part of life.
>
> The light dawned at our table after the fifth move, that we must help the community rather than concentrate on our own family's welfare. However, we learned the hard way (wasting valuable "energy") and we aren't likely to forget it.
>
> This shows problems that arise in a state of emergency: (1) lack of organization (2) lack of calmness (3) lack of a planned program in disaster. I would like to take this back to Colorado. This would show just what will happen in an emergency.

The broader perspective gained in the game is suggested by Table 10, an analysis of the number of different areas of life or career considerations mentioned by respondents in answer to an open-ended question asking them to describe how they would like to see themselves in fifteen years. Although the difference is not statistically significant in the sample of questionnaires analyzed, (a sample of 100 in each subgroup), those who played the career game mentioned, on the average, more considerations than the control group.

Table 10

MEAN NUMBER CF DIMENSIONS IN ESSAY ON "HOW YOU WOULD LIKE
TO SEE YOURSELF IN FIFTEEN YEARS"[a]

BOYS		GIRLS	
EXPERIMENTAL	CONTROL	EXPERIMENTAL	CONTROL
2.2	1.7	3.0	2.3
(100)	(100)	(100)	(100)

[a] "Before" data not available.

Summary and Discussion

Certain structural characteristics of secondary education—a focus upon future needs which are not made real to students, a rigid system of assignments and grading which does not reward high levels of achievement or effort, and emphasis upon the "judging" aspect of the teacher's role—seem to discourage optimum academic performance. Games with simulated environments are seen as a means of correcting these structural defects. Experimentation with three games indicates that they are powerful motivators and that students can learn from them. In addition to specific information acquired from playing a particular game, there seems to be a general effect, in the nature of gaining a broader or more accurate image of the kinds of environments which students will face as adults. This can take the form of a realization of the complexity of future social situations which players had thought little about previously, a greater sense of being able to cope with one's environment and a greater interest in trying to do so, or a greater ability to see a complex social situation as an organized whole.

The findings presented here give an overview of the kind of results which might be expected from use of games with simulated environments, but this is by no means a complete analysis of the possible effects of such games—or even of these three particular games. Many important questions have not even been considered. For example, what kinds of students learn most and are most motivated by games? We have some evidence that these games may be particularly valuable with the kinds of students who are not performing well under the present educational conditions, but this has not been studied systematically. What is the learning curve with extensive play of a game? Most of our data have been collected before and after a single play of a game. We feel that because a simulated environment must be complex to be realistic, and because this complexity can be overwhelming at the beginning, the best use of games is in a stepwise fashion, beginning with a very simple version which can be learned quickly and following with successively more complex versions. In this way, the initial hurdle of getting into a game is not too discouraging, yet learning of quite complex materials can occur as the game sessions proceed. But again this is an impression which requires further testing.

Much remains to be examined, but our experience with simulation games has already indicated something of the potential they have for changing the orientations of adolescents, and for learning generally.

References

BOOCOCK, S. S.   Effects of an election campaign game in four high school classes. Report to Carnegie Corporation. Department of Social Relations, Johns Hopkins University, 1963. Mimeographed.

BRONFENBRENNER, U.   The changing American child. In E. Ginzberg (Ed.), *Values and ideals of American youth.* New York: Columbia University Press, 1961. Pp. 71-84.

CAMBELL, A., GURIN, G. and MILLER, W. E.   *The voter decides.* Evanston: Row, Peterson, 1954.

CLARK, B. R.   *Educating the expert society.* San Francisco: Chandler, 1962.

DRUCKER, P.   The educational revolution. In A. H. Halsey, J. Floud, and C. A. Anderson (Eds.), *Education, economy and society.* New York: Free Press, 1961. Pp. 15-21.

KNIGHT, F. H.   *Risk, uncertainty and profit.* Boston: Houghton Mifflin, 1921.

KNUPFER, G.   Portrait of the underdog. In R. Bendix and S. M. Lipset (Eds.), *Class, status and power.* Glencoe: Free Press, 1953. Pp. 255-263.

MATZA, D.   Position and behavior patterns of youth. In R. E. L. Faris (Ed.), *Handbook of modern sociology.* Chicago: Rand McNally, 1964.

U.S. BUREAU OF THE CENSUS.   *Statistical abstract of the United States: 1963.* 84th edition. Washington: U.S. Government Printing Office, 1963.

It is easy to forget the importance of educational materials, especially when a social-psychological stance is taken toward matters of teaching and learning. Yet the major successful educative reforms of our time—from PSSC physics onward—have essentially been reforms in the pieces of paper with words on them which confront the learner, and which serve to guide the teacher in his management of the learning environment.

De Charms and Moeller make a fascinating psycho/historical study of the motives and values inferred from a content analysis of fourth-grade readers printed over a 150-year period. They leave inexplicit the question of the actual impact on children, but that is presumably not minor (cf. Litcher and Johnson's article in the present book).

The reader should examine closely the assumptions behind the method of content analysis of historical documents; do children's readers really meet all the conditions outlined by the authors? For example, do the authors of readers really believe what they are writing? Do children's readers offer an unrestricted site for the exercise of fantasy?

Those with interest in the question of how individual motives connect with economic and cultural shifts are referred to Hagen's *On the Theory of Social Change* (Irwin/Dorsey Press, 1962) and to selected articles in *Daedalus* (Summer, 1967), titled "Toward the Year 2000: Work in Progress." It is widely asserted that we are moving toward fundamental changes in values and belief systems (cf. Flacks in the present book); would de Charms and Moeller's methods pick up early warning signals of this in current readers? Perhaps popular song lyrics would be a better research site.

Values Expressed in American Children's Readers, 1800-1950*

Richard de Charms, Gerald H. Moeller

Students of cultural change within the United States seem to have reached some agreement as to a trend observable within the last century. This trend, which deals with some of the basic values of our culture, may be seen as a change from what Weber (1930) called "the Protestant ethic" to what has been called the "social ethic" (Whyte, 1956). Specifically, the dominant value of individual salvation through hard work, thrift, and competition is seen as being replaced by "a belief in the group as the source of creativity; a belief in 'belongingness' as the ultimate need of the individual; and a belief in the application of science to achieve the belongingness" (Whyte, 1956, p. 7). In Riesman's (Riesman, Glazer, and Denney, 1950) terminology the basic trend is from inner-direction to other-direction.

Actually this process is circular in the sense that the cultural change is probably accompanied by a change in values which starts a new cycle. The psychologist likes to conceive of the variables in human behavior as being internally determined and thus breaks this circle and concentrates on motives as basic.

The aim of the present paper is to investigate psychological variables which it seems logical to predict will be associated with the cultural changes observed in the United States over the last century and a half.

McClelland (1955) has noted striking similarity between his concept of the person with high achievement motivation and Riesman's inner-directed character type. McClelland defines achievement motivation as "success in competition with a standard of excellence" (p. 43). According to Riesman et al. (1950) "the drive instilled in the child is to *live up to ideals* and to test his ability to be on his own by continuous experiments in self-mastery" (p. 59). For the other-directed person "making good becomes almost equivalent to making friends" (Riesman et. al., 1950, p. 66). This sounds very much like the person with high affiliation motivation. Atkinson (1958) defines affiliation motivation as "concern . . . over establishing, maintaining,

* From *Journal of Abnormal and Social Psychology*, 1962, 64 (2), 136-142. Used by permission of the authors and publisher.

This study was carried out under Contract Nonr-816 (11) between the Office of Naval Research and the Small Groups Laboratory, Social Science Institute at Washington University.

We wish to thank David C. McClelland and Raymond E. Callahan for critical comments on an earlier version of the paper.

or restoring a positive affective relationship with another person. This relationship is most adequately described by the word friendship" (p. 206).

Assuming that achievement motivation is a basic component of the inner-directed character type, and that affiliation motivation is a basic component of the other-directed character type, in the context of Riesman's cultural change thesis, one would predict a decline in over-all achievement motivation and an increase in affiliation motivation in the last century of United States history. Strauss and Houghton (1960) have found evidence giving some support to these hypotheses in the period since 1924 in a study of 4-H club journals. A meaningful relationship should also be found between achievement orientation and economic and technological change according to McClelland (1955).

A further aspect of Riesman's thesis is that the stage of inner-direction is preceded by a stage of tradition-direction. During this stage strict moral codes demand behavioral conformity of the individual. The change from a tradition-directed society to an inner-directed society involves a secularization in the sense that the individual must prove himself worthy as in Weber's (1930) Protestant ethic, rather than be told what to do by categorical imperatives. One might thus predict more reliance on moral teaching early in the history of the United States.

The objective measurement of cultural orientations or values is always difficult, especially if an attempt is to be made to tap the values of the past. An intriguing attempt to measure the motives of an ancient culture has been reported by McClelland (1958). He has developed a method of assessing achievement motivation in a culture by content analysis of literary products of the culture. Using this tool he found striking confirmation for his hypothesis that achievement motivation preceded the economic and technological development of Athenian civilization in classical Greece, a culture also discussed by Riesman.

McClelland's measure of motivation was developed originally to assess the motives of individuals (McClelland, Atkinson, Clark, and Lowell, 1953). The extension of it to apply to cultures raises questions as to what is being measured. McClelland (1958) has argued that his content analysis of documents produced by the culture will give a measure of the level of specific types of motivation within the culture if the documents are carefully selected to reduce effects of other obviously important variables. The best support for this argument derives from a study which demonstrated that content analysis of American Indian folk tales relates to content analysis of stories obtained from individuals in the manner used originally to validate the measure for studying individual motives (McClelland and Friedman, 1952).

It is obvious that a measure which has been shown to be related to individual motives would be expected to reflect the motives of the writer of any document chosen from a culture. In order to use such a measure as an indication of cultural orientation one does not have to assume that the motive score of an individual author is a measure of the cultural orientation alone. One must, however, assume that a portion of the score is a measure of the cultural orientation. The problem of reducing idiosyncratic components in the measure of cultural orientation becomes one of (*a*) sampling randomly many authors (*b*) under as similar conditions as possible (i.e., writing similar material) and (*c*) choosing materials which should place few restrictions on the author's fantasy.

All of the above advantages can be obtained by careful sampling of stories written for children's readers. In addition, the stories are actually written to be used in transmitting cultural values, and information on how widely they have been used gives at once some indication of cultural acceptance of the values contained in the book and of the extent of its influence. An example of the use of children's readers to assess values in many cultures has been presented by McClelland (1961).

The schema presented above predicts a relationship betwen cultural achievement orientation and behavior of the members of the culture which would lead to technological advance. Just as one might predict that an individual with high achievement motivation might strive for some unique accomplishment, one might also predict that a culture with strong achievement orientation would produce many inventions. A measure of the inventiveness of the culture at various periods in history might be obtained from the number of patents issued per population, and one could predict a relationship between this and a measure of cultural achievement orientation.

Hypotheses

The present study is an attempt to plot the incidence of achievement and affiliation imagery and moral teaching in a sample of chldren's readers from 1800 to 1950. In addition, achievement imagery is to be related to data on the number of patents issued per population.

Hypothesis I. The incidence of achievement imagery in a sample of children's readers selected over the period 1800-1950 will decrease over the time period.

Hypothesis II. The incidence of affiliation imagery in the same sample of readers will increase over the time period.

Hypothesis III. The incidence of moral teaching in the sample will decrease over the time period.

Hypothesis IV. The incidence of achievement imagery will be positively related to the number of patents issued, corrected for changes in population.

The hypotheses assume, with Riesman, that the nineteenth century in the United States was dominated by the inner-directed character type. Riesman is not specific as to dates, but it would appear that the early period of the century witnessed the transition from the tradition-directed character type and that the United States has recently been in transition from an inner-directed phase to an other-directed phase.

Method

A bibliography of reading textbooks with copyright dates ranging from 1800 to 1952 was compiled. An attempt was made to procure at least four books from each 20-year period beginning in 1800. Readers were excluded which were not in wide use[1] during the period or which were used by religious affiliated schools. In the more recent periods from which more than four books were available, the choice of books was made randomly. In the periods in which fewer than four books were available the sample from each book was enlarged in so far as possible. Generally, the sample from each book was obtained by scoring every third page.

It was found that the number of words per page was sufficiently similar throughout the total sample to allow use of the page itself as the scoring unit. In order to equate for number of pages available the score was the number of pages containing imagery per 75 pages sampled. A raw score was thus computed for every 75 pages sampled (i.e., 25 pages scored).

The readers chosen for the study were, generally speaking, at a fourth grade level. During the nineteenth century many readers were designated in ways which had no relevance to grade level or, as in some cases, grade level was quite different from that of contemporary American readers in which the vocabulary is based on standard word lists. In some instances it was necessary to use the Dale and Chall (1948) formula[2] for predicting readability to determine whether the readers might be allowed in the study.

The pages selected from each book were scored independently by two scorers as to whether the page contained (*a*) achievement imagery, (*b*) affiliation imagery, or (*c*) a category called moral teaching. Achievement and affiliation imagery were scored according to the procedure outlined in Atkinson (1958). The subcategories usually scored in this procedure were not scored. The category Moral Teaching was developed and defined as explicit or implicit statements of judgment between right and wrong from the point of view of the author. The following (McGuffey, 1857) are examples of items which were scored for moral teaching:

> The little boy took care of his faithful dog as long as he lived and never forgot that we must do good to others, if we wish them to do the same to us (p. 42).

1. Evidence of "wide use" was fairly easy to establish in readers published after 1850 since the McGuffey readers and the readers of the major book companies enjoyed national popularity as official texts of large school systems. Prior to 1850 Johnson (1904) and Nietz (1961) provided lists of historical texts from which to choose. In the first two decades of the sample the only secular texts available were used.

The following criteria were used in this order to establish "wide use": Evidence (often cited in later editions) of number of copies sold; several editions of the same book; and knowledge of use by large school systems.

2. This readability formula which utilizes a word list and sentence length for determining grade level of reading materials was used because of evidence of its applicability to middle grade reading matter and high correlations with other formulae and criteria of readability (Chall, 1958).

Now that is the way with a great many thoughtless, quick tempered people. They try to find fault with somebody or something else, and get into a passion, and perhaps do mischief, when, if they would but reflect a little, it is their own dear selves who ought to bear the blame (p. 47).

Scorer reliabilities, based on presence of imagery only, were consistently high (Achievement Imagery = 94%, Affiliation Imagery = 96%, Moral Teaching = 97%).

The number of patents issued by the United States Patent Office and the United States Census figures were taken from governmental documents (United States Department of Commerce, 1960) and a patent index was computed by dividing the number of patents granted in a 20-year period by the population reported in the midyear of that period and multiplying by one million. This results in an index of patents issued per one million population during the period.

There are two methodological flaws in the procedure which it was felt might have had an effect on the results. In the·first place, the technique of blind scoring was not employed. The scoring was done directly from the book and it was therefore probable that the scorer knew the date of the book. The effect of this knowledge cannot be assessed. A second methodological flaw lies in the sampling procedure. Systematic samples were taken from each book and the books were chosen as representative and in wide use. However, since each score was based on 75 pages of text, some books were more heavily weighted than others and the individual values of their authors might have unduly influenced the results.

In order to correct these methodological flaws it was decided to repeat the study with a drastically smaller sample. A sample of 6 pages was chosen at random from each book. The sampling of books followed the same criteria as those used in the first sample. Four books were selected from each period except the periods 1800-1819 and 1820-1839 where only two were available. The books from these two periods were double sampled. Scores on each variable were assigned to each book giving four scores for each of the eight periods thus resolving the ambiguities of sampling in the first study.

The sample had to be drastically cut since the pages were typed and coded for blind scoring. (A total of 192 pages were scored independently by two scorers in the replication whereas 2,375 pages were scored in the first study.) The same number of typed lines were taken starting with each page which had been drawn randomly.

Whenever available different books were selected for the second sample. It was anticipated that since this was a much smaller sample than the first the results would not be as statistically significant. It was felt that general trends in the same direction would validate the statistically significant findings of the first sample. Actually, plots of the results of the two studies are almost identical and statistical significance was reached in most instances in the second study, although as anticipated, the probability levels were not as great as in the first. This comparison of the two replications gives greater confidence in the results of the first study. The data presented here come from the first study. Statistical analyses will be presented for both studies.

Results

Table 1 presents the mean imagery scores for achievement, affiliation, and moral teaching in each of the 20-year periods. Figures 1 and 2 are graphic presentations of these data.

Hypothesis I predicted a consistent decrease in achievement imagery. The data (see Table 1 and Figure 1) show a sharp decline since 1890, but a steady increase from 1800 to the peak at about 1890. The second sample showed almost an identical curve with consistent increase up to about 1890 and then a sharp decline. The data of both samples show a significant relationship between amount of imagery and date (First sample, $F = 8.09$, $df = 7/87$, $p < .0005$; Second sample, $F = 2.62$, $df = 7/24$, $p < .05$).

Table 1

MEAN SCORES FOR ACHIEVEMENT IMAGERY, AFFILIATION IMAGERY, AND MORAL TEACHING IN THE FIRST SAMPLE OF READERS

20-YEAR MIDPOINT	N^a	ACHIEVEMENT IMAGERY		AFFILIATION IMAGERY[b]		MORAL TEACHING[b]	
		$\overline{X}$	σ^2	$\overline{X}$	σ^2	$\overline{X}$	σ^2
1810	3	2.67	4.5	3.33	2.5	16.00	22.0
1830	4	2.50	1.7	4.25	11.7	16.75	9.7
1850	12	4.42	13.4	6.00	24.4	12.42	11.2
1870	3	8.33	2.5	6.33	25.5	6.00	1.0
1890	16	11.06	13.5	5.13	4.7	4.19	4.9
1910	10	9.40	5.1	6.70	12.0	4.50	2.7
1930	15	6.33	19.6	9.33	6.1	1.00	0.7
1950	32	4.25	14.8	5.50	12.7	0.06	0.1

[a] Number of samples of 25 pages scored. The raw score was the number of pages (out of 25) containing imagery.

[b] Variance heterogeneous. In no case were the variances heterogeneous in the second sample.

Hypothesis II predicted a consistent increase in affiliation imagery from 1800 to the present. The data in Table 1 and Figure 2 show no consistent increase but do show a general trend with an unexpected drop in 1950 to the 1890 level. Analysis of variance shows a significant relationship ($F = 2.41$, $df = 7/87$, $p < .05$) but the variance was heterogeneous. The Kruskal-Wallis (see Siegal, 1956) analysis of variance of ranks also shows a significant relationship ($p < .01$). In addition, a rank correlation (Kendall's tau) between affiliation imagery and date equals $+.61$ ($p < .03$).

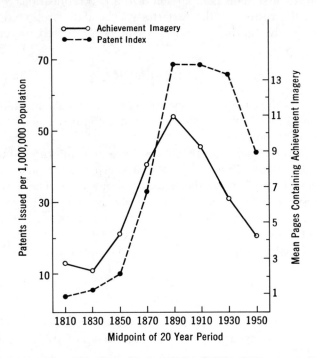

Figure 1.   Mean Number of Pages (out of 25) Containing Achievement Imagery and the Patent Index.

The data from the second sample show the same general trend with
greater variability. The correlation drops below significance and analysis of
variance does not reach significance.

Hypothesis III predicts a decrease in moral teaching from 1800 to the
present. The data show a striking confirmation (First sample, $F = 101.9$,
$df = 7/87$, $p < .0005$, heterogeneous variance; Second sample, $F = 6.95$, $df =$
$7/24$, $p < .0005$, variance homogeneous).

Hypothesis IV predicts a relationship between the amount of achievement imagery during a specific period and the index of patents issued per
population. Figure 1 shows this relationship in graphic form. A striking
relationship is apparent. The rank correlation (tau) here is $+.79$ ($p <$
$.003$). The correlation in the second sample is $+.68$ ($p < .02$).

Discussion

Achievement Imagery and Patent Index

The data on achievement imagery do not confirm the original hypothesis
which was obviously too simple. There are clear indications in both samples that achievement imagery increases to a peak around the turn of the
present century and has steadily declined since then. This relationship is

supported by the strikingly similar data from the patent index. The number of patents granted was used in preference to the number of applications for patents for two reasons: no record was kept of patents applied for until 1840 (this would have cut 39 years from the patent/population measure) and the very fact that a patent is issued is indicative of the "uniqueness" of the patent. Unique accomplishment is one of the criteria for scoring achievement imagery (Atkinson, 1958).

Affiliation Imagery

The data from both samples tend to confirm the hypothesis of increasing affiliation imagery, although the results were not statistically significant in

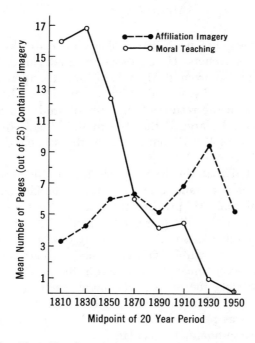

Figure 2.   Mean Number of Pages (out of 25) Containing Affiliation
Imagery and Moral Teaching Imagery.

the second sample. Certain aspects of the difference in type of affiliation imagery through time are noteworthy. Much of the early and middle nineteenth century readers' affiliation imagery, though widely scattered, was quite unsophisticated as shown by the following (Parker and Watson, 1857) example:

> I love my dear little brother and I am pleased when I see him happy. I did not intend to disobey you, dear father, and I hope you will not be displeased with me for what I have done (p. 75).

The discussion of the joys of giving to others continued unabated for the next page and a half. In contrast, affiliation imagery in the period from 1920 was considerably more subtle.

It was more difficult to score affiliation imagery in the earliest books in the study and it was in this period that interrater reliability was lowest. The difficulty lay in differentiating true affective affiliation imagery from a culturally sanctioned form of address. Thus "dear son," "dear father," and "my dear" were not scored unless affect was also demonstrated since this was often mere conventionally approved formalism.

It is possible that this scoring difficulty could account for the results found. This, in combination with the fact that the results were not significant in the second sample, suggests caution in interpretation of these results.

Moral Imagery

The decline in the religious-moral emphasis in textbooks has long been noted by various researchers. Hart (1933), in analyzing selected popular magazines of the period from 1900 to 1930, found evidence of a general decline in the status of religion and religious sanctions. These findings are in general accord with the results of the present study. In the case of the school readers it may be argued that the diminishing frequency of moral references is a result of the secularization of the schools during the nineteenth century.

It should be noted that the first schools in the colonies were church-sponsored and, in many instances, the minister of the church also served as teacher to the children. His primary purpose was not general education but simply to teach the pupils to read the Bible. The shift from church-sponsored to the public-sponsored and supported schools began about the time of the American Revolution and continued through most of the nineteenth century. However, since all the books in the present study were prepared for public schools, the decrease in moral teaching imagery indicates the cultural trend toward secularization which affected the management of the schools and was reflected in the books written for the schools even after they had become nominally secular.

The antecedent conditions of changes in values such as demonstrated here are very complex. As noted earlier, theorists such as Riesman *et al.* (1950) stress the importance of psychological factors (character type) which lead to the examination of child rearing practices. Economic historians stress political and economic factors (Rostow, 1960). The historical evidence is probably easier to marshal to support the economic interpretation.

The findings of the present study fit very well the conceptual paradigm of Rostow (1960) who stresses the economic factors. He has developed a general model of the stages of economic growth which distinguishes (*a*) precondition for take-off, (*b*) the take-off, (*c*) the drive to maturity, and (*d*) the age of high mass consumption.

In the United States, Rostow (1960) found that the traditional or agricultural society lasted until about 1840. The take-off occurred from 1843 to 1860. This appears to be the take-off period for achievement orientation also (see Figure 1). During the next period from 1860 to 1900, called by Rostow the drive to maturity, "some ten to twenty per cent of the national income was steadily invested, permitting industrial output regularly to outstrip the increase in population" (p. 9). The United States, according to Rostow's data and reasoning, reached technological maturity around 1900. This date is extremely close to the high points of achievement imagery and patent measures.

Rostow's (1960) preconditions for take-off are technological developments which might set the stage for increased social mobility, a factor mentioned by Riesman *et al.* (1950) as affecting child rearing practices. Rostow feels that during this period the idea that economic progress is possible and necessary for such ends as national dignity becomes prevalent in the culture and men come forward who are willing to mobilize savings, take risks, and engage in entrepreneurial activity.

The latter aspects have a distinctly psychological flavor. Men who take risks and engage in entrepreneurial activity are those who have high achievement motivation (McClelland, 1958). Recently economists have noted the importance of motivation and personality structure in economic growth. Thus, Hagen (1958) discusses the role of the need for achievement, for autonomy, for aggression, for dominance, for affiliation, and for dependence in the beginning of economic growth. These motivational variables interact with economic and political variables to produce cultural changes.

As noted in the introduction, evidence for the importance of psychological factors such as motives and values in cultural change and economic growth has been presented by McClelland (1955, 1958, 1961). There are, moreover, studies which have made a start in uncovering the relationship between child rearing practices and achievement and affiliation motivation. Briefly, achievement motivation appears to be associated with early parental stress on independence training and mastery, coupled with a warm acceptance of the child (Winterbottom, 1958). Affiliation motivation is related to maternal acceptance and to parental stress on interpersonal involvement of the child (Gall, 1960).

These findings appear to be in accord with Riesman's analysis of the child rearing practices which lead to the inner- and other-directed character types. The parent rearing a child in the period of transition to inner-direction must equip him with a "gyroscope" which will fit him to remain on course in a society where it is impossible to foretell, due to increasing social mobility, what role he will be called upon to play. He must be equipped to be self-reliant and independent. These are the aspects which Riesman sees in nineteenth century child rearing. The antecedents of achievement motivation seem clear.

On the other hand, with increasing urbanization and population density which result from technological advance, the child is no longer pushed to be independent, but learns the importance of other individuals in the environment. He must be taught to win approval. Although Riesman's argument is more complicated than this, the child rearing practices which he sees in contemporary United States culture seem to be ones which might lead to affiliation motivation.

In summary we propose that motivation, or cultural orientation, be conceived of as an intervening variable standing between antecedent environmental factors associated with economic and political changes and consequent behavior resulting in cultural changes such as technological growth. Such an analysis should give increased explanatory power, since it is probable that motivation is a function of factors other than economic changes. For instance, cultural values affect child rearing practices and hence motives (McClelland, Rindlisbacher, and de Charms, 1955). Thus, two cultures undergoing similar economic or political change may react quite differently due to the intervening variables of values, child rearing practices, and motives.

Summary

Content analysis of children's readers from schools in the United States demonstrated a rise in achievement imagery from 1800 to about 1900 and then a steady decline. The achievement imagery curve was related to an index of the number of patents issued. A steady decline over the period 1800-1950 was found in the amount of moral teaching in readers. There was tentative indication of an increase in affiliation imagery.

The over-all picture presented by the data corresponds very well with certain cultural trends pointed out by students of cultural change. The data illustrate an interesting technique for obtaining objective data to investigate cultural historical hypotheses.

References

ATKINSON, J. W.   *Motives in fantasy, action, and society.* Princeton: Van Nostrand, 1958.

CHALL, JEANNE.   Readability: An appraisal of research and application. *Bureau of Educational Research Monographs,* Ohio State University, 1958, No. 34.

DALE, E. and CHALL, JEANNE.   A formula for predicting readability. *Educational Research Bulletin,* 1948, 27, 11-20, 37-54.

GALL, H. S.   The development of affiliation motivation. Unpublished doctoral dissertation, University of North Carolina, 1960.

HAGEN, E. E.   How economic growth begins: A general theory applied to Japan. *Public Opinion Quarterly,* 1958, 12, 373-390.

HART, H.   Changing social attitudes and interests. In *Recent social trends in the United States.* New York: McGraw-Hill, 1933. Pp. 382-442.

JOHNSON, C.   *Old-time schools and school-books.* New York: Macmillan, 1904.

McCLELLAND, D. C.   Some social consequences of achievement motivation. In M. R. Jones (Ed.), *Nebraska symposium on motivation: 1955.* Lincoln: University of Nebraska Press, 1955. Pp. 41-65.

McCLELLAND, D. C.   The use of measures of human motivation in the study of society. In J. W. Atkinson (Ed.), *Motives in fantasy, action, and society.* Princeton: Van Nostrand, 1958. Pp. 518-552.

McCLELLAND, D. C.   *The achieving society.* Princeton: Van Nostrand, 1961.

McCLELLAND, D. C., ATKINSON, J. W., CLARK, R. A. and LOWELL, E. L.   *The achievement motive.* New York: Appleton-Century-Croft, 1953.

McCLELLAND, D. C. and FRIEDMAN, G. A.   A cross-cultural study of the relationship between child-rearing practices and achievement motivation appearing in folk tales. In G. E. Swanson, T. M. Newcomb and E. L. Hartley (Eds.), *Readings in social psychology.* (2nd ed.) New York: Holt, 1952. Pp. 243-249.

McCLELLAND, D. C., RINDLISBACHER, A. and de CHARMS, R.   Religious and other sources of parental attitudes toward independence training. In D. C. McClelland (Ed.), *Studies in motivation.* New York: Appleton-Century-Croft, 1955. Pp. 389-397.

McGUFFEY, W. H.   *New fourth eclectic reader.* New York: Wilson, Hinkle, 1857.

NIETZ, J. A.   *Old textbooks.* Pittsburgh: University of Pittsburgh Press, 1961.

PARKER, R. G. and WATSON, J. M.   *The national second reader.* New York: Barnes, 1857.

RIESMAN, D., GLAZER, N. and DENNEY, R.   *The lonely crowd.* New Haven: Yale University Press, 1950.

ROSTOW, W. W.   *The stages of economic growth.* Cambridge: Cambridge University Press, 1960.

SIEGAL, S. S.   *Nonparametric statistics for the behavioral sciences.* New York: McGraw-Hill, 1956.

STRAUSS, M. A. and HOUGHTON, L. J.   Achievement, affiliation, and cooperation values as clues to trends in American rural society, 1924-1958. *Rural Sociology,* 1960, 25, 394-403.

UNITED STATES DEPARTMENT OF COMMERCE.   *Historical statistics of the United States colonial times to 1957.* Washington: 1960.

WEBER, M.   *The Protestant ethic.* (Trans. by T. Parsons) New York: Scribner's, 1930.

WHYTE, W. H.   *The organization man.* Garden City: Doubleday, 1956.

WINTERBOTTOM, M. R.   The relation of need for achievement to learning experiences in independence and mastery. In J. W. Atkinson (Ed.), *Motives in fantasy, action, and society.* New York: Van Nostrand, 1958. Pp. 453-478.

Content analysis is a systematic procedure for describing the substance of human communication, and is most often applied to mass communication. It describes the messages, the themes, the values to which the attenders are exposed—not necessarily those they carry away. If the assumption is made that there is some correspondence between the message presented and the lesson learned, content analysis can be revealing and provocative in the study of educational phenomena. As a historical note, one of the first empirical studies to be explicitly called an investigation in the "social psychology of education" was a content analysis of the values in children's textbooks (I. L. Child *et al.*, "Children's Textbooks and Personality Development," *Psychological Monographs*, 1946, 60 (3), Whole No. 279).

This study of the De Fleurs is unique in a number of respects. It deals with a subject often deliberately taught in the schools—occupations—but in this case presented by the school's great competitor, the TV tube. It is concerned with messages about occupations that are carried incidentally to the main story line of the TV program. As the authors imply, "incidental learning" is a particularly significant form of acquiring information about society.

The study goes beyond the point where most content analyses end. Using an ingenious cartoon-like test, the investigators assessed the knowledge and attitudes children carried away with them from their contacts with TV. And as a bonus, the De Fleurs report data on developmental trends (in children from six to thirteen years of age) in understanding of occupations. Sex and social-class differences are also examined.

The Relative Contribution of Television As A Learning Source For Children's Occupational Knowledge*

Melvin L. De Fleur, Lois B. De Fleur

The literature on occupational preferences and choices of children is voluminous. However, surprisingly little research has been done to determine how much young children really *know* about various occupations or the *sources* from which they obtain their information. Similarly, only a few studies are available concerning the child's grasp of occupational prestige as a basis of social stratification. (See, for example, Stendler, 1949; Weinstein, 1956, 1958; and Simmons, 1962.) In our society, the male child is under a nearly universal requirement to select some type of occupational role which he must eventually assume. Increasingly, the female child will also eventually enter the labor force. Even if this is not the case, her destiny in adulthood will be linked to the occupational roles and statuses achieved by her husband during his lifetime. Thus, knowledge of the characteristics and consequences of occupational roles and statuses is of critical importance for children who will be our future workers and their wives.

In spite of this, our system of formal education provides children little in the way of systematic and objective information concerning occupational roles and statuses. For reasons which are not entirely clear, more time is spent by children in school memorizing the dates of ancient battles and the names of long-dead kings than in learning about the world of work to which they will have to make significant adjustments during their forty or fifty years of coping with the labor force. In short, the children of our society face the important task of selecting their place in our vast division of labor while poorly informed and ill-prepared. They formulate their occupational preferences and make their choices on the basis of information supplied for the most part by unsystematic sources of unknown validity about which we know relatively little.

One potentially important source of such knowledge, concerning which we have only limited empirical evidence, is television. At the present time, this medium has penetrated all but a few isolated segments of the American society to a point where our population now owns more than one TV set per family (M. L. De Fleur, 1966, pp. 71-73).

* From *American Sociological Review*, 1967, 32, 777-789. Used by permission of the authors and the publisher, The American Sociological Association.
This project was supported in part by NIMH grant MH 10085-01.

The merits of ordinary television content as a learning source for children have been much debated. The industry has been repeatedly criticized for providing the young audience-member with a heavy emphasis on violence, sex, and material in low cultural taste. At the same time, there seems little doubt that, through casual viewing, the child gains much information about the society in which he lives. This latter point has been documented by Wilbur Schramm in connection with the concept of "incidental learning" (Schramm, 1961.) Children, like adults, go to the television receiver primarily for entertainment rather than edification, but while being entertained they absorb much "incidental" information about their society. One of the most significant aspects of such learning may be the information children acquire concerning the labor force.

Periodic surveys of viewing habits indicate that the ordinary child spends approximately twenty hours a week watching television. While this electronic medium is by no means the only unsystematic source of occupational information, its *massive presence* demands that its contribution to the incidental learning of children concerning roles in the labor force be studied systematically. We need to replace speculation with empirical evidence. However, this is no easy task. Contemporary techniques of research provide but poor tools with which to measure and assess the influence of such a complex medium on the incidental learning process.

The present paper is the final report of a series of exploratory studies aimed at this goal. Earlier reports in the series focused on the problem of assessing occupational knowledge in young children, and on the dimensions of occupational roles as presented on television within the context of ordinary programs (See L. B. De Fleur, 1966, and De Fleur, 1964). The data reported here concern children's knowledge of selected occupational roles and the relative contribution of television as a learning source in shaping that knowledge. No claims are made that the present data provide final answers; the research is too limited in scope and too crude in its methodology. Much remains to be done in developing a research technology which will provide more rigorous approaches to this type of problem.

Purposes of the Present Research

The research project summarized in the present paper has three specific objectives: *First*, it is a study of the level of knowledge attained by young children (from 6 to 13 years of age) concerning the duties and other characteristics of eighteen selected occupational roles, including the way these roles are differentially ranked in hierarchies of prestige. *Second*, it is an attempt to probe the relationships which exist between such knowledge and membership in selected social categories. Social class, sex, and age are used as bases for hypotheses which predict that different types of children will acquire various levels of understanding of occupational roles and their prestige. *Third*, the study inquires into the relative contribution of three somewhat distinct sources of information from which children can learn about occupational roles and their social ranking.

The Sample

The data utilized were obtained in extensive interviews with 237 children and their mothers (or female family heads) in a small midwestern town (population 35,000). A five per cent systematic sample was drawn from the list of children who were currently enrolled in the metropolitan school system. The sample included children from all age levels 6 through 13 and from all socio-economic strata of the community. Since the metropolitan school district included schools in the surrounding county as well as the city, both rural and urban children were included. The interviewers were experienced school teachers who were given special training for the research task. In no case was a child interviewed by a teacher he or she had in school. Negro children were interviewed by a Negro teacher to minimize possible problems of rapport.

The Measuring Instrument

The measuring instrument used for assessing role knowledge and status knowledge was developed especially for the present project and requires explanation. This *Occupations Test* was based upon modifications of techniques developed by Lois De Fleur (L. B. De Fleur, 1966). The procedure makes use of cartoon-like representations of the various occupations to be studied. Each occupation is portrayed on a separate 4 x 5-inch card. These cards serve as stimuli in getting the children to report on the role characteristics of each occupation. The children also rank different sets of such roles by placing the cards in hierarchies. (See Figure 1.)

BANK PRESIDENT   BUTLER

Figure 1. Sample Role Representations from the Occupations Test.

The occupations included in the test are divided into three distinct *sets,* each of which contains occupations representing a hierarchy of occupational prestige. The six occupational roles of Set I are called the *personal contact occupations.* These include jobs with which the ordinary child comes into direct contact during his normal life in the community under study. These six occupations are: Minister, Teacher, Owner of Small Grocery, Mailman, Supermarket Clerk, and School Janitor.

The roles of Set II are called the *television contact* occupations. These were selected on the basis of a content analysis of six months of television broadcasts received in the local area (De Fleur, 1964). One purpose of the content analysis was to study the relative frequency with which occupations of various types were portrayed in TV drama, televised motion pictures and other ordinary television fare. The six roles in Set II were well represented in these broadcasts; they are: Judge, Lawyer, Reporter, Head Waiter, Butler, and Bell Hop.

The roles of Set III are called *general culture* occupations. They are widely understood by the adults in the community, but they are rarely seen by the child, either in person or on television. Each of these roles, however, was present in the labor force of the community. The roles included in Set III were: Bank President, Electrical Engineer, General Accountant, Skilled Printer, Shipping Clerk, and Hospital Orderly.

As is implicit in the above, these sets of occupations are drawn from three somewhat independent learning sources for children concerning knowledge of occupational roles. The control over learning sources achieved by this technique was not absolute, but it was reasonably effective. Systematic checks were made to ascertain the degree to which each child in the sample had ever seen the occupations of the three sets being performed. More than 85 per cent claimed that they had seen all roles of Set I performed. The comparable figures for Sets II and III were 1.7 per cent and 1.3 per cent, respectively.

Personal contact, television, and the general community culture are not the only sources from which occupational knowledge can be acquired, but they constitute three major sources of information. The general culture is presumably a complex of many information sources for all such occupations, and television presentations or personal contact can be considered as important additional sources.

The six occupational roles within each set represent different levels of occupational prestige. To obtain this prestige dimension, the final list of occupations was selected by a panel of "experts." These were professional sociologists who were familiar with sociological studies of occupational prestige scores and also with the structure of the labor force of the local community. On the final selections of occupations these experts were in unanimous agreement on their rankings. For the present analysis only relative rankings within sets were used, and statistical procedures were designed accordingly.

Over-all, then, the Occupations Test permits study of children's occupational *role knowledge,* the degree to which they can accurately rank occupations in *prestige hierarchies,* and the relative importance of three *sources of learning* from which they obtain ideas about the world of work.

INTERVIEWING YOUNG CHILDREN WITH THE OCCUPATIONS TEST. The materials of the test were presented to a given child one set at a time. The sets were randomly ordered and the occupations within sets were randomly ordered for each child to avoid possible serial effects.

For a given occupational role, the child was presented with the card with a cartoon-like representation of the role. He was told the name of the role and was asked (in turn) the following five questions: (1) "What kind of work does this man do?" (2) "Does he work for someone?" "Whom?" (3) "Where does he do his work?" (4) "What kinds of things does he use in his job? (5) "Does he have to prepare in some special way to get this job?" If any of these questions were not understood, they were rephrased until the child had grasped the idea. Few difficulties of this type were encountered. The interviewers probed for additional information on each question until they were convinced that they had elicited the full range of the child's knowledge. For each question the child could earn from zero to three points, representing his level of knowledge about the issue posed in the question. The first three questions were given an arbitrary weight of two and the last two were given weights of unity. Systematic criteria were used to grade the children's responses, and the interviewers were trained specifically in the use of the numerical procedures.

These techniques made it possible to represent the performance of each child on any given occupational role with a quantitative score (sum of weighted ratings). A score could be obtained for the Occupations Test as a whole concerning roles knowledge, and subscores were available for each of the three sets (representing sources of learning).

For each of the three sets, independently, the child was asked to rank the six occupations according to their relative occupational prestige. This idea had to be presented in terms understandable to the child and appropriate to his age level. The child first practiced ranking simple and obvious pairs (Army General vs. ditch-digger, truck-driver vs. airplane-pilot, scientists vs. dishwasher). He then tried his hand at a three-role hierarchy (garbageman, fireman, and doctor). No child was unable to understand the ranking principle on these practice trials. When it was clear that he had the idea, he was presented with all six cards of a set and asked to arrange them in order of prestige.

The female parent, or female responsible for rearing the child, was also interviewed concerning the major socio-economic characteristics of the family. Each of these women also ranked the three sets of occupations. A considerable variety of data was gathered but the present report is restricted to selected findings.

AGE, SEX, AND SOCIAL CLASS AS INFLUENCES ON OCCUPATIONAL KNOWLEDGE. From the foregoing it can be seen that the two major dependent variables obtained from the performance of the children on the Occupations Test were *role knowledge* and *status knowledge*. With respect to these variables, a relatively simple set of hypotheses can be tested concerning the influence of age, sex, and social class on occupational knowledge.

The first hypothesis studied was that role knowledge would increase linearly with age. This is a fairly obvious and simple hypothesis and the data of Table 1 indicate that it is generally supported within the age range studied. The findings are shown graphically in Figure 2, and it is clear that

Table 1

MEAN ROLE-KNOWLEDGE SCORES ON THREE SETS OF OCCUPATIONS FOR CHILDREN OF AGES 6–13

AGE	N	SET I	SET II	SET III	COMBINED SETS
6	29	57.86	24.21	16.48	32.85
7	37	65.89	38.95	24.71	43.18
8	44	80.93	64.77	40.75	62.15
9	42	83.76	71.24	46.52	67.17
10	35	93.57	86.40	52.94	77.64
11	34	99.23	88.47	60.50	82.73
12-13	15	108.60	98.80	71.13	92.84
All Ages	236*	82.44	65.56	42.78	65.51

Note: Total scores for role knowledge from the Occupations Test can range between 0 and 144 per set.

* One respondent had to be dropped from the analysis due to an interviewer recording error.

the children in the 12-13 age group are still acquiring information about occupational roles. Older children will have to be studied in order to determine the ages at which such acquisition begins to level off.

A second hypothesis concerning age was that as children become older, they will tend to rank occupations more and more consistently. It was also hypothesized that with increasing age, their rankings would be more and more like the hierarchies of prestige assigned to the same occupations by adults. This, of course, would reflect the increasing acquisition of culture by children with respect to the occupational world.

Table 2 lists the coefficients of concordance for children of each age group for each of the three sets of occupations (Siegel, 1956, pp. 229-238). These coefficients are indices of the degree to which the children of a given age group were consistent among themselves. This table does not indicate the degree to which the children made their rankings as adults do (which will be discussed later), but only the degree to which they ranked the occupations similarly within their age level. The degree of consistency

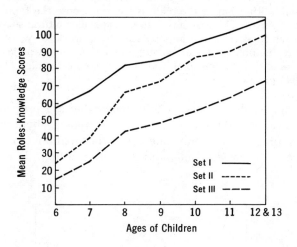

Figure 2. Mean Role-Knowledge Scores on the Three Sets of Occupations.

Table 2

COEFFICIENT OF CONCORDANCE AMONG STATUS RANKINGS OF THREE
SETS OF OCCUPATIONS, FOR CHILDREN OF AGES 6–13

AGE OF CHILD	SET I	SET II	SET III
6	.079	.128	.142
7	.323	.277	.322
8	.403	.526	.256
9	.499	.764	.420
10	.608	.831	.521
11	.602	.787	.607
12-13	.793	.778	.535
(Parents)	.736	.805	.702

Note: The coefficient of concordance equals zero when the rankings of a given group of judges are random. It equals unity when they match each other perfectly.

among parents (considered separately) is also shown for each set of occupations.

As can be seen, the children were more consistent as age increased. By the time they were 12 to 13 years old they were about as consistent with each other (except for the Set III occupations) as were their parents among themselves. The findings are shown graphically in Figure 3.

For comparisons by sex of the children's performance on the Occupations Test, there are ample grounds for predicting differences in role and status knowledge for male and female children:

In this society, with few exceptions, males must eventually chose an occupation. Within limits, the male is free to choose the type of work that he will pursue. Consequently, there is specific cultural socialization for males which stresses the importance of the world of work. Due to this cultural emphasis, it can be suggested that young males will be more aware and informed in this area than young females (L. B. De Fleur, 1966, p. 112).

Data concerning sex differences in role knowledge are presented in Table 3. At first glance, it would appear that the general hypothesis implied above is not supported. On only one set of occupations was there a significant difference between male and female children. Furthermore, for

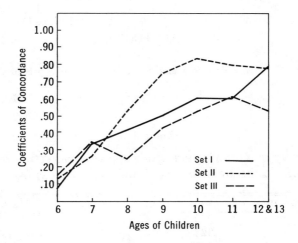

Figure 3. Consistency of Status Rankings of the Three Sets of Occupations.

Table 3

MEAN ROLE-KNOWLEDGE SCORES FOR MALE AND FEMALE CHILDREN

OCCUPATIONAL SET	MALE CHILDREN	FEMALE CHILDREN	PROBABILITY OF DIFFERENCE
Set I	83.45	81.53	.298
Set II	67.46	63.49	.206
Set III	47.01	37.19	.004
Combined Sets	196.29	181.69	.102

all three sets combined, the difference between means was not significant. This is consistent with the findings of De Fleur's earlier study (1964, p. 112) with different occupations and with a different sample of children from the same community. However, a clear difference in role knowledge occurs between the 137 males and the 99 females on the Set III occupations (Table 3). It can be suggested that it is precisely on these "general culture" occupations that the sex differences hypothesized are most likely to be apparent. That is, since both boys and girls have equal access to "personal contact" (Set I) and "television contact" (Set II) occupations, it is in the remaining set where the pressures of sex-role socialization can be expected to be most evident.[1]

In short, males and females showed no differences in knowledge about occupational roles where they each had the same opportunity to observe the roles (directly or via TV). However, boys knew significantly more than girls concerning less "visible" occupations (of Set III) in the community, suggesting that they were under greater cultural pressure to learn.

In comparing the sexes on their ability to rank the occupations of each

Table 4

MEAN COEFFICIENT OF ORDINAL ASSOCIATION BETWEEN
OCCUPATIONAL STATUS RANKINGS OF MALE AND FEMALE CHILDREN
AND RANKINGS BY TWO TYPES OF ADULTS

SEX OF CHILD	PARENTS			EXPERTS		
	SET I	SET II	SET III	SET I	SET II	SET III
Male	.434	.636	.378	.433	.654	.388
Female	.045	.056	.029	.048	.058	.031
Probability of Difference ...	.363	.062	.061	.209	.089	.081

Note: Coefficients of ordinal association (gammas) can range between zero, when no association exists, and unity, when rankings are perfectly correlated.

set, Goodman-Kruskal coefficients or ordinal association (Gammas) were computed, child by child, comparing each subject's rankings with those of adults (both parents and experts) (Freeman, 1965, pp. 79-88). On each set of occupations and for each type of adult the mean coefficient for males was higher than that for females (Table 4). However, none of the differences between means had a probability which quite reached the .05 level. While the earlier study by De Fleur showed reliable differences between males and females in this respect, the present findings do not support this generalization, although the differences are all in the hypothesized directions (L. B. De Fleur, 1966, p. 112).

There are abundant theoretical reasons for predicting differences by social class in children's conceptions of occupational roles and their relative rankings. Since occupational roles play a significant part in status achievement and upward mobility in American communities, children of the middle and upper classes should have a better command of occupational role knowledge

---

1. Schramm (1961, p. 34) notes: ". . . we find no evidence that the amount of television viewing (among children) differs significantly by sex."

and status knowledge than lower-class youngsters. Values concerning the importance of occupational achievement are an important component of middle-class ideology in particular. Social class was measured by an index of SES which took into account: (1) the occupational prestige of the male head of household; (2) family income; and (3) the educational level of both the male and female head of household. The educational variables were weighted 0.5 and the others 1.0. Six quantitative levels were provided for each of the above variables and a weighted score was computed for each family.

Table 5

MEAN ROLE-KNOWLEDGE SCORES FOR CHILDREN OF THREE
SOCIAL CLASS LEVELS

OCCUPATIONAL SET	SOCIAL CLASS LEVEL		
	I (HIGH)	II	III (LOW)
Set I	87.564	85.943	68.109
Set II	71.846	68.343	51.739
Set III	45.538	44.171	32.630
Combined Sets	203.641	196.552	152.748

On the basis of the scores, the respondents were grouped into three levels of SES.[2] Class I ($N=39$) consisted of families with professional, business-ownership or higher managerial occupations and college education or more. Class II ($N=105$) ranged from high-school-educated, white-collar or skilled workers up to lower level managerial personnel who had finished college. Class III ($N=46$) ranged from unemployed illiterates up to manual or semi-skilled workers, with less than a high school education.

In the small community under study, "upper class" by the above definition is roughly equivalent to what might be classified as "upper middle class" in a larger urban center. Thus, it was anticipated that the children of classes I and II in the present sample would share the same general values and thus would show more similarities than differences regarding the variables under study. Both, however, were expected to perform more highly than the offspring of the lower class.

Table 5 presents the mean role-knowledge scores for the children of each social class. The differences between these means for each possible class comparison were tested (one-tailed t-test). Results were obtained for each of the three sets of occupations on all such comparisons. For the children of class I compared to those of class II, these means did not differ significantly (Set I, $p=.375$; Set II, $p=.312$; Set III, $p=.341$). However, in comparing the children of classes I and III, significant differences were

2.   Complete data on all categories of SES could not be obtained for 47 of the children. This was due to the presence of families which had one or the other parent or head of household absent because of death, divorce, or other causes. These were deleted from the analysis by social class.

found on all three sets (Set I, $p=.002$; Set II, $p=.011$; Set III, $p=.010$). Finally, in comparing the children of classes II and III, significant differences between means were also found for all sets (Set I, $p=.001$; Set II, $p=.004$; Set III, $p=.002$). In short, in comparing the role-knowledge means for the social classes, the children at the bottom of the class hierarchy knew less about each set of occupational roles under study than did children higher in the socio-economic structure. No such difference was found between middle- and upper-class children.

Somewhat similar results were found concerning the children's rankings of the occupations. Table 6 shows the mean coefficients of ordinal association between the rankings of the children in each social class and those of two categories of adults (parents and experts). These means indicate the degree to which the occupational rankings of the children of a given SES category tended to agree with those of their parents and with those of the experts. The social classes can be compared on these means. For example, the means of the children of classes I and II differ with respect to both parents ($p=.134$) and experts ($p=.034$). Larger differences are in evidence when the children of classes I and III are compared. This is true of both parents ($p=.001$) and experts ($p=.006$). Classes II and III also differ on parents ($p=.001$) and experts ($p=.109$). While not completely conclusive, these data indicate that the children of the lowest social class level tended to be somewhat less consistent with both types of adults in their rankings of the occupations than children farther up the class structure. In view of the fact that lower-class children knew less about these occupations (Table 5) than children above them in the class system, it is not surprising that they ranked them more erratically, in comparison with adults.

Over-all, the comparisons by social class indicate that the middle- and upper-class children as defined in the present sample knew more about the occupational roles studied and were better able to duplicate the social rankings assigned to those occupations by adults than were lower-class children.[3] The general hypothesis that middle- and upper-class children have more facility with both role and status knowledge pertaining to occupations was clearly supported.

Table 6

MEAN COEFFICIENTS OF ORDINAL ASSOCIATION BETWEEN CHILDREN'S AND ADULTS' STATUS RANKINGS OF THE OCCUPATIONS

SOCIAL CLASS OF CHILD	PARENTS	EXPERTS
I (High)	.521	.548
II	.479	.472
III (Low)	.372	.423

3. These findings are consistent with those of Weinstein (1958, p. 283), although his index of the status of the child was based upon census tract data rather than family characteristics.

Table 7

MEAN COEFFICIENTS OF ORDINAL ASSOCIATION BETWEEN STATUS
RANKINGS OF CHILDREN OF DIFFERENT AGES AND RANKINGS
BY ADULTS

	PARENTS			EXPERTS		
AGE OF CHILD	SET I	SET II	SET III	SET I	SET II	SET III
6	.296	.273	.195	.224	.238	.147
7	.309	.455	.216	.293	.420	.149
8	.439	.639	.315	.427	.608	.306
9	.456	.763	.361	.505	.787	.475
10	.511	.820	.490	.552	.828	.573
11	.631	.865	.547	.587	.868	.602
12-13	.564	.671	.422	.689	.844	.622

The Influence of Television as a Learning Source

From the foregoing, it is clear that children in distinct social categories have
varying levels of knowledge about occupational roles and their social ranking. But what about the relative influence of the three sources of learning
represented by the selection of the three sets of occupations?

It was hypothesized that personal contact occupations (Set I) would be
best understood, television contact roles (Set II) next best, and general
culture occupations (Set III) least well understood. The findings support
this hypothesis. The means for all age levels combined (Table 1) were compared. The differences between the means of Sets I and II, I and III, and II
and III were all significantly different (with p-values less than .001 in each
case). The effects of possible correlations between arrays were taken into
account in these comparisons.

Although personal contact with an occupational role is the most effective
of the learning sources investigated in the present study, the role played by
television is clear. In connection with TV, we have already made note of
the process of "incidental learning" (Schramm, 1961, p. 75.) The present
findings suggest that a considerable amount of information about occupational roles is gained from the medium in this manner by children. The
roles of Set II, although no more "visible" to children in the community
under study through personal contact than those of Set III, were significantly better understood. The importance of TV as a learning source
can be further illustrated. Children who watched television most frequently,
according to parental reports, were compared with those who viewed in-
frequently. The mean role-knowledge scores of these groups were compared
for each set of occupations. For Set I, no significant differences were noted
($p = .75$). For Set III, the same situation prevailed ($p = .10$). For Set II
(the TV occupations), however, frequent viewers scored better than infrequent viewers ($p = .05$). Thus, knowledge of the TV occupations was

enhanced by heavy viewing, while the other two sets of occupations were not so affected.

With respect to status knowledge, the influence of television is striking. As was mentioned in connection with Tables 4 and 6, coefficients of ordinal association were computed child by child to determine how closely each child's ranking compared with his parent's rankings and with the rankings of the same occupations assigned by experts. These data are presented for each age group in Table 7. These data are shown separately in graphic form for parents (Figure 4) and for experts (Figure 5).

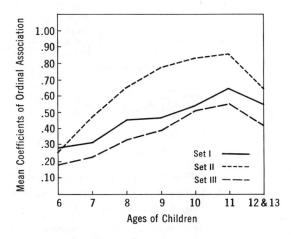

Figure 4.   Association Between Children's Status Rankings and Those of Their Parents.

The data presented in Table 7 and the curves shown in Figures 4 and 5 indicate rather clearly that the rankings of the *television* occupations (Set II) made by the children in the present sample corresponded much more closely to rankings made by adults (both parents and experts) than was the case with the personal contact occupations (Set I) and the general culture occupations (Set III). Beyond about age seven, the differences in mean coefficients of ordinal association between the television occupation rankings and those of the other sets were uniformly significant in a statistical sense (Table 8). Thus, the influence of television as a learning source was substantial concerning the social rankings of occupations. Not only did the children rank television contact occupations more consistently among themselves at earlier ages than those of other sets (Table 2 and Figure 3), but they ranked them in ways which generally more closely corresponded with both parents and experts (Table 7 and Figures 4 and 5). Given these three independent checks on the influence of television, and the data on statistical significance from Table 8, it seems safe to conclude that, within the limits

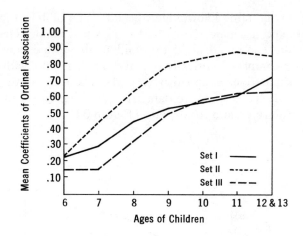

Figure 5.   Association Between Children's Status Rankings and Those of Experts.

Table 8

THE SIGNIFICANCE OF DIFFERENCES BETWEEN MEAN COEFFICIENTS
OF ORDINAL ASSOCIATION FOR THE THREE SETS
OF OCCUPATIONS, BY AGE

	OCCUPATIONAL SETS		
AGE OF CHILD	I-II	I-III	II-III
6	n.s.	n.s.	n.s.
7	<.001	n.s.	<.001
8	<.001	.010	<.001
9	<.001	<.001	<.001
10	<.001	<.001	<.001
11	<.001	<.001	<.001
12+13	<.001	<.001	<.050
All Ages	<.001	<.001	<.001

of the present samples of children and occupations, television is a more potent source of occupational status knowledge than either personal contact or the general community culture.

However, given the finding that children learn social ranking more readily from television as a source for incidental learning than from the other sources represented in the present study, what about more qualitative aspects of the information they receive? The data from the rather complex comparisons of the present study, along with other independent evidence, indicate that portrayals of occupations on television tend to be *stereotyped* in such a way that the audience is offered more uniform interpretations of their relative status. It can also be suggested that in view of the relatively high performance of the children on the role-knowledge aspects of the Set II occupations (Table 1), this generalization may apply to role-portrayals as well as to status-portrayals.

These interpretations are given support by the findings from another part of the research program of which the present study is a part. It has already been indicated that a content analysis was made of the occupational portrayals occurring in six months of ordinary television programs received in the same community just prior to the gathering of the present data. The tendency of television portrayals to be stereotyped was clearly evident

> The occupations shown were often stereotyped. Lawyers were very clever, and usually legally unorthodox. Members of artistic professions were almost always temperamental and eccentric. Police officials were generally hardened, and often brutal. Private investigators were always resourceful and clearly more clever than the police. Nurses were cold and impersonal. Salesmen were glib. Journalists were callous. Taxi, bus and truck drivers were burly and aggressive. . . . such occupational stereotypes are part of our culture and were undoubtedly incorporated into the television characters to make them "believable." However, such occupational stereotypes may correspond to reality only to the same degree as do *stereotypes of any kind* (De Fleur, 1964, p. 71).

Thus, the consistency of the findings, both from the systematic examination of occupational portrayals in the television content received in the local area, and from the analysis of the occupational interpretations of a sample of local children, appear to support the notion of a *homogenization effect* with respect to children's incidental learning about work from TV. While it would be unwise to induce elaborate generalizations about mass media influences from the conclusions of only two studies, an important possible role of television in imparting stereotyped consistency to children's beliefs about occupational status and roles is strongly suggested.

Discussion and Summary

In general, children appear to begin acquiring definite ideas about occupational roles and the social rankings among such roles at a relatively early age. Even 6-year-olds in the present sample were able to give rough accounts of the occupational activities which they had actually seen performed. Children of this age level earned an average score of 39 per cent of the possible maximum on the personal contact occupations. (Most adults would probably not reach 100 per cent.) By the age of 12 or 13, role knowledge performance had reached 73 per cent of the possible maximum on the test for personal contact occupations and 63 per cent for the "invisible" occupations of Set III (Table 1).

On the other hand, the ability to rank occupational roles into complex hierarchies of occupational prestige appeared to come at a later age. For the youngest group (6-year-olds) the coefficients of concordance, indicating inter-child agreement on occupational rankings, were near zero (Table 2). When these children's rankings were compared with those of adults, the coefficient of ordinal association on Set I (where the 6-year-olds performed best) was only 0.296 (Table 7).

We may tentatively conclude, then, that while role-knowledge begins to be acquired early, status-ranking abilities are acquired more slowly. Generally, as age increases, so does the acquisition of knowledge about the occupational system. However, the more concrete aspects of the duties of specific roles appear to be grasped first. The more abstract notion of hierarchies of prestige among roles appears to come later. This seems to describe the relationship between role-knowledge and status-knowledge in the present study and it confirms the results of the earlier study.

> These data imply clearly that role knowledge was acquired more readily than status knowledge. Therefore, one implication of the present study is that it may be possible to develop a set of *stages* or prerequisites of knowledge through which the child moves in acquiring conceptions about the occupational world (L. B. De Fleur, 1966, p. 110).

All of these findings, plus those of prior research, appear to provide an adequate basis for confirming the following general proposition: The understanding which the maturing child develops concerning the labor force as a ranked system of occupational roles follows the *general* patterns of concept formation by which he acquires understandings of many aspects of his culture. That is, learning proceeds from the simple to the complex and from the concrete to the abstract (Piaget, 1929, pp. 166-168).

However, in addition to age, it is quite clear that other category memberships of a given child mediate the degree to which he understands the occupational world. Males knew significantly more about the less "visible" roles in their community than females (Table 3). While the findings of the present study did not strongly confirm the conclusion of the pilot study that males were better able to rank *all occupations* (Table 4), the findings of Simmons (1962, p. 356) did support this generalization. In any case, the sex of the child can be said to be a significant factor in his acquisition of occupational information.

Social class played a more clear-cut influence in mediating the acquisition of occupational knowledge among the children studied. Upper- and middle-class children, as defined in the present study, had significantly more role knowledge concerning the occupations studied than did lower-class children. The results concerning social-class differences in the ability to rank occupations followed similar patterns (Tables 5 and 6). These findings are generally supported in the earlier research cited.

Not only were the occupational conceptions of the children studied influenced by their age, sex, and social-class levels, they were in part a product of the learning source from which they had acquired their information. The (admittedly imperfect) attempt to sort out the relative influences of three learning sources indicated that personal contact with an occupation constitutes the most effective source of information for learning about the role aspects of that occupation (Table 1). Vicarious contact via television, on the other hand, is a potent source of "incidental" learning for children concerning adult occupational roles. The oldest group of children studied scored, on the average, 66 per cent of the possible maximum on the roles test for televised occupations (Table 1). This may represent a level of performance nearly equal to that of adults (although adult norms are not at present available for this instrument). Clearly, the children scored significantly better on the televised roles than on those for which "general culture" was the principal learning source. These common but less visible roles in the community were the least understood.

In spite of the relative effectiveness of television as a learning source, however, there is reason to believe that the TV portrayals were stereotyped. The data indicated a homogenization effect, whereby the children were more consistent both among themselves and with parents and experts in ranking the occupations for which TV was the major learning source than for the other sets (Tables 2, 7, and 8).

The evidence concerning the homogenizing impact of TV may reinforce the claims of critics of the medium who see television as a powerful force tending to reduce individuality among the members of the audience. Even more objective analysts of the impact of mass communications have long suspected that the increased standardization of content in the several widely adopted media will eventually have some visible result in reducing the heterogeneity of the culture of the mass audience. However, the fears are probably unfounded that standardizing influences among our media are going to impose on us a "mass culture" which will eventually erode our moral convictions, reduce us to bland uniformity, or brutalize our esthetic sensibilities.[4] Given the limited amount of objective research data on incidental learning which has been assembled at present, we can do little more than note that television appears to be an important agency of socialization for children concerning the adult world. However, there is ample reason to suspect that the information it presents is often distorted in a variety of ways (Lang and Lang, 1953).

Thus, the present findings do not provide an adequate basis for settling debates concerning the role of television in producing a uniform mass culture. However, it can be suggested that TV provides children with much superficial and misleading information about the labor force of their society. From this they acquire stereotyped beliefs about the world of work.

4.   For an unusually vigorous exposition of this point of view, see Ferry (1966).

Given the deep significance of occupational roles for both the individual and his society, any learning source which distorts reality concerning this aspect of the social structure and the child's "generalized other" may be laying the foundations for difficult personal and social problems.

References

DE FLEUR, L. B.   Assessing occupational knowledge in young children. *Sociological Inquiry*, 1966, 36, 98-115.

DE FLEUR, M. L.   Occupational roles as presented on television. *Public Opinion Quarterly*, 1964, 28, 57-74.

DE FLEUR, M. L.   *Theories of mass communication.* New York: David McKay Company, Inc., 1966.

FERRY, W. H.   Mass communication as guru. In W. H. Ferry and H. S. Ashmore, *Mass communications.* Santa Barbara: Center for the Study of Democratic Institutions, 1966. Pp. 8-19.

FREEMAN, L. C.   *Elementary applied statistics.* New York: John Wiley, 1965.

LANG, K. and LANG, G. E.   The unique perspective of television and its effects: a pilot study. *American Sociological Review*, 1953, 17, 3-12.

PIAGET, J.   *The child's conception of the world.* New York: Harcourt Brace, 1929.

SCHRAMM, W.   *Television in the lives of our children.* Stanford, California: Stanford University Press, 1961.

SIEGEL, S.   *Nonparametric statistics.* New York: McGraw-Hill, 1956.

SIMMONS, D.   Children's rankings of occupational prestige. *Personnel and Guidance Journal*, 1962, 41, 332-336.

STENDLER, C. B.   *Children of Brasstown.* Urbana: University of Illinois Press, 1949.

WEINSTEIN, E.   Weights assigned by children to criteria of prestige. *Sociometry*, 1956, 19, 126-132.

WEINSTEIN, E.   Children's conceptions of occupational stratification. *Sociology and Social Research*, 1958, 42, 278-284.

6. EDUCATION AS PERSONAL CHANGE

Interestingly enough, American approaches to bringing up children, in school and out, are not holy—and are not even the only alternative. In this article, Bronfenbrenner does an uncommonly productive job of comparing socialization practices in the Soviet Union and the United States, retrieving a great deal of scientific and practical knowledge, and illuminating the opportunities for research and educational practice in this area.

The striking thing about American classrooms, from the perspective of this article, is the degree to which knowledge about group functioning is *not* explicitly used to aid learning and personal development. Intergroup competition often tends (as explained in Coleman's article in the present book) to work against school goals; socialization influences usually happen "by themselves" instead of being explicitly harnessed. There are vigorous efforts to use groups to support personal growth of *adults* (in this book, Winter, Griffith and Kolb; Miles; Schmuck on in-service education)—but when the moral development of young children is at stake, American educators hesitate to act explicitly. Bronfenbrenner shows us that we need not avoid or dismiss the ethical questions involved—and that some powerful mechanisms for personal change in school settings are at our disposal.

Perhaps then our problem in utilizing knowledge about group functioning in the classroom lies, after all, in the words of the Russian who told Bronfenbrenner: "That's one of the strange things about your system in the West. The family is separated from the rest of society. That's not good. It's bad for the family and bad for society." Is it so? And if yes, whither the American schools?

Soviet Methods of Character Education: Some Implications for Research*

Urie Bronfenbrenner

Every society faces the problem of the moral training of its youth. This is no less true of Communist society than of our own. Indeed, Communist authorities view as the primary objective of education not the learning of subject matter but the development of what they call "socialist morality." It is instructive for us in the West to examine the nature of this "socialist morality" and the manner in which it is inculcated, for to do so brings to light important differences in the ends and means of character education in the two cultures. For research workers in the field of personality development, such an examination is especially valuable, since it lays bare unrecognized assumptions and variations in approach. Accordingly, it is the purpose of this paper to provide a much-condensed account of Soviet methods of character education and to examine some of the provocative research questions that emerge from the contrast between the Soviet approach and our own.

I.   The Work and Ideas of A. S. Makarenko

To examine Soviet methods of character training is to become acquainted with the thinking and technology developed primarily by one man—Anton Semyonovich Makarenko. Makarenko's name is virtually a household word in the Soviet Union. His popularity and influence are roughly comparable to those of Dr. Spock in the United States, but his primary concern is not with the child's physical health but with his moral upbringing. Makarenko's influence extends far beyond his own voluminous writings since there is scarcely a manual for the guidance of Communist parents, teachers, or youth workers that does not draw heavily on his methods and ideas. His works have been translated into many languages and are apparently widely read not only in the Soviet Union but throughout the Communist bloc countries, notably East Germany and Communist China. Excellent English translations of a number of his works have been published in Moscow (Makarenko, 1953, 1954, 1955, 1964), but they are not readily available in this country, except for Makarenko (1967).

* From *Religious Education*, 1962, 57 (4), Research Supplement, pp. S45-S61. Used by permission of the author and the publisher, The Religious Education Association, New York City.

Makarenko developed his ideas and methods over the course of a lifetime of practical work with young people. In the early 1920's, as a young school teacher and devout Communist, Makarenko was handed the assignment of setting up a rehabilitation program for some of the hundreds of homeless children who were roaming the Soviet Union after the civil wars. The first group of such children assigned to Makarenko's school, a ramshackle building far out of town, turned out to be a group of boys about eighteen years of age with extensive court records of housebreaking, armed robbery, and manslaughter. For the first few months, Makarenko's school served simply as the headquarters for the band of highwaymen who were his legal wards. But gradually, through the development of his group-oriented discipline techniques, and through what can only be called the compelling power of his own moral convictions, Makarenko was able to develop a sense of group responsibility and commitment to the work program and code of conduct that he had laid out for the collective. In the end, the Gorky Commune became known throughout the Soviet Union for its high morale, discipline, and for the productivity of its fields, farms, and shops. Indeed, Makarenko's methods proved so successful that he was selected to head a new commune set up by the Ministry of Internal Affairs (then the Cheka, later to become the GPU and NKVD). In the years which followed Makarenko's theories and techniques became widely adopted throughout the U.S.S.R. and now constitute the central core of Soviet educational practice.

To turn to the ideas themselves, we may begin with an excerpt from what is possibly the most widely read of Makarenko's works, *A Book for Parents* (1954).

But our [Soviet] family is not an accidental combination of members of society. The family is a natural collective body and, like everything natural, healthy, and normal, it can only blossom forth in socialist society, freed of those very curses from which both mankind as a whole and the individual are freeing themselves.

The family becomes the natural primary cell of society, the place where the delight of human life is realized, where the triumphant forces of man are refreshed, where children—the chief joy of life—live and grow.

Our parents are not without authority either, but this authority is only the reflection of societal authority. The duty of a father in our country towards his children is a particular form of his duty towards society.

It is as if our society says to parents: You have joined together in good will and love, rejoice in your children and expect to go on rejoicing in them. That is your personal affair and concerns your own personal happiness. Within the course of this happy process, you have given birth to new human beings. A time will come when these beings will cease to be solely the instruments of your happiness, and will step forth as independent members of society. For society, it is by no means a matter of indifference what kind of people they will become. In delegating to you a certain measure of societal authority the Soviet State demands from you the correct upbringing of its future citizens. Particularly it relies on

you to provide certain conditions arising naturally out of your union;
namely, your parental love.

If you wish to give birth to a citizen while dispensing with parental
love, then be so kind as to warn society that you intend to do such a rot-
ten thing. Human beings who are brought up without parental love are
often deformed human beings (Makarenko, 1954, p. 29).

Characteristic of Makarenko's thought is the view that the parents'
authority over the child is delegated to him by the state and that duty to
one's children is merely a particular instance of one's broader duty towards
society. A little later in his book for parents, the author makes this point even
more emphatically. After telling the story of a boy who ran away from home
after some differences with his mother, he concludes by affirming: "I am a
great admirer of optimism and I like very much young lads who have so
much faith in the Soviet State that they are carried away and will not trust
even their own mothers" (Makarenko, 1954, pp. 37-38). In other words,
when the needs and values of the family conflict with those of society, there
is no question about who gets priority. And society receives its concrete
manifestation and embodiment in the *collective,* which is an organized
group engaged in some socially useful enterprise.

This brings us to Makarenko's basic thesis that optimal personality development can occur only through productive activity in a social collective.
The first collective is the family, but this must be supplemented early in
life by other collectives specially organized in schools, neighborhoods, and
other community settings. The primary function of the collective is to
develop socialist morality. This aim is accomplished through an explicit
regimen of activity mediated by group criticism, self-criticism, and group-
oriented punishments and rewards.

Makarenko's ideas are elaborated at length in his semi-biographical, semi-
fictional accounts of life in the collective (1943, 1955). It is in these works
that he describes the principles and procedures to be employed for building
the collective and using it as an instrument of character education. More
relevant to our purposes, however, is the manner in which these methods
are applied in school settings, for it is in this form that they have become
most systematized and widely used.

II.   Socialization in the School Collective

The account which follows is taken from a manual (Novikova, 1950) for
the training and guidance of "school directors, supervisors, teachers, and
Young Pioneer leaders." The manual was written by staff members of the
Institute on the Theory and History of Pedagogy at the Academy of
Pedagogical Sciences and is typical of several others prepared under the
same auspices and widely distributed throughout the U.S.S.R.

This particular volume carries the instructive title: *Socialist Competition
in the Schools.* The same theme is echoed in the titles of individual chapters:

"Competition in the Classroom," "Competition between Classrooms," "Competition between Schools," and so on. It is not difficult to see how Russians arrive at the notion, with which they have made us so familiar, of competition between nations and between social systems. Moreover, already in the chapter titles we see reflected the influence of dialectical materialism: conflict at one level is resolved through synthesis at the next higher level, always in the service of the communist collective.

Let us examine the process of collective socialization as it is initiated in the very first grade. Conveniently enough, the manual starts us off on the first day of school with the teacher standing before the newly-assembled class. What should her first words be? Our text tells us:

> It is not difficult to see that a direct approach to the class with the command "All sit straight" often doesn't bring the desired effect since a demand in this form does not reach the sensibilities of the pupils and does not activate them.

How does one "reach the sensibilities of the pupils" and "activate them"? According to the manual, here is what the teacher should say:

"Let's see which row can sit the straightest."

This approach, we are told, has certain important psychological advantages. In response,

> The children not only try to do everything as well as possible themselves, but also take an evaluative attitude towards those who are undermining the achievement of the row. If similar measures arousing the spirit of competition in the children are systematically applied by experienced teachers in the primary classes, then gradually the children themselves begin to monitor the behavior of their comrades and remind those of them who forget about the rules set by the teacher, who forget what needs to be done and what should not be done. The teacher soon has helpers.

The manual then goes on to describe how records are kept for each row from day to day for different types of tasks so that the young children can develop a concept of group excellence over time and over a variety of activities, including personal cleanliness, condition of notebooks, conduct in passing from one room to the other, quality of recitations in each subject matter, and so on. In these activities considerable emphasis is placed on the externals of behavior in dress, manner, and speech. There must be no spots on shirt or collar, shoes must be shined, pupils must never pass by a teacher without stopping to give greeting, there must be no talking without permission, and the like. Great charts are kept in all the schools showing the performance of each row unit in every type of activity together with their total over-all standing. "Who is best?" the charts ask, but the entries are not individuals but social units—rows, and later the "cells" of the communist youth organization which reaches down to the primary grades.

At first it is the teacher who sets the standards. But soon, still in the first grade, a new wrinkle is introduced: responsible monitors are designated in each row for each activity. In the beginning their job is only to keep track of the merits and demerits assigned each row by the teacher. Different children act as monitors for different activities and, if one is to believe what the manual says, the monitors become very involved in the progress of their row. Then, too, group achievement is not without its rewards. From time to time the winning row gets to be photographed "in parade uniforms" (all Soviet children must wear uniforms in school), and this photograph is published in that pervasive Soviet institution, the wall newspaper. The significance of the achievements is still further enhanced, however, by the introduction of competition between *classes* so that the winning class and the winning row are visited by delegates from other classrooms in order to learn how to attain the same standard of excellence.

Now let us look more closely at this teacher-mediated monitoring process. In the beginning, we are told, the teacher attempts to focus the attention of children on the achievements of the group; that is, in our familiar phrase, she accentuates the positive. But gradually, "it becomes necessary to take account of negative facts which interfere with the activity of the class." As an example we are given the instance of a child who despite warnings continues to enter the classroom a few minutes after the bell has rung. The teacher decides that the time has come to evoke the group process in correcting such behavior. Accordingly, the next time that Serezha is late, the teacher stops him at the door and turns to the class with this question: "Children, is it helpful or not helpful to us to have Serezha come in late?" The answers are quick in coming. "It interferes, one shouldn't be late, he ought to come on time." "Well," says the teacher, "how can we help Serezha with this problem?" There are many suggestions: get together to buy him a watch, exile him from the classroom, send him to the director's office, or even to exile him from the school. But apparently these suggestions are either not appropriate or too extreme. The teacher, our text tells us, "helps the children find the right answer." She asks for a volunteer to stop by and pick Serezha up on the way to school. Many children offer to help in this mission.

But tragedy stalks. The next day it turns out that not only Serezha is late, but also the boy who had promised to pick him up. Since they are both from the same group, their unit receives two sets of demerits and falls to lowest place. Group members are keenly disappointed. "Serezha especially suffered much and felt himself responsible, but equal blame was felt by his companion who had forgotten to stop in for him."

In this way, both through concrete action and explanation, the teacher seeks to forge a spirit of group unity and responsibility. From time to time, she explains to the children the significance of what they are doing, the fact "that they have to learn to live together as one friendly family, since they will have to be learning together for all of the next ten years, and that for this reason one must learn how to help one's companions and to treat them decently."

By the time the children are in the second grade, the responsibilities expected of them are increased in complexity. For example, instead of simply recording the evaluations made by the teacher, the monitors are taught how to make the evaluations themselves. Since this is rather difficult, especially in judging homework assignments, in the beginning two monitors are assigned to every task. In this way, our text tells us, they can help each other in doing a good job of evaluation.

Here is a third grade classroom:

> Class 3-B is just an ordinary class; it's not especially well disciplined nor is it outstandingly industrious. It has its lazy members and its responsible ones, quiet ones and active ones, daring, shy, and immodest ones.
>
> The teacher has led this class now for three years, and she has earned the affection, respect, and acceptance as an authority from her pupils. Her word is law for them.
>
> The bell has rung, but the teacher has not yet arrived. She has delayed deliberately in order to check how the class will conduct itself. In the class all is quiet. After the noisy class break, it isn't so easy to mobilize yourself and to quell the restlessness within you! Two monitors at the desk silently observe the class. On their faces is reflected the full importance and seriousness of the job they are performing. But there is no need for them to make any reprimands: the youngsters with pleasure and pride maintain scrupulous discipline; they are proud of the fact that their class conducts itself in a manner that merits the confidence of the teacher. And when the teacher enters and quietly says be seated, all understand that she deliberately refrains from praising them for the quiet and order, since in their class it could not be otherwise. . . .
>
> During the lesson, the teacher gives an exceptional amount of attention to collective competition between "links." (The links are the smallest unit of the communist youth organization at this age level.) Throughout the entire lesson the youngsters are constantly hearing which link has best prepared its lesson, which link has done the best at numbers, which is the most disciplined, which has turned in the best work.
>
> The best link not only gets a verbal positive evaluation but receives the right to leave the classroom first during the break and to have its notebooks checked before the others. As a result the links receive the benefit of collective education, common responsibility, and mutual aid.
>
> "What are you fooling around for? You're holding up the whole link," whispers Kolya to his neighbor during the preparation period for the lesson. And during the break he teaches her how better to organize her books and pads in her knapsack.
>
> "Count more carefully," says Olya to her girlfriend. "See, on account of you our link got behind today. You come to me and we'll count together at home."

In the third grade still another innovation is introduced. The monitors are taught not only to evaluate but to state their criticisms publicly.

> Here is a typical picture. It is the beginning of the lesson. In the first row the link leader reports, basing his comments on information submitted by the sanitarian and other responsible monitors: "Today Valadya did the wrong problem. Masha didn't write neatly and forgot to underline the right words in her lesson, Alyoshi had a dirty shirt collar."

The other link leaders make similar reports (the Pioneers are sitting by rows).

The youngsters are not offended by this procedure: they understand that the link leaders are not just tattle-telling but simply fulfilling their duty. It doesn't even occur to the monitors and sanitarians to conceal the shortcomings of their comrades. They feel that they are doing their job well precisely when they notice one or another defect.

Also in the third grade, the teacher introduces still another procedure. She now proposes that the children enter into competition with the monitors, and see if they can beat the monitor at his own game by criticizing themselves. "The results were spectacular: if the monitor was able to talk to only about four or five members of the row, there would be supplementary reports about their own shortcomings from as many as eight or ten pupils."

To what extent is this picture overdrawn? Although I have no direct evidence, the accounts I heard from participants in the process lend credence to the descriptions in the manual. For example, I recall a conversation with three elementary school teachers, all men, whom I had met by chance in a restaurant. They were curious about discipline techniques used in American schools. After I had given several examples, I was interrupted: "But how do you use the collective?" When I replied that we really did not use the classroom group in any systematic way, my three companions were puzzled. "But how do you keep discipline?"

Now it was my turn to ask for examples. "All right," came the answer, "let us suppose that ten-year-old Vanya is pulling Anya's curls. If he doesn't stop the first time I speak to him, all I need do is mention it again in the group's presence; then I can be reasonably sure that before the class meets again the boy will be talked to by the officers of his Pioneer link. They will remind him that his behavior reflects on the reputation of the link."

"And what if he persists?"

"Then he may have to appear before his link—or even the entire collective —who will explain his misbehavior to him and determine his punishment."

"What punishment?"

"Various measures. He may just be censured, or if his conduct is regarded as serious, he may be expelled from membership. Very often he himself will acknowledge his faults before the group."

Nor does the process of social criticism and control stop with the school. Our manual tells us, for example, that parents submit periodic reports to the school collective on the behavior of the child at home. One may wonder how parents can be depended on to turn in truthful accounts. Part of the answer was supplied to me in a conversation with a Soviet agricultural expert. In response to my questions, he explained that no matter what a person's job, the collective at his place of work always took an active interest in his family life. Thus, a representative would come to the worker's home to observe and talk with his wife and children. And if any undesirable features were noted, these would be reported back to the collective.

I asked for an example.

"Well, suppose the representative were to notice that my wife and I quarreled in front of the children (my companion shook his head). That would be bad. They would speak to me about it and remind me of my responsibilities for training my children to be good citizens."

I pointed out how different the situation was in America where a man's home was considered a private sanctuary so that, for example, psychologists like myself often had a great deal of difficulty in getting into homes to talk with parents or to observe children.

"Yes," my companion responded. "That's one of the strange things about your system in the West. The family is separated from the rest of society. That's not good. It's bad for the family and bad for society." He paused for a moment, lost in thought. "I suppose," he went on, "if my wife didn't want to let the representative in, she could ask him to leave. But then at work, I should feel ashamed." (He hung his head to emphasize the point.) "Ivanov," they would say, "has an uncultured wife."

But it would be a mistake to conclude that Soviet methods of character education and social control are based primarily on negative criticism. On the contrary, in their approach there is as much of the carrot as the stick. But the carrot is given not merely as a reward for individual performance but explicitly for the child's contribution to group achievement. The great charts emblazoned "Who Is Best?" which bedeck the halls and walls of every classroom have as entries the names not of individual pupils but of rows and links (the link is the smallest unit of communist youth organization, which of course reaches into every classroom, from the first grade on). It is the winning unit that gets rewarded by a pennant, a special privilege, or by having their picture taken in "parade uniforms." And when praise is given, as it frequently is, to an individual child, the group referent is always there: "Today Peter helped Kate and as a result his unit did not get behind the rest."

Helping other members of one's collective and appreciating their contributions—themes that are much stressed in Soviet character training—become matters of enlightened self-interest, since the grade that each person receives depends on the over-all performance of his unit. Thus, the good student finds it to his advantage to help the poor one. The same principle is carried over to the group level with champion rows and classes being made responsible for the performance of poorer ones.

Here then are the procedures employed in Soviet character education. As a result of Khrushchev's educational reforms, they may be expected to receive even wider application in the years to come, for, in connection with these reforms, several new types of educational institutions are to be developed on a massive scale. The most important of these is the "internat," or boarding school, in which youngsters are to be entered as early as three months of age with parents visiting only on weekends. The internat is described in the theses announcing the reforms as the kind of school which "creates the most favorable conditions for the education and communist upbringing of the rising generation" (Communist Party of the Soviet Union,

1958). The number of boarding schools in the USSR is to be increased during the current seven-year plan from a 1958 level of 180,000 to 2,500,000 in 1965 (figures cited in *Pravda*, November 18, 1958), and according to I. A. Kairov, head of the Academy of Pedagogical Sciences, "No one can doubt that, as material conditions are created, the usual general educational school will be supplanted by the boarding school" (Kairov, 1960).

If this prophecy is fulfilled[1] we may expect that in the years to come the great majority of Soviet children (and children in some other countries of the Communist bloc as well) will from the first year of life onward be spending their formative period in collective settings and will be exposed daily to the techniques of collective socialization we have been describing. It is, therefore, a matter of considerable practical and scientific interest to identify the salient features of these techniques and subject them to research study, insofar as this becomes possible within the framework of our own society.

III.   Guiding Principles of the Soviet Approach to Character Training

As a first approximation, we may list the following as distinguishing characteristics or guiding principles of Communist methods of character education:

1. The peer collective (under adult leadership) rivals and early surpasses the family as the principal agent of socialization.
2. Competition between groups is utilized as the principal mechanism for motivating achievement of behavior norms.
3. The behavior of the individual is evaluated primarily in terms of its relevance to the goals and achievements of the collective.
4. Rewards and punishments are frequently given on a group basis; that is, the entire group benefits or suffers as a consequence of the conduct of individual members.
5. As soon as possible, the tasks of evaluating the behavior of individuals and of dispensing rewards and sanctions is delegated to the members of the collective.
6. The principal methods of social control are public recognition and public criticism, with explicit training and practice being given in these activities. Specifically, each member of the collective is encouraged to observe deviant behavior by his fellows and is given opportunity to report his observations to the group. Reporting on one's peers is esteemed and rewarded as a civic duty.
7. Group criticism becomes the vehicle for training in self-criticism in the presence of one's peers. Such public self-criticism is regarded as a powerful mechanism for maintaining and enhancing commitment to

1. Since Khrushchev, the number of boarding schools has been reduced in favor of schools of the prolonged day, primarily for economic reasons, but also to maintain the contact of children with families and the community. U.B. 6/27/68.

approved standards of behavior, as well as the method of choice for bringing deviants back into line.

There are of course many other important features of the Soviet approach to socialization, but the seven listed above are those which present the greatest contrast to the patterns we employ in the West. It is for this reason that they are selected for special consideration here. We shall now proceed to examine each feature in greater detail with particular attention to the research ideas which it may generate.

IV.   The Family vs. the Collective

American theory and research on moral development have given almost exclusive emphasis to the family as the principal context and agent of socialization. The Soviet pattern, with its predominant emphasis on the collective, therefore raises the question of how these two socializing agents may differ in the nature and effect of the techniques they employ. To put the problem in another way: What types of socialization process and character structure emerge under the predominant influence of one or the other agent, or a combination of the two?

Stated in this form, the question seems an obvious and important one. Yet, to the writer's knowledge, research to date has little to offer in reply. True, there have been studies of personality development in several diverse types of children's groups who, for one reason or another, have grown up outside the context of the nuclear family. But for several reasons these studies do not shed much light on the problem at hand. The limitation springs in part from the highly specialized character of the groups investigated: youngsters removed to residential nurseries during war time (Burlingham and Freud, 1944), children rescued from Nazi concentration camps (Freud and Denn, 1954), delinquent gangs (Thrasher, 1936; Whyte, 1943; Cohen, 1955; Cohen and Short, 1958; Miller, 1958), and Kibbutz children (Irvine, 1952; Caplan, 1953; Faigin, 1958; Rabin, 1958; Spiro, 1958).

Second, by and large these investigations take the form of clinical or case studies focusing on the particular problem at hand; they lack the structured design and comparative frame of reference which enhance the possibility of recognizing important differences, distinguishing characteristics, functional relationships. The advantages of these strategic devices are evidenced in the researches which employ them. Thus, in a comparative ethnographic study. Eisenstadt (1956) demonstrated that peer collectives are most likely to develop in a society when there is marked discontinuity between values and role allocations in the family and in the adult world. Exploiting another kind of naturalistic experiment, two investigations (Rosen, 1955; Haire and Morrison, 1957) have studied situations in which parental values conflict with those of the peer group, and have found in each instance that although both sources are influential, the peer group tends to outweigh the parent in the age range studied (12 to 18). The research bearing most directly on the problem at hand is Boehm's comparative study (1957) of conscience development in Swiss and American children. She finds that the latter transfer parent dependence to peer dependence at an earlier age, and that

> One result of this earlier transferring appears to be that the American child's conscience becomes less egocentric and interiorizes earlier than does that of the Swiss child. There is, however, some indication that the content of conscience differs in these two types of societies. Whereas the American child's conscience is turned, primarily, toward social adjustment, the Swiss child's is geared toward character improvement (pp. 91-92).

The principal shortcoming of all these studies for the issue at hand, however, is their failure to examine and analyze their data from the point of view of the group processes of socialization that may be occurring in the collective setting outside the family. To the extent that socialization is dealt with at all in these investigations, it is treated in conventional fashion with attention accorded primarily to the behavior of a parent or a parent surrogate toward the child. Such a restricted focus is of course understandable, given the traditional emphasis in Western culture, reflected in scientific work, on the centrality of the parent-child relationship in the process of upbringing. It is this circumscribed conception which probably accounts for the fact that Western personality theory and research, highly developed as they are in comparison with their Russian counterparts (Bronfenbrenner, 1961c) offer little basis for ready-made hypotheses bearing on processes and effects of socialization in collective settings.

Nevertheless, despite their limitations, the existing researches have considerable potential value. To begin with, many of them, especially the clinical and case studies, contain excellent descriptive data that could be re-examined from our new perspective to discover whether they might not shed some light on phenomena of collective socialization. Second, the more structured investigations suggest research designs that might profitably be employed in future work. The first research paradigm, exemplified by both the Eisenstadt and Boehm studies, makes use of groups with contrasting degrees of exposure to socialization in family *vs.* collective settings. Such contrasts are understandably found most readily in different cultures, but under these circumstances interpretation is complicated by the presence of other factors associated with each culture that might account for the observed differences in character development. Eisenstadt endeavors to circumvent this difficulty by using data from a large number of societies in which other factors besides those under immediate investigation may be expected to vary widely. While highly useful, particularly in the exploratory stages of research, this approach has its serious limitations. Either one must make do with only partially-adequate data gathered by other investigators with other objectives in mind, or one must carry out new specially-designed cross-cultural studies in a substantial number of different settings.

But there is an alternative strategy which, to the writer's knowledge, has hardly been exploited to date. It involves finding groups exposed to different agents of socialization within the same or closely comparable cultural contexts. Such comparable groups may be difficult to discover, but once identified they offer rich opportunities for research on differential processes and outcomes of character training in familial *vs.* peer-group settings. The ideal contrast in this regard would be two groups of children from the same social milieu, one group having attended boarding school from an early age, the other raised at home with minimal and relatively late exposure to group influences in school or peer group. Obviously this ideal would be almost impossible to achieve but it can certainly be approximated, especially in such countries as England, Switzerland, or, should the opportunity arise, the Soviet Union, where boarding schools are relatively common; or in Israel, with a focus on the comparison between children raised in the *kibbutz,* where the young are reared primarily outside the family in collective settings, and the *moshav,* where adult life is collectively organized but children are brought up in the nuclear family. The last contrast should be particularly instructive since collective ideology would be present in both settings but the principal agent of socialization would differ.

Another research opportunity found more easily outside the United States is that provided by families living in relative geographic isolation. An extreme example in a modern Western country occurs in Norway, where some families live in mountainous areas that remain isolated during a large part of the year. A current study of this group by Aubert, Tiller, and their associates at the Oslo Institute for Social Research should shed light on the character development of children raised in a nuclear family under conditions of minimal contact with others outside the home.

The American scene is of course not without its possibilities for research along the same lines, even if over a somewhat more restricted range. Thus, we too have our boarding schools, and although their enrollment tends to be limited to children who are highly selected on socio-economic, religious, or psychological characteristics, an appropriately-matched sample of controls not attending boarding school can usually be found. Indeed, to minimize differences in family values and background one could make use of those private schools which enroll both boarding and day pupils. Similarly, instances of families living in geographic isolation can still be found especially in the receding remnants of the American frontier in mountains, deserts, and north country; moreover, with the occasional influx of skilled technicians to such areas, the possibility arises of studying families who are living in an isolation which is primarily physical and not cultural as well. Finally, among the run-of-the-mill families in any American community there is likely to be an appreciable range of variation in the amount of socialization children experience outside the nuclear family. Some youngsters participate from an early age in nursery schools, camps, clubs, gangs, and other peer-group settings both with and without adult supervision. Others remain relatively isolated from peers until they enter kindergarten or first grade, and even thereafter extra-familial associations may be minimal. A study of differences in character development in children exposed to varying degrees of familial *vs.* extra-familial socialization could be illuminating.

The last proposal highlights a difficulty plaguing all of the research designs outlined above. It is obvious that families in which contact with peers is postponed and minimized are likely to exhibit different value systems and techniques of socialization from those in which children are permitted or encouraged to have early associations outside the home. Such differences will be found also even in the "cleanest" and most closely-matched comparisons. Thus, day and boarding pupils in the same school will still differ in family background, values, and child-rearing practices. The fact that particular values and techniques may be functionally linked to the setting in which they occur does not remove the necessity of identifying them and taking them into account in the interpretation of results and in the design of subsequent studies.

Comparing groups with differing socialization experience is not the only strategy available for studying the differential influence of the family *vs.* the peer collective. The researches of Rosen and Haire mentioned above suggest still another gambit: that of comparing the relative effects of both types of influence on the same children. The strategy here involves finding instances in which familial and peer-group standards conflict in varying degrees and to observe which influence prevails under what circumstances.

The last strategy focuses even more sharply the question of what dependent variables should be investigated in studies of this kind. Quite naturally one thinks first of the variables that have been emphasized in American studies of moral development; namely, projective measures of conscience and guilt of the type employed by Allinsmith (1957, 1960), Aronfreed (1959, 1960), Hoffman (1961), and Miller and Swanson (1960), or the behavorial measures of similar variables growing out of the work of Whiting and Sears and their colleagues at the Harvard Laboratory of Human Development (Whiting and Child, 1953; Whiting, 1954; Sears, Maccoby, and Levin, 1957) and implemented most recently in a study of antecedents of resistance to temptation conducted by Burton, Maccoby, and Allinsmith (undated).

It would clearly be a matter of considerable theoretical and practical interest whether children experiencing different ratios of exposure to socialization within the family *vs.* within the peer-group exhibit differences in types and degrees of self-blame, tendency to blame others, resistance to temptation or in any of the other patterns of moral judgment commonly examined in current research on this topic. The psychoanalytic theories on which most of these instruments are based would lead one to expect stronger internalization and self-blame among children raised primarily within the nuclear family, and this prediction receives at least indirect support from the one study we have found (Boehm, 1957) that comes near to dealing with the problem. But much depends on the particular socialization processes employed in one or another collective setting. In the absence of adequate data or theory dealing directly with this issue, we can only resort to speculation on the basis of what knowledge we do have about socialization processes generally. And since this knowledge is based almost entirely on studies of the family, we are forced into the risky expedient of arguing by analogy. Accordingly, in order to try to become aware both of the possibilities and pitfalls of this approach, we shall begin by assuming isomorphism and then call the assumption into question.

What are the principal generalizations, then, to be drawn from existing studies of factors in the nuclear family affecting the moral development of the child? A growing number of independent researches (Sears, Maccoby, and Levin, 1957; Miller and Swanson 1958, 1960; Bronfenbrenner, 1961a, 1961b, 1961d; Hoffman, 1961) point to the conclusion that the internalization of moral standards is a function of the degree and ratio of parental affection and discipline. Specifically, internalization appears to be maximized when both affection and discipline are high. When parents rely primarily on the assertion of power in a relatively non-affectionate context, the child is likely to be responsive only to external controls (i.e., fear of punishment). When both affection and discipline are low, or when the former appreciably outweighs the latter, moral standards tend to be weak or ineffective and the child resorts to distortive mechanisms such as denial or displacement (for example, unjustly blaming others). But internalization can also take non-adaptive forms characterized by inflexibility or excessive self-blame. Such rigid or self-deprecatory standards are especially likely to arise when parents are generally affectionate but rely on discipline techniques which "involve ego attack and depreciation of the child" (Hoffman, 1961, p. 5). In contrast, parents of children whose moral standards are more realistic and responsive to extenuating circumstances tend to "appeal more to approach motives." Hoffman, in the most recent and extensive study of this problem, elaborates on the differences between the two groups of parents as follows:

> . . . The two groups are similar in that their parental discipline relies primarily on the frequent use of inductive techniques within an affectionate context, and the infrequent use of power assertion. What mainly characterizes and differentiates [that adaptive group] is that they report their parents as more frequently using techniques that communicate disappointment in the child for not living up to the parent's expectations and less frequently as using ego attack and love withdrawal techniques. It seems to us that the expression of disappointment, while it indicates that the parent has in a sense hurt the child, also conveys the feeling that the child is capable of living up to an ideal (Hoffman, 1961, pp. 37-38).

Pursuing our argument by analogy and shifting the context from the family to the school-collective, we may ask whether any of these patterns of socialization apply to the Soviet case and, if so, what kinds of consequences in moral development we might expect. With due regard to the tentative and largely impressionistic character of this initial comparison, it is nevertheless striking to note the correspondence between the techniques recommended in our Soviet manual and Hoffman's description of the pattern of socialization most likely to lead to the internalization of realistic and appropriately flexible moral standards. Both situations involve high levels of discipline and support with the primary emphasis on an appeal to motives of approach rather than of avoidance (e.g., "How can we help Serezha with his problem?"). Also in both instances, there is infrequent use of power assertion. Finally, the many examples of group criticism appearing in the Soviet manual are surely more appropriately described in Hoffman's terminology not as an "ego attack and depreciation of the child" but precisely as statements "that communicate disappointment in the child for not living up to expectations," which "convey the feeling that the child is capable of living up to an ideal."

If the analogy is a valid one, and *if* the Russians actually practice what they preach, we should therefore expect that the pattern of socialization in the peer collective would lead to the development of the same quality of moral standards achieved by an optimal balance of support and control in the American nuclear family. The two *if's*, however, can hardly be allowed to stand unquestioned. To consider the purely empirical question first, it seems likely that, as in every society, actual practice in Soviet society falls somewhat short of the ideal, or at least deviates from it. The nature of this deviation must await the results of systematic objective observations in Soviet schoolrooms. And it may be some time before such data are made available by either Soviet or Western behavioral scientists. In the meanwhile, however, there is nothing to prevent American workers from initiating a systematic program of research on group atmospheres in the classroom or other peer-collective settings and observing, through naturalistic or contrived experiments, the differential effects of various ratios of support and control on the development of moral standards and behavior. Indeed, the prototype of such research already exists in the classic experiment of Lewin, Lippitt, and White (1939), and it is both regrettable and surprising that this study has not been followed up by others in a systematic program of research on socialization processes in peer group settings. Perhaps White and Lippitt's (1960) recently published reanalysis of their data will help stimulate a renewed interest in this neglected area.

Our second *if* gives rise to even more questions and complexities. It seems hardly likely that generalizations derived from studies of the American family could be applied directly to the analysis of socialization processes in the classroom, and a Soviet classroom at that. To begin with, such an analogy assumes that the teacher and the classroom group have re-enforcement power equivalent to that of the parent. This assumption can be challenged from both directions. On the one hand psychoanalytic theory, and probably common belief as well, discounts the possibility that any other social group could approach the family in the strength of its affectional and controlling influences. Yet, a growing body of research stemming from the work of Asch (1956) demonstrates that the group is capable of exerting tremendously powerful forces toward conformity, even to the extent of inducing distortions in reality perception. The question of the relative potential of the family and the peer-group as agents of socialization therefore remains an open one resolvable only through empirical research.

The issue is complicated further by the fact that, to a greater or lesser degree, the child is usually exposed to some measure of socialization within the family before he enters the collective. In fact, the responsiveness of the child to socialization in a group setting may even depend on prior experience in the family. It is noteworthy in this connection that, up until now, most of the children who have been exposed to Soviet methods of character education in school have spent the first seven years of their lives in the bosom of the family. Should the preceding speculation be valid, the Russians may experience some difficulty with their methods once they begin, as they propose, to place children in collectives during the first five years of life.

Apart from questions about the relative socializing power of the family and the collective, there are of course important differences in the social structure of the two systems. Yet, while influential theorists like Freud (1948) and Parsons and Bales (1955) have stressed the analogy between parent and children on the one hand and group leader and group members on the other, to this writer's knowledge little attention has been given to the theoretical implications for the process of socialization of such obvious differences as group size, range of role differentiation, specificity of function, duration through time, and their psychological consequences in degree of ego involvement. At the same time, so far as Soviet society is concerned, we must take note of the two-way theme constantly reiterated in Russian writings on character education that the family must become a collective and the collective must take on the characteristics of a family. As a result, it is conceivable that over time the differences between these two types of social structure in Soviet society will become attenuated and the similarities maximized. This possibility highlights the value of comparative longitudinal studies of the changing character of Western and Communist family and peer-group structures. Such studies would of course have special significance as necessary background for research on character development.

The preceding consideration points directly to the most important difference between American and Soviet socialization practice, whether in the family or out. This is the matter of ideological content and the special procedures which this content inspires. It is this content and procedure which are the burden of the remaining six of the guiding principles we have listed earlier.

V. Group Incentives

Principles 2-4 emphasize the importance of the collective over the individual as the frame of reference for evaluating behavior and distributing punishments and rewards. As the principles indicate, there are three elements to the pattern: desired behavior is motivated through competition between groups rather than between individuals; behavior is judged in terms of its implication for the achievement and reputation of the group; and rewards and punishments are given on a group basis so that all members of the group stand to gain or lose from the actions of each individual.

The arousal of motivation through competition between groups is certainly not an unfamiliar phenomenon in American society or in the American schoolroom. But even without the support of systematic evidence, one could confidently assert that this motivating device used to be employed far more frequently three or more decades ago than it is today. This same trend is dramatically reflected in the character of research studies being carried out in the late twenties and thirties as compared with the present time. Thus, Murphy, Murphy, and Newcomb in the 1937 revision of their *Experimental Social Psychology* (pp. 476-493) tabulate as many as twenty-five studies dealing with competition in children's groups, many of them focusing directly on the issue of group *vs.* individual incentive. In contrast, a contemporary survey of group research (Thibaut and Kelley, 1959) scarcely mentions the topic. Even though the earlier studies of group incentives focus almost entirely on motor and intellectual tasks rather than attitude formation, the results are instructive. Group competition generally increases output but is less effective as an incentive than self-oriented or individual competition. As Murphy, Murphy, and Newcomb properly caution, however, "Any discussion of . . . studies of the effects of incentives must be seen in relation to the cultural background which has set so much store by individual achievement, and has nourished this movement to find ways of stimulating the greatest achievement in the individual" (p. 501).

This caveat carries implications for a potentially fruitful research design in which children with contrasting individualistic *vs.* collectivistic backgrounds would be exposed to both types of competitive situations and their performance observed. Although one's first impulse is to discount such a proposal on the practical ground that it would be virtually impossible to find children with such diverse backgrounds in the same culture, further consideration suggests that good research opportunities do exist. The most obvious example is Israel, where both types of orientation are common even within the same ethnic and socio-economic sub-groups. Furthermore, the contrast can be approximated in our own society, since many private schools differ widely precisely along this continuum. For example, many progressive schools are ultra-individualistic in their philosophy and practice whereas others would probably be shocked to learn that their emphasis on sub-group solidarity and competition is properly described as collectivistic.

But in view of the dearth of research studies of the phenomenon over the last twenty-five years, there would be much to learn from research on the effects of group incentives even with children coming from the predominantly-individualistic background characteristic of American society. On the independent side, these researches should give attention to such specific variables as the motivating power of inter-group *vs.* inter-individual competition, evaluation of individual behavior in terms of its contribution to the status of the group as a whole, and the giving of punishments and rewards on a group basis. On the dependent side, the spectrum of variables should be broadened beyond problem-solving to include personality measures such as the indices of moral standards employed in much current research as well as other relevant social attitudes and behaviors. These important additions are more appropriately discussed after we have completed examination of the last three of the distinguishing characteristics of Soviet methods of character education—these having to do with group criticism and self-criticism.

VI. Group Criticism and Self-Criticism

The feature of Soviet socialization practices which clashes most sharply with the American pattern is the Russians' widespread resort to the procedure of criticizing others and one's self in public. The practice is common throughout all levels of Soviet society from school, farm, and factory to the highest echelons of the party. Thus, by being taught these techniques in early childhood, Soviet youth are being prepared in patterns of response that will be expected and even required of them throughout their life span. Since such practices are uncommon in American society, it is not surprising that they have not been subjected to research study in any direct way. As already noted, however, the work of Asch and others (Asch, 1956; Berenda, 1950) testifies to the power of an overwhelming majority forcing the deviant individual to conform. In these rigged experiments members of the majority do not engage in criticism but simply give responses which conflict with the reality perceptions of the experimental subject. The effect on the subject is to lead him, in an appreciable number of instances, to change his own response in the direction of the majority. In a sense, such alteration represents a confession of his own previous "error." Obviously, the experiments cannot be said to reproduce explicit features of Soviet group criticism and self-criticism but the fit could be made much closer by instructing confederates to engage in criticism and by asking the subject to admit that his previous responses had not been correct. Such variations would of course make even more salient questions of scientific ethics that invariably arise when experiments of this kind are viewed from the perspective of the Western Judeo-Christian moral tradition. (It is doubtful, incidentally, that such questions would ever be raised in a Communist society.) Still, ways can probably be found to conduct experiments on the processes of group criticism and self-criticism without doing serious violence to our own ethical traditions.

The fact remains, however, that such socialization procedures as group criticism and self-criticism have moral implications and hence may be expected to have moral consequences; that is, they are likely to influence the moral attitudes, actions, and character structure of the individual on whom they are employed. Moreover, it is doubtful whether such consequences are fully or even adequately reflected by the measures of conscience and guilt currently employed in research on moral development. Certainly it would be important to know about the nature of conscience and guilt in the "new Soviet men" who have been exposed to a lifetime of experience in group criticism and self-criticism. But in building "socialist morality" Soviet educators are less concerned with such questions as whether the individual tends to blame others or himself as with his sense of commitment to the collective, especially in the face of competing individualistic values and preferences.

Accordingly, perhaps the most important research implication to be drawn from our examination of Soviet methods of character education is the necessity of expanding the spectrum of what we conceive as moral development beyond the characteristically Judeo-Christian concern with personal responsibility and guilt to a consideration of the broader moral issues inherent in the relation of man to man and of the individual to his society.

We have tried to take some beginning steps in this direction in the research on character development being conducted at Cornell by Bronfenbrenner, Devereux, and Suci. Specifically, as a point of departure we have distinguished five hypothetical extreme types of character structure representing the presumed products of five divergent patterns of socialization and moral development in children and adolescents. These five are tentatively designated as *self-oriented, adult-oriented, peer-oriented, collective-oriented,* and *objectively-principled* character structures.[2]

The *self-oriented* child is motivated primarily by impulses of self-gratification without regard to the desires or expectations of others or to internalized standards. Such an asocial and amoral orientation is presumed to arise when the child's parents are so permissive, indifferent, inconsistent, or indulgent that immediate self-indulgence becomes the practicable and, in the long run, most rewarding course of action for the child. The development of this personality type is further facilitated by participation in peer groups which encourage self-indulgence and exact neither loyalty nor discipline from their members.

The *adult-oriented* child is one who accepts parental strictures and values as final and immutable. He is completely submissive to parental authority and the moral standards imposed by the parent. This orientation generalizes to adult authority outside the home in school and community. In other words, here is the over-socialized "good child," already a little adult, who causes no trouble but is relatively incapable of initiative and leadership. He is presumed to be the product of intensive socialization within the nuclear family but with minimal experience outside the home.

In contrast, the *peer-oriented* child is an adaptive conformist who goes along with the group and readily accepts every shift in group opinion or

2. A similar typology, but unlinked to particular patterns and agents of socialization, has recently been proposed by Peck and Havighurst (1960).

conduct. This is the "outer-directed" character-type of Riesman's (1950) typology or the future "organization man" described by Whyte (1956). His values and preferences reflect the momentary sentiments of his social set. The optimal circumstances for the development of this personality type involve a combination of parents who are either permissive or actively encourage conformity to group norms, accompanied by early and extensive participation in peer groups requiring such conformity as the price of acceptance. The norms of such groups, however, are ephemeral in character and imply no consistent standards or goals.

The prototype of the *collective-oriented* personality is of course the "new Soviet man"—a person committed to a firm and enduring set of values centering around the achievement of enduring group standards and goals. These group values take precedence over individual desires or obligations of particular interpersonal relationships. Such an orientation presumably springs from a developmental history in which from the very outset the parents place the needs and demands of the collective above those of the child or of particular family members. Affection and discipline are bestowed in the name and interests of the social group and the child spends most of his formative years in collective settings under the guidance of adults and leaders who train him in the skills and values of collective living.

Finally, the behavior of the *objectively-principled* child is guided by values which, although learned through experience in the family and in peer groups, do not bind him to undeviating conformity to the standards of the one or the other. This is the "inner-directed" personality of Riesman's (1950) typology. On one occasion he may act in accordance with the standards of his parents; on another with the mores of the peer group; or in still a third instance he may take a path which deviates from the preferences of both parents and peers. There is, however, a consistency in pattern of response from one situation to the next which reflects the child's own now-autonomous standards of conduct. The developmental history posited for this type of character structure assumes a strong, differentiated family organization with high levels of affection and discipline but at the same time considerable opportunity granted to the child to participate in selected but varied peer-group experiences both with and without adult supervision. These peer groups, in turn, are also characterized by high levels of affectional involvement and their own particular disciplinary codes. The hypothesis implicit in this developmental sequence is that an autonomous set of moral standards is developed from having to cope with different types of discipline in a variety of basically-accepting social contexts, so that the child is forced to compare and come to terms with different codes of behavior imposed by different persons or groups each of whom is supportive and wins his liking and respect. This hypothesis, though highly speculative, derives in part from some of our research results (Bronfenbrenner 1961a, 1961b, 1961d) which suggested that children who are rated by teachers and peers as high in social responsibility and initiative tend to come from families where parental affection and discipline are relatively strong, parental roles are moderately differentiated (e.g., one parent tends to exercise authority slightly more than the other), but the child also participates in many group activities outside the home. Unfortunately, in these initial studies very little information was obtained about the child's experiences in peer group settings.

We are currently in the process of devising instruments for measuring the five types of character structure outlined above as these are manifested both in attitudes and behavior. Several of our instruments have yielded promising results in pilot studies but have also brought to light shortcomings in theory and method. The principal value of the approach in its present stage of development is its capacity to generate fruitful hypotheses and research designs for the investigation of character development as a social process.

The last consideration brings us back to the main objective of this paper. Its primary purpose is not to argue for a particular theoretical orientation or methodology; the sole and central aim is to encourage and assist behavioral scientists and educators to give careful attention to the problems and processes implicit in collective methods of character education such as those employed in the Soviet Union and elsewhere in the Communist bloc. We have tried to show that these problems and processes have considerable social relevance and theoretical importance far beyond their immediate social context. We have also attempted to demonstrate that they can be made amenable to empirical investigation. The paper will have served its purpose if it contributes to a renewal of research interest in the study of extra-familial groups as socializing agents, for such scientific study should do much to enhance our understanding of intriguing social processes through which human character is formed.

References

ALLINSMITH, W. Conscience and conflict: the moral force in personality. *Child Development,* 1957, 28, 469-476.

ALLINSMITH, E. The learning of moral standards. In D. R. Miller and G. E. Swanson, *Inner conflict and defense.* New York: Holt, 1960, Pp. 141-176.

ARONFREED, J. Internal and external orientation in the moral behavior of children. Paper read at the American Psychological Association meetings, Cincinnati, September, 1959.

ARONFREED, J. Moral behavior and sex identity. In D. R. Miller and G. E. Swanson, *Inner conflict and defense.* New York: Holt, 1960. Pp. 177-193.

ASCH, S. E. Studies of independence and conformity: a minority of one against a unanimous majority. *Psychological Monographs,* 1956, 70(9, Whole No. 416).

BERENDA, R. W. *The influence of the group on the judgments of children.* New York: King's Crown Press, 1950.

BOEHM, L. The development of independence: a comparative study. *Child Development,* 1957, 28, 85-92.

BRONFENBRENNER, U.   The changing American child. In E. Ginsberg (Ed.), *Values and ideals of American youth*. (Also in *Merrill-Palmer Quarterly*, 1961, 7, 73-84.) New York: Columbia University Press, 1961. Pp. 71-84. (a)

BRONFENBRENNER, U.   Some familial antecedents of responsibility and leadership in adolescents. In L. Petrullo and B. M. Bass (Eds.), *Leadership and interpersonal behavior*. New York: Holt, Rinehart and Winston, 1961. Pp. 239-272. (b)

BRONFENBRENNER, U.   Soviet studies in personality development and socialization. Ithaca, N.Y.: Cornell University, Department of Child Development and Family Relationships, 1961. (c) (Ditto)

BRONFENBRENNER, U.   Toward a theoretical model for the analysis of parent-child relationships in a social context. In J. C. Glidewell (Ed.), *Parental attitudes and child behavior*. Springfield, Ill.: Charles C. Thomas, 1961. Pp. 90-109. (d)

BURLINGHAM, D. and FREUD, A.   *Infants without families*. London: George Allen and Unwin, 1944.

BURTON, R. V., MACCOBY, E. E., and ALLINSMITH, W.   Antecedents of resistance to temptation. Washington, D.C.: National Institute of Mental Health, United States Department of Health, Education, and Welfare, undated. (Mimeo)

CAPLAN, G.   Clinical observations on the emotional life of children in the communal settlements in Israel. In M. J. Senn (Ed.), *Transactions of the Seventh Conference on Problems of Infancy and Childhood*. New York: Josiah Macy, Jr., Foundation, 1953.

COHEN, A. K.   *Delinquent boys—the culture of the gang*. Glencoe, Ill.: Free Press, 1955.

COHEN, A. K. and SHORT, J. F., JR.   Research in delinquent subcultures. *Journal of Social Issues*, 1958, 14, 23-37.

COMMUNIST PARTY OF THE SOVIET UNION.   *Ob ukreplenii svyazi shkoli s zhiznyu i o dalneishem razvitii sistemi naraodnogo obrazovaniya v strane* [On the strengthening of ties between school and life and the further development of the system of public education in the country]. (Theses of the Central Committee of the Communist Party of the Soviet Union) Moscow: Gospolitizdat, 1958.

EISENSTADT, S. N.   *From generation to generation*. Glencoe, Ill.: Free Press, 1956.

FAIGIN, H.   Case report: social behavior of young children in the kibbutz. *Journal of Abnormal and Social Psychology*, 1958, 56, 117-129.

FREUD, A. and DANN, S.   An experiment in group upbringing. In W. E. Martin and C. B. Stendler (Eds.), *Readings in child development*. New York: Harcourt Brace, 1954.

FREUD, S.   *Group psychology and the analysis of the ego*. London: Hogarth Press, 1948.

HAIRE, M. and MORRISON, F. School children's perceptions of labor and management. *Journal of Social Psychology*, 1957, 46, 179-197.

HOFFMAN, M. L.   Techniques and processes in moral development. Detroit: Merrill-Palmer Institute, 1961. (Mimeo)

IRVINE, E. E.   Observations on the aims and methods of child-rearing in communal settlements in Israel. *Human Relations*, 1952, 5, 247-275.

KAIROV, I. A.   [Long range plans for the development of pedagogical sciences and coordination of the work of the Academy and Chairs of Pedagogy of Pedagogical Institutes, USSR.] (Translation of an article in *Sovetsk. Pedag.*, 1960, 24(2), 16-44.) New York: United States Joint Publications Research Service, 1960.

LEWIN, K., LIPPITT, R. and WHITE, R. K. Patterns of aggressive behavior in experimentally created "social climates." *Journal of Social Psychology*, 1939, 10, 271-299.

MAKARENKO, A.   *Pedagogicheskaya poema* [A pedagogical poem]. (Available in English under the title *The road to life*, translated by Ivy and Tatiana Litvinov. Moscow: Foreign Languages Publishing House, 1955.) Leningrad: Leningradskoye gazetno-zhurnalnoye i knizhnoye izdatelstvo [Leningrad Newspaper-Periodical and Book Publishing House], 1949.

MAKARENKO, A. S.   *Learning to live*. Moscow: Foreign Languages Publishing House, 1953.

MAKARENKO, A. S.   *Kniga dlya roditelei* [A Book for Parents]. (Available in English. Moscow: Foreign Languages Publishing House, 1954.) Petrozavodsk: Gosudarstvennoye Izdatel'stvo Karel'skoi ASSR [State Publishing House of the Karelian Autonomous Soviet Socialist Republic], 1959.

MAKARENKO, A. S.   *The collective family: a handbook for Russian parents.* Garden City, N.Y.: Doubleday & Co., 1967. *Makarenko, his life and work.* (articles, talks, reminiscences) Moscow: Foreign Languages Publishing House, 1964.

MILLER, D. R. and SWANSON, G. E.   *The changing American child.* New York: Wiley, 1958.

MILLER, D. R. and SWANSON, G. E.   *Inner conflict and defense.* New York: Holt, 1960.

MILLER, W.   Lower class culture as a generating milieu of gang delinquency. *Journal of Social Issues,* 1958, 24, 5-19.

MURPHY, G., MURPHY, L. B. and NEWCOMB, T. M.   *Experimental social psychology.* (Rev. ed.) New York: Harper, 1937.

NOVIKOVA, L. E. (Ed.)   *Sotsialisticheskoye sorevnovaniye v shkole* [Socialist competition in the school]. Moscow: Uchpedgiz, 1950.

PARSONS, T. and BALES, R. F.   *Family, socialization and interaction process.* Glencoe, Ill.: Free Press, 1955.

PECK, R. F. and HAVIGHURST, R. J.   *The psychology of character development.* New York: Wiley, 1960.

RABIN, A. I.   Kibbutz children—research findings to date. *Children,* 1958, 5, 179-184.

RIESMAN, D. (with N. Glazer and R. Denney).   *The lonely crowd: a study of the changing American character.* New Haven: Yale University Press, 1950.

ROSEN, B. C.   Conflicting group membership: a study of parent-peer group cross pressures. *American Sociological Review,* 1955, 20, 155-161.

SEARS, R. R., MACCOBY, E. E. and LEVIN, H.   *Patterns of child rearing.* Evanston, Ill.: Row, Peterson, 1957.

SPIRO, M. E.   *Children of the kibbutz.* Cambridge, Mass.: Harvard University Press, 1958.

THIBAUT, J. W. and KELLEY, H. H.   *The social psychology of groups.* New York: Wiley, 1959.

THRASHER, F. M.   *The gang.* Chicago: University of Chicago Press, 1936.

WHITE, R. K. and LIPPITT, R.   *Autocracy and democracy.* New York: Harper, 1960.

WHITING, J. W. M.   Fourth presentation. In J. M. Tanner and B. Inhelder (Eds.), *Discussions on child development.* Vol. 2. London: Tavistock Publications, 1954.

WHITING, J. W. M. and CHILD, I. L.   *Child training and personality.* New Haven: Yale University Press, 1953.

WHYTE, W. F.   *Street corner society.* Chicago: University of Chicago Press, 1943.

WHYTE, W. H.   *The organization man.* New York: Doubleday, 1956.

⁂ ⁂ ⁂ ⁂ ⁂

The Thematic Apperception Test was adapted a number of years ago by the author of this article to measure the strength of a person's psychological need to achieve. The test asks the person to write short stories about rather vague pictures that are shown to him, and the stories are carefully analyzed for the "achievement imagery" contained in them. Like other projective tests, it is designed to reveal deep-lying aspects of personality. Is it believable that by teaching a person the "correct" answers to the test—i.e., how to write stories containing achievement imagery—one can alter his basic motivations? In this article, McClelland says it can be done. But as the reader will soon see, that is only a small part of the story.

By addressing himself to the task of strengthening the achievement motive, McClelland is going to the roots of one of the most serious educational problem of our time. It is an empirical fact that the most subjugated, deprived members of our society have, on the average, little motivation to achieve, and there is good reason to believe that success in our middle-class school system requires such motivation. Establishing equality in educational opportunity will come to nothing if people are uninterested in seizing the opportunities.

While the report deals with McClelland's work in training businessmen in need achievement, the twelve general propositions he outlines hold such blatant lessons for education that they need no translation. A number of social psychologists around the country have picked up McClelland's implications and, at this writing, are actively testing the theory with school children of the slums.

Toward a Theory of Motive Acquisition*

David C. McClelland

Too little is known about the processes of personality change at relatively complex levels. The empirical study of the problem has been hampered by both practical and theoretical difficulties. On the practical side it is very expensive both in time and effort to set up systematically controlled educational programs designed to develop some complex personality characteristic like a motive, and to follow the effects of the education over a number of years. It also presents ethical problems since it is not always clear that it is as proper to teach a person a new motive as it is a new skill like learning to play the piano. For both reasons, most of what we know about personality change has come from studying psychotherapy where both ethical and practical difficulties are overcome by the pressing need to help someone in real trouble. Yet, this source of information leaves much to be desired: It has so far proven difficult to identify and systematically vary the "inputs" in psychotherapy and to measure their specific effects on subsequent behavior, except in very general ways (cf. Rogers and Dymond, 1954).

On the theoretical side, the dominant views of personality formation suggest anyway that acquisition or change of any complex characteristic like a motive in adulthood would be extremely difficult. Both behavior theory and psychoanalysis agree that stable personality characteristics like motives are laid down in childhood. Behavior theory arrives at this conclusion by arguing that social motives are learned by close association with reduction in certain basic biological drives like hunger, thirst, and physical discomfort which loom much larger in childhood than adulthood. Psychoanalysis, for its part, pictures adult motives as stable resolutions of basic conflicts occurring in early childhood. Neither theory would provide much support for the notion that motives could be developed in adulthood without somehow recreating the childhood conditions under which they were originally formed. Furthermore, psychologists have been hard put to it to find objective evidence that even prolonged, serious, and expensive attempts to introduce personality change through psychotherapy have really proven successful (Eysenck, 1952). What hope is there that a program

* From *American Psychologist*, 1965, 20, 321-333. Used by permission of the author and publisher.

I am greatly indebted to the Carnegie Corporation of New York for its financial support of the research on which this paper is based, and to my collaborators who have helped plan and run the courses designed to develop the achievement motive—chiefly George Litwin, Elliott Danzig, David Kolb, Winthrop Adkins, David Winter, and John Andrews. The statements made and views expressed are solely the responsibility of the author.

to introduce personality change would end up producing a big enough effect to study?

Despite these difficulties a program of research has been under way for some time which is attempting to develop the achievement motive in adults. It was undertaken in an attempt to fill some of the gaps in our knowledge about personality change or the acquisition of complex human characteristics. Working with n Achievement has proved to have some important advantages for this type of research: the practical and ethical problems do not loom especially large because previous research (McClelland, 1961) has demonstrated the importance of high n Achievement for entrepreneurial behavior and it is easy to find businessmen, particularly in underdeveloped countries, who are interested in trying any means of improving their entrepreneurial performance. Furthermore, a great deal is known about the origins of n Achievement in childhood and its specific effects on behavior so that educational programs can be systematically planned and their effects evaluated in terms of this knowledge. Pilot attempts to develop n Achievement have gradually led to the formulation of some theoretical notions of what motive acquisition involves and how it can be effectively promoted in adults. These notions have been summarized in the form of 12 propositions which it is the ultimate purpose of the research program to test. The propositions are anchored so far as possible in experiences with pilot courses, in supporting research findings from other studies, and in theory.

Before the propositions are presented, it is necessary to explain more of the theoretical and practical background on which they are based. To begin with, some basis for believing that motives could be acquired in adulthood had to be found in view of the widespread pessimism on the subject among theoretically oriented psychologists. Oddly enough we were encouraged by the successful efforts of two quite different groups of "change agents"—operant conditioners and missionaries. Both groups have been "naive" in the sense of being unimpressed by or ignorant of the state of psychological knowledge in the field. The operant conditioners have not been encumbered by any elaborate theoretical apparatus; they do not believe motives exist anyway, and continue demonstrating vigorously that if you want a person to make a response, all you have to do is elicit it and reward it (cf. Bandura and Walters, 1963, pp. 238 ff.). They retain a simple faith in the infinite plasticity of human behavior in which one response is just like any other and one can be "shaped up" (strengthened by reward)— presumably even an "achievement" response as produced by a subject in a fantasy test. In fact, it was the naive optimism of one such researcher (Burris, 1958) that had a lot to do with getting the present research under way. He undertook a counseling program in which an attempt to elicit and reinforce achievement-related fantasies proved to be successful in motivating college students to get better grades. Like operant conditioners, the missionaries have gone ahead changing people because they have believed it possible. While the evidence is not scientifically impeccable, common-sense observation yields dozens of adults whose motivational structure has seemed to be quite radically and permanently altered by the educational efforts of Communist Party, Mormon, or other devout missionaries.

A man from Mars might be led to observe that personality change appears to be very difficult for those who think it is very difficult, if not impossible, and much easier for those who think it can be done. He would certainly be oversimplifying the picture, but at the very least his observation suggests that some theoretical revision is desirable in the prevailing views of social motives which link them so decisively to early childhood. Such a revision has been attempted in connection with the research on n Achievement (McClelland, Atkinson, Clark, and Lowell, 1953) and while it has not been widely accepted (cf. Berelson and Steiner, 1964), it needs to be briefly summarized here to provide a theoretical underpinning for the attempts at motive change to be described. It starts with the proposition that all motives are learned, that not even biological discomforts (as from hunger) or pleasures (as from sexual stimulation) are "urges" or "drives" until they are linked to cues that can signify their presence or absence. In time clusters of expectancies or associations grow up around affective experiences, not all of which are connected by any means with biological needs (McClelland *et al.*, 1953, Ch. 2), which we label motives. More formally, motives are "affectively toned associative networks" arranged in a hierarchy of strength or importance within a given individual. Obviously, the definition fits closely the operations used to measure a motive: "an affectively toned associative cluster" is exactly what is coded in a subject's fantasies to obtain an n Achievement score. The strength of the motive (its position in the individual's hierarchy of motives) is measured essentially by counting the number of associations belonging to this cluster as compared to others that an individual produces in a given number of opportunities. If one thinks of a motive as an associative network, it is easier to imagine how one might go about changing it: The problem becomes one of moving its position up on the hierarchy by increasing its salience compared to other clusters. It should be possible to accomplish this end by such tactics as: (*a*) setting up the network—discovering what associations, for example, exist in the achievement area and then extending, strengthening, or otherwise "improving" the network they form; (*b*) conceptualizing the network—forming a clear and conscious construct that labels the network; (*c*) tying the network to as many cues as possible in everyday life, especially those preceding and following action, to insure that the network will be regularly rearoused once formed; and (*d*) working out the relation of the network to superordinate associative clusters, like the self-concept, so that these dominant schemata do not block the train of achievement thoughts—for example, through a chain of interfering associations (e.g., "I am not really the achieving type").

This very brief summary is not intended as a full exposition of the theoretical viewpoint underlying the research, but it should suffice to give a rough idea of how the motive was conceived that we set out to change. This concept helped define the goals of the techniques of change, such as reducing the effects of associative interference from superordinate associate clusters. But what about the techniques themselves? What could we do that would produce effective learning of this sort? Broadly speaking, there are four types of empirical information to draw on. From the animal learning experiments, we know that such factors as repetition, optimal time intervals between stimulus, response, and reward, and the schedule of rewards are very important for effective learning. From human learning experiments, we know that such factors as distribution of practice, repetitions, meaningfulness, and recitation are important. From experiences with psychotherapy (cf. Rogers, 1961), we learn that warmth, honesty, nondirectiveness, and the ability to recode associations in line with psychoanalytic or other personality theories are important. And, from the attitude-change research literature, we learn that such variables as presenting one side or two, using reason or prestige to support an argument, or affiliating with a new reference group are crucial for developing new attitudes (cf. Hovland, Janis, and Kelley, 1953). Despite the fact that many of these variables seem limited in application to the learning situation in which they were studied, we have tried to make use of information from all these sources in designing our "motive acquisition" program and in finding support for the general propositions that have emerged from our study so far. For our purpose has been above all to produce an effect large enough to be measured. Thus, we have tried to profit by all that is known about how to facilitate learning or produce personality or attitude change. For, if we could not obtain a substantial effect with all factors working to produce it, there would be no point to studying the effects of each factor taken one at a time. Such a strategy also has the practical advantage that we are in the position of doing our best to "deliver the goods" to our course participants since they were giving us their time and attention to take part in a largely untried educational experience.[1]

Our over-all research strategy, therefore, is "subtractive" rather than "additive." After we have demonstrated a substantial effect with some 10–12 factors working to produce it, our plan is to subtract that part of the program that deals with each of the factors to discover if there is a significant decline in the effect. It should also be possible to omit several factors in various combinations to get at interactional effects. This will obviously require giving a fairly large number of courses in a standard institutional setting for the same kinds of businessmen with follow-up evaluation of their performance extending over a number of years. So obviously it will be some time before each of the factors incorporated into the propositions which follow

---

1. Parenthetically, we have found several times that our stated desire to evaluate the effectiveness of our course created doubts in the minds of our sponsors that they did not feel about many popular courses for managers that no one has ever evaluated or plans to evaluate. An attitude of inquiry is not always an asset in education. It suggests one is not sure of his ground.

can be properly evaluated so far as its effect on producing motive change is concerned.

The over-all research strategy also determined the way the attempts to develop the achievement motive have been organized. That is to say, in order to process enough subjects to permit testing the effectiveness of various "inputs" in a reasonable number of years, the training had to be both of *short duration* (lasting 1–3 weeks) and *designed for groups* rather than for individuals as in person-to-person counseling. Fortunately these requirements coincide with normal practice in providing short courses for business executives. To conform further with that practice, the training has usually also been *residential* and *voluntary.* The design problems introduced by the last characteristic we have tried to handle in the usual ways by putting half the volunteers on a waiting list or giving them a different, technique-oriented course, etc. So far we have given the course to develop n Achievement in some form or another some eight times to over 140 managers or teachers of management in groups of 9–25 in the United States, Mexico, and India. For the most part the course has been offered by a group of 2–4 consultant psychologists either to executives in a single company as a company training program, or to executives from several different companies as a self-improvement program, or as part of the program of an institute or school devoted to training managers. The theoretical propositions which follow have evolved gradually from these pilot attempts to be effective in developing n Achievement among businessmen of various cultural backgrounds.

The first step in a motive development program is to create confidence that it will work. Our initial efforts in this area were dictated by the simple practical consideration that we had to "sell" our course or nobody would take it. We were not in the position of an animal psychologist who can order a dozen rats, or an academic psychologist who has captive subjects in his classes, or even a psychotherapist who has sick people knocking at his door every day. So we explained to all who would listen that we had every reason to believe from previous research that high n Achievement is related to effective entrepreneurship and that therefore business executives could expect to profit from taking a course designed to understand and develop this important human characteristic. What started as a necessity led to the first proposition dealing with how to bring about motive change.

Proposition 1. The more reasons an individual has in advance to believe that he can, will, or should develop a motive, the more educational attempts designed to develop that motive are likely to succeed. The empirical support for this proposition from other studies is quite impressive. It consists of (*a*) the prestige-suggestion studies showing that people will believe or do what prestigeful sources suggest (cf. Hovland *et al.,* 1953); (*b*) the so-called "Hawthorne effect" showing that people who feel they are especially selected to show an effect will tend to show it (Roethlisberger and Dickson, 1947); (*c*) the "Hello-Goodbye" effect in psychotherapy showing that patients who merely have contact with a prestigeful medical authority improve significantly over waiting list controls and almost as much as those who get prolonged therapy (Frank, 1961); (*d*) the "experimenter bias" studies which show that subjects will often do what an experimenter wants them to do, even though neither he nor they know he is trying to influence them (Rosenthal, 1963); (*e*) the goal-setting studies which show that setting goals for a person particularly in the name of prestigeful authorities like "science" or "research" improves performance (Kausler, 1959; Mierke, 1955); (*f*) the parent-child interaction studies which show that parents who set higher standards of excellence for their sons are more likely to have sons with high n Achievement (Rosen and D'Andrade, 1959). The common factor in all these studies seems to be that goals are being set for the individual by sources he respects—goals which imply that his behavior should change for a variety of reasons and that it *can* change. In common-sense terms, belief in the possibility and desirability of change are tremendously influential in changing a person.

So we have used a variety of means to create this belief: the authority of research findings on the relationship of n Achievement to entrepreneurial success, the suggestive power of membership in an experimental group designed to show an effect, the prestige of a great university, our own genuine enthusiasm for the course and our conviction that it would work, as expressed privately and in public speeches. In short, we were trying to make every use possible of what is sometimes regarded as an "error" in such research—namely, the Hawthorne effect, experimenter bias, etc., because we believe it to be one of the most powerful sources of change.

Why? What is the effect on the person, theoretically speaking, of all this goal setting for him? Its primary function is probably to arouse what exists of an associative network in the achievement area for each person affected. That is, many studies have shown that talk of achievement or affiliation or power tends to increase the frequency with which individuals think about achievement or affiliation or power (cf. Atkinson, 1958). And the stronger the talk, the more the relevant associative networks are aroused (McClelland *et al.*, 1953). Such an arousal has several possible effects which would facilitate learning: (*a*) It elicits what exists in the person of a "response" thus making it easier to strengthen that response in subsequent learning. (*b*) It creates a discrepancy between a goal (a "Soll-lage" in Heckhausen's (1963) theory of motivation) and a present state ("Ist-lage") which represents a cognitive dissonance the person tries to reduce (cf. Festinger, 1957); in common-sense terms he has an image clearly presented to him of something he is not but should be. (*c*) It tends to block out by simple interference other associations which would inhibit change—such as, "I'm too old to learn," "I never learned much from going to school anyway," "What do these academics know about everyday life?" or "I hope they don't get personal about all this."

After the course has been "sold" sufficiently to get a group together for training, the first step in the course itself is to present the research findings in some detail on exactly how n Achievement is related to certain types of successful entrepreneurial performance. That is, the argument of *The Achieving Society* (McClelland, 1961) is presented carefully with tables, charts, and diagrams, usually in lecture form at the outset and with the help of an educational TV film entitled *The Need to Achieve*. This is followed by discussion to clear up any ambiguities that remain in their minds as far as the central argument is concerned. It is especially necessary to stress that not all high achievement is caused by high n Achievement—that we have no evidence that high n Achievement is an essential ingredient in success as a research scientist, professional, accountant, office or personnel manager, etc.; that, on the contrary, it seems rather narrowly related to entrepreneurial, sales, or promotional success, and therefore should be of particular interest to them because they hold jobs which either have or could have an entrepreneurial component. We rationalize this activity in terms of the following proposition.

Proposition 2. The more an individual perceives that developing a motive is consistent with the demands of reality (and reason), the more educational attempts designed to develop that motive are likely to succeed. In a century in which psychologists and social theorists have been impressed by the power of unreason, it is well to remember that research has shown that rational arguments do sway opinions, particularly among the doubtful or the uncommitted (cf. Hovland *et al.*, 1953). Reality in the form of legal, military, or housing rules does modify white prejudice against Negroes (cf. Berelson and Steiner, 1964, p. 512). In being surprised at Asch's discovery that many people will go along with a group in calling a shorter line longer than it is, we sometimes forget that under most conditions their judgments conform with reality. The associative network which organizes "reality"—which places the person correctly in time, place, space, family, job, etc.—is one of the most dominant in the personality. It is the last to go in psychosis. It should be of great assistance to tie any proposed change in an associative network in with this dominant schema in such a way as to make the change consistent with reality demands or *"reasonable"* extensions of them. The word "reasonable" here simply means extensions arrived at by the thought processes of proof, logic, etc., which in adults have achieved a certain dominance of their own.

The next step in the course is to teach the participants the n Achievement coding system. By this time, they are a little confused anyway as to exactly what we mean by the term. So we tell them they can find out for themselves by learning to code stories written by others or by themselves. They take the test for n Achievement before this session and then find out what their own score is by scoring this record. However, we point out that if they think their score is too low, that can be easily remedied, since we teach them how to code and how to write stories saturated with n Achievement; in fact, that is one of the basic purposes of the course: to teach them to think constantly in n Achievement terms. Another aspect of the learning is discriminating achievement thinking from thinking in terms of power or affiliation. So usually the elements of these other two coding schemes are also taught.

Proposition 3. The more thoroughly an individual develops and clearly conceptualizes the associative network defining the motive, the more likely he is to develop the motive. The original empirical support for this proposition came from the radical behaviorist Skinnerian viewpoint: If the associative responses are the motive (by definition), to strengthen them one should elicit them and reinforce them, as one would shape up any response by reinforcement (cf. Skinner, 1953). But, support for this proposition also derives from other sources, particularly the "set" experiments. For decades laboratory psychologists have known that one of the easiest and most effective ways to change behavior is to change the subject's set. If he is responding to stimulus words with the names of animals, tell him to respond with the names of vegetables, or with words meaning the opposite, and he changes his behavior immediately and efficiently without a mistake. At a more complex level Orne (1962) had pointed out how powerful a set like "This is an experiment" can be. He points out that if you were to go up to a stranger and say something like "Lie down!" he would in all probability either laugh or escape as soon as possible. But, if you say "This is an experiment! Lie down!" more often than not, if there are other supporting cues, the person will do so. Orne has demonstrated how subjects will perform nonsensical and fatiguing tasks for very long periods of time under the set that "This is an experiment." At an even more complex level, sociologists have demonstrated often how quickly a person will change his behavior as he adopts a new role set (as a parent, a teacher, a public official, etc.). In all these cases an associative network exists, usually with a label conveniently attached which we call set and which, when it is aroused or becomes salient, proceeds to control behavior very effectively. The purpose of this part of our course is to give the subjects a set or a carefully worked out associative network with appropriate words or labels to describe all its various aspects (the coding labels for parts of the n Achievement scoring system like Ga$^+$, I$^+$, etc.; cf. Atkinson, 1958). The power of words in controlling behavior has also been well documented (cf. Brown, 1958).

It is important to stress that it is not just the label (n Achievement) which is taught. The person must be able to produce easily and often the new associative network itself. It is here that our research comes closest to traditional therapy which could be understood as the prolonged and laborious formation of new associative networks to replace anxiety-laden ones. That is, the person over time comes to form a new associative network covering his relations, for example, to his father and mother, which still later he may label an "unresolved Oedipus complex." When cues arise that formerly would have produced anxiety-laden associations, they now evoke this new complex instead, blocking out the "bad" associations by associative interference. But all therapists, whether Freudian or Rogerian, insist that the person must learn to produce these associations in their new form, that teaching the label is not enough. In fact, this is probably why so-called directive therapy is ineffective: It tries to substitute new constructs ("You should become an achiever") for old neurotic or ineffective ones ("rather than being such a slob") without changing the associative networks which underlie these surface labels. A change in set such as "Respond with names of vegetables" will not work unless the person has a whole associative network which defines the meaning of the set. The relation of this argument is obvious both to Kelly's (1955) insistence on the importance of personal constructs and to the general semanticists' complaints about the neurotic efforts of mislabeling or overabstraction (Korzybski, 1941).

But, theoretically speaking, why should a change in set as an associative network be so influential in controlling thought and action? The explanation lies in part in its symbolic character. Learned acts have limited influence because they often depend on reality supports (as in typewriting), but learned thoughts (symbolic acts) can occur any time, any place, in any connection, and be applied to whatever the person is doing. They are more generalizable. Acts can also be inhibited more easily than thoughts. Isak Dinesen tells the story of the oracle who told the king he would get his wish so long as he never thought of the left eye of a camel. Needless to say, the king did not get his wish, but he could easily have obeyed her prohibition if it had been to avoid *looking* at the left eye of a camel. Thoughts once acquired gain more control over thoughts and actions than acquired acts do because they are harder to inhibit. But why do they gain control over actions? Are not thoughts substitutes for actions? Cannot a man learn to think achievement thoughts and still not act like an achiever in any way? The question is taken up again under the next proposition, but it is well to remember here that thoughts are symbolic acts and that practice of symbolic acts facilitates performing the real acts (cf. Hovland, 1951, p. 644).

The next step in the course is to tie thought to action. Research has shown that individuals high in n Achievement tend to act in certain ways. For example, they prefer work situations where there is a challenge (moderate risk), concrete feedback on how well they are doing, and opportunity to take personal responsibility for achieving the work goals. The participants in the course are therefore introduced to a "work" situation in the form of a business game in which they will have an opportunity to show these characteristics in action or more specifically to develop them through practice and through observing others play it. The game is designed to mimic real life: They must order parts to make certain objects (e.g., a Tinker Toy model bridge) after having estimated how many they think they can construct in the time allotted. They have a real chance to take over, plan the whole game, learn from how well they are doing (use of feedback), and show a paper profit or loss at the end. While they are surprised often that they should have to display their real action characteristics in this way in public, they usually get emotionally involved in observing how they behave under pressure of a more or less "real" work situation.

Proposition 4. The more an individual can link the newly developed network to related actions, the more the change in both thought and action is likely to occur and endure. The evidence for the importance of action for producing change consists of such diverse findings as (*a*) the importance of recitation for human learning, (*b*) the repeated finding that overt commitment and participation in action changes attitudes effectively (cf. Berelson and Steiner, 1964, p. 576), and (*c*) early studies by Carr (cf. McGeoch and Irion, 1952) showing that simply to expose an organism to what is to be learned (e.g., trundling a rat through a maze) is nowhere near as effective as letting him explore it for himself in action.

Theoretically, the action is represented in the associative network by what associations precede, accompany, and follow it. So including the acts in what is learned *enlarges* the associative network or the achievement construct to include action. Thus, the number of cues likely to trip off the n Achievement network is increased. In common-sense terms, whenever he works he now evaluates what he is doing in achievement terms, and whenever he thinks about achievement he tends to think of its action consequences.

So far the course instruction has remained fairly abstract and removed from the everyday experiences of businessmen. So, the next step is to apply what has been learned to everyday business activities through the medium of the well-known case-study method popularized by the Harvard Business School. Actual examples of the development of the careers or firms of business leaders or entrepreneurs are written up in disguised form and assigned for discussion to the participants. Ordinarily, the instructor is not interested in illustrating "good" or "bad" managerial behavior— that is left to participants to discuss—but in our use of the material, we do try to label the various types of behavior as illustrating either n Achievement and various aspects of the achievement sequence (instrumental activity, blocks, etc.), or n Power, n Affiliation, etc. The participants are also encouraged to bring in examples of managerial behavior from their own experience to evaluate in motivational terms.

Proposition 5. The more an individual can link the newly conceptualized association-action complex (or motive) to events in his everyday life, the more likely the motive complex is to influence his thoughts and actions in situations outside the training experience. The transfer-of-training research literature is not very explicit on this point, though it seems self-evident. Certainly, this is the proposition that underlies the practice of most therapy when it involves working through or clarifying, usually in terms of a new, partially formed construct system, old memories, events from the last 24 hours, dreams, and hopes of the future. Again, theoretically, this should serve to enlarge and clarify the associative network and increase the number of cues in everyday life which will rearouse it. The principle of symbolic practice can also be invoked to support its effectiveness in promoting transfer outside the learning experience.

For some time most course participants have been wondering what all this has to do with them personally. That is to say, the material is introduced originally on a "take it or leave it" objective basis as something that ought to be of interest to them. But, sooner or later, they must confront the issue as to what meaning n Achievement has in their own personal lives. We do not force this choice on them nor do we think we are brain-washing them to believe in n Achievement. We believe and we tell them we believe in the "obstinate audience" (cf. Bauer, 1964), in the ultimate capacity of people to resist persuasion or to do in the end what they really want to do. In fact, we had one case in an early session of a man who at this point decided he was not an achievement-minded person and did not want to become one. He subsequently retired and became a chicken farmer to the relief of the business in which he had been an ineffective manager. We respected that decision and mention it in the course as a good example of honest self-evaluation. Nevertheless, we do provide them with all kinds of information as to their own achievement-related behavior in the fantasy tests, in the business game, in occasional group dynamics session—and ample opportunity and encouragement to think through what this information implies so far as their self-concept is concerned and their responsibilities to their jobs. Various devices such as the "Who am I?" test, silent group meditation, or individual counseling have been introduced to facilitate this self-confrontation.

Proposition 6. The more an individual can perceive and experience the newly conceptualized motive as an improvement in the self-image, the more the motive is likely to influence his future thoughts and actions. Evidence on the importance of the ego or the self-image in controlling behavior has been summarized by Allport (1943). In recent years, Rogers and his group (Rogers, 1961; Rogers and Dymond, 1954) have measured improvement in psychotherapy largely in terms of improvement of the self-concept in relation to the ideal self. Indirect evidence of the importance of the self-schema comes from the discussion over whether a person can be made to do things under hypnosis that are inconsistent with his self-concept or values. All investigators agree that the hypnotist can be most successful in getting the subject to do what might normally be a disapproved action if he makes the subject perceive the action as consistent with his self-image or values (cf. Berelson and Steiner, 1963, p. 124).

The same logic supports this proposition. It seems unlikely that a newly formed associative network like n Achievement could persist and influence behavior much unless it had somehow "come to terms" with the pervasive superordinate network of associations defining the self. The logic is the same as for Proposition 2 dealing with the reality construct system. The n Achievement associations must come to be experienced as related to or consistent with the ideal self-image; otherwise associations from the self-system will constantly block thoughts of achievement. The person might be thinking, for example: "I am not that kind of person; achievement means judging people in terms of how well they perform and I don't like to hurt people's feelings."

Closely allied to the self-system is a whole series of networks only half conscious (i.e., correctly labeled) summarizing the values by which the person lives which derive from his culture and social milieu. These values can also interefere if they are inconsistent with n Achievement as a newly acquired way of thinking. Therefore, it has been customary at this point in the course to introduce a value analysis of the participants' culture based on an analysis of children's stories, myths, popular religion, comparative attitude surveys, customs, etc., more or less in line with traditional, cultural anthropological practice (cf. Benedict, 1946; McClelland, 1964). For example, in America we have to work through the problem of how being achievement oriented seems to interfere with being popular or liked by others which is highly valued by Americans. In Mexico a central issue is the highly valued "male dominance" pattern reflected in the patriarchal family and in the *macho* complex (being extremely masculine). Since data show that dominant fathers have sons with low n Achievement and authoritarian bosses do not encourage n Achievement in their top executives (Andrews, 1965), there is obviously a problem here to be worked through if n Achievement is to survive among thoughts centered on dominance. The problem is not only rationally discussed. It is acted out in role-playing sessions where Mexicans try, and often to their own surprise fail, to act like the democratic father with high standards in the classic Rosen and D'Andrade (1959) study on parental behavior which develops high n Achievement. Any technique is used which will serve to draw attention to possible conflicts between n Achievement and popular or traditional cultural values. In the end it may come to discussing parts of the *Bhagavad Gita* in India, or the *Koran* in Arab countries, that seem to oppose achievement striving or entrepreneurial behavior.

Proposition 7. The more an individual can perceive and experience the newly conceptualized motive as an improvement on prevailing cultural values, the more the motive is likely to influence his future thoughts and actions. The cultural anthropologists for years have argued how important it is to understand one's own cultural values to overcome prejudices, adopt more flexible attitudes, etc., but there is little hard evidence that doing so changes a person's behavior. What exists comes indirectly from studies that show prejudice can be decreased a little by information about ethnic groups (Berelson and Steiner, 1963, p. 517), or that repeatedly show an unconscious link between attitudes and the reference group (or subculture) to which one belongs—a link which presumably can be broken more easily by full information about it, especially when coupled with role-playing new attitudes (cf. Berelson and Steiner, 1963, pp. 566 ff.).

The theoretical explanation of this presumed effect is the same as for Propositions 2 and 6. The newly learned associative complex to influence thought and action effectively must somehow be adjusted to three superordinate networks that may set off regularly interfering associations— namely, the networks associated with reality, the self, and the social reference group or subculture.

The course normally ends with each participant preparing a written document outlining his goals and life plans for the next 2 years. These plans may or may not include references to the achievement motive; they can be very tentative, but they are supposed to be quite specific and realistic; that is to say, they should represent moderate levels of aspiration following the practice established in learning about n Achievement of choosing the moderately risky or challenging alternative. The purpose of this document is in part to formulate for oneself the practical implications of the course before leaving it, but even more to provide a basis for the evaluation of their progress in the months after the course. For it is explained to the participants that they are to regard themselves as "in training" for the next 2 years, that 10-14 days is obviously too short a time to do more than conceive a new way of life: It represents the residential portion of the training only. Our role over the next 2 years will be to remind them every 6 months of the tasks they have set themselves by sending them a questionnaire to fill out which will serve to rearouse many of the issues discussed in the course and to give them information on how far they have progressed toward achieving their goals.

Proposition 8. The more an individual commits himself to achieving concrete goals in life related to the newly formed motive, the more the motive is likely to influence his future thoughts and actions.

Proposition 9. The more an individual keeps a record of his progress toward achieving goals to which he is committed, the more the newly formed motive is likely to influence his future thoughts and actions. These propositions are both related to what was called "pacing" in early studies of the psychology of work. That is, committing oneself to a specific goal and then comparing one's performance to that goal has been found to facilitate learning (cf. Kausler, 1959), though most studies of levels of aspiration have dealt with goal setting as a result rather than as a "cause" of performance. At any rate, the beneficial effect of concrete feedback on learning has been amply demonstrated by psychologists from Thorndike to Skinner. Among humans the feedback on performance is especially effective if they have high n Achievement (French, 1958), a fact which makes the relevance of our request for feedback obvious to the course participants.

The theoretical justification for these propositions is that in this way we are managing to keep the newly acquired associative network salient over the next two years. We are providing cues that will regularly rearouse it since he knows he is still part of an experimental training group which is supposed to show a certain type of behavior (Proposition 1 again). If the complex is rearoused sufficiently often back in the real world, we believe it is more likely to influence thought and action than if it is not aroused.

As described so far the course appears to be devoted almost wholly to cognitive learning. Yet this is only part of the story. The "teachers" are all clinically-oriented psychologists who also try to practice whatever has been learned about the type of human relationship that most facilitates emotional learning. Both for practical and theoretical reasons this relationship is structured as warm, honest, and nonevaluative, somewhat in the manner described by Rogers (1961) and recommended by distinguished therapists from St. Ignatius[2] to Freud. That is to say, we insist that the only kind of change that can last or mean anything is what the person decides on and works out by himself, that we are there not to criticize his past behavior or direct his future choices, but to provide him with all sorts of information and emotional support that will help him in his self-confrontation. Since we recognize that self-study may be quite difficult and unsettling, we try to create an optimistic relaxed atmosphere in which the person is warmly encouraged in his efforts and given the opportunity for personal counseling if he asks for it.

Proposition 10. Changes in motives are more likely to occur in an interpersonal atmosphere in which the individual feels warmly but honestly supported and respected by others as a person capable of guiding and directing his own future behavior. Despite the widespread belief in this proposition among therapists (except for operant conditioners), one of the few studies that directly supports it has been conducted by Ends and Page (1957) who found that an objective learning-theory approach was less successful in treating chronic alcoholics than a person-oriented, client-centered approach. Rogers (1961) also summarizes other evidence that therapists who are warmer, more empathic, and genuine are more successful in their work. Hovland *et al.* (1953) report that the less manipulative the intent of a communicator, the greater the tendency to accept his conclusions. There is also the direct evidence that parents of boys with high n Achievement are warmer, more encouraging and less directive (fathers only) than parents of boys with low n Achievement (Rosen and D'Andrade, 1959). We tried to model ourselves after those parents on the theory that what is associated with high n Achievement in children might be most likely to

2. In his famous spiritual exercises which have played a key role in producing and sustaining personality change in the Jesuit Order, St. Ignatius states: "The director of the Exercizes ought not to urge the exercitant more to poverty or any promise than to the contrary, nor to one state of life or way of living more than another . . . [while it is proper to urge people outside the Exercizes] the director of the Exercizes . . . without leaning to one side or the other, should permit the Creator to deal directly with the creature, and the creature directly with his Creator and Lord."

encourage its development in adulthood. This does not mean permissiveness or promiscuous reinforcement of all kinds of behavior; it also means setting high standards as the parents of the boys with high n Achievement did but having the relaxed faith that the participants can achieve them.

The theoretical justification for this proposition can take two lines: Either one argues that this degree of challenge to the self-schema produces anxiety which needs to be reduced by warm support of the person for effective learning to take place, or one interprets the warmth as a form of direct reinforcement for change following the operant-conditioning model. Perhaps both factors are operating. Certainly there is ample evidence to support the view that anxiety interferes with learning (cf. Sarason, 1960) and that reward shapes behavior (cf. Bandura and Walters, 1963, pp. 283 ff.).

One other characteristic of the course leads to two further propositions. Efforts are made so far as possible to define it as an "experience apart," "an opportunity for self-study," or even a "spiritual retreat" (though that term can be used more acceptably in India than in the United States). So far as possible it is held in an isolated resort hotel or a hostel where there will be few distractions from the outside world and few other guests. This permits an atmosphere of total concentration on the objectives of the course including much informal talk outside the sessions about Ga^+, Ga^-, I^+, and other categories in the coding definition. It still comes as a surprise to us to hear these terms suddenly in an informal group of participants talking away in Spanish or Telugu. The effect of this retreat from everyday life into a special and specially labeled experience appears to be twofold: It dramatizes or increases the salience of the new associative network and it tends to create a new reference group.

Proposition 11. Changes in motives are more likely to occur the more the setting dramatizes the importance of self-study and lifts it out of the routine of everyday life. So far as we know there is no scientific evidence to support this proposition, though again if one regards Jesuits as successful examples of personality change, the Order has frequently followed the advice of St. Ignatius to the effect that "the progress made in the Exercizes will be greater, the more the exercitant withdraws from all friends and acquaintances, and from all worldly cares." Theory supports the proposition in two respects: Removing the person from everyday routine (*a*) should decrease interfering associations (to say nothing of interfering appointments and social obligations), and (*b*) should heighten the salience of the experience by contrast with everyday life and make it harder to handle with the usual defenses ("just one more course," etc.). That is to say, the network of achievement-related associations can be more strongly and distinctly aroused in contrast to everyday life, making cognitive dissonance greater and therefore more in need of reduction by new learning. By the same token we have found that the dramatic quality of the experience cannot be sustained very long in a 12–18-hour-a-day schedule without a new routine attitude developing. Thus, we have found that a period somewhere between 6 to 14 days is optimal for this kind of "spiritual retreat." St. Ignatius sets an outside limit of 30 days, but this is when the schedule is less intensive (as ours has sometimes been), consisting of only a few hours a day over a longer period.

Proposition 12. *Changes in motives are more likely to occur and persist if the new motive is a sign of membership in a new reference group.* No principle of change has stronger empirical or historical support than this one. Endless studies have shown that people's opinions, attitudes, and beliefs are a function of their reference group and that different attitudes are likely to arise and be sustained primarily when the person moves into or affiliates with a new reference group (cf. Berelson and Steiner, 1963, pp. 580 ff.). Many theorists argue that the success of groups like Alcoholics Anonymous depends on the effectiveness with which the group is organized so that each person demonstrates his membership in it by "saving" another alcoholic. Political experience has demonstrated that membership in small groups like Communist or Nazi Party cells is one of the most effective ways to sustain changed attitudes and behavior.

Our course attempts to achieve this result (*a*) by the group experience in isolation—creating the feeling of alumni who all went through it together; (*b*) by certain signs of identification with the group, particularly the language of the coding system, but also including a certificate of membership; and (*c*) by arranging where possible to have participants come from the same community so that they can form a "cell" when they return that will serve as an immediate reference group to prevent gradual undermining of the new network by other pressures.

In theoretical terms a reference group should be effective because its members constantly provide cues to each other to rearouse the associative network, because they will also reward each other for achievement-related thoughts and acts, and because this constant mutual stimulation, and reinforcement, plus the labeling of the group, will prevent assimilation of the network to bigger, older, and stronger networks (such as those associated with traditional cultural values).

In summary, we have described an influence process which may be conceived in terms of "input," "intervening," and "output" variables as in Table 1. The propositions relate variables in Column A via their effect on the intervening variables in Column B to as yet loosely specified behavior in Column C, which may be taken as evidence that "development" of n Achievement has "really" taken place. The problems involved in evaluation of effects are as great and as complicated as those involved in designing the treatment, but they cannot be spelled out here, partly for lack of space, partly because we are in an even earlier stage of examining and classifying the effects of our training 1 and 2 years later preparatory to conceptualizing more clearly what happens. It will have to suffice to point out that we plan

Table 1

VARIABLES CONCEIVED AS ENTERING INTO THE MOTIVE
CHANGE PROCESS

A INPUT OR INDEPENDENT VARIABLES	B INTERVENING VARIABLES	C OUTPUT OR DEPENDENT VARIABLES
1. Goal setting for the person (P1, P11)	Arousal of associative network (salience)	Duration and/or extensiveness of changes in:
2. Acquisition of n Achievement associative network (P2, P3, P4, P5)	Experiencing and labeling the associative network	1. n Achievement associative network
3. Relating new network to superordinate networks	Variety of cues to which network is linked	2. Related actions: use of feedback, moderate risk taking, etc.
reality (P2)		3. Innovations (job improvements)
the self (P6)	Interfering associations assimilated or by-passed by reproductive interference	4. Use of time and money
cultural values (P7)		5. Entrepreneurial success as defined by nature of job held and its rewards
4. Personal goal setting (P8)		
5. Knowledge of progress (P3, P4, P9)	Positive affect associated with network	
6. Personal warmth and support (P10)		
7. Support of reference group (P11, P12)		

Note: P1, P11, etc., refer to the numbered propositions in the text.

extensive comparisons over a 2-year period of the behaviors of our trained subjects compared with matched controls along the lines suggested in Column C.

What the table does is to give a brief over-all view of how we conceptualize the educational or treatment process. What is particularly important is that the propositions refer to *operationally defined* and *separable* treatment variables. Thus, after having demonstrated hopefully a large effect of the total program, we can subtract a variable and see how much that decreases the impact of the course. That is to say, the course is designed so that it could go ahead perfectly reasonably with very little advanced goal setting (P1), with an objective rather than a warm personal atmosphere (P11), without the business game tying thought to action (P9), without learning to code n Achievement and write achievement-related stories (P3), without cultural value analysis (P7), or an isolated residential setting (P1, P11, P12). The study units are designed in a way that they can be omitted without destroying the viability of the treatment, which has never been true of other studies of the psychotherapeutic process (cf. Rogers and Dymond, 1954).

But is there any basis for thinking the program works in practice? As yet, not enough time has elapsed to enable us to collect much data on long-term changes in personality and business activity. However, we do know that businessmen can learn to write stories scoring high in n Achievement, that they retain this skill over 1 year or 2, and that they like the course—but the same kinds of things can be said about many unevaluated management training courses. In two instances we have more objective data. Three courses were given to some 34 men from the Bombay area in early 1963. It proved possible to develop a crude but objective and reliable coding system to record whether each one had shown *unusual* entrepreneurial activity in the 2 years prior to the course or in the 2 years after course. "Unusual" here means essentially an unusual promotion or salary raise or starting a new business venture of some kind. Of the 30 on whom information was available in 1965, 27% had been unusually active before the course, 67% after the course ($x^2 = 11.2, p < .01$). In a control group chosen at random from those who applied for the course in 1963, out of 11 on whom information has so far been obtained, 18% were active before 1963, 27% since 1963.

In a second case, four courses were given throughout 1964 to a total of 52 small businessmen from the small city of Kakinda in Andhra Pradesh, India. Of these men, 25% had been unusually active in the 2-year period before the course, and 65% were unusually active immediately afterwards ($x^2 = 17.1, p < .01$). More control data and more refined measures are needed, but it looks very much as if, in India at least, we will be dealing with a spontaneous "activation" rate of only 25%–35% among entrepreneurs. Thus, we have a distinct advantage over psychotherapists who are trying to demonstrate an improvement over a two-thirds spontaneous recovery rate. Our own data suggest that we will be unlikely to get an improvement or "activation" rate much above the two-thirds level commonly reported in therapy studies. That is, about one-third of the people in our courses have remained relatively unaffected. Nevertheless the two-thirds activated after the course represent a doubling of the normal rate of unusual entrepreneurial activity—no mean achievement in the light of the current pessimism among psychologists as to their ability to induce lasting personality change among adults.

One case will illustrate how the course seems to affect people in practice. A short time after participating in one of our courses in India, a 47-year-old businessman rather suddenly and dramatically decided to quit his excellent job and go into the construction business on his own in a big way. A man with some means of his own, he had had a very successful career as employee-relations manager for a large oil firm. His job involved adjusting management-employee difficulties, negotiating union contracts. etc. He was well-to-do, well thought of in his company, and admired in the community, but he was restless because he found his job increasingly boring. At the time of the course his original n Achievement score was not very high and he was thinking of retiring and living in England where his son was studying. In an interview, 8 months later, he said the course had served not so much to "motivate" him but to "crystallize" a lot of ideas he had vaguely or half consciously picked up about work and achievement all through his life. It provided him with a new language (he still talked in terms of standards of excellence, blocks, moderate risk, goal anticipation, etc.), a new construct which served to organize those ideas and explain to him why he was bored with his job, despite his obvious success. He decided he wanted to be an n-Achievement-oriented person, that he would be unhappy in retirement, and that he should take a risk, quit his job, and start in business on his own. He acted on his decision and in 6 months had drawn plans and raised over $1,000,000 to build the tallest building in his large city to be called the "Everest Apartments." He is extremely happy in his new activity because it means selling, promoting, trying to wangle scarce materials, etc. His first building is partway up and he is planning two more.

Even a case as dramatic as this one does not prove that the course produced the effect, despite his repeated use of the constructs he had learned, but what is especially interesting about it is that he described what had happened to him in exactly the terms the theory requires. He spoke not about a new motive force but about how existing ideas had been crystallized into a new associate network, and it is this new network which *is* the new "motivating" force according to the theory.

How generalizable are the propositions? They have purposely been stated generally so that some term like "attitude" or "personality characteristic" could be substituted for the term "motive" throughout, because we believe the propositions will hold for other personality variables. In fact, most of the supporting experimental evidence cited comes from attempts to change other characteristics. Nevertheless, the propositions should hold best more narrowly for motives and especially the achievement motive. One of the biggest difficulties in the way of testing them more generally is that not nearly as much is known about other human characteristics or their specific relevance for success in a certain type of work. For example, next to nothing is known about the need for power, its relation to success, let us say, in politics or bargaining situations, and its origins and course of development in the life history of individuals. It is precisely the knowledge we have about such matters for the achievement motive that puts us in a position to shape it for limited, socially and individually desirable ends. In the future, it seems to us, research in psychotherapy ought to follow a similar course. That is to say, rather than developing "all-purpose" treatments, good for any person and any purpose, it should aim to develop specific treatments or educational programs built on laboriously accumulated detailed knowledge of the characteristic to be changed. It is in this spirit that the present research program in motive acquisition has been designed and is being tested out.

References

ALLPORT, G. W.   The ego in contemporary psychology. *Psychological Review,* 1943, 50, 451-478.

ANDREWS, J. D. W.   The achievement motive in two types of organizations. *Journal of Personality and Social Psychology,* 1965, in press.

ATKINSON, J. W. (Ed.)   *Motives in fantasy, action and society.* Princeton, N.J.: Van Nostrand, 1958.

BANDURA, A. and WALTERS, R. H.   *Social learning and personality development.* New York: Holt, Rinehart & Winston, 1963.

BAUER, R. A.   The obstinate audience: The influence process from the point of view of social communication. *American Psychologist,* 1964, 19, 319-329.

BENEDICT, RUTH.   *The chrysanthemum and the sword.* Boston: Houghton Mifflin, 1946.

BERELSON, B. and STEINER, G. A.   *Human behavior: An inventory of scientific findings.* New York: Harcourt, Brace, 1964.

BROWN, R. W.   *Words and things.* Glencoe, Ill.: Free Press, 1958.

BURRIS, R. W.   The effect of counseling on achievement motivation. Unpublished doctoral dissertation, University of Indiana, 1958.

ENDS, E. J. and PAGE, C. W.   A study of three types of group psychotherapy with hospitalized male inebriates. *Quarterly Journal on Alcohol,* 1957, 18, 263-277.

EYSENCK, H. J.   The effects of psychotherapy: An evaluation. *Journal of Consulting Psychology,* 1952, 16, 319-324.

FESTINGER, L.   *A theory of cognitive dissonance.* New York: Harper and Row, 1957.

FRANK, J.   *Persuasion and healing.* Baltimore: Johns Hopkins Press, 1961.

FRENCH, E. G.   Effects of the interaction of motivation and feedback on task performance. In J. W. Atkinson (Ed.), *Motives in fantasy, action and society.* Princeton, N.J.: Van Nostrand, 1958. Pp. 400-408.

HECKHAUSEN, H.   Eine Rahmentheorie der Motivation in zehn Thesen. *Zeitschrift für experimentelle und angewandte Psychologie,* 1963, X/4, 604-626.

HOVLAND, C. I.   Human learning and retention. In S. S. Stevens (Ed.), *Handbook of experimental psychology.* New York: Wiley, 1951.

HOVLAND, C. I., JANIS, I. L. and KELLEY, H. H.   *Communication and persuasion: Psychological studies of opinion change.* New Haven: Yale University Press, 1953.

KAUSLER, D. H.   Aspiration level as a determinant of performance. *Journal of Personality,* 1959, 27, 346-351.

KELLY, G. A.   *The psychology of personal constructs.* New York: Norton, 1955.

KORZYBSKI, A.   *Science and sanity.* Lancaster, Pa.: Science Press, 1941.

McCLELLAND, D. C.   *The achieving society.* Princeton, N.J.: Van Nostrand, 1961.

McCLELLAND, D. C.   *The roots of consciousness.* Princeton, N.J.: Van Nostrand, 1964.

McCLELLAND, D. C., ATKINSON, J. W., CLARK, R. A. and LOWELL, E. L.   *The achievement motive.* New York: Appleton-Century, 1953.

McGEOCH, J. A. and IRION, A. L.   *The psychology of human learning.* (2nd ed.) New York: Longmans, Green, 1952.

MIERKE, K.   *Wille und Leistung.* Göttingen: Verlag für Psychologie, 1955.

ORNE, M.   On the social psychology of the psychological experiment: With particular reference to demand characteristics and their implications. *American Psychologist,* 1962, 17, 776-783.

ROETHLISBERGER, F. J. and DICKSON, W. J.   *Management and the worker.* Cambridge: Harvard University Press, 1947.

ROGERS, C. R.   *On becoming a person.* Boston: Houghton Mifflin, 1961.

ROGERS, C. R. and DYMOND, R. F. (Eds.)   *Psychotherapy and personality change.* Chicago: University of Chicago Press, 1954.

ROSEN, B. C. and D'ANDRADE, R. G.   The psychosocial origins of achievement motivation. *Sociometry,* 1959, 22, 185-218.

ROSENTHAL, R.   On the social psychology of the psychological experiment: The experimenter's hypothesis as unintended determinant of experimental results. *American Scientist,* 1963, 51, 268-283.

SARASON, I.   Empirical findings and theoretical problems in the use of anxiety scales. *Psychological Bulletin,* 1960, 57, 403-415.

SKINNER, B. F.   *Science and human behavior.* New York: Macmillan, 1953.

The actual findings in this study of a human relations workshop are not as important as the model it provides for educational evaluation. One might not expect an evaluation model to emerge from as "soft-headed" an enterprise as the T-group laboratory, but perhaps it is precisely because of the difficulties in this domain—defining outcomes, saying what the treatment is, and coping with all the social and personal factors conditioning the outcomes—that a highly comprehensive, systematic evaluation procedure did emerge from it.

In going through the article, the reader might ask himself how the various facets of Miles' procedure would translate into the common task of evaluating classroom practices and methods. Some facets would be part of any good evaluation—the use of pre- and post-measures, of experimental and control groups, and maybe even of extra groups to check the reactive effects of the pre-test. But other facets may raise questions about the conventional procedures and suggest improvements in them.

Classroom evaluation, of course, has the advantage of carefully developed, standardized achievement tests against which practices can be evaluated. But how much of an advantage is this? Achievement tests correspond to Miles' proximate criteria of short-run changes during training. What if anything corresponds to his more ultimate criteria? Even for the short run, the reader might ask whether achievement tests relate as directly to the objectives of particular educational practices as Miles' measures did to his objectives. Maybe they do, but it is also possible that the ubiquitous standardized tests have led educators to define purposes in terms of what the tests measure.

What do Miles' "treatment participation variables" translate to in the conventional curriculum evaluation? Nothing, as far as we know, but it seems reasonable that evidence on students' engagement in learning activities, or some other counterpart, could help explain outcomes (compare Kounin's ideas on learner commitment in this book). And what about Miles' elaborate ordering of predictor variables? It contains the rudiments, at least, of an explanatory system, and it enables us to analyze the differential effects of treatment on those exposed to it. Both are often missing in "hard-headed" educational evaluation.

Changes During and Following
Laboratory Training:

A Clinical Experimental Study*

Matthew B. Miles

Introduction

Research on any form of treatment is classically difficult, unrewarding, and infrequent. When the product of a process is change in persons, the criterion problem is ordinarily a major one, whether the treatment occupies the domain of education, mental health, or social functioning. Goals are vaguely stated (partly because of ignorance and partly, it has been suggested, to protect the practitioner against charges of malpractice). Often, it is claimed that "real" change may not be assessable until long after the treatment has occurred. Even if goals are precisely and operationally defined, treatment programs themselves are usually hard to describe accurately enough for later replication. Furthermore, test-treatment interaction is quite likely; subjects are easily sensitized by pre-measures. Even more crudely, it is frequently difficult to locate anything like a meaningful control group, let alone establish its equivalence. Finally, numbers are usually small, and the treatment population is often biased through self-selection.

Thus it is not surprising that perhaps 95 per cent of all treatment efforts go unstudied,[1] and that even the 5 per cent typically show serious defects in design, measurement, or data analysis stemming from insufficient attention to the problems alluded to above. And, methodological problems aside, most treatment studies have a central substantive weakness: being relatively atheoretical, they lead to no coherent additions to *either* science or practice. The variables presumed to *explain* the amounts of change in subjects are rarely specified, and change processes during treatment are hardly ever studied.

* From *Journal of Applied Behavioral Science*, 1965, 1 (3), 215-242. Used by permission of the author and publisher.

This report is based on research conducted by the author with Sanci K. Michael, Frederick L. Whitam, and Thomas M. Harris.

1. This is probably conservative. A recent study (Johnson, 1964) showed that only one-half of 1 per cent of over 1,500 NDEA grants made in a large state for experimental educational programs—grants which *required* evaluation—were evaluated in any systematic manner.

Yet these problems and dissatisfactions are not insuperable. The present study indicates some ways in which they can be realistically approached.[2] A population of persons, all occupying the same occupational role, was studied before, during, and after a particular form of treatment—a human relations training laboratory. Our aim was to assess precisely the contributions of personality, organizational press, and involvement in treatment processes to final outcome. Major effort was put into the development of sensitive, durable criterion measures. Carefully selected control groups were employed. Most basically, perhaps, we attempted the explanation of learning outcomes during training by specifying certain components of the treatment—variables thought to explain amounts and types of received change —within a reasonably systematic theoretical network. Finally, the attempt was made to exploit a small population intensively by the use of multiple measures and correlational methods.

The Study

Subjects

Thirty-four elementary school principals attending a two-week human relations training laboratory at Bethel, Maine, in the summer of 1958 were used as the experimental population. Two control groups were used: a matched-pair group nominated by the experimental participants, and a random group ($N = 148$) drawn from a national directory of principals. Comparisons across these groups, and with a national survey of elementary principals conducted by the NEA, indicated that the experimental group members, as might be expected from a self-selected population, had slightly more work experience, were more mobile, and had slightly more independence from their superiors, in comparison with samples of populations not appearing for training. The differences are not large, but the flavor, perhaps predictably, is one of "cosmopolitanism" rather than localism. Older women were also slightly overrepresented.

Procedure

Criterion measures for the experimental group and the two control groups included the following instruments (all administered to each participant *and* to an average of five of his associates on the job):

1. The Ohio State Leader Behavior Description Questionnaire, which measures "initiating structure" or task-oriented behavior, and "consideration" or warm socio-emotional behavior.

2. See also the thorough discussion of these problems, and inventive solutions to them, offered by Hyman, Wright, and Hopkins (1962), using survey methods. For reviews of research on human relations training specifically, see Stock (1964) and Buchanan (1964).

2. The Group Participation Scale, a peer nomination form originally developed by Pepinsky, Siegel, and Van Alta (1952) as a counseling criterion measure.
3. An open-end perceived change measure; as described below, this combined the perceptions of participant and job associates to get a kind of "verified change" score.

These were administered in a modified Solomon four-group design[3] prior to, three months after, and eight months after the laboratory. At the laboratory itself three additional criterion instruments were administered:

1. A performance test, administered early and late in the laboratory, in which randomly composed groups of participants carried out a discussion task, then filled out ratings and sociometric devices. Observer data were also collected.
2. Anchored trainer ratings, filled out early and late in the laboratory by the two different trainers who worked with the participant in his T-group and in an exercise group.
3. A self-perceived learning measure. Late in the laboratory, the participant was asked to list his learnings, then rate their clarity and relevance to his job on a semantic differential form, and indicate specific actions he felt he might carry out upon his return.

The three variables underlying these instruments were labeled *sensitivity* (perceptiveness re social phenomena), *diagnostic ability* (use of relevant, appropriate explanatory categories in assessing social behavior of self and others), and *action skill* (effective intervention in social situations). The initial number of criterion measurements for each participant was 38; combination and purification operations reduced this to six.

We approached the problem of prediction and explanation by hypothesizing that the learner's organizational position and situation, his personality, and his participation in learning processes during the laboratory would all be relevant to his net change on the criterion variables.

The organizational measures collected included:

1. Security, as measured by length of tenure in present job.
2. Power, as measured by number of teachers in the participant's school (of which he was the principal, it will be remembered).
3. Autonomy, as measured by length of time between required reports to immediate superior.
4. Perceived power, as measured by a Likert scale.
5. Perceived adequacy of organization's functioning, as measured by a Likert scale.

3.   In this design, half of the experimental group and half of the control group are given pre- and post-measures; the remaining halves receive post-only measures. This permits the assessment of changes caused (in effect) by the acts of filling out the instruments as such and separating of these from the actual effects of the treatment. See Campbell (1957) for a thorough discussion of this design, and others.

We expected these organization-level variables (*a*) to condition the strength of desire for change prior to the treatment and (*b*) to mediate or condition the degree to which laboratory-caused change would show up in the home organization afterward. Figures 1 and 2 indicate these predicted relationships graphically.

Heavy lines with arrows show predictions. Light lines show where significant (or near-significant) relationships were found, but without prediction. Figures by lines of both sorts are obtained correlations.

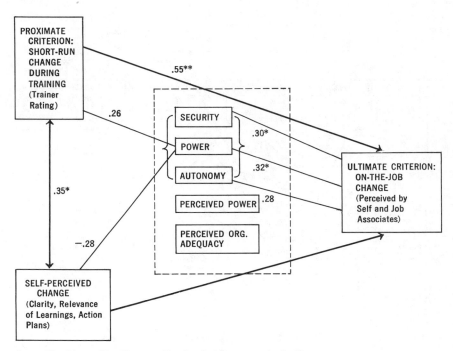

*p < .05   **p < .01   Figures without asterisks approach significance.

Figure 1.   Predicted and Obtained Relationships Among Criterion
Measures and Mediating Organizational Variables.

Participation (training-process) measures included:

1. Desire for change, as measured by participant ratings prior to coming to the laboratory, and a Likert scale administered early in the training period.
2. Unfreezing, or reduction of defensiveness. This too was measured by a Likert scale administered twice during the laboratory.
3. Involvement, or degree to which the participant became actively involved in the give-and-take of the T-group. This was measured by a trainer instrument in which behaviors were checked as being more or less characteristic of each participant.

4. Received feedback, as measured by an instrument in which the participant outlined the feedback he felt he had received during the preceding week of training, then rated its clarity, helpfulness, relevance, and pleasurableness on a semantic differential form.

Heavy lines with arrows show predictions. Light lines show where significant (or near-significant) relationships were found, but without prediction. Figures by lines of both sorts are obtained r's.

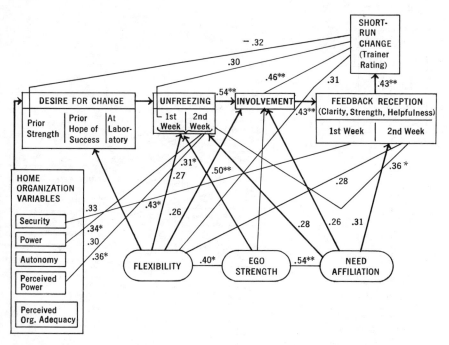

*p < .05   **p < .01   Figures without asterisks approach significance.

Figure 2.   Predicted and Obtained Relationships Among Organizational, Personality, Treatment Participation Variables, and Short-Run Change.

These predictor variables were expected to operate in a cumulative-sequential manner during the laboratory (see Figure 2).

The personality predictor variables measured were:

1. Ego strength, as measured by items from Barron's scale (restandardized by us for normal rather than clinical population).
2. Flexibility, as measured by Barron's Rigidity scale, reverse scored, and restandardized as above.
3. Need affiliation, as measured by French's Test of Insight, a sentence-completion form.

We did *not* expect these personality measures to predict improvement on the criterion measures directly; practical experience in training suggests rather clearly that people of a wide range of personality types can profit from laboratory training. In addition, back-home organization factors are likely to exert as much or more influence (as hypothesized above) on net changes on the job as do personality factors. Therefore, we predicted that the personality measures would relate mainly to the participant's scores on the *training-process* variables (see Figure 2). For example, a participant with high ego strength and high need affiliation would presumably be more likely to have a high received-feedback score.

A total of 41 predictor variables was measured for each participant; this was reduced to 19 via index construction.

Data reduction and analysis were primarily accomplished through zero-order, partial, and multiple correlation using the raw data and resulting indices; analysis of variance; and McQuitty-type cluster analysis.

Results

Criterion changes measured at the laboratory itself were examined via a multitrait-multimethod matrix, following Campbell and Fiske (1959). This method compared measures of the variables made on five different instruments (ratings by trainers and peers); we found that the three variables could not be successfully discriminated. Thus, a weighted "over-all effectiveness" score drawn from five different pre-post trainer ratings was used as the basic short-run change measure. Seventy-six per cent of the experimental group showed gain over the two weeks of the laboratory on this measure. These scores correlated .35 ($p < .05$) with the index of participant self-perceived learning.

The explanatory theory, as inspection of Figure 2 and Table 1 will indicate, was generally supported, with the exception of the first variable (desire for change) which, as measured before the laboratory, showed a negative relationship to gain. Ceiling effects and the apparent social desirability of professing a wish for change seemed to be at work.[4] Organizational factors, contrary to prediction, showed no significant correlation with desire for change.

However, the three remaining factors—unfreezing, involvement, and reception of feedback—did appear to operate roughly as we had expected. A sequential arrangement is suggested by the fact (see Figure 2) that feedback and involvement are each more closely related to the just-preceding variable than to any other in the supposed chain. There appears, in addition, to be a warm-up effect; the relationship between received feedback and change does not appear until the second week, as if the training

---

4. For example, female, older, and less flexible Ss tended to have higher desire-for-change scores, yet tended to show less net change than male, younger, more flexible Ss.

Table 1

CORRELATES OF CHANGE, DURING AND AFTER TREATMENT

	CHANGE MEASURE		
	SHORT-RUN: SELF-PER- CEIVED, AT LABORATORY	SHORT-RUN: TRAINER RATING, AT LABORATORY	ON-THE-JOB: SELF- AND JOB ASSOCIATE- PERCEIVED, AFTER LABORATORY
Personality Factors			
1. Ego Strength (revised Barron)	.09	.09	.05
2. Flexibility (revised Barron) ..	.27	.31*	−.01
3. Need Affiliation (French)	.30*	.22	.13
4. Personality Index (Comb. of #1, #2, & #3)	.28	.26	.08
Age	−.41***	−.17	.07
Sex (male)	.25	.45***	.33*
Organizational Factors			
1. Security (years as a principal)	−.23	−.09	.30*
2. Power (number of teachers) ..	−.17	.26	.32*
3. Autonomy (infreq. of mtgs. with superior)	−.15	−.04	−.03
4. Index combining #1, #2, & #3	−.28	.03	.28
5. Perceived power of self in org.	.26	.11	−.06
6. Perceived flex. adequacy of org.	.06	.10	−.15
7. Index combining #5 & #6	.18	.12	−.11
Participation Factors			
1. Desire for change			
a. Prior need	−.03	−.32*	−.14
b. Prior anticipation of success	−.08	−.28	−.39**
c. During laboratory	−.15	−.03	−.15
2. Unfreezing			
a. First week	.10	.22	.08
b. Second week	.18	.30*	.33*
c. Index combining a & b ..	.16	.36**	.34**
3. Involvement	.17	.46***	.25
4. Feedback reception			
a. First week (clear- strong-helpful)	.00	−.02	.04
b. First week (pleasurableness)	−.09	.10	.03
c. Second week (clear- strong-helpful)	.45***	.43***	.04
d. Second week (pleasurableness)	.27	.23	.12

Table 1

CORRELATES OF CHANGE, DURING AND AFTER TREATMENT *(Cont.)*

	CHANGE MEASURE		
	SHORT-RUN: SELF-PER-CEIVED, AT LABORATORY	SHORT-RUN: TRAINER RATING, AT LABORATORY	ON-THE-JOB: SELF- AND JOB ASSOCIATE-PERCEIVED, AFTER LABORATORY
Change During Treatment			
1. Short-run (trainer rating composite)	.35**	–	.55**
2. Self-perceived change	–	.35**	.06

* $p<.10$ ** $p<.05$ *** $p<.01$ For simplicity, these are two-tailed significance levels, since not all relationships were predicted.

were beginning to "take hold." However, an index of the last three participation variables constructed to take account of sequence effects proved no better a predictor of gain ($r=.51$) than a multiple R (.49).

As predicted, the personality variables did not correlate with gain during treatment, but *did* relate to some of the training-process variables above. Ego strength appeared to support unfreezing, both early and late in the laboratory;[5] flexibility related to unfreezing (first week), and approached significance with unfreezing (second week), involvement, and feedback (second week); and need affiliation was associated with reception of feedback (second week), approaching significance with unfreezing (second week) and involvement.

Our analysis so far has dealt solely with measures internal to the training experience and has emphasized understanding of the effects of psychological components of training on a short-run criterion measure (trainer ratings). Any evaluation study must also deal with the longer-term, more basic criterion problem.

Analysis of variance showed no pre-post experimental-control differences (and no test-treatment interaction) on the LBDQ or on the Group Participation Scale (on which both experimental and control scores rose). In retrospect, the LBDQ in particular seems unsuitable as a change-measuring instrument, since each participant's score comes from the summation of a number (averaging five) of his associates' scores; thus, averaging effects occur and score stability is likely. The criterion measure we developed was essentially primitive—and effective in avoiding this problem. Both S and his associates were asked to describe any behavior changes which had occurred

5. Ego strength was also related (r's of .33 and .48) to the tendency to perceive feedback as pleasurable rather than painful. However, pleasure/pain is independent of the clarity, strength, and helpfulness of feedback, and of net change as a result of the laboratory experience.

during the period under scrutiny, and extra scoring weight was given to "verified" changes—ones on which S and an associate, or two associates, agreed. The experimental/control differences on the eight-month post administration of this instrument are shown in Table 2. The various measures derived from the data indicate that experimental participants appear to have changed with about three times as much frequency as control Ss,

Table 2

RETROSPECTIVE CHANGES IN BEHAVIOR REPORTED BY SELF
AND WORKING ASSOCIATES, EIGHT MONTHS AFTER TRAINING PERIOD

	EXPERIMENTAL GROUP (N=34)	MATCHED CONTROL GROUP (N=29)		RANDOM CONTROL GROUP (N=148)
Median change score†	3.5	1		1
Mean change score	4.4	1.2	*	1.7
Standard deviation of change scores	3.93	1.44		2.10
Per cent of persons above control group base rate (score 2)	73	17	*	29
Per cent mentioning a behavior change in the person:				
—By self	82	33	*	21‡
—By associates	30	10		12‡
Per cent of persons who have at least *two* associates mentioning a behavior change in them:	47	0	*	12‡
(Associate N)	178	140		155‡

† Score derived by totaling discrete changes mentioned, and adding 1 unit for each instance of associate-associate or self-associate agreement.

* Matched versus random differences significant at .05 level. All experimental versus control differences significant at .01.

‡ N is 34 randomly selected subjects from the random control group.

even when the base rate of control group change (yes, people do improve their behavior without recourse to laboratory training!) is allowed for. It is interesting to note in passing that *self*-mentioned changes in all samples, laboratory participants included, outnumber associate-identified changes by two or three to one. Behavior change looks bigger "from the inside out," perhaps.

A preliminary content analysis of the changes reported more frequently in experimental than control data indicated that they fell mostly in the areas of increased sensitivity to others, equalitarian attitudes, skills of communication and leadership, and group task and maintenance skills. Personal traits, such as "more considerate," "relaxed," account for about a quarter of the reported changes in the experimental group, with organization-relevant changes (such as "delegates more") and group-relevant changes (such as "aids group decision making") making up the remainder. This rough balance also occurred in the participants' self-reported learnings at the close of the training period[6] and is congruent with the laboratory staff's statements of objectives.

This basic on-the-job criterion measure gains added validity when we note that the short-run change measure (derived from pre-post ratings made by the T-group trainer, who saw the participant longest and most intensively during the laboratory) correlates .55 ($p < .01$) with it (Figure 1). Interestingly enough, the self-perceived learning measure taken at the end of the treatment period shows *no* relationship with change on the job eight months later. Apparently, a competent professional can see changes in participants during the laboratory, changes which are associated with later improvements on the job—while the changes noted by participants themselves, though phenomenologically real, are *not* predictive of later changes.

It appears, as we expected, that some objective organizational factors may mediate to some extent between short-run and on-the-job criterion changes. (Interestingly, *perceived* organizational factors seem not to have any mediating effects.) Table 1 and Figure 1 indicate that participants with high security (longer experience) are among the higher changers on the job ($r = .30$). If amounts of change during training are held constant by partial correlation, the relationship rises to .42. Figured the other way, the correlation of .55 between short-run and on-the-job change becomes .61, when the factor of security in own organization is held constant. The factor of own power (number of teachers in school) correlates .32 with change on the job, but this is reduced to .22 by holding amount of short-run change constant. The short-run versus on-the-job change correlation is relatively unaffected by power (.55 to .51). Partial correlations can conceal the nature of relationships, however; Table 3 gives some indication of how the mediation actually works. The majority of high changers during training who have high or moderate power and security at home also show high job change; low changers with low power and security change less when they return. And the middle group (high short-run changers with low organizational support and low short-run changers with high support) seem about a 50-50 bet for net change on the job.

Finally, as predicted, personality variables did *not* show a relationship with change in job behavior of these subjects (Table 1).

---

6. Bunker and Knowles (1967) have since employed this measure in a study of the effects of six different training laboratories; similar experimental-control differences were found. The scoring method and the content analysis scheme have been considerably developed and refined; the measure now seems eminently suitable and usable for any treatment aiming at behavior change, including psychotherapy.

Table 3

SHORT-RUN AND ON-THE-JOB CRITERION CHANGES, AS MEDIATED
BY OWN POWER AND SECURITY IN HOME ORGANIZATION

		POWER/ SECURITY	ON-THE-JOB CRITERION CHANGE (SELF- AND JOB ASSOCIATE-PERCEIVED)	
			LOW	HIGH
SHORT-RUN CRITERION CHANGE (TRAINER RATINGS)	*High*	Moderate and high	$2/2*$	$10/9$
		Low	$3/3$	$2/3$
	Low	Moderate and high	$7/5$	$5/4$
		Low	$5/7$	$0/1$

* In each cell, the figure above the / refers to persons categorized by *power;* the figure below refers to persons categorized by *security*.

Case Studies of Learning[7]

The material discussed above is highly analytic in nature. That is, we have broken down the responses of 34 persons to a learning experience in considerable detail. We have often been more interested in how a particular variable (such as unfreezing or feedback) behaved than in what the meaning of the laboratory experience was to any single participant.

What we need now is a synthesis. How do all the pieces of the laboratory picture fit together, when we look at specific persons? This section presents case studies of four laboratory participants. Names are, of course, fictional; and possibly-identifying data are omitted or altered to protect anonymity.

The first participant was one for whom the laboratory experience had little relevance or helpfulness, both during the training period and back on the job. The second experienced considerable impact both during the two weeks and in terms of improved job performance. The third participant appeared to experience a good deal of learning while at the laboratory, but little durable job change seems to have ensued. The fourth case study describes a participant who seemed to learn little at the laboratory, but in fact changed a good deal on the job.

In addition to giving more of the "flavor" of the laboratory as it was experienced by participants, these case studies may give the reader additional impressions of how well the model of learning presented above seems

7.   This section is based on material originally prepared by Frederick L. Whitam.

to work out when it is applied to specific individuals. He will be able to detect exceptions to as well as confirmations of the theory we have explored in this study.

An Unsuccessful Learner

Bernice Johnson is an example of a principal on whom the laboratory, as far as it is possible to tell, seems to have had little impact. According to her trainer's ratings, she seems not to have improved in effectiveness at all. Eight months after returning to her job, Bernice felt that she had not changed any of her behavior as a result of the training, and three of four associates concurred. One associate mentioned that this participant had become "more active in all educational circles," a rather vaguely described change only peripherally related to the types of change hoped for as a result of laboratory training. Why was Bernice Johnson hardly touched by it?

Bernice's school is located in a suburban town of 5,000 in a Middle Atlantic state. Her school is small—nine teachers. Bernice, in her middle fifties, has been in this school system for nearly 20 years and has held her present job for 10 years. In responding to the pre-laboratory instrument measuring desire for change, Bernice indicated that many of the needs for change she felt had to do wtih a community which was *resistant* to change. She wanted to learn "how to initiate change in a community" and "how to work in situations where there is resistance to change"; as an administrator she wanted to see "changes in teachers' attitudes toward and understanding of a community undergoing change."

Our measure of organizational climate indicated that Bernice perceived her school system as only moderately adequate and flexible. She saw her own power as rather low. Bernice's goals for change seemed to center in changing the community situation; she was less concerned with change in herself (though she did mention feelings of "inadequate skills for group participation and leadership").

Turning to personality measures, we find that Bernice's change-relevant personality characteristics were those we predicted would be unfavorable to learning at the laboratory and to the initiation of change on the job. Her scores on instruments measuring ego strength, flexibility, and need affiliation were low. To the degree the instruments have validity, her scores suggest a person who would have difficulty in coping productively with the emotional stresses of learning at the laboratory, would have difficulty in changing attitudes and behavior patterns, and would tend not to get closely involved with other people.

At the laboratory, Bernice's scores on the "unfreezing" instrument were very low at the start of the training; when the instrument was administered the second week, her scores still suggested difficulty in "loosening up." Her replies at the start of the laboratory, for instance, indicate that she saw herself as reluctant to try out new behavior in the group, as hesitating to offer ideas of her own, and as not feeling free to admit an ineffective or undesirable behavior of her own. Her trainer saw her as withdrawn from group interaction and not actively involved.

For the most part, feedback was not a comfortable or profitable experience for Bernice at the laboratory; even less so as it progressed. During the first week she perceived feedback as fairly strong and gainful, but at the same time as relatively unclear and nonrewarding (unpleasurable). During the second week her feedback, she felt, became much less strong, slightly less helpful, and remained unclear and nonpleasurable. The only feedback she mentioned receiving during the first week was resentment of others toward a suggestion she had made. At the end of the second week she mentioned no specific feedback at all in answer to the same question.

At the laboratory's end, Bernice's scores on the self-perceived learnings instrument indicated that her learnings were neither clear nor relevant to her. When asked to describe feelings about her work situation that had changed or improved, she said: "I have changed, but I am not sure in what ways." When asked to mention things which she understood better about human relations in her work, she wrote:

> People relate to each other because of the image they see, each to the other. The knowledge, status, experiences, attitudes, feelings, and so on that each individual has is the person. It is a task to change them!

When asked to name things which she intended to do to improve human relations on the job back home, she listed only three possible actions, fewer than almost anyone else. One improvement mentioned was cautious indeed: "I intend to go very slowly in introducing to the group any idea I have received here."

When Bernice's over-all performance was rated by trainers in her skill-practice group and her T-group, the results corresponded with her own subjective view of the laboratory experience. She scored in the lowest quarter on the skill-group rating, and at the bottom of the range on the T-group rating. Her improvement in the performance task situation as measured by ratings was average.

When Bernice returned to her school, little new seems to have happened. She had been confronted at the outset by a community situation resistant to change and an organizational structure where she felt she had little power; she brought to the laboratory low ego strength, low flexibility, and low need affiliation; she seemed to find it difficult to become actively involved; and subsequent laboratory experiences were not meaningful to her.

This is a saddening but realistic picture of a participant for whom the experience provided no gain. Let us turn to an example of a participant whose job performance showed clear improvement.

A Successful Learner

Tom Leonard is a participant who seemed to learn a good deal at the laboratory, and was able to work with people more effectively when he returned to his school. He felt that after returning he had a greater tolerance for others, more insight into others' motives, and a better understanding of his role as a principal and of group functioning. Four of seven job associates felt that he had changed his behavior; they regarded him as being happier, less reserved, more relaxed, more willing to accept teachers' ideas, more friendly, and easier to work with.

Tom's school is located in a Southwestern city of 60,000, and is relatively large—about 25 teachers. Tom, a man in his late fifties, has been principal of this school for over 30 years. Examination of instruments filled out before the laboratory suggests that he had rather direct, positive motivations for coming. As to why he decided to attend, Tom wrote: "To grow in my understanding of working with others." Generally, he wanted to "help groups [in which he worked] define goals and have common goals and to grow in my understanding of ways of working with others." Specifically, he wanted to "overcome difficulties I am experiencing in working with people on higher levels of authority than my own." On the organizational climate instrument, Tom indicated that he perceived the flexibility and adequacy of his organization, and his own power in the organization, to be low.

On instruments designed to measure personality variables relevant to the laboratory experience, Tom scored slightly above the mean. His scores on ego strength, flexibility, and need affiliation are all moderate plus.

Tom scored fairly high on the unfreezing instrument given at the start of the laboratory. He rated himself as feeling free to admit an ineffective or undesirable behavior of his own and to ask for comments on his behavior; he rated himself as not being reluctant to try out new behavior in the group and as not feeling apprehensive in the situation. His unfreezing score was even higher in the second week than at the beginning. His T-group trainer saw him as being actively involved.

Tom's scores indicate that during the first week he was not very much aware of feedback. He saw it as having an average amount of strength and helpfulness and as being moderately clear. He was not able to remember and/or describe any feedback which he had received during the week. By the second week, he had, however, become considerably more sensitive to feedback. He came to see his feedback as being considerably more strong, helpful, clear, and pleasurable. He wrote: "I requested feedback about my contributions to the group; the group was willing to discuss these contributions." "I got feedback from the trainer about my contribution in specific situations." "I felt the group was friendly toward one another and toward me."

On the self-perceived learnings instrument, administered at the end of the laboratory, Tom's learnings seem to have been fairly clear and relevant to him. He mentioned several kinds of understandings and learnings: "the wide variety of interpretations which may be placed upon what is said and the feelings expressed in groups"; "the importance of participation in the group by every member"; "how to more effectively analyze forces which contribute to growth and inhibit growth in the group"; "how to better play my role as a group member so as to make my best contribution"; "I will be more cautious in appraising the motives and feelings of other group members."

In answer to the question, "What things will you do to improve human relations situations you are in on the job?" Tom replied that he would suspend judgment until he had fully tested any assessment of motive or feeling of group members; be aware of the full range of contributions he could make to the group in terms of task and group maintenance; actively participate in all groups of which he is a member; more completely analyze problems and situations before formulating plans for actions or conclusions.

Tom's ratings by other persons at the laboratory—both trainers and members—tend to substantiate this impression of him as a successful learner. The trainer in his T-group gave Tom a very high rating on his improvement in over-all performance in the group. In the skill group, Tom scored slightly above the mean. When rated by trainer and members during the performance test, Tom showed much improvement in effectiveness. In general, then, other persons observing Tom's behavior at the laboratory agreed with his view that it was a profitable learning experience for him.

From this summary, then, we get some insight into the conditions which eventually may lead to initiation of change on the job following laboratory training. Tom Leonard is a person who—despite the fact that he saw his own power and the "flexible adequacy" of his organization as low—was able to bring about some improvement in his working behavior in his school. His relatively high motivation in going to the laboratory, his personality adequacy in terms of ego strength, flexibility, and need affiliation, his ability to unfreeze, his high degree of involvement, and his reception of helpful feedback all interacted to improve his working relationships when he returned to the job.

Not all laboratory participants fall so neatly into the two categories represented by Bernice Johnson and Tom Leonard. One can imagine at least two other types of participants: those who seemed to learn while there, but on returning to their jobs showed no improvement in their working behavior; and those who gave little evidence of learning at the laboratory, but *did* effect change back on the job. Examination of the data showed that there were no participants who unambiguously fitted these two types. The participants who are nearest to these "ideal types" are Jack Martin (who scored high on gain at the laboratory and then scored at about the mean on job change) and Alice West (who scored at about the mean on gain and then high on job change).

A Quasi-Learner

Jack Martin impressed his trainers sufficiently to get a high score on his performance improvement while at the laboratory, but when he returned to his home situation he did not show more than average improvement in his working effectiveness. Most people who scored as high as Jack on laboratory change showed above-average change on the job, but Jack himself reported that in the eight months since the laboratory he had not changed his behavior in any way. Four of his seven describers agreed that he had not changed, and the three who did mention change reported vague changes not clearly related to human relations training: "He is more skillful in doing desirable things"; "He tries to develop social activities and interest in the school"; "He has a more progressive approach"; "He has a greater maturity of perception and greater understanding." Only the last change seems to relate to the aims of the laboratory, and it remains very general.

Given this lack of transfer from laboratory to job, we ought to look at some other factors to see whether this inconsistency can be explained.

Jack is a principal in a small school in the Middle West. Prior to the laboratory, he saw as his major goals on his job: "Establishing a sound program of human relations within the school community," and "developing more community interest in school activities and making the school a community center." He felt that the major obstacles confronting him in his work were "helping the general public understand the total school program, the philosophy of the school, and why we are doing what we are doing," and "establishing a good system of communication to include teachers, pupils, parents, board of education, and lay public." These comments suggest that, like Bernice Johnson, he tended to be oriented toward the larger community rather than toward human relations problems within the school system. It is possible that learnings at this laboratory were not highly relevant for this category of problem.

Further statements by Jack indicate generally positive but diffuse motivation: "I have applied for another position and feel that this workshop would better qualify me for it. I would like to share common problems and form some plans for overcoming them. I am a firm believer in the group process and feel that many problems can be solved by its use. I would like to make new friends, get fruitful ideas for a good program of human relations, and become a better person with this experience."

A somewhat different emphasis on change is indicated if we turn to the desire-for-change instrument Jack completed before his training. He focuses on changes in other persons with whom he works. In answer to the question, "What things would you like to learn to do better in your work situation?" he replied: "To create conditions within the school to stimulate teachers and students to learn desired behavior and to act accordingly." To the item, "Feelings in your work situation which you would like to change or improve," he responded in terms of improving others: "I would like to be looked upon as a leader or coordinator and not a boss. I would like for my co-workers to understand my belief in the worth of individuals and the things they do." Under "Changes which I as an administrator would like to see made in my work situation," he listed. "To be able to spend more time with my teachers and help them to see the value in some of the newer methods of teaching instead of not saying anything about the outdated ones." Skills he wanted to get were: "To come back with the ability and know-how to lead teachers to see the necessity of self-improvement and to help them to want to accept constructive criticism without thinking of me as a boss."

These two emphases on change, i.e., changing the relations of school with community, and changing others on the job, are most prominent in Jack's motivation for going to the laboratory. It may be that such motivation, though appropriate, is less likely to lead to changes in one's own behavior.

Within his school organization, Jack perceived both his own power and the flexible adequacy of the organizational structure to be moderate. This suggests that the organizational climate of his school was seen by him to be reasonably favorable to—or at least not as impeding—change. Measures of personality variables relevant to the laboratory situation suggest that Jack possessed moderate ego strength and high personal flexibility and that he had above-average strength of need affiliation. Theoretically, these personality attributes would enhance his learnings at the laboratory.

Jack did, in fact, do well. His scores on the unfreezing instrument in the first week indicate that he was ready to unfreeze and involve himself with others. As the program progressed, he seems to have become even more willing to unfreeze—during the second week his unfreezing score was in the top quartile. His T-group trainer felt his involvement in group discussion was about average. At the beginning, feedback did not come across to him well: he perceived it as not particularly strong, helpful, clear, or pleasurable. Progressively, feedback became more meaningful. By the second week, his feedback scores had risen from slightly below the mean at the outset to several points above the mean. He felt that feedback became considerably stronger, more helpful, clearer, and more pleasurable.

Jack's perceived learnings instrument indicates that he saw his learnings at the laboratory as only moderately clear and relevant. His over-all self-perceived learning score was slightly above the mean, and he mentioned a number of changes he intended to make after getting back on the job:

> Begin to modify my own behavior as it affects co-workers.
> Be on the lookout for every good thing I can see in the work of others.
> Give honest praise whenever possible.
> Reorganize staff meetings to meet the needs of teachers. Begin with their problems.
> Be as informal and friendly to everyone as much as possible.
> Be sincere in all phases of my job.
> Communicate to teachers the reasons for all decisions made which affect them.

Some other comments by Jack on this instrument retain part of the flavor of the pre-laboratory instrument, in which he indicated a desire to change others:

I think I've learned how to better initiate change in people.

I realize now that it is a long, slow process and that the leader cannot do this through autocratic methods. Begin where teachers are!

I feel that group work can solve many problems, but some things must be decided by the principal without help of staff.

I would like my teachers to recognize the need for improvement and ask my help in making these changes.

I think I've learned how groups work successfully and how to organize and supervise proper operation of all types of groups.

In the skill group and in the T-group, Jack's trainers rated him high in improvement in over-all effectiveness—in both cases well above the mean. His improvement in the performance task situation when measured by ratings was well above average.

Why Jack did not improve human relations in his school setting more than he did remains, of course, highly speculative. It is possible that his own motivations—he thought laboratory participation would put him in a position to get a better job; he wanted to improve school-community relations; he wanted to change others rather than himself—intervened to reduce the high potential for improving his own job effectiveness with which he left. We need to know much more than we do now about the problem of laboratory-to-job transfer.

A *"Late Bloomer"*

Finally, let us consider Alice West, whose score on T-group trainer ratings was at about the mean, while her job change score was well above the mean. Alice, herself, felt that she had "become more relaxed in groups"; that she "takes more time in planning and listening"; and that she "uses others' suggestions more." Two of her six describers felt that she had changed. They said that she had "grown professionally"; that she "listens more"; that she "helps groups function more effectively"; that she had "greater skill in getting group participation in discussion." Nearly all these changes are related quite closely to the aims of the laboratory.

Alice, in her early fifties, is a principal in a suburban school in New England. Her school has 19 teachers, and she has held this job for nearly 20 years. When applying for admission, she indicated that her major goals were: "Teacher growth and effectiveness; understanding human relations and their importance; mental health and child development with parents." She mentioned, as obstacles in her work: "Leading group discussions for full participation; inability to recognize and encourage contributions and apply them to the topic; working with emerging leadership; need for skills and techniques to do these things." These goals and obstacles seem closely related to the kinds of learnings which are supposed to take place at the laboratory; the obstacles refer mainly to her own behavior rather than the behavior of others. The impression that Alice's needs and problems were laboratory-relevant is substantiated by her desire-for-change instrument. She wanted to understand better: "How to recognize needs and feelings of individuals in a group and to help each to contribute to the problem at hand"; "How to help group members recognize these things in one another and to respect the contributions of others." Things which she wanted to learn to do better were: "To guide discussion groups for fuller participation and better group decisions; to be able to develop self-confidence in more retiring members; and to deal more effectively and tactfully with over-aggressive members." She wanted to improve "feelings of inadequacy in dealing with classroom teachers and others who are more intelligent and perhaps stronger than I," and "to develop leadership techniques to better cope with the great variety of situations which I face." She wanted to be able to "do more classroom observation and still be able to do the counseling and conference work which is needed." She added, "I think the change must come in me rather than in the work situation itself." In answer to an item about skills which she hoped to get at the laboratory, she said in conclusion: "I don't think I can list them. I need better skills in dealing with all personnel. I am sure there are attitudes and understandings which may be intangible which I can acquire, and I am looking forward to this workshop experience."

In contrast to Jack Martin—whose goals and needs were somewhat diffuse and less clearly related to human relations in the school—Alice seems to have been highly motivated to acquire human relations skills to cope with ongoing demands of work in her school. In addition, she perceived her own power in her organizational structure as high and the organizational structure itself as flexible and adequate. However, on examining Alice's laboratory-related personality scores, we find that her ego strength and flexibility, as measured by our instruments, are below the mean and that her need affiliation score is at the mean. Before coming to the laboratory, then, there were factors which might facilitate change on the job and at the same time factors which might inhibit change at the laboratory.

On arriving at the laboratory, Alice seemed quite willing to involve herself in its activities. On the unfreezing measure, taken early, she scored very high and appeared to maintain her willingness to loosen up—indicated by her second-week unfreezing score, which was also quite high. Her T-group trainer saw her as being actively involved.

Feedback during the training period, however, seems not to have been a fully helpful experience for Alice. She scored above the mean only on clarity of feedback; while relevance, strength, helpfulness, and pleasurableness of feedback were lower. During the second week her feedback scores improved only slightly; she scored slightly above the mean on clarity and pleasurableness.

On the self-perceived learnings instrument, Alice's scores suggest that her learnings were not very clear or relevant. Her description of her own learnings gives an impression of their being somewhat general and vague. She better understood, for example, "the many forces that are present in each individual in any group that each may contribute or restrain; that many problems are the result of lack of understanding of human relations and ineffective leadership." She learned to "better use the human resources available to me in my job, encourage more teacher participation in staff meetings, do better planning." A change she would like to see made was: "more group-centered activities—fewer principal-centered." Skills she felt she had acquired were: "better understanding of group processes; skills in communication, diagnosis, planning, and interviewing ability."

When asked to name things which she would actually do to improve human relations in her school, she was more specific:

> Try to understand my own behavior in relation to those with whom I work.
>
> Try to use some of the skills which have been presented, discussed, and practiced in improving staff meetings—specifically: I will use sub-groups to encourage freer participation; watch communication, trying to make it two-way—fewer bulletins, more face-to-face contact; ask for reactions to my own behavior in specific situations; try to help people understand themselves better.

Her final comment suggests a picture of as-yet-incomplete learning: "I must first sort out and try to assimilate the learnings which have been packed into the two weeks. I can't say for sure how many will stick."

The image we get from these scores is mixed, but coherent, one feels. Alice West's willingness to unfreeze was extremely high, yet her received feedback was not particularly potent and her learnings were somewhat uncertain. Ratings by her trainers tend to support this picture; in her T-group, her improvement score on over-all effectiveness was about at the mean. In the skill group, her score was in the lowest quartile. Her improvement in the performance task situation was below average when measured by ratings. It is as if shorter-term learning situations leave her at a disadvantage.

What emerges from this overview of Alice's comments and scores, then, is a picture of a highly motivated person, with real, specific needs for improving human relations in her school, and an organizational structure which might support change. At the laboratory, it is as if her personality characteristics operated to delay change, in spite of her active involvement in learning. Judging from her comments and her performance eight months later, she actually *had* learned a good deal, but it was in storage, so to speak, and needed sorting out. With strong motivation and organizational support, she did improve her performance considerably. In laboratories as in schools, we need not expect that all the consequences of new learning will be immediately apparent.

Implications and Conclusions

The methodological problems of treatment studies can be at least partially overcome, given care in design, measurement, and data analysis. The main strategies employed in this study were those of careful criterion measurement and refinement, the use of a role-homogeneous population, the location of plausible control groups, the assessment of possible test-treatment interaction, the predictive analysis of components thought to cause change on criterion measures, and the use of large numbers of measures.[8]

Substantively, we have found valid experimental-control differences as a result of a human relations training experience; the gains by participants were primarily predicted by variables connected with actual participation in the treatment—unfreezing, active involvement, and reception of feedback. The personality variables studied—ego strength, flexibility, and need affiliation—did not affect laboratory outcomes directly, but did seem to influence behavior during training. Finally, the organizational variables studied— personal security, autonomy and power, and organizational problem-solving adequacy—had less impact on the participants' stance at the beginning of training than expected, but did appear to affect their subsequent use of learnings on the job. The case studies reviewed suggest that a reasonable degree of confidence can be placed in the findings.

8.   With so many relationships to be examined, the question of capitalizing on randomly distributed "significant" correlations becomes important. A check on the *initial* (not reduced) matrix indicated that, of the 595 relationships among the 27 nonconfounded predictors and 8 criteria, 54 reached the .05 level (two-tailed test), when 30 would have appeared by chance, and 23 reached the .01 level, when 6 might have appeared by chance. The majority of these relationships had been predicted.

References

BUCHANAN, P.   Evaluating the effectiveness of laboratory training in industry. Paper read at American Management Association seminar, New York, Feb. 24-26, 1964.

BUNKER, D. R. and KNOWLES, E.   Comparison of behavioral changes resulting from human relations training laboratories of different lengths. *Journal of Applied Behavioral Science,* 1967, 3(4), 505-523.

CAMPBELL, D. T.   Factors relevant to the validity of experiments in social settings. *Psychological Bulletin,* 1957, 54, 297-312.

CAMPBELL, D. T. and FISKE, D. W.   Convergent and discriminant validation by the multitrait-multimethod matrix. *Psychological Bulletin,* 1959, 56, 81-105.

HYMAN, H. H., WRIGHT, C. R. and HOPKINS, T. K.   *Applications of methods of evaluation.* University of California Publications in Culture and Society, Vol. 7, Berkeley and Los Angeles: University of California Press, 1962.

JOHNSON, D. W.   Title III and the dynamics of educational change in California schools. In M. B. Miles (Ed.), *Innovation in education.* New York: Teachers College Press, 1964. Pp. 157-182.

PEPINSKY, H. B., SIEGEL, L. and VAN ALTA, E. L.   The criterion in counseling: A group participation scale. *Journal of Abnormal and Social Psychology,* 1952, 47, 415-419.

STOCK, DOROTHY (WHITAKER, D. S.).   A summary of research on training groups. In L. P. Bradford, K. D. Benne and J. R. Gibb (Eds.), *T-group theory and laboratory method: Innovation in re-education.* New York: Wiley, 1964.

꙰ ꙰ ꙰ ꙰ ꙰

Does learning require a teacher? Quite clearly not. All learning environments are "teacher-less" in some important respects: even the young child, ultimately, must make his way alone through learning tasks. Yet few researchers have attempted to move beyond a naive Couéism ("every day in every way, I am getting better and better" as a self-exhortation) to examine the phenomena of self-directed learning.

Winter and her colleagues here analyze the personality characteristics of learners who were more and less successful in inducing self-reported (and expert-judged) change, primarily in the area of interpersonal relations.

The sample is small, and the failure of some of the content-analytic dimensions to replicate on the second sample gives pause. However, the findings on the importance of treating yourself both as "conditional," in flux, *and* as having a reasonably firm identity—as paradoxical as that sounds —are clearly echoed in Smith's Peace Corps study in the present volume. It looks as if some good theories of self-operated learning situations may be within our grasp—and that they can be meaningfully linked to existing theory (e.g., cognitive dissonance). As is so often the case, sophisticated practice (here, Winter *et al.*'s adaptation of T-group techniques) has preceded theory-building. Perhaps this study will help both researchers and practitioners to push further into this area.

Capacity for Self-Direction*

Sara K. Winter,
Jeffery C. Griffith, David A. Kolb

The idea that people can change themselves has been unfashionable among psychologists for some time. Since Freud and his followers cast doubt on the will psychology of William James, psychologists have generally accepted the notion that present behavior is rooted in the past and in the unconscious. As Allport (1960) noted, contemporary psychological theories focus heavily on the ways in which men respond reactively to external stimuli and pay little attention to man's proactive, self-directing capacities. There is a corresponding assumption that an individual cannot by his own efforts effect personal change.

In the popular mind, however, self-directed personal change has consistently been recognized as difficult but worthy of consideration. Self-improvement books are commercially successful, and New Year's resolutions, although often broken, continue to be made. Moreover, in recent years members of the treatment professions are increasingly questioning Freudian assumptions about personality change. The growing and widespread interest in behavior therapy (Grossberg, 1964) suggests a return to the belief that isolated symptoms can be accepted more or less at face value and can be treated without probing for "deeper" problems. One publication (Goldiamond, 1965) addressed itself directly to "the application of self-controlled procedures to the solution of certain limited behavioral problems." It appears that many psychologists are increasingly willing to explore the possibility that an individual can identify his own problems and work to effect a change.

The study reported here is part of a research program aimed at developing a method for self-directed personal change and at understanding the psychological processes involved in successful personal change efforts. The simple change method employed in the research provides a paradigm for studying factors and processes which presumably are also important in other situations where people work to change themselves.

* From *Journal of Consulting and Clinical Psychology*, 1968, 32, 35–41. Used by permission of the authors and publisher.

This research was in part supported by the Sloan Research Fund, Massachusetts Institute of Technology. The authors are indebted to the MIT students who devoted time and energy to reporting their self-directed change projects and to John Aram, Michael Fulenwider, Douglas Hall, David Meredith, William McKelvey, and Irwin Rubin, who served as T-group trainers.

The major emphasis of the method is on self-research. The individual is given responsibility for diagnosing his own problem, setting his own goal, and accomplishing change by his own efforts. When business-school students used this method to change themselves as part of their participation in self-analytic groups (Kolb, Winter, and Berlew, 1968), two factors were found that predicted their success in changing. Change was found to be related to the individual's commitment to his change goal and the amount of feedback he received from other group members. Improving the change method to increase goal commitment and feedback increased the percentage of students successfully attaining their goals from 5% to 61%.

This gave no attention, however, to the question of individual differences in ability to achieve personal change goals. The purpose of the study reported here is to gain further insight into the self-directed change process by learning more about the attributes of individuals who are and are not able to achieve personal change. The approach is inductive, since so little is known about personality factors important in self-directed change.

In the present paper, self-descriptive essays written by subjects who later prove to be successful in their change efforts are compared with the essays of subjects who later prove unsuccessful in changing. Through content analysis, features of the essays which distinguish between the two groups will be isolated. These findings will then be cross-validated for a second sample of successful and unsuccessful subjects.

Procedure

SETTING. The study was conducted in a one-semester course in Psychology and Human Organization, required of candidates for a master's degree in Management at MIT. As a part of the course, students participated in 15-man training groups (T-groups) which met twice weekly throughout the semester (see Bradford, Gibb, and Benne, 1964, for a general description of T-groups). The self-directed change projects were required as a part of the student's T-group participation, but were ungraded. The study reported here was carried out during two successive semesters.

SUBJECTS. High-change and low-change Ss were selected as described below from among the 51 students in Semester 1 (85% of the total course enrollment of 60) and the 70 students in Semester 2 (92% of the total course enrollment of 76) who completed self-directed change projects. All students were male undergraduates or master's degree candidates in Industrial Management at MIT. They ranged in age from 20 to 35, with most in their early 20s.

CHANGE METHOD. The self-directed change technique employed by all Ss in Semesters 1 and 2 can be summarized as follows: In the first week of the course, before hearing of the change projects, each student wrote a brief essay on "How I would ideally like to be in a group." This essay (referred to below as the ideal self paper) was followed in the third week of the course by a brief essay on "How I am actually perceived in groups" (the real self paper). These two essays were assigned to increase students' thoughtfulness about themselves and their goals, preparatory to the actual change projects. In Semester 2 the Rokeach Dogmatism scale (Rokeach, 1960) was administered, since it seemed that this measure of cognitive openness might predict ability to change by the self-directed method.

The change technique was introduced in the fifth week of the course with a lecture by the course instructor. After a discussion of factors influencing behavior change (McClelland, 1965) and a presentation of individual case studies of self-directed change (Schwitzgebel, 1964; Zachs, 1965), the instructor explained the procedure for carrying out the change projects. Students were asked to spend the next two T-group meetings considering and discussing possible personal change goals. They were encouraged, though not required, to select goals relevant to their participation in the T-group sessions.

In the seventh week of the course, each student selected a personal change goal and noted how he planned to measure progress toward his goal. Goals varied widely; some students selected global objectives (e.g., "to become more sensitive to others' feelings"), while other students chose more discrete behavior-change goals (e.g., "I would like to speak more slowly and clearly"). In successive group meetings (9 meetings in Semester 1, 10 in Semester 2), the student rated his progress toward his goal after each session. The basis for these ratings again varied widely; some students made subjective personal judgments, while others kept objective counts of the behavior in question or asked other group members to provide peer ratings. Ratings were entered on a graph, so that the student could examine a visual record of his progress toward the goal from meeting to meeting Group members were encouraged to give one another feedback on their progress.

At the end of the semester each student evaluated his over-all progress in a short final paper which included his estimate of the degree to which he had achieved his change goal and a discussion of factors contributing to change or lack of change.

SELECTION OF HIGH-CHANGE AND LOW-CHANGE SAMPLES.   From the total group of students completing change projects, two samples of Ss were selected for comparison—a high-change group, whose members were clearly successful in achieving their change goals, and a low-change group, whose members were clearly unsuccessful in this task. An S's degree of success in achieving his change goal was determined by two criteria—a subjective change rating and a trainer rating of change. The subjective change rating was assigned on the basis of S's own evaluation of the success of his project, as reported in his final paper. The rating was based on the final paper rather than on the meeting-by-meeting record of progress, because meeting-by-meeting records were difficult to compare due to the wide variety of indexes of progress employed by different Ss. Two raters, unacquainted with the Ss, read each final paper and assigned a subjective change rating using a 5-point scale ranging from utter failure (1) to great success (5). In 75% of the cases, raters independently assigned ratings within one point of each other. For one-point discrepancies, the two ratings were averaged. For papers where disagreement was greater than one point, the two raters conferred and assigned a common rating. The trainer rating of change used the same 5-point scale and was provided by each S's T-group leader at the close of the semester. Trainers did not read the final papers or self-descriptive essays.

The high-change sample consisted of Ss who by both criteria were successful in achieving their change goals (both ratings were 4 or 5). Low-change Ss were those who failed to achieve their change goals by both criteria (both ratings were 1 or 2). Among the 51 students in Semester 1 there were 13 high-change and 11 low-change Ss by these criteria. In Semester 2, the total sample of 70 included 9 high-change and 22 low-change Ss.

Change projects of the remaining Ss, who received moderate ratings of change by either criterion or who rated themselves higher or lower in change than did the T-group trainer, were excluded from the present analysis. Trainer ratings of change were significantly, although not highly, correlated with subjective change ratings in both semesters (Semester 1, $r = .36$, $N = 51$, $p < .01$; Semester 2, $r = .26$, $N = 70$, $p < .05$). Discrepancies between the two ratings are difficult to interpret, since they could be due to (*a*) Ss' biased perceptions of degree of change, (*b*) trainers' difficulty in observing change for Ss whose goals involved changes in feelings or internal states, or (*c*) the fact that Ss and trainers may have used quite different data as the basis for their ratings. Since it was difficult to determine whether Ss or trainers were in a better position to estimate change "accurately," it was decided that both types of ratings should be used to select high-change and low-change Ss for the present analysis.

CONTENT ANALYSIS OF IDEAL SELF AND REAL SELF PAPERS. The students' ideal self and real self essays represent samples of the way high-change and low-change Ss thought about personal goals and described their interpersonal behavior, before the change technique had influenced them. It was hypothesized that analysis of these data on ideal self and real self conceptualizations would reveal personality differences that would explain success or lack of success with a self-directed change project, although no specific predictions were made. In examining the essays, the content-analysis method used by McClelland and his associates for developing new scoring systems for written TAT protocols (Atkinson, 1958) was employed. In this method, two groups of protocols are compared in order to discover content and/or stylistic features which are more frequent in one group than in the other. After categories differentiating the two groups are inductively derived, the investigator writes category definitions which specify scoring criteria for these categories. Scoring criteria should be sufficiently objective so that interscorer reliability exceeds 75%. The second stage of data analysis is to cross-validate the obtained intergroup differences by blind scoring of protocols from a second sample of Ss.

Results

In the present study the essays of the 13 high-change and 11 low-change subjects in Semester 1 were used for the inductive phase of data analysis. Blind scoring of the essays by the authors revealed six categories for which high-change and low-change subjects' scores were significantly different ($p < .05$, two-tailed) by the Mann-Whitney U test. These findings were cross-validated by blind scoring of the essays of the 9 high-change and 22 low-change subjects in Semester 2. Only the three categories which did cross-validate successfully in Semester 2 will be discussed in detail.[1] These categories are as follows.

Ideal Self Essay

CONDITIONAL DESIRE (CD). This category was more frequent in the essays of high-change subjects. CD scores those statements which indicate a desire for a goal with the implicit recognition that this goal has not yet been achieved. The most common statement in this category is a statement beginning, "I would like. . . ." The category is an index of the degree to which the student thinks conditionally about himself, in the sense that he indicates awareness of and desire for a goal which has not yet been attained.

DESCRIPTION OF ESSENCE (DE). This category was more frequent in the essays of low-change subjects. DE scored those instances where the individual gave an unconditioned description of his present or future self. There is no recognition of separation between the ideal and the current state.

Real Self Essay

IDENTITY DIFFUSION (ID). This category was more frequent in the essays of low-change subjects. ID scores statements from which one can

---

1. The remaining three categories, for which there are statistically significant differences in Semester 1 but not in Semester 2, were as follows: (a) In the ideal self essay, high-change subjects exceeded low-change subjects in number of different goals named; (b) in the ideal self essay, high-change subjects' goals dealt with cooperation with other group members more often than did goals of low-change subjects; (c) in the ideal self essay, low-change subjects mentioned social inadequacy or fear of failure more frequently than did high-change subjects. A complete scoring manual is available from the authors.

infer confusion about the self or about the relationship of the self to others and to the outside world. It seems to be related to Erikson's (1959) definition of the term. Four types of statements are included: (*a*) concern with reality—all phrases that stress that one thing is more real or less real than another; (*b*) feelings of playing a role—statements which indicate lack of congruence between the way the person acts and the way he feels, with no stated desire to resolve the contradiction; (*c*) vagueness about others' perceptions of the self—expressions of uncertainty about how the self is perceived by others or doubts about how the person wants others to perceive him; (*d*) indecisiveness and lack of conviction—any statement indicating uncertainty, tentativeness, or lack of conviction about one's own ideas or actions.

Interscorer reliability for the content-analysis categories was calculated in the following way. The original scores assigned by the authors were compared with the scoring of another rater unaware either of the hypotheses of the study or of the identity of the essays. This rater scored 10 essays, conferred with the authors about cases where her scores differed from the original scores, and then independently scored 25 essays. The percentage agreement on scoring these 25 essays was 90% for both CD and DE and 84% for ID.

COMPARISON OF HIGH-CHANGE AND LOW-CHANGE SUBJECTS' SCORES ON CONTENT-ANALYSIS VARIABLES IN SEMESTERS 1 AND 2. In Table 1 are mean values and significance levels of high-change/low-change comparisons for the three content-analysis categories described above. Data for Semester 1 appear in the left-hand portion of the table, while the cross-validation data from Semester 2 are presented in the right-hand portion of the table. Significance of differences between high-change and low-change subjects was tested by the Mann-Whitney U test.

Contrary to prediction, high-change and low-change subjects' scores on the Rokeach Dogmatism scale were not significantly different. Within the Semester 2 samples as a whole, the Rokeach score was unrelated to degree of change (r with subjective change rating $= -.07$, r with trainer rating of change $= -.19$), but was significantly correlated with the DE score ($r = .28$, $p < .05$). This finding is discussed below.

There are some interesting relationships among the three content-analysis categories. The notion that the CD and DE categories appear to reflect psychologically opposite approaches to the ideal self essay is supported by the negative correlation between these two variables in both semesters. For the entire sample of students completing change projects, CD correlated with DE $-.38$ in Semester 1 ($p < .05$) and $-.37$ in Semester 2 ($p < .01$).

Since these variables are negatively correlated, it may be meaningful to think of the CD:DE ratio as a psychologically significant variable in its own right. An ideal self essay in which CD statements exceed DE statements would indicate a well-developed ability to look beyond the present self and think conditionally about possibilities for change, while an essay with more

Table 1

CONTENT-ANALYSIS CATEGORY SCORES OF HIGH- AND LOW-CHANGE
SUBJECTS IN ORIGINAL AND CROSS-VALIDATION SAMPLES

	SEMESTER 1			SEMESTER 2		
	M SCORE		p^a	M SCORE		p^b
CATEGORY	HIGH	LOW		HIGH	LOW	
	$N = 11$	$N = 13$		$N = 9$	$N = 22$	
Conditional desire[c]	6.91	3.69	$<.02$	8.22	3.59	$<.02$
Description of essence[c]	3.18	8.46	$<.002$	4.22	6.36	$<.02$
Identity diffusion[d]	2.64	4.23	$<.05$	2.12	4.00	$<.004$

[a] Mann-Whitney U test, two-tailed. This statistic tests the difference between two sets of ranked scores; mean values are presented for descriptive purposes only.

[b] Mann-Whitney U test, one-tailed.

[c] Ideal self essay.

[d] Real self essay.

DE than CD would suggest that the subject attends less to the discrepancy between goal and present self than he does to the present state of being. This ratio of CD to DE differentiates the high-change and low-change subsamples in both semesters more strongly than does either category alone. In Semester 1 all high-change subjects included more CD than DE statements in their ideal self essays, while all low-change subjects showed the reverse pattern (χ^2 corrected for continuity $= 20.14$, $p<.001$). In the cross-validation sample the change classifications of 24 of the 31 subjects can be predicted correctly from the CD:DE ratio (χ^2 corrected for continuity $= 6.06$, $p<.015$).

The ID category does not appear to be related consistently to either CD or DE. In Semester 1, ID is significantly correlated with DE ($r=.37$, $p<.05$), but not with CD ($r= -.09$). In the cross-validation sample neither of these correlations is significant (ID with DE, $r=.06$; ID with CD, $r=.02$).

Discussion

The results suggest that two relatively independent personality characteristics are related to the ability to attain personal change goals. The first important characteristic, measured by the CD:DE ratio, is the ability to think conditionally about oneself. The high-change subject is one who displays the ability to postulate future possibilities for himself with the implicit recognition that these have not yet been attained. The low-change subject appears deficient in this ability; his high DE score suggests that future possibilities are less salient for him than is his present behavior and/or convictions about what he will be like in the future.

The second characteristic is confusion or tentativeness about the present self, as reflected in the ID code for the real self essay. The low-change subject's concern with defining "reality," his sense of playing an artificial role, his vagueness about how he is perceived by others, and his indecisiveness about his own thoughts and actions appear to be incompatible with successful self-directed change. The similarity of this personality syndrome to identify diffusion, as described by Erikson (1959), has already been noted.

Why should these particular personality characteristics be important for the outcome of an individual's self-directed change project? In earlier research with the self-directed change method (Kolb *et al.*, 1968) an individual's commitment to his goal was found to be related to degree of change. Moreover, the over-all percentage of high-change subjects increased when the change technique was modified so as to encourage more thoughtful consideration of goals. Thus, it appears that the goal-setting process is a central element in successful self-directed change, perhaps because the establishment of a goal is crucial in arousing motivation for the difficult struggle to achieve a change. Cognitive dissonance theory (Brehm and Cohen, 1962; Festinger, 1957) would suggest that the self-directed change effort is motivated by an individual's desire to reduce the dissonance which he has created for himself by establishing and attaching value to a personal goal which he has not yet achieved.

There are several possible ways to resolve this dissonance between present self and goal. One way is to retract commitment from the goal and to decide that the present behavior is satisfactory after all. Another possible solution is to change one's perception of the present self without changing present behavior, so that one becomes convinced that the goal has already been attained. The third and often most difficult avenue of dissonance reduction is to change the present behavior until it becomes congruent with the valued goal.

The present self-directed change method includes mechanisms which discourage individuals from reducing dissonance in either of the first two ways. First, the method makes abandonment of the goal difficult by forcing the individual to focus attention on the goal over a protracted period of time. Not only has he committed himself to his goal publicly before other T-group members, but he must consider the goal anew at each group meeting when he assigns himself his progress ratings from week to week. Second, dissonance reduction via an inaccurate perception that the goal is being attained is made difficult by the change method's emphasis on objective feedback. The person gives himself weekly feedback through his meeting-by-meeting ratings, and feedback is provided by other members of the group. Through emphasis on the goal and through feedback, the self-directed change method makes it difficult for the individual to reduce real-self—ideal-self dissonance by the quick and easy methods which presumably short circuit many personal change efforts in everyday life. The probability is thereby increased that dissonance will be reduced by bringing behavior into closer approximation to the goal.

It now becomes clearer why CD, DE, and ID are important personality variables for the self-directed change process. These categories appear to reflect individual differences in ability to create and maintain awareness of dissonance in the goal-setting phase of a self-directed change project.

CD seems to reflect the student's natural tendency to phrase personal goals in a manner which implies dissonance between the goal and present behavior. By phrasing goal statements conditionally, the person demonstrates simultaneous awareness of two dissonant elements—the present self and the goal. Such clearly recognized dissonance motivates the individual in his change effort.

If the high-change subject is one who is able to create and maintain dissonance between his present self-concept and his goal, the low-change subject, in contrast, seems to be one who does not create dissonance for himself when he sets goals. A consideration of the two content-analysis categories characteristic of the papers of low-change subjects suggests reasons why this may be so. First, the low-change subject's goals may be imperfectly differentiated in his mind from his present behavior. Low-change subjects' ideal self essays are characterized by high DE, and by a CD:DE ratio of less than one. In other words, when the low-change subject is asked to think of goals, he concentrates heavily on what he is and appears to be unable to postulate for himself clearly different behaviors or feelings. He appears closed-minded to possibilities for himself that do not exist at the present time. The positive correlation between DE and the Rokeach Dogmatism scale may indicate that this closed-mindedness extends to other areas of such individuals' functioning as well. In any case, this inability to clearly articulate differences between present behavior and future goal reduces the probability of experiencing dissonance between these two elements. Accordingly, little motivation to change behavior is likely to be present.

The ID category can be interpreted in a similar manner. As Brown (1965) pointed out, a dissonant relationship between two cognitive elements exists not when the elements are logically contradictory, but when the elements are psychologically incompatible for the particular individual in question. The classical dissonance experiments in the psychological literature work because most people share certain suppressed premises about themselves —"I say what I believe," "I do things that are worthwhile," and so on. But "since dissonance derives from premises about oneself and the world, it must vary with self-concept and world-view" (Brown, 1965, p. 598). Thus, there may be individuals for whom the usual premises do not hold. For such persons elements which we generally term dissonant can coexist without creating motivation to change.

A person high in ID would appear to be one who tolerates internal ambiguity and contradiction without experiencing dissonance. The high ID score suggests that the person ordinarily conceives of himself in contradictory terms. It is reasonable to suppose that for him no contradiction is necessarily implied by the fact that present behavior and valued goal are different from one another. For low-ID subjects, dissonance between present self and valued goal is created because of the presence of the unspoken premise, "I do what I value." For subjects high in ID, however, this premise appears to be directly refuted in the real self essay. High-ID subjects will experience as consonant discrepancies between the ideal self and the real self which would be felt as dissonant by low-ID individuals.

If the above reasoning is correct, it may be possible to increase an individual's success in self-directed change by creating conditions which will increase his awareness of dissonance between his self-concept and his ideal-self-concept. Future research should investigate this possibility.

References

ALLPORT, G. *Personality and social encounter.* Boston: Beacon Press, 1960.

ATKINSON, J. W. (Ed.) *Motives in fantasy, action and society.* Princeton: Van Nostrand, 1958.

BRADFORD, L. P., GIBB, J. and BENNE, K. *T-group theory and laboratory method.* New York: Wiley, 1964.

BREHM, J. W. and COHEN, A. R. *Explorations in cognitive dissonance.* New York: Wiley, 1962.

BROWN, R. *Social psychology.* Glencoe, Ill.: The Free Press, 1965.

ERIKSON, E. Identity and the life cycle. *Psychological Issues,* 1959 1(1), 1-171.

FESTINGER, L. *A theory of cognitive dissonance.* Evanston, Ill.: Row-Peterson, 1957.

GOLDIAMOND, I. Self-control procedures in personal behavior problems. *Psychological Reports,* 1965, 17, 851-868.

GROSSBERG, J. M. Behavior therapy: A review. *Psychological Review,* 1964, 62, 73-88.

KOLB, D. A., WINTER, S. K. and BERLEW, D. E. Self-directed change: Two studies. *Journal of Applied Behavioral Science,* 1968, 4(4), 453-472.

McCLELLAND, D. C. Toward a theory of motive acquisition. *American Psychologist,* 1965, 20, 321-333.

ROKEACH, M. *The open and closed mind.* New York: Basic Books, 1960.

SCHWITZGEBEL, R. A simple behavioral system for recording and implementing change in natural settings. Unpublished doctoral dissertation, Harvard School of Education, 1964.

ZACHS, J. Collaborative therapy for smokers. Unpublished manuscript, Harvard University, 1965.

※ ※ ※ ※ ※

What is competence, and how do we get it? We know a good deal about how to cure, how to remediate, and how to teach people specific subject matter—but little about the production of "self-actualized," productive, creative human beings.

Smith takes a thoughtful and fascinating look at this problem in his study of Peace Corps volunteers—able young people who voluntarily took a "moratorium" from more usual educational pursuits. They were a remarkable group, sharing some values with Flacks' student protesters described elsewhere in this book, and were by and large committed to the personal and social challenge of their two years' teaching in Ghana.

The article is an excellent exhibit of how to deal with complex, rich data in a coherent way. Smith takes us behind the methodological scenes in a comfortably relaxed manner. Research is much more like this picture than it is like the official "Problem . . . Hypotheses . . . Methods . . . Findings . . . Discussion" format. The article shows well how intensive interview data can be treated meaningfully via Q-sort methods and factor analysis. The reader without background in factor analysis should not worry, but concentrate on the meaningfulness of the patterns or clusters Smith reviews.

Substantively, we see once again (as with Winter, Griffith, and Kolb and Kounin, Gump, and Ryan, that the learner's forward projections (his goal-setting and goal-seeking activity) are of intense relevance to his own growth. It is of special interest that the "mock autobiography" technique used to assess orientation toward the future did an excellent job of predicting performance when a standardized test of authoritarianism, and psychiatric judgments, failed. Might mock autobiographies be used in ordinary school settings?

Explorations in Competence:
A Study of Peace Corps Teachers in Ghana*

M. Brewster Smith

One of the hopeful aspects of our affluent society—and I persist in believing that there are many—is our increasing concern with psychological effectiveness and fulfillment. Like the hierarchy of needs that Abraham Maslow (1954) has proposed, there seems to be a hierarchy of human goals that underlie fashions of value-oriented research. When people are undernourished and die young, as they still do in much of the world, research and action on public health is the first order of business. Achievements in this initial sphere have brought us to realize belatedly that successful attack on the "underdeveloped syndrome" requires knowledge and action on two additional fronts: economic development, to provide a better livelihood for the growing and now impatient numbers who survive; and population control, lest economic gains dissolve into net losses. Psychologists are beginning to find a challenge for research in the former topic (McClelland, 1965); they have still to rise to the need and the opportunity in regard to the second.

The basic problems of human survival and maintenance are never permanently solved, but social priorities do shift. Over the last generation American psychologists have found a good deal of social support in their preoccupation with derangements of conduct and social relations among physically healthy people—a concern that would have seemed an unwarranted luxury in a society where the more exigent problems of health and hunger had not been substantially tamed. These problems are still with us, and as we extend our attention to the submerged and essentially underdeveloped sectors of our own society, they will rank high in our scheme of priorities for a good while longer.

* From *American Psychologist*, 1966, 21(6), 555-566. Used by permission of the author and publisher.

Invited address, Division 8, American Psychological Association, Chicago, September, 1965; written during tenure as Fellow of the Center for Advanced Study in the Behavioral Sciences and Special Research Fellow of the National Institute of Mental Health. The data reported are based on a study at the Institute of Human Development, University of California, Berkley, under contract No. PC-(W)-55 with the Peace Corps, which of course is not responsible for the opinions and judgments that I have ventured to express. A fuller report of the study will be presented in a book in preparation, to be published by John Wiley and Sons. I am especially indebted to my closest associates in this research, Raphael S. Ezekiel and Susan Roth Sherman; to George Carter, the initial Peace Corps Representative in Ghana; and to the volunteers themselves whose tolerance and hospitality made my research both possible and gratifying.

All the same, psychologists are beginning to bring psychological research to bear upon the forms and conditions of more positive aspects of human functioning, under such rubrics as "positive mental health," psychological effectiveness, creativity, and competence. These may still be middle-class luxuries, but it is now politically astute, not merely visionary, to conceive of a "great society" in which such phrasings of the good life become relevant for everybody.

When we turn from the bottom of the hierarchy of social goals, where consensus on values is easily had in regard to the minimal essentials of life in society, to the unimagined variety of paths along which people may seek fulfillment, it is easy to lose our bearings, to confuse tendentious pleading for our own versions of the good life with the explorations of empirical fact. I have done my own share of floundering in these waters, fishing from the armchair in discussions of "positive mental health" (Smith, 1959, 1961). From the armchair, the critical need seemed to me to be for more adequate mapping of facts and relationships concerning widely valued modes of behavior.

I therefore grasped the opportunity to make an intensive study of a group of promising young people who were faced with a challenging assignment: the first group of Peace Corps volunteers to go overseas, who trained in Berkeley in the summer of 1961 and served for two years as secondary school teachers in Ghana. The combined idealistic-practical auspices of the Peace Corps seemed right, and Nicholas Hobbs (then Director of Selection and Research for the Peace Corps) was encouraging. I saw the study as an investigation of psychological effectiveness (let us put aside the awkward terminology of "mental health"). More recently, the cogency of Robert White's (1959, 1963) conceptions to my emerging data has become increasingly apparent, so that I now think of myself as having been engaged in "explorations in competence."

There were 58 young people who entered training in Berkeley, 50 of whom completed one year[1] and 45 completed two years of overseas service. Our most intensive data are for 27 men and 17 women who finished the two-year term. I met my obligations to the Peace Corps with a technical report (Smith, 1964), and since then have been working on a volume that intends to illuminate the statistical findings with a series of illustrative case studies.

Here I must be selective. I shall draw on our findings to develop several themes that represent things I think I have learned about competence in this special Peace Corps setting.

My major points will be four. First, in regard to the nature of competence in this group, time, and setting: Our data support the view that competence has a coherent core of common psychological attributes. But, second,

---

1. Their mean age of entry was 24.0 (range, 19–34); subsequent groups averaged about a year younger. Forty-six per cent had had a year or more of teaching experience; subsequent groups were less experienced.

competent performance takes various forms, which people reach by different psychological routes. Third, in regard to the prediction of competent
performance: Two reasonable possibilities, grounded in the respective
thought patterns of social psychologists and of psychiatrists and clinical
psychologists, turn out not to work at all, while a third predictor, introduced on a hunch, shows promise. Both the failures and the relative success
have something to say about the psychological nature of competence.
Finally, we have some evidence about the maturing effects of Peace Corps
service, which lends itself to speculation about motivational aspects of the
Peace Corps experience.

From Field Interviews to *Q* Sort Patterns

Before I can turn to the first of these topics, a word is needed about the
kind of data that we will be dealing with. Of course we had a kit of pencil-
and-paper tests, some of them administered both before and after overseas
experience. We also had various staff ratings from the training period and
from the field. Our central information about the experience and performance of the volunteers, however, came from long and detailed interviews
that R. S. Ezekiel and I recorded with the volunteers at their schools in the
early summer of 1962 and 1963.

Our reliance on informal interviews made a virtue of necessity. Practical
considerations excluded the systematic use of classroom observation, or of
data from students, fellow teachers, or headmasters. The spirited touchiness
of the volunteers themselves in regard to psychological assessment procedures—partly a residue of their experience during selection-in-training at
Berkeley—required us to establish an essentially collaborative relationship
with them if we were to do the study at all. Fortunately, the volunteers
liked to talk about their lives and jobs, and we were able to gain a satisfying
degree of rapport with them—which still continues.

We planned the guide for the first-year interviews on the basis of my
quick reconnaissance during the volunteers' first Christmas in Ghana. As it
turned out, the roughly 4 hours of interviewing apiece the first year, and
2½ the second, gave a highly informative picture of what the volunteer had
made of his job and Peace Corps role and of his qualities as a person as they
were brought out in this novel and challenging setting. We were well satisfied
with the quality of our interviews. But how to process them to preserve
their richness yet assure the maximum degree of objectivity that we
could attain?

Our first and crucial decision on behalf of objectivity was made at the
onset: to record and transcribe the interviews in full. Following the lead
of my colleague Jack Block (1961), we then invested major effort in constructing two decks of *Q* sort items that "judges" could use to extract
and quantify the meat of the interview transcripts. One deck, of 65 items
in the final version, dealt with the volunteer's role perceptions, personal

agenda, and role performance. The second, of 64 items, permitted judges to characterize the volunteer's personality structure and processes.[2] These sets of items were in development over much of a year. Our procedure was to hold "clinical" conferences in the attempt to formulate what the interviews could tell us about the personality and performance of particular volunteers, then to translate our intuitive insights into items. There followed the usual tedious process of trial use by the research staff and by naive judges, and endless editing and revision.

Once the decks had been refined to our satisfaction, we had 12 advanced graduate students in psychology use them to characterize each volunteer after studying the transcript of his interviews. The judges were given a brief orientation to the setting and special terminology of "Peace Corps—Ghana" and discussed their discrepancies in the rating of a practice case—the investigator carefully holding back his own version of "the truth"—but they were otherwise unfamiliar with the volunteers and with the preconceptions of the investigator. Their task in each case was to sort the items of a given deck in a prescribed 9-point distribution, ranging from the three items that appeared to be most saliently characteristic or newsworthy about the volunteer (given a rating of 9) down to the three that seemed most saliently uncharacteristic of him (a rating of 1). Clearly, normative considerations about what might be expected of people in general and of Peace Corps volunteers in particular intrude into these ipsative ratings. The advantage of the ipsative task over normative ratings would seem to lie, rather, in its focus on the *patterning* of personality and performance, thus reducing the potency of general halo effects that might otherwise obscure patterned differences among volunteers.

We will be concerned here with Q sorts made on the basis of reading *both* years' interviews with a particular volunteer (giving precedence to status as of the final year in cases of evident change). Depending on the extent of interjudge agreement achieved by the first pair of raters to Q sort a case, from two to six judges contributed to each of the composite Q sort ratings that constitute our central data. On the basis of the average interjudge correlations for each case, appropriately transformed,[3] the role performance Q set was judged with a mean estimated reliability of .76; the personality set with a mean estimated reliability of .68.

The composite ratings of each volunteer on the two Q sets allow us to identify distinguishable major patterns of personal orientation and performance in Peace Corps service. The first step was to compute the matrix of interperson correlations for each of the two sets. We could then carry out a Q oriented principal-components factor analysis on each matrix. The

2. A third Q deck characterizing the volunteer's view of his situation, its challenges and limitations, and aspects of morale and job satisfaction was also developed; results depending on this deck are drawn upon in the larger study, but will not be cited here.

3. Average r's were computed via Fisher's z transformation, and corrected by the Spearman-Brown formula according to the number of judges contributing to a given composite.

first principal component that was produced from each of the two analyses, which accounted for 41% and 44%, respectively, of the communality of the role performance and the personality matrices, defined a highly evaluative dimension, as we could see from the items that received high or low factor scores, and from our acquaintance with the volunteers who received high or low factor loadings. Loadings on these factors thus provided us with measures of general competence as reflected in the interviews, and refracted through the Q sorts for role performance and for personality. Volunteers' loadings on these factors correlated .26 and .35, respectively, with administrative ratings of over-all performance as of the end of the second year—modest correlations to be sure, but better than 0 at $p < .05$ for the personality factor. Loadings on the first personality and first performance factors were closely intercorrelated: $r = .89$.

The evaluative halo extracted in the first principal component factors was thus of interest to us in its own right, for its item content and for the evaluative criteria that the factor loadings provided against which to test predictor variables. But we were also interested in penetrating and dissecting this halo, insofar as possible, to distinguish recurrent patterns of role performance and of personality functioning overseas: coherent ways in which volunteers resembled or differed from one another in their handling of the Peace Corps role and in their traits and coping styles as inferred from the field interviews. To this end we carried out varimax rotations of the factors obtained through the principal-components analysis. Three clearly interpretable patterns of role performance and six of personality emerged from this analysis—much to our surprise after months of delayed gratification while interview tapes were transcribed, Q decks built, transcripts judged, and cards punched. But now it is time to look at the data.

Some Patterns of Competence

A Picture of General Competence

Let us first look at the evaluative first principal components, beginning with the one based on Q sorts with the personality deck. Table 1 lists the items that were especially characteristic of volunteers who received high loadings on this factor: items with factor scores a standard deviation or more above the mean. The items defining what is *un*characteristic of these volunteers—those with distinctively low factor scores, are given in Table 2. Inspection of the tables shows a pattern of self-confidence, high self-esteem, energy, principled responsibility, optimistic realism, and persistence with flexibility, among other virtues. We felt justified in labelling this P-1 pattern "Self-Confident Maturity."

The corresponding first factor based on the role performance deck really gives us an alternative perspective on the same facts, since it is based on the same interviews and much the same people obtained high loadings.

Table 1

ITEMS WITH HIGH FACTOR SCORES ON PERSONALITY
FACTOR P-1: SELF-CONFIDENT MATURITY

ITEM	FACTOR SCORE
Generally self-confident	73
A genuinely dependable and responsible person.	69
The values and principles which he holds directly affect what he does.	65
Feels his own life is important, that it matters what he does with his life.	65
Open to experience, ready to learn.	62
Tolerant and understanding.	61
Characteristically maintains a highly articulate, intellectual formulation of his situation and problems.	60

Table 2

ITEMS WITH LOW FACTOR SCORES ON PERSONALITY
FACTOR P-1: SELF-CONFIDENT MATURITY

ITEM	FACTOR SCORE
Feels a lack of worth; has low self-esteem.	24
Basically a dependent person; characteristically leans upon others for support.	33
Has had a characteristically high level of anxiety during the time in Ghana.	33
Tends to expect little of life, pessimistic.	33
Seems generally to lack energy, to operate at a markedly low key. ...	35
Tends to be suspicious of others.	35
Tends to give up easily when faced with setbacks.	36
Would be unable to accept help from others when in need.	37
When things go badly, would tend to let them drift.	37
Tends to be preoccupied with matters of physical health.	38
Irritable and overresponsive to petty annoyances.	38
Engages in "posturing" to self and others; concerned with maintaining "face."	39
Tends unrealistically to minimize or deny the difficulties that he faces.	40

Table 3 shows the items that have high scores on this factor. Commitment to and competence in the teaching role top the list, with liking for one's students a close third. Other items emphasize qualities both of the volunteer's teaching and of his involvement with Africa. In Table 4 are given the *uncharacteristic* items, with low factor scores. These items paint a picture of low competence and commitment, and of a variety of ways in which a volunteer might perform his role less than well. We label this P-1 performance pattern "Competent Teaching in Africa."

The pictures that emerge from the two Q sort decks readily coalesce. We find a pattern defined on its good side by qualities of warranted self-confidence, commitment, energy, responsibility, autonomy, flexibility, and

Table 3

ITEMS WITH FACTOR SCORES ON PERFORMANCE

FACTOR P-1: COMPETENT TEACHING IN AFRICA

ITEM	FACTOR SCORE
Committed to carrying out his job as Peace Corps teacher to the best of his ability.	72
Is, all-in-all, a good competent teacher.	71
Generally likes his students, treats them with warmth and understanding.	66
Values his Peace Corps assignment as relevant to his career plans.	63
Views his teaching in terms of its contribution to the personal welfare or development of his students.	62
In his appraisal of Ghanaian life and institutions, is sympathetically critical; forms his own judgments with due regard to historical and cultural differences.	62
As a teacher emphasizes challenging students to think.	61
His African experiences have increased his concern with race relations in the United States.	61
Judges Ghanaian governmental policies and actions in terms of the needs of Ghana (regardless of approval or disapproval).	61
His approach to teaching integrates the formal curricular and examination requirements with his own sense of proper educational objectives.	60
Has shown consideration in his dealings with adult Ghanaians.	60

Table 4

ITEMS WITH LOW FACTOR SCORES ON PERFORMANCE

FACTOR P-1: COMPETENT TEACHING IN AFRICA

ITEM	FACTOR SCORE
Incompetent in his understanding of the major subject matter that he has to teach.	25
Feels mostly negative about Ghanaians he has met, really doesn't like them very much.	27
Overidentified with Ghana, attempts to "go native."	30
Has little real interest in Ghana.	31
Shows a lack of tact in relations with students.	33
Imposes own educational objectives at expense of preparing student for formal curricular and examination requirements.	34
Sees his school job as one restricted almost entirely to the classroom— the "9 to 5" attitude.	36
Tends to be condescending toward his students.	36
His personal problems of finding himself take priority for him over the tasks of the Peace Corps assignment.	37
Reacts to his students as a category or as types, rather than as individuals (N.B. regardless of degree of warmth or liking).	39

hopeful realism together with other skills and attitudes more specifically appropriate to the role of Peace Corps teacher. The pattern has psychological coherence, in that having some of these virtues should make it easier to have the others. (If you lack most of them, it is very hard to get a start on acquiring any of them—as we are learning from efforts to relaunch culturally deprived youth.) Undoubtedly, raters' halo exaggerates the coherence of our data: To a degree that we cannot ascertain, raters will have attributed miscellaneous virtues to the volunteers of whom they came to think well, on whatever grounds. We will assume, all the same, that this syndrome of general competence rests on underlying psychological fact. Other coherences in our data tend to lend to this assumption at least some support.

Patterns of Role Performance

Turn now to the discriminable patterns of role performance that emerge from varimax rotation. For the sake of economy, we will look only at the items with distinctively high factor scores. Under rotation, the generally evaluative dimension of Competent Teaching in Africa pulls apart into two distinct patterns, one emphasizing involvement with Africa, the other an exclusive commitment to teaching.

Table 5 shows the items with high scores on Factor V-1, "Constructive Involvement with Africa." They emphasize good personal relations with students and with other Africans, and a thoughtful integration of the experience of Africa, coupled with commitment to the teaching job.

Quite in contrast is the picture of Factor V-2, "Exclusive Teaching Commitment" (Table 6). Volunteers who loaded high on this factor were skillfully devoted to their teaching almost to the exclusion of other involvements with Africa: their contact with Africa was deep but narrow, through their school and students.

Our third varimax performance factor looks the opposite of "gung-ho." From the items with high factor scores in Table 7, we see that this pattern characterizes volunteers who, by and large, were good teachers, but were low in commitment both to modern Africa and to the teaching job. They were "9-to-5ers" who nevertheless often made a substantial contribution to their schools. The negative correlation of $-.50$ between factor loadings on "Limited Commitment" and on the P-1 competence factor reflects the relatively low evaluation they tended to receive from the Q sort judges; they did not fare so badly in administrative evaluation.

The results so far carry a message of some practical importance. They show that although a syndrome of general competence in the Peace Corps role can be identified, two quite different patterns of competent performance emerged, both "good." We will see that different personality patterns accompanied these distinctive performance styles. Selection policies based on a stereotyped conception of the ideal volunteer could readily go astray.

Table 5

ITEMS WITH HIGH FACTOR SCORES ON PERFORMANCE
FACTOR V-1: CONSTRUCTIVE INVOLVEMENT WITH AFRICA*

ITEM	FACTOR SCORE
His African experiences have increased his concern with race relations in the United States.	68
Generally likes his students, treats them with warmth and understanding.	65
Has established intimate, continuing relationships with adult Africans.	64
Enjoys or admires Ghanaian style of living.	64
In his appraisal of Ghanaian life and institutions, is sympathetically critical; forms his own judgments with due regard to historical and cultural differences.	63
Is on friendly terms with many Ghanaians (apart from his students). (N.B. Disregard depth of the relationship.)	63
Has developed close, personal relationships with some of his students.	61
Committed to carrying out his job as Peace Corps teacher to the best of his ability.	61
In anticipating his return he is concerned with interpreting Ghana and/or West Africa to Americans.	61
Judges Ghanaian governmental policies and actions in terms of the needs of Ghana (Regardless of approval or disapproval).	61
Views his teaching in terms of its contribution to the personal welfare or development of his students.	60
Views his teaching in terms of its contribution to the development of Ghana.	60
As a result of his experience in Ghana, his thoughts and feelings about America show increased depth and perspective.	60

* Note.—Twenty-seven per cent of communality; r with P-1 (performance) = .84, r with P-1 (personality) = .68.

Personality Patterns in the Field Interviews

Since six intelligible patterns appeared in the varimax analysis of the personality Q sorts, I must hold myself to a summary treatment. The labels we gave them appear in Table 8, together with the correlations between loadings on each of them and loadings on the evaluative first principal components. The table also shows their relationships to the varimax performance factors, again correlating factor loadings taken as scores.

Three of the patterns are associated with competent performance. V-1, Interpersonally Sensitive Maturity, differs little from the P-1 factor based on the same Q sort, except that it gives greater emphasis to interpersonal openness, nurturance, empathy, and intensity of self-involvement. Women were more likely than men to fit this pattern. The other two "good" patterns were more characteristic of men: V-2, Intellectualizing Future Orientation, and V-5, Controlling Responsibility.

Table 6

ITEMS WITH HIGH FACTOR SCORES ON PERFORMANCE

FACTOR V-2: EXCLUSIVE TEACHING COMMITMENT*

ITEM	FACTOR SCORE
His whole life has centered on the school compound.	78
Absorbed in his work.	70
Committed to carrying out his job as Peace Corps teacher to the best of his ability.	69
Is, all-in-all, a good competent teacher.	69
Spends much time preparing lessons, correcting papers, etc.	67
As a teacher emphasizes challenging students to think.	64
Has well defined teaching goals and objectives.	62
Has worked out a balance between informality and closeness to students, on the one hand, and the requirements of discipline and authority on the other.	62
Generally likes his students, treats them with warmth and understanding.	61
His approach to teaching integrates the formal curricular and examination requirements with his own sense of proper educational objectives.	61
Concerned with setting Ghanaians a good personal example.	61

* Note.—Nineteen per cent of communality; r with P-1 (performance) = .32, r with P-1 (personality) = .31.

Table 7

ITEMS WITH HIGH FACTOR SCORES ON PERFORMANCE

FACTOR V-3: LIMITED COMMITMENT*

ITEM	FACTOR SCORE
Most of his time outside of class is spent in reading, recreation, or other activities unrelated to work.	71
Establishing relationships with the opposite sex has been an important aspect of his period of Peace Corps service.	68
Is, all-in-all, a good competent teacher.	67
Sees his school job as one restricted almost entirely to the classroom—the "9 to 5" attitude.	66
His approach to teaching integrates the formal curricular and examination requirements with his own sense of proper educational objectives.	65
Was quick to become aware of difficulties in communicating with students in the classroom and to adapt his teaching accordingly.	65
Has many, or close, contacts with expatriates (off school compound).	63
Interested in traditional Ghanaian life and customs.	61
Meets his teaching obligations day-by-day with little long-term planning.	61
Concerned with introducing American educational approaches and techniques.	60

* Note.—Nine per cent of communality; r with P-1 (performance) = −.50, r with P-1 (personality) = −.39.

One pattern, when it appeared, strongly tended to be incompatible with good performance: V-4, Dependent Anxiety. Finally, there were two well-defined patterns that showed little correlation with loadings on the evaluative P-1 factors: V-3, Self-Reliant Conventionality, and V-6, Self-Actualizing Search for Identity.

The right-hand column of the table shows the main lines of relationship between these personality patterns and the varimax performance factors. Let us note the major correlates of each of these performance patterns in turn. We see that performance factor V-1, Constructive Involvement with Africa, is positively linked with Interpersonally Sensitive Maturity and with Intellectualizing Future Orientation—alternative routes toward getting involved with Africa—and negatively with Dependent Anxiety. V-2, Exclusive Teaching Commitment, is closely tied with Controlling Responsibility, and negatively linked with Self-Actualizing Search for Identity. Finally, V-3, Limited Commitment, is associated with both Self-Reliant Conventionality and with Dependent Anxiety, as alternative psychological bases, and is negatively related to Interpersonally Sensitive Maturity and to Controlling Responsibility. Diverse personal styles are indeed involved in the patterns of performance that our method has discerned in the interviews.

We can put a little meat on these bones by looking at the items that define patterns V-5 and V-6, to which we will have occasion to refer subsequently. Factor V-5, Controlling Responsibility, is presented in Table 9. Volunteers who were high on this factor tended, we remember, also to be high on Exclusive Teaching Commitment. They were steady, somewhat rigid people, self-contained but given to intense involvement. Highly *un*characteristic items (not shown) indicate that self-control was as important to them as control over the situations that they faced. They tended to be low in emphatic sensitivity but high in nurturance. They had considerable personal resources.

In contrast to them are the interesting volunteers who showed the pattern to which we have given the perhaps pretentious but nevertheless descriptive label, Self-Actualizing Search for Identity. The defining items with high factor scores appear in Table 10. These volunteers, like those who were high on V-2 (Intellectualizing Future Orientation), appear to have been in good communication with themselves and to have found the topic interesting; the search for identity was still a prominent part of their agenda of young adulthood. But whereas the volunteers who were high on Intellectualizing Future Orientation seem in general to have gained the upper hand in the struggle for self-definition, those who were high on V-6 were clearly in the midst of a postadolescent turmoil. The Q sort items describe them as intense, unconventional, and impulsive, a bit confused and chaotic, not at all sure of themselves or of what the future might offer. But they were working hard and constructively, if somewhat erratically, on the problem: Self-cultivation and improvement stood high on their personal agenda.

Table 8

PERSONALITY PATTERNS DERIVED FROM INTERVIEW Q SORTS AND
SOME OF THEIR CORRELATES

PATTERN	% COMMUNALITY	r WITH P-1 LOADINGS		CLOSEST CORRELATES AMONG ROLE PERFORMANCE FACTORS
		PERF.	PERS.	
V-1, Interpersonally sensitive maturity	27%	.80	.82	V-1 (Involv. in Afr.): .74
				V-3 (Limited commit.): -.43
V-2, Intellectualizing future orientation	13%	.48	.57	V-1 (Involv. in Afr.): .40
V-3, Self-reliant conventionality	12%	-.07	.08	V-3 (Limited commit.): .50
V-4, Dependent anxiety	11%	-.76	-.87	V-1 (Involv. in Afr.): -.58
				V-3 (Limited commit.): .40
V-5, Controlling responsibility	11%	.46	.50	V-2 (Exclus. teach.): .62
				V-3 (Limited commit.): -.51
V-6, Self-actualizing search for identity	7%	-.15	-.11	V-2 (Exclus. teach.): -.38

Table 9

ITEMS WITH HIGH FACTOR SCORES ON PERSONALITY
FACTOR V-5: CONTROLLING RESPONSIBILITY*

ITEM	FACTOR SCORE
Control of his situation is important to him.	75
A genuinely dependable and responsible person.	69
Engages in "posturing" to self and others; concerned with maintaining "face."	67
Preoccupied with the power aspects of relations.	66
Intense, tends to involve self deeply.	65
Is uneasy when the situation is not clearly defined.	65
The values and principles which he holds directly affect what he does.	65
High in initiative; active rather than reactive.	65
Nurturant; enjoys helping the younger or less adequate.	62
A major component of his stance has been his assumption that one meets one's daily obligations as a matter of course.	61
Generally self-confident.	60

* Note.—Eleven per cent of communality; r with P-1 (personality) = .50, r with P-1 (performance) = .46.

Table 10

ITEMS WITH HIGH FACTOR SCORES ON PERSONALITY FACTOR V-6:
SELF-ACTUALIZING SEARCH FOR IDENTITY*

ITEM	FACTOR SCORE
Feels his own life is important, that it matters what he does with his life.	73
Devotes much of his energy to a deliberate program of self-improvement (creative activity, study, etc.).	73
Intense, tends to involve self deeply.	72
Is aware of his own feelings and motives.	68
The values and principles which he holds directly affect what he does.	65
Copes with the novelty of the Ghanaian experience by seeking relationships, activities and settings that let him continue important personal interests.	64
Unsure just who he is or who he ought to be or how he fits into the world.	63
Impulsive; undercontrolled (N.B. opposite implies over-controlled).	60
Is actively striving toward a clearer, more complex or mature sense of identity.	60

* Note.—Seven per cent of communality; r with P-1 (personality) = $-.11$, r with P-1 (performance) = $-.15$.

Some Problems of Prediction

It is one thing to explore, as we have been doing, the relationship between patterns of role performance and of personality overseas, both derived from judgments of the same field interviews. This is to extract, as objectively and sensitively as we can, what the interviews have to say. To do so has obviously been informative. But to *predict* performance from independent measures of personality is quite another matter, in regard to which the entire experience of personnel psychology must caution us against optimism. I now turn to three attempts at prediction of competence, two of them failures, one a qualified success. For criterion variables we will use factor loadings on the evaluative first principal component factors, and also second-year evaluative ratings, made on a 5-point scale by the Peace Corps Representative in Ghana. We will also refer to loadings on some of the varimax patterns that we have just examined.

Authoritarianism

Since I will be having some sharp things to say about the predictive value of mental health assessments, it is only tactful to begin with a failure of a prediction made on what I thought were good social psychological grounds. Persons high in authoritarianism, I would have supposed, should be hampered by traits of ethnocentrism and rigidity, among others, from performing well as teachers in Africa. To make a long story short,[4] we employed two measures of authoritarianism: one, a 24-item version identical to that used by Mischel (1965) and closely similar to the versions employed in *The Authoritarian Personality* (Adorno, Levinson, Sanford, and Frenkel-Brunswik, 1950); the other a more sophisticated 100-item instrument carefully balanced to eliminate the effect of response sets. We obtained surprisingly good evidence that these measures, particularly the more sophisticated one, sorted the volunteers out at the time they were in training along a composite dimension, the ingredients of which were essentially as the authors of *The Authoritarian Personality* had claimed, including intolerance of ambiguity, over-control, moralism, projectivity, conservatism, distrustfulness of others, and repressiveness. Yet scores on authoritarianism showed essentially null correlations with loadings on the general competence patterns and with administrative evaluations. The only appreciable correlations involving our better measure of authoritarianism were with V-2, Intellectualizing Future Orientation ($-.38$, $p<.05$) and with V-6, Self-Actualizing Search for Identity ($-.26$, $p<.10$), both patterns that involved good communication with and about the self.

Second thoughts after direct experience in the field suggest that the prediction was naive in giving insufficient weight to a job analysis of the requirements on a teacher in an essentially authoritarian educational setting.[5] In any case, it is apparent that although our measure did relate sensibly to certain personality patterns overseas, it did *not* contribute to the prediction of competent performance.

4.   A full account of methods and results is given in Smith (1965a).

5.   It would be particularly interesting to know the predictive values of measures of authoritarianism for performance in community development settings, where higher levels of flexibility and tolerance for ambiguity would seem to be essential than in classroom teaching.

Psychiatric Ratings

Early in the training period at Berkeley, each volunteer was seen in two 50-minute appraisal interviews by psychiatrists from the Langley-Porter Neuropsychiatric Institute.[6] Each of the seven participating psychiatrists made a variety of predictive ratings. The most reliable of these required the psychiatrist to rate the "predicted psychological effectiveness" of the 16 or 17 trainees that he had seen, on a 7-point scale with a prescribed distribution. The correlation between ratings given by first and second interviewers was .41.

On what did the psychiatrists base their predictive ratings? We were able to find out, since they also wrote 2- or 3-page freehand summaries of each interview. We had these summaries translated into ratings by independent judges on Jack Block's (1961) California Q set for the general dynamic description of personality, and performed an item analysis by t test looking for Q sort items that discriminated between the 20 volunteers whom the psychiatrists rated highest in "psychological effectiveness" and the 20 rated lowest. Not surprisingly in view of the psychiatrists' professional training, their responsibility for weeding out disqualifying pathology, and their essential ignorance of the criterion situation, the discriminating items corresponded closely with the ones listed by Block (1961, pp. 144-145) as defining, positively or negatively, "the optimally adjusted personality" as viewed by clinical psychologists—what amounts to a "mental health stereotype." The mean item Q sort ratings for the group regarded more favorably by the psychiatrists correlated (rho = .78) with Block's item data for the mental health stereotype; for the less favorably regarded group, the corresponding rho was .07. The items ordered in much the same way with respect to discriminatory power (t) as they did with respect to the degree to which they were seen by clinical psychologists as characterizing the "optimally adjusted personality" (rho = .83).

The psychiatrists' "mental health" ratings had a close to 0 correlation with our criterion measures of competent performance. Within the admittedly restricted range of volunteers actually sent overseas, the degree to which a person's adjustment as appraised by the psychiatrists approximated the "optimal" pattern simply had nothing to do with the adequacy with which he performed in the Peace Corps role.[7]

---

6. This procedure was tried out by the Peace Corps for experimental purposes, and does not represent current practice. I am grateful to M. Robert Harris for making the results of the psychiatric interviews available to me.

7. Apart from self-selection by the volunteers and pre-selection by the Peace Corps on the basis of letters of reference, 8 of 58 volunteers in training were not sent overseas. Of these, 1 fled training in panic; for 4 others, judgments regarding personal adjustment played a substantial role in deselection. My present hunch, for what it is worth, is that 2 or 3 of these would have been quite successful had they been sent to Ghana. The really dubious case would have been deselected by nonprofessionals relying on the naked eye.

An intriguing footnote to this convincingly null over-all relationship emerges when we divide the volunteers according to whether their schools were located in the major cities, in provincial towns, or in more remote "bush" settings. The groups are small, but striking differences in correlation appear. In relation to second-year administrative evaluations, for example, where the over-all correlation with psychiatric ratings is −.02, there is a positive correlation of .54 for the city teachers, a correlation of −.02 for the intermediate ones, and one of −.36 for those with bush assignments! Other data support the view that this is not a chance finding. Clearly the implications of the psychiatrists' ratings were situationally specific, rather than pertaining to general competence. I will forego speculation about what situational factors were involved, except to suggest that city assignments, which diverged greatly from the volunteers' expectations, seemed to give rise to certain special morale problems among this initial Peace Corps group.

Dimensions of the Personal Future

After this dismal but familiar story of predictive failure, now for a modest success! At the time the Ghana volunteers were in training at Berkeley, Raphael Ezekiel, then a beginning graduate student, was working with me on the psychology of time perspectives. It occurred to him that a subject's view of his own personal future should have a clearer psychological significance than indices derived from Thematic Apperception Test stories and the like. We adapted a procedure that he was currently trying on other groups, and included in the battery for the trainees the assignment of writing three essays: one about their alternative immediate plans if they were not accepted in the Peace Corps, one a brief "mock autobiography" covering the three years after return from Peace Corps service, and the third a similar mock autobiography covering the year in which they would be 40 years old.[8]

These essays were rated with satisfactory reliability by independent judges (Spearman-Brown r's of .70 to .80 for the several dimensions, once the protocols of certain volunteers who were independently judged to have rejected the task had been eliminated) on three 7-point scales: *Differentiation*, the extent to which each essay showed complex and detailed mapping of the future; *Agency*, the extent to which the essays as a whole showed the future self as the prime agent in determining the course of the person's future life; and *Demand*, the extent to which they described a life viewed by the respondent as demanding long-term continuing effort. Each of these correlated dimensions has its own distinctive pattern of correlates, but we will be concerned here only with correlates of a sum score across all of them.

The sum score correlated .41 ($p < .01$) with the over-all administrative evaluation of the volunteers' effectiveness as of the second year. As for our Q

---

8. A fourth essay, an imaginary letter from Ghana to a friend describing the volunteer's life and activities, was dropped from analysis when it appeared to evoke a highly stereotyped regurgitation of official doctrine received in training.

sort dimensions based on the field interviews, correlations with the generally evaluative P-1 factors were insignificant but positive. The stronger correlations were with loadings on two particular personality patterns, both moderately correlated in turn with the measures of over-all competence derived from the interviews: V-2, Intellectualizing Future Orientation ($r=.41$, $p < .05$), and V-5, Controlling Responsibility ($r=.43$, $p < .01$). We have already seen the items defining the latter factor. Those that define Intellectualizing Future Orientation include: "Characteristically maintains a highly articulate intellectual formulation of his situation and problems," "Has long term goals," "Has a complex, well-differentiated picture of his own future," "Feels his own life is important, that it matters what he does with his life"—items that correspond strikingly to the dimensions on which the mock autobiographies were rated.

Table 11

ITEMS THAT ARE CHARACTERISTIC OF VOLUNTEERS
WITH HIGH SUM SCORES ON MOCK AUTOBIOGRAPHIES

ITEM	p^a
Personality Q sort	
Envisions a challenging and demanding personal future.	.05
Characteristically maintains a highly articulate intellectual formulation of his situation and problems.	.05
Shows inventiveness, ingenuity.	.05
Has developed a well-balanced, varied, and stable program for self of work, relaxation, relief or escape.	.05
Devotes much of his energy to a deliberate program of self-improvement (creative activity, study, etc.).	.10
High in initiative; active rather than reactive.	.10
Performance Q sort	
Elaborates his performance of teaching duties in non-routine imaginative ways; invests self creatively in teaching job in and out of class.	.01
Values his Peace Corps assignment as relevant to his career plans.	.05
Actively employs self in useful, school-related activities outside of class.	.10
Concerned with using his Peace Corps experience to test himself.	.10

[a] By t test comparing extreme thirds of distribution.

We may gain a fuller picture of the psychological meaning of the sum scores by looking at the Q sort items from the personality and role performance decks that discriminate high scorers from low scorers significantly by t test. The ones that are more characteristic of high scorers are given in Table 11. Apart from items that constitute further construct validation of the index, the picture of inventiveness, initiative, job-elaboration, and self-testing or responsiveness to challenge indicates that the procedure has indeed tapped qualities that should contribute to a more than routine performance.

But it is time to introduce a note of qualification that has its own substantive interest. When, on a hunch, Ezekiel looked separately at data for Protestants and Catholics, who performed equally well on the average, he found that the predictive relationship is entirely concentrated in the Protestant group. For them, the correlation with second-year evaluation is .64 ($p<.01$), while it is only .13 for Catholics. Furthermore, the subordinate dimensions of which the sum score is composed do not intercorrelate as highly for the Catholics as they do for the Protestants. We are of course dealing with such small numbers here that in the absence of replication one can have little confidence. Speculatively, however, exposure to the Protestant Ethic may be required to consolidate the variables on which the mock autobiographies were rated into a coherent psychological dimension.

With this qualification, Ezekiel interprets his measures as tapping the volunteer's readiness to commit himself to demanding tasks and to take active initiative in bringing about desired futures, the pathways to which he sees with some clarity—dispositions exceedingly relevant to the core content of competence as we are beginning to conceive of it. True, there is a bias toward the intellectualizer; but our small sample of strategically evoked verbal behavior does seem to have caught some of the motivational basis for response to the challenge of the Peace Corps assignment with commitment, initiative, and effort. We seem to be on the right track here.[9] Maybe mental health or adjustment (except at the sick extreme) and authoritarianism really were blind alleys.

The Peace Corps and Personality Change

Since our data concerning personality change over the period of Peace Corps service are complex and untidy, I will summarize them cavalierly. In regard to short-run changes, analysis of the field interviews indicated a degree of shift from initial all-out enthusiasm in the first year to more of a "veteran" mentality in the second, in which the volunteers came to be sustained more by their principles than by sheer enthusiasm. In the second year there seems to have been some decrease in involvement on all fronts, a partial withdrawal from full engagement with the opportunities and challenges of the situation. But there were also indications of greater self-insight and raised aspirations for the future. As for the longer run, comparisons are available on two pencil-and-paper questionnaires taken in training and at termination. Consistent shifts in response would appear to indicate that the volunteers became more tough-minded and realistic, more autonomous and independent of authority, and much more concerned with the plight of the American Negro. This was at the time of Birmingham; in the absence of a control group, we cannot assess the importance of the fact that it was from Africa that the volunteers were indignantly viewing events at home.

Messy data aside, my personal impression from knowing a number of the volunteers rather well was that important personality changes in the direc-

9. For a full discussion and analysis of the mock autobiography technique as used in this research, see Ezekiel (1964).

tion of maturity were frequent. I think I know why. My reconstructed account is at least consistent with our data, though it goes considerably beyond what I could use them to establish. It will also serve to put in context some of the themes with which we have been concerned.

When they joined the Peace Corps, many of this initial group of volunteers were not very clear as to why they did so: This was one of the reasons why they prickled when psychologists, psychiatrists, journalists, friends, and casual passers-by insistently asked them the question. Toward the end of their service, one could get a better and I think more accurate answer. The most frequent motivational mix, as I intepret it, was composed in varying proportions to two major ingredients and some minor ones. First, they needed a "psychosocial moratorium," in Erikson's (1956) sense. They were more often than not somewhat unclear about where they were heading, perhaps somewhat dissatisfied with their current directions. Two years' time out for reassessment and self-discovery was welcome, not a major sacrifice. (How the volunteers resented talk of the sacrifices they were making!) But second, and this must be stressed in almost the same breath to give a fair picture, the volunteers wanted to earn and justify this moratorium by doing something that seemed to them simply and intrinsically worthwhile, cutting through the complexities and hypocrisies of modern life and international relations. The Peace Corps as an opportunity for direct personal action toward good ends was strongly appealing. And third—less important—the appeal of adventure and foreign exposure was a factor for some, and the possibility of career-relevant experience for others.

But this account of the volunteers' private motives for joining the Peace Corps does not fairly describe the motivation that *sustained* them in their efforts. Once in, most of them saw and were captured by the challenges of the job and role: students and schools that needed everything they could give, a window on Africa that invited exploration. Their effective motivation was emergent: a response to opportunities and difficulties as challenges to be met, not as frustrations to be endured or "adjusted" to. If this reaction was typical of the group as a whole, it was truest of volunteers who were rated high in competence, and least true of those rated low or characterized by the Limited Commitment pattern.

How did the volunteers' particularly engrossing commitment to the job come about? It was not prominent in their motivation for joining, although their attraction to worthwhile activity as such obviously foreshadows it. Partly, to be sure, it must have been induced by the example and precept of the excellent training staff and Peace Corps leadership in the field. Given the volunteers' initial need to find themselves while doing something valuable intrinsically in simple human terms, however, I think the definite 2-year limit may have been important, though for most it was not salient. One can afford to make a fuller, less reserved or cautious investment of self in an undertaking if the demand is explicitly time limited.

It was this high degree of committed but disinterested investment in a challenging undertaking, I think, that was so auspicious for psychological change in the direction of maturity. Experiences from which the self is held in reserve do not change the self; profit in growth requires its investment.

Largely by self-selection, the volunteers who came to training fortunately contained a majority who were predisposed to respond to the Peace Corps challenge with high commitment. Our experimental mock autobiographies seem to have sampled this predisposition, though only crudely. In contrast, the "mental health" orientation, which received considerable weight during selection-in-training, turned out to be essentially irrelevent to the prediction of competent performance—and even of the volunteers' ability to carry on as teachers given the unforeseen press of stresses and supports that Ghana presented. Psychologists who assume responsibility for Peace Corps selection: please note!

This opportunistic study in the Peace Corps has suggested certain common strands in competence, and also illustrated that in this setting, there were various psychological routes to competent performance. We have not asked, how can young people be raised and educated to cultivate the emergence of competence? What social innovations are needed to capitalize upon existing potentials of competence? How can social and psychological vicious circles be reversed to allow the socially deprived to gain in competence? These questions should stand high on our agenda.[10] Our experience with the Peace Corps as an imaginative social invention carries some suggestions worth pursuing.

10. For a preliminary scouting of these questions, see Smith (1965b), where I report on a conference at which these topics were discussed.

References

ADORNO, T. W., LEVINSON, D. J., SANFORD, R. N. and FRENKEL-BRUNSWIK, E. *The authoritarian personality.* New York: Harper, 1950.

BLOCK, J.   *The Q-sort method in personality assessment and psychiatric research.* Springfield, Ill.: Charles C. Thomas, 1961.

ERIKSON, E. H.   The problem of ego identity. *Journal of the American Psychoanalytic Association,* 1956, 4, 55-121.

EZEKIEL, R. S.   *Differentiation, demand and agency in projections of the personal future: A predictive study of the performance of Peace Corps teachers.* Unpublished doctoral dissertation, University of California, Berkeley, 1964.

MASLOW, A. H.   *Motivation and personality.* New York: Harper, 1954.

McCLELLAND, D.C.   Toward a theory of motive acquisition. *American Psychologist,* 1965, 20, 321-333.

MISCHELL, W.   Predicting the success of Peace Corps volunteers in Nigeria. *Journal of Personality and Social Psychology,* 1965, 1, 510-517.

SMITH, M. B.   Research strategies toward a conception of positive mental health. *American Psychologist,* 1959, 14, 673-681.

SMITH, M. B.   Mental health reconsidered: A special case of the problem of values in psychology. *American Psychologist,* 1961, 16, 299-306.

SMITH, M. B.   Peace Corps teachers in Ghana. Final report of evaluation of Peace Corps project in Ghana. University of California, Institute of Human Development, Berkeley, 1964 (Mimeo).

SMITH, M. B.   An analysis of two measures of "authoritarianism" among Peace Corps teachers. *Journal of Personality*, 1965, 33, 513-535.   (a)

SMITH, M. B.   Socialization for competence. *Items* (Social Science Research Council), 1965, 19, 17-23.   (b)

WHITE, R. W.   Motivation reconsidered: The concept of competence. *Psychological Review*, 1959, 66, 297-333.

WHITE, R. W.   Ego and reality in psychoanalytic theory: A proposal regarding independent ego energies. *Psychological Issues*, 1963, 3, No. 3.

7. COLLEGE CONSEQUENCES

This study by Siegel and Siegel is retained from the first edition as a "classic." The work is a brilliant example of the systematically-conceived and executed field experiment. Other field experiments in this book either deal with more limited settings (Thomas *et al.*), are limited to a short slice of time (Feshbach and Devor), or—more crucially—study settings in which some or all of the subjects were *aware* that some social process was being studied (Bridges *et al.*, Litcher and Johnson).

The Siegels took great pains to be sure that the process of reference-group choice was studied unobtrusively. (They also minimized the manipulation and deception of subjects which is so frequent in experimental social psychology.) If you are interested in the problem of how to measure something without influencing the very thing you are trying to measure—a serious and deep problem in any science and particularly social psychology —you should look at Webb *et al.'s* fascinating book *Unobtrusive Measures* (Rand McNally, 1966).

The other notable feature is the classic clarity with which the essential variables (membership group and reference group) were conceptualized and turned into operational measures.

The reader should note that all subjects were "high status oriented," and had higher E-F scale scores than the general college population; thus, there may be some problems in generalizing the results. Most research on "persuasibility" says that persons with an authoritarian orientation are easier to influence.

Two final plus marks for this article: the raw data are shown so you can perform your own analyses if you wish, and a powerful and little-used test of significance was used. The late Sidney Siegel made a substantial contribution through his book of nonparametric statistical tests; this article shows that he cared about the clarification of substantive problems as well.

Reference Groups, Membership Groups, and Attitude Change*

Alberta Engvall Siegel, Sidney Siegel

In social psychological theory, it has long been recognized that an individual's *membership groups* have an important influence on the values and attitudes he holds. More recently, attention has also been given to the influence of his *reference groups,* the groups in which he aspires to attain or maintain membership. In a given area, membership groups and reference groups may or may not be identical. They are identical when the person aspires to *maintain* membership in the group of which he is a part; they are disparate when the group in which the individual aspires to *attain* membership is one in which he is not a member. It has been widely asserted that both membership and reference groups affect the attitudes held by the individual (See Sherif and Sherif, 1953).

The present study is an examination of the attitude changes which occur over time when reference groups and membership groups are identical and when they are disparate. The study takes advantage of a field experiment which occurred in the social context of the lives of the subjects, concerning events considered vital to them. The subjects were not aware that their membership and reference groups were of research interest; in fact, they did not know that the relevant information about these was available to the investigators.

The field experiment permitted a test of the general hypothesis that both the amount and the direction of a person's attitude change over time depends on the attitude norms of his membership group (whether or not that group is chosen by him) and on the attitude norms of his reference group.

This hypothesis is tested with subjects who shared a common reference group at the time of the initial assessment of attitudes. They were then randomly assigned to alternative membership groups, some being assigned to the chosen group and others to a nonchosen group. Attitudes were reassessed after a year of experience in these alternative membership groups with divergent attitude norms. During the course of the year, some subjects came to take the imposed (initially nonpreferred) membership group as

* From *Journal of Abnormal and Social Psychology,* 1957, 55, 360-364. Used by permission of the authors and publisher. This study was supported by grants from the Committee for the Study of American Values at Stanford University and from the Stanford Value Theory Project.

their reference group. Attitude change after the year was examined in terms of the membership group and reference group identifications of the subjects at that time.

The Field Experiment

The Ss of this study were women students at a large private coeducational university. The study was initiated shortly before the end of their freshman year, when they all lived in the same large freshman dormitory to which they had been assigned upon entering the university. At this university, all women move to new housing for their sophomore year. Several types of housing are available to them: a large dormitory, a medium-sized dormitory, several very small houses which share common dining facilities, and a number of former sorority houses which have been operated by the university since sororities were banished from the campus. These latter are located among the fraternity houses on Fraternity Row, and are therefore known as "Row houses." Although the Row houses are lower in physical comfort than most of the other residences for women, students consider them higher in social status. This observation was confirmed by a poll of students (Siegel, 1954) in which over 90 per cent of the respondents stated that Row houses for women were higher in social status than non-Row houses, the remaining few disclaiming any information concerning status differences among women's residences.

In the Spring of each year, a "drawing" is held for housing for the subsequent year. All freshmen must participate in this drawing, and any other student who wishes to change her residence may participate. It is conducted by the office of the Dean of Women, in cooperation with woman student leaders. Any participant's ballot is understood to be secret. The woman uses the ballot to rank the houses in the order of her preference. After submitting this ballot, she draws a number from the hopper. The rank of that number determines the likelihood that her preference will be satisfied.

In research reported earlier (Siegel, 1954) a random sample was drawn from the population of freshman women at this university, several tests were administered to the Ss in that sample, and (unknown to the Ss) their housing preferences for the forthcoming sophomore year were observed by the investigator. The Ss were characterized as "high status oriented" if they listed a Row house as their first choice, and were characterized as "low status oriented" if they listed a non-Row house as their first choice. The hypothesis under test, drawn from reference group theory and from theoretical formulations concerning authoritarianism, was that high status orientation is a correlate of authoritarianism. The hypothesis was confirmed: freshman women who listed a Row house as their first choice for residence scored significantly higher on the average in authoritarianism, as measured by the E-F scale (Adorno *et al.*, 1950; Gough, 1951), than did women who listed a non-Row house as their first choice. The present study is a continuation of the one described, and uses as its Ss only those members of the original sample who were "high status oriented," i.e., preferred to live in a Row house for the sophomore year. In the initial study, of the 95 Ss whose housing choices were listed, 39 were "high status oriented," i.e., demonstrated that the Row was their reference group by giving a Row house as their first choice in the drawing. Of this group, 28 were available to serve as Ss for the follow-up or "change" study which is the topic of the present paper. These women form a homogeneous subsample in that at the conclusion of their freshman year they shared a common membership group (the freshman dormitory) and a common reference group (the Row). These Ss, however, had divergent experiences during their sophomore year: nine were Row residents during that year (having drawn sufficiently small numbers in the housing drawing to enable them to be assigned to the group of their choice) and the other 19 lived in non-Row houses during that year (having drawn numbers too large to enable them to be assigned to the housing group of their choice).

E-F scores were obtained from each of the 28 Ss in the course of a large-scale testing program administered to most of the women students at the university. Anonymity was guaranteed to the Ss, but a coding procedure permitted the investigators to identify each respondent and thereby to isolate the Ss and compare each S's second E-F score with her first.

To prevent the Ss from knowing that they were participating in a follow-up study, several procedures were utilized: (*a*) many persons who had not served in the earlier study were included in the second sample, (*b*) the testing was introduced as being part of a nation-wide study to establish norms, (*c*) the test administrators were different persons from those who had administered the initial tests, (*d*) Ss who informed the test administrator that they had already taken the "Public Opinion Questionnaire" (E-F scale) were casually told that this did not disqualify them from participating in the current study.

The Ss had no hint that the research was in any way related to their housing arrangements. Testing was conducted in classrooms as well as in residences, and all procedures and instructions were specifically designed to avoid any arousal of the salience of the housing groups in the frame of reference of the research.

The annual housing drawing was conducted three weeks after the sophomore-year testing, and, as usual, each woman's housing ballot was understood to be secret. In this drawing, each S had the opportunity to change her membership group, although a residence move is not required at the end of the sophomore year as it is at the end of the freshman year. If an S participated in this drawing, the house which she listed as her first choice on the ballot was identified by the investigators as her reference group. If she did not, it was evident that the house in which she was currently a member was the one in which she chose to continue to live, i.e., was her reference group. With the information on each S's residence choice at the end of her freshman year, her assigned residence for her sophomore year, and her residence choice at the end of her sophomore year, it was possible to classify the subjects in three categories:

   A. Women ($N = 9$) who had gained assignment to live on the Row during their sophomore year and who did not attempt to draw out of the Row at the end of that year;

   B. Women ($N = 11$) who had not gained assignment to a Row house for the sophomore year and who drew for a Row house again after living in a non-Row house during the sophomore year; and

   C. Women ($N = 8$) who had not gained assignment to a Row house for the sophomore year, and who chose to remain in a non-Row house after living in one during the sophomore year.

For all three groups of Ss, as we have pointed out, membership group (freshman dormitory) and reference group (Row house) were common at the end of the freshman year. For Group A, membership and reference groups were disparate throughout the sophomore year. For Group B, membership and reference groups were disparate throughout the sophomore year. For Group C, membership and reference groups were initially disparate during the sophomore year but became identical because of a change in reference groups.

As will be demonstrated, the Row and the non-Row social groups differ in attitude norms, with Row residents being generally more authoritarian than non-Row residents. From social psychological theory concerning the influence of group norms on individuals' attitudes, it would be predicted that the different group identifications during the sophomore year of the three groups of Ss would result in differential attitude change. Those who gained admittance to a Row house for the sophomore year (Group A) would be expected to show the least change in authoritarianism, for they spent that year in a social context which reinforced their initial attitudes. Group C Ss would be expected to show the greatest change in authoritarianism, a change associated not only with their membership in a group (the non-Row group) which is typically low in authoritarianism, but also with their shift in reference groups, from Row to non-Row, i.e., from a group normatively higher in authoritarianism to a group normatively lower. The extent of attitude change in the Ss in Group B would be expected to be intermediate, due to the conflicting influences of the imposed membership group (non-Row) and of the unchanged reference group (Row). The research hypothesis, then, is that between the time of the freshman-year testing and the sophomore-year testing, the extent of change in authoritarianism will be least in Group A, greater in Group B, and greatest in Group C. That is, in extent of attitude change, Group A < Group B < Group C.

Results

Group Norms

From the data collected in the large-scale testing program, it was possible to determine the group norms for authoritarian attitudes among the

Row and the non-Row women at the university. The E-F scale was administered to all available Row residents ($N=303$) and to a random sample of residents of non-Row houses ($N=101$). These Ss were sophomores, juniors, and seniors. The mean E-F score of the Row women was 90, while the mean E-F score of the non-Row was 81. The E-F scores of the two groups were demonstrated to differ at the $p<.001$ level ($\chi^2=11.1$) by the median test (Siegel, 1956), a nonparametric test, the data for which are shown in Table 1.

Table 1

FREQUENCIES OF E-F SCORES ABOVE AND BELOW
COMMON MEDIAN FOR ROW AND NON-ROW RESIDENTS

	RESIDENTS OF NON-ROW HOUSES	RESIDENTS OF ROW HOUSES	TOTAL
Above Median	36	166	202
Below Median	65	137	202
Total	101	303	404

Attitude Change

The central hypothesis of this study is that attitude change will occur differentially in Groups A, B, and C, and that it will occur in the direction which would be predicted from knowledge of the group norms among Row and non-Row residents in general. The 28 Ss of this study had a mean E-F score of 102 at the end of their freshman year. The data reported above concerning authoritarianism norms for all women residing on campus would lead to the prediction that in general the Ss would show a reduction in authoritarianism during the sophomore year but that this reduction would be differential in the three groups; from the knowledge that Row residents generally are higher in authoritarianism than non-Row residents, the prediction based on social group theory would be that Group A would show the smallest reduction in authoritarianism scores, Group B would show a larger reduction, and Group C would show the largest reduction. The data which permit a test of this hypothesis are given in Table 2. The Jonckheere test (1954), a nonparametric k-sample test which tests the null hypothesis that the three groups are from the same population against the alternative hypothesis that they are from different populations which are ordered in a specified way, was used with these data. By that test, the hypothesis is confirmed at the $p<.025$ level.

Discussion

Substantively, the present study provides experimental verification of certain assertions in social group theory, demonstrating that attitude change over time is related to the group identification of the person—both his membership group identification and his reference group identification. The hypothesis that extent of attitude change would be different in the three subgroups of Ss, depending on their respective membership group and reference group identifications, is confirmed at the $p<.025$ level; in extent of change in authoritarianism, Group A<Group B<Group C, as predicted.

Another way of looking at the data may serve to highlight the influence of membership groups and reference groups. At the end of the freshman year, the Ss in Groups A, B, and C shared the same membership group and the same reference group. During the sophomore year, the Ss in Group A shared one membership group while those in Groups B and C together shared another. From membership group theory, it would be predicted that the extent of attitude change would be greater among the latter Ss. This hypothesis is supported by the data (in Table 2); by the Mann-Whitney test, (Siegel, 1954, pp. 116-117), the change scores of these two

Table 2

FRESHMAN-YEAR AND SOPHOMORE-YEAR E-F SCORES OF SUBJECTS

GROUP	END OF FRESHMAN YEAR	END OF SOPHOMORE YEAR	DIFFERENCE
	108	125	−17
	70	78	−8
	106	107	−1
	92	92	0
A	80	78	2
	104	102	2
	143	138	5
	110	92	18
	114	80	34
	76	117	−41
	105	107	−2
	88	82	6
	109	97	12
	98	83	15
B	112	94	18
	101	82	19
	114	93	21
	104	81	23
	116	91	25
	101	74	27
	121	126	−5
	87	79	8
	105	95	10
	97	81	16
C	96	78	18
	108	73	35
	114	77	37
	88	49	39

sets of Ss (Group A versus Groups B and C together) differ in the predicted direction at the $p < .025$ level. This finding illustrates the influence of *membership* groups on attitude change. On the other hand, at the conclusion of the sophomore year, the Ss in Groups A and B shared a common reference group while those in Group C had come to share another. From reference group theory, it would be predicted that attitude change would be more extensive among the subjects who had changed reference groups (Group C) than among those who had not. This hypothesis is also supported by the data (in Table 2); by the Mann-Whitney test, the change scores of these two sets of Ss (Groups A and B together versus Group C) differ in the predicted direction at the $p < .05$ level. This finding illustrates the influence of *reference* groups on attitude change. Any inference from this mode of analysis (as contrasted with the main analysis of the data, by the Jonckheere test) must be qualified because of the nonindependence of the data on which the two Mann-Whitney tests are made, but it is mentioned here to clarify the role which membership and reference groups play in influencing attitude change.

The findings may also contribute to our understanding of processes affecting attitude change. The imposition of a membership group does have some effect on an individual's attitudes, even when the imposed group is not accepted by the individual as his reference group. This relationship is shown in the case of Group B. If the person comes to accept the imposed group as his reference group, as was the case with the Ss in Group C, then the change in his attitudes toward the level of the group norm is even more pronounced.

Methodologically, the study has certain features which may deserve brief mention. First, the study demonstrates that it is possible operationally to define the concept of reference group. The act of voting by secret ballot for the group in which one would like to live constitutes clear behavioral specification of one's reference group, and it is an act whose conceptual meaning can be so directly inferred that there is no problem of reliability of judgment in its categorization by the investigator. Second, the study demonstrates that a field study can be conducted which contains the critical feature of an experiment that is usually lacking in naturalistic situations: randomization. The determination of whether or not a woman student would be assigned to the living group of her choice was based on a random event: the size of the number she drew from the hopper. This fact satisfied the requirement that the treatment condition be randomized, and permitted sharper inferences than can usually be drawn from field studies. Third, the test behavior on which the conclusions of this study were based occurred in a context in which the salience of membership and reference groups was *not* aroused and in which no external sanctions from the relevant groups were operative. This feature of the design permitted the interpretation that the E-F scores represented the Ss' internalized attitudes (Sherif and Sherif, 1953, p. 218). Finally, the use of a paper-and-pencil measure of attitude and is of attitude change, rather than the use of some more behavioral measure, is a deficiency of the present study. Moreover, the measure which was used suffers from a well-known circularity, based on the occurrence of pseudo-low scores (Adorno, 1950, p. 771; Siegel, 1954, pp. 221-222).

Summary

In the social context of the lives of the subjects, and in a natural social experiment which provided randomization of the relevant condition effects, the influence of both membership and reference groups on attitude change was assessed. All subjects shared a common reference group at the start of the period of the study. When divergent membership groups with disparate attitude norms were socially imposed on the basis of a random event, attitude change in the subjects over time was a function of the normative attitudes of both imposed membership groups and the individuals' reference groups. The greatest attitude change occurred in subjects who came to take the imposed, initially nonpreferred, membership group as their reference group.

References

ADORNO, T., *et al.* *The authoritarian personality.* New York: Harper and Row, 1950.

GOUGH, H. G. Studies of social intolerance: I, Some psychological and sociological correlates of anti-Semitism. *Journal of Social Psychology*, 1951, 33, 237-246.

JONCKHEERE, A. R. A distribution-free, k-sample test against ordered alternatives. *Biometrika*, 1954, 41, 133-145.

SIEGEL, S. Certain determinants and correlates of authoritarianism. *Genetic Psychology Monographs*, 1954, 49, 187-299.

SIEGEL, S. *Nonparametric statistics for the behavioral sciences.* New York: McGraw-Hill, 1956.

SHERIF, M. and SHERIF, C. *Groups in harmony and tension.* New York: Harper and Row, 1953.

❊ ❊ ❊ ❊ ❊

Student protest is very much a central feature of our time. In an interesting way, the political/social/cultural confrontations now involving students and educational institutions (more and more of them high schools, currently) can serve as a useful barometer of one's own deep-lying attitudes toward change.

To wit: when you learn from a study like Flacks' that student protesters are, essentially, our best young people, how do you react?

> —The empire must really be doomed, then.
> —It's tragic, then, that they are so misguided.
> —We should support their aims, if not always their methods.
> —They're right: our educational system and the society surrounding it
> are rotten.

Flacks' study represents a thoughtful integration of social/psychological with historical and political modes of thought. His analysis of why student protest was so unexpected by social scientists is particularly interesting.

Like Kandel and Lesser in the present book, he is able to show that the Western nuclear family is not dead, but very much contributory to the values and hopes of students. The analysis of values presented can be profitably compared with what Newcomb and his colleagues found at Bennington. (See article following this one.)

In the last analysis, it may very well turn out that colleges and high schools (and elementary schools?) will be the primary interaction arenas where revised value and belief systems for our "post-industrial" society will be developed, reinforced, and diffused. If so, the question for educators is: will this happen in spite of us, or with our aid?

The Liberated Generation: An Exploration of the Roots of Student Protest*

Richard Flacks

As all of us are by now aware, there has emerged, during the past five years, an increasingly self-conscious student movement in the United States. This movement began primarily as a response to the efforts by southern Negro students to break the barriers of legal segregation in public accommodations —scores of northern white students engaged in sympathy demonstrations and related activities as early as 1960. But as we all know, the scope of the student concern expanded rapidly to include such issues as nuclear testing and the arms race, attacks on civil liberties, the problems of the poor in urban slum ghettoes, democracy and educational quality in universities, the war in Vietnam, and conscription.

This movement represents a social phenomenon of considerable significance. In the first place, it is having an important direct and indirect impact on the larger society. But secondly it is significant because it is a phenomenon which was unexpected—unexpected, in particular, by those social scientists who are professionally responsible for locating and understanding such phenomena. Because it is an unanticipated event, the attempt to understand and explain the sources of the student movement may lead to fresh interpretations of some important trends in our society.

Radicalism and the Young Intelligentsia

In one sense, the existence of a radical student movement should not be unexpected. After all, the young intelligentsia seem almost always to be in revolt. Yet if we examine the case a bit more closely I think we will find that movements of active disaffection among intellectuals and students tend to be concentrated at particular moments in history. Not every generation produces an organized oppositional movement.

* From *Journal of Social Issues*, 1967, 23 (3), 52-75. Used by permission of the author and publisher.

The research reported here stemmed from a coalescence of interests of the author and Bernice Neugarten of the Committee on Human Development of the University of Chicago. The research has been supported in part by grant #MH 08062, National Institute of Mental Health, in part by grants from the Carnegie Fund for the Advancement of Teaching and the Survey Research Center of the University of Michigan. I wish to thank Prof. Neugarten, Charles Derber and Patricia Schedler for their help in preparing this manuscript; its flaws are entirely my own responsibility.

In particular, students and young intellectuals seem to have become active agents of opposition and change under two sets of interrelated conditions:

> When they have been marginal in the labor market because their numbers exceed the opportunities for employment commensurate with their abilities and training. This has most typically been the case in colonial or underdeveloped societies; it also seems to account, in part, for the radicalization of European Jewish intellectuals and American college-educated women at the turn of the century (Coser, 1965; Shils, 1960; Veblen, 1963).
>
> When they found that the values with which they were closely connected by virtue of their upbringing no longer were appropriate to the developing social reality. This has been the case most typically at the point where traditional authority has broken down due to the impact of Westernization, industrialization, modernization. Under these conditions, the intellectuals, and particularly the youth, felt called upon to assert new values, new modes of legitimation, new styles of life. Although the case of breakdown of traditional authority is most typically the point at which youth movements have emerged, there seems, historically, to have been a second point in time—in Western Europe and the United States—when intellectuals were radicalized. This was, roughly, at the turn of the century, when values such as gentility, laissez-faire, naive optimism, naive rationalism and naive nationalism seemed increasingly inappropriate due to the impact of large-scale industrial organization, intensifying class conflict, economic crisis and the emergence of total war. Variants of radicalism waxed and waned in their influence among American intellectuals and students during the first four decades of the twentieth century (Aaron, 1965; Eisenstadt, 1956; Lasch, 1965).

If these conditions have historically been those which produced revolts among the young intelligentsia, then I think it is easy to understand why a relatively superficial observer would find the new wave of radicalism on the campus fairly mysterious.

In the first place, the current student generation can look forward, not to occupational insecurity or marginality, but to an unexampled opening up of opportunity for occupational advance in situations in which their skills will be maximally demanded and the prestige of their roles unprecedentedly high.

In the second place, there is no evident erosion of the legitimacy of established authority; we do not seem, at least on the surface, to be in a period of rapid disintegration of traditional values—at least no more so than a decade ago when sociologists were observing the *exhaustion* of opportunity for radical social movements in America (Bell, 1962; Lipset, 1960).

In fact, during the Fifties sociologists and social psychologists emphasized the decline in political commitment, particularly among the young, and the rise of a bland, security-oriented conformism throughout the population, but most particularly among college students. The variety of studies conducted then reported students as overwhelmingly unconcerned with value questions, highly complacent, status-oriented, privatized, uncommitted (Jacob, 1957; Goldsen, *et al.*, 1960). Most of us interpreted this situation as one to be expected given the opportunities newly opened to educated youth, and given the emergence of liberal pluralism and affluence as the characteristic features of postwar America. Several observers predicted an intensification of the pattern of middle-class conformism, declining individualism, and growing "other-directedness" based on the changing styles of childrearing prevalent in the middle class. The democratic and "permissive" family would produce young men who knew how to cooperate in bureaucratic settings, but who lacked a strongly rooted ego-ideal and inner control (Miller and Swanson, 1958; Bronfenbrenner, 1961; Erikson, 1963). Although some observers reported that some students were searching for "meaning" and "self-expression," and others reported the existence of "subcultures" of alienation and bohemianism on some campuses (Keniston, 1965a; Trow, 1962; Newcomb and Flacks, 1963), not a single observer of the campus scene as late as 1959 anticipated the emergence of the organized disaffection, protest and activism which was to take shape early in the Sixties.

In short, the very occurrence of a student movement in the present American context is surprising because it seems to contradict our prior understanding of the determinants of disaffection among the young intelligentsia.

A Revolt of the Advantaged

The student movement is, I think, surprising for another set of reasons. These have to do with its social composition and the kinds of ideological themes which characterize it.

The current group of student activists is predominantly upper middle class, and frequently these students are of elite origins. This fact is evident as soon as one begins to learn the personal histories of activist leaders. Consider the following scene at a convention of Students for a Democratic Society a few years ago. Toward the end of several days of deliberation, someone decided that a quick way of raising funds for the organization would be to appeal to the several hundred students assembled at the convention to dig down deep into their pockets on the spot. To this end, one of the leadership, skilled at mimicry, stood on a chair, and in the style of a Southern Baptist preacher, appealed to the students to come forward, confess their sins and be saved by contributing to SDS. The students did come forward, and in each case the sin confessed was the social class or occupation of their fathers: "My father is the editor of a Hearst newspaper, I give $25"! "My father is Assistant Director of the ———— Bureau, I give $40." "My father is dean of a law school, here's $50"!

These impressions of the social composition of the student movement are supported and refined by more systematic sources of data. For example, when a random sample of students who participated in the anti-Selective Service sit-in at the University of Chicago Administration Building was compared with a sample composed of non-protesters and students hostile to the protest, the protesters disproportionately reported their social class to be "upper middle," their family incomes to be disproportionately high, their parents' education to be disproportionately advanced. In addition, the protesters' fathers' occupations were primarily upper professional (doctors, college faculty, lawyers) rather than business, white collar, or working class. These findings parallel those of other investigators (Braungart, 1966). Thus, the student movement represents the disaffection not of an underprivileged stratum of the student population but of *the most advantaged* sector of the students.

One hypothesis to explain disaffection among socially advantaged youth would suggest that, although such students come from advantaged backgrounds, their academic performance leads them to anticipate downward mobility or failure. Stinchcombe, for example, found high rates of quasi-delinquent rebelliousness among middle-class high school youth with poor academic records (Stinchcombe, 1964). This hypothesis is not tenable with respect to college student protest, however. Our own data with respect to the anti-draft protest at Chicago indicate that the grade point average of the protesters averaged around B to B+ (with 75% of them reporting a B − or better average). This was slightly higher than the grade point average of our sample of nonprotesters. Other data from our own research indicate that student activists tend to be at the top of their high school class; in general, data from our own and other studies support the view that many activists are academically superior, and that very few activists are recruited from among low academic achievers. Thus, in terms of *both* the status of their families of origin *and* their own scholastic performance, student protest movements are predominantly composed of students who have been born to high social advantage and who are in a position to experience the career and status opportunities of the society without significant limitations.

Themes of the Protest

The positive correlation between disaffection and status among college students suggested by these observations is, I think, made even more paradoxical when one examines closely the main value themes which characterize the student movement. I want to describe these in an impressionistic way here; a more systematic depiction awaits further analysis of our data.

ROMANTICISM: There is a strong stress among many Movement participants on a quest for self-expression, often articulated in terms of leading a "free" life—i.e., one not bound by conventional restraints on feeling, experience, communication, expression. This is often coupled with aesthetic interests and a strong rejection of scientific and other highly rational pursuits. Students often express the classic romantic aspiration of "knowing" or "experiencing" "everything."

ANTI-AUTHORITARIANISM: A strong antipathy toward arbitrary rule, centralized decision-making, "manipulation". The anti-authoritarian sentiment is fundamental to the widespread campus protests during the past few years; in most cases, the protests were precipitated by an administrative act which was interpreted as arbitrary, and received impetus when college administrators continued to act unilaterally, coercively or secretively. Anti-authoritarianism is manifested further by the styles and internal processes within activist organizations; for example, both SDS and SNCC have attempted to decentralize their operations quite radically and members are strongly critical of leadership within the organization when it is too assertive.

EGALITARIANISM, POPULISM: A belief that all men are capable of political participation, that political power should be widely dispersed, that the locus of value in society lies with the people and not elites. This is a stress on something more than equality of opportunity or equal legal treatment; the students stress instead the notion of "participatory democracy"—direct participation in the making of decisions by those affected by them. Two common slogans—"One man, one vote"; "Let the people decide."

ANTI-DOGMATISM: A strong reaction against doctrinaire ideological interpretations of events. Many of the students are quite restless when presented with formulated models of the social order, and specific programs for social change. This underlies much of their antagonism to the varieties of "old left" politics, and is one meaning of the oft-quoted (if not seriously used) phrase: "You can't trust anyone over thirty."

MORAL PURITY: A strong antipathy to self-interested behavior, particularly when overlaid by claims of disinterestedness. A major criticism of the society is that it is "hypocritical." Another meaning of the criticism of the older generation has to do with the perception that (a) the older generation "sold out" the values it espouses; (b) to assume conventional adult roles usually leads to increasing self-interestedness, hence selling-out, or "phoniness." A particularly important criticism students make of the university is that it fails to live up to its professed ideals; there is an expectation that the institution ought to be *moral*—that is, not compromise its official values for the sake of institutional survival or aggrandizement.

COMMUNITY: A strong emphasis on a desire for "human" relationships, for a full expression of emotions, for the breaking down of interpersonal barriers and the refusal to accept conventional norms concerning interpersonal contact (e.g., norms respecting sex, status, race, age, etc.). A central positive theme in the campus revolts has been the expression of the desire for a campus "community," for the breaking down of aspects of impersonality on the campus, for more direct contact between students and faculty. There is a frequent counterposing of bureaucratic norms to communal norms; a testing of the former against the latter. Many of the students involved in slum projects have experimented with attempts to achieve a "kibbutz"-like community amongst themselves, entailing communal living and a strong stress on achieving intimacy and resolving tensions within the group.

ANTI-INSTITUTIONALISM: A strong distrust of involvement with conventional institutional roles. This is most importantly expressed in the almost universal desire among the highly involved to avoid institutionalized careers. Our data suggest that few student activists look toward careers in the professions, the sciences, industry or politics. Many of the most committed expect to continue to work full-time in the "movement" or, alternatively, to become free-lance writers, artists, intellectuals. A high proportion are oriented toward academic careers—at least so far the academic career seems still to have a reputation among many student activists for permitting "freedom."

Several of these themes, it should be noted, are not unique to student activists. In particular, the value we have described as "romanticism"— a quest for self-expression—has been found by observers, for example Kenneth Keniston (1965b), to be a central feature of the ideology of "alienated" or "bohemian" students. Perhaps more important, the disaffection of student activists with conventional careers, their low valuation of careers as important in their personal aspirations, their quest for careers outside the institutionalized sphere—these attitudes toward careers seem to be characteristic of other groups of students as well. It is certainly typical of youth involved in "bohemian" and aesthetic subcultures; it also characterizes students who volunteer for participation in such programs as the Peace Corps, Vista and other full-time commitments oriented toward service. In fact, it is our view that the dissatisfaction of socially advantaged youth with conventional career opportunities is a significant social trend, the most important single indicator of restlessness among sectors of the youth population. One expression of this restlessness is the student movement, but it is not the only one. One reason why it seems important to investigate the student movement in detail, despite the fact that it represents a small minority of the student population, is that it is a symptom of social and psychological strains experienced by a larger segment of the youth—strains not well understood or anticipated heretofore by social science.

If some of the themes listed above are not unique to student activists, several of them may characterize only a portion of the activist group itself. In particular, some of the more explicitly political values are likely to be articulated mainly by activists who are involved in radical organizations, particularly Students for a Democratic Society, and the Student Non-violent Coordinating Committee. This would be true particularly for such notions as "participatory democracy" and deep commitments to populist-like orientations. These orientations have been formulated within SDS and SNCC as these organizations have sought to develop a coherent strategy and a framework for establishing priorities. It is an empirical question whether students not directly involved in such organizations articulate similar attitudes. The impressions we have from a preliminary examination of our data suggest that they frequently do not. It is more likely that the student movement is very heterogeneous politically at this point. Most participants share a set of broad orientations, but differ greatly in the degree to which they are oriented toward ideology in general or to particular political positions. The degree of politicization of student activists is probably very much a function of the kinds of peer group and organizational relationships they have had; the underlying disaffection and tendency toward activism, however, is perhaps best understood as being based on more enduring, pre-established values, attitudes and needs.

Social-Psychological Roots of Student Protest: Some Hypotheses

How, then, can we account for the emergence of an obviously dynamic and attractive radical movement among American students in this period? Why should this movement be particularly appealing to youth from upper-status, highly educated families? Why should such youth be particularly concerned with problems of authority, of vocation, of equality, of moral consistency? Why should students in the most advantaged sector of the youth population be disaffected with their own privilege?

It should be stressed that the privileged status of the student protesters and the themes they express in their protest are not *in themselves* unique or surprising. Student movements in developing nations—e.g., Russia, Japan and Latin America—typically recruit people of elite background; moreover, many of the themes of the "new left" are reminiscent of similar expressions in other student movements (Lipset, 1966). What is unexpected is that these should emerge in the American context at this time.

Earlier theoretical formulations about the social and psychological sources of strain for youth, for example the work of Parsons (1965), Eisenstadt (1956), and Erikson (1959), are important for understanding the emergence of self-conscious oppositional youth cultures and movements. At first glance, these theorists, who tend to see American youth as relatively well-integrated into the larger society, would seem to be unhelpful in providing a framework for explaining the emergence of a radical student movement at the present moment. Nevertheless, in developing our own hypotheses we have drawn freely on their work. What I want to do here is to sketch the notions which have guided our research; a more systematic and detailed exposition will be developed in future publications.

What we have done is to accept the main lines of the argument made by Parsons and Eisenstadt about the social functions of youth cultures and movements. The kernel of their argument is that self-conscious subcultures and movements among adolescents tend to develop when there is a sharp disjunction between the values and expectations embodied in the traditional families in a society and the values and expectations prevailing in the occupational sphere. The greater the disjunction, the more self-conscious and oppositional will be the youth culture (as for example in the situation of rapid transition from a traditional-ascriptive to a bureaucratic-achievement social system).

In modern industrial society, such a disjunction exists as a matter of course, since families are, by definition, particularistic, ascriptive, diffuse, and the occupational sphere is universalistic, impersonal, achievement-oriented, functionally specific. But Parsons, and many others, have suggested that over time the American middle-class family has developed a structure and style which tends to articulate with the occupational sphere; thus, whatever youth culture does emerge in American society is likely to be fairly well-integrated with conventional values, not particularly self-conscious, not rebellious (Parsons, 1965).

The emergence of the student movement, and other expressions of estrangement among youth, leads us to ask whether, in fact, there may be families in the middle class which embody values and expectations which do *not* articulate with those prevailing in the occupational sphere, to look for previously unremarked incompatibilities between trends in the larger social system and trends in family life and early socialization.

The argument we have developed may be sketched as follows:

FIRST,   on the macro-structural level we assume that two related trends are of importance: one, the increasing rationalization of student life in high schools and universities, symbolized by the "multiversity", which entails a high degree of impersonality, competitiveness and an increasingly explicit and direct relationship between the university and corporate and governmental bureaucracies; two, the increasing unavailability of coherent careers independent of bureaucratic organizations.

SECOND,   these trends converge, in time, with a particular trend in the development of the family; namely, the emergence of a pattern of familial relations, located most typically in upper middle-class, professional homes, having the following elements:

(a) a strong emphasis on democratic, egalitarian interpersonal relations
(b) a high degree of permissiveness with respect to self-regulation
(c) an emphasis on values *other than achievement;* in particular, a stress on the intrinsic worth of living up to intellectual, aesthetic, political, or religious ideals.

THIRD, young people raised in this kind of family setting, contrary to the expectations of some observers, find it difficult to accommodate to institutional expectations requiring submissiveness to adult authority, respect for established status distinctions, a high degree of competition, and firm regulation of sexual and expressive impulses. They are likely to be particularly sensitized to acts of arbitrary authority, to unexamined expressions of allegiance to conventional values, to instances of institutional practices which conflict with professed ideals. Further, the values embodied in their families are likely to be reinforced by other socializing experiences—for example, summer vacations at progressive children's camps, attendance at experimental private schools, growing up in a community with a high proportion of friends from similar backgrounds. Paralleling these experiences of positive reinforcement, there are likely to be experiences which reinforce a sense of estrangement from peers or conventional society. For instance, many of these young people experience a strong sense of being "different" or "isolated" in school; this sense of distance is often based on the relative uniqueness of their interests and values, their inability to accept conventional norms about appropriate sex-role behavior, and the like. An additional source of strain is generated when these young people perceive a fundamental discrepancy between the values espoused by their parents and the style of life actually practiced by them. This discrepancy is experienced as a feeling of "guilt" over "being middle class" and a perception of "hypocrisy" on the part of parents who express liberal or intellectual values while appearing to their children as acquisitive or self-interested.

FOURTH, the incentives operative in the occupational sphere are of limited efficacy for these young people—achievement of status or material advantage is relatively ineffective for an individual who already has high status and affluence by virtue of his family origins. This means, on the one hand, that these students are less oriented toward occupational achievement; on the other hand, the operative sanctions within the school and the larger society are less effective in enforcing conformity.

It seems plausible that this is the first generation in which a substantial number of youth have both the impulse to free themselves from conventional status concerns *and can afford to do so*. In this sense they are a "liberated" generation; affluence has freed them, at least for a period of time, from some of the anxieties and preoccupations which have been the defining features of American middle-class social character.

FIFTH, the emergence of the student movement is to be understood in large part as a consequence of opportunities for prolonged interaction available in the university environment. The kinds of personality structures produced by the socializing experiences outlined above need not necessarily have generated a collective response. In fact, Kenneth Keniston's recently published work (1965a) on alienated students at Harvard suggests that students with similar characteristics to those described here were identifiable on college campuses in the Fifties. But Keniston makes clear that his highly alienated subjects were rarely involved in extensive peer-relationships, and that few opportunities for collective expressions of alienation were then available. The result was that each of his subjects attempted to work out a value-system and a mode of operation on his own (Keniston, 1965b).

What seems to have happened was that during the Fifties, there began to emerge an "alienated" student culture, as students with alienated predispositions became visible to each other and began to interact. There was some tendency for these students to identify with the "Beat" style and related forms of bohemianism. Since this involved a high degree of disaffiliation, "cool" non-commitment and social withdrawal, observers tended to interpret this subculture as but a variant of the prevailing privatism of the Fifties. However, a series of precipitating events, most particularly the southern student sit-ins, the revolutionary successes of students in Cuba, Korea, and Turkey, and the suppression of students demonstrations against the House Un-American Activities Committee in San Francisco, suggested to groups of students that direct action was a plausible means for expressing their grievances. These first stirrings out of apathy were soon enmeshed in a variety of organizations and publicized in several student-organized underground journals—thus enabling the movement to grow and become increasingly institutionalized. The story of the emergence and growth of the movement cannot be developed here; my main point now is that many of its characteristics cannot be understood solely as consequences of the structural and personality variables outlined earlier—in addition, a full understanding of the dynamics of the movement requires a "collective behavior" perspective.

SIXTH, organized expressions of youth disaffection are likely to be an increasingly visible and established feature of our society. In important ways, the "new radicalism" is *not* new, but rather a more widespread version of certain subcultural phenomena with a considerable history. During the late 19th and early 20th century a considerable number of young people began to move out of their provincial environments as a consequence of university education; many of these people gathered in such locales as Greenwich Village and created the first visible bohemian subculture in the United States. The Village bohemians and associated young intellectuals shared a common concern with radical politics and, influenced by Freud, Dewey, etc., with the reform of the process of socialization in America—i.e., a restructuring of family and educational institutions (Lash, 1965; Coser, 1965). Although many of the reforms advocated by this group were only partially realized in a formal sense, it seems to be the case that the values and style of life which they advocated have become strongly rooted in American life. This has occurred in at least two ways: first, the subcultures created by the early intellectuals took root, have grown and been emulated in various parts of the country. Second, many of the *ideas* of the early twentieth century intellectuals, particularly their critique of the bourgeois family and Victorian sensibility, spread rapidly; it now seems that an important defining characteristic of the college-educated mother is her willingness to adopt child-centered techniques of rearing, and of the college-educated couple that they create a family which is democratic and egalitarian in style. In this way, the values that an earlier generation espoused in an abstract way have become embodied as *personality traits* in the new generation. The rootedness of the bohemian and quasi-bohemian subcultures, and the spread of their ideas with the rapid increase in the number of college graduates, suggests that there will be a steadily increasing number of families raising their children with considerable ambivalence about dominant values, incentives and expectations in the society. In this sense, the students who engage in protest or who participate in "alienated" styles of life are often not "converts" to a "deviant" adaptation, but people who have been socialized into a developing cultural tradition. Rising levels of affluence and education are drying up the traditional sources of alienation and radical politics; what we are now becoming aware of, however, is that this same situation is creating new sources of alienation and idealism, and new constituencies for radicalism.

The Youth and Social Change Project

These hypotheses have been the basis for two studies we have undertaken. Study One, begun in the Summer of 1965, involved extensive interviews with samples of student activists and non-activists and their parents. Study Two, conducted in the Spring of 1966, involved interviews with samples of participants, non-participants and opponents of the tumultuous "anti-ranking" sit-in at the University of Chicago.

Study One—The Socialization of Student Activists

For Study One, fifty students were selected from mailing lists of various peace, civil rights, and student movement organizations in the Chicago area. An additional fifty students, matched for sex, neighborhood of parents' residence, and type of college attended, were drawn from student directories of Chicago-area colleges. In each case, an attempt was made to interview both parents of the student respondent, as well as the student himself. We were able to interview both parents of 82 of the students; there were two cases in which no parents were available for the interview; in the remaining 16 cases, one parent was interviewed. The interviews with both students and parents averaged about three hours in length, were closely parallel in content, and covered such matters as: political attitudes and participation; attitudes toward the student movement and "youth"; "values", broadly defined; family life, child-rearing, family conflict and other aspects of socialization. Rating scales and "projective" questions were used to assess family members' perceptions of parent-child relationships.

It was clear to us that our sampling procedures were prone to a certain degree of error in the classification of students as "activists" and "non-activists." Some students who appeared on mailing lists of activist organizations had no substantial involvement in the student movement, while some of our "control" students had a considerable history of such involvement. Thus, the data to be reported here are based on an index of activism constructed from interview responses to questions about participation in seven kinds of activity: attendance at rallies, picketing, canvassing, working on a project to help the disadvantaged, being jailed for civil disobedience, working full-time for a social action organization, serving as an officer in such organizations.

Study Two—The "Anti-Ranking" Sit-in

In May, 1966, about five hundred students sat in at the Administration Building on the campus of the University of Chicago, barring the building to official use for two and a half days. The focal issue of the protest, emulated on a number of other campuses in the succeeding days, was the demand by the students that the University not cooperate with the Selective Service System in supplying class standings for the purpose of assigning student deferments. The students who sat in formed an organization called "Students Against the Rank" (SAR). During the sit-in, another group of students, calling themselves "Students for a Free Choice" (SFC) circulated a petition opposing the sit-in and supporting the University Administration's view that each student had a right to submit (or withhold) his class standings—the University could not withhold the "rank" of students who requested it. This petition was signed by several hundred students.

Beginning about 10 days after the end of the sit-in, we undertook to interview three samples of students: a random sample of 65 supporters of SAR (the protesters); a random sample of 35 signers of the SFC petition (the anti-protesters); approximately 60 students who constituted the total population of two randomly selected floors in the student dormitories. Of about 160 students thus selected, 117 were finally either interviewed or returned mailed questionnaires. The interview schedule was based largely on items used in the original study; it also included some additional items relevant to the sit-in and the "ranking" controversy.

Some Preliminary Findings

At this writing, our data analysis is at an early stage. In general, however, it is clear that the framework of hypotheses with which we began is substantially supported, and in interesting ways, refined, by the data. Our principal findings thus far include the following:[1]

Activists tend to come from upper-status families. As indicated earlier, our study of the Chicago sit-in suggests that such actions attract students predominantly from upper-status backgrounds. When compared with students who did not sit in, and with students who signed the anti-sit-in peti-

---

1. A more detailed report of the procedures and findings of these studies is available in Flacks (1966).

tion, the sit-in participants reported higher family incomes, higher levels of education for both fathers and mothers, and overwhelmingly perceived themselves to be "upper-middle class." One illustrative finding: in our dormitory sample, of 24 students reporting family incomes of above $15,000, half participated in the sit-in. Of 23 students reporting family incomes below $15,000, only 2 sat in.

Certain kinds of occupations are particularly characteristic of the parents of sit-in participants. In particular, their fathers tend to be professionals (college faculty, lawyers, doctors) rather than businessmen, white-collar employees or blue-collar workers. Moreover, somewhat unexpectedly, activists' mothers are likely to be employed, and are more likely to have "career" types of employment, than are the mothers of non-activists.

Also of significance, although not particularly surprising, is the fact that activists are more likely to be Jewish than are non-activists. (For example, 45% of our SAR sample reported that they were Jewish; only about one-fourth of the non-participants were Jewish.) Furthermore, a very high proportion of both Jewish and non-Jewish activists report no religious preference for themselves and their parents. Associated with the Jewish ethnicity of a large proportion of our activist samples is the fact that the great majority of activists' grandparents were foreign born. Yet, despite this, data from Study One show that the grandparents of activists tended to be relatively highly educated as compared to the grandparents of non-activists. Most of the grandparents of non-activists had not completed high school; nearly half of the grandparents of activists had at least a high school education and fully one-fourth of their maternal grandmothers had attended college. These data suggest that relatively high status characterized the families of activists over several generations; this conclusion is supported by data showing that, unlike non-activist grandfathers, the grandfathers of activists tended to have white-collar, professional and entrepreneurial occupations rather than blue-collar jobs.

In sum, our data suggest that, at least at major Northern colleges, students involved in protest activity are characteristically from families which are urban, highly educated, Jewish or irreligious, professional and affluent. It is perhaps particularly interesting that many of their mothers are uniquely well-educated and involved in careers, and that high status and education has characterized these families over at least two generations.

Activists are more "radical" than their parents; but activists' parents are decidedly more liberal than others of their status. The demographic data reported above suggest that activists come from high-status families, but the occupational, religious and educational characteristics of these families are unique in several important ways. The distinctiveness of these families is especially clear when we examine data from Study One on the political attitudes of students and their parents. In this study, it should be remembered, activist and non-activist familes were roughly equivalent in status, income and education because of our sampling procedures. Our data quite clearly demonstrate that the fathers of activists are disproportionately liberal. For example, whereas forty per cent of the non-activists' fathers said that they were Republican, only thirteen per cent of the activists' fathers were Republicans. Only six per cent of non-activists' fathers were willing to describe themselves as "highly liberal" or "socialist," whereas sixty per cent of the activists' fathers accepted such designations. Forty per cent of the non-activists' fathers described themselves as conservative; none of the activists' fathers endorsed that position.[2]

In general, differences in the political preferences of the students paralleled these parental differences. The non-activist sample is only slightly less conservative and Republican than their fathers; all of the activist students with Republican fathers report their own party preferences as either Democrat or independent. Thirty-two per cent of the activists regard themselves as "socialist" as compared with sixteen per cent of their fathers. In general, both nonactivists and their fathers are typically "moderate" in their politics; activists and their fathers tend to be at least "liberal," but a substantial proportion of the activists prefer a more "radical" designation.

A somewhat more detailed picture of comparative political positions emerges when we examine responses of students and their fathers to a series of 6-point scales on which respondents rated their attitudes on such issues as: U.S. bombing of North Vietnam, U.S. troops in the Dominican Republic, student participation in protest demonstrations, civil rights protests involving civil disobedience, Lyndon Johnson, Barry Goldwater, congressional investigations of "un-American activities," full socialization of all industries, socialization of the medical profession.

Table 1 presents data on activists and nonactivists and their fathers with respect to these items. This table suggests, first, wide divergence between the two groups of fathers on most issues, with activist fathers typically critical of current policies. Although activists' fathers are overwhelmingly "liberal" in their responses, for the most part, activist students tend to endorse "left-wing" positions more strongly and consistently than do their fathers. The items showing strongest divergence between activists and their fathers are interesting. Whereas activists overwhelmingly endorse civil disobedience, nearly half of their fathers do not. Whereas fathers of both activists and nonactivists tend to approve of Lyndon Johnson, activist students tend to disapprove of him. Whereas activists' fathers tend to disapprove of "full socialization of industry," this item is endorsed by the majority of activists (although fewer gave an extremely radical response on this item than any other); whereas the vast majority of activists approve of socialized medicine, the majority of their fathers do not. This table provides further support for the view that activists, though more "radical" than

2. For the purposes of this report, "activists" are those students who were in the top third on our Activism index; "nonactivists" are those students who were in the bottom third—this latter group reported virtually no participation in any activity associated with the student movement. The "activists" on the other hand had taken part in at least one activity indicating high commitment to the movement (e.g. going to jail, working full-time, serving in a leadership capacity).

Table 1

STUDENTS' AND FATHERS' ATTITUDES ON CURRENT ISSUES

ISSUE	ACTIVISTS		NONACTIVISTS	
	STUDENTS	FATHERS	STUDENTS	FATHERS
Per cent who approve:				
Bombing of North Vietnam	9	27	73	80
American troops in Dominican Republic	6	33	65	50
Student participation in protest demonstrations	100	80	61	37
Civil disobedience in civil rights protests	97	57	28	23
Congressional investigations of "un-American activities"	3	7	73	57
Lyndon Johnson	35	77	81	83
Barry Goldwater ː...............	0	7	35	20
Full socialization of industry	62	23	5	10
Socialization of the medical profession	94	43	30	27
N		34	30	37	30

their fathers, come predominantly from very liberal homes. The attitudes of nonactivists and their fathers are conventional and supportive of current policies; there is a slight tendency on some items for nonactivist students to endorse more conservative positions than their fathers.

It seems fair to conclude, then, that most students who are involved in the movement (at least those one finds in a city like Chicago) are involved in neither "conversion" from nor "rebellion" against the political perspectives of their fathers. A more supportable view suggests that the great majority of these students are attempting to fulfill and renew the political traditions of their families. However, data from our research which have not yet been analyzed as of this writing, will permit a more systematic analysis of the political orientations of the two generations.

Activism is related to a complex of values, not ostensibly political, shared by both the students and their parents. Data which we have just begun to analyze suggest that the political perspectives which differentiate the families of activists from other families at the same socioeconomic level are part of a more general clustering of values and orientations. Our findings and impressions on this point may be briefly summarized by saying that, whereas nonactivists and their parents tend to express conventional orientations toward achievement, material success, sexual morality, and religion, the activists and their parents tend to place greater stress on involvement in intellectual and esthetic pursuits, humanitarian concerns, opportunity for self-expression, and tend to de-emphasize or positively disvalue personal achievement, conventional morality, and conventional religiosity.

When asked to rank order a list of "areas of life," nonactivist students and their parents typically indicate that marriage, career, and religion are most important. Activists, on the other hand, typically rank these lower than the "world of ideas, art, and music" and "work for national and international betterment"—and so, on the whole, do their parents.

When asked to indicate their vocational aspirations, nonactivist students are typically firmly decided on a career and typically mention orientations toward the professions, science, and business. Activists, on the other hand, are very frequently undecided on a career; and most typically those who have decided mention college teaching, the arts or social work as aspirations.

Such responses suggest, somewhat crudely, that student activists identify with life goals which are intellectual and "humanitarian" and that they reject conventional and "privatized" goals more frequently than do nonactivist students.

Four Value Patterns

More detailed analyses which we are just beginning to undertake support the view that the value patterns expressed by activists are highly correlated with those of their parents. This analysis has involved the isolation of a number of value patterns which emerged in the interview material, the development of systems of code categories related to each of these patterns, and the blind coding of all the interviews with respect to these categories. The kinds of data we are obtaining in this way may be illustrated by describing four of the value patterns we have observed:

Romanticism: Esthetic and Emotional Sensitivity

This variable is defined as: "sensitivity to beauty and art—appreciation of painting, literature and music, creativity in art forms—concern with esthetic experience and the development of capacities for esthetic expression—concern with emotions deriving from perception of beauty— attachment of great significance to esthetic experience. More broadly, it can be conceived of as involving explicit concern with experience as such, with feeling and passion, with immediate and inner experience; a concern for the realm of feeling rather than the rational, technological or instrumental side of life; preference for the realm of experience as against that of activity, doing or achieving." Thirteen items were coded in these terms: for each item a score of zero signified no mention of "romanticist" concerns, a score of one signified that such a concern appeared. Table 2 indicates the relationship between "romanticism" and activism. Very few activists received scores on Romanticism which placed them as "low"; conversely, there were very few high "romantics" among the nonactivists.

Intellectualism

This variable is defined as: "Concern with ideas—desire to realize intellectual capacities—high valuation of intellectual creativities—appreciation of theory and knowledge—participation in intellectual activity

Table 2

SCORES ON SELECTED VALUES BY ACTIVISM (PERCENTAGES)

	ACTIVISTS	NONACTIVISTS
(a) *Romanticism*		
High	35	11
Medium	47	49
Low	18	40
(b) *Intellectualism*		
High	32	3
Medium	65	57
Low	3	40
(c) *Humanitarianism*		
High	35	0
Medium	47	22
Low	18	78
(d) *Moralism*		
High	6	54
Medium	53	35
Low	41	11
N	34	37

(e.g., reading, studying, teaching, writing)—broad intellectual concerns." Ten items were scored for "intellectualism." Almost no activists are low on this variable; almost no nonactivists received a high score.

Humanitarianism

This variable is defined as: "Concern with plight of others in society; desire to help others—value on compassion and sympathy—desire to alleviate suffering; value on egalitarianism in the sense of opposing privilege based on social and economic distinction; particular sensitivity to the deprived position of the disadvantaged." This variable was coded for ten items; an attempt was made to exclude from this index all items referring directly to participation in social action. As might be expected, "humanitarianism" is strongly related to activism, as evidenced in Table 2.

Moralism and Self Control

This variable is defined as: "Concern about the importance of strictly controlling personal impulses—opposition to impulsive or spontaneous behavior—value on keeping tight control over emotions—adherence to conventional authority; adherence to conventional morality—a high degree of moralism about sex, drugs, alcohol, etc.—reliance on a set of external and inflexible rules to govern moral behavior; emphasis on importance of hard work; concern with determination, 'stick-to-itiveness,' antagonism toward idleness—value on diligence, entrepreneurship, task orientation, ambition." Twelve items were scored for this variable. As Table 2 suggests, "moralism" is also strongly related to activism; very few activists score high on this variable, while the majority of nonactivists are high scorers.

These values are strongly related to activism. They are also highly intercorrelated, and, most importantly, parent and student scores on these variables are strongly correlated.

These and other value patterns will be used as the basis for studying value transmission in families, generational similarities and differences, and several other problems. Our data with respect to them provide further support for the view that the unconventionality of activists flows out of and is supported by their family traditions.

Activists' parents are more "permissive" than parents of nonactivists. We have just begun to get some findings bearing on our hypothesis that parents of activists will tend to have been more "permissive" in their child-rearing practices than parents of equivalent status whose children are not oriented toward activism.

One measure of parental permissiveness we have been using is a series of rating scales completed by each member of the family. A series of seven-point bipolar scales was presented in a format similar to that of the "Semantic Differential." Students were asked to indicate "how my mother (father) treated me as a child" on such scales as "warm-cold," "stern-mild," "hard-soft"—10 scales in all. Each parent, using the same scales, rated "how my child thinks I treated him."

Table 3

SONS' AND DAUGHTERS' RATINGS OF PARENTS BY
ACTIVISM (PERCENTAGES)

| | MALES | | FEMALES | |
TRAIT OF PARENT	HI ACT	LOW ACT	HI ACT	LOW ACT
mild-stern				
per cent rating mother "mild"	63	44	59	47
per cent rating father "mild"	48	33	48	32
soft-hard				
per cent rating mother "soft"	69	61	60	57
per cent rating father "soft"	50	50	62	51
lenient-severe				
per cent rating mother "lenient"	94	61	66	63
per cent rating father "lenient"	60	44	47	42
easy-strict				
per cent rating mother "easy"	75	50	77	52
per cent rating father "easy"	69	44	47	37
N	23	24	27	26

Table 3 presents data on how sons and daughters rated each of their parents on each of four scales: "mild-stern"; "soft-hard"; "lenient-severe"; and "easy-strict." In general, this table shows that activist sons and daughters tend to rate their parents as "milder," "more lenient," and "less severe" than do nonactivists. Similar data were obtained using the parents' ratings of themselves.

A different measure of permissiveness is based on the parents' response to a series of "hypothetical situations." Parents were asked, for example, what they would do if their son (daughter) "decided to drop out of school and doesn't know what he really wants to do." Responses to this open-ended question were coded as indicating "high intervention" or "low intervention." Data for fathers on this item are reported in Table 4. Another hypothetical situation presented to the parents was that their child was living with a member of the opposite sex. Responses to this item were coded as "strongly intervene, mildly intervene, not intervene." Data for this item for fathers appear in Table 5. Both tables show that fathers of activists

Table 4

FATHER'S INTERVENTION—"IF CHILD DROPPED OUT OF SCHOOL"
(PERCENTAGES)

DEGREE OF INTERVENTION	ACTIVISM OF CHILD	
	HIGH	LOW
Low	56	37
High	44	63
N	30	30

Table 5

FATHER'S INTERVENTION—"IF CHILD WERE LIVING WITH MEMBER OF OPPOSITE SEX" (PERCENTAGES)

DEGREE OF INTERVENTION	ACTIVISM OF CHILD	
	HIGH	LOW
None	20	14
Mild	50	28
Strong	30	58
N	30	30

report themselves to be much less interventionist than fathers of nonactivists. Similar results were obtained with mothers, and for other hypothetical situations.

Clearly both types of measures just reported provide support for our hypothesis about the relationship between parental permissiveness and activism. We expect these relationships to be strengthened if "activism" is combined with certain of the value patterns described earlier.

A Concluding Note

The data reported here constitute a small but representative sampling of the material we have collected in our studies of the student movement. In general, they provide support for the impressions and expectations we had when we undertook this work. Our view of the student movement as an expression of deep discontent felt by certain types of high-status youth as they confront the incongruities between the values represented by the authority and occupational structure of the larger society and the values inculcated by their families and peer culture seems to fit well with the data we have obtained.

A variety of questions remains which, we hope, can be answered, at least in part, by further analyses of our data. Although it is clear that value differences between parents of activists and nonactivists are centrally relevant for understanding value, attitudinal and behavioral cleavages among types of students on the campus, it remains to be determined whether differences in family status, on the one hand, and child-rearing practices, on the other, make an independent contribution to the variance. A second issue has to do with political ideology. First impressions of our data suggest that activists vary considerably with respect to their degree of politicization and their concern with ideological issues. The problem of isolating the key determinants of this variation is one we will be paying close attention to in further analysis of our interview material. Two factors are likely to be of importance here—first, the degree to which the student participates in radical student organizations; second, the political history of his parents.

At least two major issues are not confronted by the research we have been doing. First, we have not examined in any detail the role of campus conditions as a determinant of student discontent. The research reported here emphasizes family socialization and other antecedent experiences as determinants of student protest and leads to the prediction that students experiencing other patterns of early socialization will be unlikely to be in revolt. This view needs to be counterbalanced by recalling instances of active student unrest on campuses where very few students are likely to have the backgrounds suggested here as critical. Is it possible that there are two components to the student protest movement—one generated to a great extent by early socialization; the second by grievances indigenous to the campus? At any rate, the inter-relationships between personal dispositions and campus conditions need further detailed elucidation.

A second set of questions unanswerable by our research has to do with the future—what lies ahead for the movement as a whole and for the individual young people who participate in it? One direction for the student movement is toward institutionalization as an expression of youth discontent. This outcome, very typical of student movements in many countries, would represent a narrowing of the movement's political and social impact, a way of functionally integrating it into an otherwise stable society. Individual participants would be expected to pass through the movement on their way to eventual absorption, often at an elite level, into the established institutional order. An alternative direction would be toward the development of a full-fledged political "left," with the student movement serving, at least initially, as a nucleus. The potential for this latter development is apparent in recent events. It was the student movement which catalyzed professors and other adults into protest with respect to the Vietnam war. Students for a Democratic Society, the main organizational expression of the student movement, has had, for several years, a program for "community organizing," in which students and ex-students work full-time at the mobilization of constituencies for independent radical political and social action. This SDS program began in poverty areas; it is now beginning to spread to "middle-class" communities. These efforts, and others like them, from Berkeley to New Haven, became particularly visible during the 1966 congressional elections, as a wave of "new left" candidates emerged across the country, often supported by large and sophisticated political organizations. Moreover, in addition to attempts at political organizations, SDS, through its "Radical Education Project" has begun to seek the involvement of faculty members, professionals and other intellectuals for a program of research and education designed to lay the foundations for an intellectually substantial and ideologically developed "new left."

At its convention in September, 1966, SDS approached, but did not finally decide, the question of whether to continue to maintain its character as a campus-based, student organization or to transform itself into a "Movement for a Democratic Society." Characteristically, the young people there assembled amended the organization's constitution so that anyone regardless of status or age could join, while simultaneously they affirmed the student character of the group by projecting a more vigorous program to organize uncommitted students.

The historical significance of the student movement of the Sixties remains to be determined. Its impact on the campus and on the larger society has already been substantial. It is clearly a product of deep discontent in certain significant and rapidly growing segments of the youth population. Whether it becomes an expression of generational discontent, or the forerunner of major political realignments—or simply disintegrates—cannot really be predicted by detached social scientists. The ultimate personal and political meaning of the student movement remains a matter to be determined by those who are involved with it—as participants, as allies, as critics, as enemies.

References

AARON, D.   *Writers on the left.* New York: Avon, 1965.

BELL, D.   *The end of ideology.* New York: The Free Press, 1962.

BRAUNGART, R. G.   Social stratification and political attitudes. Pennsylvania State University, 1966. (unpublished ms.)

BRONFENBRENNER, U.   The changing American child: a speculative analysis. *Merrill-Palmer Quarterly,* 1961, 7, 73-85.

COSER, L.   *Men of ideas.* New York: The Free Press, 1965.

ERIKSON, E.   Identity and the life-cycle. *Psychological Issues,* 1959, 1, 1-171.

ERIKSON, E.   *Childhood and society.* New York: Norton, 1963, 306-325.

EISENSTADT, S. N.   *From generation to generation.* Glencoe: The Free Press, 1956.

FLACKS, R.   The liberated generation. University of Chicago, 1966. (mimeo)

GOLDSEN, R., ROSENBERG, M., WILLIAMS, R. and SUCHMAN, E.   *What college students think,* Princeton: Van Nostrand, 1960.

JACOB, P.   *Changing values in college.* New York: Harper, 1957.

KENISTON, K.   *The uncommitted.* New York: Harcourt Brace, 1965a.

KENISTON, K.   Social change and youth in America. In E. Erikson (Ed.), *The challenge of youth.* Garden City: Doubleday Anchor, 1965b.

LASCH, C.   *The new radicalism in America.* New York: Knopf, 1965.

LIPSET, S. M.   *Political man, the social bases of politics.* Garden City: Doubleday Anchor, 1960.

LIPSET, S. M.   University students and politics in underdeveloped countries. *Comparative Education Review,* 1966, 10, 132-162.

LIPSET, S. M. and ALTBACH, P.   Student politics and higher education in the United States. *Comparative Education Review,* 1966, 10, 320-349.

MILLER, D. R. and SWANSON, G. E.   *The changing American parent.* New York: Wiley, 1958.

NEWCOMB, T. M. and FLACKS, R.   *Deviant subcultures on a college campus.* U.S. Office of Education, 1963.

PARSONS, T.   Youth in the context of American society. In E. Erikson (Ed.), *The challenge of youth.* Garden City: Doubleday Anchor, 1965.

SHILS, E. A.   The intellectuals in the political development of new states. *World Politics,* 1960, 12, 329-368.

STINCHCOMBE, A.   *Rebellion in a high school.* Chicago: Quadrangle, 1964.

TROW, M.   Student cultures and administrative action. In Sutherland, R. *et al.* (Eds.), *Personality factors on the college campus.* Austin: Hogg Foundation for Mental Health, 1962.

VEBLEN, T.   The intellectual pre-eminence of Jews in modern Europe. In B. Rosenberg (Ed.), *Thorstein Veblen.* New York: Crowell, 1963.

꙼ ꙼ ꙼ ꙼ ꙼

The social-psychological story is familiar: groups, over time, tend to build up norms or standards for conduct, and apply sanctions to deviating behavior. The IBM man who doesn't wear a white shirt gets jokes from his colleagues, and thus appears the next day with a white shirt. In short, group members get pushed (or jump) into uniform behavior.

But is this necessarily so? Wouldn't it be possible for a group to have a norm favoring creative, *divergent* behavior? Suppose a group began to give allegiance to the standard of "do your own thing"? In principle, it would seem possible for such norms to develop. They would in effect be "meta-norms," operating at a second level. By "doing your thing," though apparently deviating from the behavior of others, you would be conforming to a higher-level norm, that of originality and creativity. This theoretical possibility offers a way out for those disturbed by "conformity" and "group pressure" as features of educational environments.

Newcomb and his colleagues, in their study of student culture in the 1960's at Bennington College, have been able to show that this possibility can in fact exist. "Do your thing" subcultures do seem to be viable.

We do not really know what the long-term effects of such norms are. Newcomb *et al.* (*Persistence and Change*, chapters 4, 5, 6) *did* find that the politically liberalizing norms of Bennington in the 1930's had durable effects twenty-five years later on the lives of alumnae, partly supported via the liberal attitudes of friends and husbands. Perhaps a 1985 follow-up can show us whether the specter of 1984 uniformity has or hasn't materialized for Bennington's creative individualists.

Group Norms and Creative Individualism

A Case Study*

Theodore M. Newcomb,
Richard Flacks, Donald P. Warwick

The aim of this article is to explore the informal atmosphere or "student culture" found at Bennington College, a small liberal arts college for women, in the early 1960's.

We shall focus upon only one aspect of student culture—the prevailing social norms in the college community. For present purposes we may define norms as *standards on which there is acknowledged consensus within a group and to which sanctions are attached.*

The discussion will focus specifically upon what seemed to be the dominant social norms at that time, and will introduce data of various kinds to show the extent of consensus about these norms, the nature of the sanctions used to make them effective and how individuals adapted to these norms.

The Setting

The student culture found on a campus at any given time is the product of many historical, geographical, ecological, and cultural forces, but certainly three of the most important are: (1) the history of the college and its formal traditions, (2) its current administrative policies, and (3) the background characteristics of the students who find themselves attracted to it.

Like many "experimental" colleges, Bennington came into being with a sense of educational mission which it retains to this day, and which seems to leave its mark upon many of its graduates.

The following statement taken from the Bennington College Catalogue for the years 1962-1963 summarizes the basic educational policies followed by the college since its foundation:

> The college encourages the students to engage voluntarily in learning, to acquire lasting interests and an objective understanding of the world in which they live. To this end, the student is encouraged to work at tasks which have meaning to her, to learn the inherent discipline of good work, and to take an active part in her own education. External

* Adapted from T. M. Newcomb, K. E. Koenig, R. Flacks and D. P. Warwick, *Persistence and change: Bennington College and its students after twenty-five years.* New York: John Wiley and Sons, 1967. Chs. 9, 10, 11, 12. Used by permission of the authors and publisher.

discipline, such as compulsory courses, competitive grades, formal examinations, the numerical accumulation of credits, and other mechanical devices are avoided as seriously interfering with real incentives and active learning.

As we shall later show, these policies are more than a mere set of catalogue ideals; they are closely related to the norms of intellectuality and individualism in the student community.

Bennington takes positive steps to incorporate direct experience and active participation into the learning process. In the general curriculum of the college this policy is reflected in the fact that the creative and performing arts rank equally with the more traditional disciplines. Similarly, the college encourages direct experience in learning through small seminars, encourages the student to discover her interests and abilities, and provides her with a maximum amount of freedom to develop them. Social rules, academic distinctions, and formal requirements are viewed as potential barriers to intellectual and social development, and are kept to a minimum.

Another factor which undoubtedly reinforces the "unconventional" atmosphere of Bennington College is self-selection on the part of the students themselves. Bennington has now been in existence for more than 30 years, and has achieved a national reputation as one of the foremost "progressive-experimental" colleges.

The analysis to follow will show that norms favoring individualism, unconventionality, and intellectuality are central in Bennington student culture. It is also important to note that entering freshmen appear to be aware of these norms, even before they arrive on campus. In questionnaire data collected in 1960 (Newcomb *et al.*, 1967, p. 111), these three norms were seen most frequently by entering freshmen as "distinctive characteristics" of Bennington.

Certain background characteristics of the Bennington student body must also be noted. An oversimplified but reasonably accurate picture of the typical student entering Bennington at the time of this study would be: Eastern, upper-middle class, Protestant or Jewish, but with little inclination toward formal worship, liberal in political beliefs, and more unconventional or rebellious in her attitudes than a freshman entering a more "traditional" college.

We are saying, then, that matters of student expectation and (probably) self-selection are at work in influencing student attitudes and behavior, as well as the forces stemming from the norms themselves.

Consensus on Community Norms

The definition of norms given above immediately suggests two relevant questions: (1) Are there any standards on which a majority of Bennington students seem to be in agreement? and (2) Are there rewards for those who adhere to these standards, or punishments for those who do not?

Our evidence for consensus about a somewhat distinctive set of standards comes in two forms: direct statements from interviews with members of the student body, and statistical indicators such as the percentage of agreement on various adjectives describing the college.

The Words of the Students

One of the most fruitful sources of information about norms was a set of interviews with 101 students during 1961 and 1962. During these sessions the students were asked about a variety of topics relating to their experience at the college, including the ways in which they had changed, the major types of social pressures in the community, and the effects of Bennington upon their lives. An analysis of their responses suggests the following as the most salient norms in the Bennington community: (1) individualism, (2) unconventionality, (3) intellectuality, and, somewhat less prominently, (4) tolerance of differences in others' behavior.

The two themes that seemed to generate the most ardent and lengthy discussion in the interviews were those dealing with individualism and unconventionality. Although there was some variation in the meaning attached to these terms, the following definitions would be accurate in most cases:

> *Individualism:* a striving for self-awareness and self-expression and for a synthesis of values and beliefs that is unique to each person.
>
> *Unconventionality:* a total or partial rejection of certain values, norms, and behavior patterns associated with the larger society, and especially the middle class and eastern "society."

We shall attempt to go beyond these terms to the pattern of expectations that they represent in the student community.

A close examination of the interview material suggests that both a striving for individualism and a rejection of conventional norms are expected at Bennington College, and are very closely related. In a sense they are two sides of the same coin, one positive and one negative. The negative side includes a widespread expectation that students who come to the community will seriously question their previous values and beliefs and will reject at least some forms of behavior that are considered conventional in the larger society. But the real point of this "minimal" norm, according to the ideals expressed by many of the respondents, is to set the stage for a positive striving for self-discovery and self-expression or, in short, for individualism. Let us consider this process in the words of the students themselves.

Individualism

First, there are many indications that individualism as reflected in self-awareness and self-expression, is a positive ("ideal") norm at the college, whereas there are only a few signs that unconventionality is valued in itself. Consider these statements indicating the salience of "being an individual."

> They expect you to be yourself, think for yourself. There is a premium on being yourself—don't conform.
>> You should think individualistic, don't think like the rest . . . if you don't want to conform it's your own business.

The following excerpts suggest that there are community pressures toward both self-awareness and self-expression:

> There is a pressure to find out what you are. This is a completely new kind of thing—measured against what you should be.
>> There are many things here that expose you to yourself. This is a very egocentric school in some ways.

Many of the students interviewed noted that an attitude of questioning and doubting one's initial values was not only encouraged in the community but also expected, especially in the earlier years.

> Precedent is tabooed. Don't rest on your previous background.
>> Bennington is conducive to breaking away from values of your family.

Unconventionality

The comments cited thus far point up the complex nature of the norm of individualism at Bennington College, and also suggest its close relationship with unconventionality—the process of self-discovery often leads to doubts about earlier values and about conventional norms in general. From here it is only a short step to an outright rejection of conventions and to patterns of behavior widely regarded as unconventional. The following statements suggest that a good number of the students take this step at some point in their careers:

> To be not conventional, to not conform, to do something bizarre is OK.
>> To follow what is accepted on the outside is bad.
>> There is a freedom for eccentricity and variety.

Perhaps the most commonly mentioned form of unconventionality at Bennington is in the area of dress and appearance.

> It seems that you're almost supposed to be a bit weird in dress just to say you're not bound by tradition or custom.

But another way of manifesting one's unconventionality seems to lie in the rejection of certain groups considered by the students to embody "convention."

There is a definitive feeling against Ivy League, preppy **Smith College.**

(Pressures on) people who read *Life* magazine . . . and anything to do with Society or the Junior League or "coming out."

Finally, it is worth noting that the community norms regarding individualism and unconventionality are closely related to an expectation of tolerance among the students. Tolerance, in the sense in which it is used at Bennington, usually means an attitude of "live and let live," a willingness to let others discover themselves and engage in unconventional behaviors.

Intellectuality

The second major cluster of norms found in the Bennington community is that of *intellectuality*—a commitment to intellectual pursuits in general and to the development of basic intellectual skills. In one sense it should not be surprising to find that students in a college community are dedicated to serious study. But it must also be admitted that there are wide differences in the extent to which this objective is reached, and that on some campuses the average level of intellectuality is reported to be low. Our argument, then, is not that Bennington is unique in possessing the qualities mentioned earlier, but that the entire area of intellectuality is more salient here than on many campuses, and that it is recognized as one of the major community norms.

The interview material is particularly clear in showing the extent of apparent intellectual involvement among the present generation of Bennington students.

There is a great emphasis upon intellectualism.

One thing I've noticed when I go home and talk to my friends from Radcliffe and Smith is that I was the only one in the group who was excited about what we are doing academically.

One of the specific ways in which the college contributes to intellectual involvement is by encouraging the development of an individualistic approach to study.

You are allowed to think for yourself in the classroom. You can digest things for yourself. Teachers encourage you to find your own meaning.

I doubt that in any other college I could explore a field from my own viewpoint. Students from other colleges can spit back information, but they haven't thought things through as well. Bennington prepares you better for life.

Another facet of intellectuality is the development of critical and analytic skills.

It's a very critical atmosphere. Nothing comes up that isn't challenged.

It's a training period in how to evaluate things critically.

Finally, Bennington students more than many others seem to make a point of the long-term implications of their education. As the following students point out:

> Bennington prepares you to keep a learning process going. It's so much centered about having you help yourself.

> It has opened up an intellectual world for me. I will continue to be well informed and to know how to do it.

In summary, interviews with about one-third of the Bennington student body point to individualism, unconventionality and intellectuality as the most distinctive norms in the community.[1]

1. The themes that emerge from these interviews are quite different from those seen in the 1930s at Bennington, when norms about public affairs were highly salient, and there were community pressures against political conservatism (Newcomb, 1943, 1952). Bennington students in the early 1960s, on the other hand, seem to encounter many pressures to discover themselves and to become involved in intellectual affairs, but not necessarily to change political views.

Supporting Data

The interview material considered thus far is not the only source of information about norms at Bennington College. Several other sets of data are available from the present study.

Adjective Check List

One of the simplest and most direct indicators of consensus in the community consists of data obtained from the students in the fall of 1959. Respondents were asked to consider Bennington College students in general and then to check the adjectives which distinguished them from women in other colleges. Table 1 shows those characteristics which were regarded as distinctive by at least 70% of the 320 students who completed the questionnaire.

Even a quick inspection of this list shows that the adjectives form clusters which approximate the pattern of norms in the interviews. Without undue strain on the data it is possible to group these eighteen adjectives under the headings used earlier, with the following result:

> *Individualism-unconventionality:* creative, independent, individualistic, introspective, liberal, progressive, unconventional, outspoken.

> *Intellectuality:* esthetic, alert, capable, critical, interests wide, original, resourceful, serious, versatile.

Although the fit between the characteristics and the categories is not perfect, the classification does underscore the salience of the themes of

Table 1

ADJECTIVES REPORTED TO BE DISTINCTIVE OF THE STUDENTS AT
BENNINGTON COLLEGE ($N = 320$)

ADJECTIVE	PER CENT OF STUDENTS	ADJECTIVE	PER CENT OF STUDENTS
Creative	95	Liberal	75
Independent	91	Serious	73
Individualistic	91	Unconventional	73
Original	83	Versatile	73
Progressive	83	Capable	72
Sensitive	77	Alert	71
Critical	76	Esthetic	70
Introspective	76	Interests wide	70
Resourceful	76	Outspoken	70

individualism-unconventionality and intellectuality in the Bennington
culture.

Students' Descriptions of Themselves

Finally, when students were asked to rate a series of nineteen questionnaire items as to how "characteristic of me" they were, the first four items
were as follows:

Table 2

ITEMS RATED AS CHARACTERISTIC OF SELF

ITEMS	PER CENT ENDORSING
Question things about myself	62
Individualistic—try to be myself	55
Able to continue the learning process after college	54
Express myself—what I think and feel	46

These results show again that a significant proportion of the Bennington
student body considers its main traits to be individualism and a long-term
commitment to intellectual growth.

Sanctions and Community Norms

The specific sanctions used to enforce any set of community norms will depend upon the type of group involved and upon ecological factors such as
size, isolation, and opportunities for members to interact and to monitor
each other's behavior. In tightly controlled institutions such as armies,
prisons, convents, and mental hospitals there is a marked tendency to rely
upon sanctions deriving from prescribed rules and formal authority. In the

American college community, on the other hand, the really effective sanctions are usually not those meted out by the Dean of Students or other officials, but the subtle rewards and punishments administered informally by peers and faculty. At Bennington these informal sanctions are made especially powerful by the frequency and intimacy of student interaction and by the relative absence of the usual formal rules governing conduct in the community.

In order to demonstrate that there are sanctions attached to the standards of individualism, unconventionality, intellectuality, and tolerance we shall present evidence showing that: (1) non-conformity with the prevailing standards is punished by isolation, ridicule, and other negative sanctions; and (2) rewards such as admiration and respect go to those individuals who reflect the dominant norms in their attitudes and behavior.

Negative Sanctions

In the 101 interviews obtained in this study the students themselves gave at least some indications of the types of negative sanctions used at Bennington, and of the types of behavior to which these were applied. The most common types of negative sanctions are listed here, together with relevant statements from the interviews.

1. *Direct steps: harassment, face-to-face discussion of faults, etc.*
   I have had no connection with my house. Lately they have been aroused and bother me. I don't want to play a game. The minute they get in a group they have destructive tendencies. Individually they are fine. The names they would call me! A lot of people have this happen.
2. *Isolation from the community*
   I think there is a lack of tolerance in a sense . . . girls a little more shy and not being able to really step up—they have been shoved into the background since other girls feel they don't have anything to offer. So you could go into a room and die and no one would know.
3. *Gossip, denial of respect, other indirect measures*
   I'm sort of tolerant. When people sit around and gossip and tear people apart I get angry. This is a good part of the life around here.

One striking conclusion that emerges from a close analysis of the interview responses is that the negative sanctions are most frequently applied to behavior defined here as "conventional": identification with eastern Society and the Junior League, "collegiate" clothes, frequent dating, and a failure to question one's initial values and beliefs.

People who read Life magazine—you just don't do this. Precedent is tabooed—don't rest on your previous background.

Dating a lot is looked down on, especially if you look the type (conventional).

To follow what is accepted on the outside is bad.

Some kids go to church every Sunday and there are snickers around.

The interviews imply, then, that the tolerance often cited by the students as characteristic of Bennington is essentially a tolerance for behavior and attitudes which are considered unconventional in the society at large and not for infractions of norms within the community itself. Thus, in order to gain at least minimal acceptance, the entering freshman must divest herself of the more visible marks of conventionality, especially in her moral values, dress, and dating behavior, and must further show a tolerance for unconventional behavior on the part of others.

A Typology of Students

Before continuing to a discussion of positive sanctions, we wish to explain the methods we used to establish a typology of students at Bennington, according to their acceptance of the going norms.

We assumed that the two clusters of norms we had isolated, "individualism," and "intellectualism" were independent dimensions, each constituting a fundamental basis of differentiation and association among the students. If so, some students would be high on both dimensions, some low on both, and some high on one, but not the other (see Figure 1).

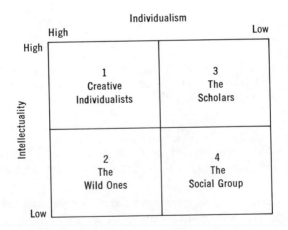

Figure 1. A hypothetical typology of norm acceptance—individualism.

Analysis of students' questionnaire responses (see Newcomb *et al.*, 1967, pp. 171-173) showed that these four types were most frequently mentioned by students.

Occasionally, it was also mentioned that there were groups of students who were active in student government, as well as "political activists" who engaged themselves in various social movements. We were particularly interested in these types, even though they were rarely mentioned—first, because they provided a link to the thirties when community participation and political activism were dominating norms on the campus; and, second, because we were interested to see what kinds of students held power and rank in the formal structure of student organization at Bennington, and how this structure related to informal patterns of influence and status. We expected that these two types would not necessarily be independent of the four principal types.

Thus, we emerged with six types of students who seemed to be fairly prevalent at the college.

Our next task was to construct brief descriptions of each of these types so that these could be "fed back" to the students in order to enable us to classify particular students with respect to these categories.

The descriptions which we used for this purpose were developed according to the following criteria:

1. The description should reflect the hypothesized source of the type; for example, the description of a "high individualism-high intellectuality" type should clearly suggest both dimensions to those exposed to it.
2. Each description should use direct quotes from the students' questionnaire responses.
3. All descriptions should be as nearly equivalent as possible in "social desirability."

With these requisites in mind, we formulated the following descriptions taken mainly from students' own phrasing.

1. *Creative Individualists* [*High Individualism-High Intellectuality*]— girls who sincerely believe in certain principles and who stick by those though they are usually opposed by society in general . . . people who feel they are superior intellectually and more sophisticated than other people . . . intellectual snobs according to some . . . seem very dedicated to creative pursuits . . . imaginative and free-thinking.
2. *Wild Ones* [*High Individualism-Low Intellectuality*]—wild, free, bizarre girls caring little about work and a lot about excitement . . . uninhibited, generally unkempt . . . try to be as different from everyone else as they can . . . love having wild parties . . . may feel they are misunderstood.
3. *Scholars* [*Low Individualism-High Intellectuality*]—those who seem to concentrate only on their work . . . seem to do little but study . . . come-out-for-air group . . . definite scholars . . . sublimate social interests . . . seem to spend most of their time in the library.
4. *The Social Group* [*Low Individualism-Low Intellectuality*]—very interested in their social life and talk about little else . . . do enough

work to pass their courses, but main interest is in having as much
fun as possible ... concentrate on dating and meeting boys ...
because of interest in social life, may mask their intelligence ...
characterized as "preppy" by some ... generally neat in appearance.

And, in addition, student government and political activist types were
described as follows.

> 5. *Leaders*—particularly interested in Bennington College government
>   ... organize committees or groups ... may be characterized by
>   friendliness among major part of the student body.
> 6. *Political Activists*—people interested in public affairs, interested in
>   civil rights, sane nuclear policy—circulate petitions ... civic-minded
>   reformists either of campus politics or of social conditions in the
>   country as a whole.

In the spring of 1961 the foregoing descriptions were given to each of the
40 students who were interviewed at that time. Each interviewee was presented with descriptions of each of the six types and a list of names of
students at her own year level (juniors and seniors were given the names
of students at both year levels). Instructions were to indicate, for each
type, the names of those students who fitted, to some degree, part or all of
the description. Thus, each student at the college was rated by at least ten
(and in the case of juniors and seniors, 20) panelists.

With this explanation of a student typology and its measurement in mind,
let us return to the question of the *positive* sanctions applied in support of
the norms of unconventionality and intellectuality.

Positive Sanctions

Both the interviews and the questionnaires suggest that there are also
positive sanctions at work in the Bennington community, and that the most
potent of these are the respect and admiration of student peers. Here we
will show that such sanctions are related to the prevailing norms in general,
but that they are most closely related to the "ideal" norms of individualism
and intellectuality than to the "minimal" norms of unconventionality and
tolerance.

Our major source of evidence is a series of sociometric nominations in
response to the following instructions:

COMMUNITY REPRESENTATIVE (FALL, 1959)

Suppose there was to be an important gathering of representative students from every type of American college during the coming winter.
Each of the colleges selected is to be represented by three students
who are to be chosen by their fellow students—not for ability to speak
in public nor for any other special ability, but merely as worthy representatives of their institutions. ... It is fair to assume that Bennington

College will be judged, to a greater or less extent, by the students who represent it. List three students whom you consider most worthy to serve as such representatives.

ADMIRATION (FALL, 1960)

Please enter below the names of at least two students (and no more than five) whom you *particularly admire,* no matter for what reasons.

With these two measures of respect and admiration it was possible to analyze the relationship between positive sanctions and standards.

INDIVIDUALISM. Three sets of statistical data indicate the extent to which the norm of individualism is supported with the sanctions of respect and admiration. In brief, these are as follows:
1. Students frequently mentioned by the panel as Creative Individualists received more nominations as "Community Representative" (average 3.9) and "Most Admired" (5.6) than those listed as members of the Social Group (1.6, and 1.6, respectively); these differences were statistically significant.
2. Students with high scores on an index of individualism[2] received more nominations as Community Representative than those with low scores, and the results were statistically significant. There was no significant relationship, however, between this index and nominations as Most Admired.
3. A statistically significant relationship ($r = .60$) was found between nominations as Most Admired and as "Creative and Original."[3] (In this study creativity and originality are considered to be aspects of individualism and, more specifically, of self-expression. It is obvious, however, that these traits are also bound up with intellectuality.)

These results thus provide rather convincing evidence that individualism is related to the positive sanctions in the Bennington community. On all of the available measures, those who show many signs of individualistic attitudes or behavior receive more nominations as Community Representative and Most Admired than those who show few such signs; in almost every instance the differences are statistically significant.

INTELLECTUALITY. Similar kinds of data are available concerning the relationship between intellectuality and the positive sanctions of respect and admiration.

Two personality measures, drawn from the Omnibus Personality Inven-

2. The measure of individualism was constructed by combining items measuring the perception of individualism as a distinctive feature of the college, scores on a six-item scale of Individual Orientation, and the ranking of "Opportunity to Be Creative and Original" as a career requirement.

3. The nominations as "Creative and Original" were obtained from a questionnaire administered in the fall of 1960 to all of the students but the freshmen. The specific item used was an open question which read as follows:
Please enter below the names of at least two students (and no more than five) whom you consider to be *unusually creative* or original.

tory,[4] were considered measures of intellectuality; they were called Estheticism and Theoretical Orientation. Both were significantly related to the indices of positive sanctions. The Estheticism Scale was significantly related to both nominations as Community Representative ($p < .01$) and as Most Admired ($p < .05$). Theoretical Orientation, on the other hand, was significantly related to Community Representative ($p < .01$), but not to Most Admired.

4. A measure of intellectuality was shown to be significantly related to nominations as Community Representative ($p < .05$), but not to Most Admired. This index of intellectuality consisted of a combination of the following items: ranking of estheticism as a value; frequency of nonassigned reading; number of books owned; extent of reading of "serious" magazines.

These findings suggest that intellectuality is associated with the positive sanctions of respect and admiration in the student community.

UNCONVENTIONALITY. The norm is more closely related to negative than to positive sanctions in the Bennington community. Although students who show signs of unconventionality do seem to receive more respect and admiration than those who do not, the relationship between unconventionality and these sanctions is generally weak.

Perhaps the best measure of unconventional attitudes available in this study is the Developmental Status Scale of the Omnibus Personality Inventory. This is an empirically developed scale which contains attitude items differentiating freshmen from seniors, and which seems to reflect a kind of "Rebellious Independence" (Webster and Heist, 1959). The scores on this scale were related to the number of nominations as Community Representative and Most Admired, in the expected direction, but neither of the comparisons was statistically significant.

Students who are repeatedly nominated as Creative Individualists also show significantly higher scores on the Developmental Status Scale than those classified as members of the Social Group. It was shown earlier that nominations as Creative Individualists are significantly related to respect and admiration (and negatively so for nominations as Social).

Those who enjoy a high degree of respect and admiration are above average in their unconventionality, but not everyone who is highly unconventional is rewarded with respect and admiration. Thus, unconventionality appears to be a facilitating but not a sufficient condition for high prestige in the student community.

To summarize the findings so far: several distinctive norms appear in the student community at Bennington College; they center about the themes

4. This instrument was constructed at the Center for the Study of Higher Education (University of California, Berkeley) for purposes of identifying "nonintellective" or personality factors related to the observed or anticipated effects of colleges upon their students. See Newcomb *et al* (1967, pp. 273-279) for further discussion.

of individualism, unconventionality, intellectuality, and to a lesser degree, tolerance. Evidence both from interviews with 101 students and from questionnaire responses by larger populations at different times indicates that there is a substantial degree of consensus on these standards.

There also appear to be differences in the functions that these four norms serve in the community, differences which we have attempted to capture with the concepts of *ideal* and *minimal* norms. The minimal standards for acceptance in the student body at large include at least a modicum of unconventionality in one's attitudes and a tolerance for unconventional attitudes and behavior on the part of others.

Students who do not comply with these standards are likely to be subjected to some of the more painful negative sanctions used at Bennington, especially direct criticism, isolation, and gossip. The ideal norms, on the other hand, lie in the areas of intellectuality and a striving for individualism, and these more than the others are rewarded with the positive sanctions of admiration and respect in the community.

Adapting to Community Norms

The study of group norms leads naturally to the question of the ways in which individuals adapt to these norms. This is an especially relevant question at Bennington College, where two of the most prominent standards in the community, individualism and unconventionality, are essentially "anti-adaptive" in character. The aim of this section is to examine the most common reactions to the norms outlined earlier, both for the students in general and for specific groups within the college.

Perhaps the key proposition underlying the entire discussion which follows is that the student's reaction to community norms will depend upon the extent to which they have become a personal problem for her, and the type of problem that they present. In the Bennington setting, for instance, it is extremely important to consider the student's own views at the time of her entrance into college. Some appear on campus with attitudes that show great discrepancy with the prevailing norms, whereas others seem to have been thoroughly "prepped" for Bennington through high school experiences, conversations with alumnae, and reading. The first group is often profoundly shocked early in its stay, whereas the second makes the transition with little difficulty.

Even those who enter with "congruent" attitudes may experience their own brand of problems at Bennington. Their very congruence, for example, may free them from some of the usual pressures toward "unconventionality," but also makes them more susceptible to pressures issuing from the "ideal" norms of individualism and intellectuality. Across the community, there tend to be similarities as well as differences in student adaptations to the prevailing norms and it is essential to consider both.

Data Concerning Directions of Change

There are two sources of information about the directions of change that we shall note: (1) interviews with a total of 101 students in 1961 and 1962, and (2) various questionnaires administered to almost the entire student body.

The Words of the Students

The most striking feature of the interview responses on change is that they strongly reflect the dominant norms. The most prominent themes of change are identical with the most important norms: individualism and intellec-

Table 3

MAJOR DIRECTIONS OF CHANGE OBSERVED IN INTERVIEWS WITH
BENNINGTON STUDENTS ($N = 101$)

AREA OF CHANGE*		PER CENT
1. Individualism, any mention		73
(a) Increased self-awareness	49	
(b) Increased self-confidence, strength, independence	42	
(c) Increased self-expression	11	
2. Intellectuality, any mention		73
(a) Increased intellectual awareness, broadening	37	
(b) Development of basic intellectual skills	33	
(c) Increased intellectual involvement	31	
(d) Long-term intellectual commitment	13	
3. Tolerance, any mention		48
(a) Less irritation, annoyance with peers	16	
(b) Increased understanding, acceptance of differences	15	
(c) Development of relativistic viewpoint	5	
4. Unconventionality, any mention		24
(a) Cyclical change	14	
(b) Increased unconventionality	10	
5. Other, any mention		46
(a) Changes in interpersonal attitudes	17	
(b) Changes in psychological adjustment	14	
(c) Changes in political attitudes	8	
(d) Changes in religious commitment	5	
(e) Changes in social life and dating	5	
(f) Other	9	

* The main headings (Individualism, Intellectuality, etc.) include the percentage of students who mentioned *at least one* statement in the area under consideration. These categories include statements that fell under the more specific headings of individualism, for example, as well as certain general statements that could not be classified under these headings. It should also be noted that it was possible for any individual to give statements that fell into more than one of the subheadings. Therefore, the percentages for the general categories (for example, 73%) should not be interpreted as sums of the more specific figures.

tuality. Almost three-fourths of the students interviewed (73%) report an increase on at least one of the specific dimensions of individualism or intellectuality, and many report change on more than one dimension.

Questionnaire Data and Directions of Change

The results of the first set of 40 interviews (in 1961) were so clear in suggesting directions of change that they were used as the basis of a series of items in a 1962 questionnaire administered to nearly all students. The aim here was to structure the items in the students' own words to the extent possible, and then obtain responses in more uniform ways about these areas of change from the entire student body. We tried to include not only those changes mentioned by a majority of the students, such as "more individualistic," but also those mentioned only occasionally, such as "committed to religious beliefs."

The patterns of change emerging from these responses and from the interview data are very similar. The predominating themes again are individualism, intellectuality, and tolerance.

The "minor" areas of change receive relatively greater attention in the questionnaires than in the interviews. In the questionnaire, students were asked directly about their changes in each of the areas, and thus were almost forced to give a response, but in the interviews they were given considerable freedom to comment upon the areas most salient for them.

It is the similarities between the two sets of data, however, that are most striking. In particular, both sets of data indicate that the main directions of attitude and value change are approximately the same as those of the prevailing norms in the Bennington college community. Table 4 shows the questionnaire results.

Variations in the Patterns of Change

The discussion thus far has emphasized the similarities in the patterns of change among Bennington students, but we shall show that there are individual differences in the observed patterns of change, and that these differences are related both to the initial characteristics of the students themselves, and to their experiences while in college.

The Initial Characteristics of the Student

One crucial stimulus to change for many students is a painful discrepancy between their initial views and those expected in the community.

We shall examine certain patterns of initial characteristics in terms of *congruence*. A student's attitudes are considered congruent if they are generally consistent with the principal norms in the student community—

Table 4

PROPORTION OF BENNINGTON STUDENTS REPORTING SIGNIFICANT
CHANGE ON SELECTED CHARACTERISTICS ($N = 309$)

ITEMS	"MUCH MORE THIS WAY NOW"	INTER-MEDIATE	"MUCH LESS THIS WAY NOW"
I. Individualism			
Question things about myself ...	51%	47%	2%*
Express myself—what I think and feel	46	52	2
Approach and explore material from my own viewpoint	44	54	2
Individualistic—try to be myself	43	55	2
II. Intellectuality			
Able to continue the learning process after college	59	40	1
Absorbed in studies and academic work	58	37	5
Critical and analytic in my approach to material	50	49	1
Committed to learning for its own sake	38	54	8
III. Tolerance			
Tolerant of behaviors that may violate my standards	43	52	5
Bothered by ideas very different from my own	4	63	33
IV. Unconventionality			
Unconventional in opinions and beliefs	28	68	4
Disapprove of the style of life in Ivy League colleges	20	69	11
V. Other			
Willing to support my convictions with action	32	66	2
Absorbed in social life and dating	12	70	18
Question or doubt the beliefs and values I brought to college ...	11	62	27
Similar to my parents in values and beliefs	11	63	26
Self-centered: not concerned with others' problems and needs ...	9	69	22
Committed to religious beliefs ...	6	74	20
Conservative in political and economic views	4	77	19

* Each row totals to 100%.

individualism-unconventionality, intellectuality, and tolerance. They are called incongruent when they are inconsistent with these norms. Students entering with congruent attitudes are often nominated as "creative individualists" in sociometric rankings, whereas those with incongruent views are frequently dubbed "conventional," "preppy," or "social."

Through the use of this concept it is possible to test two hypotheses:

1. Increases in tolerance and unconventionality will be more frequent among those initially incongruent in their attitudes, values, and beliefs than among those initially congruent.
2. Increases in individualism and intellectualism will be more frequent among students initially congruent in their views than among those initially incongruent.

Hypothesis 1 is based upon the assumption that the principal problem facing the incongruent group is that of meeting the "minimal" norms for acceptance in a community which include unconventionality and tolerance toward those with opposing views.

Hypothesis 2 follows from the notion that the congruent group will be less concerned than others with meeting the "minimal" standards for acceptance, and will thus be freer to work toward the ideal norms of individualism and intellectualism. Students in this group will thus have to spend less of their energy trying to win the acceptance and support of their peers, and will have greater freedom to become aware of themselves, consolidate their values, achieve a greater sense of self-confidence, and pursue their intellectual interests.

The index of congruence that seemed most appropriate was the student's score on the first administration of the Developmental Status Scale. This scale, administered shortly after the students arrived on campus, seemed to be a good measure of initial attitudes. As indicated earlier, it seems to be tapping a general factor of "rebellious independence" which corresponds quite closely to the concept of "unconventionality" used in this study. We have therefore considered the 49 students who fell into the top third of the distribution of scores on the first administration of this scale as congruent, and the 55 in the lowest third as incongruent.

The data relevant to our hypotheses came from two sources: (1) questionnaires administered to the entire group of 104 students classified as congruent or incongruent; and (2) statements from the 46 members of this group who also were in the interview sample.

HYPOTHESIS 1: CHANGES IN TOLERANCE AND UNCONVENTIONALITY. The findings in Table 5 support the hypothesis that an increase in tolerance will be more frequent among students who are initially incongruent than among those initially congruent. Of the 19 incongruent respondents, 14 (74%) report an increase in tolerance of views that differ from their own, whereas only 10 (37%) of the 27 listed as congruent report such a change.

Table 5

CHANGE IN TOLERANCE ACCORDING TO INITIAL CONGRUENCE:

INTERVIEW DATA

	INCREASE IN TOLERANCE REPORTED	NO INCREASE IN TOLERANCE REPORTED	N
Students initially incongruent	14	5	19
Students initially congruent	10	17	27
N	24	22	46

$\chi^2 = 4.62; p < .05$

Table 6, based on questionnaire data, shows non-significant results, but in the predicted direction.

Table 6

CHANGE IN TOLERANCE ACCORDING TO INITIAL CONGRUENCE:

QUESTIONNAIRE DATA

	"TOLERANT OF BEHAVIORS THAT MAY VIOLATE MY STANDARDS"		
	"MUCH MORE THIS WAY NOW"	LESSER DEGREE OF CHANGE	N
Students initially incongruent	26	28	54
Students initially congruent	17	32	49
N	43	60	103

$\chi^2 = NS$

It was also predicted in the first hypothesis that the incongruent group would show more change in unconventionality than the congruent group; the data presented in Table 7 also tend to confirm this observation. Students who enter the college with incongruent attitudes show significantly more change toward unconventionality than those who enter with congruent attitudes.

HYPOTHESIS 2: CHANGES IN INDIVIDUALISM AND INTELLECTUALISM. According to this hypothesis, there should be a similar relationship between congruence and change in individualism and intellectualism. Table 8 provides clear support for this hypothesis. The two groups differ significantly in change toward community norms in respect to *both* individualism and intellectualism.

EXPERIENCE DURING THE COLLEGE YEARS.   There are undoubtedly many experiences on and off the campus which can have a significant impact upon the student's views, most notably interactions with family, student peers, faculty members, and other "reference groups"; periods of questioning, doubting, and emotional upsets; academic successes and fail-

Table 7

CHANGE IN UNCONVENTIONALITY ACCORDING TO INITIAL
CONTINUITY IN ATTITUDES

	55 STUDENTS INITIALLY INCONGRUENT	49 STUDENTS INITIALLY CONGRUENT
1. Mean change on two administrations of the Developmental Status Scale .... $t = 4.68; p < .001$	+4.73	+0.65*
2. Questionnaire item: "Unconventional in opinions and beliefs"		
Much more this way now	18	9
Lesser degree of change	37	40
	55	49

$\chi^2 = $ NS

* It is possible that the differences observed here may be the result of a "ceiling effect" for the congruent group; its initially congruent scores leave little room for change toward further congruence.

Table 8

CHANGES IN INDIVIDUALISM AND INTELLECTUALISM ACCORDING TO
INITIAL CONGRUENCE OF ATTITUDES

	REPORTED INCREASE IN BOTH INDIVIDUALISM AND INTELLECTUALISM		
	YES	NO	N
Students initially incongruent	2	17	19
Students initially congruent	19	8	27
N	21	25	46

$\chi^2 = 13.77; p < .001$

ures; various types of reading; work experiences during vacations or non-resident terms; and participation in programs such as those sponsored by Civil Rights or Peace groups. There are two among these which seem to be especially important in accounting for change: (1) the questioning and doubting of attitudes, values, and beliefs; and (2) relationships with reference groups, especially family and student peers.

A. *Questioning and Doubting*

Here it was possible to test two hypotheses:

1. In general, change in the direction of community norms will be greater among students who question their values than among those who do not.
2. The relationship between questioning and change toward community norms will be closer for students initially incongruent in their views than for those initially congruent.

In the second hypothesis, our assumption is that when a student enters with incongruent views, and later questions these attitudes, the road to change is clearly marked should she be prepared to take it. Actual changes, in her case, are often the means of winning the support of student peers, and will ordinarily be in the direction of the norms held by these peers.

The situation is somewhat different, on the other hand, for the student who enters with congruent attitudes and later questions her initial positions. For her there is no clearly marked path to change, mainly because she already possesses enough of the valued attitudes to be accepted by the majority group. She is, in a sense, freer—free to move toward the dominant norms of intellectualism, free to become *less* individualistic and unconventional if she feels that she has gone too far in these directions, or free to change in other ways. Hence the change for the incongruent group should be more predictable.

Table 9 tends to support both of the hypotheses about questioning and doubting of values. Change in the direction of community norms, in this instance toward unconventionality, is greater among those, initially incongruent, who question their values and beliefs than among those who do not or who do so only slightly.

Table 9

QUESTIONING OF MORAL STANDARDS AND CHANGE IN
"REBELLIOUS INDEPENDENCE"

	MEAN CHANGE IN "REBELLIOUS INDEPENDENCE"			
	STUDENTS		STUDENTS	
DEGREE OF QUESTIONING	INITIALLY		INITIALLY	
MORAL STANDARDS	INCONGRUENT	N	CONGRUENT	N
Low questioning*	+3.61	33	−0.11	28
High Questioning	+6.41	22	+1.67	21
N		55		49
	$t = 2.20$		$t = 1.56$	
	$p < .05$		$p = $ NS	

* The category listed as "low questioning" includes those students who reported no questioning, slight questioning, or moderate questioning. The category of "high questioning" includes students reporting "intense questioning" of moral standards.

B. *Relationships with Reference Groups*

One of the most important factors in attitude change is the individual's relationships with "reference groups," which have been defined as follows:

> A group functions as a normative reference group for a person to the extent that its evaluations of him are based upon the degree of his conformity to certain standards of behavior or attitudes, and to the extent that the delivery of rewards and punishments is conditional upon these evaluations (H. H. Kelley, 1952).

For the college student two of the most important reference groups seem to be the family and campus peers, especially friends.[5] The typical freshman, for instance, may feel strongly attracted to her new-found friends on the campus, and may also feel that the views of her family are at least mildly antiquated.

The specific hypotheses tested here were the following:

1. Change in the direction of unconventionality will be directly related to the reported unconventionality of Bennington friends.
2. The relationship between change in unconventionality and reported unconventionality of Bennington friends will be closer for those initially incongruent in their views than for those initially congruent.

Table 10 supports both of these hypotheses: friends' unconventionality is directly related to amount of change, and this relationship is stronger for students with initially incongruent views.

Table 10

REPORTED UNCONVENTIONALITY OF BENNINGTON FRIENDS AND
CHANGE IN "REBELLIOUS INDEPENDENCE"

REPORTED UNCONVENTIONALITY OF BENNINGTON FRIENDS	MEAN CHANGE IN "REBELLIOUS INDEPENDENCE"			
	STUDENTS INITIALLY INCONGRUENT	N	STUDENTS INITIALLY CONGRUENT	N
Low unconventionality	+3.50	10	−0.50	4
Medium unconventionality	+4.32	31	−0.14	21
High unconventionality	+6.50	14	+1.54	24
Total	+4.75	55	+0.65	49

$\chi^2 = 6.75, p < .05$ (2 df)

product-moment correlation (unconventionality and change) . . .	$r = .30$ (p < .05)	$r = .19$ (NS)

To summarize briefly: we have shown that Bennington students do change in the direction of the dominant norms of individualism, intellectuality, tolerance, and to a lesser extent, unconventionality. Those entering with initially incongruent attitudes show a greater tendency to change in tolerance and unconventionality than in individualism and intellectuality, whereas the pattern is reversed for those entering with congruent attitudes. Both the process of questioning one's values and beliefs, and the effects of one's friends, serving as a "reference group" also induced changes toward unconventionality; these effects were stronger for those with views initially incongruent with the norms.

5. See also Newcomb (1952).

Student Types, Subgroups and Subcultures

Finally, it may be useful to return to our earlier typology of students, constructed according to their acceptance of the norms. When students were asked to nominate others as falling into the categories described above, the results were as follows.

Table 11

PERCENTAGES BELONGING TO CATEGORIES, BY YEAR LEVEL*

	51 FRESH- MEN	62 SOPHO- MORES	58 JUNIORS	52 SENIORS	TOTAL	N
Creative individualists ...	17	17	30	35	99%	46
Scholars	16	36	32	16	100	25
Wild ones	40	34	14	11	99	35
Social group	27	33	27	13	100	45
Leaders	0	27	37	36	100	30
Political activists	31	24	21	24	100	42

* Rounded to nearest integer.

The data suggest that students tend to perceive seniors as more likely to be Creative Individualists and freshmen as more likely to be Social. This perception makes sense in terms of the attitude change results reported above: over time Bennington students tend to move toward the Creative Individualist ideal, and away from the conventional, non-intellectual "anti-ideal" embodied in the Social Group.

The data also reflect a related finding: the Social Group has a significantly higher drop-out rate than any other category. For example, 11 (24%) of the 45 students in the Social Group dropped out after the spring semester in 1961. This was two and one-half times the college average (10%). No other group exceeded the college average in drop-out rate.

But do students seen as belonging to various stereotyped categories by other students really differ in their acceptance of the Bennington norms?

Differences among the Types with Respect to Norm Acceptance

The students assigned to the various categories were compared on a wide variety of indices relating to norm acceptance. We expected that these comparisons would show the Creative Individualists to be highest in norm acceptance, since they were hypothesized to be high in both individualism and intellectualism, and that the Social Group would be lowest, since they were hypothesized to be low on both dimensions. The Scholars and the Wild Ones were expected to fall between these categories, with Scholars relatively high on intellectualism and low on individualism, and the Wild Ones high on individualism and low on intellectualism.

In general, the results bore out these predictions. The most striking and most consistent findings had to do with differences between the Creative Individualists and the Social Group.

On all seven scales of the Omnibus Personality Inventory, the Creative Individualists fell on one side of the all-college mean, and the Social Group on the other (Newcomb *et al.*, 1967, p. 178). The Creative Individualists were more atheistic, more rebellious, more esthetically and theoretically-oriented, less authoritarian, more original, and more liberal.

Table 12 presents the means of self-ratings by the Creative Individualists and the Social Group on each of 12 seven-point rating scales.

Table 12

MEAN SELF-RATINGS OF "CREATIVE INDIVIDUALISTS" AND "SOCIAL GROUP" ON SELECTED TRAITS

	TOTAL COLLEGE ($N = 297$)	CREATIVE ($N = 37$)	SOCIAL ($N = 40$)	SIG. LEVEL*
Traits related to individualism†				
Conventional in dress or appearance	3.8	3.0	4.8	.01
Conventional in opinion or belief ..	3.1	2.3	3.7	.01
Conservative	3.1	2.2	3.5	.01
Compliant	3.9	3.3	4.0	NS
Absorbed in social life and dating ..	4.0	3.1	5.4	.01
Traits related to intellectualism†				
Intellectual	5.6	6.1	5.5	NS
Absorbed in studies and academic work	5.9	6.5	6.2	NS
Interested in national and international affairs	5.6	5.8	5.6	NS
Traits unrelated to norms†				
Tenseness	5.0	4.8	5.1	NS
Impulsiveness	4.8	4.6	5.1	NS
Interested in religion	4.2	3.4	4.8	.01
Dedicated to a special field	5.6	6.3	5.7	NS

* Significance determined by *t*-test between means for Creative Individualist and Social Group; probabilities above .05 are regarded as not significant (NS). The higher the score, the closer the respondent is to the pole indicated by the phrase at the left.

† Factor-analytically derived.

Clearly, there are important differences in the "self-images" of these two groups, particularly in what we have called "individualism": those nominated for membership in the Social Group saw themselves as much more conservative, conventional, and date-conscious than did the Creative Individualists.

Results for the groups other than Creative Individualists and the Social Group were as follows:

> The Wild Ones were particularly high in such traits as unconventionality in dress and appearance, and opinions and beliefs, intellectualism, tenseness, impulsiveness, and interest in social life, and were the lowest group in self-rating of "absorption in academic life and studies."
>
> The Scholars did not present a picture of high intellectualism, but tended to be low in "absorbed in social life" and in "critical of rules."
>
> The Leaders' self-ratings were very close to those of the Social Group, except that they saw themselves as highly "critical of rules."
>
> The Political Activists presented no major differences from the college average, except that they were uniquely high in "interest in international and national affairs," and uniquely low in "compliance."

In general, then, the results of these self-ratings tend to conform to the images of these people which others held of them: the Creative Individualists saw themselves as high in all traits connected with the norms of the college, and the Social Group saw themselves as relatively low in most of these traits. Not all of the expected traits of the Wild Ones and the Scholars were reflected in their scores, although the former did see themselves as both highly unconventional and highly social, whereas the latter tended to regard themselves as somewhat aloof from social life. As expected, Political Activists were high in traits reflecting their political interest and noncompliant, activist behavior. It is interesting, and not expected, that the Leaders should tend to see themselves as somewhat divergent from the Bennington norms on many traits.

Table 13 provides some further data on differences between Creative Individualists and the Social Group on indices of norm acceptance.

Table 13

SCORES OF "CREATIVE INDIVIDUALISTS" AND "SOCIAL GROUP" ON
MISCELLANEOUS INDICES OF NORM ACCEPTANCE

	CREATIVE INDIVIDUALISTS		SOCIAL GROUP	
	MEAN	N	MEAN	N
Index of conventionality*	0.2	23	4.2	26
"Small talk" index	4.2	30	5.9	36
"Serious conversation" index	4.8	30	4.2	36
Number of weekends on campus	16.0	34	12.5	41

* This item was not given to freshmen.

The "index of conventionality" is a scale based on the average number of conventional adjectives ("collegiate," "preppy," "social") checked as "favorable."

The other indices are intended to be measures of "intellectualism." The "small-talk" index is based on the amount of time the respondent reported that she spent in conversations having to do with social life, personal problems, gossip, and so on. The "serious conversation" index represents the reported amount of time the respondent spent in discussing the arts, public affairs, philosophical issues, and other intellectual matters. "Number of weekends on campus" refers to the mean number of weekends the respondents said they had remained at Bennington (this gives some indication of the amount of dating and off-campus interests that the respondent engaged in). On all of these variables, with the exception of the "serious conversation" index, the Creative Individualists were significantly more "intellectual" than the Social Group ($p < .05$ for differences between means).

If Bennington's norms are indeed concerned with what we have called "individualism" and "intellectuality," then our data rather clearly suggest the existence of categories of students who differ in the degree to which they accept these norms. At one extreme are the Creative Individualists who tend to score at or near the top of the population on all indices related to these norms. In their self-descriptions, their attitudes, and their reported activities the students reputed to fall into this category seem to embody the dominant norms of the college. At the other extreme is the Social Group, whose self-images, attitudes, and activities consistently run counter to the prevailing norms of the student body. These students, to a surprising degree, seemed to respond to our questionnaire in ways that fitted the stereotype which others have of them. Between these extremes there are apparently pockets of students who, reputedly, accept only partially the norms embodied by the Creative Individualists.

The Scholars and the Wild Ones, however, in terms of our measures, failed to present fully coherent pictures; they failed to fit their stereotypes to the same degree as the Creative Individualists and the Social Group fitted theirs. Perhaps the clearest thing that emerges about these types is that, although both the Scholars and the Wild Ones are at or above the college average in norm acceptance, they differ from the norms in this respect: the Scholars are below average in their social interest, whereas the Wild Ones are substantially above average in their participation in social life.

The two remaining types, the Leaders and the Political Activists, are even less consistent in their orientation to the norms. The Political Activists tend generally to be high in norm acceptance, but, true to their reputation, are above average in political interest. More interesting is the fact that students reputed to be community Leaders (in the sense that they are most active in student government) tend to emerge as more conventional, more socially minded, and less intellectual than the college average.

The Typology and Social Structure

The data just reviewed demonstrate that students identified by other students as belonging in various stereotyped categories differed substantially in their orientation to the norms of the student culture. But such evidence is not sufficient to establish that a student subculture existed. The categories we had isolated might consist simply of sets of students with similar attitudes whose orientations and actions are independent of one another. We might regard these as *types* of students, but a *subculture* implies more than a collection of people holding similar attitudes; it implies, too, that they are mutually attracted to one another, and that they are aware of their common orientation. The data collected in the spring of 1961 provided some initial clues about which of the various types we had isolated had subcultural attributes.

Table 14 reports data on the extent to which the friendship choices of the students within each category were accorded to others in that category.

Table 14

WITHIN-GROUP FRIENDSHIP CHOICES BY TYPES

	N	WITHIN-GROUP CHOICES AS PER CENT OF TOTAL CHOICES	
		EXPECTED	OBTAINED
Creative individualists	46	15%	35%
Scholars	25	7	26
Wild ones	35	10	5
Social group	45	14	45
Leaders	30	9	28
Political activists	42	12	28

The actual number of within-group choices divided by the total number of choices made by the group members is compared with the expected proportion of within-group choices. The expected proportion of within-group choices is equal to the size of the category relative to the total N of the student body.

Table 14 indicates that there is a substantial degree of within-group choice among persons named as Creative Individualists and as Social, and that Scholars, Leaders, and Political Activists show some degree of intragroup attraction. The Wild Ones, on the other hand, do not seem to be a subcultural group; the degree of intragroup attraction was approximately at the chance level. Thus, as with our previously reported findings on attitudinal differences, the most clearly defined groups were the Creative Individualists and the Social Group.

Table 15 further indicates that the status order of the college as a whole rather neatly fitted our expectations. The Creative Individualists were ranked first, the Social Group received the lowest rank.

The entire rank order was: Creative Individualists, Scholars, Leaders, Political Activists, Wild Ones, and Social Group. This rank ordering fits the hypothesis that a group will be ranked according to its degree of acceptance of the norms of the community.

Note, too, the interesting evidence that the members of each category tended to identify themselves with the category—they tended to give their own category a higher rank than that assigned by others.

Table 15

RANK ORDER OF THE TYPES

PREFERENCES EXPRESSED BY	N	MEAN PREFERENCES FOR					
		CREATIVE INDIVID- UALISTS	SCHOLARS	LEADERS	POLITICAL ACTIVISTS	WILD ONES	SOCIAL GROUP
Total college	291	1.8	3.0	3.2	3.4	4.8	4.9
Creative individualists	35	1.5(1)*	2.5(2)	3.7(4)	3.1(3)	4.9(5)	5.5(6)
Scholars	24	1.8(1)	2.4(2)	3.7(4)	3.1(3)	4.6(5)	5.4(6)
Leaders	27	2.5(2)	2.9(3)	2.2(1)	3.0(4)	5.4(6)	5.0(5)
Political activists	36	2.1(1)	2.7(2)	3.1(3)	2.9(4)	4.9(5)	5.4(6)
Wild ones	32	1.4(1)	3.5(3)	4.0(5)	2.4(2)	3.6(4)	4.2(6)
Social group	39	2.3(1)	3.7(4)	2.6(2)	3.5(3)	4.7(6)	4.0(5)

* Numbers in parentheses indicate rank orders of preference expressed by the type described at the left.

To summarize: we developed "ideal types," descriptions of students who differed in their orientation to the norms, and used the language of the students in developing the descriptions of these types. We then found that students could identify actual firls who fitted each of these types. And, finally, we found certain marked, even striking, differences among the girls so identified.

Particularly striking and coherent were the differences between the Creative Individualists (those hypothesized to be high on the normative patterns of "individualism" and "intellectualism") and the Social Group (those who, in our model, were expected to be low with respect to the same norms). These two groups differed widely in their degree of norm acceptance, and in the expected directions. They differed markedly in the amount of prestige accorded them by the rest of the college, again in the directions one would expect. Finally, unlike the other categories we developed, there was a strong tendency for those identified in each of these ways to interact with one another and to choose each other as friends, thus suggesting that their similar orientations were not fortuitous, but shared.

Concluding Comments

Our findings with respect to the emergence of divergent subcultures at Bennington were somewhat unexpected. The original study (Newcomb, 1943) indicated that most Bennington students shared a common set of attitudes, and that nonconforming students tended to be isolated, "negativistic," or peripheral individuals. Moreover, the small and highly selected character of the student body had led us to expect that the social structure and interaction processes in the 1960s would not be very different from those observed 25 years earlier. What we found, however, was that students who did not accept the prevailing norms at the college no longer appeared to be isolated and uninvolved; instead, a large proportion of such students had clustered together to create an identifiable "subculture."

This change, though unanticipated, is readily intelligible when viewed from the perspective of sociological and social-psychological theory about "deviant behavior" and nonconformity. Considerable prior research and theoretical formulation with respect to nonconformity tends to converge with respect to the following generalizations.

First, when attitudes become normative in a group or organization, participants who do not, at the outset, share the dominant attitudes are likely to experience considerable psychological "strain."

Second, this stress occurs for at least two reasons. On the one hand, any discrepancy between one's own attitudes and the attitudes of people with whom one regularly interacts and finds attractive is likely to produce discomfort or "cognitive imbalance" (Heider, 1958; Newcomb, 1961). In addition, insofar as the nonconformist becomes visible as such, other group members are likely to communicate disapproval and accord him low status.

A good demonstration of the latter is the isolated position of many conservative students at Bennington in the 1930s.

Third, there are several ways in which the deviant member can cope with this situation. One way is to reduce his participation or withdraw entirely from the group. This was a typical response of the deviants at Bennington in the 1930s; as we noted in the previous chapter, "dropping out" was quite prevalent among "Social" types in the 1960s. But other responses are possible as well. In particular, nonconformists can seek the support of like-minded individuals. Such a process of group formation among deviants can reduce the degree of psychological stress arising from attitudinal discrepancy. In addition, the developing deviant subgroup is likely to place high value on the kinds of behavior which the deviants *can* enact, standards which they *are* capable of achieving, and attitudes which they *can* accept. Thus, those who are status-deprived in the larger system can achieve approval within the subgroup (Cohen, 1955, 1959).

Our decision to try to interpret the "Social Group" as a "deviant subculture" led us to a number of hypotheses about the consequences of the group for its members. The most important hypothesis was that the Social Group served to insulate participants from pressures to change toward the dominant norms of "individualism" and "intellectuality." Another function that participation performed, we hypothesized, was to provide opportunities for friendship, acceptance, and prestige which would not otherwise be available to the participants. Furthermore, despite the finding that a large proportion of Social Group members dropped out, we speculated that the rate of departure would have been even higher for girls with initially deviant attitudes had they not had the opportunity to participate in the subculture. The function of the subculture was thus to enable relatively conventional and unintellectual Bennington students to remain at the college while successfully avoiding substantial disruption of their basic values and style of life.

In these terms, the Social Group at Bennington was seen as not very different from "collegiate" subcultures found in studies of a number of other campuses (for example, Trow, 1959, 1960; Coleman, 1961; Goldsen *et al.*, 1960; Bushnell, 1962; Freedman, 1956). In all such studies, the "collegiate-Greek-social" subculture is seen as composed of students relatively indifferent to intellectual concerns, effectively insulating such students from pressures toward academic seriousness emanating from the faculty.

An apparent difference, however, between the situation at Bennington and other well-studied schools (Vassar, for instance) is that at Bennington the "collegiate" subculture is deviant rather than dominant. At Vassar, the collegiate type is said to dominate; intellectuals and nonconformists tend to drop out or form closely knit subgroups (Freedman, 1956, p. 20). At Bennington, the situation is exactly reversed. This striking contrast between Bennington and Vassar suggests that the adaptation of students cannot be understood on the basis of individual predispositions only; rather, we need to place such dispositions in the context of the larger student culture and social structure. The relationship between individual attitudes and the dominant normative structure is a key to understanding both interpersonal relations on the campus and the ways in which students respond to the college and the values it transmits.

References

BUSHNELL, J. H.   Student culture at Vassar. In N. Sanford (Ed.), *The American college*. New York: John Wiley and Sons, 1962, pp. 489-514.

COHEN, A. K.   *Delinquent boys: the culture of the gang*. New York: The Free Press, 1955.

COHEN, A. K.   The study of social disorganization and deviant behavior. In R. K. Merton, L. Broom, and L. Cottrell (Eds.), *Sociology today*. New York: Basic Books, 1959, Ch. XXI.

COLEMAN, J. S.   *The adolescent society*. New York: The Free Press, 1961.

FREEDMAN, M.   Studies of college alumni. In N. Sanford (Ed.), *The American college*. New York: John Wiley and Sons, 1962, pp. 847-886.

GOLDSEN, R. K., ROSENBERG, M., WILLIAMS, R. M. and SUCHMAN, E. A. *What college students think*. Princeton: D. Van Nostrand, 1960.

HEIDER, F.   *The psychology of interpersonal relations*. New York: John Wiley and Sons, 1958.

KELLEY, H. H.   Two functions of reference groups. In G. E. Swanson, T. M. Newcomb, and E. L. Hartley. (Eds.), *Readings in social psychology* (Rev. Ed.), New York: Holt, Rinehart, and Winston, 1952.

NEWCOMB, T. M.   *Personality and social change*. New York: Dryden, 1943.

NEWCOMB, T. M.   Attitude development as a function of reference groups: The Bennington study. In G. E. Swanson, T. M. Newcomb, and E. L. Hartley (Eds.), *Readings in Social Psychology* (Revised Edition). New York: Holt, Rinehart and Winston, 1952.

NEWCOMB, T. M.   *The acquaintance process*. New York: Holt, Rinehart and Winston, 1961.

NEWCOMB, T. M., KOENIG, K. E., FLACKS, R. and WARWICK, D. P.   *Persistence and change: Bennington College and its students after twenty-five years*. New York: John Wiley and Sons, 1967.

TROW, M.   Cultural sophistication and higher education. Unpublished paper. Berkeley: Center for the Study of Higher Education, University of California, 1959.

TROW, M.   The campus viewed as a culture. In H. T. Sprague (Ed.), *Research on college students*. Boulder, Colorado: WICHE, 1960, pp. 106-123.

WARWICK, D. P., Socialization and value change in a college community. Unpublished doctoral dissertation. University of Michigan, 1963.

WEBSTER, H., FREEDMAN, M. and HEIST, P.   Personality changes in college students. In N. Sanford (Ed), *The American college*. New York: John Wiley and Sons, 1962, pp. 811-846.

WEBSTER, H. and HEIST, P.   Construction of a multiple trait personality test for use with college populations. Unpublished paper. Berkeley: Center for the Study of Higher Education, University of California, 1959.

※ ※ ※ ※ ※

Can adults—even young adults—change? Classical Freudian psychology and right-wing views of "human nature" say no. Most of our daily experience says yes, as does a good deal of sociological data.

In this article, Gottlieb defines socialization as "the modification of the self through acquisition of personality characteristics through contact with significant others," and shows that graduate students do change during their graduate-school careers on a dimension classically important to the professor: motivation toward research, or toward teaching. He is able to show that such changes depend not only on the over-all orientation of the student's department, but on the nature and intensity of the student's contact with "significant others"—professors. The findings on "cues" the faculty member emits, and their consequences, are interestingly parallel to Beez' findings in this book on teacher expectations.

Methodologically, the article is an excellent exhibit of how a sociologist goes about the patient, sequential task of extracting meaning from a set of survey data.

The reader is also referred to Wallace's *Student Culture* (Aldine, 1966) for a fascinating account of how the peer "interpersonal environment" of students moved them in directions similar to those observed in the Gottlieb study. And, teachers become socialized as they enter school systems (cf. Hoy in this book), even though school systems are not supposed to teach teachers anything. Or are they?

Processes of Socialization in American Graduate Schools*

David Gottlieb

In recent years, increasing attention has been paid in the literature of occupations and professions to the phenomenon of adult socialization.[1] Starting with the assumption that the personality is a growing, changing, plastic structure that is subject to modification throughout life by the social influences that surround the individual at given stages, the analysts of adult socialization have attempted to show the influence of the occupational subculture on the nature of the individual who has, at this stage of his life, committed himself irrevocably to the environment which this occupation represents. While the ratio of speculation to empirical findings in this field is high, the study of adult socialization promises to produce important generalizations about the development of the social individual through the life cycle.

Although—as will be shown below—the concept of adult socialization is really a very traditional orientation of sociology, the great bulk of studies of recent years has emphasized child socialization, and the term *socialization* has come to mean the process by which the individual is originally inducted into the social organization (see Child, 1954, p. 655).

Under the influence of this orientation, investigators of socialization have concentrated their attention on such phenomena as child-rearing practices, family structure, parental values, and the effect of the peer-group culture as contrasted with the home culture.

Perhaps under the influence of the Freudian theory of the relative completeness of the personality structure at the conclusion of puberty (cf. Miller and Swanson, 1956) the study of socialization has been more or less banished to the domain of child psychology. The contemporary students of adult socialization take a somewhat more generalized view of socialization than the one noted above, a view which makes the concept of socialization applicable to later development of personality structure.

* From *Social Forces*, 1961, 40, 124-131. Used by permission of the author and publisher.

The data for this analysis are taken from a national survey of American graduate students conducted by the National Opinion Research Center. The writer is indebted to James A. Davis, study director, for his many helpful comments.

1. Cf. especially Becker and Strauss (1956), and Merton, Reader and Kendall (1957, pp. 40-42, 287-293).

> Socialization . . . refers to the learning of social roles. In its application to the medical student, socialization refers to the process through which he develops his professional self, with its characteristic values, attitudes, knowledge, and skills, fusing these into a more or less consistent set of dispositions which govern his behavior in a wide variety of professional (and extra-professional) situations. Socialization takes place primarily through social interaction with people who are significant for the individual—in the medical school, probably with faculty members above most others, but also with fellow students, with the complement of associated personnel (nurses, technicians, case workers, etc.) and with patients. (Merton *et al.*, 1957, p. 287.)

From this point of view, socialization is seen as any development which entails the modification of the self through the acquisition of personality characteristics through contact with "significant others." It assumes that the "professional self" is an important aspect of the total self, and that the professional school and the personnel directly and indirectly associated with it are significant influences in the formation of the professional self. Because the professional school attendance must of necessity come after adolescence, it follows that professional socialization constitutes a form of post-adolescent modification of the self.

Frame of Reference

This paper concerns itself with the development of the professional self of the academic scholar and the part played in that development by the graduate school faculty with which the student comes in contact during the course of his graduate training. In this analysis the faculty is cast in the role of the socializer and the graduate student in the role of socializee. We assume that the graduate student enters school with a tentative orientation toward either a career in research or a career in teaching. We assume that the graduate faculty is also possessed of an orientation toward one of these alternatives. This is not to say that it is either *teaching or research* but rather a stronger preference for one as opposed to the other. We hypothesize that when the orientation of the student and the faculty are in substantial agreement the student's orientation will be reinforced, and he will be relatively less amenable to change than the student whose orientation is not similar to that of the faculty. We further predict that the student whose orientation is different from that of the faculty will tend to alter his view in the direction of that held by the faculty rather than away from it.

The Sample

The National Opinion Research Center's sample of graduate students, which is the source of this analysis, is a two-stage stratified cluster sample of the enrollment of American graduate schools which offered the Ph.D. in the "traditional arts and sciences" in the autumn of 1958. A total of 2,842 students from 25 graduate schools participated in this survey.[2]

Changes in Career Preferences

The first question we seek to answer is a most basic one: Do graduate students report changes in their career preferences as they progress through their professional training? In order to obtain an answer to this question, each of the respondents was asked the following:

> Please rank the following in terms of your personal preference as a future occupation:
> a. Teaching undergraduates   _____
> b. Teaching graduates   _____
> c. Doing research in your field   _____
> d. Academic administration   _____
>
>   Have your opinions on these alternatives changed since you first decided to go to graduate school? Please write the letter or letters of any alternatives which seem more desirable to you now.

The responses to this set of questions were used as the basis for a change index. Persons who indicated that any alternative was more desirable to them are considered "changers"; persons who indicated no change in preference are considered "non-changers." We found that 41 per cent of the graduate students in our sample do report a change of some kind in their career preferences.

Given that two out of every five graduate students do indicate a career preference change, we want to understand how this change phenomenon is tied in with the graduate student faculty. More specifically, our concern here will be with how interpersonal relationships between student and faculty operate to bring about changes in career preferences.

There are, of course, a number of ways in which student-faculty contacts take place and are maintained over time. The classroom, the informal session, the work period where the student assistant has an opportunity to meet with his faculty sponsor, etc. Each of these interaction situations differs and each, we suggest, will produce a different degree of socialization potential.

We begin with the hypothesis that the greater the degree of integration between student and faculty the greater the probability of reported change in the career preferences of the graduate student.

In order to determine the level of integration with the faculty, responses to the following question were used:

2.   A more detailed review of the sample and how it was structured is on file at the National Opinion Research Center and is available for inspection on request.

How many members of the graduate faculty in your department do you know well enough to drop in at their offices without a formal appointment?

Given this information, integration can be viewed as the number of faculty members known well enough to drop in on without an appointment, expressed as a proportion of the total number of faculty members in the department. Categories were then obtained so that the index of integration would give the following:

No integration: no faculty members known well.

Low integration: one or more, less than .33 of all members in the department.

High integration: more than .33 of all members in the department.

Table 1

INTEGRATION WITH THE FACULTY AND CAREER PREFERENCE CHANGE

INTEGRATION	HIGH	LOW	NONE
Per cent	44	42	34
Base	(613)	(1762)	(467)

From Table 1 we see that there is a relationship between integration with the faculty and reported changes in career preferences. It will be noted from Table 1 that it does not seem to matter whether the student is highly integrated or not, but the fact that the student is integrated does appear to raise his probability of changing.

Prior to any discussion of the actual process of student socialization and how faculty climates and cues operate to bring about changes in career preferences, it is important that we look at the relationship between faculty integration, change in career preferences, and number of years which the student has spent in his current department. This table is crucial to our argument since the objection might be raised that the relationship between integration and change would tend to disappear with time, that the nonintegrated population is made up largely of persons who are in the first year or even the first term of study in their department, and that they have not as yet had time to change the career preferences they brought with them into the graduate school system. Table 2 shows that this is not the case. When we control for time in the department, the effect does not disappear. The people who are integrated with the faculty change more than those who are not, and this effect accelerates with the passage of time up to the end of the fourth year of graduate study. In this group of departmental veterans the trend to change, with years, levels off, but the integrated still change more than do those who are not integrated with the faculty. In fact, the difference reaches its maximum with this group of students. While there is a significant relationship between student-faculty integration and changes

Table 2

YEARS IN CURRENT DEPARTMENT, INTEGRATION WITH THE FACULTY,
AND CHANGE IN CAREER PREFERENCES

YEARS	INTEGRATION		
	HIGH	LOW	NONE
1 or less	40	38	33
Base	(184)	(476)	(308)
2 years	47	42	36
Base	(126)	(326)	(99)
3 to 4 years	49	47	40
Base	(134)	(362)	(93)
5 or more years	44	41	29
Base .....·.............	(90)	(199)	(53)

in career preferences, this variable does not differentiate direction of change in career preferences. In other words, we find that integrated students who report changes are not any more likely to report changes in a given direction than are students who are not integrated with their faculty. It would appear then that knowledge of contact between student and faculty is not sufficient to account for variations in the kinds of career changes made by the graduate student. In line with our original hypothesis, it was felt that the explanation of the variation in the direction of career change might be found in the content of the interaction of the student and the faculty— with change in career preference going in a direction consistent with the conceptions of the professional self held by the faculty.

The operational procedure for determining the faculty value climate was based on a series of items which the student could select as those "which gave a student high prestige with the faculty." The items and percentage of students who chose each item are produced in Table 3.

It should be recognized that we are dealing here with only one side of the academic coin: the student's view of what the faculty holds as being important. Whether there is realistic consensus between what the faculty

Table 3

ITEMS WHICH GIVE STUDENTS HIGH PRESTIGE WITH THE FACULTY*

ITEM	PER CENT
Demonstrating research or scholarly capacity	96
Being original and creative	76
Dedication to the field	74
Teaching ability	47
Pleasing personality	42
Interest in things outside the discipline	22
Application of the discipline to the non-academic world ..	21
Not being too critical	18

* Base N's range from 508 to 2,622.

sees and what the student perceives is not crucial to this discussion. Rather, our concern is with how the student's image of the faculty is tied in with patterns of career change. The distribution of answers to this question tells us some interesting things about the values of the faculty as perceived by the graduate student. First of all, virtually every student sees the faculty of his department as interested in research. The emphasis on research is true regardless of school quality or division of study within the university. Secondly, only about one-half of the students see reward in the display of teaching ability to the faculty. Third, the faculty, it would appear—at least from the student's viewpoint—is only a little interested in the outside world. Finally, we see that displays of professional interest are much more effective in getting prestige with the faculty than "well roundedness" or a pleasant personal facade.

If faculty values are to be used to account for change in career preferences, we should expect that it would be much more likely that a student will change, if he changes at all, in the direction of research as opposed to teaching. We find that this is the case: of the changers, 51 per cent move to research; 32 per cent to teaching; and 17 per cent are "ambiguous."[3] But we want to be more specific than this. We wish to determine the impact of the graduate department on the student's career preferences; in other words, we want to see if certain academic departments are more likely to "move" students to research than are other academic departments. To accomplish

Table 4

DEPARTMENTAL TYPE AND DIRECTION OF CHANGE IN
CAREER PREFERENCES

CHANGING TO....	RESEARCH PER CENT	TEACHING PER CENT	AMBIGUOUS PER CENT	N	TOTAL
Single-minded	54	28	18	557	100
Eclectic	45	39	16	456	100

$\chi^2 = 13.45, p < .005.$

this it was necessary to develop some measure of departmental climate which would tell us what departments to look at in order to find the ones in which research is especially favored. A glance at the marginals in Table 3 tells us that we will not find any department in which research is not emphasized; thus, we will not be able to produce any clean-cut dichotomy of teaching *versus* research departments.

3.   The changers were further broken down into three categories: (1) those who indicated that teaching had become more desirable to them; (2) those who reported they now had a greater preference for research; (3) an "other" category of mixed and ambiguous changers who may have preferred both research and teaching, or changers who expressed greater preference for one of these in combination with academic administration or some other activity which they were free to select in addition to the alternatives which were given.

The fact that the prestige items do overlap in departments suggested a different type of approach, that of the cumulation of items. For example, some departments may encourage research alone, while other departments encourage teaching, and still other departments encourage both of these *plus* application of the field to non-academic areas. This situation suggested the use of the Guttman scalogram technique which serves as a model to any cumulative phenomenon. Through the employment of the Guttman technique and a method by which graduate departments could be classified we were able to establish two different departmental types. The first department type was interested only in research and dedication to the field, while the second departmental type was interested—in addition to research and the field—in teaching and application of the discipline to the nonacademic world. We called the first type "single-minded" departments and the latter type "eclectic."[4] The actual distribution of the two departmental types was fairly even: 49 per cent fell in the single-minded grouping, 38 per cent in the eclectic, and 13 per cent were undefinable.

We can hardly expect that any given departmental type will be able to completely halt the trend in change toward research. Since every academic department encourages research, it is our position that the expected influence of the departments is such that single-minded departments might be expected to accentuate the trend toward research, since research and the advancement of the field are the only aspects the department is interested in, while the eclectic departments might be expected to expose students to a more varied set of cues and stimuli and thus be significantly lower in its output of changers toward research. In Table 4 we see the direction of change in the two departmental types. Our hypothesis about the differential production of changers is confirmed. The single-minded departments do produce a significantly greater number of changers towards research than do the eclectic departments. We may now ask what is the relationship between departmental climate, student-faculty integration, and direction of career preference change.

When we examine Table 5, we see departmental type again: regardless of level of integration, the single-minded departments produce more change towards research; but the relationship to integration within departments is not so clear. One would expect that the greatest shift to research would occur among students who are highly integrated within the single-minded departments. We find, however, that integration per se has little to do with direction of career preference change. It would seem, then, that the type of interpersonal relationship represented by our integration variable is not a reasonable predictor of the direction of change in career preference. This would suggest the use of some other integration variable, one that will not only tell us if the student is close to a faculty member but, in addition, will supply us with some clue as to the content of the particular interpersonal

4. A detailed description of the error types and the criteria for establishing the departmental types can be found in Gottlieb (1960).

Table 5

DEPARTMENTAL TYPE, INTEGRATION WITH THE FACULTY,

AND CHANGE IN CAREER PREFERENCES

INTEGRATION	CHANGE TO RESEARCH PER CENT	CHANGE TO TEACHING PER CENT	AMBIGUOUS PER CENT	N	TOTAL
	SINGLE-MINDED DEPARTMENTS				
High	52	37	11	87	100
Low	53	28	19	336	100
None	53	28	19	103	100
	ECLECTIC DEPARTMENTS				
High	44	34	22	118	100
Low	50	35	15	266	100
None	43	38	19	49	100

relationship. The question in our schedule which seems to meet this requirement is one that deals with opportunities to discuss career plans. Each of the respondents was asked this question:

> Do you feel you have enough opportunities to discuss your career plans formally or informally with members of the faculty in your department? (Yes or No).

The response was 62 per cent yes and 38 per cent no. When opportunities to discuss career plans are introduced as an intervening variable, a further spread in the percentage differential among changers in different types of departments is produced.

Table 6 shows the double effect of departmental climate and opportunities to discuss career plans. Change to research is more pronounced in the single-minded departments than in the eclectic departments, regardless of opportunities to discuss; but within each departmental type the change to research is greater among those who feel they have opportunities to discuss their career plans. The opposite trend is observable among those who have changed toward teaching and those whose career plans are ambiguous. The conclusion suggested here is that opportunities to discuss career plans with the faculty does have a discernible effect but that this effect depends on the kind of faculty members one does his discussing with.

Our picture of integration and socialization begins to take on a more specific pattern. We said earlier that there was no apparent relationship between integration with the faculty and the direction of change, thus casting doubt on the importance of the integration mechanism in the process of the socialization of the graduate student. Interpersonal friendship is not a necessary condition of socialization; socialization can take place in the classroom or the laboratory session as well as through informal contacts in the faculty member's office. What we have shown is that the graduate

Table 6

DEPARTMENTAL TYPE, OPPORTUNITIES TO DISCUSS CAREER
PLANS, AND CHANGE IN CAREER PREFERENCES

OPPORTUNITY TO DISCUSS	CHANGE TO RESEARCH PER CENT	CHANGE TO TEACHING PER CENT	AMBIGUOUS PER CENT	N	TOTAL
SINGLE-MINDED DEPARTMENTS					
Yes	56	26	18	292	100
No	50	33	17	263	100
ECLECTIC DEPARTMENTS					
Yes	45	34	21	267	100
No	40	39	21	184	100

student and the faculty do not, on the whole, form a single social system although the values of the faculty are influential on the actions of changers.

So it seems that the really important element in the interaction variables we have been discussing thus far is opportunity to discuss career plans with the faculty, and it is here that we introduce faculty integration as a secondary variable which will predict opportunities to discuss career plans. When we examine the relationship between integration with the faculty and opportunities to discuss, we see that it is much more likely that the person with high faculty integration will have the better chance to discuss his career plans with a faculty member.

After discussion, however, it is believed that high integration may act as a deterrent to change. This may take place for a variety of reasons: (1) the fact that a person is highly integrated may provide social support for him to stick to his original plans; (2) the person who is highly integrated may receive cues from a variety of faculty members, each with his own interests and his own impressions of the student, the net effect of which is to cancel out the aggregate of advice and leave the student in a mental state conducive to adherence to his own original plans. On the other hand, we may examine the reason why the low integrated change more than the high integrated from the standpoint of the low integrated student: (1) the low integrated may have contact with only one member of the faculty or a small corps of faculty members, therefore, faculty advice on career plans might be more likely to be uniform in content and, hence, more effective in bringing about change; in a research department it is more likely that the advice the student will get will incline him towards research; (2) the low integrated may perceive that they are low on the integration ladder and change more often in order to increase the amount of their integration with the faculty; since all faculties appear to value research skills, it is more likely that the low integrated can increase his interpersonal status with the faculty by changing his career interests in the direction of research, especially if he is a totally nonresearch person to begin with.

The nonintegrated student, not having had sufficient opportunity to discuss his career plans, and being least likely to get that chance, is the least changeable, and this intractability persists regardless of the number of years he spends in the department. This would seem to argue the importance of integration, for if it were simply a matter of exposure to a "message" contained in the doctrine preached in departmental classes, seminars, and laboratories, one would expect that the passage of time would bring the "message" to all graduate students. As we noted earlier, this is not the case; regardless of years in the current department, it is the integrated student who is most likely to report a change in his career preferences.

Faculty Encouragement

Having considered the importance of departmental climates, integration with the faculty, and the passing of time on changes in career preferences, we will conclude our discussion of the socialization process with the investigation of one further area of faculty-student interaction. Here we will be dealing with how students, in both single-minded and eclectic departments, respond to the verbal cues of faculty members.

Each of our respondents was asked a set of questions dealing with specific things they had been told by the faculty. The responses to four of these items in this set of questions were used to formulate a "specific encouragement" index. The specific encouragement index sorts the respondents into four categories: (1) those who have been told by at least one faculty member that they have a flair for teaching: (2) those who have been told by at least one faculty member that they have a flair for research; (3) those who have had both experiences (1) and (2), that is, they have been told by one or more faculty members that they have both a flair for teaching and a flair for research; (4) those who have been given no specific encouragement regarding either teaching or research.

The relationship between direction of change and specific encouragement is as one would expect. Persons who have been told that they are potentially good researchers are the most likely to change to research, while those who have been given a mixed cue in the direction of research and teaching are the next most likely; those who have been told nothing encouraging them either in the direction of teaching or research fall in the middle, while those who have been specifically encouraged in the direction of teaching are the least likely to change to research.

When, however, departmental climate is controlled (Table 7), the same effect appears among students in the eclectic departments, the order of productivity of changers to research being: (1) research encouragement only, (2) research-teaching, (3) no specific encouragement, and (4) encouragement towards teaching. It will be noted that encouragement of any kind in eclectic departments produces less change toward research than the same kind of encouragement in single-minded departments. The beauty of

Table 7, however, lies in the following: Students in the eclectic departments change in the direction of specific faculty cues. The strongest changers toward research are found among those students who have been told they will make good researchers. The lowest percentage of research changers among students in the eclectic departments is found in the group who has been given only teaching encouragement. The "nones" show more change to research than do the students who received only the teaching cue, and those who received the combined cues of teaching and research show more change to research than either the "nones" or the teaching only group. Among the single-minded departments the situation is different. Here we find that no matter what he has been told the student changes in the direc-

Table 7

DEPARTMENTAL TYPE, SPECIFIC ENCOURAGEMENT, AND
CHANGE IN CAREER PREFERENCES

DEPARTMENTAL TYPE	PER CENT CHANGING TO RESEARCH				
	T[a]	R[b]	TR[c]	NONE[d]	*N*
Single-minded	59	55	62	50	563
Eclectic	36	54	52	46	438
Total					1001

[a] T = students who have been told by at least one faculty member that they have a flair for teaching.

[b] R = students who have been told by at least one faculty member that they have a flair for research.

[c] TR = students who have been told by at least one faculty member that they have a flair for both teaching and research.

[d] None = students who have been told none of the above.

tion of research. In fact, the impact of being told you will make a good teacher by a faculty member of a research-oriented department is sufficient to bring about a greater change to research than being told nothing at all. Being told you will make a good teacher by a faculty member who values research is, it would appear, most likely viewed as the "kiss of death" and seen not so much as praise but as a cue that the student is on the wrong track.

Summary and Conclusions

In this paper we have explored some of the byways of socialization in the American graduate school with particular emphasis on the departmental climate, faculty-student integration, and changes in career preferences. We have shown that graduate students do alter their career preferences and that these changes do not appear to be so much a result of a selectivity process as they are a function of the graduate school system itself. We have seen that integration with the faculty disposes one toward change and raises the probability that he will have opportunities to discuss his career plans with faculty members. Finally, we have noted that cues imparted to the students by the faculty have a significant effect on the direction of changes in career preferences.

References

BECKER, H. S. and STRAUSS, A.   Careers, personality and adult socialization. *American Journal of Sociology*, 1956, 42, 253-263.

CHILD, I. L.   Socialization. In G. Lindzey (Ed.). *Handbook of social psychology.* Cambridge: Addison-Wesley, 1954.

GOTTLIEB, D.   Processes of socialization in American graduate schools. Ph.D. dissertation, University of Chicago, 1960.

MERTON, R. K., READER, G. and KENDALL, P. (Eds.).   *The student physician: Introductory studies in the sociology of medical education.* Cambridge: Harvard University Press, 1957.

MILLER, D. R. and SWANSON, G. E.   *The changing American parent.* New York: Wiley, 1956.

Table 1

PROFILES OF ATTENDANCE AREAS AND NUMBERS OF RESPONDENTS*

	MEDIAN FAMILY INCOME	% IN WHITE-COLLAR OCCUPATIONS	MEDIAN YRS. OF SCHOOL COMPLETED	% NEGRO	% INCREASE IN SCHOOL POP. (1960-1963)	NUMBER OF INTERVIEWS			
						MOTH-ERS	TEACH-ERS	STU-DENTS	PRIN-CIPALS
City neighborhoods									
White middle-class (el.)	$10,000	55%	12	<5%		92	13	0	1
White working-class (el.) ...	$6,000	40%	8	<5%		92	18	0	1
Mixed Negro and white (el.).	$4,500	20%	8	40%		84	9	0	1
Negro (el.)	$4,500	15%	8	90%		66	16	0	1
Cross-section (high school)						138	29	157	1
Suburbs									
Stable middle-class	$15,000	75%	13	<1%	5%	131	22	59	2
Growing middle-class	$10,000	70%	13	<1%	15%	128	31	48	2
Stable working-class	$6,000	30%	9	<1%	1%	111	25	49	3
Growing working-class	$7,000	35%	11	<1%	41%	142	48	45	2
Small towns									
Middle-class (pop. 4,000) ...	$6,300	50%	12			154	23	45	2
Working-class (pop. 6,000) ..	$6,200	40%	10			125	30	56	2
Rural community (pop. 2,500)**						127	19	49	2

* All census figures are approximate in order to preserve community anonymity. The 1960 U.S. Census was used.

** Census data not provided.

8. THE PEOPLE WHO EDUCATE

When the student fails, whose fault is it? An old Russian saying holds that there are no stupid pupils, only teachers too stupid to teach them.

This study suggests, however, that given the chance to do so, teachers will attribute the success of an "improving" student to their own efforts, but place the causality for non-improvement at the student's door.

The study is also methodologically interesting, and represents a thoughtful use of the laboratory experimental setting to test some well-formulated predictions. Much rests on whether or not the subjects actually believed that they were really teaching real fourth-graders. While it is possible they did, the authors did not debrief subjects in a way that would let us know.

All in all, however, the success of the predictions is convincing. In part, this may be because Johnson and his colleagues have taken hold of variables (see Heider, *The Psychology of Interpersonal Relations*, Wiley, 1958) of a basic, even "primitive" sort. For example, judgments as to whether a student or a teacher "can" do something, or "wants" to do it, are at the heart of the day-to-day transactions of the classroom. The particular conjunction of "can" and "not want" which appears in this study can also be noted in Beez' study of teacher expectancy in this volume—and perhaps was even felt by Feshbach and Devor's four-year-olds as they struggled with their sometimes intractable three-year-old pupils.

Some Determinants and Consequences of the Teacher's Perception of Causation*

Thomas J. Johnson,
Rhoda Feigenbaum, Marcia Weiby

Although teachers tend to acknowledge motivating students to be among their most important problems and frequently complain about the lack of motivation in certain students or classes, the motive construct itself is generally invoked to explain or account for a pupil's behavior. Yet, at present, little is known about the cues (from a child's behavior) which form the basis for a teacher's inferences of motivation or other "causes" underlying a student's behavior. Moreover, there is little evidence of how a teacher's subsequent behavior toward a child is influenced by her perceptions of what guides, directs, or causes the child's behavior. The basic problem then was to investigate some of the determinants and consequences of the teacher's perceptions of causation.

According to Heider (1944) general perception is characterized by a tendency toward a state of balance or harmony among the elements accepted into perception. In the absence of harmony, there is a preference for a balanced state, tension will arise, and reorganization will occur to regain the state of balance. Since events in the social field gain meaning from the sources to which they are attributed, causal units consisting of a person and his act are formed, and these obey the laws of perceptual unit formation.

Heider (1958) provides an analysis of the manner in which these general principles of perception govern the perception of other persons and their behaviors. If the characteristics of an actor are positive (origin) and his act is positive (effect), the cause will tend to be located in the actor (i.e., his characteristics), and the observer will perceive the situation as balanced. However, if the characteristics are positive and the act is negative, a state of imbalance exists since the person (as origin) does not fit the effect. On these occasions the locus of causality will tend to be perceived as external to the actor (bad luck, etc.). By locating the cause outside the actor, the observer creates, by reorganization, a state of balance. Assimilation can also occur, and the act will be changed to fit the qualities of the person as in "halo" phenomena.

* From *Journal of Educational Psychology*, 1964, 55 (5), 237-246. Used by permission of the authors and publisher.

In a similar vein, qualities, which are consistent with the qualities of acts, will be attributed to persons. If an act is perceived as negative, we tend to attribute negative characteristics to the actor, thus creating a balanced causal unit. The cause of the negative behavior resides in the negative characteristics that are attributed to the individual.

The concept of the balanced state also designates a situation in which the perceived causal units and the experienced sentiments (e.g., like, dislike, trust, sympathy, etc.) coexist without stress. Thus, initial perceptions of other persons and their behavior provide a basis for the development and expression of positive and negative sentiments toward them. Conversely, if positive and negative sentiments already exist, they influence the judgments we make about other persons and their acts.

The intent of this study was to investigate a number of Heider's hypotheses in a classroom context, although Festinger's (1957) "dissonance" theory and Osgood's (1955) "congruence" theory would yield equivalent predictions. The main focus was in discovering how the characteristics and/or actions of the student (the actor and his act) differentially affect the teacher's (*a*) attribution of characteristics, (*b*) perceptions of causation, and (*c*) expressions of sentiment.

Method

Subjects

Eighty volunteer female subjects, enrolled in educational psychology courses, were randomly placed into one of four experimental groups. All subjects had had previous teaching experience in regular classes as part of their earlier professional training.

Apparatus

The experiment was conducted in a learning laboratory suitable for small groups research. A speaker system provided one- or two-way communication between the laboratory and an adjacent room. A control panel with an on-off switch and three other switches clearly labeled A, B, C was mounted on a wall to the left of where the subject was to be seated; and a large speaker was mounted on the wall behind the subject. During the experiment, the subject heard only the feedback from her own voice as she spoke into the microphone.

Procedure

Each subject was tested individually by one of two female graduate students. The subjects were seated at a table in front of a microphone and were handed two 1-page arithmetic instructional units to look over. These units (previously prepared by the experimenter) dealt with the concepts involved in multiplying numbers by 10 or by 20. After reading the two units, the subjects were asked to read the first paragraph from the 10s unit into the microphone to relax them prior to the experiment proper (and to facilitate the subsequent deception).

General Instructions

The subjects were told they were participating in a government-supported study in cooperation with the city school system, and that the purpose of the experiment was to learn more about the teacher's role in the teaching-learning process. They would be teaching the arithmetic concepts to two fourth-grade boys (actually fictitious) who had volunteered to participate with the understanding that they would be given free time from school for their part in the experiment. However, these "students" were only to receive their free time if they cooperated with the subject. Thus, the subject could take away some or all of their free time if they did not pay close attention to her or did not follow instructions. (This was done to enhance the superordinate-subordinate relationship.) The subjects were told the anonymity of the two students would be preserved by referring to them only as A and B.

The mechanics of the speaker system were then explained to the subject. Communication between the subject and the two students was to be controlled by the experimenter, who would turn on the microphone during the times that the subject would be talking to the students. If the switch was on C, the subject could talk to both students; if the switch was on A or B, the subject could only talk to that student. Communication was to be only one way, i.e., the students could not talk to the subject.

After the subject presented a unit, the students would work on some problems based on the concept the subject had presented. The subjects were told that examples of the students' work would be brought to the subject during the course of the experiment, and the subject would be given the opportunity to talk to the students periodically. The subject was then shown the work sheets that would be given to the students. One sheet contained five sets of 10 problems each dealing with multiplying by 10s, and the other sheet was similar except that it dealt with multiplying by 20s. Answers to the problems were supplied.

The subjects were told that their teaching ability would be evaluated in part on the basis of how well their students performed on the tasks, and that they should caution their students to listen carefully and follow instructions.

Phase I. The experimenter turned the microphone on and set the switch to C. The subject was then given the standard unit on the 10s concept to present, and the experimenter left the room to pass out the work sheets to the students. After the subject had finished the presentation, the experimenter returned and informed the subject that the students were working on the problems. After a short time the experimenter left to get the work of one of the students and returned with a previously prepared work sheet purporting to be B's work up to that point. Of the 10 problems in the first set, B had 2 correct out of 4 completed. In the second set, 1 was correct out of 3 completed. On the third set, B had attempted to play ticktacktoe. The experimenter told the subject, "You'd better get after B," and handed her the sheet. The experimenter then turned the microphone switch to B, and the subject was allowed to talk with B for 30 seconds. (Although no attempt was made to monitor these conversations, they generally tended to be admonishments for B to pay attention, followed by recapitulations of the previous presentation.) The experimenter left again to get A's work on the five sets and the rest of B's work on the remaining two sets. The experimenter returned and handed the sheets to the subject. A had completed from between 4 to 6 problems on each of the five sets and all of them were correct. B continued to complete 3 or 4 with 1 or 2 correct. The experimenter turned the microphone switch to A, and the subject was permitted to talk to him for 30 seconds. The subjects were then given the first of the two experimental questionnaires.

Phase II. After the subjects had completed the questionnaire, they were randomly assigned to *positive* or *negative* groups and were given two cumulative folders purporting to contain the personal histories of A and B. The data for Student A had been previously prepared to make him appear to have "positive" characteristics (IQ above 130, previous achievement high, father was a professional, etc.) B's data were varied to make him appear to have either positive characteristics (equivalent to A) or "negative" characteristics (IQ below 100, past achievement poor, father unskilled laborer, etc.), depending on the experimental treatment. The subjects were allowed to familiarize themselves with the histories, and were then given the unit on multiplying by 20s to present to the students who would then work on problems related to the 20s concept.

Phase III. The subjects began the presentation, and the experimenter left to pass out the work sheets. The experimenter returned after the subjects had finished the presentation and asked them to indicate whose work they would like to see.

At this point in the experiment, *PosHi, PosLo, NegHi,* and *NegLo* groups were formed. The first term refers to the nature of B's characteristics in the folder (positive or negative) and the second refers to B's performance on the second (20s) task (high or low). In the PosLo and NegLo groups, B's performance remained three or four completed with one or two correct. A's performance continued to be four to six completed, all correct. In the PosHi and NegHi groups, B's performance was equal to A's, i.e., four to six completed, all correct. Table 1 depicts the over-all design of the study. The experimenter left and returned with three sets of problems from the appropriate work sheet, and the subjects were allowed to communicate briefly with whomever they had chosen. Then the subjects were again asked whose work they would like to see, and the experimenter left and returned with the remaining work sheets for A and B. After checking the papers, the subjects were permitted to communicate briefly with the student whose work they had requested and were then given a second form of the experimental questionnaire. The experiment was terminated, a plausible (but irrelevant) purpose for the experiment was explained to the subjects, and

Table 1

EXPERIMENTAL DESIGN

STUDENT B	PosHi	PosLo	NegHi	NegLo
Performance on first task				
First questionnaire Y_1	Lo	Lo	Lo	Lo
Ascribed characteristics	Pos	Pos	Neg	Neg
Performance on second task				
Second questionnaire Y_2	Hi	Lo	Hi	Lo

they were requested not to communicate with other classmates. None of the subjects indicated that she was aware of the deception.

Questionnaire Instrument

The experimental questionnaire was first administered after the two students had completed the first task, before the positive and negative characteristics had been ascribed to A and B via the cumulative folder. The instrument contained a number of different measures. On 5-point scales the subjects rated the adequacy (5) or inadequacy (1) of their presentation. Each student was assigned separate grades for effort, skills, and understanding, using a letter-grading system of E, G, M, P, F (excellent, good, medium, poor, failure). Two completion items which asked the subject to account for the performance of A and B provided a measure of the perception of causation. To assess the attribution of characteristics, a seven-item "characteristics" subscale forced the subject to choose either A or B on the following: higher IQ, higher achieving, more motivated, more ambitious, least dependable, more troublesome, and comes from a lower social class. Four forced-choice items (would check on more, would rate presentation higher, would do more if not checked on, should lose free time) formed a "sentiment" subscale. Several filler items also were included in an attempt to mask the purpose of the experiment. A second form of the questionnaire (minus the characteristics subscale) was administered after the second task had been completed.

Results and Discussion

Effectiveness of the Experimental Manipulation

On the first task A's actual performance was higher than B's in all experimental groups. On the second task A's performance remained higher than B's in the PosLo and NegLo groups. In the PosHi and NegHi groups B improved, so A and B were equally high. Since the subjects were required to evaluate the performance of A and B after each task by assigning individual letter grades for effort, skills, and understanding, these evaluations should reveal whether these experimental specifications were met. Mean evaluations in each group are presented in Table 2. Analysis of second task grades alone is sufficient to demonstrate that A is graded significantly higher than B in the PosHi and PosLo groups ($t = 4.73$, $df = 39$, $p < .005$) as well as in the NegHi and NegLo groups ($t = 6.31$, $df = 39$, $p < .005$). When the relevant groups are compared, the second task grades given to

Table 2

MEAN GRADES ON EFFORT (E), SKILLS (S), AND UNDERSTANDING (U), ACCORDING TO TASK AND EXPERIMENTAL GROUP

TASK		PosLo			PosHi		
		E	S	U	E	S	U
First	A	4.20	4.60	4.60	4.30	4.55	4.75
	B	2.55	2.00	1.85	2.80	2.25	2.35
Second	A	4.30	4.50	4.45	4.35	4.45	4.70
	B	3.10	2.75	2.75	4.50	4.35	4.65
		NegLo			NegHi		
First	A	4.20	4.65	4.75	4.50	4.70	4.75
	B	2.80	2.25	2.20	2.70	2.20	1.95
Second	A	4.55	4.80	4.80	4.60	4.45	4.75
	B	3.60	2.40	2.45	4.65	4.15	4.55

both A and B are significantly higher in the PosHi group than in the PosLo group ($t = 4.90$, $df = 38$, $p < .005$), and the NegHi grades are higher than the NegLo grades ($t = 9.81$, $df = 38$, $p < .005$). Thus, the manipulation of performance was apparently successful.

An interesting and unexpected phenomenon that occurs in these evaluations is the tendency for A's effort grades to be lower and for B's effort grades to be higher than the grades given on the other dimensions. To test this effect each letter grade was assigned a value from 5 to 1, and the difference between the effort grade and the "skill-understanding" grade given by the subject to each student was determined. (If A's effort grade on the first task were 3 and his mean skill-understanding grade we:e 3.5, A's difference on this task would be .5. If B's effort grade were 3 and his mean skill-understanding grade were 2.5, B's difference on this task would be −.5.) Each subject was then assigned a "discrepancy" score based on the algebraic value of the difference between these two differences. (A .5 for A and a −.5 for B yielded a discrepancy score of 1.0.) Mean discrepancies appear in Table 3. The existence of differential effort grading for A and B on the first task is reflected in the highly significant mean discrepancies which occur in the PosHi and PosLo groups ($t = 10.0, df = 39, p < .005$), as well as in the NegHi and NegLo groups ($t = 8.04, df = 39, p < .005$). When relevant group comparisons are made on the second task grades, the mean discrepancy in the PosLo group is greater than in the PosHi group ($t = 3.61, df = 38, p < .005$), and the NegLo mean is greater than in the

Table 3

MEAN DISCREPANCY BETWEEN EFFORT GRADES AND COMBINED
SKILL-UNDERSTANDING GRADES ACCORDING TO TASK
AND EXPERIMENTAL GROUP

TASK	PosLo	PosHi	NegLo	NegHi
First	1.075	1.125	1.125	.950
Second	1.200	.325	1.425	.475

NegHi group ($t = 4.32, df = 38, p < .005$). Thus, the phenomenon appears to have been affected by the variation of performance on the second task. Although halo, logical error, and leniency effects do occur in the evaluation of others, none of these phenomena seems to explain these findings adequately. The results could be interpreted as a "compensation" effect related to the separate grading system for achievement and industry that some teachers informally employ. The compensation occurs when the quality of the effort augments, reduces, or replaces the actual quality of the achievement.

Attribution of Characteristics

Based on the earlier reasoning, it was hypothesized that positive characteristics would be inferred from positive actions, and negative characteristics would be inferred from negative actions. Since the experimental manipulation was apparently successful, the subjects were aware that A had done better work than B on the first task, and consequently they would be expected to perceive A as having positive characteristics and to perceive B as having negative characteristics.

Data relevant to this hypothesis were derived from the characteristics scale of the first questionnaire. Scores were number of choices of A on the four positive characteristics and B on the three negative characteristics.

Table 4

MEAN CHARACTERISTICS SCORES ACCORDING TO EXPERIMENTAL GROUP

	PosLo	PosHi	NegLo	NegHi
	6.85	6.55	6.58	6.85

Mean characteristics scores for each group appear in Table 4. The data reveal that means for all experimental groups are above 6.5 (7.0 maximum), and the groups do not differ significantly ($F = 1.42$, $df = 3/75$, $p > .20$). The very high means indicate that Student A is the dominant choice on the positive items and Student B on the negative items in accordance with the hypothesis.

Although a number of studies have demonstrated the manner in which superficial external cues (i.e., appearance, etc.) affect judgments of others (e.g., Bruner and Tagiuri, 1954; Thornton, 1944) less is known of the manner in which behavioral cues affect the observer. The relative importance of external and behavioral cues has been investigated by Lippitt, Polansky, and Rosen (1952), who compared two boys' camps on judgments of fighting ability. In one camp where very little fighting occurred, judgments were based primarily on physical size. In the other camp where a great deal of fighting took place, these judgments were based on performance. However, in the latter situation external cues were also present. In the present experiment external cues (other than productivity) were not available during the student's initial performance. Thus, the results demonstrate the manner in which "pure" performance has provided specific behavioral cues for attributing characteristics to others.

Perception of Causation

According to Heider (1958) the cause of an act will tend to be perceived as internal when actions are congruent with the characteristics of the actor and tend to be perceived as external to the actor when the actions are non-congruent with his characteristics. If the characteristics of the actor are not known, the cause will tend to be perceived as internal, and characteristics will be attributed which are congruent with the actions.

Data relevant to the perception of causation were obtained on both questionnaires using open-ended items which asked the subjects to account for the performances of A and B. Responses to each item were categorized as to the perceived cause, using the following criteria:

1. A *positive internal* cause was scored if the performance was explained as due to the student's understanding of the concept, attentiveness, greater interest or motivation, higher abilities, etc.
2. A *negative internal* cause was scored if the performance was explained by a lack of understanding, inattentiveness, disinterest, lower ability, etc.

3. A *positive external* cause was scored if the performance was attributed to the subject's presentation, influence attempts, punitive threats, etc.

4. A *negative external* cause was scored if the performance was attributed to the subject's poor presentation, poor explanation, etc.

Mixed responses were scored according to the majority of statements in a given category. Per cent agreement among judges using these criteria was .95.

The theoretical expectation was that the perceived cause of A's first and second performance would be positive internal and B's first performance would be negative internal. To test the effects of the experimental treatment, the subjects who responded according to the theoretical expectations were classified as criterion subjects and were assigned two new scores based on their perception of the cause of B's second performance. A "perceived productivity" score of 1 was assigned if their response had been placed in either positive category (positive internal, positive external), and −1 if the response was placed in either negative category (negative internal, negative external). A "causation" score of 1 was assigned for either external category and −1 for either internal category. The remaining subjects (those who failed to respond as predicted on the initial criteria) received scores of zero on each of these dimensions and were included in the data analysis.

Mean perceived productivity scores for each group appear in Table 5. Analysis of variance yielded a highly significant main effect of B's performance on perceived productivity, ($F = 56.37$, $df = 1/76$, $p < .001$), as expected. The effect of the experimenter's ascribing positive or negative characteristics to B fell just short of the customary 5% level of significance ($F = 3.68$, $df = 1/76$, $p < .08$), and reflects the tendency for some subjects in the PosLo group to misperceive B's low, second performance as improved. This latter result suggests that perceptual facilitation may have been operating to a certain extent,[1] due to the positive characteristics ascribed to B, or the subject's efforts to influence B's behavior.

Mean causation scores for each group appear in Table 6. Analysis of variance on these data yielded a significant main effect of B's second performance on the external-internal dimension of perceived cause ($F = 18.12$, $df = 1/76$, $p < .001$). When B improves, the subjects tend to perceive themselves as responsible for his improvement, but perceive B as responsible when his performance does not improve. In view of the subject's consistent efforts throughout the experiment to influence B's performance, it is not surprising that some subjects would perceive themselves as the causative agent when B does improve. However, since B's second performance was equal to A's in the PosHi and NegHi groups, it is worth noting that in contrast A's high performance had been attributed to A's interest, motivation, eagerness, etc.

---

1. A separate analysis indicates that there was significantly less difference between the A and B grades given by these subjects on the second task ($t = 2.79$, $df = 18$, $p < .01$).

Table 5

RELATION BETWEEN B'S SECOND PERFORMANCE AND ASCRIBED
CHARACTERISTICS AND PERCEIVED PRODUCTIVITY

ASCRIBED CHARACTERISTICS	SECOND PERFORMANCE	
	LOW	HIGH
Positive	−.15	.80
Negative	−.55	.65

Table 6

RELATION BETWEEN B'S SECOND PERFORMANCE AND ASCRIBED
CHARACTERISTICS AND EXTERNAL-INTERNAL CAUSATION

ASCRIBED CHARACTERISTICS	SECOND PERFORMANCE	
	LOW	HIGH
Positive	−.55	.10
Negative	−.65	.15

Additional insight into the perception of causation can be derived from analyzing the subjects' evaluations of their own performance. If the subjects in any group perceived themselves as responsible for B's improvement on

Table 7

RELATION BETWEEN B'S SECOND PERFORMANCE AND ASCRIBED
CHARACTERISTICS AND PERCEIVED ADEQUACY
OF SECOND PRESENTATION

ASCRIBED CHARACTERISTICS	SECOND PERFORMANCE	
	LOW	HIGH
Positive	2.5	3.7
Negative	2.8	3.5

the second task, this ought to be reflected in their evaluations of their second presentation. Mean perceived adequacy scores for each group are shown in Table 7. Analysis of covariance revealed a highly significant main effect of B's second performance on perceived adequacy ($Fy = 17.73$, $df = 1/76$, $p < .001$). Thus, the subjects perceived their second presentations to be more adequate when B improved.

Expression of Sentiment

According to Heider (1958) sentiment and causal unit formation tend toward a balanced state, hence sentiments should be expressed which are congruent with the characteristics and actions of the actor. Consequently, after the first task, the sentiments expressed for A should be different from those expresssed for B. After the second task, a reduction in this difference might be expected to occur in the PosHi and NegHi groups as B's performance is seen to improve.

Table 8

RELATION BETWEEN B'S SECOND PERFORMANCE AND ASCRIBED
CHARACTERISTICS AND DIFFERENCE IN SENTIMENT

| ASCRIBED | SECOND PERFORMANCE | |
CHARACTERISTICS	LOW	HIGH
Positive	3.55	2.50
Negative	3.30	2.60

In order to test this hypothesis, the sentiment subscale was scored according to the number of "correct" choices of A or B. On the first questionnaire the two A items were, (*a*) would rate presentation higher, and (*b*) would do more if not checked on; and the two B items were, (*c*) would check on more, and (*d*) would take free time from. On the second questionnaire the A items were, (*a*) would rate second presentation higher, and (*b*) would prefer to teach; and the two B items were, (*c*) would check on more for third task, and (*d*) would expect to misbehave. The maximum score on each questionnaire was 4, with a larger score representing greater difference in sentiment toward the students.[2]

Mean sentiment scores for each group after the second task appear in Table 8. Analysis of covariance revealed a significant main effect of performance on sentiment ($Fy = 19.35$, $df = 3/76$, $p < .001$), indicating that the difference in sentiment toward the two students has been reduced in the two high performance groups.

Heider's hypothesis that sentiment and causal unit formation tend toward a balanced state appears to be based on the well-documented finding that judgments of others tend to be highly unified (e.g., Asch, 1952; Ichheiser, 1949; Spiegel, 1950). The results of this investigation have indicated that the particular sentiments expressed tended to be related to the characteristics and actions of the two students.

Although these findings could be due to organizing factors in perception, an alternative explanation would seem to lie in the type of superordinate-subordinate relationship that had been established. According to Thibaut and Kelley (1959) power in the form of fate control exists when X can effect Y's outcomes regardless of what Y does. When fate control is used by X to influence a subordinate's behavior, this can be done by either augmenting

---

2.   *Sentiment* in Heider's (1958) terms refers to the way a person feels about or evaluates something. It is assumed that a number of different sentiments might underlie the particular choice of A or B on an item, e.g., like, sympathy, trust, etc. Consequently, specific inferences concerning the quality or nature of these sentiments have been left to conjecture.

Y's outcomes when he complies, or by reducing Y's outcomes when he does not comply. When augmentation is the mode of control, Y will present evidence of his compliance to X and thereby validate his claim to reward. However, when reduction of outcome is used, X must keep Y's compliance under surveillance. In this experiment the student (Y) had been promised free time which the subject-teacher (X) could take away for noncooperation. Consequently, the only direct means of control would be via reduction of outcomes. Since Y had given evidence of noncompliance on the first task through his performance, it might be expected that Y would be closely monitored on the second task.

That this type of interaction situation can have negative effects on the subordinate has been demonstrated by Kahn and Katz (1953), who found an inverse relationship between productivity and morale. Strickland (1958) studied the perceptions of the superordinate in a study very similar to the present one. In his study the subject supervisor demanded a high output from two (fictitious) workers whom he could monitor and influence by reduction of outcomes. The objective output of the two workers was held equal, but the subject was forced to monitor A more than B. His subjects chose to continue to monitor A for a second work period, expressed negative sentiments toward A, and perceived the locus of causality for A's compliance as external to A (residing in their own application of influence).

An important methodological consideration in this investigation was the use of a simulated teaching situation to manipulate the independent variables of interest. Although the particular strategy of simulation employed in this study required the subjects to teach an arithmetic unit to two students, alternative types of teaching-learning situations seem equally amenable to controlled experimentation using the simulation format. One apparent advantage of this type of research would seem to lie in generalizing the results directly to the real-life classroom.

References

ASCH, S. E. *Social psychology.* New York: Prentice-Hall, 1952.

BRUNER, J. S. and TAGIURI, R. The perception of people. In G. Lindzey (Ed.), *Handbook of social psychology.* Cambridge, Mass.: Addison-Wesley, 1954. Pp. 634-654.

FESTINGER, L. *A theory of cognitive dissonance.* Evanston, Ill.: Row, Peterson, 1957.

HEIDER, F. *The psychology of interpersonal relations.* New York: Wiley, 1958. 51, 358-374.

HEIDER, F. *The psychology of interpersonal relations.* New York: Wiley, 1958.

ICHHEISER, G. Misunderstandings in human relations. Part II. *American Journal of Sociology,* 1949, 55 (Part 2).

KAHN, R. L. and KATZ, D. Leadership practices in relation to productivity and morale. In D. Cartwright and A. Zander (Eds.), *Group dynamics.* Evanston, Ill.: Row, Peterson, 1953. Pp. 612-628.

LIPPITT, R., POLANSKY, B. N. and ROSEN, S.   The dynamics of power. *Human Relations*, 1952, 5, 37-64.

OSGOOD, C. E. and TANNENBAUM, P. H.   The principle of congruity in the prediction of attitude change. *Psychological Review*, 1955, 62, 42-55.

SPIEGEL, L. A.   The child's concept of beauty: A study in concept formation. *Journal of Genetic Psychology*, 1950, 77, 11-23.

STRICKLAND, L. H.   Surveillance and trust. *Journal of Personality*, 1958, 26, 200-215.

THIBAUT, J. and KELLEY, H. H.   *The social psychology of groups.* New York: Wiley, 1959.

THORNTON, G. R.   The effect of wearing glasses upon judgments of personality traits of persons seen briefly. *Journal of Applied Psychology*, 1944, 28, 203-207.

※ ※ ※ ※ ※

It is the rare mother who does not have pretty definite ideas about how children should be taught and classrooms run. Teaching is one occupation about which nearly everyone feels he is an expert. In this unusual study, Sieber and Wilder explore the ideas of mothers, teachers, principals, and even students.

The study is unusual not only because of the extensiveness of the data collected—2200 open-ended interviews lasting over an hour each—but also because of the study-design that enabled interviewers to match each mother with her child's teacher. Thus, they could study the *specific* agreements and disagreements between mother-teacher pairs. (In doing so, they found disagreement to be the rule: 69 per cent of the mothers preferred a teaching style different from the one reportedly used by the teacher of her child.) This detailed examination has been called "micro-analysis of role consensus" by Gross, Mason, and McEachern in their remarkable study of the school superintendent-school board relationship (*Explorations in Role Analysis,* Wiley, 1958). The conventional method, called "macro-analysis," involves comparing group averages between mothers and teachers. The reader should consult the book by Gross and his colleagues to get the distinction in mind and discover the advantages of "micro-analysis." Kandel and Lesser provide us with another example of it in the present book.

Teaching Styles: Parental Preferences and Professional Role Definitions*

Sam D. Sieber, David E. Wilder

All aspects of public education are matters of public interest and concern both by law and by tradition. Public participation in school-related activities, however, has often been shown to vary from one social setting to another. Generally, whether the activity is voting in school elections or membership in the PTA, participation is higher in communities or among individuals with relatively high socioeconomic status.[1] This tendency has been interpreted by some observers as reinforcement for inequalities which already exist in the schools and as a barrier to improved education in working-class settings. In recent years, civil rights leaders and poverty area workers have attempted to provoke higher participation from parents, particularly in urban slum areas; and school protests (such as the ones in New York City during 1966–1967) have been one of the outgrowths of this movement. Some schools, in turn, have gone on record as favoring decentralization of administration and direct public involvement in school matters.[2] These recommendations are directed at the improvement both of education and of school-community relations. However, it is possible that there are differences in the values and expectations of parents and educators which will lead to open conflict as parental involvement in the schools increases, and as parents and educators become more aware of their differences.[3]

One area of potential conflict between parents and educators is that of the appropriate role behavior of teachers. The role behavior of teachers can

*From *Sociology of Education*, 1967, 40 (4), 302-15. Used by permission of the authors and publisher, The American Sociological Association.

This study was made possible by a grant from the U.S.O.E. We are indebted to Professor William J. Goode for his helpful comments on the first draft of this article.

1. For a summary statement of the social characteristics of voters and non-voters in school elections, see Carter (1960). For evidence regarding differential participation in P.T.A., see especially Sexton (1961), and Herriott and St. John (1966). A doctoral dissertation by Friedman (1968) based on data from this study further elaborates and corroborates these relationships, and investigates some of the consequences of differential parental observability and participation in the schools.

2. Two notable examples are the New York City schools (see the minutes of the Board of Education, December 21, 1966), and the recommendation made to the schools of Washington, D.C. by A. Harry Passow (1967), as a result of an extensive and much publicized study.

3. The larger study of which this is part will explore several of the areas of possible conflict in a forthcoming report. Some of the normative differences between teachers and parents have been described by Jenkins and Lippitt (1951) and Foskett (1967).

be regarded as reflecting instrumental processes as distinguished from terminal goals or the eventual outputs desired from education. It seems probable that the purposes of education must be diffuse in order to accommodate the different values and expectations of the different interested groups. Indeed, the ultimate goals of education are often stated in platitudes. As a result, there are seldom public disputes between parents and teachers over the purposes of education. In contrast, instrumental processes concern the daily behavior of teachers and students. Both parents and teachers may have rather specific ideas about what this should be like, and open disputes may more readily result.[4]

The preferences and images of parents regarding instructional practices has been a subject of considerable debate in the past ten years. Spokesmen on both sides of the "great debate" concerning the most suitable kind of education for the post-Sputnik era have imputed attitudes to the community to support their own preferences. Thus, the critics of progressive education have claimed that parents are dismayed by the poverty of instruction in the basic subjects, while the defense has argued that current instructional approaches reflect the desires of local publics, and that parents are highly concerned about the school's contribution to the emotional and social development of their children.[5]

In the midst of this controversy, some educators have become worried that teachers themselves have been misled by a vocal minority of prominent critics. They fear that teachers wrongly believe that parents favor more academic pressure on pupils at the expense of other kinds of growth.[6] By examining how parents feel about various styles of teaching, we hope to furnish a partial answer to the practical question of what sorts of instruction are preferred by what types of parents. And by juxtaposing self-images of teachers against the expectations of parents, we should be able to see how parents' desires compare with teachers' own role-definitions.

Methods

Styles of teaching can be thought of in many ways—for example, authoritarian versus permissive, pupil-directed versus content-oriented, or business-

---

4. Traditionally, educators have maintained that the purposes or terminal goals of education should be determined by the citizenry, but that professional educators should be left to decide how subject matter will be taught. Citizens have not always shared this definition of the situation judging from the controversies over methods of teaching reading, for example, and the pronouncements of popular critics of American education, including Admiral Rickover and Martin Mayer. The limits of lay authority become especially relevant when parents participate in school activities; and in New York, parents have recently demanded the right to participate in the selection of professional school personnel.

5. See, for example, Scott, Hill and Burns (1959).

6. This study of parents' and teachers' opinions about the roles and goals of education was originally prompted by precisely this concern on the part of officials in one of the State Education Departments.

like versus unplanned. Several writers have developed lists of teaching styles.[7] But just what teachers actually do is still very much an open question. (See Wallen and Travers, 1963.) The main reason for the lack of research evidence on what teachers do in the classroom is the difficulty of measuring classroom behavior. But despite the absence of empirically documented styles, a number of ideal-constructs have been derived from "philosophies" of teaching, from controversies over progressive versus traditional education, and from the everyday discourse of practitioners and parents.

Two especially important aspects of the teaching role are widely discussed in the literature: (1) the extent to which subject matter is emphasized, and (2) the extent to which adult authority is exercised. By dichotomizing and combining these two dimensions, we obtain four distinct styles of teaching:

		Emphasis on subject matter	
		High	*Low*
Relations	*Adult* *centered* (authori- tarian)	Content- oriented	Control- oriented
between *teacher* *and* *child*	*Child-* *centered* (permis- sive)	Discovery- oriented	Sympathy- oriented

The four styles singled out for study are not exhaustive of the popular conceptions of teaching and are not wholly accurate reflections of behavior patterns, but they do represent some of the most common images that are held of teaching at the elementary and secondary levels.

The four styles of teaching were presented to first, fifth, and tenth grade *teachers*, to the *mothers* of many of these teachers' pupils, to the *pupils* of selected tenth grade English teachers, and to the *principals* of the schools where the teachers were located. (The sample design is discussed below.) The questions that were posed were the following:

> *Mothers and Students*—Although teachers have to concern themselves with many different things in their jobs, some teachers emphasize certain things more than others. Suppose there were four first (fifth, or tenth) grade teachers in (school) and you could choose the one you wanted to be (M: child's teacher; S: your 10th grade English teacher). Which of these would be your first choice?

7.   The most extensive list of dimensions for classifying teacher behavior has been developed by Ryans (1960). More sociologically oriented conceptualizations can be found in Brim (1958); Charters (1963, pp. 715-813); and Bidwell (1965). Bidwell's recent restatement of Waller (1932) in terms of two conflicts faced by teachers, the use or non-use of affect in controlling students, and whether to emphasize nurturance or student achievement, produces four types very similar to those we have used.

Which of these best describes (M: child's teacher; S: name of English teacher)?

Teachers—Although teachers have to concern themselves with many different things in their jobs, some teachers emphasize certain things more than others. We would like to know which one of the following four types of teachers you think best describes you.

Which of these four types of teachers do you think most of the mothers of the students in your class prefer?

How about your principal? Which type do you think he (she) prefers?

Principals—(Same basic question as above, but:) Which of these four types of teachers do you prefer having as a teacher in (school)?

The four teaching styles were described as follows:

(Control-oriented)   Teacher #1 is most concerned with maintaining discipline, seeing that students work hard, and teaching them to follow directions.

(Content-oriented)   Teacher #2 feels it's most important that students know their subject matter well, and that he (she) cover the material thoroughly and test their progress regularly.

(Discovery-oriented)   Teacher #3 stresses making the class interesting and encourages students to be creative and to figure things out for themselves.

(Sympathy-oriented)   Teacher #4 thinks it's most important that a teacher be friendly and well liked by students and able to understand and to handle their problems.

School attendance areas were selected in order to maximize the homogeneity of certain social and ecological characteristics. (See Table 1 for profiles of the communities and numbers of respondents.) A city school system provided four elementary attendance areas. Three of these were predominantly working-class areas: one was mostly white, one was mostly Negro, and one was mixed. The fourth elementary attendance area in the city was mainly composed of white middle-class residents. In the same city a high school which received the students from the schools already mentioned was also selected. Outside of the city, four suburbs, two small towns, and one rural community were chosen. The suburbs were selected according to both SES of the residents (middle versus working class) and rate of growth (stable versus growing). The two small towns were selected according to SES and commuting rate.

All the mothers of pupils in the classrooms of two teachers in each school building at each of three grade levels (first, fifth, and tenth) were in the sample. Wherever possible, the two teachers in each grade represented a slow and a fast track, on a non-college and a college track. The tenth grade teachers were teachers pf English. All teachers in the elementary schools

Table 1

PROFILES OF ATTENDANCE AREAS AND NUMBERS OF RESPONDENTS*

	MEDIAN FAMILY INCOME	% IN WHITE-COLLAR OCCUPATIONS	MEDIAN YRS. OF SCHOOL COMPLETED	% NEGRO	% INCREASE IN SCHOOL POP. (1960-1963)	NUMBER OF INTERVIEWS			
						MOTH-ERS	TEACH-ERS	STU-DENTS	PRIN-CIPALS
City neighborhoods									
White middle-class (el.)	$10,000	55%	12	<5%		92	13	0	1
White working-class (el.) ...	$6,000	40%	8	<5%		92	18	0	1
Mixed Negro and white (el.).	$4,500	20%	8	40%		84	9	0	1
Negro (el.)	$4,500	15%	8	90%		66	16	0	1
Cross-section (high school) ...						138	29	157	1
Suburbs									
Stable middle-class	$15,000	75%	13	<1%	5%	131	22	59	2
Growing middle-class	$10,000	70%	13	<1%	15%	128	31	48	2
Stable working-class	$6,000	30%	9	<1%	1%	111	25	49	3
Growing working-class	$7,000	35%	11	<1%	41%	142	48	45	2
Small towns									
Middle-class (pop. 4,000)	$6,300	50%	12			154	23	45	2
Working-class (pop. 6,000) ..	$6,200	40%	10			125	30	56	2
Rural community (pop. 2,500)**						127	19	49	2

* All census figures are approximate in order to preserve community anonymity. The 1960 U.S. Census was used.
** Census data not provided.

were also interviewed; all English teachers were interviewed in each high school. All principals and all tenth grade English students were also respondents.[8]

Results

Before looking at the correlates of preferred teaching styles, it needs to be emphasized that the expectations that mothers hold are by no means of minor importance to them. For if mothers do not believe that teachers are meeting their role expectations, they tend to be dissatified with the teacher.

As noted above, the mothers were asked to select the style that they preferred and also the style that "best describes" the teacher. By matching the mothers' *preferences* with their *perceptions* of teachers, we are able to designate mothers who desire a teaching style that is at odds with what they believe the teacher is actually doing in the classroom. As a measure of satisfaction with the teacher's performance, we have employed the following question:

> Are there any things that you think it is important for (teacher) to be doing differently than he (she) is in order to help (child) get the most out of school?

Table 2 shows that mothers who perceive the teachers as deviating from their expectations much more often desire some modification in the teacher's behavior. Only 15 per cent of those who perceive *conformity* desire other behavior, contrasted with 40 per cent of those who perceive *deviance*. These figures at once lend credibility to the responses of mothers about preferred teaching styles, and demonstrate the practical value of studying parental preferences.

Perceived deviance with respect to two of the four styles is especially highly related to dissatisfaction. These styles are the two *intellectual* ones: content-orientation and discovery orientation. Almost half of the mothers who see the teacher as failing to conform to these desired styles would welcome a change in the teacher's behavior. As we shall see in a moment, these are also the two patterns of teaching that are most commonly preferred at all three grade levels.

Preferred Teaching Styles at Different Grade Levels

It is generally assumed that elementary and secondary teachers are expected to perform their teaching roles quite differently. As the pupil passes from

8. For a detailed discussion of the sample design, including problems in its development, see Wilder and Friedman (1965). Response rates for the various groups were as follows: mothers, 83%; teachers, 99%; principals, 100%; and students, 97%. Interviews with mothers were conducted in the homes by Roper Associates. The interviews lasted 90 minutes on the average. Teachers and students were interviewed in the schools, and interviews averaged 60 minutes.

Table 2

MOTHERS' DISSATISFACTION WITH TEACHERS, ACCORDING TO MOTHERS'
PERCEPTION OF TEACHERS' CONFORMITY TO PREFERRED
STYLES OF TEACHING

				DISSATISFACTION			
		TEACHING STYLES		(% MOTHERS WHO SAY THAT TEACHER SHOULD BE DOING SOMETHING DIFFERENTLY)			
		PREFERRED	PERCEIVED				
Perceived Conformity		Control	Control	16%	(140)*	15%	(680)
		Content	Content	16%	(251)		
		Discovery	Discovery	14%	(228)		
		Sympathy	Sympathy	13%	(61)		
Perceived Deviance		Control	(Not control)	27%	(134)	40%	(614)
		Content	(Not content)	44%	(227)		
		Discovery	(Not discovery)	48%	(181)		
		Sympathy	(Not sympathy)	33%	(72)		

* Numbers in parentheses are the N on which the percentage is based.

lower to higher grade levels, he is expected to become more intellectually serious, and especially so if he wishes to enter college. One would therefore predict that parents with children in the higher grades would place greater emphasis on teaching of *content*. Also, one would expect parents of younger children to desire greater support or sympathy from teachers.

Despite these common impressions, our data show only a slight trend in the direction of parents' placing greatest emphasis on *content*-orientation from lower to higher grade levels, and practically no difference with respect to preferences for the *sympathy*-oriented teacher. As shown in Table 3, 33 per cent of the mothers of first graders would choose a teacher who was content-oriented, compared with 38 per cent of the mothers of fifth graders, and 43 per cent of the mothers of tenth graders. There is a clear trend, but it is much less pronounced than common sense would predict. The sympathy-oriented style was favored by only 11 per cent of first grade mothers, 11 per cent of fifth grade mothers, and eight per cent of tenth grade mothers.

The greatest difference occurs with respect to preferences for the *control*-oriented teacher: 26 per cent of the first grade mothers, 22 per cent of the fifth grade mothers, and 13 per cent of the tenth grade mothers desire this teaching style. Thus, the younger the child, the more likely are their mothers to want a non-intellectual authoritarian style. This would appear to be in direct conflict with the professional educational ideology that stresses the importance of a permissive classroom climate in the early grades.

To sum up thus far, mothers of older children more often desire the two styles of teaching that emphasize *subject matter*, content-orientation and discovery-orientation. But the over-all difference between first and tenth grade mothers is not very pronounced, suggesting that variations in the expectations of parents with children in different grade levels has been overestimated by professional educators.

Table 3

TEACHING STYLES PREFERRED BY MOTHERS WITH CHILDREN IN
DIFFERENT GRADE LEVELS

	% MOTHERS		
	GRADE LEVEL OF CHILD		
TEACHING STYLES	1ST	5TH	10TH
Control	26%	22%	13%
Content	33	38	43
Discovery	30	29	36
Sympathy	11	11	8
	100%	100%	100%
N mothers	(453)	(494)	(424)

Perhaps of greater significance is the observation that *within each grade level,* the mothers prefer the *content*-oriented teacher first and the *discovery*-oriented teacher second in order of frequency. Only a small percentage of the mothers opted for the *sympathy*-oriented teacher. In short, it is not true that mothers are only secondarily concerned with the intellectual maturation of their children. Even in the elementary grades, only about a tenth of the mothers prefer a teacher who is primarily oriented to playing a nurturance role with pupils (i.e., the sympathy-oriented teacher.) The critics of educational practices who claim that parents are mainly concerned about the intellective aspects of education are by and large correct in their assessment, and especially with reference to the higher grade levels.

Preferred Teaching Styles and Social Position

The sample design permits us to examine the expectations of teachers that prevail in different social contexts. In the following discussion we shall use the features of the community to define the characteristics of respondents. In other words, instead of classifying the mothers according to their own socio-economic position and race, we shall classify them according to the socio-economic and racial composition of their community. Further analysis will draw upon both sources of classification simultaneously, but for the purposes of this paper it is sufficient to note variations according to community characteristics alone.[9]

9. For stylistic convenience we shall occasionally refer to mothers residing in the various types of social context as "middle-class" or "working-class" mothers; but it should not be overlooked that we are really speaking of mothers who reside in certain types of communities. As previously mentioned, the communities were selected partly on the basis of internal homogeneity of socio-economic characteristics, and therefore this characterization of mothers is accurate in the vast majority of cases.

Table 4

TEACHING STYLES PREFERRED BY MOTHERS WITH CHILDREN IN
DIFFERENT GRADE LEVELS, ACCORDING TO SES OF COMMUNITY

	1ST AND 5TH GRADES		10TH GRADES*	
	COMMUNITY SES		COMMUNITY SES	
	WORKING	MIDDLE	WORKING	MIDDLE
TEACHING STYLES	CLASS	CLASS	CLASS	CLASS
Control	30%	17%	12%	8%
Content	32	39	55	40
Discovery	23	38	25	47
Sympathy	15	6	8	5
	100%	100%	100%	100%
N mothers	(495)	(372)	(114)	(129)

* Excludes the city high school because it contains a mixture of social class backgrounds.

The variation in preferences of mothers by the social class composition of the communities is at least as great as the variation by grade level; and with respect to certain styles of teaching it is much greater. The most consistent difference between working-class and middle-class communities, controlling for grade level of child, relates to the preference of the middle-class for the *discovery*-oriented style. As shown in Table 4, mothers in the middle-class communities much more often prefer this style of teaching. Thus, 23 per cent of the working-class residents compared with 38 per cent of the middle-class residents with grade school children prefer the discovery-oriented teacher; and the respective figures for mothers of tenth graders are 25 per cent and 47 per cent.

Evidently, the middle-class emphasis on training for independent effort reasserts itself in the preferences of mothers regarding their children's formal education.[10] One important implication of this finding is that teachers who actually use the "discovery method" will be more successful with middle-class than with working-class children, because of the cultural support for independent effort that middle-class students receive in the home. This is a possibility that has so far been overlooked in the psychological literature on the subject (for example, see Bruner, 1963).

Mothers located in working-class communities prefer the *control*-oriented and the *sympathy*-oriented styles of instruction more often than do mothers in middle-class communities. (This is mainly the case among grade school mothers.) As mentioned earlier, these two images refer to non-intellectual mechanisms of socialization. Indeed, the two styles refer to socialization sanctions employed by mothers themselves, namely, disciplining and giving affective support. It appears then that working-class mothers, and especially

10. For a review of research on "independence training" according to social class of parents, see Bronfenbrenner (1958).

those with grade school children, are more likely to desire a teacher who is a prototypical parent-surrogate. This tendency to expect teachers to perform in ways that are similar to informal socialization of the young might stem from the working-class tendency to view the world in more simplistic and personal terms (see Lipset, 1959). Isolation from the internal workings of formal organizations and from professional role-playing might limit their understanding of the extent to which teachers are prepared to play a specialized role in dealing with children.

Of the two images more often preferred by working-class mothers of grade school children, it is a preference for the 'control-oriented teacher which more clearly differentiates the two social classes. Seventeen per cent of the middle-class mothers of grade school children prefer this teaching style compared with 30 per cent of the working-class mothers. At the tenth grade level, however, it is the *content*-oriented style that most clearly distinguishes the working class from the middle class (55 per cent vs. 40 per cent, respectively). These apparent differences between grade levels mask an important underlying similarity. It will be recalled that control- and content-orientation are the two styles which we have designated as *authoritarian*. The proportion of working-class, tenth grade mothers choosing *both* of these styles remains high in comparison with first and fifth grade mothers. Thus, there is simply a shift from one authoritarian stance (control-orientation) to another (content-orientation), although this shift of emphasis crosses the boundary from the non-intellectual, parent-surrogate styles to the intellectual realm of teaching. Stated in relation to the preferences of middle-class mothers, the difference between the two social classes shifts from the question of *whether* subject matter should be emphasized to the question of the appropriate *manner* of emphasis. To sum up, when the working-class mothers choose an intellectual style at the tenth-grade level, they choose "authoritarian intellectualism" (content) rather than "permissive intellectualism" (discovery).

These results are in accord with research that reports a tendency among working-class members to value authoritarian social relationships (Christie, 1954), and particularly the child-rearing studies that show greater emphasis on parental dominance among working-class mothers (Bronfenbrenner, 1958).

The social class differences we have observed are not confounded by the different racial compositions of working- and middle-class schools. Table 5 makes this quite clear. In this table we show the styles of teaching preferred by mothers of grade school children who are located in the one city in our sample. (As mentioned earlier, the three working-class grade schools in the city were selected according to their racial composition.) Table 5 shows that the mothers' desires do not differ systematically according to the proportion of Negroes in the school. But what is more significant, all of the major differences previously noted between middle-class and working-class mothers of grade school children *persist* regardless of racial composition. Working-class mothers more often prefer the control-oriented and the sympathy-oriented

Table 5

TEACHING STYLES PREFERRED BY MOTHERS OF GRADE SCHOOL
CHILDREN IN THE CITY, ACCORDING TO RACIAL COMPOSITION AND
SES OF SCHOOL ATTENDANCE AREA

	WORKING CLASS			MIDDLE CLASS
TEACHING STYLE	WHITE	MIXED	NEGRO	(MOSTLY WHITE)
Control	40%	41%	35%	21%
Content	33	25	26	40
Discovery	17	13	22	30
Sympathy	10	21	17	9
	100%	100%	100%	100%
N mothers	(81)	(92)	(65)	(91)

teachers, while middle-class mothers more often prefer the content-oriented and the discovery-oriented teachers.[11]

But we have not yet looked at the teachers themselves. In order to determine the amount of consensus between teachers and mothers on styles of classroom teaching, we need to compare the expectations of mothers with the role-definitions of teachers. This question is especially important if we wish to see whether teachers are more likely to conform to the expectations prevailing in the world of professional education than they are to the expectations flowing from outside the system.

Consensus on Styles of Teaching between Teachers and Parents

We saw earlier that mothers who believe that teachers are *not* teaching the way they would like them to teach are much more often dissatisfied with teachers. Apparently there is much room for dissatisfaction, for when we compare the teaching styles preferred by parents with the teacher's definitions of their role, we find considerable discrepancy. For example, as we see in Table 6, only 30 per cent of the grade school mothers desire the *discovery*-oriented style, but 56 per cent of the teachers claim that this is the style that best describes them. And even a larger gap occurs between tenth grade mothers and teachers.

Teachers also diverge widely from parents' expectations in the category of *content*-oriented teaching. Thus, 43 per cent of the tenth grade mothers prefer this style, but only 16 per cent of the teachers describe themselves in

11. It is clear from comparing Tables 4 and 5 that working-class mothers of grade school children in the city prefer the control-oriented style of teaching over the content-oriented style, while the opposite is true for elementary school mothers in working-class settings which are not in the city.

Table 9

PREFERENCES OF TENTH GRADE MOTHERS, STUDENTS, AND
PRINCIPALS FOR VARIOUS STYLES OF TEACHING, AND TENTH GRADE
TEACHERS' OWN ROLE-DEFINITIONS

TEACHING STYLES PREFERRED	MOTHERS	STUDENTS	TEACHERS[*]	PRINCIPALS
Control	13%	7%	10%	. .
Content	43	22	16	14%
Discovery	36	57	72	86
Sympathy	8	14	2	. .
	100%	100%	100%	100%
N[**]	(424)	(418)	(104)	(7)

* Percentages refer to own role-definitions.
** This table contains only 10th grade teachers, mothers of 10th grade students, and principals of high schools, so that results can be compared with the students.

prefer a content-oriented style more often than any other, while a majority of teachers see themselves as discovery-oriented. In addition, over two-thirds of the mothers expressed role preferences that were not in accord with the self-descriptions of their child's teacher. A higher proportion of the mothers of 10th graders than mothers of first and fifth graders were found to prefer the two subject matter oriented styles, but somewhat larger differences were found between mothers in communities with different socio-economic composition. Working-class mothers had a higher preference for the two authoritarian styles of teaching, while middle-class mothers tended to share the preference for a discovery-oriented style with teachers. The latter finding was interpreted as suggesting compatibility between the independence training stressed by middle-class parents and the teaching styles advocated by teachers. It is not clear whether the preference of teachers for the discovery-oriented style is a reflection of professional socialization or a functional requirement of the teaching role in American schools. The high consensus on teaching styles among teachers, however, and especially the even higher consensus among principals suggest a pervasive educational ideology.

Evidence that instrumental goals of education are potential sources of conflict was shown by the higher dissatisfaction among mothers whose perceived and preferred teaching styles were dissimilar. This demonstrates the importance of studying what teachers do, and are thought to do, in the classroom, as distinct from the more diffuse purposes of education.

In view of the current agitation for increased parental participation in the schools in working-class areas, the especially high preference for the control-oriented teaching style among the mothers of the elementary school children in such areas might be a potential source of parent-teacher conflict. If increased participation results in increased awareness among mothers of

Table 8

PREFERENCES OF MOTHERS AND PRINCIPALS FOR VARIOUS STYLES OF
TEACHING, AND TEACHERS' OWN ROLE-DEFINITIONS

TEACHING STYLES PREFERRED	MOTHERS	TEACHERS*	PRINCIPALS
Control	22%	16%	5%
Content	38	17	5
Discovery	30	62	90
Sympathy	10	5	..
	100%	100%	100%
N	(1334)	(271)	(20)

* Percentages refer to own role-definition.

family and school is the large minority of mothers (23 per cent of the entire sample) who expect the teacher to be *content*-oriented but whose teachers describe themselves as *discovery*-oriented.

The discrepancy between parental and professional role expectations becomes even larger when we compare mothers with *principals*. Table 8 shows that teachers occupy a position midway between parents and principals with respect to the proportion espousing the discovery-oriented style. This style, which we earlier characterized as "permissive intellectualism," is preferred by 30 per cent of the mothers, 62 per cent of the teachers, and 90 per cent of the principals. In short, the degree of integration into the educational sub-system determines the extent to which the value of "permissive intellectualism" is held.

The differences observed might not be only due to background differences among the three status-groups. The importance of *degree of involvement in the educational structure* is suggested when we examine the role-expectations of *students,* who occupy the overlapping status of "client within the organization." Thus, students stand with one foot in the community and the other in the organization. And as shown in Table 9, the teaching styles favored by students reflect their degree of involvement in the educational system.

Whether the emphasis on *discovery* and deemphasis on *content* of professional educators reflects a functional requirement of our educational system or merely an educational fad cannot be determined here. But whatever the source, "permissive intellectualism" is clearly a part of the value system of education, as shown by our data, and is differentially espoused according to the degree of involvement in the educational structure.

Conclusions

By comparing the preferences of mothers among four typical teaching styles with the self-images of their children's teachers, it was found that mothers

Table 6

TEACHING STYLES PREFERRED BY MOTHERS COMPARED WITH
TEACHERS' OWN ROLE-DEFINITIONS (BY GRADE)

| | 1ST AND 5TH GRADES | | 10TH GRADE | |
| | % MOTHERS WHO PREFER | % TEACHERS WHO DESCRIBE | % MOTHERS WHO PREFER | % TEACHERS WHO DESCRIBE |
TEACHING STYLE	TYPE	SELVES	TYPE	SELVES
Control	24%	20%	13%	10%
Content	35	18	43	16
Discovery	30	56	36	72
Sympathy	11	6	8	2
	100%	100%	100%	100%
N	(947)	(175)	(424)	(104)

this fashion. In short, mothers most often prefer the content-oriented style, while teachers tend to espouse the discovery-oriented style. This contrast confirms the critics of public education who claim that parents want more attention devoted to the basic content of school subjects while school personnel favor a more permissive intellectual approach stressing "independent discovery."

Regardless of the merits of these two instructional patterns, it is obvious that many parents and teachers have quite different educational philosophies. Specifically, *69 per cent of the mothers in our study have a teacher for their child whose role-definition is not in accord with their preferences.* The proportions of mothers with various role-preferences whose teachers describe themselves in various ways are shown in Table 7.

Mothers whose expectations are most often violated (at least with respect to the teacher's definition of her role) are those who favor a *sympathy-*oriented style. Only five per cent of these mothers have teachers who describe themselves as sympathy-oriented. But only a small proportion of mothers prefer this style. More serious in terms of possible strain between

Table 7

TEACHERS' ROLE-DEFINITIONS ACCORDING TO THE EXPECTATIONS OF
THEIR PUPILS' MOTHERS

| | | STYLES PREFERRED BY MOTHERS | | | |
		CONTROL	CONTENT	DISCOVERY	SYMPATHY
TEACHERS'	Control	27%	24%	17%	21%
SELF-	Content	16	13	12	17
DESCRIPTIONS	Discovery	55	59	67	57
	Sympathy	2	4	4	5
		100%	100%	100%	100%
N mothers		(278)	(510)	(401)	(136)

their differences with teachers, then the likelihood of conflict should also increase unless (a) the schools are able to legitimize teacher behavior which is not in accord with parental expectations, for example, by persuading parents in working-class areas of the virtues of discovery-oriented teaching, or (b) teachers change their role definitions in accord with the expectations held by the constituency of parents.

References

BIDWELL, C. E.   The school as a formal organization. In J. G. March (Ed.), *Handbook of organizations*. Chicago: Rand McNally, 1965. Pp. 972-1022.

BRIM, O.   *Sociology and the field of education*. Philadelphia: Russell Sage, 1958.

BRUNER, J. S.   The act of discovery. *Harvard Educational Review*, 1963, 33, 124-135.

BRONFENBRENNER, U.   Socialization and social class through time and space. In E. E. Maccoby, T. M. Newcomb and E. L. Hartley (Eds.), *Readings in social psychology*, 3rd edition. New York: Henry Holt, 1958. Pp. 400-425.

CARTER, R. F.   *Voters and their schools*. Stanford: Stanford University Press, 1960.

CHARTERS, W. W. JR.   The social background of teaching. In N. L. Gage (Ed.), *Handbook of research on teaching*. Chicago: Rand McNally, 1963. Pp. 715-813.

CHRISTIE, R.   Authoritarianism re-examined. In R. Christie and M. Jahoda. *Studies in the scope and method of "The authoritarian personality."* Glencoe: The Free Press, 1954. Pp. 123-196.

FOSKETT, J. M.   *The normative world of the elementary school principal*. Eugene, Ore.: Center for the Advanced Study of Educational Administration, University of Oregon, 1967.

FRIEDMAN, N. S.   Observability in school systems: a problem of inter-system integration. Unpublished Ph.D. dissertation, Columbia University, 1968. Cooperative Research Project #6-8967.

HERRIOTT, R. E. and ST. JOHN, N. H.   *Social class and the urban school*. New York: Wiley, 1966.

JENKINS, D., and LIPPITT, R.   Interpersonal perception of teachers, students and parents. Washington: National Education Association, 1951.

LIPSET, S.M.   Democracy and working-class authoritarianism. *American Sociological Review*, 1959, 24, 482-501.

PASSOW, A. H.   *Toward creating a model urban school system: A study of the Washington, D.C. schools*. New York: Teachers College, Columbia University, 1967.

RYANS, D. G.   *Characteristics of teachers*. Washington, D.C.: American Council on Education, 1960.

SCOTT, W. C., HILL, C. M. and BURNS, H. W.   *The great debate—our schools in crisis*. Englewood Cliffs, N.J.: Prentice Hall, 1959.

SEXTON, P. C.   *Education and income*. New York: Viking Press, 1961.

WALLEN, N. E. and TRAVERS, R. M. W.   Analysis and investigation of teaching methods. In N. L. Gage (Ed.), *Handbook of research on teaching*. Chicago: Rand McNally, 1963. Pp. 448-505.

WALLER, W.   *The sociology of teaching*. New York: Wiley, 1932.

WILDER, D.E. and FRIEDMAN, N.S.   Projection Memorandum #1—Selecting ideal-typical communities and gaining access to their schools for social research purposes. New York: Bureau of Applied Social Research, Columbia University, 1965.

※ ※ ※ ※ ※

Role is one of the oldest and most useful terms in social psychology. The fundamental insight the word captures is that the beliefs people around you have about how you should act are powerful forces affecting your behavior. These beliefs, or expectations, are organized around societal *positions* that you and others may occupy—positions like policeman, basketball referee, father, and teacher. Theories have arisen around role conflict and its resolution, role consensus, role learning, role enactment, and so on.

Biddle and associates take the occasion of their large-scale study of the teacher's role to examine a special but important problem of role analysis: the case in which people think others hold expectations that in fact they do not. "Shared inaccuracies" are especially intriguing because they usually must be spotted by an outside observer, like a social scientist. By definition the participants themselves are unaware of them.

Two decades ago in a classic paper, T. M. Newcomb described the universality of misperceptions even in the intimacy of the family, and saw the roots of the problem in the communication barriers people erect between themselves. ("Autistic Hostility and Social Reality," *Human Relations*, 1947, 1, 69-86.) The invention of techniques for reducing communication barriers has been one of the most valuable contributions of social psychology to human affairs. Several articles in this book deal directly with the matter (for example, those by Schmuck on in-service education, Miles, and Winter, Griffith, and Kolb).

Shared Inaccuracies in the Role of the Teacher*

Bruce J. Biddle, Howard A. Rosencranz,
Edward Tomich, J. Paschal Twyman

It is often assumed in social theories that social stability depends on the accuracy with which roles are perceived. Thus, persons are presumed both to be aware of, and to share, standards for behaviors that are appropriate for persons who are members of social positions. Should people disagree, by chance, about what behaviors are appropriate, they must at least be aware of the others' thinking in order to plan intelligent activity with those others.

In contrast with this broad assumption, a small group of commentators has stressed the usefulness of deception (Bettelheim, 1943; Goffman, 1959), ignorance (Moore and Tumin, 1949), and partial information (von Neumann and Morgenstern, 1947). In the view presented by these latter authors, social relations may often be designed around or benefit from inaccuracies of role perception. At the very least, inaccurate and non-shared perceptions are not only indigenous to some forms of social relationships, they are often necessary or desirable.

Despite these latter assertions, clear empirical studies of situations involving shared distortions of role are difficult to find in the literature. Perhaps the first such study was that of Schanck (1932) who discovered in an isolated community evidence for agreed-upon norms which were attributed widely to members of the community but which were not matched by the privately held norms of individuals nor by their actual (secret) behaviors. A different example was provided by Wheeler (1961). In this study, the author demonstrated that inmates and prison officials both inaccurately judged norms held by the other group for themselves—both tending to exaggerate normative disparities.

In the Schanck and Wheeler studies it is assumed that shared inaccuracies on role concepts attributed are a social phenomenon, that they are the results of processes acting jointly on a number of individuals, and that they are stable despite the problems they imply for persons involved. Thus,

* From B. J. Biddle and E. J. Thomas (Eds.). *Role theory: Concepts and research.* New York: Wiley, 1966. Pp. 302-310.

Used by permission of the authors and publisher. The research reported herein was performed pursuant to contracts with the Cooperative Research Program, Office of Education, Department of Health, Education, and Welfare and the Office of Naval Research (Group Psychology Branch) at the Universities of Kansas City and Missouri.

these examples are distinct from studies of "social perception" in which the misperception of social events is treated as an individual phenomenon (see Gage and Cronbach, 1955; and Cronbach, 1958).

The purpose of this paper is to examine and interpret evidence for the existence of shared inaccuracies in the role of the public school teacher. It will be shown that teachers and those with whom they interact have distorted ideas of one another's norms and that those distortions imply problems for all concerned.

Shared Inaccuracies in Role

In order to discuss the problem of shared inaccuracies in role attribution, it is necessary that we adopt certain verbal conventions. *Shared inaccuracy of role attributions will be said to exist whenever two or more subject persons share mistaken concepts about covert processes characterizing an object person or position.* Several implications of this definition are worth noting. First, while people may often be mistaken about the overt performance of others—particularly when they don't have a chance to observe the performances in question—we focus on the mistaken concepts people have of covert processes taking place in others (mistaken concepts of others' norms, values, or concepts, etc.).

Second, there are usually two or more classes of object persons referenced in role attributions. It is easiest to demonstrate this property with an example: "Americans hold mistaken concepts about the norms held by Russians for women." Such a statement has the logical form of a statement about a norm; thus it exhibits three classes of persons. The *subjects* are those persons who share the attributed concepts in question (Americans). The *objects* are those persons to whom are attributed covert processes (Russians). Finally, the *secondary objects* are those persons for whom covert processes attributed to object persons are presumably held (women). Subjects must of course be real persons, while objects and secondary objects are but referenced and may be either real or fictitious. However, in order to judge the accuracy of an attributed concept it is necessary to find a real group of object persons who match the object designation appearing in the attribution.

This brings up the problem of operationalizing a shared inaccuracy. In order to judge accuracy of role attributions it is necessary to obtain an overt expression from both subject and object persons. The accuracy of an attributed norm, for instance, may only be judged when we have an expression of both the norm attributed by the subject and the norm actually held by the object person.

Finally, it should be clear that norms held by subjects, norms attributed by subjects to object persons, norms held by objects, and actual performances by secondary object persons are all independently defined and independently measurable. Whether these phenomena are related—and how—

depends on the nature of the relationships among subject, object, and secondary object persons. For instance, groups of persons who are separated
from one another by physical or social distance may often hold quite distorted views of one another without engendering immediate problems.
However, when subject and object persons are called upon to interact with
each other, distortions of one anothers' views are likely to pose problems for
both parties and to be maintained only through systemic activity. In the
study described here, public school teachers constitute the secondary object
position, and norms are attributed and reported by persons representing
various positions that interact with teachers.

Shared Inaccuracies in Teacher Role Attribution

The data to be reported here were gathered as part of a two-and-one-half
hour group interview study consisting of five different instruments that were
administered to 927 respondents from the Kansas City metropolitan area.[1]
Respondents represented a number of social positions defined in relationship
with the public school systems and were sampled through schools. In this
paper, we report data from four subject groups: 98 teachers, 261 parents,
237 pupils, and 67 school officials.

Among other tasks, respondents were asked to give their own norms and
then to attribute norms to three object positions: People in General, Teachers, and School Officials. Each respondent was given a set of ten situations in
which a teacher (secondary object) performance was placed. For instance,
Item 1 read, "Watching pupils during a study period." Five alternate degrees
of teacher performance were then specified ranging from: (1) Teachers
should do little or no "watching pupils" (or other behavior specified), to (5)
Teachers should do a great deal of "watching pupils." Respondents were
asked to choose one of the five scaled behavioral alternatives to indicate
their own norms, the norms of People in General, and so on. In all, four
normative responses were collected for each behavioral item from each
respondent—one that was their own and three that were attributed to others.
Finally, teacher respondents (only) were asked to give an additional
response in which they reported their *own* performance for the item.

In order to cover a broad spectrum of teacher performance, three different forms were used. Thus, a total of thirty performance items was covered
in all, while any given item was seen by only a third of the total group of
respondents. Items were derived from prior studies in which respondents
had volunteered their concerns for teacher role. Items were chosen to represent regions of inter-positional conflict.

Analysis of these data was performed on a computer. For each type of
comparison (for instance, norms attributed by parents to School Officials

1. Additional reports of this study may be found in Biddle (1961, 1964); Biddle,
Rosencranz, and Rankin (1961); Biddle, Twyman, and Rankin (1962); Rosencranz and
Biddle (1964); and Twyman and Biddle (1963, 1964).

versus norms revealed by school officials) the difference in central tendency was assessed by the Mann-Whitney z_u. This statistic is roughly equivalent to a t test of mean differences but is appropriate for use with rank-order data. It should be noted that all findings reported in this paper were significant at $p < .05$ or less (using the Mann-Whitney z_u), but that numerical differences reported are mean differences.

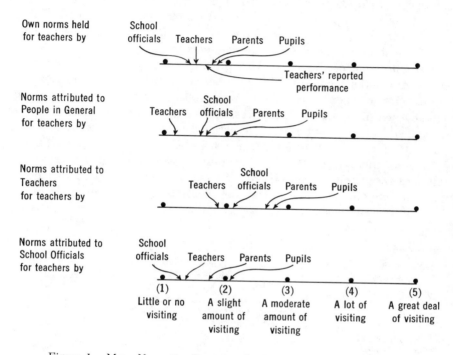

Figure 1.   Mean Normative Responses for Item 11, "Visiting with other Teachers During Study Period."

Examples of Inaccurate Attributions

It is best to begin with two items exemplifying distinct patterns of shared inaccuracy in the attribution of norms. Figure 1 displays the mean own and attributed norms given by respondents for Item 11—Visiting with Other Teachers During Study Period. Figure 2 presents similar information for Item 12—Watching for Cheaters During a Classroom Test. On the first lines of these two figures are displayed the mean responses of the four respondent positions when giving their own norms. On the second line, norms attributed to People in General are displayed; on the third, norms attributed to Teachers; on the fourth, norms attributed to School Officials. Mean teacher reported performance is indicated by an entry underneath the first line.

If we turn first to Figure 1, it will be seen that norms attributed to People in General (line 2) and School Officials (line 4) are within the same general range as the norms actually held by these groups (line 1). By way of contrast, however, norms attributed to Teachers (line 3) are displaced to the right; that is, towards the self-indulgent end of the scale. As a generalization, respondents attributed to Teachers norms for greater amounts of self-indulgence than teachers revealed in norms they held for themselves (line 1). Moreover, the performances reported by teachers (underneath line 1) matched the own norms reported by teachers rather than the norms erroneously attributed to Teachers by respondents.

The third line of Figure 1, thus, provides an example of shared, inaccurate attribution of norms. Respondents generally attributed to Teachers norms (for teachers) that were more self-indulgent than were norms actually held by teachers themselves. It should also be noted that teachers responded to the "problem" of differential standards by conforming to their own norms rather than to the norms attributed to them by others. Finally, pupil respondents were the least accurate in norms attributed to Teachers, followed by parent, school official, and teacher respondents in that order.

A somewhat more complex picture of shared inaccuracy appears in Figure 2. In this latter figure it will be seen that while respondents generally

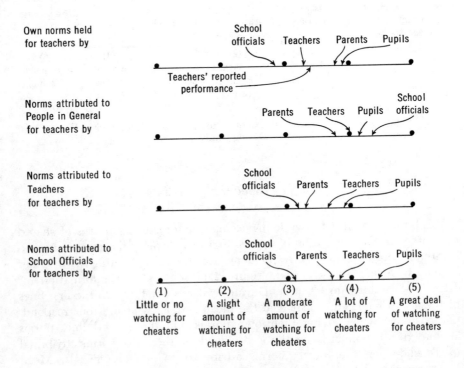

Figure 2.   Mean Normative Responses for Item 12, "Watching for Cheaters During a Classroom Test."

assigned to Teachers (line 3) norms that were similar both to their own and those actually held by teachers (line 1), the norms attributed to People in General and School Officials show a different story. Norms attributed to People in General (line 2) are displaced in a conservative direction— towards the right—by all respondents execept parents. Additionally, all respondents except school officials attributed similar, conservative norms to School Officials. If we compare these two sets of attributed norms with the own norms held by parents[2] and school officials, respectively, it is evident that both are distorted. Figure 2 thus exhibits two examples of shared inaccuracies in role attribution: respondents were generally mistaken about norms held by both People in General and School Officials; moreover, the mistakes made about these two object positions were similar. Note, however, that parents made the least error in attributing norms to People in General; and school officials, who made the greatest error in attributing to People in General, were the least inaccurate in attributing norms to School Officials.

The Extent of Shared Inaccuracies

But how significant and wide-spread were these findings of shared inac- curacies in teacher role? Tables 1 and 2 attempt to answer this question by presenting significances and mean differences for selected items that show clear patterns similar to those of items 11 and 12. (Items not included in these tables presented little evidence of shared inaccuracies in teacher role, although they were productive of other findings. Altogether, 23 per cent of all comparisons checked for shared inaccuracy were statistically significant at $p < .05$; while 38 per cent of all comparisons for shared inaccuracy reported in Tables 1 and 2 are similarly significant.)

Table 1 presents findings for items involving teacher self-indulgence. The reader will note that significant differences appear in this table between norms attributed to Teachers and those actually held by teachers (part A) and between norms attributed to Teachers and the performances reported by teachers (part B). Interestingly enough, although distorted when com- pared with teacher-held norms, norms attributed to Teachers are not gen- erally significantly different from norms actually held by subjects (part C). Again, it must be concluded that (particularly parental and pupil) respond- ents are incorrectly convinced that Teachers hold self-indulgent norms for themselves—norms that are not matched by teacher reported performances, and that are reasonably similar to norms actually held by respondents themselves.

Table 2 presents findings for items involving teacher discipline and control of pupils. The major pattern appearing in Table 2 is of shared inaccuracy

2. The equivalence of parents (a subject position) with People in General (an object position) is questionable. The parental sample was obviously not a demographic sample of the public. However, it may well have been a sample of "the public that takes action on school matters." In addition, in a pilot study we were unable to find *any* significant differences between attributions to Parents and to People in General.

Table 1

MEAN DIFFERENCES AND LEVELS OF SIGNIFICANCE FOR ITEMS INVOLVING TEACHER SELF-INDULGENCE

	NORMS ATTRIBUTED TO PEOPLE IN GENERAL BY				NORMS ATTRIBUTED TO TEACHERS BY				NORMS ATTRIBUTED TO SCHOOL OFFICIALS BY			
	TEACHERS	PARENTS	PUPILS	SCHOOL OFFICIALS	TEACHERS	PARENTS	PUPILS	SCHOOL OFFICIALS	TEACHERS	PARENTS	PUPILS	SCHOOL OFFICIALS
A. Differences between Norms Attributed to Object Persons and Norms Actually Held by Them												
Item 9. Visiting with other teachers on the playground	−.48 *					.54 **	.78 **	.71 **	−.58 *		.63 *	
Item 11. Visiting with other teachers during study period	−.50 *				.48 *	1.00 ***	1.11 ***	.94 **				
Item 21. Reading own books during study period	−.97 **		.82 *			1.15 ***	1.70 ***				1.59 **	
Item 22. Leaving the room during a classroom test						.33 *	.58 *					
Item 23. Grading papers during a classroom singing period						.84 **	1.13 **				1.02 *	
B. Differences between Norms Attributed to Object Persons and Reported Teacher Performances												
Item 9. Visiting with other teachers on the playground									−.58 *			
Item 11. Visiting with other teachers during study period			.61 *			.95 ***	1.05 ***	.89 **				

Note: All figures to be found in Tables 1 and 2 are signed mean differences that were statistically significant. Significance was computed using the Mann-Whitney z_U and is indicated as follows:

$* = .01 < p < .05$, $** = .001 < p < .01$, $*** = p < .001$.

Table 1 (Continued)

MEAN DIFFERENCES AND LEVELS OF SIGNIFICANCE FOR ITEMS INVOLVING TEACHER SELF-INDULGENCE

	NORMS ATTRIBUTED TO PEOPLE IN GENERAL BY				NORMS ATTRIBUTED TO TEACHERS BY				NORMS ATTRIBUTED TO SCHOOL OFFICIALS BY			
	TEACHERS	PARENTS	PUPILS	SCHOOL OFFICIALS	TEACHERS	PARENTS	PUPILS	SCHOOL OFFICIALS	TEACHERS	PARENTS	PUPILS	SCHOOL OFFICIALS
Item 21. Reading own books during study period			1.75*			1.31*	1.85*				1.60*	
Item 22. Leaving the room during a classroom test												
Item 23. Grading papers during a classroom singing period						.98*						
C. Differences between Norms Attributed to Object Persons and Norms Held by Subjects												
Item 9. Visiting with other teachers on the playground				−.54*								
Item 11. Visiting with other teachers during study period					.48*	.51**	.59**	.76*				
Item 21. Reading own books during study period												
Item 22. Leaving the room during a classroom test												
Item 23. Grading papers during a classroom singing period						.38*						

Note: All figures to be found in Tables 1 and 2 are signed mean differences that were statistically significant.
Significance was computed using the Mann-Whitney z_U and is indicated as follows:
* $= .01 < p < .05$, ** $= .001 < p < .01$, *** $= p < .001$.

Table 2

MEAN DIFFERENCES AND LEVELS OF SIGNIFICANCE FOR ITEMS INVOLVING DISCIPLINE AND PUPIL CONTROL

	NORMS ATTRIBUTED TO PEOPLE IN GENERAL BY				NORMS ATTRIBUTED TO TEACHERS BY				NORMS ATTRIBUTED TO SCHOOL OFFICIALS BY			
	TEACHERS	PARENTS	PUPILS	SCHOOL OFFICIALS	TEACHERS	PARENTS	PUPILS	SCHOOL OFFICIALS	TEACHERS	PARENTS	PUPILS	SCHOOL OFFICIALS
A. Differences between Norms Attributed to Object Persons and Norms Actually Held by Them												
Item 1. Watching pupils during study period				.76 ***			.90 ***			.53 *	.59 *	
Item 7. Policing the halls	−.51 *			.65 *		.60 *	1.21 ***			.89 **	.80 **	
Item 8. Disciplining pupils during basketball games in gym						.52 *				.74 *	1.05 ***	
Item 12. Watching for cheaters during a classroom test			.60 **	.65 *					1.20 **	1.11 **	1.46 ***	
Item 14. Telling misbehaving pupils in classroom to stop talking						.43 *	.86 ***			.90 **	1.15 ***	
Item 19. Supervising on the playground				.51 *			.72 **			.88 **		
Item 24. Threatening pupils misbehaving in classroom						.87 **				1.22 **	1.45 **	
B. Differences between Norms Attributed to Object Persons and Reported Teacher Performances												
Item 1. Watching pupils during study period				.85 **						.43 *	.49 *	
Item 7. Policing the halls		.67 **	.61 *	1.44 ***			.78 **		.58 *	1.04 ***	.95 ***	

Note: All figures to be found in Tables 1 and 2 are signed mean differences that were statistically significant. Significance was computed using the Mann-Whitney z_U and is indicated as follows:

* = .01 < .05 ** = .001 < .01 *** = p < .001

Table 2 (Continued)

	NORMS ATTRIBUTED TO PEOPLE IN GENERAL BY				NORMS ATTRIBUTED TO TEACHERS BY				NORMS ATTRIBUTED TO SCHOOL OFFICIALS BY			
	TEACHERS	PARENTS	PUPILS	SCHOOL OFFICIALS	TEACHERS	PARENTS	PUPILS	SCHOOL OFFICIALS	TEACHERS	PARENTS	PUPILS	SCHOOL OFFICIALS
Item 8. Disciplining pupils during basketball games in gym		** .95	** 1.08			* .61	** 1.20			** 1.05	*** 1.36	
Item 12. Watching for cheaters during a classroom test	* .65		** .77	* .83			** .63		* .61	* .53	*** .87	
Item 14. Telling misbehaving pupils in classroom to stop talking		* .54	* .63				** .72				** .71	
Item 19. Supervising on the playground	* .60	*** .83		*** 1.10						** .68	** .71	** .85
Item 24. Threatening pupils misbehaving in the classroom			* 1.25			* 1.17						
C. Differences between Norms Attributed to Object Persons and Norms Held by Subjects												
Item 1. Watching pupils during study period			* .60	* .77			* .52			** .34	*** .80	
Item 7. Policing the halls			* .55	*** 1.21			** .72		** .70		*** .89	* .58
Item 8. Disciplining pupils during basketball games in gym										* .39		
Item 12. Watching for cheaters during a classroom test				** 1.28								
Item 14. Telling misbehaving pupils in classroom to stop talking			* .37	* .93					** .75			
Item 19. Supervising on the playground						** -.62	* .45	* 1.05	** .77		* .45	
Item 24. Threatening pupils misbehaving in the classroom	** .87		* .42					* .83			*** .72	

in norms attributed to School Officials, primarily by parents and pupils. These respondents are in agreement that School Officials hold conservative norms for teacher disciplining and controlling of pupils—norms that are not in fact held by school officials. It should also be noted that school-official respondents (and to a lesser extent others) attributed similar, inaccurate, conservative norms to People in General. Finally, performances reported by teachers did not match the inaccurate, conservative norms attributed to School Officials and People in General (part B); and, interestingly, the falsely inaccurate norms attributed tended to be significantly more conservative than norms actually held by subjects themselves (part C).

Interpretation

An understanding of these findings requires that one answer several questions. How did these shared inaccuracies get set up? By what means are these inaccuracies maintained? What problems do these inaccuracies impose on teachers and those with whom they interact?

The appearance of inaccurate attributions to teachers favoring self-indulgence would appear to pose few problems of origin or effect. It may be assumed that most occupations or professions will be judged, by outsiders, to be self-indulgent; if only as a means of ego defense for those who are not members. If this interpretation is correct, we will find similar norms approving self-indulgence attributed to doctors, lawyers, coal miners, policemen, indeed anyone with a defined occupation. It should also be noted that our data show few significant differences between norms attributed to Teachers for self-indulgence and norms actually held by subjects themselves —suggesting that respondents are for the most part attributing to Teachers but a modification of their own norms. Attributed norms involving self-indulgence would pose a problem for the teacher only if associated with a general denigration of the profession. There seems to be little evidence for this here.

The problem of conservative standards for the teacher-pupil relationship is considerably more complex. One must assume that education today is faced with rapid social change paired with the legitimizing of public outcry from heel-draggers. Many persons may assume that the public continues to think of teachers in terms of the values of small-town America when they listen to the criticisms of the super-patriots and those interested in a "classical" education. Assuming this explanation, similar conservative inaccuracies should be observable for many public values (such as sexual mores), particularly when they are supported by public outcry from but a single faction (as in the case of Southern Whites speaking on desegregation of schools).

It may also be true that teachers are particularly vulnerable to conservative inaccuracies due to their ambiguous position of giving personal service in a public institution and their inability to form strong professional organizations that would set and enforce standards for their profession. This latter interpretation suggests that conservative inaccuracies would be likely to appear for nurses, social workers, government officials, and other professions having similar liabilities.

Whatever its etiology, conservative inaccuracies for the teacher are probably maintained through restriction of both communication and performance observation. It may be noted that teacher performance in the school is rarely observed by anyone other than the teacher herself and her pupils. School officials and teachers must rely upon hearsay for a description of (other) teachers' classroom performance, while parents depend upon the reporting of their own children. Many schools are also notable in the slight degree to which they discuss standards for teacher performance.

It is also probable that the conservative inaccuracy attributed to School Officials is facilitated by duplicity. It should be noted that school officials are the most mistaken of all respondents in the norms they attribute to People in General. The school official, then, is faced with the problem of "representing" a public whose standards run counter to his own. This should result in a double standard of performance; conservative values for teacher behavior supported and enforced in public—liberal standards held in private. Thus, through lack of information about actual public opinion on teacher role, the school official is not only forced into upholding standards he does not share, but he adds to his burdens by appearing as an authoritarian "fuddy-duddy" in the eyes of teachers, parents, and pupils alike.

But not only the school official suffers from conservative, mistaken, attributed norms. Parents and teachers are constrained from expressing opinions which they believe run counter to norms of school officials and (sometimes) public opinion. (Note the number of significant differences between the own norms of subjects and those attributed to others.) Teachers, also, who in fact share many norms with school officials, appear unaware of this commonality of role and are burdened with satisfying a set of standards which they don't believe in and which are not shared by school officials.

It is possible that shared inaccuracies of a conservative type are endemic to the maintenance of authority within an hierarchically ordered institution. It is also possible that contemporary leaders will generally tend to underestimate the degree to which their constituents are ready for change. One wonders, however, what would happen if school officials were apprised that public opinion was generally more liberal than they gave credit for; or a serious attempt was made by the school system to sample public opinion regarding teacher role on a regular basis. It is possible that changes might be wrought for the role of teacher, and that the professions of teacher and school administrator might become more attractive.

Forms of Shared Inaccuracy

The example of shared inaccuracy presented here differs from those of both the Schanck and Wheeler examples previously cited. In Schanck's original study shared inaccuracies were presented for the case in which subjects attributed to a position of which they were members norms for themselves (which were in error). In the Wheeler example, subjects attributed to a different object position norms for themselves (which were in error). In our example, subjects (for instance, parents) attributed to a different object position (for instance, School Officials) norms for a third position (teachers).

Certain logical properties differentiate these cases from one another. For instance, in both the Wheeler and our examples, it is possible to study the effect of social distance between subjects and objects on the prevalence of shared inaccuracy. In our data (See Tables 1 and 2, Part A), note that there is not a single significant case in which parents attributed inaccurate norms to People in General nor school officials to themselves, and there is but one case where teachers were mistaken about Teacher norms. In addition, but two cases exist where pupils were mistaken about the norms of People in General, but two in which school officials were mistaken about Teachers, and but two in which teachers misjudged School Officials. In contrast, pupils and parents were often in error about Teacher and School Official norms, while school officials were in error about the norms of People in General. Note also that the greatest number of mistakes was made by pupils. It would seem from these data that shared inaccuracies were more likely with immature subjects and with increased social distance between subject and object positions. (Wheeler reports related findings.)

Despite differences among these three studies, Schanck, Wheeler, and we have suggested that not only do shared inaccuracies pose problems for those who interact but also that stable patterns of inaccuracy may persist in some situations. In fact, where shared inaccuracies are supported through deception and the hiding of one's true norms, it would appear that shared inaccuracies are generating the very conditions that would guarantee their perpetuation. This suggests that stable social forms may sometimes be organized around the perpetuating of partial or distorted communication systems. To the best of our knowledge, no systematic discussion has yet appeared of the forms of distortion-protecting interaction.

It should be clear, for instance, that the Schanck, Wheeler and our examples do not exhaust the forms of shared inaccuracy; nor are we yet informed about the conditions creating or supporting such forms, nor the extent to which they create problems for participants. Shared inaccuracies exist, nevertheless, in many role relationships. Investigators should be sensitized to recognize shared, inaccurate role attributions and to seek out the various ways in which they affect our lives.

References

BETTELHEIM, B.   Individual and mass behavior in extreme situations. *Journal of Abnormal and Social Psychology,* 1943, 38, 417-452.

BIDDLE, B. J.   *The present status of role theory.* Columbia, Mo.: University of Missouri Press, 1961 (mimeographed).

BIDDLE, B. J.   Roles, goals and value structures in organizations. In W. W. Cooper, J. J. Leavitt, and M. Shelly (Eds.), *New perspectives in organization research.* New York: Wiley, 1964.

BIDDLE, B. J., ROSENCRANZ, H. A. and RANKIN, E. F., JR. *Studies in the role of the public school teacher* (5 volumes) Columbia, Mo.: University of Missouri Press (mimeographed), 1961.

BIDDLE, B. J., TWYMAN, J. P., and RANKIN, E. F., JR.   The role of the teacher and occupational choice. *School Review,* 1962, 70, 191-206.

CRONBACH, L. J.   Proposals leading to analytic treatment of social perception scores. In R. Tagiuri and L. Petrullo (Eds.), *Person perception and inter-personal behavior.* Stanford, Calif.: Stanford University Press, 1958.

GAGE, N. L. and CRONBACH, L. J.   Conceptual and methodological problems in interpersonal perception, *Psychological Review,* 1955, 62, 411-422.

GOFFMAN, E.   *The presentation of self in everyday life.* New York: Doubleday, 1959.

MOORE, W. E. and TUMIN, M. M.   Some social functions of ignorance, *American Sociological Review,* 1949, 14, 787-795.

ROSENCRANZ, H. A. and BIDDLE, B. J.   The role approach to teacher competence evaluation. In B. J. Biddle and W. J. Ellena (Eds.), *Contemporary research on teacher effectiveness.* New York: Holt, 1964.

SCHANCK, R. L.   A study of a community and its groups and institutions conceived of as behaviors of individuals. *Psychological Monograph,* 1932, 43, No. 2.

TWYMAN, J. P. and BIDDLE, B. J.   Role conflict for public school teachers, *Journal of Psychology,* 1963, 55, 183-198.

TWYMAN, J. P. and BIDDLE, B. J.   *The uses of role conflict.* Stillwater, Okla.: Oklahoma State University Monographs in Social Science, 1964.

VON NEUMANN, J. and MORGENSTERN, O.   *Theory of games and economic behavior* (2nd. ed.). Princeton, N.J.: Princeton University Press, 1947.

WHEELER, S.   Role conflict in correctional communities. In D. R. Cressey (Ed.), *The prison: Studies in institutional organization and change.* New York: Holt, 1961.

✳ ✳ ✳ ✳ ✳

It is a widely held belief in our society that the experienced teacher is a better teacher than the novice. He is presumed to have a certain self-assurance, to have skills in handling students and in organizing lessons, and generally to have learned things that only first-hand exposure to classrooms full of live children can teach. Teacher certification laws and the practice teaching programs of training institutions reflect this belief. School districts base their salary schedules on it. In the labor market, teachers with experience are worth more than those without.

What, precisely, does classroom experience teach? Research provides no general answer, but several recent studies, Hoy's among them, have begun to show consistency with respect to one kind of learning that may take place: teachers seem to concern themselves more with classroom management and less with instruction. Whether this learning is merely a matter of gaining a better balanced perspective on the realities of teaching cannot be determined through these studies. And what the data show may not even be "learning," at least in any sense that represents a difference in teaching behavior. The evidence rests entirely on paper-and-pencil responses.

Hoy can be faulted for not tying this study to similar investigations in the research literature, most of which used the Minnesota Teacher Attitude Inventory (MTAI) to identify the changes in responses associated with teaching experience. He and the others who worked with him in developing the measure of Pupil Control Ideology (see his footnote 3) can be criticized for not showing that their instrument measures something different from the well-known MTAI, especially considering the fact that they borrowed items from it. This is only to say, though, that they have left research for others (including students) to do.

The Influence of Experience on the Beginning Teacher*

Wayne K. Hoy

Since a primary task of the teacher is to define and evaluate student levels of accomplishment, some restraint upon individual student behavior is inevitable. In fact, the political organization of the school has been described as a despotic structure which emphasizes dominance of teachers and subordination of students (Waller, 1932).

The problem of pupil control is not new, nor is there any lack of opinion or prescription on the subject, but unfortunately there is little systematic study of pupil control in schools, and much less study which begins from the perspective of the school as a social system. Such a view calls attention to both the structural and the normative aspects of the school. Studies which have focused upon the school as a social system have described antagonistic student subcultures and attendant conflict and control problems (Coleman, 1961; Willower and Jones, 1967; Gordon, 1957; and Waller, 1932).

Control of students—"discipline"—is a major concern of all teachers, but it is especially acute for beginning teachers. Likewise, teaching experience has impact upon all teachers, but for new recruits, initial teaching experience may be a sudden confrontation with conflicting role demands of teaching, especially with regard to pupil control and learning goals of the school. Teachers' orientations toward pupil control may be studied in terms of behavior or in terms of ideology. The present inquiry focuses upon the relationship between teaching experience and the pupil control ideology of beginning teachers.

A Conceptualization of Pupil Control Ideology[1]

The importance and centrality of pupil control in the organizational life of the school should not be surprising, especially in light of the involuntary nature of student participation. In fact, selectivity in the relationship

* Reprinted from *School Review*, 1968, 76 (3), 312-323, by permission of the author and the publisher, The University of Chicago Press. Copyright 1968 by the University of Chicago.

This research was supported by a grant from the Oklahoma State University Research Foundation.

1. For a more complete discussion of pupil control ideology, and the development of an operational measure of pupil control ideology, see Willower, Eidell, and Hoy (1967).

between the organization and the client has been used to develop a useful typology of service organizations (Carlson, 1964). Public schools fall into the same category of organizations as prisons and public mental hospitals, in that clients have no choice in their participation in the organization; and conversely, the organization has no control in the selection of clients. A word of caution seems necessary when comparing schools to prisons and public mental hospitals. Most prisons and public mental hopitals are coercive organizations, while most public schools are normative organizations (Etzioni, 1961, pp. 3-66). Further, prisons and public mental hospitals are "total institutions" and schools are not (Goffman, 1961). Nevertheless, the similarity of the selectivity in the client-organization relationship should have important consequences for certain aspects of organizational life.

Relevant conceptualization is a necessary prerequisite for fruitful analysis and study of pupil control ideology. A classification of client control ideology employed by Gilbert and Levinson (1957, pp. 20-34) to study staff ideology in mental hospitals has been adapted for use in the study of pupil control ideology in public schools. Prototypes of custodial and humanistic orientations toward pupil control were developed, and a brief schematic formulation of each ideological orientation is presented below.

The model of the custodial orientation is the traditional school which provides a rigid and highly controlled setting concerned primarily with the maintenance of order. Students are stereotyped in terms of their appearance, behavior, and parents' social status. Teachers who hold a custodial orientation conceive of the school as an autocratic organization with a rigid pupil-teacher status hierarchy; the flow of power and communication is unilaterally downward. Students must accept the decision of their teachers without question. Teachers do not attempt to understand student behavior, but instead view misbehavior as a personal affront. Students are perceived as irresponsible and undisciplined persons who must be controlled through punitive sanctions. Impersonality, pessimism, and "watchful mistrust" pervade the atmosphere of the custodial school.[2]

The humanistic orientation, on the other hand, conceives of the school as an educational community in which students learn through co-operative interaction and experience. Learning and behavior are viewed in psychological and sociological terms, not moralistic terms. Self-discipline is substituted for strict teacher control. A humanistic orientation leads teachers to desire a democratic atmosphere with open channels of two-way communication between pupils and teachers and increased self-determination. In brief, a humanistic orientation is used in the sociopsychological sense suggested by Fromm (1948); it indicates an orientation which stresses the importance of the individuality of each student and the creation of an atmosphere to meet the wide range of student needs.

---

2. It is of interest to note that a genotypically similar prototype of the custodial orientation in the prison setting is given by Powelson and Bendix (1961).

The Teacher and Organizational Socialization

The particular part of the learning process which deals with the acquisition of the requisite orientations for satisfactory functioning in a role is referred to as the process of socialization (Parsons, 1951, p. 205). Socialization is an ongoing process which begins early in childhood and continues throughout life. Primary socialization, the formation of the "basic personality structure," usually is well completed by adulthood; that is, the major value-orientation patterns of an individual are not, on a large scale, subject to drastic change in later life (Parsons, 1951, pp. 208, 236-248). However, as Etzioni (1961, p. 142) indicates, "Learning of specific skills and role orientations continues with every change of status, in particular with membership in new social units, such as organizations."

Organizational socialization is concerned with the processes by which the requisite role orientation of offices, statuses, and positions is acquired by participants in the organization. Formal organizations are partial systems in that they do not affect all the basic needs of their members; however, few members can escape the formative influence of the values, expectations, incentives, and sanctions of the organization. Organizations mold role ideology and role performance of personnel through a variety of procedures and mechanisms designed to make individual beliefs, values, and norms correspond with those of the organization. The period before and/or shortly after new participants join an organization is highly significant in terms of socialization; it is a time "when efforts to induce consensus between newcomers and the rest of the organization are comparatively intense" (Etzioni, 1961, p. 142).

Public school teachers go through a double socialization process. Initial socialization to professional norms and values occurs during college preparation, where teaching and learning are likely to focus on ideal images and practices. The second phase of the socialization process begins as new teachers enter the "real" teaching world as full-time members of a school organization. Here neophytes may suddenly be confronted with a set of organizational norms and values at variance with those acquired in formal preparation; that is, the internalized ideal images of the teacher role may be in conflict with the norms and values of the school subculture.

During socialization, both before and after entrance into the profession, each teacher forms his own version of the necessary orientation for effective pupil control. It appears likely that as the new, idealistic teacher comes to his first position, he will be confronted with a conflicting set of norms and values concerning the control of students. During the initial phase of the socialization of the prospective teacher, professors of education stress the desirability of permissive pupil control, while "discipline" as it is actually practiced in the public schools emphasizes the need for more authoritarian controls (Ausubel, 1961). More experienced teachers tend to oppose permissiveness and embrace a more custodial pupil control ideology than do inexperienced teachers (Willower, Eidell and Hoy, 1967; Willower and Jones, 1967). In fact, in some schools, the ability to control is often equated with the ability to teach. Willower, Hoy and Eidell (1967) furnish a few illustrations of this kind of conflict experienced by newer teachers in one school:

> Newer teachers reported that a major problem was to convince the older, more experienced teachers that their younger colleagues were not soft on discipline. The older teachers, dominant in the informal structure of the school, seldom hesitated to communicate their views to the younger, newer teachers whom they often thought of as being lax about maintaining sufficient social distance with regard to pupils. Teachers viewed as weak on control had marginal status among their colleagues and others. Situations of high visibility such as the assembly or school library furnished special testing grounds where teachers made valiant efforts to "look good." Thus, in assemblies, some of the most striking performances emanated from the audience.

The significance of the attitudes of experienced teachers for beginning teachers, during a period when the latter are especially vulnerable to formal and informal organizational demands, is succinctly described by Waller (1932, p. 389): "The significant people for a school teacher are other teachers, and by comparison with good standing in that fraternity, the good opinion of students is a small thing and of little price. A landmark in one's assimilation to the profession is that moment when he decides that only teachers are important."

If beginning teachers are confronted with a relatively custodial pupil control ideology on the part of experienced teachers, and if these experienced teachers constitute a group of "significant others," then it seems reasonable to predict a positive relationship between teaching experience and a change toward a more custodial pupil control ideology. More specifically, two major hypotheses guided the empirical phase of this study: (1) The pupil control ideology of beginning public school teachers will be significantly more custodial after one year of teaching. (2) The pupil control ideology of prospective teachers who do *not* teach the year after graduation will *not* be significantly more custodial after one year.

Procedures

Instrument.[3]—Pupil control ideology was measured by a twenty-item instrument, the Pupil Control Ideology Form (hereafter called the PCI Form). Responses to each item were made on a five-point Likert-type scale and are scored from 5 ("strongly agree") to 1 ("strongly disagree"); the higher the over-all score on the instrument, the more custodial the ideology of the respondent.

3. See Willower, Eidell and Hoy (1967).

Examples of items used include: "A few pupils are just young hoodlums and should be treated accordingly," "It is often necessary to remind pupils that their status in schools differs from that of teachers," and "Pupils can be trusted to work together without supervision" (score reversed).

Split-half reliability coefficients, in two samples, were .95 ($N=170$) and .91 ($N=55$) with application of the Spearman-Brown formula. Validity of the measure was supported by principals' judgments of certain of their teachers. Teachers judged to be most custodial by their principals had significantly higher ($p < .01$ using t-test procedures) PCI Form scores than a like number of teachers judged to be most humanistic. Further evidence of the validity was established by a comparison of PCI Form scores of personnel from schools known by reputation to be humanistic with scores of personnel from other schools at the same grade levels.

Subjects.—Eighty-two elementary and ninety-three secondary teachers comprised the original sample of this study. These 175 subjects represented virtually the entire set of student teachers who completed their practice teaching during the 1966 spring semester at Oklahoma State University. All subjects completed the PCI Form in group meetings on campus just prior to the commencement of their practice teaching. Upon the conclusion of their eight weeks of practice teaching, again on campus and in group sessions, the subjects responded to the PCI Form for the second time. Approximately one year later, in the spring of 1967, the same 175 subjects were contacted by mail and asked to respond to the PCI Form once again. One hundred sixty-two of the 175 participants (92.6 per cent) returned usable PCI Forms and other information concerning their present status. Of these 162 respondents, all fifty-eight elementary teachers returning usable forms were female, while forty-two of the fifty-eight (73.4 per cent) secondary teachers were female; twenty-eight out of thirty-nine (71.8 per cent) respondents who had not taught during the 1966-67 year were female, and seven female respondents were graduate assistants.

Findings

The major hypotheses of this study were confirmed by t-tests for the difference between means of correlated samples. The pupil-control ideology of beginning teachers was significantly more custodial after their first year of teaching. Separate tests of this hypothesis were made and confirmed on both elementary and secondary levels, since previous research had indicated that the pupil control ideology of secondary teachers was significantly more custodial than pupil control ideology of elementary teachers (Willower, Eidell, and Hoy, 1967). In addition, as predicted, there was no significant custodial change in pupil control ideology for individuals who did not teach during the first year after graduation. The results of the t-tests are summarized in Table 1.

It is also instructive to examine the progressive changes in pupil control ideology of subjects in the present sample as they began and completed

Table 1

A COMPARISON OF THE PUPIL CONTROL IDEOLOGY OF TEACHERS
BEFORE AND AFTER STUDENT TEACHING AND AFTER THE FIRST
YEAR OF TEACHING

POSITION	N	EXPERIENCE	PCI FORM MEAN SCORE	STANDARD ERROR	t
Public school teacher	116	Before student teaching	44.56	.560	......
		After student teaching	48.93	.704	6.569*
		After first year teaching	51.48	.766	3.783*
Elementary teacher .	58	Before student teaching	42.36	.593	......
		After student teaching	45.90	.759	4.336*
		After first year teaching	48.05	.950	2.446*
Secondary teacher ..	58	Before student teaching	46.76	.862	......
		After student teaching	51.97	1.050	4.971*
		After first year teaching	54.91	1.026	2.871*
Graduate assistant ..	7	Before student teaching	43.86	1.471	......
		After student teaching	48.00	1.363	2.008
		After first year teaching	43.14	2.283	2.303
Not teaching	39	Before student teaching	44.80	.932	......
		After student teaching	47.31	1.553	2.404*
		After first year	47.05	1.278	.270

* $p < .01$.

student teaching[4] and then completed their first year of teaching. Groups
of teachers at both the elementary and secondary levels showed significantly
more custodial pupil control ideology after each successive period of teaching experience; however, the PCI mean scores for the group of thirty-nine
teachers who did *not* teach the year subsequent to graduation remained
virtually the same during that year, although a significant change in the
custodial direction had occurred during student teaching.[5] Furthermore, the

4.   Earlier research, using a larger sample of participants, indicated that a significant
change in the pupil control ideology of student teachers also occurred during student
teaching; student teachers were significantly more custodial in their pupil control ideology
after student teaching. See Hoy (1967).

5.   All elementary teachers in the present sample were female; however, there were sixteen men and forty-two women in the group of secondary teachers. A comparison of mean
PCI scores indicated that both men and women become increasingly more custodial in
their orientation after each successive period of experience. Their respective mean scores
as they began and completed student teaching and then completed their first year of
teaching were 45.0, 50.3, and 53.5 for the women and 51.3, 56.4, and 58.6 for the men.
A separate analysis of male and female respondents who did not teach the year subsequent to graduation indicated similar patterns of change regardless of sex. The before
student teaching, after student teaching, and after one year PCI means were 43.4, 45.6,
and 45.8, respectively, for twenty-eight women respondents and 48.4, 51.5, and 50.2,
respectively, for eleven men respondents.

pupil control ideology of a group of seven participants became substantially more custodial during student teaching but returned to nearly the prior level when they returned to college the following year as graduate assistants. The results of this statistical analysis are also summarized in Table 1.

Participants teaching during the 1966-67 school year were also asked to respond to several other statements concerning their preparation and teaching. In response to the statement, "Teacher education programs tend to focus on ideal images and situations rather than the 'harsh' realities of teaching," 71.14 per cent of the secondary teachers and 67.24 per cent of the elementary teachers agreed. In addition, 81.03 per cent of the secondary teachers and 84.48 per cent of the elementary teachers agreed with the statement, "In the school in which I am teaching, good teaching and good classroom control tend to be equated."[6] In brief, approximately 94 per cent (109 out of 116) of all the teachers completing their first year of teaching agreed with one of the above two statements. It is also of interest to note that none of the 116 teachers planned to leave the profession permanently, although thirteen planned a temporary departure. Most teachers claimed they were relatively satisfied with teaching after one year; in fact, only thirteen teachers expressed dissatisfaction.

Discussion

Although the hypothesis that teacher socialization results in the adoption of a more custodial pupil control ideology has been tested using cross-sectional data (Willower, Eidell, and Hoy, 1967), the results of this study are based on longitudinal data. The findings suggest that the pupil control ideology of beginning teachers is affected by teaching experience. The process of socialization within the school subculture seems important in reshaping the control ideology of organizational newcomers. New, idealistic teachers appear to be confronted with a relatively custodial control orientation as they become a part of the organization; in fact, the vast majority of teachers in the present study at both elementary and secondary levels described their school subculture as one in which good teaching and good discipline were

6. It should be noted that earlier research indicated that teachers were significantly more custodial than principals or counselors. The relevant comparisons are as follows. For teachers ($N = 945$) the PCI mean was 58.8 and for principals ($N = 181$) it was 54.4 ($t = 5.693, p < .001$). A 52.3 mean PCI score for counselors ($N = 180$) was significantly less custodial than the mean PCI score for teachers ($t = 9.902, p < .001$). Further, principals taken as a group were more custodial in pupil control ideology than counselors ($t = 2.190, p < .05$); however, these data must be interpreted with care, since there were significant differences between elementary and secondary school principals. Elementary principals ($N = 84$) had a mean PCI score of 50.9, lower than that of the counselors in the sample, and secondary principals ($N = 97$) had a substantially higher mean score of 57.4. A significant difference also existed between the mean score of elementary teachers ($N = 468$, mean $= 55.3$) and secondary teachers ($N = 477$, mean $= 62.3$). Thus, secondary school teachers were highest on custodial orientation, followed in order by secondary principals, elementary teachers, counselors, and elementary principals. See Willower, Hoy, and Eidell (1967).

equated. Again, the saliency of pupil control in public schools, organizations in which participation is mandatory and clients are unselected, is underscored. Although only seven graduates returned to college as graduate assistants, it is interesting to note an increase in the custodialism of their pupil control ideology during student teaching but a return to a relatively humanistic control ideology as they returned to the university subculture, a setting described by most respondents as one which focused on ideal images and situations rather than the "harsh" realities of teaching. In brief, the significant increase in custodialism of first-year teachers along with a virtually constant pupil control ideology for non-teaching graduates supported the theoretical formulation from which these predictions were generated.

Student teaching is strategically located in terms of the socialization of teachers. Usually occurring at the conclusion of formal classroom education and immediately preceding the first field assignment, practice teaching provides a transitional phase in the socialization process. The student-teaching experience appears to be functional for prospective teachers in terms of mitigating the potential role strain with respect to control of students that tends to be created as they become official members of a school faculty. Recall that student teachers become significantly more custodial during practice teaching, as they are confronted with the realities of teaching and the relatively custodial teacher subculture of the public schools. This kind of anticipatory socialization, that is, adopting the norms and values of the teacher subculture to which practice teachers aspire but do not fully belong, should facilitate their acceptance by teachers and make for easier adjustment to the teacher group.[7]

Since the concept of socialization refers to learning specific skills and orientations associated with various status positions, a change from teacher to principal or teacher to counselor implies further resocialization. Although the socialization of beginning teachers is stressed in the present study, the resocialization of public school professional personnel as they change status positions within public schools is an area for further research.

It seems appropriate to raise the question as to what extent the concepts of custodialism and humanism are useful in identifying different types of schools. If student control is central in the organizational life of public schools and if statements concerning ideology correspond relatively well with behavior, then the pupil control ideology of a school may be an important first step in identifying the "social climate" of the school.

The results of this study should be interpreted with some care. The entire sample of subjects completed their formal education at one university. Moreover, the proportion of female teachers in the group of teachers completing their first year of teaching was relatively high. This was in part due to the world situation; many of the young men were drafted into the armed services upon graduation. Nevertheless, all predictions were confirmed and

---

7. For a more detailed discussion of anticipatory socialization, see Merton (1957, pp. 262-280).

the findings of this study complement well the results of earlier research which dealt with status relations, role, personality, and pupil control ideology of public school professional personnel (Willower, Eidell, and Hoy, 1967).

References

AUSUBEL, D. P.   New look at classroom discipline. *Phi Delta Kappan*, 1961, 18, 26-28.

CARLSON, R. O.   Environmental constraints and organizational consequences: The public school and its clients. In D. E. Griffiths (Ed.), *Behavioral science and educational administration*. Chicago: University of Chicago Press, 1964. Pp. 262-276.

COLEMAN, J. S.   *The adolescent society*. New York: The Free Press, 1961.

ETZIONI, A.   *A comparative analysis of complex organizations*. New York: Free Press, 1961.

FROMM, E.   *Man for himself*. New York: Farrar & Rinehart, 1948.

GILBERT, D. and LEVINSON, D. J.   "Custodialism" and "humanism" in mental hospital structure and in staff ideology. In M. Greenblatt, D. J. Levinson and R. H. Williams (Eds.), *The patient and the mental hospital*. Glencoe: The Free Press, 1957.

GOFFMAN, E.   *Asylums*. Garden City, N.Y.: Doubleday, 1961.

GORDON, C. W.   *The social system of the high school*. Glencoe: The Free Press, 1957.

HOY, W. K.   Organizational socialization: The student teacher and pupil control ideology. *Journal of Educational Research*, 1967, 51, 153-155.

MERTON, R. K.   *Social theory and social structure*. Glencoe: The Free Press, 1957.

PARSONS, T.   *The social system*. Glencoe: The Free Press, 1951.

POWELSON, H. and BENDIX, R.   Psychiatry in prison. *Psychiatry*, 1961, 14, 73-86.

WALLER, W.   *The sociology of teaching*. New York: Wiley, 1932.

WILLOWER, D. J.   Hypotheses on the school as a social system. *Educational Administration Quarterly*, 1965, 1, 45-51.

WILLOWER, D. J., EIDELL, T. L. and HOY, W. K.   *The school and pupil control ideology*. University Park, Pa.: Penn. State Studies Monograph, 1967.

WILLOWER, D. J., HOY, W. K. and EIDELL, T. L.   The counselor and the school as a social organization. *Personnel and Guidance Journal*, 1967, 46, 228-234.

WILLOWER, D. J. and JONES, R. G.   Control in an educational organization. In J. D. Raths (Ed.), *Studying teaching*. Englewood Cliffs, N.J.: Prentice-Hall, 1967.

✵ ✵ ✵ ✵ ✵

School administration is not a field in which one would expect to find much use of the controlled experiment, and indeed little of the research is experimental. The following study shows us, however, that this state of affairs is not due to some inherent intractability of the problems or subject matter in school administration.

Edwin Bridges and his colleagues worked with the oldest of all problems in experimental social psychology. The study of group problem-solving had its genesis in Triplett's laboratory back in 1897, where he had ten- and twelve-year-old children winding fishing reels under alone and together conditions. Children in the group situation excelled, a finding that led to seventy years of research to uncover the bases of group superiority (at least in certain kinds of task). For a good discussion of this research, see Collins and Guetzkow, *A Social Psychology of Group Processes for Decision-making* (Wiley, 1964).

Drawing on the accumulated research and theory, Bridges predicted—and demonstrated—that groups of teachers without their building principal performed better in a problem-solving task than groups which included the principal as a participating member. Though the task is a puzzle-type or "Eureka" task, and is thus less rich than the usual problems faced by teachers and administrators, the findings seem potentially applicable to daily life in the school.

But note! The investigators went to considerable pains to test the accuracy of the *reasoning* back of their predictions. To their surprise, the underlying assumptions did not stand up. Apparently they had made the right predictions for the wrong reasons. Seventy years of research has not provided all the answers.

Effects of Hierarchical Differentiation on Group Productivity, Efficiency, and Risk-Taking*

Edwin M. Bridges,
Wayne J. Doyle, David J. Mahan

Administrators are frequently admonished to solve their organizational problems through the medium of groups. This exhortation is based largely on the body of research that demonstrates the superiority of groups over individuals in solving certain kinds of problems. Recently, however, organizational theorists have begun to point out that the superiority of groups over individuals may be found only in undifferentiated groups, i.e., peer groups (See Blau and Scott, 1963; Katz and Kahn, 1966; Smith and Keith, 1967). Those theorists contend that in hierarchically differentiated groups, the stimulation of social interaction is restricted. The validity of this contention can be tested by studying group functioning in hierarchically differentiated and undifferentiated groups.

The main purposes of the experiments reported in this paper were to determine whether hierarchically differentiated groups would be as productive on a problem-solving task as hierarchically undifferentiated groups, and to examine the effects of formally based status differences on group efficiency and risk-taking.

Hypotheses

Hypothesis 1

Hierarchically differentiated groups will be less productive than hierarchically undifferentiated groups. Some theorists maintain that groups are superior to individuals on certain types of problem-solving tasks, because social interaction (1) provides an error-correcting mechanism, (2) furnishes social support to individual members, and (3) fosters competition for respect (Blau and Scott, 1963, pp. 121-124). The relationship of these factors to increased group productivity is indicated in the discussion that follows and is drawn principally from the work of Blau and Scott (1963).

* From *Administrative Science Quarterly*, 1968, 13 (2), 305-319. Used by permission of the authors and publisher.

It is not easy for an individual to detect mistakes in his thinking. He brings a set perspective to the problem-solving situation, which militates against his seeing the problem from another perspective. When a number of individuals are working on a common task, the chances that an error in thinking will be detected are increased, because the other people bring different assumptions, frames of references, experiences, and knowledge to bear on the problem. This facilitates the detection of false reasoning and tends to result in a rejection of ideas and suggestions based on illogical inferences.

Second, social interaction furnishes social support to group members. A problem-solving situation creates a condition of uncertainty for individual members, and this leads to mental blocks that interfere with the development of their ideas. When an individual works with a group on a task, his good suggestions are likely to receive the approval of others. Such social approval reduces his anxieties and encourages him to develop his ideas further.

Third, the presence of others motivates members of a group to make good suggestions in order to win the respect and esteem of the other members.

The presence of status differences in a group, however, curtails these three group processes, according to Blau and Scott. Formally instituted status differences undermine the competition for respect that mobilizes the energies of group members. In the face of organizationally induced status differences, there is little incentive to compete for respect, since a person's standing in the group is not based on the respect of others, but is prescribed by the formal organization. Formally instituted status differences also distort the error-correction mechanism. Subordinates are likely to be reluctant to criticize the opinions of persons with superior status or to find fault with their suggestions and ideas. Finally, formally instituted status differences affect the distribution of social support. Low-status members do not receive their share of the group's support, and it is support that relieves anxiety and stimulates thinking.

Using this line of reasoning, it is hypothesized that hierarchically differentiated groups will be less productive than undifferentiated or peer groups. The differences in the productivity of these two types of groups are accounted for by the curtailment of the three group processes in hierarchically differentiated groups.

Hypothesis 2

Hierarchically differentiated groups will be less efficient than hierarchically undifferentiated groups. When a collection of individuals comes together in a group, the individuals have the potential to produce more in concert than separately; however, the potential is not realized until a pattern of interpersonal relations is developed (Collins and Guetzkow, 1964, p. 60).

Status differences among the group members constitute an obstacle that delays the development of a pattern of interpersonal relationships. Low-status members of hierarchically differentiated groups hesitate to become actively involved in solving the problem, until the superordinate indicates through his behavior the kind of role he will play in the problem-solving situation. The low-status members define their roles in the group and develop their pattern of behavior only after the superordinate has made clear how he will behave in this situation. In hierarchically undifferentiated groups, members can begin immediately to develop a pattern of interpersonal relationships, since they are not hindered by the need to adjust and readjust their behavior to a person with higher formal status. This means that the process of developing interpersonal relationships will require more time in hierarchically differentiated groups than in undifferentiated groups. As a result, the hierarchically differentiated groups will be slower than undifferentiated groups and, therefore, less efficient in successfully moving toward the goal.

Hypothesis 3

Hierarchically differentiated groups will exhibit less risk-taking behavior than hierarchically undifferentiated groups. In this study, risk-taking was measured as the willingness of group members to subject ideas to a test. The presence of a superordinate among a group of subordinates tends to inhibit the tendencies of subordinates to expose their ideas to possible failure. In order for an idea to be acted upon by the group, the person who generates the idea must defend his view and advocate the idea before the rest of the group. By attempting to promote the idea, the person becomes identified with it. If the group acts upon the idea and the idea is subsequently proven unsound, the individual who advanced the idea experiences failure in the eyes of his superior, a risk few subordinates are willing to take. It might be expected, therefore, that hierarchically differentiated groups will present fewer of their generated solutions to the research worker than the undifferentiated groups. The research worker is an immediate source of feedback concerning the worth of the idea.

Method

Sample

In order to test the three hypotheses, 20 groups were formed, each with four subjects drawn from the staffs of 10 elementary schools in the St. Louis metropolitan area. Of the 80 subjects, 10 were principals (5 male and 5 female), and 70 were teachers (68 female and 2 male). With the exception of the principals, subjects were randomly selected from staff rosters provided to the investigators. In each of the 10 schools, two groups were formed, each with four members. One group included the principal and three of his teachers, while the other group consisted of four teachers. All teachers were randomly assigned to their groups.

The groups with the principal were designated as hierarchically differentiated groups. Status differences between the principal and his teachers were prescribed by the formal organization. The groups composed exclusively of teachers were designated as hierarchically undifferentiated groups. According to the organizational chart in these schools, teachers held positions that were equivalent in organizational status; therefore, formally based status differences were present only in the hierarchically differentiated groups.

Procedures

The small-group experiments were conducted in each of the ten participating schools prior to and immediately following the regular school day. Hierarchically differentiated and undifferentiated groups were randomly assigned to morning and afternoon problem-solving sessions. Each session was conducted in a section of the building free of interruption. This location varied from building to building, though within each school, the location was the same for both groups.

Each subject was provided with a copy of the problem. Subjects were told to work together on it and to discuss their ideas on the solution to the problem among themselves. Participants were free to ask the experimenter questions. The only restriction imposed on their method of operation was that they had to use a parliamentarian constitutional arrangement[1] in deciding whether a solution generated by the group should be presented to the experimenter as a possible correct solution. As long as a majority of the members present agreed to present a generated solution, groups could present as many solutions as they wished, until the problem was correctly solved. Each session was tape-recorded. In addition, the experimenter noted when the group overcame each one of the three beliefs, and when the group generated and presented a solution.[2] The procedure was the same for all groups.

1. The concept of constitutional arrangement refers to the procedures by which the group is to arrive at a decision. The three most frequently mentioned constitutional arrangements are the parliamentarian, the participant-determining, and the centralist. In groups using either the participant-determining or parliamentarian modes for reaching decisions, every group member has relatively equal power and influence over the decision. The major distinction between these modes is that under the participant-determining arrangement consensus is required. Groups using parliamentarian procedures for making and executing decisions can exercise a choice that is binding on the group whenever a majority agrees that a particular course of action is desirable. Groups operating under a centralist constitutional arrangement are bound by a decision whenever one is reached by the person in final authority. Cf. Swanson (1959).

2. Since each session was tape-recorded, the investigators were able to verify the accuracy of the information recorded by the experimenter during the session as to (1) the time required to overcome the first belief (the efficiency measure), (2) the number of beliefs overcome and whether the group solved the problem (the productivity measures), and (3) the number of solutions generated by the group versus the number presented as a correct solution (the risk-taking measure).

The problem to be solved was "the doodlebug problem," a problem devised by M. Ray Denny and subsequently revised by Denny and Rokeach.[3] The problem is nonideological and is essentially a problem in logic involving an imaginary insect named Joe Doodlebug, who operates in an environment under unusual governing conditions. Solution of the problem includes analysis and synthesis phases. During the analysis phase, subjects have to overcome certain presently held beliefs. In the synthesis phase subjects have to integrate the beliefs into a new system. Productivity was measured in each phase.

A time limit of 30 minutes was set for the group to solve the problem. At the close of the experimental session, subjects were given a copy of the solution and asked not to discuss what had occurred with anyone until the day after the last scheduled experimental session.

Results

To test hypothesis 1, the differences in productivity between hierarchically differentiated and undifferentiated groups were examined in both the analysis and synthesis phases of the problem. Only three of the twenty groups solved the problem. Two of the correct solutions were generated by hierarchically undifferentiated groups; the other by a hierarchically differentiated group. The number of correct solutions was therefore too small to test differences in productivity in the synthesis phase of the task.

The hypothesis was then tested by looking at the productivity of the two kinds of groups during the analysis phase. The measure of productivity for this phase was the total number of beliefs overcome by the group in the time allotted. For each belief overcome, the group was awarded a score of one. Since there were only three beliefs—a facing belief, a direction belief, and a movement belief—to be overcome, the range on the productivity index in the analysis phase was 0 to 3.[4] The mean productivity score was 2.2 for the hierarchically differentiated groups and 2.8 for the undifferentiated groups. A test of the significance of the difference between these means resulted in a t of 2.52. For a one-tailed test with 18 df, this value is significant at the .05 level. The hypothesis is confirmed at the analysis phase of the task, the only phase that could be tested. That is, the hierarchically differentiated groups were less productive than the hierarchically undifferentiated groups.

3. For a full description of "the doodlebug problem," see Rokeach (1960, pp. 171-181).

4. In the "Joe Doodlebug Problem" the subject is given the end result (that Joe must jump four times to reach his food) and is asked to tell why Joe reaches the conclusion he does. In order to reach a correct solution the subject must overcome three basic beliefs. In everyday life we face the food we are about to eat, but Joe need not face his food in order to eat it. He can land on top of it (*the facing belief*). In everyday life we can change our direction at will. Joe, however, can change direction only by jumping sideways or backwards (*the direction belief*). In everyday life we can change direction immediately, but Joe must make four jumps in one direction before he changes. Subjects have difficulty with this belief because they assume that Joe is at the end rather than possibly in the middle of a sequence (*the movement belief*).

Hypothesis 2, comparing efficiency, was tested by examining the length of time required to overcome the first belief. The mean number of minutes required to overcome the first belief was 2.7 for the undifferentiated groups and 4.8 for the hierarchically differentiated groups. This difference is significant at the .05 level for a one-tailed test with a t of 1.745 and df of 18. The hierarchically differentiated groups were less efficient than the undifferentiated groups.

For hypothesis 3, the operational definition of risk-taking behavior for each group was the difference between the number of solutions generated by the group and the number presented to the experimenter. The smaller the discrepancy between the number of generated solutions and presented solutions, the greater was the risk-taking. The mean risk-taking score was .8 for the hierarchically undifferentiated groups and 1.8 for the hierarchically differentiated groups. The difference between the two means is significant at the .05 level for a one-tailed test, with a t of 1.754 and df of 18. Forty-four per cent of the generated solutions were presented to the experimenter in the hierarchically differentiated groups, in contrast to 71 per cent in the undifferentiated groups. When the administrator-generated solutions were excluded, and only the teacher-generated and presented solutions are used, the difference in risk-taking for the two types of groups is even more pronounced. Only 36 per cent of the solutions generated by teachers in the hierarchically differentiated groups were presented to the experimenter, in contrast to 71 per cent in the undifferentiated groups. The presence of formally based status differences among group members did inhibit the risk-taking behavior of subordinates, as was hypothesized.

Although the investigators randomly assigned groups to morning and afternoon sessions, an analysis was made of the differences between before-school and after-school groups on each of the three dependent variables. None of the three analyses approached significance at the .05 level. The t-values for productivity, risk-taking, and efficiency were all less than 1.00. The differences between the means on these three measures for morning and afternoon groups were .2 for productivity, 0 for risk-taking, and .45 for efficiency.

In order to determine whether there was a significant relationship among any of the dependent variables, correlations were run on the productivity, efficiency, and risk-taking scores. None of the correlations was significant at the .05 level. The correlation coefficient for productivity and efficiency was $-.15$; for productivity and risk-taking it was $-.19$. The correlation (.38) between the efficiency and the risk-taking scores does approach significance, however, and suggests that efficient groups are also high risk-taking groups.[5]

---

5.   The reader is reminded that the higher the efficiency score the more inefficient the group is and the higher the risk-taking score the fewer the risks taken by the group.

Discussion

Although the results of this experiment are consistent with the hypotheses elaborated at the beginning of this paper, some questions arose during the analysis of the data. One of these questions has to do with the validity of the risk-taking index. In the hierarchically differentiated groups, although only 36 per cent of the teacher-generated solutions were presented by the groups to the experimenter, 78 per cent of the administrator-generated solutions were presented. One might argue that in groups with a history of association and development that the suggestions of members of lower rank are passed over more often than the suggestions of higher-ranked members.[6] If this line of reasoning is valid, then the lower proportion of solutions presented to the experimenter in the hierarchically differentiated groups was not due to a reluctance by subordinates to take risks, but rather to the tendency of ideas advanced by low-ranking group members to be over-looked. Differences between differentiated and undifferentiated groups on the risk-taking measure could be attributed to the passing over of the ideas of low-ranking members in groups having formally based status differences among the members, rather than to the hypothesized inhibition of risk-taking.

In order to determine which of these two explanations might have accounted for the differences on the risk-taking index between the two types of groups, a second experiment was conducted using 18 groups, each including five subjects. Subjects for the groups were drawn from the staffs of eight elementary schools and one junior high school in the St. Louis metropolitan area. With the exception of the principals, subjects were randomly selected from staff rosters provided the investigators. In each of the nine schools, two groups were formed, each with five members. One group included four teachers and the principal, with the principal acting solely as an *observer*, whereas the other group consisted of five teachers, with one of the five designated as an observer. All teachers were randomly assigned to the two groups and to their roles as observer or participant. In both groups the observer was instructed to watch the group as it worked on the problem, to refrain from making any comments even if called upon by a member of the group, and to withhold any expression of emotion during the session. Though informed of the identity of the person who was desig-nated as observer, subjects were told only that he could not participate in the problem-solving activity. No other information about the observer's role was given. The procedures during the problem-solving session were iden-tical in other respects to the procedures followed in the first experiment.

Although information was gathered on all three measures for each group, the measure of chief interest was the scores of the two types of groups on the risk-taking measure. If this measure really represented the willing-

6. This argument was suggested in a paper by Heinicke and Bales (1953).

ness of group members to subject ideas to a test, then the groups with a superordinate (in this case the principal) present as an observer should offer fewer of their generated solutions to the experimenter than groups with a peer serving as the observer. On the other hand, if the two types of groups did not differ on the risk-taking measure, this would argue for the interpretation that the differences on this index in the first experiment were due to the ideas of teachers (lower-status members) being overlooked when in competition with the ideas of the principal (a higher-status member).

The results of this second experiment confirmed the interpretation of the risk-taking index as a measure of the willingness of group members to subject their ideas to a test. The mean score on the risk-taking measure for groups observed by a superordinate was 1.56, while the mean score for groups observed by a peer was .56, a low score indicating high risk-taking. A test of the significance of the difference between these two means resulted in a t of 2.947. For a two-tailed test with 16 df, this value is significant at the .01 level. The rival explanation for the findings in the first experiment with respect to the differences between the risk-taking scores of hierarchically differentiated and undifferentiated groups was, therefore, rejected by the investigators.

A second question emerged from an analysis of the social interaction in the hierarchically differentiated groups. Since the authors had reasoned that productivity would be lower in the hierarchically differentiated groups because the stimulation of social interaction would be curtailed, the investigators studied certain aspects of the group processes to determine if these had been curtailed in the differentiated groups. Although ten such groups were tape recorded, it was possible to study the interaction processes in only eight differentiated groups because of excessive background noise. The focus of the analysis was on the extent to which the error-correction mechanism and the distribution of social support were distorted.

Distortions in the error-correction mechanism and the distribution of social support were studied by looking at what happened to ideas emanating from the principal and from one teacher randomly selected from each group. A statement by a participant was classified as an idea if it was any one of the following: (1) an interpretation of the problem not already mentioned in the written problem presented to the group, (2) a possible cause of the problem, (3) a possible solution of the problem, (4) a relationship between a cause and a problem, and (5) a criterion for judging the appropriateness of any of the preceding.[7] Two investigators, working from typed transcripts of the eight sessions, independently traced what happened to each idea by looking at the three responses made immediately following the introduction of the idea.[8] The fate of each idea was classified

7. These criteria were drawn from Glidewell (1953, pp. 175-176).

8. Degree of agreement between the two coders was determined by a procedure recommended by Bales (1950, pp. 103-111). The extent of the agreement between coders was determined for both administrator and teacher ideas by means of the chi-square test.

Table 1

DISPOSITION OF IDEAS OF TEACHERS AND ADMINISTRATORS IN
THE HIERARCHICALLY DIFFERENTIATED GROUPS*

	DISPOSITION OF IDEAS							
INITIATION OF IDEA	CRITICIZE		USE		ACCEPTANCE WITHOUT USE		IGNORE	
	%	N	%	N	%	N	%	N
Administrators	51	27	20	11	10	5	19	10
Teachers	37	20	13	7	26	14	24	13

* Chi-square test shows no significant differences at .05 level.

in one of the following categories: criticized, ignored, used, accepted without being used.[9] Criticisms were considered to be the functional equivalent of error-correcting behavior, on the assumption that criticisms represented the rejection of false leads and unproductive ideas. Supportive behavior was signified by the use of an idea or the acceptance of an idea without use, on the assumption that these behaviors reinforced the behavior of the person who initiated the idea, thus making him feel more secure and less anxious. An individual who set forth an idea but had it overlooked or ignored could have had his anxiety increased, if he interpreted the lack of response as representing a lack of confidence in his reasoning ability.

The disposition of administrator and teacher ideas in the hierarchically differentiated groups is reported in Table 1. A chi-square test of these data is not significant at the .05 level.

Since the disposition of an idea in the hierarchically undifferentiated groups might have differed from the disposition of an idea in the hierarchically differentiated groups, an analysis was made of what happened to the

---

Bales considers a chi-square value which has a probability of .50 or greater as evidence of acceptable agreement among coders. The investigators preferred to use a more conservative estimate of agreement, and set a chi-square value with a *p* of .80 or greater as the acceptable level. For both the administrator and teacher ideas, the probability of a chi-square value with four degrees of freedom (unclassified responses also were included in this analysis) was in excess of .90.

9. A response was classified as *criticized* if another participant disagreed with the idea. Disagreement could include personal judgment and/or reference to instructions and conditions. For example, a participant advances the idea that Joe will take three jumps north and then one west. Another participant then points out that Joe cannot jump diagonally. Ideas were classified as *ignored* if there was no further reference to it. An idea was classified as *used* if another participant employed the idea in developing the same or another idea or in generating a solution. For example, a participant presents the idea that Joe jumps sideways. Another participant uses this idea by developing a solution that Joe jumps four times, sideways to the west. An idea was coded in the *acceptance without use* category if another participant agreed with the idea, but did not use it. For example, a participant states that the size of the food is probably important. Another participant remarks, "That's right," but does not make any further comments. Slightly less than 20 per cent of the ideas were clarified by the experimenter before they were used or criticized; in these cases the ideas were not classified.

Table 2

DISPOSITION OF IDEAS OF TEACHERS AND ADMINISTRATORS IN THE
HIERARCHICALLY DIFFERENTIATED AND UNDIFFERENTIATED GROUPS*

| | DISPOSITION OF IDEAS | | | | | | | |
| | CRITICIZE | | USE | | ACCEPTANCE WITHOUT USE | | IGNORE | |
INITIATION OF IDEA	%	N	%	N	%	N	%	N
Administrators in differentiated groups ..	51	27	20	11	10	5	19	10
Teachers in differentiated groups ..	37	20	13	7	26	14	24	13
Teachers in undifferentiated groups	35	33	23	22	22	20	20	19

* Chi-square test shows no significant differences at .05 level.

ideas emanating from a teacher randomly selected from each of eight undifferentiated groups. The results of this analysis then were contrasted with the disposition of ideas proposed by teachers and administrators in the differentiated groups in the same eight schools (see Table 2). This chi-square test also showed no significant differences in the disposition of ideas.

Differences in the level of productivity between the hierarchically differentiated and undifferentiated groups apparently were not caused by a reluctance of subordinates to criticize the ideas of superordinates, as maintained by Blau and Scott (1963) in their discussion of how the error-correction mechanism operates in differentiated groups. Nor was social support, as operationally defined in this study, unevenly distributed between subordinates and superordinates in the differentiated groups, as contended by Blau and Scott. Since these two conditioning variables did not operate as hypothesized, the question remains as to what accounted for the differences in the productivity of the two types of groups.

One possible explanation is that the competition for respect, a third beneficial characteristics of group processes, was curtailed by the presence of formally based status differences, as Blau and Scott contend. To summarize their line of reasoning, hierarchical differentiation undermines the competition for respect. Status in the group is accorded on the basis of the person's organizational rank, rather than on the basis of the person's contribution to goal attainment. One consequence of this is that members of the differentiated groups do not mobilize their energies fully, and this low level of mobilization reduces group productivity.

The data in this study which suggests that members of the undifferentiated groups had more fully mobilized their energies were the number of ideas initiated by members of the two types of groups while working on the problem. This indicator, unlike the ones used to examine distortions in the error-correction mechanism and the distribution of social support, emerged from an analysis of the data. Therefore, the data on idea initiation rates are used *post hoc* to support the competition for respect argument advanced by Blau and Scott.

Data in Table 2 indicated that a greater number of ideas were being initiated in the undifferentiated groups. To examine this possibility more systematically, an idea rate was computed for each of the groups. This idea rate was based on the total number of ideas initiated by a group divided by the amount of time the group worked on solving the problem. Significantly higher idea initiation rates were found in the hierarchically undifferentiated groups ($\overline{X} = 1.35$) than in the differentiated groups ($\overline{X} = 1.08$). This difference was significant at the .05 level for a two-tailed test ($t = 2.250$; $df = 14$).

The significantly higher idea initiation rates in the hierarchically undifferentiated groups may have been a function of the greater mobilization of energy engendered by the competition for respect in these groups. Hierarchically differentiated groups, on the other hand, may have had lower idea initiation rates because a person's standing in the group was not based upon respect gained from performance on the task. Rather, a person's standing in the group was prescribed by the formal organization. Under these conditions, competition for respect, a major determinant of a person's motivation to initiate ideas and to participate fully in accomplishing the task, was not operating.

Concluding Remarks

The findings reported in this paper tend to confirm the notion of a number of organizational theorists that hierarchical differentiation has its dysfunctional as well as its functional consequences. Specifically, formally based status differences were found to inhibit group productivity at the analysis phase of problem solving, efficiency, and risk-taking. Hierarchical differentiation also seemed to attenuate one of the beneficial characteristics of group processes—competition for respect—as evidenced by the lower idea initiation rates.

At the same time, some doubt was cast upon two of the assumptions with which this study began, that is, that the presence of formally based status differences among group members distorts the error-correction mechanism and the distribution of social support. A more direct empirical test of these Blau and Scott postulates appears warranted, since the fate of ideas initiated by administrators and teachers in the hierarchically differentiated groups did not differ as hypothesized. It is still a question whether differences in the productivity and efficiency of the two types of groups would be found if a centralist constitutional arrangement were used.[10] Since this type of constitutional arrangement is typically used by formal organizations in reaching decisions, a study of this variable and its effects on group performance would be meaningful. Finally, the investigators were unable to test the consequences of hierarchical differentiation at the synthesis phase of problem solving; this too represents a fruitful question for further research. Hopefully, these problems will provide productive leads for subsequent studies in this area.

References

BALES, R. F.   *Interaction process analysis.* Cambridge, Mass.: Addison-Wesley, 1950.

BLAU, P. M. and SCOTT, W. R.   *Formal organizations.* San Francisco: Chandler, 1963.

COLLINS, B. E. and GUETZKOW, H.   *A social psychology of group processes for decision-making.* New York: Wiley, 1964.

GLIDEWELL, J. C.   Group emotionality and productivity. Unpublished Ph. D. dissertation, The University of Chicago, 1953.

HEINICKE, C. and BALES, R. F.   Developmental trends in the structure of small groups. *Sociometry,* 1953, 16, 7-38.

KATZ, D. and KAHN, R. L.   *The social psychology of organizations.* New York: Wiley, 1966.

ROKEACH, M.   *The open and closed mind.* New York: Basic Books, 1960.

SMITH, L. M. and KEITH, P. M.   *Social psychological aspects of school building design.* Washington, D.C.: Bureau of Research, U.S. Office of Education, 1967.

SWANSON, G. E.   The effectiveness of decision-making groups. *Adult Leadership,* 1959, 8, 48-52.

10.   It is conceivable that the productivity of the hierarchically differentiated groups was inhibited not by formally based status differences alone, but rather by a combination of formally based status differences and the constitutional arrangement chosen by the investigators. In the first experiment, the investigators used a parliamentarian type of constitutional arrangement. This placed the elementary school principal in a decision-making situation with his teachers, in which the decision was to be reached by majority vote. By selecting a constitutional arrangement not customarily used in this type of organization, yet not specifying the role of the principal, the investigators may have inadvertently created a situation where the teachers did not know the appropriate status of the principal. As a result, the teachers may not have known how to behave toward the principal *in this situation.* This ambiguity may have threatened the low-power persons, leading to increased anxiety, which in turn lowered productivity. The same line of reasoning could also account for the differences between hierarchically differentiated and undifferentiated groups on the efficiency measure.

✳ ✳ ✳ ✳ ✳

We live in a time of uprisings. The idea that people on the bottom side of a social system "ought" to have more influence is spreading vigorously, even if many of its advocates have never read Karl Marx. And after student power and black power, it is not surprising that teacher power has become more and more salient.

Are teachers an oppressed class? Moeller and Charters began this study with a central hypothesis: that those teachers working in highly bureaucratized school systems would feel less powerful than those where rules, defined authority channels, and all the properties of rational organizations which Max Weber defined were somehow less in evidence.

The study is of special methodological interest on two counts. First, what do you do when an "obvious" prediction fails, and the converse is decidedly apparent? Secondly, the authors do a particularly thoughtful job of specifying "control" variables—the "other things" which are always supposed to be equal, but never are—and analyzing the data in their light.

Relation of Bureaucratization to Sense of Power Among Teachers*

Gerald H. Moeller, W. W. Charters, Jr.

The present investigation concentrated on the feelings of powerlessness among classroom teachers in the social organization of the school as those feelings derived from the school's bureaucratic structure.

Although powerlessness has usually been studied in the larger societal context, this investigation. like Pearlin's (1962) and Clark's (1959), narrowed the context to a particular organization. Such narrowing gives rise to several problems about the concept of powerlessness, defined by Seeman (1959) as a person's "expectancy . . . that his own behavior cannot determine the occurrence of the outcomes, or reinforcements, he seeks."

Introduction

Source of "Sense of Power"

One issue is the extent to which a person's sense of powerlessness in the organizational context is a generalized attitude derived from his early socializing experiences or elsewhere and brought by him to the organizational setting. Treatment of the concepts of alienation and powerlessness in the literature imply that these are highly pervasive attitudes. Dean (1961) reported substantial correlations between measures of powerlessness, normlessness, and social isolation on a sample of residents in a Midwestern city, while Douvan and Walker (1956) believed they had traced sense of effectiveness in public affairs to fundamental personality attributes:

> The fact that the sense of effectiveness has been shown to be in many people part of a general way of looking at the world—that governmental affairs become a vehicle for the expression of a personal orientation—suggests that whatever external factors enter as determinants of this attitude are at least to some extent mediated through a screen of stable personality characteristics. [p. 19]

Shipton and Belisle (1956, p. 307), too, regarded the feelings of local inefficacy which they found among school patrons to stem from a more

---

* From *Administrative Science Quarterly*, 1966, 10, 444-465. Used by permission of the authors and publisher.

basic phenomenon; they suggested that powerlessness reflected "some generalized feelings of futility and dissatisfaction which are projected upon either local government or public education in general." The present study, on the other hand, assumed that powerlessness, or "sense of power" as it is termed here, is in some degree situationally specific—that it would vary with the bureaucratic character of the teacher's work setting. Clearly, tenability of the assumption must be examined closely in the data.

A second issue, especially salient in a study of teaching personnel, is the particular realms of organizational life in which powerlessness is experienced. In his study of the mental hospital, Pearlin (1962) measured the nurse's feeling of powerlessness principally over her immediate work situation. Clark's (1959) study of members of a farm cooperative, on the other hand, measured their feelings of powerlessness to control major organizational policies. In the case of teachers, a sense of power may be examined with regard to affairs of the classroom or with regard to affairs of the school. Teachers in today's schools typically are accorded a great deal of autonomy in their classrooms, an autonomy protected by their physical insulation from observability and fortified by strong professional norms. With respect to school policies, however, teachers traditionally have lacked power. Subordinated to administrators, school boards, and vocal citizens, largely unorganized for (and even unsympathetic to) collective action on their own behalf, teachers frequently have been prey to arbitrary manipulations of their conditions of work. In consequence, a teacher might well feel fully in command of the classroom learning process, but feel essentially powerless to control his fate in the larger organizational setting. This study measured sense of power from the standpoint of the ability of the teachers to influence the larger organizational forces that importantly shape their destiny.

A final issue is the relationship between feelings of powerlessness and the objective situation of power. In a sense, this is the other side of the coin of the first issue—concerning alienation as a generalized attitude—but it draws attention to a different problem. If a measure of sense of power were nothing more than a report on a person's location in a power structure, the concept would have little significance. A psychological feeling of power or powerlessness must carry implications which transcend the fact of power position. Indeed, it is precisely the far-reaching implications of the concept which most of the published studies of alienation have documented.[1] At the same time, the studies consistently indicate that experienced powerlessness is not independent of objective circumstances. Campbell, Gurin, and Miller (1954), for example, showed that males had a higher sense of political efficacy than females, and persons with higher incomes, more extensive educational training, and higher social status felt greater power with respect to public affairs than less advantaged people. A subjective sense of

---

1. Browning, Farmer, Kirk and Mitchell (1961) propose that powerlessness is the first of a series of stages leading to global alienation.

power, then, must be rooted in both situational determinants and personal responses, as Douvan and Walker (1956) emphasized. In this study, "sense of power" scores reflected variations in teachers' access to the decision-making arena, to some extent, thereby providing evidence on construct validity of the measure.

The organizational structure of the school provides the arena where teachers' orientations to power and the realities of power meet. This structure may be described in terms of the degree of bureaucracy exhibited. The bureaucratic model describes organizations designed to accomplish large administrative tasks by systematically coordinating the work of many individuals. The bureaucratic organization, according to Blau (1956), includes a definite division of labor, a hierarchy of authority with carefully prescribed responsibilities, a system of rules or policy, impersonality in the interaction of its members, employment based on technical qualifications, and efficiency from a technical standpoint. These aspects of bureaucracy are the basis of the analysis of the organizational structure of the school systems studied.

Hypothesis and Design

The primary hypothesis of the study was that teachers in highly bureaucratized school systems would have a much lower "sense of power" than teachers in less bureaucratic systems. The hypothesis assumed that the teacher, constrained by rules and regulations in whose establishment he had but a small voice, would respond to the impersonality, the magnitude, and the complexity of the bureaucratic system with a distinct feeling of impotence to control events which would affect his interests. The teacher in the small, structurally simple system, on the other hand, was expected to feel less ineffectual.

A second hypothesis was introduced to demonstrate the situational specificity of teachers' sense of power. If sense of power derives from exposure to the particular organizational setting in which teachers work rather than from previous experience in the society at large or from other sources, then it should follow that the difference between sense of power among teachers in highly bureaucratic school systems and less bureaucratic systems would increase with the length of exposure to their respective environments.

To test the hypotheses, 20 school systems employing from 37 to 700 full-time classroom teachers were selected from the St. Louis metropolitan area exclusive of the city of St. Louis itself.[2] The systems were rated by panels of schoolmen in such a way that scores of degree of bureaucratization were available for each. For most of the statistical analyses, the systems were

---

2. Details of the study, of which this article is a partial summary, are given in Moeller (1962). This study was part of a larger project, Project No. 929, U.S. Office of Education, Cooperative Research Program, "Teacher Perceptions of Administrator Behavior," in which W. W. Charters, Jr. was the principal investigator.

categorized on the basis of the scores as highly bureaucratic and less bureaucratic. Superintendents of the systems were visited by the research staff for authorization to contact teachers, who, once approval was given, were randomly selected from faculty rosters. Twenty elementary school and twenty secondary school teachers were chosen, whenever faculty size permitted. They were given a questionnaire, which included measures of sense of power, and obtained information on length of service in the school and a number of other variables. By follow-up procedures, the final return rate reached 88 per cent of all teachers sampled, or 692 responses, of which 30 had to be discarded for lack of sufficient data and other reasons.

The primary analysis compared the sense of power scores of teachers in systems varying in the degree of bureaucratization. Although the school systems were alike in several gross features—for example, all were public systems with twelve grades—it was necessary to conceptualize and measure a number of additional features of the environments and of the teachers which could affect sense of power and render spurious the relationship expected between bureaucratization and sense of power. Most of the statistical analyses for testing the principal hypothesis involved only teachers who had been teaching in the particular school system four years or longer. This limitation was based on the assumption that issues of power with respect to school system affairs become salient only after teachers had come to terms with the procedures and problems of classroom instruction.

Method

Measure of Sense of Power

Sense of power was conceived as a continuum. At one end are teachers who feel unlimited in the degree to which they can affect school system policy, and at the other end are those who feel totally powerless to influence its direction in any way. A set of Likert-form questionnaire items was prepared, tested in a pilot group of 100 classroom teachers, and subjected to a Guttman scale analysis. Six items with marginal distributions well distributed over a range between 0.2 and 0.8 and with low error counts were selected for the final measure. These six items constituting the sense of power scale are:

In the school system where I work, a teacher like myself . . .
a. Believes he has some control over what textbooks will be used in the classrooms.
b. Feels he does not know what is going on in the upper levels of administration.
c. Never has a chance to work on school committees which make important decisions for the school system.
d. Considers that he has little to say over what teachers will work with him on his job.

    e. Usually can find ways to get system-wide policies changed if he feels strongly enough about them.

    f. Feels he has little to say about important system-wide policies relating to teaching.

Teachers responded to each item by choosing "strongly agree," "agree," "maybe and maybe not," "disagree," or "strongly disagree."

For the purpose of scoring, responses to each item were dichotomized: a "disagree" or "strongly disagree" response was assigned a positive value and one of the other three alternatives a negative value. (In Items *a* and *e* the procedure was reversed; "agree" and "strongly agree" alternatives had the positive value.)

Later, using the responses of the teachers in the main study, scale analysis was again conducted to determine whether unidimensionality could be cross-validated. The six items were scaled in the same order as before and gave a coefficient of reproducibility of 0.93, when chance reproducibility would have given 0.85.

Measure of Bureaucratization

Development of a measure of the degree of bureaucratization among public school systems was hindered by the fact that American schools are typically highly bureaucratic organizations, governed by a complex body of law, and characterized by an elaborate division of labor and formal structure of administrative authority. Teachers are certified for their jobs on criteria of technical competence and usually are promoted on the basis of seniority. Consequently, distinctions drawn among school systems must necessarily be within a relatively narrow range on a continuum of bureaucratization.[3]

Using an eight-item forced-choice instrument, based on Blau's characterization of bureaucracy, a group of persons with first-hand knowledge of school systems in the area made judgments which provided the data for ordering the twenty systems on a scale of bureaucratization. The method of scaling followed, in general, the procedures outlined by Riley, Riley, and Toby (1954, chapter 5) for object scales based upon collective responses. Each of the twenty systems was rated by three, four, or five judges. If a majority of judges chose the bureaucratic alternative on a given item when rating a school, a positive entry was made in the scaling matrix; otherwise a negative entry was made. In this way a single set of ratings over the eight items was obtained for each system based upon the majority response of the system's judges. A Guttman scale analysis was performed, but with reference to the objects of the ratings, the school systems.

---

3. For this reason, a measure such as Udy's (1958), which covers a far wider band on the continuum, was not suitable.

The scaling procedure arranged the pairs of items from most to least bureaucratic, as shown in Table 1. The bureaucratic and nonbureaucratic alternatives are listed separately in the table. In the forms used by judges, however, the alternatives were intermixed and the pairs of items were listed in a different order.

Table 1

FORCED-CHOICE MEASURES OF BUREAUCRATIZATION OF SCHOOL
SYSTEMS WITH SCALE WEIGHTS.

BUREAUCRATIC ALTERNATIVE	NONBUREAUCRATIC ALTERNATIVE	SCALE WEIGHT
A uniform course of study is developed or specified for the system, and teachers are expected to follow it.	If there is a course of study recommended in the system, teachers may depart from it or alter it to suit their own tastes.	8
The superintendent or school board members are likely to communicate with their employees only through established channels.	The superintendent or school board members are likely to talk directly to any person in their employ about school business.	7
Uniform procedures are set up for hiring and dismissing teachers and are applied in all cases.	Procedures for hiring or dismissing teachers depend upon the circumstances and may vary from one case to another.	6
It is next to impossible for administrators or nonteaching personnel to lose their jobs unless they violate a specific regulation regarding their job performance.	Administrators and nonteaching personnel may be dismissed for a variety of reasons other than incompetency in performing their job.	5
Decisions tend to be made by administrators on the basis of established, written school policies.	Decisions tend to be made by administrators on the merits of issues as they arise, without reliance on established policy.	4
The job of each member of the school system is clearly defined, and he knows exactly where his responsibility begins and where it ends.	In defining his job, each member of the school system is likely to "play by ear" and fill in where needed.	3
Each member in the school system is directly responsible to someone higher in authority for his work.	Little emphasis is placed on laying out the lines of authority in the system.	2
A standard policy determines where on a salary schedule the new teacher will be placed.	Starting salaries and other conditions of employment for new teachers vary from one case to another, depending on how badly the system needs them.	1

The limited number of objects (school systems) used in the scale analysis makes the coefficient of reproducibility meaningless, but interrater reliability, following the analysis of variance design proposed by Ebel (1951) when several raters are used, was computed to be 0.47. This statistic, however, underestimates the interrater correlation, since it does not permit the removal of between-rater variance.

A parallel scale analysis was followed with the same data to determine the bureaucratic bias of the various judges. A school system might achieve a high score by having as its judges persons who were inclined to see a great deal of bureaucracy in any school they rated. The subject scale of bureaucracy[4] (in which judges rather than school systems were ranked) indicated that systematic differences existed among judges in their inclinations to choose the bureaucratic alternative in rating school systems. Crosstabulations of subject and object scores, however, showed the correlation, as estimated by the contingency coefficient, to be essentially zero; therefore school system scores on bureaucratization appeared to be independent of the bureaucratic bias of the judges who rated them.

The scale analyses of bureaucracy ratings violated one of the principal assumptions underlying the method—that there be sufficient cases to afford stability to the scale patterns—but they were pursued as an alternative to an even more arbitrary procedure, the construction of a simple index. Only a study conducted on a far larger sample of ratings could verify the unidimensionality which was assumed for this measure.

Control Variables

A number of attributes of school systems, of individual teachers, and of teachers' positions within school systems were also measured, so that they could be introduced as controls in the study. The following variables, suspected of affecting the sense of power of teachers, were singled out as especially relevant.

1. CLIMATE OF REPRESSIVE AUTHORITY. The investigators believed that feelings of powerlessness could be generated in the relatively nonbureaucratized systems under a superintendent whose leadership style was coercive and oppressive. Consequently, a rough measure of teachers' perceptions of the repressiveness of the administrative climate was developed and used to control for this factor. Four items were selected from the Leadership Behavior Description Questionnaire (Halpin, 1957), asking teachers to describe the frequency with which their superintendent—"Rules teachers with an iron hand," "Speaks to teachers in a manner not to be questioned," "Refuses to explain his actions to teachers," and "Acts without

---

4. Again a collective scale was used: judges were scored positive or negative on each item according to the proportion of school systems to which they attributed the "bureaucratic" alternative.

consulting his teachers." A simple index was contrived by weighting the frequency categories and summing teacher responses over the school system.

2. TEACHERS IN POSITIONS OF RESPONSIBILITY. Teachers who hold positions of substantial responsibility in the system might well manifest higher scores on sense of power than their colleagues without such assignments. This variable would have a spurious influence on the results if, in addition, positions of responsibility were more widely distributed among teachers in the less bureaucratic systems. The difference in sense of power between the school systems created thereby could be mistakenly attributed to the more pervasive environmental influence under investigation. Items on the teacher questionnaire asked about extra-classroom responsibilities, and responses were coded according to their significance in the school's power structure.

3. RELATIONS WITH SCHOOL OFFICIALS. Even in the absence of formal positions of responsibility, teachers might have personal access to school board members, superintendents, and other officials by virtue of extra-school friendship ties which could enhance their feelings of power. Such informal avenues to policymakers almost certainly would be more common in the less bureaucratic systems, typical of small towns or rural communities, and this advantage would render spurious any relationship observed between degree of bureaucratization and teachers' sense of power. An index of particularistic relations was obtained through the teacher questionnaire by responses indicating a visiting relationship and/or a first-name relationship between the teacher and school officers.

4. LENGTH OF SERVICE. Although the investigators intended to limit the study principally to teachers of relatively long tenure in the schools—four years or more—it seemed important to exercise even closer control over length of service. Teachers who remain in the systems for extensive periods of time should find themselves favorably situated in the informal if not the formal power structure. Seniority is a significant fact in most American public schools, bringing not only higher salaries but rights and privileges and usually greater responsibility in policy decisions. It is highly probable that older teachers have served under several sets of school officers, or if not, that they are known intimately by the officials and parents in the community. Length of service was expected to operate in two ways to affect sense of power: first, to enhance directly teachers' feelings of capability to influence affairs of the school, and second to expose the teachers longer to the diffuse influence of the organizational environment, increasing the difference between those in the highly bureaucratic systems and those in the less bureaucratic systems with respect to sense of power.

5. SEX, SOCIAL CLASS, AND TEACHING LEVEL. Teachers' sex and social class (measured by father's occupation) were introduced as controls

since, as noted earlier, they are known to correlate with alienation. Teaching level was examined because of the evidence that elementary and secondary teachers constitute markedly different populations.[5]

Role of Teachers' Organizations

A final factor, not strictly a control variable, which entered into the analysis was evidence about teachers' organizations in the various school systems. One consequence of teachers' position in the power hierarchy of the school is the emergence of associations through which they seek to redress the power imbalance. Bureaucratization of the school may well lead to feelings of powerlessness among teachers, but it may also lead to the development of groups which effectively restore the sense of power. The hypothesized differences in sense of power could be obscured by such a countervailing force.

Evidence was obtained, therefore, on the existence and nature of associations to which the teacher could turn to reverse an unfavorable administrative decision. Teacher responses indicated the availability of three types of association: (1) local groups affiliated with the National Education Association, (2) "teacher welfare committees," members of which usually are chosen by popular vote of classroom teachers in a particular school system, and (3) labor union locals affiliated with the American Federation of Teachers. Following Lieberman (1956, pp. 281-296), the investigators assumed the most effective association in providing redress of power for teachers would be the teachers' union, the least effective the local professional association of the N.E.A., with the welfare committees falling between the other two. The investigators hypothesized that the more highly bureaucratized systems would have the more effective teachers' associations and, where they did not, the sense of power among the teachers would be inordinately low.

Results

Control Variables

The relationship between teachers' sense of power and the control variables generally followed expectations.

1. CLIMATE OF REPRESSIVE AUTHORITY. The climate of repressive authority, measured by teacher responses to a four-item description of the superintendent's leadership style, was found to be related to sense of power. School systems characterized by an arbitrary, oppressive style of administration (high mean scores on repressive authority) also tended to be those in

5. See, for example, Ryans (1960).

which teachers' mean scores on sense of power were low. Contrary to expectation, repressive authority was as common in the highly bureaucratic as in the less bureaucratic schools.

2. TEACHERS IN POSITIONS OF RESPONSIBILITY. These showed significantly higher scores in sense of power than teachers without such responsibilities, but highly bureaucratic and less bureaucratic systems did not differ in the proportions of their staffs occupying responsible positions.

3. RELATIONS WITH SCHOOL OFFICIALS. Teachers reporting relations of friendship with school officials also scored higher on sense of power than those lacking personal contacts; in this case, however, particularistic relationships with school officials were reported considerably more frequently in the less bureaucratic than in the highly bureaucratic systems, and it was clear that this variable would have to be introduced as a control.

4. LENGTH OF TEACHERS' SERVICE. This variable was found to be closely related to sense of power. Moreover, systems differed greatly in the proportion of high-seniority teachers in their faculties, with the highly bureaucratic systems having more teachers of long service. Length of service, therefore, had to be controlled so that its effects would not obscure the expected difference between the two organizational types.

5. SEX, SOCIAL CLASS, AND TEACHING LEVEL. Males felt a greater sense of power than females, a finding in accord with other studies; and elementary school teachers felt a greater sense of power than secondary school teachers. A cross-tabulation of sex and teaching level revealed one subgroup with a strikingly high sense of power—the male elementary school teacher (although male elementary teachers were very few in number). The two types of systems did not differ, however, in the proportions of either males or elementary school teachers on their staffs. Also in accord with previous studies, social class origin was found to be directly associated with sense of power; teachers from professional homes were highest and those with labor origins lowest, while the business-managerial and the clerical-white collar groups fell in this order in between. Teachers from farm families, surprisingly, were second highest in their feelings of sense of power. Since highly bureaucratic systems drew more heavily from the upper social class levels and less heavily from farm origins for their staffs than the less bureaucratic systems, this variable, too, had to be controlled in tests of the principal hypothesis.

In brief, all of the control variables measured in this study were significantly related to teachers' sense of power. The only variables to which a difference between highly and less bureaucratic systems might be attributed, however, were particularistic relations, length of service, and social class. There was a disproportionate distribution between the two types of school system on these variables, but an equal distribution on the other variables. (Analyses, nevertheless, were carried out with all control variables in an attempt to discover interaction effects with bureaucratization.)

Primary Hypothesis

With respect to the primary hypothesis, analyses demonstrated a significant difference between types of systems in sense of power, but in a direction opposite to that hypothesized. Teachers in highly bureaucratic systems had a significantly higher, not lower, sense of power than those in less bureaucratic systems. A rank correlation between degree of bureaucratization and sense of power means over the twenty systems was .40

Table 2

TEACHERS' SENSE OF POWER IN HIGHLY BUREAUCRATIC AND LESS
BUREAUCRATIC SCHOOL SYSTEMS WITH LENGTH OF SERVICE, SOCIAL
CLASS ORIGINS, AND PARTICULARISTIC RELATIONS CONTROLLED.

	MEAN SENSE OF POWER	
CONTROL VARIABLES	HIGHLY BUREAUCRATIC	LESS BUREAUCRATIC
Length of Service (years)	N = 329	N = 317
1	3.76	2.61
2-3	2.48	2.33
4-5	2.79	2.18
6-7	2.63	2.41
8-9	3.20	2.63
10-19	3.48	2.71
20 and over	3.61	3.04
Mean	3.14	2.51
Social class origin	N = 328	N = 313
Professional	3.29	2.81
Business, managerial	3.15	2.41
Clerical, white collar	3.32	2.25
Labor	2.75	2.21
Farm	3.23	2.83
Mean	3.15	2.50
*Particularistic relations**	N = 220	N = 178
Visiting relation	3.73	2.65
First-name basis, no visits	2.91	2.20
No visits, no first-name basis ...	3.03	2.61
Mean	3.19	2.56

* Data for teachers with 4 or more years of service.

$(p<.05)$.[6] Furthermore, the greater sense of power in highly bureaucratic schools was not affected by the introduction of statistical controls on the three variables requiring it. The means in Table 2 show, for example, that teachers in the highly bureaucratic systems exceeded teachers in the less bureaucratic systems at every level of length of service, as was true for social class and for particularistic relations with school officials. In all cases the main effect of bureaucratization was statistically significant well beyond the .01 level (see Table 3). Thus, the principal hypothesis was unequivocally refuted.

In exploring effects of the other control variables on scores of sense of power, positions of extra-classroom responsibility revealed a significant interaction with bureaucratization. This variable was related to teachers'

Table 3

ANALYSES OF VARIANCE OF SENSE OF POWER SCORES FOR
BUREAUCRATIZATION BY LENGTH OF SERVICE, SOCIAL CLASS
ORIGINS, AND PARTICULARISTIC RELATIONS.

SOURCE	SUM OF SQUARES	df	MEAN SQUARE	F
Length of Service				
Bureaucracy	2.05	1	2.05	26.93**
Length of Service	1.50	6	0.25	3.29**
Among lengths of service	1.33	5	0.26	3.57**
First year vs. other service ...	0.16	1	0.16	2.24
Error		634	0.07	
Bureaucracy × service	0.75	6	0.12	1.64
Social Class Origin				
Bureaucracy	1.02	1	1.02	20.51**
Social class	0.46	4	0.12	2.40*
Bureaucracy × Class	0.13	4	0.03	0.57
Error		604	0.05	
Particularistic Relations				
Bureaucracy	0.81	1	0.81	26.26**
Particularistic relations	0.41	2	0.20	6.55**
Bureaucracy × Particularistic relations	0.11	2	0.06	1.77
Error		392	0.03	

  * $p < .05$.
  ** $p < .01$.

Note: Numerals beyond the second decimal place used in the calculations are omitted in the table. Since subclass frequencies are unequal, the approximation procedure recommended by Walker and Lev was followed; see Walker and Lev (1953, pp. 381-382).

6. A plot of sense of power means against the score indicating degree of bureaucratization for each school showed the relationship to be essentially linear.

sense of power only in the highly bureaucratic systems; it had no effect on sense of power in the less bureaucratic schools.

The climate of repressive authority failed to reveal an anticipated inter-action with bureaucratization. In highly bureaucratic administrations where reliance is placed upon rationality and impersonal structures to achieve organizational objectives, the investigators expected that repressive author-ity would only rarely be reported; and if it were reported, the personal style of a single administrative official would have little effect upon sense of power. Neither prediction was supported by the findings.[7] As already noted, climates of repressive authority were reported as often in the highly bureaucratic as in the less bureaucratic systems, and the impact of adminis-trative style on sense of power scores was observed in both types of schools. Apparently, rationality in bureaucratic organization does not preclude the use of restrictive and coercive measures. As Gouldner (1959, p. 403) has noted, bureaucracies may be punishment-centered, using compulsion and sanctions; or bureaucracies may be representative, using human relations techniques, information feedback, and education to attain compliance with organizational objectives.

Secondary Hypothesis

In spite of the lack of confirmation of the principal hypothesis, it is still reasonable to examine the second hypothesis and ask whether the difference in sense of power between teachers in highly bureaucratic and less bureau-cratic systems was induced by exposure to the organizational environment or whether it was due to some differential in the selection of teachers. On the assumption that a feeling of sense of power was the result of the situation, it was hypothesized that the longer persons are exposed to the two environments the more their scores of sense of power would diverge. The plots of scores of sense of power among teachers with varying lengths of service in the two types of system displayed in Figure 1 (based upon the means in Table 2) provide a rough test of the hypothesis. The test is limited, of course, by the fact that the data are cross-sectional rather than longitudinal. It is clear that the difference in sense of power does not become magnified with length of exposure to the contrasting environments. Especially noteworthy is the fact that in their first year of teaching respon-dents in the two types of systems differed as much in sense of power as any

---

7. Half of the highly bureaucratic systems were above the median of all systems ranked on degree of administrator repressiveness. When systems were ranked simultane-ously on administrator repressiveness and teacher sense of power, using system means of teachers' reports, the rank-order correlation between the two was $-.43$ for the highly bureaucratized schools, and $-.57$ for the less bureaucratized schools ($N = 10$ in each case). For the second prediction to be confirmed, the correlation for highly bureaucratized schools would have had to be substantially closer to zero than the correlation for less bureaucratized systems.

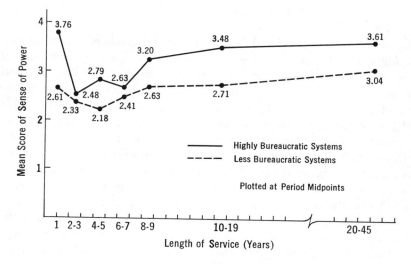

Figure 1. Mean Scores of Sense of Power by Length of Service in Highly Bureaucratic and Less Bureaucratic Systems.

other tenure group. A t test showed this difference to be statistically significant beyond the .05 level. These data were obtained after the first-year respondents had been teaching for five months, and it is possible that the scores of teachers in the two types of systems would have been more similar had they been measured earlier in the year. On the other hand, new teachers normally are so engrossed in coping with problems of classroom teaching in their first few years that they probably have little inclination to consider their position with respect to the school system.

Since the difference between highly bureaucratic and less bureaucratic systems did not increase with longer exposure to the system (longer tenure), the higher scores in sense of power in highly bureaucratic systems may be a function of the tendency of these systems to recruit teachers with initially greater feeling of power. The basis of differential selectivity was not clear, even after the investigators conducted further analyses on the first-year teachers alone. There were attributes measured in this study which distinguished beginning teachers in highly bureaucratic systems from beginners in the less bureaucratic systems and which, simultaneously, related to their scores on sense of power. Examined were such variables as sex, prior teaching experience, size of the building unit in which teachers worked, teaching level, social-class origins, home-town teaching, as well as positions of responsibility, repressive authority, particularism, and the like. In no instance, however, did the difference between first-year teachers in the two types of systems disappear when they were equated on these variables.

Role of Teachers' Organizations

Remaining to be considered is the role of the teachers' organizations in affecting sense of power. Earlier it was proposed that the emergence of a strong association of classroom teachers could offset the feelings of powerlessness among teaching staffs in the highly bureaucratic school systems. None of the available evidence, however, supports this conjecture. First, what the investigators considered on *a priori* grounds to be the most effective association in enhancing teachers' sense of power—the teachers' union—was found to be the least effective. Highest scores on sense of power were associated with the existence of teacher welfare committees, next highest with the professional associations. Furthermore, such organizations did not appear to be the result of a high degree of bureaucratization. Five of the ten less bureaucratic systems and six of the ten highly bureaucratic systems had either a union or welfare committee. (All but one of the twenty systems had NEA-affiliated professional associations.) Finally, considering only the highly bureaucratic schools, scores of sense of power clearly were not higher in the systems with a welfare committee or union than in systems where these supposedly powerful organizations were absent (see Table 4). The overriding influence of the bureaucratization variable is obvious irrespective of the teachers' associations.

Discussion

Bureaucratization of school systems in this study was assumed to vary over a narrow band of a unidimensional continuum. While results of the scale analyses of the bureaucratization measure were not inconsistent with the assumption of unidimensionality, the number of cases was insufficient for the scale analyses to test it. Certain of Udy's (1959) data challenge the assumption, although he dealt with a far broader spectrum of organizations than modern American school systems. Several anomalies in the relation of bureaucratization and size of schools are worth noting. The largest school system of all, with nearly 700 teachers and an administrative and clerical staff of 160 persons, was one of the three lowest on the measure of bureaucratization. It had the same position as a system with 38 teachers and an administrative-clerical staff of 7 and another system with 74 teachers and 18 administrators and clerks. Two small, quasi-rural systems had bureaucratization scores above the median. The rank correlation between degree of bureaucratization and school system size was a modest 0.43. Patently, the measure of bureaucratization used in the present study demands further examination in a larger sample of systems in which objective indicators of bureaucratization are also employed.[8]

8. For the development of objective indicators of the complexity of work structures in public school systems, see Keene (1962, ch. 2).

What of the finding that teachers' sense of power was greater, contrary to expectations, in the highly bureaucratic than in the less bureaucratic

Table 4

SENSE OF POWER MEANS IN HIGHLY BUREAUCRATIC AND LESS
BUREAUCRATIC SCHOOL SYSTEMS AS RELATED TO TYPES OF
TEACHERS' ORGANIZATIONS.

TYPE OF ORGANIZATION*	HIGHLY BUREAUCRATIC			LESS BUREAUCRATIC		
	N OF SCHOOLS	SENSE OF POWER	(N OF TEACHERS)	N OF SCHOOLS	SENSE OF POWER	(N OF TEACHERS)
Union	1	2.65	(33)	1	2.19	(23)
Welfare committee ..	5	3.25	(167)	4	2.89	(124)
Local professional only	4	3.34	(131)	5	2.40	(170)

* Nineteen of the 20 school systems had local professional associations affiliated with the National Education Association. The one exception, a highly bureaucratic system, had a labor-affiliated union instead. With that exception, existence of a union or welfare committee in a system is in addition to the presence of a local professional association.

schools? It clearly challenges the conception of the nature of bureaucratic organizations with which the investigators began the study.[9] But the various analyses also bring into question the assumption that the difference is traceable to the character of the organizational environment in which the teachers perform their work. Taking all the analyses into consideration, the evidence on the situational specificity of teachers' sense of power is mixed. On the one hand, it may be that teachers in the highly bureaucratic systems bring a strong sense of power into the schools at the time of their employment, although the personal attributes associated with the selectivity remain obscure in the present data. Differences in scores of sense of power were as great among first-year teachers as for any group of longer service.

On the other hand, the remarkable drop in sense of power in the second through the seventh year of teaching, observable in Figure 1 for both types of systems, suggests that perhaps some specific organizational phenomenon operates across school systems to eliminate those with a high sense of power at the end of the first year of teaching. It is difficult to attribute this striking pattern of findings to forces which are not associated with the organizational setting, but longitudinal data are required to clarify the issue.[10] Still other evidence supports the proposition of situational specificity. When the super-

9. Implications of the findings for the conception of bureaucracy were elaborated by the senior author in the principal report; see Moeller (1962b, ch. 4). An abbreviated consideration of the implications appeared in Moeller (1962a, p. 4).

10. Longitudinal data have recently become available. By identifying which of Moeller's first-year teachers remained to teach in their school systems in the second year, Charters (1964) demonstrated that selective resignations could not account for the apparent drop in sense of power.

Hopson (1966) failed to confirm the unusually high sense of power scores among new groups of first-year teachers but showed a substantial decline in scores of Moeller's first-year teachers when they were re-measured after four years in their systems. Hopson's data also replicated the sense of power differences by level of bureaucratization.

intendent produced a climate of repressive authority, sense of power was low; when the climate was less restrictive, sense of power was higher. When teachers engaged in a visiting relationship with school officials, their sense of power was higher than when they did not. And when teachers were in positions of responsibility, their sense of power scores responded correspondingly, albeit only in the highly bureaucratic systems. Thus, it seems that feelings of power are sensitive to some organizational circumstances.

That scores of sense of power were related to teachers' extra-classroom positions of responsibility only in the highly bureaucratic systems suggests that these positions of responsibility did not constitute avenues to power in the less bureaucratic systems. Perhaps the greater visibility of the teacher in the smaller less bureaucratic school reduced the importance of the formal committee structure as a source of influence with respect to educational policies. The informal road to influence, at least as captured in the measure of particularistic relations with school officials, may have made the extra-classroom position of responsibilities less important sources of influence. This speculation is based upon the assumption that the scores of sense of power reflect in part the objective circumstances of power in the organization.

In sum, teachers' feelings of power to influence school system policies appear to be affected by variables lying within the teachers themselves and in the organizational structure of the school systems. The initial hypothesis on the impact of a diffuse bureaucratic ethos upon sense of power was not upheld, but several specified attributes of organizational structure were shown to enhance or depress the scores of sense of power. In some degree, teachers' feelings of power seem to reflect their objective positions of power within the schools' social system. In some degree, too, feelings of power may reflect more general attitudes associated with the teachers' sex, social-class origins, and still unspecified attributes which served to differentiate teachers selected for employment in the highly bureaucratic from those in the less bureaucratic school systems.

References

BLAU, P. M.   *Bureaucracy in modern society.* New York: Random House, 1956.

BROWNING, C. J., FARMER, M. E., KIRK, H. D. and MITCHELL, G. D.   Letter to the editor, *American Sociological Review*, 1961, 26, 780-781.

CAMPBELL, A., GURIN, G. and MILLER, W. E.   *The voter decides.* Evanston: Row, Peterson, 1954.

CHARTERS, W. W., Jr.   Sense of power and length of service among public school teachers: some further analyses. Unpublished manuscript, 1964.

CLARK, J. P.   Measuring alienation within a social system. *American Sociological Review*, 1959, 24, 849-852.

DEAN, D. G.   Alienation: its meaning and measurement. *American Sociological Review,* 1961, 26, 753-758.

DOUVAN, E. and WALKER, A. M.   The sense of effectiveness in public affairs. *Psychological Monographs,* 1956, 70 (22, Whole No. 429).

EBEL, R. L.   Estimation of the reliability of ratings. *Psychometrika,* 1951, 16, 407-424.

GOULDNER, A. W.   Organizational analysis. In Merton, R. K. and Cottrell, L. S. (Eds.) *Sociology today.* New York: Basic Books, 1959. Pp. 400-427.

HALPIN, A. W.   *Leadership behavior of school superintendents.* School-Community Development Study Monograph No. 4. Columbus: Ohio State University, 1957.

HOPSON, J. A.   The sense of power of short-tenure teachers. Ph. D. dissertation, Washington University, 1966.

LIEBERMAN, M.   *Education as a profession.* Englewood Cliffs, N.J.: Prentice-Hall, 1956.

MOELLER, G. H.   Bureaucracy and teachers' sense of power. *Administrator's Notebook,* 1962, 9, 4. (a)

MOELLER, G. H.   The relationship between bureaucracy in school system organization and teachers' sense of power. Unpublished doctoral dissertation, Washington University, 1962. (b)

PEARLIN, L. I.   Alienation from work: A study of nursing personnel. *American Sociological Review,* 1962, 27, 314-326.

RILEY, M. W., RILEY, J. W. and TOBY, J.   *Sociological studies in scale analysis.* New Brunswick, N.J.: Rutgers University, 1954.

RYANS, D. G.   *Characteristics of teachers: Their description, comparison and appraisal.* Washington: American Council on Education, 1960.

SEEMAN, M.   On the meaning of alienation. *American Sociological Review,* 1959, 24, 783-791.

SHIPTON, J. M. and BELISLE, E. L.   Who criticizes the public schools? *Phi Delta Kappan,* 1956, 37, 303-307.

UDY, S. Jr.   "Bureaucratic" elements in organizations: Some research findings. *American Sociological Review,* 1958, 23, 415-418.

UDY, S. Jr.   "Bureaucracy" and "rationality" in Weber's organization theory: An empirical study. *American Sociological Review,* 1959, 24, 791-795.

WALKER, H. M. and LEV, J.   *Statistical inference.* New York: Holt, Rinehart and Winston, 1953.

※ ※ ※ ※ ※

The French sociologist Tarde wrote in 1903:

> To innovate, to discover, to awake for an instant, the individual must escape, for the time being, from his social surroundings. Such unusual audacity makes him super-social rather than social.

Outsiders, cosmopolitans, strangers *do* have a restless, magical, change-bringing quality to them. The newcomer farmer tries hybrid corn sooner; the local civil rights disturbance is often erroneously attributed to "outside agitators" (i.e., who among us insiders could even *consider* agitating?).

Carlson explores these matters in relation to a focal role in education—that of superintendent. It turns out that those who enter this almost unreasonably demanding position from inside their own school systems are quite different—and are treated quite differently—in most respects from those coming from outside.

The study shows well how a variety of field research methods can be used to examine a powerful variable. Carlson employs observation, interviews, and the analysis of data available through documents and other research projects to explore the ramifications of the inside/outside distinction.

In passing, the reader may wish to reflect on the personality orientations that may underlie the active, seeking behavior of the "career-bound" outsider, as compared with the waiting, passive behavior of the "place-bound" insider. Do they apply to the behavior of children in school as well? Smith's article in this book says they may be relevant to the way college students grow in the Peace Corps.

Succession and Performance Among School Superintendents*

Richard O. Carlson

All enduring organizations must cope with succession. To minimize dependence on individuals as such, organizations are structured around roles, offices, or jobs. Replacement of an individual, however, is potentially a significant event in the development of an organization, particularly when a key office is involved. Beyond its developmental significance, succession can be stressful for members and clients of an organization; therefore organization theory should deal with succession and organizational responses to succession.[1] This paper develops and tests some propositions about succession of the chief executive in public school systems, taking the origin of the successor as a variable. Although the data have a specific setting, they may carry important implications for succession in other organizations.

With few exceptions, school superintendents are drawn from the ranks of those already employed in public schools. To obtain the superintendent's credential, they must provide evidence of successful experience as a classroom teacher. Usually by the time the credential is earned, some administrative experience has also been gained. Ultimately two alternatives are open to the would-be superintendent. One is to wait for the superintendency to become available in his own school system; the other is to seek a superintendency in some other school system.

The man who waits simply remains in his school system until the superintendency is his. His career is one of ascent up the hierarchy in one school system, although he may have changed school systems prior to becoming superintendent. The man who waits can be called an insider. He has been promoted from within. Ordinarily the insider completes his career as superintendent in the one home system. If he is removed from the superintendency before retirement age has been reached, he often takes an existing or frequently new lower-level administrative position in the same home district.

* From *Administrative Science Quarterly*, 1961, 6, 210-227. Used by permission of the author and publisher.

1. The meager systematic literature on succession and its consequences is largely descriptive in nature and tends to overemphasize the disruptive aspects. Propositions are seldom developed or tested. There are, however, notable exceptions. Trow (1960) has tested some propositions about succession rates in small groups, and Scheff (1960) has attempted to account for individual differences in the resistance to change that frequently follows succession.

The man who does not wait, but seeks a superintendency wherever it is to be found, can be called an outsider. His career is always spread over two or more school systems. He has never served the district in which he is superintendent in any capacity other than superintendent. Ordinarily his career does not stop with one superintendency.

Insiders and outsiders differ in the importance they assign to career and place. Both have made sacrifices to obtain the superintendent's credential. The insider, however, seems to want the career of superintendent only if it can be had in a specific place, his home school system. He puts place of employment above career as superintendent. The insider is place-bound. The outsider puts career above place. He leaves the home school system and takes a superintendency elsewhere. The outsider is career-bound.

Whether to wait for the superintendency or seek it is a major decision in the career of an individual. The differences that are suggested by the commitments of place-bound and career-bound superintendents are so basic that they should be apparent in the ways in which these two types relate to their organizations. This paper, taken from a larger study on administrative succession in public schools,[2] presents some evidence of these differences.

Some of the data presented relate to the job to be done by insiders and outsiders as defined by the employers. These data spell out the conditions of a successful performance in office. Other data bear on relevant personality factors of superintendents with different origins.[3] Still other data bridge the gap between personality and job, and deal with action in office. Significant events in the cycle of succession are used as the analytic scheme. This facilitates an intertwining of factors that pertain to the job to be done, personality factors, and the superintendent's acts as successor. First, attention is given to the conditions of employment of inside and outside successors. Then the concern shifts to the early activities of successors and the differences between insiders and outsiders. After the prominence gained by the two types is examined, the analysis centers on tenure of employment and succession patterns.

Continuous observations and interviews were made over a nine-month period in four school systems that had new superintendents. Leads gained from these observations and interviews were followed in lengthy interviews with an additional twenty superintendents. Data were taken from selected reports and documents, and a secondary analysis was made of raw data collected for two published studies dealing with superintendents.

2.   The larger study (Carlson, 1962) was supported by a post-doctoral fellowship from the Administrative Science Center, University of Pittsburgh. I am indebted to my colleagues at the Administrative Science Center for their counsel.

3.   Several researchers have gathered data on the personalities of individuals having commitments similar to those of place-bound and career-bound individuals. Marvick (1954) has written about "institutionalists" and "specialists" in a federal agency. Some differences between "locals" and "cosmopolitans" on a college faculty have been pointed to by Gouldner (1957, 1958). And Avery (1959) has gathered data on potential "passive" and "active" managers. There seems to be a likeness among institutionalists, locals, passive managers, and insiders as well as among specialists, cosmopolitans, active managers, and outsiders.

Conditions of Employment

When a school board chooses a superintendent it has a free hand. Seniority rights do not infringe on the appointment. It is not reviewed at a higher level. The board can make the appointment solely in the light of what it believes will be best for the board and the school system. Under what conditions then does a school board deem it best to appoint an insider as the new superintendent? When does it prefer an outsider?

Observations and interviews in the four school systems indicate that, if the administration of the school system is perceived as satisfactory, the appointment will go either to an insider or outsider.[4] If the school board perceives the administration as unsatisfactory, the appointment will go to an outsider. This trend was evident in the districts under observation, and in histories collected on thirty-six other successions. No insider reported that the school board was unhappy with the way the schools were being administered at the time he was appointed. Typical of their responses were: "I succeeded a very successful man," "I think they were satisfied," "Now you'll always have an individual who is dissatisfied with a particular part of a school system but generally they seemed to be proud." On the other hand, in no case where the administration was considered unsatisfactory was an insider appointed.

The conditions of employment indicate that the school board will be satisfied if the insider "keeps things as they are," but they expect an outsider to make changes and are only satisfied when he does. School boards expect a creative performance from outsiders and are happy with a stabilizing performance from insiders.

It appears that the insider, because of his history in the organization, is so bound up by the internal and external interpersonal structure that if appointed at a time when changes are desired he will be unable or unwilling to make the desired changes. To gain the job as an insider, he had to give more than token support to his predecessor and his predecessor's program. To depart from this program in any major way would signal a change of "face." Such pressures seem to ensure that with an insider the organization will continue along its present path.

Not only is the school board free of a number of important constraints in the selection of the superintendent, but also it is free to determine the salary. The commitments of the insider suggest that it will be easier for the board to come to terms with him than with an outsider, since he appears more interested in making a career in the particular school system

4. It might appear natural for school boards always to appoint an insider when things are going well. After all, the insider knows the school system's background and its history and undoubtedly is well versed in the present programs, problems, sources of support, philosophy, and personnel in the organization and its environment. Sometimes no insider has the necessary experience or credential to be given the superintendency. Or there may be too many qualified insiders, so that selecting one from among them might invite unnecessary grievances or might deepen already-existing factions. In both these cases an outsider is sought.

than in making a career as a superintendent. Further, from what has been said above it appears that the school board is purchasing a service requiring less creativity from the insider than from the outsider. Linking the differences in services expected with the insider's commitments, we should find that insiders accept the job on the terms of the school board while outsiders tend to take the appointment on their own terms. The outsider is in a position to bargain and win; the insider is not interested in bargaining and would probably lose if he did. Table 1 indicates the extent to which out-

Table 1

MEAN SALARIES OF FIRST OR SECOND YEAR: INSIDE AND OUTSIDE
SUCCESSORS BY SCHOOL DISTRICT POPULATION.*

POPULATION OF DISTRICT	MEAN SALARY OF INSIDERS (NUMBER)	MEAN SALARY OF OUTSIDERS (NUMBER)	DIFFERENCE IN FAVOR OF OUTSIDERS
500,000 and over	$19,750 (2)	$22,250 (1)	$2,500
100,000 to 499,999	14,200 (7)	19,200 (8)	5,000
30,000 to 99,999	12,400 (14)	15,000 (15)	2,600
10,000 to 29,999	10,300 (9)	11,500 (42)	1,200
5,000 to 9,999	9,450 (5)	10,450 (21)	1,000
2,500 to 4,999	6,900 (3)	8,100 (15)	1,200

* These data were obtained by a secondary analysis of raw data gathered by the American Association of School Administrators (A.A.S.A.) and the National Education Association (N.E.A.). I wish to express thanks to the N.E.A. and the A.A.S.A. for permission to use raw data from their study (1960).

siders are able to command higher salaries than insiders. The beginning outsider receives from $1,000 to $5,000 more a year than the beginning insider. A similar but less marked difference holds true regardless of time in service.[5]

5. The differences in pay, conditions of employment, and other areas are not necessarily related to the quality of insiders and outsiders. The differences seem to be a function of the definition of the situation. There is no reason to expect that outsiders are more capable administrators than insiders. This explanation is given support by recent research in another setting (McGee, 1960), which suggests that while the University of Texas discriminates against those on the faculty with Ph.D. degrees from the University of Texas as opposed to Ph.D. degrees from other institutions in academic rank, class load, and so on, there is no difference between these two groups in scholarly production. Noting the restriction due to the sample, the author concludes, "There is no reason to believe that the differential treatment of the inbred product is the result of inferior quality on his part."

Further, in a sample of 745 superintendents, 38 marked as appropriate the response that a willingness to accept the salary was a reason for being selected for the superintendency they now held. Nine per cent of the insiders and 3 per cent of the outsiders made this acknowledgment.[6]

Administrative Responses of Successor

The definition of the situation under which insiders are appointed suggests that they will be inclined to keep things pretty much as they are, for after all the employers are happy. The limited evidence available demonstrates that the insider conforms to the expectation that he will not make great changes.

The tendency for new chief executives to become preoccupied with rules and rule making[7] has been noted in at least two other settings—penal (Grusky, 1959), and industrial (Gouldner, 1954). New school superintendents show the same tendency. Rules formalize internal or external commitments of an organization. They are instrumental in establishing the course of an organization and in determining its character. Insiders acted in ways that did not alter the course or establish new commitments. Their rule activities preserved and tightened what existed. In the case of the outsiders observed, about 85 per cent of the effort expended in rule making was in the area of new rules—rules that filled in gaps or rules that took the place of existing ones. Insiders, on the other hand, did not devote any significant amount of time to new rules. Their concern for rules was in publicizing and reinforcing old rules and assessing the extent to which old rules were being followed.

Barnard (1938, p. 159) has cited the "propensity of all organizations to expand," and it has been noted that as organizations expand the administrative component tends to constitute a larger and larger per cent of those employed in the organization (Terrien and Mills, 1955). There is every reason to expect that the addition of individuals to an administrative staff will be related to potentially identifiable organization variables, and no reason to expect that such conditions will take place at random. Leadership change or stability appears to be such a variable. The new chief executive is faced with the problem of loyalty and of building goals into the social structure of the organization. It is somewhat commonplace to see old organizations abandoned or bypassed and new ones created to handle marked changes in orientation and goal. An old agency or organization embodies precedents for action, alliances, and personal loyalties and can muster resistance capable of drastically restricting the full development of a new program. But often, even though new goals are sought or weak ones emphasized, the organization cannot be cast aside; it must be maintained.

6. Secondary analysis of data in A.A.S.A. and N.E.A. (1960).

7. The term "rule" is being used here in a broad way to include such items as definition of work day, procedures for handling paper work and people, and policy statements.

If this is the case, as it is with public schools, the alternative is to cast aside people, bring in new ones, or both.

The conditions of employment suggest that the outsider has reason to "retool" the school system and that the insider does not. Success for the outsider tends to be defined in terms of change. For change to be realized loyalty and commitment to an idea or person must, to some extent, be diffused throughout the organization. The insider does not need to alter loyalties and commitments. For him success lies in keeping the organization committed as it is.

Such reasoning underlies two hypotheses about successors and expansion of the administrative staff. The first hypothesis is that during the early stages of the succession cycle the number of outside successors who add to their central office administrative staff will be greater than the number of inside successors who add to their central office administrative staff.[8] To test the hypothesis the succession and staffing histories of the one hundred largest school districts in California were gathered for the period from 1952 to 1956. The size of the administrative staff of the central office inherited by a new superintendent was compared with the size of the staff two years later. The administrative staff of the central office was taken as the index, for its size is less responsive to increases in numbers of pupils, and therefore more responsive to the wishes of the superintendent than is the size of the total administrative staff. If the pupil enrollment of a district is growing, as was the case with all of these districts, it must provide additional administrative personnel in its new schools. If a district adds a new school, it is not compelled to add certified administrative staff at the central office level, but when an addition is made to the *central* office administrative staff, such an addition is not as directly related to external forces as it is to the discretion of the administrative officers of the school district.

The one hundred districts had a total of thirty-five new superintendents during the four-year period. Twelve of the new superintendents were insiders and twenty-three were outsiders. Three of the twelve insiders and fourteen of the twenty-three outsiders increased the size of their central office administrative staff during their first two years in office. The statistical significance of the difference is beyond the .05 level of confidence[9] and therefore supports the hypothesis that during the early stages of the succession cycle the number of outside successors who add to their central office staff will be greater than the number of inside successors who add to their central office staff.

This hypothesis is based on the assumption that expansion of the administrative hierarchy involves discretion and that it is not directly related to the growth in enrollment. This assumption can be tested by comparing the

8. A somewhat similar but untested proposition to the effect that an outsider as a top executive will utilize an "assistant-to" more frequently than an insider has been advanced by Whisler (1960).

9. This difference yielded a probability of .024 on a one-tailed test using the Fisher Exact Probability Test.

number of additions made to the central office staff over a specified time in school systems of "identical" size and growing at the same rate. The assumption can be considered valid if it can be demonstrated that such school districts do not exhibit an "identical" pattern in the additions to the central office administrative staff.

The second hypothesis relating successors and expansion of the administrative staff is concerned with the impact of the successor on the rate at which positions are added to the administrative staff. It tests the assumption just made and states that during the early stages of the succession cycle, outside successors will add more positions to the central office administrative staff than will "old" superintendents in comparable districts during the same time span, and vice versa for insiders. Each of the thirty-five districts with new superintendents was paired with another district in which: (a) the type of district was the same (i.e., elementary, high school, unified) and the size and pupil growth figures corresponded year by year for the relevant time span with a difference of less than 10 per cent of the enrollment of the district with a new superintendent, (b) the superintendent had been in office at least four years and was therefore "old." Four districts were lost from the sample because these conditions could not be met. If more than one district met the conditions from the total population of the one hundred largest districts, the "twin" was drawn at random from among those in the qualifying group. Eleven districts with inside successors and twenty districts with outside successors could be matched with a "twin."

The eleven districts with new insiders added a total of five positions at the central office level, an average of 0.45 positions per district within two years after the succession, and their "twin" districts of the same size and growth rate with "old" superintendents added fourteen such positions, an average of 1.27 positions per district over the same time span. The twenty districts with new outsiders added thirty-nine positions, an average of 1.9 positions per district within two years of the succession, and their "twin" districts with "old" superintendents added twenty-five positions, an average of 1.25 positions per district over the same time.[10]

The findings support the assumption that newness of the superintendent is a factor bearing on the discretionary act of adding to the central office administrative staff, and further substantiate the notion that outsiders increase the administrative staff more than insiders.

But the findings raise a question. What happens to the rates after the first two years in office? If the rate of additions to the staff remained the same over an extended period, it is obvious that the central office staffs of districts with insiders would become significantly smaller than central office staffs of districts with outsiders.

Ultimately there are two possibilities. One is that over the long run insiders and outsiders create about the same number of new positions, but

---

10. Both differences are statistically significant beyond the .01 level of confidence. The Wilcoxon Matched-Pairs Signed-Ranks Test was used to determine significance.

the positions are created at different times in the succession cycle. It could be argued that, given the needs of the outsider, he creates most of the new positions early in his stay in office, whereas the insider creates them throughout his term of office.

The second possibility is that outsiders create more administrative positions in the central office than insiders. Perhaps given the conditions of employment and commitments of the two types of successors and the head start of the outsider, as shown by the data, the insider would never catch up with the outsider in the number of new administrative staff positions he creates during his term in office. The expansion rates of each may converge toward a mean, but this would still mean that there would be a difference between the number of positions added over time in "identical" districts. This suggestion further implies that, in continually growing school districts, a district might reduce the difference between the size of its central office staff and the mean size for comparable districts as it replaces an insider with an outsider, and the other way around. These explanations are speculative since data are lacking.

Prominence Among Colleagues

Insiders and outsiders are called on to render different types of services to school systems. The data on rule making and staff changes indicate that the two types tend to conform to the expectations formed at the time of employment. Insiders and outsiders also differ in their prominence among colleagues.

The phrase "a comedian's comedian" is a rating one step above superior or excellent. It means that the individual has mastered the important subtleties that are most readily recognized by his colleagues. An insider is not a superintendent's superintendent.

Twenty superintendents, recommended by two knowledgeable judges as being perceptive about the experiences and careers of superintendents, were each asked to name five prominent superintendents within their state. Several factors should be considered before looking at the responses. About one-third of the superintendents in the United States are insiders. They are found in districts of all sizes but hold about one-half of the superintendencies in cities of 100,000 or larger.[11] Their disproportionate representation in large systems might cause a skewing effect in the ratings. On the other hand, insiders usually complete their careers in one school district. This might, to some extent, limit their acquaintance with other superintendents.

The responses of the twenty superintendents were heavily in favor of outsiders. Eighty-three of the one hundred votes were for twenty-nine outsiders, seventeen votes were for three insiders. (One insider received fourteen votes.)

11.   Secondary analysis of data in A.A.S.A. and N.E.A. (1960).

Change and Succession Patterns

The careers of many superintendents are marked by movement from district to district, and school superintendents, like city managers (Floro, 1955), assert that they can hurt the profession and fail to provide proper service by moving too soon or staying too long. One highly regarded elder statesman among superintendents has remarked that he is most proud of the fact that he never left a superintendency voluntarily; he always managed to stir up enough controversy over innovations that he was asked to leave. Another superintendent (Bell, 1955, p. 149) has written: "If a man stays in one administrative post for very many years, he must be tremendously efficient and capable, or else resort to the practice of maintaining his job at the expense of any creditable educational performance in his district."

The commitment of the insider to the community and the school district is made obvious by the fact that he stays and waits for the superintendency. It is to be expected, then, that he places lower value on mobility than the outsider and further that he is more likely to remain in the superintendency longer than the outsider.

A secondary analysis of data gathered by Seeman (1958) shows that insiders' and outsiders' attitudes toward mobility differ significantly.[12] On a scale "whose purpose was to distinguish those for whom mobility interest takes precedence over a wide range of more 'intrinsic' interests (for example, health, family, community)" (Seeman, 1958, p. 642) eleven insiders scored a mean of 69.8 and thirty outsiders a mean of 78.5.[13] The higher the score the greater the interest in mobility. Sample items state: "I wouldn't let my friendship ties in a community stand in the way of moving on to a higher position," "The executive who has his eye on the jobs up the line, just can't go all out for the group he is serving at the moment," "My goal has always been to wind up as head of a small organization that I could guide over the long pull," "If you've got a worthwhile program developing in your present position, I don't think you ought to be really tempted if a bigger job comes your way," "If you stay quite a while in one executive position, you become too concerned with keeping things as they are" (Seeman, 1958, p. 635).

Table 2 shows length of incumbency and origin of 792 superintendents. About 14 per cent of the insiders have held the job twenty or more years and about 6 per cent of the outsiders have been in one job this long. The mean time in office for insiders is ten years and for outsiders eight years. Medians are eight years for insiders and six years for outsiders.

12. I wish to express thanks to Professor Seeman for granting me access to the data gathered for his study.

13. The differences in scores on the scale of attitude toward mobility produced a z-score of 2.44 on the Mann-Whitney Test, which is significant beyond the .01 level of confidence on a one-tailed test.

Table 2

ORIGIN OF SUPERINTENDENT AND LENGTH OF INCUMBENCY*

| | ORIGIN OF SUPERINTENDENT | |
YEARS IN OFFICE	% INSIDERS $N = 279$	% OUTSIDERS $N = 513$
1-2	14.3	19.8
3-4	16.5	17.7
5-9	25.1	28.2
10-14	23.6	21.4
15-19	6.8	6.8
20-24	7.2	1.8
over 25	6.5	4.0

* Secondary analysis of raw data gathered for A.A.S.A. and N.E.A., (1960).

Greater commitment to community and school district, the attitude against mobility, and the longer stay in office suggest that the insider, more than the outsider, tends to practice job perpetuation.[14]

The various comparisons between insiders and outsiders suggest the hypothesis that an organization would not be able to adapt itself and operate successfully under the impact of two successive insiders. A reputation would develop that the system was not developing an adequate program and able personnel could not be attracted. The community would complain about outmoded procedures and practices. Institutional integrity would be damaged, for the commitments of the insider suggest that he is more willing to make compromises than the outsider. In time, this could reflect on the professional standing of all administrators in the system and on the school board.

There are four possible succession patterns in school systems: insider to insider, insider to outsider, outsider to outsider, and outsider to insider. On the basis of the facts discussed above, it was expected that the pattern of insider to insider would occur rarely. In 103 successions taking place over some thirty-two years in forty-eight city school systems in California the least frequent pattern was from insider to insider; this pattern occurred only

14. A similar relation between performance and tenure in office has been observed about mental hospital superintendents. Belknap (1956, pp. 79-80) has written: "The superintendents have been confronted, as medical men, with a dilemma. If they conformed to the structure of the hospital as they found it, they could carry out a reasonably good, routine custodial administration. If, however, they attempted to establish modern psychiatric treatment of patients, the procedures necessary called for changes in the traditional routines. . . . But the professional training of any physician has been for at least the past hundred years in the direction of seeking and finding improvement in the condition of his patients. . . . The superintendents . . . found themselves confronted with a choice between being good doctors and poor administrators, or good administrators and poor doctors. . . . The superintendents with the longest tenure were those who apparently accepted the second horn of the dilemma and became efficient administrators."

seven times. A study of succession patterns in school districts of Pennsylvania replicated the finding.[15] Table 3 gives the findings of both samples.

Table 3

SUCCESSION PATTERNS.

TYPE OF CHANGE	CALIFORNIA*	PENNSYLVANIA†
Outsider to outsider	58	43
Insider to insider	7	9
Outsider to insider	22	31
Insider to outsider	16	23
Total	103	106

* Data gathered for all (48) city school districts in California from the annual directory of California Association of Secondary Administrators, *California Schools,* for the period 1926 to 1958.

† Data gathered for all (24) first- and second-class school districts and 17 third-class districts in Pennsylvania drawn at random from personnel files in the State Department of Public Instruction for the period 1922 to 1959.

Since insiders show (1) high commitment to community and school district, (2) low commitment to specialized skills of the profession, (3) appointment for a stabilizing performance, (4) administrative activity tending toward maintenance of the organization, (5) lack of proportionate place among prominent members of the profession, and (6) long tenure in office, suggesting the tendency to practice job perpetuation, it would seem that a school system cannot afford to have an insider follow an insider into the superintendency. Succession patterns support this assumption.

Successor's Program and Counteracting Forces

The preceding discussion has shed some light on the differences between place-bound and career-bound school superintendents. Any full understanding of how these two types relate to their organizations must include a study of the responses of organizations to the successors. Though highly influential, the chief executive is not the master of the organization's course. A good deal is known (Lipset, 1950; Gouldner, 1954) about counteracting forces within organizations undergoing change—change that is frequently

15. Because there are a number of cases of insider to insider succession, even though fewer than chance would indicate, and because of the high possibility of detrimental consequences of such a succession pattern, it would seem fruitful to explore the conditions under which such a succession pattern occurs. Three conditions suggest themselves: (1) A lack of separation of municipal politics and school board functions may alter the setting of appointments. (2) The term in office of the first insider may not run its full course, because of death or other natural reason. (3) The insider may be a deviant member of his class. In addition, it would be fruitful to come to a better understanding of the consequences of following the succession pattern of insider to insider.

initiated by outside successors. When the new leadership is committed to system maintenance, as with insiders, the tracing out of counteracting forces has been ignored, although there is no reason to expect that counteracting forces will be absent.

For example, inside successors may be unwilling to press for advances in salary and welfare benefits for teachers. The lower salary of an insider is not as far "out of line" with respect to teachers' salaries as is the salary of the outsider. The insider, therefore, feels less pressure to bring teachers' salaries "into line." Also, some judge school systems by how much they pay teachers. To raise teachers' salaries may be a side payment bargained for and won by outsiders, but not by insiders. Furthermore, insiders may know the teachers too well to be concerned over their salaries. In contrast, the outsider knows only the salary figures for the district, and if salaries are low he will raise them without thought of teachers as individuals.

This may have been the basis of teacher resentment in one system observed. In one of the systems involving an insider, the teachers' organization took on a more aggressive attitude than had been customary on salaries and welfare benefits. The teachers' organization assumed that to gain welfare benefits and salary increases it must work around the superintendent (which was contrary to past procedures) and deal directly with the school board. Members of the teachers' organization felt the superintendent would not "fairly" represent their case. He was disturbed. The development established a precedent and a new definition of the relationship between teachers, superintendent, and school board with possible far-reaching consequences. The consequences of the precedent, however, could not be adequately assessed during the time given to this research.

Summary and Further Implications

The basic proposition explored here is that the origin of the successor is a major variable in the study of administrative succession—that insiders, those promoted from within, and outsiders, those brought in from outside, relate to their organizations in dissimilar ways during the cycle of succession. One of the distinctive differences in the two types of school superintendents is the value put on career and place of work. Insiders are place-bound; they put place of employment above career. Outsiders are career-bound; they put career above place of employment. Insiders are called on for a stabilizing performance when employers wish to maintain the system. They are paid less and gain less prominence than the outsiders, who are called on for a creative performance when the employers desire changes in the system. Similarly, insiders act in a way that does maintain the system: they do not develop new rules and policies that alter the course of the organization; they do not prepare the organization for new ways of functioning by expanding the administrative staff. Outsiders, on the other hand, look more favorably upon mobility and occupy a superintendency for a shorter period of time. Such differences suggest that a school system, under normal circumstances, would not employ two successive insiders in the superintendency. Succession patterns over thirty years in eighty-nine school systems support this proposition.

These differences permit a tentative characterization of the two types. Their performances label the insider as an adaptive man and the outsider as an innovator. Both are conformists in the sense that their performance conforms to the expectations of their employers. The insider, however, adapts or modifies his performance to fit the office. He aims at preserving the office as it has been, which negates the possibility of bringing added status to the role. The place-bound superintendent seems to derive status from the office; he does not bring status to it. The insider is like an understudy, or a stand-in. He performs within the framework established by the predecessor rather than by creating a new framework. The performance of the outsider, on the other hand, does add something to the role. The office is modified rather than the person. His performance changes the office and the relations of others to the office; such a performance holds possibilities of increasing the status of the office.

The variable or origin used here is gross and unrefined. However, such a gross distinction is probably useful in many organizational settings. It is not necessary to leave a firm, government agency, army, or labor union to become an outsider. An outsider is simply a "stranger" in Georg Simmel's use of the term: a man unacquainted with the social realities of the particular setting. Thus, the new manager from the home office is an outsider with reference to his new field office position, just as is the army officer taking command of a new post. Gouldner's "Mr. Peele" is a case in point. Peele was not an outsider with respect to the General Gypsum Company, but he was an outsider with reference to the Oscar Center Plant (Gouldner, 1954).

School systems belong to a class of organizations that can be called "domesticated"; that is, they are not compelled to attend to all of their needs. A steady flow of clients is assured, and although they do compete for resources, support is not closely tied to quality of performance. The business firm in a competitive industry, on the other hand, can be seen as existing in a "wild" setting. It is not protected at vulnerable points as is the school system. There is probably less demand for adaptation to the environment in the protected setting and, therefore, more place-bound chief executives would be found in "domesticated" than in "wild" organizations. It should follow that the succession pattern of place-bound to place-bound executive would occur less frequently in "wild" than in "domesticated" organizations. These are purely speculative ideas, however, for adequate data are not available.

References

AMERICAN ASSOCIATION OF SCHOOL ADMINISTRATORS and NATIONAL EDUCATION ASSOCIATION. *Profile of the school superintendent.* Washington: American Association of School Administrators, 1960.

AVERY, R. W.   Orientation toward careers in business: A study in occupational sociology. Unpublished doctoral dissertation, Harvard University, 1959.

BARNARD, C. I.   *The functions of the executive.* Cambridge: Harvard University Press, 1938.

BELKNAP, I.   *Human problems of a state mental hospital.* New York: McGraw-Hill, 1956.

BELL, T. H.   *The prodigal pedagogue.* New York, 1955.

CARLSON, R. O.   *Executive succession and organizational change.* Chicago: Midwest Administration Center, University of Chicago, 1962.

FLORO, G. K.   Continuity in city manager careers. *American Journal of Sociology,* 1955, 61, 204-246.

GOULDNER, A. W.   *Patterns of industrial bureaucracy.* Glencoe: The Free Press, 1954.

GOULDNER, A. W.   Cosmopolitans and locals: Toward an analysis of latent social roles (I). *Administrative Science Quarterly,* 1957, 2, 281-306.

GOULDNER, A. W.   Cosmopolitans and locals: Toward an analysis of latent social roles (II). *Administrative Science Quarterly,* 1958, 2, 444-480.

GRUSKY, O.   Role conflict in organizations: A study of prison camp officials. *Administrative Science Quarterly,* 1959, 3, 452-472.

LIPSET, S. M.   *Agrarian socialism.* Berkeley: University of California Press, 1950.

MARVICK, D.   *Career perspectives in a bureaucratic setting.* (Michigan Governmental Studies No. 27) Ann Arbor: University of Michigan Press, 1954.

McGEE, R.   The function of institutional inbreeding. *American Journal of Sociology,* 1960, 65, 483-488.

SCHEFF, T. J.   Perceptual orientation of staff members toward patients in a mental hospital ward. Paper presented at the meeting of the American Sociological Association, 1960.

SEEMAN, M.   Social mobility and administrative behavior. *American Sociological Review,* 1958, 23, 633-642.

TERRIEN, F. W. and MILLS, D. L.   The effect of changing size upon the internal structure of organization. *American Sociological Review,* 1955, 20, 11-13.

TROW, D. B.   Membership succession and team performance. *Human Relations,* 1960, 13, 259-268.

WHISLER, T. L.   The "assistant-to" in four administrative settings. *Administrative Science Quarterly,* 1960, 5, 181-216.

9. CHANGING THE SCHOOLS

What accounts for the mysterious phenomenon of educational innovation? How does it happen that modern math or team teaching diffuses through 30,000 school districts, each one in principle autonomous?

In this study, Carlson points us toward the behavior of the chief decision-maker in school systems: the superintendent. It turns out that adoption of educational innovations—as with farmers and hybrid corn, doctors and penicillin, males and turtleneck shirts—is a kind of social chain reaction, in which adopters influence each other. Thus, matters of relative social status and friendship among adopters assume a good deal of importance.

So yes, Virginia, superintendents do have friends (among other superintendents, at least), and their standing with each other influences how soon they decide to adopt innovations.

Some matters for the reader to ponder: how would Carlson's results have been different if he had used a slower-moving innovation (see Figure 3); how are his results affected by the fact that no "outsider" superintendents who took office during the turbulent, post-Sputnik years were included? (See Carlson on "outsiders" in the preceding article.)

Interestingly, too, superintendents seem to judge each other somewhat differently in different states. In West Virginia, the "professional superintendent" is seen as someone with more education; in Pennsylvania, he is the man with a higher salary. The interested reader may want to refer to Carlson's complete monograph to explore such differences further.

The Adoption of
Educational Innovations*

Richard O. Carlson

This inquiry seeks explanation—explanation of varying rates of adoption of new educational practices by school systems and superintendents.

Because they are self-conscious about their significant purposes, and exist in a rapidly developing culture in which knowledge is greatly expanding and technological advances are commonplace, school systems are pressed to and do seek change in their educational practices.

Adoption of new educational practices is only one means by which school systems attempt to adjust to their environment. The educational enterprise also changes its structure, size, and support; alters its definition of purpose or mission; and adjusts the number, competencies, and characteristics of its personnel. But, the adoption of new educational practices, practices which alter the instructional program, seems to be at the center of the issue as school systems attempt to provide an adequate education for their clients.

An educational innovation has a natural history and, in a sense, a life cycle. The full account of the life cycle of an innovation is the story of its invention, development and promotion, adoption, diffusion, and demise, along with an account of the problems encountered and solutions developed in introducing and maintaining the innovation in specific settings, and the unanticipated consequences growing out of its use. No attempt is made here to analyze the full life cycle of an educational innovation; the discussion focuses only on adoption and diffusion.

Varying Rates of Adoption:
An Explanatory Framework

This inquiry into the varying rates of adoption of educational innovations takes its orientation from the following scheme of factors in the adoption of new ideas. It is assumed that the rate of acceptance of a new practice or idea by individuals or adopting groups depends on (1) the characteristics of the adopting unit (individual and/or group), (2) the way the adopting unit is joined to communication channels and sources of informa-

* Adapted from *Adoption of educational innovations* (Eugene, Oregon: Center for the Advanced Study of Educational Administration, 1965) Chs. 1, 2, 4 and 5. Used by permission of the author and publisher.

tion, and (3) the position the adopting unit holds in the social structure of like units.

This explanatory framework draws its support from two main sources. The first source is research on mass communications, through which the hypothesis of the two-step flow of communications has been developed. The hypothesis in the original form proposed that "... influences stemming from mass media first reach 'opinion leaders' who, in turn, pass on what they read and hear to those of their every-day associates for whom they are influential" (Katz, 1957, p. 61; see also Riley and Riley, 1959). This is called a two-step flow because much of the "traditional" research on mass communication concentrated on the flow of the communication to the recipient and the recipient's response to the communication.

Over-all, the two-step flow hypothesis suggests that mass communication messages are mediated by the reference groups of the recipient and the social structure in which they are imbedded. When a school superintendent reads or hears about modern math, for example, the hypothesis suggests that his response is not directly determined by the message but is determined by his relationships with other persons whom he sees as important to him.

The second source of support for the explanatory framework used here comes from the nature and shape of the curve that usually depicts the course of the diffusion of an innovation. When the cumulative percentage of adopters of an innovation is graphed from the time of its first acceptance until it is completely diffused, the curve produced has an S-shape similar to that shown in Figure 1.

Note that there is a sharp rise in the per cent of adoption, preceded and followed by slow rises. What notions about the adoption process best explain this diffusion pattern?

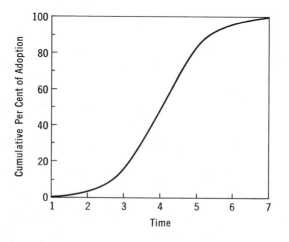

Figure 1. The Normal Diffusion Curve.

Let's start with the assumption that adoption is an *individual process,* meaning that the number of adopters accepting the innovation in each time unit would remain a fixed percentage of those who have not already accepted the practice. The dotted line in Figure 2 depicts the diffusion curve assuming that adoption is an *individual process.* Note that this dotted line in Figure 2 is an inadequate representation of the normal diffusion curve shown in Figure 1.

Now let's make the assumption that adoption is not an individual process, but rather that it is a *chain reaction* process. The solid line in Figure 2 shows a curve representing a chain reaction process, wherein the number of adopters in each unit of time increases in proportion to the number that has already accepted the new practice. Note that the solid line in Figure 2 is a better representation of the normal diffusion curve than is the dotted line.

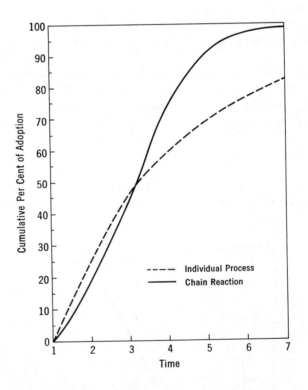

Figure 2. Chain Reaction and Individual Process Curves.

The diffusion curve, in its similarity to a chain reaction, suggests that there is intercommunication among adopters—that potential adopters learn from each other, and that the act of adoption by some acceptors is itself a means of influencing others to adopt the practice.

Social Structure and Rate of Adoption

This study of the diffusion and adoption of educational innovations takes the school system as the adopting unit; however, the *major emphasis is placed on the school superintendent* as an element of the school system; only rather incidental attention is given to other elements of the school system. Though it is true that a school system as a whole accepts or rejects innovations, the school superintendent is at the focal point in the decision process regarding innovations. Whether he convinces his staff or is convinced by them, the superintendent is in a position to make the final decision.

It is the purpose of this section to examine the relationship between a superintendent's position in the social structure of his peers and his rate of adoption of an innovation. The background discussion above has indicated the rationale for choosing this class of explanation.

AN ALTERNATIVE EXPLANATION: MONEY. Since the 1930's, the late Paul Mort and his students have carried out over 200 studies of school system "adaptability" (Ross, 1958), defined as the ability of a school to take on new practices and discard outmoded ones.

In summarizing the findings of these studies, Ross said:

> If but one question can be asked, on the basis of the response to which
> a prediction of adaptability [adoption of innovations] is to be made,
> the question is: How much is spent per pupil? (1958, p. 15).

Because this statement characterizes and summarizes past research on adoption of new educational practices, the relationship between expenditure per pupil and adoption and diffusion of educational innovations was also examined in the present study.

Research Methods

The Innovation Studied: Modern Math

The innovations about which diffusion rate data were gathered in the larger study (Carlson, 1965) of which this article is part were modern mathematics, programmed instruction, team teaching, foreign language labs, foreign language instruction in elementary grades, and accelerated programs in secondary schools.

Because modern math was the most widely diffused of the selected innovations and because it was among the most recently accepted innovations, it is the most appropriate single innovation on which to base the analysis.

As an innovation, modern math does not call upon the school system to provide a completely new service or teach a new subject. Modern math is a new way of ordering and teaching a firmly established part of the school program. To adopt modern math a school system generally accepts new textbooks and other instructional material and provides some retraining of teachers.

To put modern math into the context of other educational innovations, it may be useful to look briefly at comparative adoption rates (Fig. 3), in the two school system samples of this study (West Virginia and Allegheny County, Pennsylvania).

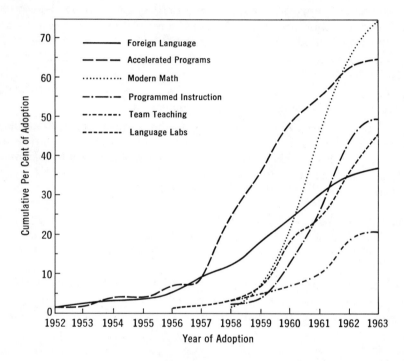

Figure 3.   Diffusion Curves of Six Innovations.

At the extremes, this figure shows that foreign language instruction in the elementary grades, after first being accepted in 1952, had been adopted by 37 per cent of the school districts in both samples by 1963. And, that modern math, after first being accepted in 1958, had been adopted by 75 per cent of the school districts in both samples by 1963.

Among the two populations of school superintendents studied, modern math had been adopted by about 75 per cent of the men at the time of the interviews. It was first accepted as a new practice in Allegheny County in 1958 and by 1963 had been adopted by 51 of the 61 superintendents interviewed. Modern math was first adopted in West Virginia in 1959 and by 1964 it had been accepted by 29 of the 46 men interviewed.

In short, we are dealing with an innovation which had diffused relatively more rapidly than any of the other five innovations studied, a fact which might have been predicted from the comments made above about the character of modern math as an innovation.

The Research Sites

The innovations selected for attention, the explanatory framework, and the concentration on the school superintendent imposed restrictive conditions for the research sites. Since the innovations studied, including modern math, were taking place in both elementary and secondary schools, it was necessary that the school superintendents in the sample be in control of both elementary and secondary programs; this meant that unified school systems had to be chosen.

A greater restriction was imposed in connection with the assumption that varying rates of adoption are, in part, accounted for by varying positions of adopters in the social structure of school superintendents. In the attempt to determine a man's position in the social structure, questions were posed which could be answered only if sample members knew each other. For this condition to be met, it was necessary to select research sites containing relatively few superintendents, and sites wherein those superintendents involved had frequent opportunities to see, talk to, and interact with one another about problems common to all.

Two research sites were selected that met these conditions: Allegheny County, Pennsylvania, and the state of West Virginia. (Two sites were selected instead of one in order to provide a broader base on which to judge the utility of the explanatory framework.) Allegheny County was selected as a matter of convenience since a number of counties met the above stated conditions. The selection of a state which met the specified conditions, however, was a more difficult matter. On the one hand, most states have not unified all of their school districts, and on the other, some states with all unified districts contain so many superintendents that any given superintendent cannot be knowledgeable about the other superintendents. Three states—West Virginia, Utah, and Florida—have all unified school districts and contain relatively few superintendents (55, 40, and 67, respectively). Some school superintendents in Florida are elected to office by popular vote and some are appointed by boards of education. Florida was eliminated from consideration because of this possible contaminating factor. West Virginia was selected over Utah because its greater number of superintendents would enhance the statistical treatment of the data.

At the time the data were gathered there were 68 superintendents in Allegheny County. Assuming that men in position less than two years would not have been in position at the time of adoption of innovations of interest, no attempt was made to include them in the sample. Four of the 68 superintendents had been in position less than two years. Two men would not grant interviews and one was on extended sick leave. Thus, data were collected from 61 of the 68 superintendents in Allegheny County.

The data collection figures for West Virginia are as follows: total number of superintendents—55; number in position less than two years—8; number refusing interviews—1; number of superintendents interviewed—46.

All told, 107 school superintendents were interviewed to obtain data on varying rates of adoption of educational innovations.

Sample and Data Collection

Before proceeding with an examination of the relationship between position in social structure and rate of adoption, it is necessary to specify the sample involved and the way in which it was determined *if* modern math had been adopted and if so, *when* it was adopted.

Because school superintendents frequently move from superintendency to superintendency, a difficulty arises in assigning a score to each superintendent in a geographical area which adequately reflects his rate of acceptance of an innovation. A score for rate of adoption of an innovation has a time base, and to have meaning, each superintendent should have equal opportunity to obtain each score. The difficulty arises with superintendents who take their positions after the first acceptance of the innovation, for no matter how quickly they adopt the practice, they do not have a chance to obtain all scores. Said another way, unless all superintendents are in position at the time of the first adoption, a score reflecting rate of adoption which has as its base the date of the first adoption is distorted for some adopting units.

The sample, therefore, includes only those men who were in position at least one year prior to the introduction of the innovation. Of the 61 superintendents interviewed in Allegheny County, only 38 of the adopters of modern math were in position at least one year before the first adoption of modern math in the county. Of the 46 superintendents interviewed in West Virginia, only 16 of the adopters of modern math were in position one year prior to the first acceptance of modern math in the state.

Rate of acceptance (time at which a program of modern math was adopted) is the dependent variable, and was determined by asking each superintendent if there was a modern math program in his school system, and if so, when it was first adopted. This measurement of rate of adoption was dependent on the superintendent's recall ability, since the superintendent's word was taken as the only evidence of adoption or non-adoption and of the time of first adoption. Thus, the dependent variable is subject to error corresponding to the superintendents' inability to recall accurately an event which took place in the past. It seems important to note that the recall period was not excessively long, and that all of the superintendents responded unhesitatingly and categorically regarding the presence or absence of a modern math program. It should also be pointed out that the notation of the year of adoption as the rate of adoption does not take into account the *amount of use* of the new practice.

The rate of adoption for the 54 adopters of modern math who had been in position at least one year prior to the first adoption in their geographical area was set in relation to the year of first acceptance of modern math in the geographical area. Table 1 shows how the two sets of data were combined.

Table 1

RATE OF ADOPTION OF MODERN MATH:
ALLEGHENY COUNTY AND WEST VIRGINIA

YEAR OF ADOPTION	NO. OF ADOPTERS IN ALLEGHENY COUNTY ($N = 38$)	NO. OF ADOPTERS IN WEST VIRGINIA ($N = 16$)	COMBINED NO. OF ADOPTERS ($N = 54$)
First	1	1	2
Second	4	3	7
Third	10	4	14
Fourth	12	4	16
Fifth	8	3	11
Sixth	3	1	4

The data on which this work is based, then, consist mainly of (1) the dates on which the above innovations—including modern math—were adopted (if they were adopted) by the selected school systems; and (2) characteristics of the superintendents, including (a) personal characteristics, (b) habits of communication, and (c) positions in the social structure of superintendents. Detailed measures will be explained as the data are presented. These data were collected via interviews with the superintendent in each school system. Data on expenditure were collected from state and county school records.

Findings

The Explanatory Power of School Expenditure

First, it may be useful to examine data bearing on the financial explanation for school system innovativeness.

Inasmuch as the mean expenditure per child in West Virginia school systems was only about 63 per cent of that in Allegheny County school systems,[1] the findings of the Mort studies would indicate that the innovations should be more widely accepted in Allegheny County than in West Virginia. Table 2, which shows amount of diffusion of each of the six innovations in the two geographical areas, suggests that even though school systems in

---

1. The mean expenditure per child in West Virginia school systems was $216 in 1957-58 and rose to $275 in 1962-63. The corresponding figures for school systems in Allegheny County were $349 and $440.

Allegheny County spent considerably more per child than schools in West
Virginia, the innovations were not more widely diffused in Allegheny
County than they were in West Virginia.

Table 2

DIFFUSION OF INNOVATIONS BY GEOGRAPHICAL AREA

INNOVATION	PER CENT OF DISTRICTS HAVING ADOPTED INNOVATION IN ALLEGHENY COUNTY	PER CENT OF DISTRICTS HAVING ADOPTED INNOVATION IN WEST VIRGINIA
Accelerated Programs in Secondary Schools	70	62
Foreign Language Instruction in Elementary Schools	44	28
Language Labs	39	53
Modern Math	84	62
Programmed instruction	43	55
Team Teaching	18	26

A second vantage point on the relation between expenditure per child
and adoption of new practices can be seen in Table 3, which reports the
mean expenditure level of school districts arranged according to the number
of the six innovations adopted (including modern math). Note that the
mean expenditure level was not related in a consistent manner to the number of innovations adopted. Expenditure per child is correlated with the
number of innovations accepted to the extent of —.24 in Allegheny County.
The correlation between these variables in the West Virginia data is .25.

By looking at the amount of acceptance of the various innovations in the
two geographical areas and at the relationship between the number of new

Table 3

NUMBER OF SELECTED INNOVATIONS ADOPTED
AND EXPENDITURE PER CHILD

ALLEGHENY COUNTY, PENNSYLVANIA			WEST VIRGINIA		
NO. OF INNOVATIONS ADOPTED	NO. OF DISTS.	MEAN EXPENDITURE PER CHILD (1962-63)	NO. OF INNOVATIONS ADOPTED	NO. OF DISTS.	MEAN EXPENDITURE PER CHILD (1962-63)
6	3	$405	6	4	$285
5	6	$420	5	7	$288
4	13	$411	4	9	$285
3	13	$423	3	6	$257
2	15	$404	2	9	$273
1	10	$482	1	6	$266
0	1	$585	0	5	$282

practices accepted and expenditure levels it becomes clear that expenditure level is not a powerful predictor of *amount* of acceptance of new educational practices, at least as far as the sample of school systems and innovations reported here is concerned.

In addition to the notation of relation between expenditure and *amount* of acceptance reported above, the data permit an examination of the way in which expenditure per child was related to *rate* of adoption of new educational practices. Other analyses (not shown) examined the correlation between rate of adoption of three innovations (modern math, programmed instruction, and team teaching) and the amount of money spent per pupil. In the sample of West Virginia school systems, the correlation was .303; in Allegheny County the correlation was .346. Thus, the amount of money spent per child accounted for about nine per cent of the variation in rates of adoption of these three new practices in West Virginia and about twelve per cent in Allegheny County.

In respect to the power of the variable of expenditure per child to account for *rate* of adoption and *amount* of adoption of new educational practices, Ross' statement summarizing past research on adoption of educational innovations is not supported by these data.

The remainder of this article presents evidence bearing on the explanatory power of social structural variables in predicting the adoption and diffusion of innovations.

Adoption Patterns Among Sociometric Pairs

The explanatory framework used here was in part drawn from the two-step flow of communication hypothesis, as has been indicated above. This hypothesis specifies that responses to communications received by an individual are regulated or mediated by the relationship and interaction that the individual has with his reference groups or those persons who are important to him. And, it is this hypothesis that directs attention to the position a superintendent occupies in the social structure of his peers and the relationship between this position and his rate of adoption of new practices.

The regulating or mediating function of reference groups can be seen partially in the patterns of adoption of modern math by sociometric pairs. [Sociometric pairs were determined by asking each respondent to name his three best friends from among the superintendents in his geographical area (i.e., Allegheny County or West Virginia). Among the adopters of modern math who had been in position at least one year prior to its first acceptance in the geographical area, there were five first choice sociometric pairs, and twenty sociometric pairs when all three choices were counted.]

The mediating function of the sociometric reference group suggested by the two-step flow hypothesis is apparent in the fact that three of the five first choice pairs (60%) adopted modern math simultaneously (i.e., in the same year) when chance alone would indicate that simultaneous adoption among randomly selected pairs would occur in 6 out of 21 cases (29%). In addition, adoption occurred either simultaneously or in consecutive years more frequently among first choice pairs than chance occurrence. All five of the first choice sociometric pairs adopted modern math simultaneously or in consecutive years whereas chance alone would indicate this happening in 52 per cent of the cases.

The same pattern holds among sociometric pairs indicated by all three choices of friends. With respect to simultaneous adoption, chance again indicates occurrence in 28.6 per cent of the cases, while simultaneous adoption took place with 45 per cent of the twenty "all choices" pairs. And, whereas chance indicates that simultaneous or consecutive years adoption would occur in 52 per cent of the cases, it occurred in 80 per cent of the twenty pairs.

Further, it is apparent that the *order* of choice of friends forming sociometric pairs influenced the timing of adoption. First choice sociometric pairs apparently influence one another in respect to time of adoption more than did "all choice" sociometric pairs. Simultaneous adoption occurred in 60 per cent of the first choice pairs and in 45 per cent of the all choice pairs. Similarly, adoption either simultaneously or in consecutive years occurred in 100 per cent of the first choice pairs and in 80 per cent of the all choice pairs.

These data on patterns of adoption of modern math among sociometric pairs give concrete meaning to the regulating or mediating function of reference groups, and show quite clearly that adoption of a new practice among school superintendents is not carried out by them in total isolation from one another.

The Social Itinerary of Modern Math

Even though the specific *time* of adoption of modern math is patterned among sociometric pairs, the over-all *rate* of adoption among pairs is not significantly different from the over-all rate of adoption among non-pairs. The explanatory framework, however, suggests that rate of adoption is related to the way in which a superintendent fits into the general order of friendship choices and friendship groups.

The friendship choices among the subjects in the Allegheny County sample have been pictured in Figure 4. This figure is based on responses to the question: "Among the chief school administrators in Allegheny County, who are your three best friends?"

Only choices to and from adopters of modern math are shown. Similarly, the friendship choices of sociometric isolates are not shown.

The purpose of the figure is to provide a map on which to trace the social itinerary of the innovation; to see the way in which the innovation moves through friendship choices and friendship groups from year to year.

Note that the sociogram shows what appears to be a six-member friendship group which has been encircled in the center of the figure. All of the superintendents within the circle received at least two choices from those within the circle, while no one outside the circle received two choices from those within the circle. Also, fifteen of the seventeen friendship choices made by these six men were directed to those within the circle. This central friendship group played a major role in the diffusion of modern math.

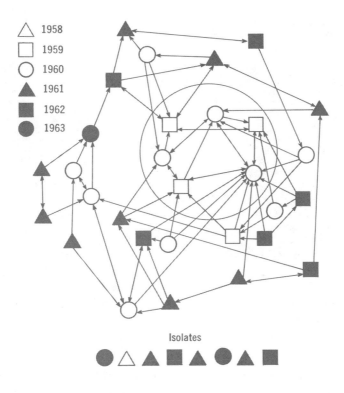

△ 1958
□ 1959
○ 1960
▲ 1961
■ 1962
● 1963

Isolates

Figure 4.   Friendship Choices and Rate of Adoption.

As to the social itinerary of modern math in Allegheny County, the first stop was with a sociometric isolate shown at the bottom of the figure. The second stop on the itinerary was mainly within the central friendship group. The third stop was again within the central friendship group and with a number of superintendents who made friendship choices to those in the central friendship group but were not of the group. The fourth and fifth itinerary stops were made with about an equal number of men who made friendship choices to the central group but were not of it, and men who did not choose as friends those in the central group. No superintendent on the sixth stop of the itinerary made a friendship choice to anyone in the central group. Over-all, the social itinerary of modern math in Allegheny County moved, after the initial adoption, to the central friendship group and from there to superintendents who were progressively less and less associated with the central friendship group.

Table 4 aids in respect to clarity and precision of the social itinerary and shows the decreasing association with the central group as the innovation was diffused.[2]

Table 4

ASSOCIATION WITH CENTRAL FRIENDSHIP GROUP AND RATE OF ADOPTION

YEAR OF ADOPTION	NUMBER OF ADOPTERS	NO. IN CENTRAL GROUP	NO. OUTSIDE GROUP WITH A CHOICE TO CENTRAL GROUP	NO. OUTSIDE GROUP WITHOUT A CHOICE TO CENTRAL GROUP
1958	1	0	0	1
1959	4	3	1	0
1960	10	3	5	2
1961	12	0	5*	7
1962	8	0	4	4
1963	3	0	0	3

* Fig. 4 shows only four 1961 adopters as making a friendship choice to the central group. This table, however includes isolates, and one isolate who adopted in 1961 made a choice to the central group.

In general, then, we have shown that time of adoption of modern math is clearly a function of the friendship patterns among school superintendents in Allegheny County. The next section extends this analysis by examining the superintendent's position in the social structure formed by his peers.

Social Structure and Adoption

Social structure has to do with the relations that exist among people. It is defined in terms of the distribution and differentiation of statuses and roles and patterns of interaction or communication among members of a social system. Because the spread of new ideas takes place in a social network in which the act of acceptance by an individual seems to influence others, knowledge of a superintendent's position in the social structure of superintendents can be used to explain, in part, varying rates of adoption of new ideas.

SOCIAL NETWORK INVOLVEMENT. One indication of a superintendent's position in the social structure is the extent to which he is immersed in the social system. Does he interact with other superintendents or stay apart from them, either from personal preference or for other reasons?

2. For a similar analysis, in a study of the diffusion of the use of a new drug by physicians, Menzel and Katz (1956) accounted for "spurts" of adoption through an examination of the the sociometric contacts of the physicians.

One measure of such involvement is the extent to which he is chosen as a friend by fellow superintendents (who were asked in the interview to name their three best friends from among the population of school superintendents in their geographical area).

The number of *friendship choices received* by the superintendents varied from those who received no choices, to one who received fourteen. The number of friendship choices received by a superintendent was found to have a relationship to his rate of acceptance of modern math.

The rate of acceptance was accelerated among those superintendents who received a high number of choices and it was decelerated among those who received a low number of friendship choices. (Data not shown.)

An alternate way to measure a superintendent's involvement in the social structure is to ask him for his own *perception of the amount of his interaction* with other superintendents as compared to that of his colleagues. This was done by presenting each respondent with a continuum representing amount of interaction ranging from less than average to more than average, and asking him to indicate his perceived standing. The results indicated that those who perceived their amount of interaction to be above average accepted modern math more readily than those who perceived their interaction to be less than average.

At best, perception of interaction is only a fair indicator of actual interaction. Measurement of actual interaction seemed out of the question so we reasoned that if a superintendent had high interaction with his colleagues he would be able to make an *accurate judgment* of the general rate of adoption of new practices in his school district as compared to the rate of adoption of new practices in other districts in the geographical area. This measure was obtained by asking each superintendent if his school system had adopted each of six new educational practices. From the responses the median number of adoptions was determined for the sample in his geographical area. Coupling this median number with each superintendent's judgment as to whether the adoption rate in his system on these innovations was above or below average produced a criterion for evaluating the accuracy of his judgment and, as was reasoned, an indirect measure of the amount of his interaction or involvement.

Table 5 shows the intercorrelations of these three measures; they are not high. If we combine them, Fig. 5 shows how the resulting measure is related to the rate of adoption of modern math.

Superintendents who scored above the median of those in the geographical area on all three measures of involvement are designated as "high," those who scored below the medians are "low," and the middle group which had a combination of high and low scores are "mixed."

It seems sufficient to say that, when combined, these three measures of social network involvement are directly related to rate of adoption of modern math and, as can be seen, achieve a fair separation of early and late adopters.

Table 5

INTERCORRELATIONS OF MEASURES
OF SOCIAL NETWORK INVOLVEMENT†

	2.	3.
1. Friendship choices	.38*	−.27
received	.43	.40
2. Perception of amount		.13
of interaction		−.08
3. Accuracy of perception		
of innovativeness		

* $p < .05$

† Italic figures represent West Virginia data $(N = 15)$; the others are Allegheny County $(N = 38)$.

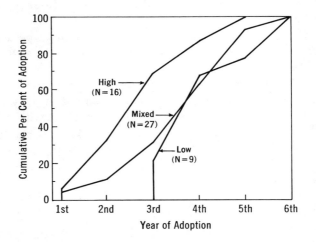

Figure 5.   Cumulative Percentage of Superintendents Adopting Modern Math Over Time by Composite of High and Low Scores on Three Measures of Social Network Involvement.

STATUS.   Another indicator of a superintendent's position in the social structure is his status. Status makes reference to a person's rank or position along some continuum. Status scores were obtained for the sample of superintendents along four continua: education, professionalism, prestige, and opinion leadership.

Amount of education was scored directly: a B.A. degree scored 1, an M.A. scored 2, graduate work beyond the M.A. scored 3, and a Ph.D. or equivalent scored 4.

Professionalism was measured by means of the superintendents' judgments of each other. Each superintendent was asked to "indicate the characteristics of the truly professional school superintendent." Then, after some discussion and examination of the suggested characteristics, each superintendent was given a deck of cards containing the names of all of the superintendents in his geographical area, one name per card, and asked to sort the cards on the basis of his own definition of the professional superintendent and his judgment of the individual superintendents. Six piles, numbered one through six, were used. Pile number one was a "no opinion" pile; from there on the higher the number a superintendent was assigned, the greater the degree of professionalism was ascribed to him by his judges. In addition, the respondents were instructed to place no more than a specific number of cards in any one pile.[3] This necessitated an almost complete use of each category if the respondent made a judgment about each of his colleagues.

The scoring was achieved by recording for each superintendent the number of times his name was placed in the various piles, multiplied by the number of the pile, and dividing this total by the number of times he had been placed in any one of the piles numbered from two to six.[4] The "no opinion" pile was omitted in the above scoring procedure.

Prestige was measured indirectly. Mason and Gross (1955, p. 330) have reported that salary alone accounted for 79 per cent of the variance in prestige among school superintendencies in a large sample they studied. The superintendent's salary, compared to other superintendents in his geographical area, was used as an indicator of the prestige of his office in the status system.

Opinion leadership was measured by asking each superintendent to name all persons from whom he had sought advice or information regarding new educational practices during the preceding ten months and recording the number of times sample members were mentioned.

Table 6 shows the intercorrelations of these measures; only professionalism and opinion leadership are highly correlated in both samples.

Table 6

INTERCORRELATIONS OF MEASURES OF STATUS†

	2.	3.	4.
1. Amount of education	.59**	.12	.42**
	.15	*.04*	*−.05*
2. Professionalism		.06	.65**
		*.68***	*.76***
3. Prestige			.09
			*.85***
4. Opinion leadership			

** $p < .01$

† Italic figures are from West Virginia data ($N = 15$); the others are Allegheny County ($N = 38$).

3. In Allegheny County this number was 12, and in West Virginia it was 9. The different numbers exist because of a numerical difference in the population of superintendents in the two geographical areas.

4. The percentage of raters who placed a superintendent in the model category or pile ranged from a low of 30 to a high of 93. The mean rater agreement was 45 per cent.

The relationship between the combined status variables of amount of education, professionalism, prestige, and opinion leadership and rate of adoption of modern math can be seen in Figure 6.

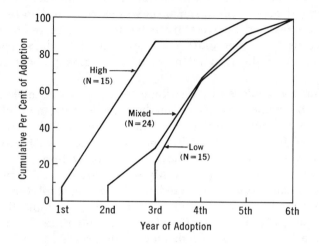

Figure 6. Cumulative Percentage of Superintendents Adopting Modern Math Over Time by Composite High and Low Scores on Four Measures of Status.

As in the preceding figure, there are three curves: one for those men who scored above the median for their geographical area on all four status measures, another for those who scored below the median on all four measures, and another curve for those who had high and low scores. The figure demonstrates that a direct relationship exists between a superintendent's position in the status structure and his rate of adoption of modern math.

INVOLVEMENT AND STATUS COMBINED.   When the seven social structure variables, three concerning involvement and four relating to status, are combined, their total relationship to rate of adoption of modern math can be seen in Figure 7.

The figure clearly indicates the utility of variables dealing with the superintendent's position in the social structure for explaining the rate of adoption of modern math among the school districts. It is evident from the figure that early adopters of modern math tended to score higher than late adopters on measures of social network involvement and position in the status structure.

Of the twenty-three superintendents who adopted the new practice in either the first, second, or third year, *ten* superintendents had scores above the median on all seven social structure measures. Of the thirty-one superintendents who adopted the practice in either the fourth, fifth, or sixth year, *no* superintendent scored above the median on all seven social structure measures.

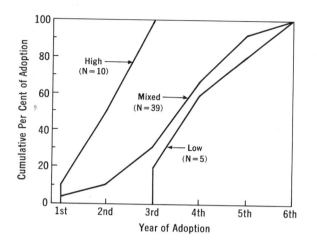

Figure 7. Cumulative Percentage of Superintendents Adopting Modern Math Over Time by Composite of High and Low Scores on Seven Social Structure Variables.

Concluding Comment

This study indicates that the adoption of educational innovations is a social process: interaction, communication and relative position among potential adopting units are crucial matters. More generally, the scheme used in this research suggests that the rate of acceptance of a new practice by individuals or adopting units is dependent on (1) the characteristics of the adopting unit, (2) the way the adopting unit is joined to communication channels and sources of information, and (3) the position the adopting unit holds in the social structure of like units. Formulations which stress only the characteristics of adopting units (such as their financial resources), or the properties of the innovation as such, will not explain enough variance in adoption rates to be useful.

References

KATZ, E.   The two-step flow of communication: An up-to-date report on an hypothesis. *Public Opinion Quarterly,* 1957, 21, 61-78.

MASON, W. S. and GROSS, N.   Intra-occupational prestige differentiation: The school superintendency. *American Sociological Review,* 1955, 20, 326-331.

MENZEL, H. and KATZ, E.   Social relations and innovation in the medical profession: The epidemiology of a new drug. *Public Opinion Quarterly,* 1956, 19, 337-352.

RILEY, J. W., Jr. and RILEY, M. W.   Mass communication and the social system. In R. K. Merton *et al.* (Eds.), *Sociology today.* New York: Basic Books, 1959, Pp. 537-578.

ROSS, D. H.   *Administration for adaptability.* New York: Metropolitan School Study Council, Teachers College, Columbia University, 1958.

The name of Socrates has been widely invoked—as has that of John Dewey—in support of the idea that instruction ought to be "individualized." Learners' experiences should be custom-tailored, depending on each client's individual educational and psychological measurements.

This is an attractive and plausible idea; yet (in spite of valiant efforts like those represented in the Eight Year Study sponsored by the Progressive Education Association in the 1930's) it never seems to have diffused into the mainstream of any educational system.

This study by Gross and his colleagues suggests some reasons why. Substantial problems arise when innovations, once "adopted" by the management of a school system, must be implemented. Users of the innovation must be clear about its properties, learn to use it, be rewarded in new ways for their efforts, and be able to communicate promptly and clearly with administrators about the problems they are encountering.

Perhaps most fundamentally of all, as the authors' book acknowledges, the innovation they studied was not a single "thing," but a complex, diverse bundle of teacher and student role expectations. Implementation failure is especially likely under such circumstances, not just because of user unclarity, but because different aspects of the bundle make different demands, and are reacted to differentially.

As the authors are aware, case studies can generate and illustrate, but not really test, theoretical frameworks. This one does draw our attention to some relatively ignored aspects of the social psychology of educational innovation—the post-adoption behaviors which occur in the context of an ongoing organization.

Failure to Implement a Major Organizational Innovation*

Neal Gross,

Joseph B. Giacquinta, Marilyn Bernstein

In his incisive paper on "The Bearing of Empirical Research on Social Theory," Merton (1957, pp. 85-117) points out that one of the ways in which empirical research invites the extension of theory is through observation of neglected facts. In his words (p. 108), "When an existing conceptual scheme commonly applied to a subject-matter does not adequately take these facts into account, research presses insistently for its reformulation. It leads to the introduction of variables which have not been systematically included in the scheme of the analysis."

A case study we conducted of an elementary school attempting to implement a major organizational innovation led us to identify a set of facts that were of critical importance in explaining why the implementation effort failed; they appear to have been neglected in schemes of analysis proposed to account for the success or failure of efforts to implement changes in organizations. In this paper we shall report selected findings of that case study and attempt to spell out their theoretical implications.

The Implementation of Organizational Innovations: The Way the Problem Has Been Conceptualized

In their attempts to account for the success or failure of deliberate or planned organizational change, social scientists have generally tended to conceptualize the problem as one of overcoming organizational members' resistance to change. (For examples see Argyle, 1967, pp. 87-101; Coch and French, 1948, pp. 512-532; Lawrence, 1954; and Zander, 1961, pp. 543-548.) Argyle's consideration of change in organizations provides a good illustration of this type of formulation. He states:

* Adapted from a paper read at the American Sociological Association meetings, Boston, August 1968, and from a forthcoming book by the authors, Neal Gross, Joseph B. Giacquinta, and Marilyn Bernstein, to be published in 1970 by Basic Books, Inc., tentatively entitled *The Implementation of Educational Innovations* (New York: Basic Books, 1970). Used by permission of the authors and publisher.

> In the first place, there is usually resistance to change of any sort. . . .
> In social organizations, patterns of behaviour become established and
> are of great stability because individuals work out drive-reducing ways
> of adapting, and fear that any change will be to their disadvantage in
> some way. Changes in industry are resisted by workers because they
> are afraid that they will be paid less or will have to work harder to earn
> the same amount. Wage-incentive schemes have often foundered for
> this reason. Changes are resisted by managers because they are afraid
> that their position will be weakened somehow or that they will be
> further from the center of power. Current changes in prisons are
> resisted by prison officers and prisoners alike because they have no
> desire to be associated with each other . . . There is anxiety either about
> possible material loss or about the disruption of a well-established and
> satisfying social system.

As a consequence of this definition of the problem, many efforts to account
for the success or failure of attempts to implement organizational change
have focused on the ability of management or a change-agent to overcome
members' initial resistance to change.[1] Thus, Argyle, after his enumeration
of a number of reasons why organizational members will resist change
(1967, p. 95) states, "It may be impossible to bring about change in the
teeth of such resistance, and it is usually possible only if the new scheme
can be shown to be advantageous. This may be achieved by means of
financial incentives, honorific ranks, training courses, or by sheer persuasive
skill."

The premise of organizational members' resistance to change appears to
be linked to the power-equalization concept,[2] which has been frequently
invoked to account for the differential success of organizations in implementing innovations. This theory can be construed as assuming that members who must implement innovations will offer resistance to them unless
they have been involved in formulating the innovation in the first place. It
is further assumed that this resistance constitutes the major obstacle to the
implementation of innovations. Thus, to overcome this resistance, management must share its power with those who must implement innovations by
allowing them to participate in decisions about the change to be made.
Implementers will then presumably perceive the innovation as self-imposed
and thereby become committed to it.

---

1.   For example, see Warren G. Bennis (1966, p. 176). He views the following conditions as necessary elements for successful implementation. The client system needs to have
as much influence as possible in developing and controlling the fate of the change; it must
have trust in the initiator; the client system must perceive the change effort as being as
self-motivated and voluntary as possible; the change program must include emotional and
value elements as well as cognitive elements. Bennis emphasizes that the quality of the
relationship between the change agent and client system is "pivotal to the success of a
change program" because the change agent "can be crucial in reducing the resistance to
change by providing consultation and psychological support during the *transitional* phase
of the change." (Italics ours.)

2.   For a detailed discussion of this concept and its use in the planned organizational
change literature, see Leavitt (1965).

Thus, in discussing styles of administration as they bear on organizational change, Argyle (1967, p. 95) maintains:

> The main principle here is that subordinates should be persuaded and motivated rather than ordered—so that they actually want to behave in the new way. This persuasive and democratic style means allowing people to take part in discussion and decisions.

And Leavitt, in his review of the power equalization approaches to organizational change (1965, p. 1159) notes:

> Power equalization has thus become a key concept in several of the prevalent people theories, a first step in the theoretical causal chain leading toward organizational change. It has been constructed as an initial subgoal, a necessary predecessor to creative change in structure, technology, task-solving, and the task implementation. Although the distances are unmarked, there is no obscurity about direction: a more egalitarian distribution is better.

The theme of resistance to change on the part of organizational members also is stressed in the body of group dynamics literature that deals with the problem of organizational change. It is asserted that through human relations training in sensitivity or T-groups, organizational members' resistance to change can be "unfrozen" and a positive orientation to change can be instilled.[3] (Such training also deals with other matters, such as efforts to improve communication, trust, and problem-solving skills. Resistance to change, however, never becomes a minor factor.)

Formulations that tend to view the problem of implementing organizational innovations as primarily one of overcoming organizational members' *initial* resistance to change appear to be too simplistic. Three general and interrelated conditions that they underplay, and that seem to us to be of critical importance are: (1) organizational members who are *not* resistant to change may encounter obstacles in their efforts to implement an innovation; (2) individuals in organizations are in part dependent upon members of their role set to overcome these obstacles, and these members may or may not provide aid; and (3) members who are *initially* favorable to organizational change may develop a negative orientation to an innovation, as a consequence of the frustrations they have encountered in attempting to carry it out.

To explore these notions, we embarked on a study of an organization attempting to implement a major innovation in which members had an initial positive orientation to change. We reasoned that if our reservations about the "resistance to change" explanations were groundless, then we should find that the implementation effort would be successful. If the imple-

3. For specific examples see Argyris (1962); Bradford, Gibb and Benne (1964); Jacques (1951); Miles (1959); Lewin (1947); and Schein and Bennis (1965). For reviews of work related to this general area, see Greiner (1967); Katz and Kahn (1966, pp. 390-451); Leavitt (1965); and Miles (1965).

mentation effort failed, then this might offer support for our contention that more complex schemes are needed to account for the success or failure of the implementation of organizational innovations. In this event, such a study also would provide evidence about the *specific* obstacles that confront organizational members as they attempt to implement organizational changes, and *specific* ways in which they are dependent on members of their role set.

An opportunity to conduct such a case study arose in the summer of 1966. We now turn to that study and its findings. In the final section of this paper we will propose a tentative theory of the implementation of organizational innovations, suggested by the results of our inquiry.

The Innovations and the Educational Setting

The innovation, a new definition of the teacher's role, was described by its originator to the teachers in an official document in November of 1966 as follows:

1. Teachers were expected to behave in ways that would assist children to learn according to *their* interests rather than in terms of a pre-scribed curriculum;
2. Teachers were expected to emphasize the process, not the content, of learning, and to allow pupils maximum freedom in choosing their own activities;
3. Teachers were expected to see that the classroom was saturated with a variety of educational materials, primarily self-instructional in nature, so that children could pursue their own interests;
4. Teachers were expected to act as facilitators of learning between children and materials and to encourage teaching of children by other children;
5. Teachers were expected to allow pupils to decide the materials they wished to work with, how long they would work with them, and with whom they wished to relate;
6. Teachers were expected to give pupils primary responsibility for directing their own learning and to assist them only when they perceived that their help was desired or needed.

The elementary school contained nearly 200 pupils and 11 full-time teachers, and was located in a lower-class urban area of the central city of an eastern metropolitan area of the United States. Nearly 60 per cent of the residents of this area were Negro, and they had encountered serious finan-cial, housing, transportation, and educational problems. In 1965, in response to pressure from citizens in this and other sections of the city for new schools and improvements of the quality of education in existing schools, the Board of Education created a Bureau for Educational Change, financed by a large Federal grant. It was charged with the responsibility of creating and administering laboratory schools; the school we studied was one of them. They were expected to focus primarily on developing and testing new programs to improve means of educating "disadvantaged students." An educational specialist brought from outside the school system was appointed as the Director of the Bureau, and became Director of the school as well. He was the originator of the innovation.

The laboratory school into which he introduced the innovation in November 1966 contained a very positive external and internal climate for educational change. The parents and higher administrative officials had expressed a strong interest in obtaining improvements in the educational program of the school. The Director was well known as an educational innovator and as a person who had strong beliefs about the necessity of educational change. He was given considerable autonomy in the operation of the laboratory school and freedom in selecting its faculty. He had attempted to secure a staff who were dissatisfied with the existing educational program offered to children in the ghetto and who had evinced a strong interest in educational change. Because of support by Title III funds, the financial and personnel resources of the laboratory school were substantially greater than those of other elementary schools. In addition to the teaching faculty, there were three subject specialists, student teachers, and teacher aides. Teachers received an additional payment of about 15 per cent of their base salaries to compensate them for the additional time and energy they would be required to expend as members of a laboratory school staff.

In the fall of 1966, a basic norm of the school was that teachers should accept and promote educational change. Our interviews revealed that all teachers recognized and accepted the need for major educational innovations in slum schools, and our field observations showed that they were using new types of instructional materials and that the administration was rewarding innovative behavior. Therefore, it was not surprising that the interviews showed that no teachers were resistant to attempting to implement the innovation at the outset. When it was first announced, all indicated that they were willing to make efforts to carry it out, even though 4 of the 11 teachers in the school had negative reactions to the innovation.

In a forthcoming book, *The Implementation of Educational Innovations,* we present a detailed description of the research methods used in conducting the study, the problems that were encountered in carrying it out, and how we attempted to resolve them. An extensive body of data was collected on the basis of daily field observations conducted over nearly a seven-month period, the examination of public and private documents, and informal and formal interviews with the teachers, their administrators, and other school personnel. Evidence from several sources indicated that a high degree of rapport had been developed between the field worker and the faculty. The formal interviews with the teachers, averaging three hours in length, were carried out in the spring of 1967 just prior to three weeks of intensive daily classroom observations. These observations were conducted in an effort to assess the degree to which the innovation had been implemented.

Findings of the Case Study and Their
Theoretical Implications

Despite the set of apparently positive antecedent and prevailing conditions that existed in the school system, community, and school in November 1966, when the innovation was first introduced to the teachers, six months later we found that practically no effort was being made to implement the innovation. In May 1967, all teachers were still behaving, for the most part, in accord with the traditional role model.[4] They were devoting very little time to trying to implement the innovation and, within that small period of time, their performance did not conform to key expectations of the new role model. We concluded that this was a case of a failure to implement a major organizational innovation.

A "resistance to change" explanation could not account for the failure of the teachers to implement the innovation; all the teachers had been positively predisposed to accept major organizational changes in the school when the innovation was presented to them.

The findings suggested that the failure of the teachers to implement the innovation in May could be traced to a set of unresolved problems or barriers to which they were exposed after they attempted to carry it out.

Barriers to Organizational Members'
Implementing Innovations

One barrier to which organizational members can be exposed is *lack of clarity* about the innovation that they are being requested to implement.

4.   Our assessment of the degree of implementation focused on both the quantity and quality of the effort teachers made to carry it out in May, 1967. To determine the quantity of staff effort, we observed and then calculated the proportion of (their) time that teachers behaved in accord with the traditional role model as compared to the new role model. This required the observer to make repeated "rounds" each day to check all classes and to keep running records of the amount of time teachers devoted to performance in line with each role model. Analysis of data collected for this aspect of the assessment showed that the staff over-all during this period spent nearly 85 per cent of the total time available to them in their classrooms behaving in accord with the *old* role model. To determine the quality of the teachers' performance during the time that they did devote to making "innovative efforts," the observer conducted in-depth systematic observations using an observation schedule of teacher performance in classrooms randomly selected for observation to guard against observer bias. Analysis of data collected for this purpose revealed that within the 15 per cent of time which teachers allotted to "innovative effort," their performance typically did not conform to key expectations of the new role model (for example, their obligation to act as catalysts between children and materials, and among children). Moreover, interviews with many teachers, as well as teachers-in-training who were present in the classrooms and who understood the innovation, corroborated these two findings: (1) that teachers were spending most of their time in classrooms behaving according to the traditional role model and (2) that their relatively small amount of "innovative performance" had serious deficiencies. A detailed discussion of the rationale underlying the evaluation, the assessment procedures employed, and our analysis of the data are presented in Chapter Five of the previously mentioned book.

Our observations of teachers suggested that most of them did not have a clear image of the role performance expected of them. Our formal interviews confirmed these field observations. They revealed that most teachers were confused about the innovation when it was first described to them in November, when they initially attempted to implement it in January, and just prior to our assessment of the degree of implementation in May.

In reporting our findings we shall present the responses of 10 of the 11 teachers, since the validity of the replies of one teacher to the formal and informal interviews is highly questionable.[5] When we asked the teachers, "After you first heard about the innovation did you have a clear picture of what you were expected to do in carrying it out?," nine of the ten responded in the negative. Here are some typical responses to the follow-up question, "In what respects was the innovation unclear?" One teacher replied, "At that time, *and still*, what methods would best implement it . . .;" a second responded, "It's unclear in most ways; how are you supposed to get a new idea across to children when he [the Director] didn't want us to call children together; I am unclear as to my role!" A third said, "How should the classroom teacher behave in this situation? The brochure never spelled out the teacher's job!" And a fourth replied, "What is the teacher's role? Should she outline daily activities? Should she spur children on? Would the activity period be all or part of the day?"

When these teachers were asked about their understanding of the innovation just before they were requested to make their first efforts to implement it in January, eight of the ten teachers again indicated confusion about it. As one teacher put it, "I still really don't have a clear understanding of the innovation, and I can assure you that I'm not the only one." Probe questions directed at the two teachers who felt they were clearer about the new role model in January than November indicated that they, too, had at best hazy notions about what was expected of them. And when we asked the teachers about the clarity of the innovation in May, just prior to our assessment of its degree of implementation, eight of the ten teachers indicated that they still had an ambiguous notion of what was expected of them.

Our findings suggest, in short, that the *clarity* of an innovation as perceived by organizational members needs to be taken into account in conceptual schemes designed to explain the success or failure of implementation efforts.

A second potential obstacle to the implementation of an organizational innovation is that members may lack the *capabilities* required to carry it out.

All teachers reported that serious problems arose when they made their initial efforts to implement the innovation in January. They all indicated that these problems persisted during the following months when they at-

---

5. The decision was made for two reasons. First, several teachers reported in confidence to the field worker that this teacher was intentionally misinforming him. They quoted him as saying privately that he was telling the field worker what he thought the field worker wanted to hear. Second, there were serious discrepancies between what this teacher reported about his behavior and the field worker's observations of that behavior.

tempted to carry it out, and furthermore, that new problems, with which they could not cope, also arose. In the words of one teacher, "I never was able to instigate enthusiasm in these kids while keeping the noise level down, and I never knew how to get them to use their time for learning instead of playing. The children were beginning to abuse freedom; they wouldn't do any work; they wouldn't record what they had done; many became discipline problems who weren't in the beginning. I just didn't know what to do." All teachers reported that they had encountered serious problems in maintaining discipline. Nine out of ten said that their pupils had "just played around with materials" or "made no effort to learn something from the materials." Eight out of ten mentioned related problems: difficulties in keeping children interested, in motivating them, in stimulating them to pursue their own interests, and in getting them to help each other with their learning problems. Most reported that large numbers of their pupils were continually demanding "direction" from them. This evidence, and much more that could be cited, indicates that the teachers were beset with a host of serious and unresolved difficulties during their attempts to implement the new role model. In this sense they were incapable of performing in accord with the new role model. We, therefore, concluded that their abandonment of efforts to implement the innovation in May was in part because they lacked the skill and knowledge to perform the new role.

A third obstacle is that organizational members may lack the *tools and equipment* required to carry innovations out. In a brochure prepared for the teachers by the administration, they were told that teachers should "transfer as much of the instructional and 'motivational' responsibilities as possible from the teacher to the total classroom environment—and to the greatly enhanced materials with which the room should be filled."

But our observations in the classrooms revealed that "highly motivating self-instructional materials" were never made available to teachers in their efforts to carry out the innovation. For example, the list of materials available to teachers in the primary grades for reading consisted of independent work sheets, word games such as "Spill and Spell," vocabulary flash cards, riddles, a set of telephones and some library books. For mathematics, there were Cuisenaire rods, an abacus, "Count the Beads," a scale, math card games, math flash cards, a printing set for numerals; for art, the materials available consisted of paper and various media like crayons and water paints; and for writing, a typewriter was available.

Most of these materials represent the kind of *supplementary* materials that can be found in a well-stocked suburban elementary school. They did not appear to, nor did they in fact, represent instructional materials that permitted pupils to progress very far in a meaningful way on their own, that is, without *instruction* from the teacher. These materials were not only of dubious quality in terms of their intended educational objectives, but were also in short supply when the teachers attempted to implement the innovation. Eight of the ten teachers complained bitterly about the paucity of curriculum materials when they described their earlier efforts to implement the innovation. These findings suggest a third variable, the *availability of tools and equipment,* that needs to be taken into account in explaining the success or failure of efforts to implement innovations.

A fourth obstacle is *organizational conditions* existing prior to and during an innovation's introduction that are *incompatible* with the innovation. Although we were able to isolate many circumstances of this kind, we shall consider here only two of them.

The first is that although the nature of the innovation required a highly flexible educational environment, most aspects of the rigid school schedule that existed prior to its introduction were retained. All children were kept out of the school building in the morning until the 8:30 bell rang and released in the afternoon by the 2:20 bell; a second bell rang in the morning before classes began. Bells were also rung for recess and lunch; all classes were expected to participate in recess from 10:30 to 11:00 and lunch from 12:00 to 12:30. Teachers were expected to adhere to this schedule. Children were taken in groups to lavatories at lunch and recess; they were required to walk up and down stairs in single lines, and were dismissed at the end of the day in a similar fashion. Moreover, children were required to participate in certain types of activities regardless of their interests. These included reading in the morning, art, music, sewing, gym, and field trips. The continuation of these school procedures clearly served to block the teachers' efforts to implement the innovation.

The second illustration is the retention of the old system of evaluating pupils. At the time of the announcement of the innovation, the school was using a report card system requiring teachers to "give grades" to each child for his mastery of different skills and subjects. However, the innovation specified that teachers should focus on the *process* of learning and the "operational competencies" involved, such as defining problems, organizing evidence and information, comparing and differentiating phenomena, and developing hypotheses. The system of evaluating pupils, therefore, would require alteration if teachers were to encourage these new types of behaviors in their pupils. However, the old report card system was retained. The teachers were not only acutely aware of the lack of congruence between the ostensible purposes of the innovation and the "outmoded" criteria they were being asked to apply to their pupils; they also became increasingly upset about this discrepancy over time. The extent to which organizational properties are compatible with innovations introduced into an organization, then, is a fourth important variable in explaining the implementation of organizational innovations.

Finally, our study suggested another important variable: the influence that *management,* as an important segment of the subordinate's role set, can have on the implementation process. We do not question the proposition that if organizational members are resistant to change, power equalization efforts by management *may* be one means by which their resistance may be reduced. However, the performance of management can have a critical bearing on the implementation of innovations in *other* ways, most notably in establishing the conditions that will permit subordinates to implement innovations, and in rewarding them for their efforts.

In our case study, we asked why the barriers teachers encountered when they attempted to implement the innovations were never removed. The evidence indicated that the teachers' lack of clarity about the new role model could largely be attributed to the following conditions: ambiguities in the minds of the Director and his administrative subordinates about the specific nature of the new role requirements for teachers; the failure of the administrators to provide effective mechanisms for teachers to obtain clarification about their role expectations; and the failure of the staff to secure clarification about the innovation, because of their lack of confidence in the capabilities of their administrators. In attempting to account for the staff's lack of capability in its attempts to implement the innovation, we concluded that this condition could be largely explained by the failure of the administration to recognize that the teachers needed to be resocialized if they were to conform to the new definition of their role, and its failure to provide them with the type of retraining they required. The lack of self-instructional materials which the teachers needed to implement the innovation was attributed in part to bureaucratic regulations about purchasing them. But more important was the unwillingness of the administration to face up to the reality that teachers had neither the skills nor time required to develop new instructional materials on the job. The failure to make modifications in organizational arrangements was traced back to the administration's unawareness that existing organizational elements were incompatible with the implementation of the innovation, and to a lack of commitment on the part of the Director's key administrative subordinate to it.

These findings led us to conclude that teachers were unable to implement the innovation largely because the administration failed to recognize or to cope effectively with the problems to which it exposed teachers when it asked them to carry it out. This condition, we would contend, was a consequence of the Director's simplistic view of the process of the implementation of organizational innovations and his lack of awareness of his role obligations to his subordinates when he initiated this process.

The Director's view of the steps required to implement the innovation, as evidenced by the strategy he employed, may be described as follows: (1) explain the philosophy and objectives of the innovation through several written documents to the staff; (2) give teachers maximum freedom to carry it out; and (3) delegate responsibility to an administrative subordinate (the Assistant Director) to see that the innovation is implemented.

The Director's strategy was inadequate, for two basic reasons. First, it failed to take account of *difficulties* to which teachers would probably be exposed when they attempted to implement the innovation. Second, it contained no provisions for *mechanisms* to identify and cope with unanticipated problems that might emerge during the period of attempted implementation.

The Director's strategy for implementing the innovation gave practically no consideration to the kinds of obstacles that were likely to confront the teachers as they attempted to implement the new role model. Since the Director's strategy essentially ignored these potential problems, no efforts were instituted *prior to the introduction of the innovation* to attempt to remove these barriers, nor was consideration given to ways to cope with them if they emerged during the period of attempted implementation.

The second major deficiency in the Director's strategy was its *lack of feedback mechanisms.* The Assistant Director had a number of reservations about the innovation, as did the subject specialists and a number of the teachers. But the Assistant Director was never given adequate opportunity to communicate his feelings to the Director about this matter, and the teachers and subject specialists never spoke frankly about them to their superiors. And, for still other interpersonal and organizational problems that occurred during the period of attempted implementation, open and frank discussion never occurred.

The Director made numerous assumptions about the innovation and the operation of the school that were in fact tenuous. He assumed that the Assistant Director and he were in agreement about the nature of the innovation. He assumed that the teachers did not need outside assistance in coping with their classroom problems, and that those that did arise could be effectively handled by the Assistant Director or the subject specialists. But these and other assumptions he made were in fact erroneous, and since he did not provide for feedback mechanisms in his strategy of implementation, he had no way of obtaining "the facts" and thereby could not identify or cope with these unrecognized implementation barriers.

This suggests that subordinates may be unable or find it difficult to make changes in their role performance unless management conforms to a set of expectations that subordinates "have a right to hold" for its performance. More specifically, subordinates have a right to expect management (1) to take the steps necessary to provide them with a *clear* picture of their new *role requirements,* (2) to adjust organizational arrangements to make them *compatible* with the innovation, (3) to provide subordinates with the *resocialization* experiences required to develop the capabilities needed to cope with the difficulties involved in implementing the innovation, (4) to provide the *resources* necessary to carry out the innovation, and (5) to provide the appropriate *supports and rewards* to maintain subordinates' willingness to make implementation efforts.

Furthermore, subordinates have a right to expect management to be committed to the implementation of the innovation, and to provide effective mechanisms and decision-making procedures to cope with anticipated and unanticipated problems that may arise during attempted implementation. Our findings, in short, suggest that the extent to which these expectations are recognized by management, built into its strategy, and conformed to, will have a direct bearing on the degree to which subordinates implement organizational innovations. The role of management in the implementation process needs to be brought to center stage in theoretical formulations of the problem.

The Time Dimension

Our third reservation about "resistance" explanations was that they minimize the fact that resistance can *develop* over time among organizational members who are positively predisposed to change, as a consequence of frustrations they have encountered in attempting to implement an innovation.

As noted earlier, there was a general acceptance of the need for change at the school in November 1966, and a general willingness to make the efforts needed to carry out the innovation. Furthermore, the data showed that although four of the teachers had negative reactions to the innovation at the time of its announcement, all reported a willingness to try to make implementation efforts.

The general picture, however, changed between the time of the innovation's announcement by management in the fall and our assessment the following spring. We found then that most staff members were no longer willing to make the necessary effort to try to implement the new role.

The following statements illustrate the reactions of teachers to the innovation at that time. After a brief absence from school, one teacher noted sardonically, "Ya know, I was sitting home the last two days saying that it can't really be that way, and that this school can't be as bad as I think it is; then I came back. Ya know, it really *is* that mixed up, confused, and nutty!" Another said, "I wonder whether it's worth the effort one has to put into it [the innovation] . . . . I can't really tell how much they're learning nor how many are learning . . . ." In a statement revealing more openly the frustrations teachers were facing with the innovation, a third exclaimed, "I'm just getting tired; I can't take it with the kids any more; I can't see what good it's [the innovation] doing; it's not worth it . . . . I go home and I've got a headache; I bite my nails . . . ." A fourth teacher reacting to the lack of discipline in children, which she felt was caused by their response to the innovation, exclaimed, "The kids are getting really fresh now . . . . Yesterday I had to go home and take two tranquilizers. The worst class is the second grade . . . ; what one child said to me I couldn't repeat . . . . I really hated coming to school today; I am sick of this place . . . ."

Our findings thus suggest that resistance to making implementation efforts can develop over time among members originally positive to changing, because of problems and ensuing frustrations encountered during the period when they attempt to carry an innovation out.

A Tentative Theory of the Implementation of Organizational Innovation

The findings of our case study thus indicate a number of conditions and circumstances that appeared to account for the failure of the implementation efforts. These are not taken into consideration by theoretical formulations which define the problem of implementing organizational changes as primarily one of overcoming resistance to change.

We would suggest that an explanation of the process of implementation of organizational innovations needs, as a start, to be based on the five following assumptions:

The first is that the degree to which members of an organization have a clear understanding of the innovation will be positively related to their ability to implement it. If they have an ambiguous understanding of the innovation, then they will be unclear about what is expected of them. If they have an erroneous interpretation of the innovation, then their efforts at implementation will be misguided.

The second assumption is that a staff's ability to implement an innovation will be a function of its capacity to carry it out. If teachers lack the skills required to perform in accord with the demands of the innovation, then it will be impossible for them to carry it out.

The third condition is that their ability to carry it out will be a function of the availability of the tools and resources required by the innovation. The fourth condition is the compatibility of organizational arrangements with the innovation. If arrangements in existence prior to the introduction of the innovation are incompatible with it and are not changed, then it will be more difficult for organizational members to carry it out.

However, if all of these conditions are fulfilled, it does not follow that the staff will implement an innovation. Staff members must also be motivated to expend the time and effort required for implementation.

Our next assumption is that the extent to which these five conditions are fulfilled will be a function of the performance of management. If ambiguity or confusion exists in the minds of the staff, management is in the best position to clarify the situation. Furthermore, the authority to establish training programs and provide the materials and tools required for the innovation is lodged in management. In addition, only it has the power to make changes in organizational arrangements that are incompatible with the innovation. And management, too, is in the position to offer the types of rewards and punishments that can motivate the staff to expend the time and effort required to implement an innovation.

If, as we have assumed, the implementation by the staff of an innovation is a function of the degree to which the five conditions specified above are fulfilled; and if the extent to which these conditions are fulfilled is a consequence of management's performance, then it follows that the degree of implementation of an organizational innovation will be a function of the extent to which management fulfills these conditions.

Final Considerations

Until now we have stressed findings of the case study that suggest the need for the reformulation of "resistance" conceptualizations. Several additional reservations about these formulations can be made.

First, the assumption that organizational members are resistant to change may be tenuous in many empirical situations. It assumes that members are generally satisfied with existing organizational conditions and thus that any disturbance in them, such as a proposed change, will be met with resistance. We submit that in many organizations the empirical reality is that many members are exposed to difficult problems in their work situation, and would welcome innovations that would appear to offer solutions to their difficulties. The degree to which organizational members are resistant to change needs to be taken as problematic, rather than as "a given," in theoretical formulations of the successful implementation of organizational innovations.

Secondly, some existing conceptualizations assume that the nature or complexity of an innovation is irrelevant to its successful implementation. It may turn out, however, that different strategies of implementation tend to be more or less effective, depending upon such circumstances as the magnitude of change required of organizational members in carrying out the innovation, and the difficulties it creates for them. This suggests the need for a typology of innovations, and the possibility that different explanations will be required to account for the successful implementation of different types of organizational innovations. In this connection, it is important to note that the theoretical explanation we offer in this paper to account for the implementation of organizational innovations may be relevant for only certain kinds of major organizational innovations, for example, those involving radical changes in the role performance of organizational members.

Finally, we wish to emphasize that our reflections have led us to recognize the need to conceive of successful implementation as the result of a process which can be reversed or halted at numerous points in time. We suggest that this process must fulfill simultaneously the five conditions specified earlier if maximum implementation is to be achieved. Since these conditions are not likely to prevail in most organizations when the decision is made to introduce an innovation, they must be developed prior to or during the period of attempted implementation. It may well be that there is a sequence of stages involved in fulfilling the several conditions. Furthermore, because the conditions, even when achieved at one stage of the process, can be reversed, problems of their maintenance need to be considered as well as those of their development.

If this dynamic conception of implementation has merit, then management would need to develop a strategy which takes into account this processual view of the problem. One contribution of research could be the systematic isolation of factors in a variety of settings that block or facilitate management's efforts to lead organizations through such a process.

The implications or generalizations drawn from a single case study, of course, must be taken with many grains of salt. We would have greater confidence in our conclusions if they had emerged from studies of both successful and unsuccessful efforts to implement organizational innovations. However, we believe our study does raise a number of basic questions that have been minimized or overlooked in schemes designed to account for the success or failure of the implementation of organizational innovations, and suggests a number of variables that need to be taken into account in subsequent theoretical formulations.

References

ARGYLE, M.   The social psychology of social change. In T. Burns and S. B. Saul (Eds.), *Social theory and economic change*. London: Tavistock Publications, 1967.

ARGYRIS, C.   *Interpersonal competence and organizational effectiveness*. Homewood, Ill.: Irwin, 1962.

BENNIS, W. G.   *Changing organizations*. New York: McGraw-Hill, 1966.

BRADFORD, L. P., GIBB, J. R. and BENNE, K. D. (Eds.)   *T-group theory and laboratory method*. New York: Wiley, 1964.

COCH, L. and FRENCH, J. Jr.   Overcoming resistance to change. *Human Relations*, 1948, 4, 512-532.

GREINER, L. E.   Patterns of organizational change. *Harvard Business Review*, 1967, 45, 119-128.

JACQUES, E.   *The changing culture of a factory*. London: Tavistock Publications, 1951.

KATZ, D. and KAHN, R. L.   *The social psychology of organizations*. New York: Wiley, 1966.

LAWRENCE, P. R.   How to deal with resistance to change. *Harvard Business Review*, 1954, 32, 49-57.

LEAVITT, H. J.   Applied organizational change in industry: Structural, technological and humanistic approaches. In J. G. March (Ed.), *Handbook of organizations*. Chicago: Rand McNally, 1965. Pp. 1144-1170.

LEWIN, K.   Frontiers in group dynamics. *Human Relations*, 1947, 1, 5-41.

MERTON, R. K.   *Social theory and social structure*. Rev. ed. Glencoe: The Free Press, 1957.

MILES, M. B.   *Learning to work in groups*. New York: Teachers College Press, 1959.

MILES, R. E.   Human relations or human resources? *Harvard Business Review*, 1965, 43, 148-157.

SCHEIN, E. H. and BENNIS, W. G.   *Personal and organizational change through group methods*. New York: Wiley, 1965.

ZANDER, A.   Resistance to change—its analysis and prevention. In W. G. Bennis, K. D. Benne and R. Chin (Eds.), *The planning of change*. New York: Holt, Rinehart and Winston, 1961.

᪥ ᪥ ᪥ ᪥ ᪥

The preceding studies in this section tend to sidestep the question of the actual classroom impact of educational innovations (Carlson) or to emphasize the difficulties involved (Gross *et al.*). Schmuck's article faces the issue squarely, and is a "success story" to boot.

The approach might be labelled "modern action research," in the sense that it takes an interventionist, action-assessing stance to a crucial question: how can teachers learn to change their classroom behavior, in the light of what is known about classroom group functioning (see, for example, Schmuck's other article in this book)?

The interventions discussed here are interesting and creative—considerably more sophisticated than what usually passes for "in-service education"—and the findings make good theoretical sense. Teachers who become more cohesive among themselves as a group, *and* who have opportunity for behavioral practice and feedback, do change their classroom behavior. As in the case of psychotherapy, "insight" is not enough. Learning *about* new styles of teacher behavior does change teachers' verbalizations about what it is they are doing, or ought to be doing—but their classrooms do not change as social systems in any significant way.

The interesting finding in Project 3 (that when a school staff was helped to become more cohesive, more involved with each other via working on shared problems, the teachers tried classroom innovations, even though none had been urged) deserves more testing—the data collected were noncomparable with those of Projects 1 and 2. Also: both "successful" projects involved an intensive period of laboratory training, as contrasted with weekly on-the-job meetings. Is this perhaps the major variable?

Helping Teachers Improve Classroom Group Processes*

Richard A. Schmuck

Informal classroom group processes affect not only students' attitudes, but their academic performance. It is possible for teachers to modify these group processes constructively. But most college and university courses, and most in-service education efforts for teachers, fail to provide the help teachers need in this area. New models for professional development seem to be needed.

This article describes, and systematically evaluates, three action research interventions designed to help teachers improve the informal group processes in their classrooms: a teacher development laboratory, the provision of consulting help, and an organization development laboratory for a school faculty.

The Problem

Classroom groups, like other groups, have both formal and informal aspects. The formal aspects have to do with ways in which various members work toward carrying out the official or specified goals of the group. In the classroom, for instance, one formal feature is the way in which any child performs the role of academic student, as it is defined by the teacher, school system, and adult community at large.

The informal aspects of a group involve the manner in which each member relates to other members as persons. In the classroom, an informal aspect is the way affection, or students' friendship for one another, is dis-

* From *Journal of Applied Behavioral Science*, 1968, 4 (4), 401-435. Used by permission of the author and publisher.

This paper summarizes over three years of action research on improving classroom group processes in schools in the metropolitan areas of Detroit, Michigan, Philadelphia, Pennsylvania, and Portland, Oregon. Acknowledgments of organizational assistance are granted to the Cooperative Research Branch of the United States Office of Education and the Center for Research on the Utilization of Scientific Knowledge of The University of Michigan for Project 1; to The Mental Health Association of Southeastern Pennsylvania and the Group Dynamics Center of Temple University for Project 2; and to the Oregon Compact and the Center for the Advanced Study of Educational Administration of the University of Oregon for Project 3. Many persons from these organizations contributed to the studies reported here. Special thanks are given to Denis Carville and Mark Chesler who worked on Project 1; to Anne Edelmann and Steven Saturen, co-workers in Project 2; and to Philip Runkel who collaborated in Project 3.

tributed. These informal features often have an important bearing on the formal aspects. Many of them, such as the amount of liking members have for one another or their willingness to help and support one another, may be thought of as positive and enhancing classroom group processes.

Informal classroom group processes, in the form of peer relations and norms as well as students' perceived group statuses, can have consequences for the students' self-esteem, attitudes toward school work, and academic achievement. In previous studies (Schmuck, 1962, 1963, and 1966), we showed that classroom groups with diffuse patterns of friendship and influence, compared with those with more hierarchical patterns, had greater cohesiveness and more supportive norms for learning. Most students in these diffuse groups perceived themselves as having high group status, while in the hierarchical groups only students who actually had high status perceived themselves as having it. Students who perceived themselves as having high peer status tended to have higher self-esteem, more positive attitudes toward school work, and were applying their intellectual abilities better than other students.

Other studies have shown that teachers can influence classroom group processes. Flanders and Havumaki (1960) showed that teachers' support and constructive praise were likely to increase students' sociometric position among their classmates. In contrived classroom settings teachers interacted with and praised only students seated in odd-numbered seats, while in comparison groups all students were encouraged to speak and the teachers' praise was directed to the whole class. Students in the odd-numbered seats, in the former situation, later received more sociometric choices than students in the even-numbered seats. In the comparison classrooms, the difference between sociometric choices of students in the odd- and even-numbered seats was insignificant.

In another study (Schmuck and Van Egmond, 1965), the results of a multi-stage analysis indicated that when the variable of familial social class—perceived parental attitudes toward school, perceived peer status, and satisfaction with the teacher—were compared for their relative relationship to academic performance, pupils' satisfactions with the teacher and performance were associated when the effects of the other three variables were held constant. The results indicated that the teacher, especially as a social-emotional leader, had an effect on the academic performances of both boys and girls which was independent, to a significant degree, from the effects of parents and peers.

Further research indicated that teachers of more cohesive classroom groups, compared with other teachers, attended to and talked with a larger variety of students per hour (Schmuck, 1966). Many teachers with less positive classroom group processes tended to call on fewer students for participation and seemed especially to neglect the slower, less involved students. Teachers with more supportive peer groups tended to reward students for helpful behaviors with specific statements and to control behavioral disturbances, with general, group-oriented statements. Teachers with less positive climates tended to reward individuals less often and to publicly reprimand them more often for breaking classroom rules. All of these results indicated that teachers can and do influence classroom group processes. The three action research interventions described below illuminate how teachers might be helped to create more psychologically supportive classroom group processes.

Project 1: Teacher Development Laboratory

In Project 1 we assumed that for classroom changes to be effective and viable, teachers need to learn more than theories, research facts, and specific innovative practices or techniques. Teachers must integrate theories, facts, and techniques into their value systems, emotional styles, and role conceptions. Sensitivity training and role-playing experiences accompanied by a scientific problem-solving orientation were hypothesized to facilitate such a re-education process. These experiences aim to encourage a teacher to search for alternative ways of teaching, stimulate his trying out new ideas, and press him to collect feedback from colleagues and students on the new practices.

Seven core training activities were carried out: (1) sensitivity training and related human relations laboratory experiences, (2) didactic discussions on basic research about classroom group processes, (3) problem-solving techniques for improving group processes, (4) analyses of diagnostic data from the teachers' own classrooms, (5) discussions about useful classroom practices developed by other teachers, (6) role-play tryouts of new classroom practices, and (7) follow-up discussions during the school year.

Twenty teachers participated in all of these activities and formed Laboratory Group A. Twenty other teachers participated in all the activities except sensitivity training, related human relations laboratory experiences, and role-play tryouts, and formed Seminar Group B. Ten teachers rounded out the design, received no special treatment, and formed Control Group C.

This project began in the spring of 1965 when a brochure announcing a four-week summer laboratory for upper elementary teachers went to 12 school systems in Metropolitan Detroit. The selection of school systems was accomplished by sampling broadly across social classes, and racial and ethnic groups. Chief school officers in all systems agreed to inform their upper elementary teachers of the program. Over 75 teachers applied, and 20 teachers were placed in Laboratory Group A and were matched with 20 others who constituted Seminar Group B. The ten teachers in Control Group C were selected later from other schools in the same school systems. The final selection of the entire sample was based on principles of demographic heterogeneity of students within the experimental categories and demographic similarity among the categories. All three categories of teachers, then, had students with a full range of social characteristics, but were quite similar to one another in their constellations.

The training period lasted six months for Laboratory Group A, starting in July and ending in December, 1965. Seminar Group B met from September to December. There was no training for Control Group C. The program for Group A began with a four-week, six-hours-each-day, intensive laboratory during July, and was followed up with feedback discussions with individual teachers and bimonthly discussion sessions from September to December. The program for Group B was constituted of weekly seminar meetings and individual conferences.

Laboratory for Group A

The *first week* of the four-week laboratory consisted almost entirely of general human relations training; the T-group, focusing on personal sensitivity, was the core of this program (Bradford, Benne, and Gibb, 1964). Twenty teachers were divided randomly into two T-groups that met separately for two-hour periods twice daily. While a skilled trainer was present in each group to maximize learning, the teachers created a group with their own concepts and in their own ways. Through this semistructured process, some of the teachers became more aware of how groups are formed, some of the significant events in group development, and the kinds of functions they personally perform in groups. Many participants gained the insight that their manner of speaking and relating to others could be just as important as the content of their communication.

Theory presentations, discussions, and skill exercises supplemented these T-groups. Theoretical lecturettes and discussions dealt with topics such as "Roles persons play in groups," "Communication and feedback," and "Personal styles in groups." Often skill exercises were based on these theory sessions. For instance, the discussion on communication and feedback was followed by a skill exercise in which the teachers gave feedback to one another in small groups and, at the same time, were required to indicate that they were "hearing" by paraphrasing what another had just said. In another combination session of theory and skill training, the teachers privately completed the Edwards Personal Preference Inventory, received their own scores on ten psychological needs, were informed of what the scores meant conceptually, and then role-played how such need patterns would be expressed behaviorally in the classroom.

During the *second week* T-groups continued to meet but only once each day, as the laboratory's discussions centered on the classroom as a human relations setting. Three categories of information were presented during the second week:

1. Some basic research on classroom group processes.
2. A problem-solving scheme, including these stages:
    a. identifying classroom group problems,
    b. diagnosing the classroom problems,
    c. developing a plan of action,

      d. trying out the plan, and

      e. getting feedback and making an evaluation (Schmuck, Chesler and Lippitt, 1966).

3. Classroom diagnosis in more depth, including the following topics:

      a. assessing the classroom learning climate,

      b. social relations in the classroom,

      c. peer group norms,

      d. student-teacher interaction,

      e. outside influences on students' learning,

      f. parental influences on school adjustment,

      g. the students' self-concept, and

      h. students' attitudes toward school and teachers (Fox, Luszki, and Schmuck, 1966).

Pairs or trios of teachers took one of these diagnostic topics and were responsible for teaching the entire workshop group how to use questionnaires and other measurement procedures on that topic. The trio working on teacher-student interaction received special instruction in Flanders' Interaction Analysis and used this procedure for collecting data on the teachers' instructional styles as the others taught about the various diagnostic techniques. After all of the other teachers had completed their instruction, this group reported on interaction analysis by giving feedback to all of the instructional teams on how they behaved according to the observation categories. Discussions on diagnosis were completed by the end of the second week.

Next, the teachers were assigned to skim through a booklet containing other teachers' practices and to decide tentatively on some practices they would like to try to improve classroom group processes or, more specifically, to solve classroom peer relations problems (Kaufman, Schmuck, and Lippitt, 1963). The teachers' techniques, devices, and special procedures included in this booklet had been examined for their soundness by skilled teachers, educational administrators, and social psychologists. A few examples drawn from the booklet are:

> *Development of a classroom group government to assist in social relations management.* Early in the year the class votes for a Rules Committee which sets up a Bill of Rights for all students and presents it to the rest of the group for discussion and approval. A Judiciary Committee is constituted to enforce the rules and serves for four weeks. Every day a member of the Judiciary Committee puts a schedule of the day's activities on the board including the name of the committee member who will be responsible for supervision of behavior during each period. The Judiciary Committee and the class officers meet to arrange the class seating plans and rearrange them as necessary. Every month four students who have not been on the Judiciary Committee are elected to serve until all students have taken part.

> *Formation and clarification of peer group behavior standards.* The teacher divides the class into small subgroups for discussion of behavioral standards. The groups initially are led by sociometrically high

students who are given some leadership training before commencing the groups. Each subgroup reports its findings orally to the class, the whole class identifies the standards they like best, and these become classroom rules. These subgroups meet once every week and all students receive some leadership training and a chance to lead a group.

Teaching human relations skills. Short class meetings are held three times each week concerning human relations topics. Some of these discussions are taped so that they can be played back later and evaluated by the students. The students also are encouraged to express their opinions by answering questions such as "What did you like about today?" and "What do you like or not like about our school?" When problems are identified, role-playing situations are set up and enacted. The students suggest alternative ways of behaving during the role-plays and discuss the meaning of role-plays for their classroom group relations.

On Monday and Tuesday of the *third week* the T-groups discussed the teachers' perceptions of the classroom practices presented in the booklet. Each teacher was asked to develop at least one practice that he wished to try out as a way of improving classroom group processes. On those same days, several two-hour sessions were held on the rationale for, and some ways of using, role playing (Chesler and Fox, 1966). Also one session was given on collecting feedback from students.

From Wednesday of the third week to Wednesday of the fourth and *final week,* each teacher spent one hour simulating part of his chosen practice in a role-play enactment using the other teachers in roles as students or as outside observers.

During the last two days of the laboratory, the teachers made specific plans for how they would implement these new classroom procedures during the school year. Lewin's force-field analysis was presented so that each teacher could estimate the restraining forces that would deter him from following through with the plan (Coch and French, 1948). After considerable thought was given to implementing the plan, each teacher conferred with a staff member about his plan. This conference took the place of a final examination and was tape recorded. A schedule was formed for playing the tape early in the fall at a similar conference, as a reminder and motivational device for supporting tryouts of the plan.

From September until December of 1965, the teachers continued to be involved in the program. Early in September, data were collected on the quality of group processes in all classrooms. Some data were immediately presented to the teachers. Next, the teachers listened to their tape recordings with a person from our staff and made more realistic plans based on the new data and their summer plans. Group discussions were held bimonthly during which the teachers discussed the strong and weak points of their teaching experiences. Attempts were made to support the teachers' efforts to follow through on their plans and to help the teachers to engage continuously in problem-solving. The program of training for Laboratory Group A was ended with an informal gathering one week before winter vacation.

Seminar for Group B

Group B met weekly from September to December, 1965. They were initially presented the same problem-solving sequence used by Group A. They learned about the uses of diagnostic tools and received group processes data from their classrooms for analysis. Basic research findings about classroom group processes also were presented to them and they read about the classroom practices of other teachers and discussed ones they would like to try. The principal activities omitted from the seminar for Group B were sensitivity training and role playing.

Project 1: Data Collection

Early in the fall, during the school year, and again late in the spring, students completed self-report questionnaires on classroom group processes and their attitudes toward peers, school, self, and teacher. Teachers in Groups A and B kept diaries concerned with their planned attempts at improving group processes. Every teacher was also observed three or four times for an hour each time during the school year. Data were collected on teachers in Group C only during the spring. The assumption made was that Group C classes, in which no interventions were tried, would more nearly reflect the fall than the spring patterns of classes in Groups A and B.

We also collected before and after self-report questionnaires from the students in Groups A and B classrooms in the fall and spring of the school year. Students in Group C completed questionnaires only in the spring. Averages from the fall measure taken on students in Groups A and B were used as estimates of the before data in Group C.

In general, the questions centered on the students' perceptions of their influence and friendship statuses in the classroom group and the extent to which they supported one another and felt a part of the group. Students were asked to estimate whether they saw themselves in the highest part (quarter) of the class, the second highest part, in the third part, or in the lowest part on these two questions: (1) *Influence:* "Compared with others in the class, how often can you get others to do what you want them to do?" and (2) *Friendship:* "Where would you place yourself in judging how much the others in the class like you?" Improved group relations would be indicated by the students' feeling that they were more influential and had more friends in the spring compared with the fall.

Furthermore, we asked students to describe, through a symbolic drawing, the friendship structure of the classroom group as they saw it. Students were presented the five rectangles as shown in Figure 1. Students selected the rectangle that best represented thier view of the peer group, or drew their own version in the blank rectangle. About 40 per cent of the students

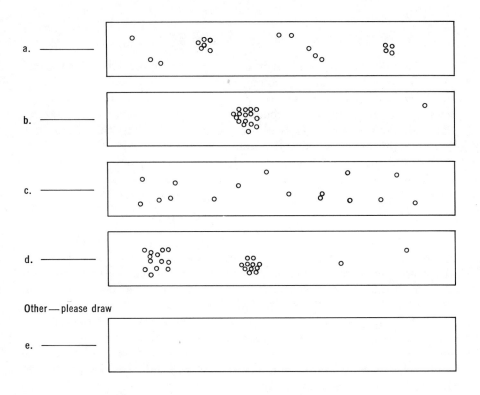

a. _____

b. _____

c. _____

d. _____

Other — please draw

e. _____

If you were to think about this class as a group, which one of these drawings would most nearly resemble your class?

Pretend that each circle stands for a person in this class. Circles that are close together stand for people who are friends. (Check the one most like your class.) Place an "X" within the circle that stands for your position in the group.

Figure 1.   The Classroom Group (A Method for Measuring Friendship Structure).

drew their own picture of the group. The students also were asked to place an "X" within one circle that would stand for their own position in the group.

We defined a friendship group as more than two circles in a cluster and compared the average number of these perceived to exist in the class early and late in the school year. We also categorized the place a student perceived his own position to be in the group during fall and spring by using these four categories: (1) at the center of a larger group, defined as more than four circles; (2) at the periphery of a large group; (3) in a smaller group, defined as four or fewer circles; and (4) alone or isolated. Finally, as a means of getting some idea of the supportive nature of the group, especially with regard to academic matters, we asked a series of questions about the frequency of supportive behaviors in the classroom. The one presented here asked: "The students in this class help one another with their school work (a) almost always, (b) usually, (c) seldom, and (d) almost never.

Results of Project 1

An overview of the results indicates that the Laboratory Group A teachers and students made more positive changes in their group processes than those in Seminar Group B and that both Groups A and B were more improved at the end of the school year than Control Group C.

Perhaps the most obvious difference between teachers in Groups A and B was their *group cohesiveness*. The *esprit de corps* in Group A was extremely positive, while almost none existed in Group B. Group A teachers telephoned one another 25 times about professional matters, while only two such calls were reported by Group B teachers. Fifteen of the 20 teachers in Group A visited socially during the school year; only three from Group B met informally. Numerous instances of sharing classroom teaching ideas occurred in Group A, while the teachers in Group B talked about their practices only during seminar time. Group A teachers talked more about their classrooms before and after class and during coffee breaks. Group A initiated a party at the end of the laboratory and many members indicated strong desires to continue or at least to keep in touch. Group B teachers showed more interest in receiving college credit than in one another.

These differences would not be very significant in themselves if they were not accompanied by *changes in classroom practices*. Evidence from diaries and observations indicated that the Group A teachers were much more innovative than the Group B teachers. Teachers in Group A produced more elaborate plans of action and attempted more practices for improving group processes than the Group B teachers. Group B teachers typically tried one or two practices during the year to improve group processes, while teachers in Group A tried from five to 17 different procedures with their students.

The most emphasized goal of the practices tried by Group A teachers was increasing openness in classroom communication between peers and between students and teacher. Communication was encouraged by summarizing data from student questionnaires and discussing their meanings, role playing difficult classroom situations, discussing critical statements placed in a suggestion box, discussing thoughts about what makes for a "good" or "bad" day in a class, and reviewing how the class had been proceeding by holding a once-weekly evaluation and review-discussion. Group B teachers used a few of these practices but tried fewer per teacher and continued using them for shorter durations.

The most widespread interest, manifested by 15 out of the 20 Group A teachers, was in raising students' participation levels in deciding upon classroom regulations and procedures. In seven Group A classrooms, student governments were formed and functioned successfully throughout most of

Table 1

STUDENT PERCEPTIONS OF INFLUENCE STATUS IN THEIR CLASSROOM GROUPS

THREE CATEGORIES OF CLASSROOMS IN FALL AND SPRING

PERCEIVED INFLUENCE STATUSES	LABORATORY GROUP A				SEMINAR GROUP B				CONTROL GROUP C (ESTIMATED)			
	FALL		SPRING		FALL		SPRING		FALL		SPRING	
	N	PER CENT	N	PER CENT	N	PER CENT	N	PER CENT	N	PER CENT	N	PER CENT
Highest part	(55)	10	(28)	5	(45)	9	(44)	9	(31)	10	(29)	9
Second part	(236)	43	(309)	56	(168)	35	(154)	32	(126)	39	(113)	35
Third part	(206)	37	(155)	28	(187)	39	(202)	42	(124)	38	(120)	37
Lowest part	(55)	10	(60)	11	(80)	17	(80)	17	(42)	13	(61)	19

Laboratory Group A:
$\chi^2 = 48.90$
$df = 3$
$p < .005$

Seminar Group B:
$\chi^2 = 2.39$
$df = 3$
$p = NS$

Control Group C:
$\chi^2 = 10.16$
$df = 3$
$p < .025$

the year. Teachers with such governments attempted to increase the diffusion of influence in the peer group by encouraging all students to take part at some point in the classroom government.

Results shown in Table 1, on the perceived influence status of each student early and late in the school year, indicated the positive significance of the laboratory experience for the Group A classrooms. The students with Group A teachers who perceived themselves as high (above the median) in peer group influence increased significantly from 53 per cent to 61 per cent during the school year. Students in Group B, on the other hand, showed no significant change from fall to spring on perceived influence. In the Control Group C classes, the results were that the students became significantly more negative in their perceptions of influence. While 49 per cent viewed themselves as high in influence during the fall, only 44 per cent perceived that they were high in the spring.

Results in Table 2 indicated that positive gains in perceived friendship status were made in all three categories of classrooms during the school year.

The positive gains made in Laboratory Group A were greater than those made in either Seminar Group B or Control Group C. Fifty-seven per cent of the students in Group A classrooms viewed themselves as highly liked early in the year. This number increased to 77 per cent in the spring, an increase of 20 percentage points. Percentage increases in Groups B and C were significantly positive also, but were only half as great as the increase in Group A. We conclude that in most classrooms students tended to perceive that they are liked by more people in the spring than in the fall, but the laboratory teachers appear to have increased this positive trend even more than the others.

Additional data indicating changes in classroom friendship patterns are summarized in Tables 3 and 4. In general, these data also supported our expectation that the laboratory would have positive benefit for Group A classroom groups. Results in Table 3 showed that positive gains in the number of friendship groups perceived by the students to exist in the class were made in all three categories. As in Table 2, comparisons of the chi-square totals as well as the percentages in Table 3 indicated that the positive gains were greatest for teachers in Laboratory Group A.

Results in Table 4 emphasized the success of the laboratory even more than those in Table 3. Here significant changes occurred in the extent to which students viewed themselves as being an integral part of either large (four or more persons) or small (three or fewer persons) friendship groups in the class. Fifty-three per cent of the Group A students saw themselves as at the center of a large or small group during the fall. This increased to 76 per cent by the spring. The comparable increase in Control Group C classes was from 58 per cent to 66 per cent, representing a minor increment compared with the laboratory classes. No significant change was made during the year in the Seminar Group B classroom groups on perception of friendship group position.

Table 2

STUDENT PERCEPTIONS OF FRIENDSHIP STATUS IN THEIR CLASSROOM GROUPS

THREE CATEGORIES OF CLASSROOMS IN FALL AND SPRING

PERCEIVED FRIENDSHIP STATUSES	LABORATORY GROUP A				SEMINAR GROUP B				ESTIMATED CONTROL GROUP C			
	FALL		SPRING		FALL		SPRING		FALL		SPRING	
	N	PER CENT	N	PER CENT	N	PER CENT	N	PER CENT	N	PER CENT	N	PER CENT
Highest part	(79)	14	(99)	18	(101)	21	(91)	19	(56)	17	(58)	18
Second part	(237)	43	(326)	59	(221)	46	(278)	58	(143)	44	(171)	53
Third part	(171)	31	(105)	19	(106)	22	(72)	15	(87)	27	(55)	17
Lowest part	(65)	12	(22)	4	(52)	11	(39)	8	(37)	12	(39)	12

$\chi^2 = 92.39$
$df = 3$
$p < .005$

$\chi^2 = 29.84$
$df = 3$
$p < .005$

$\chi^2 = 17.37$
$df = 3$
$p < .005$

Table 3

STUDENT PERCEPTIONS OF NUMBER OF CLASSROOM FRIENDSHIP GROUPS

THREE CATEGORIES OF CLASSROOMS IN FALL AND SPRING

NUMBER OF FRIENDSHIP GROUPS	LABORATORY GROUP A				SEMINAR GROUP B				CONTROL GROUP C			
	FALL		SPRING		FALL		SPRING		FALL		SPRING	
	N	PER CENT	N	PER CENT	N	PER CENT	N	PER CENT	N	PER CENT	N	PER CENT
0 or 1	(157)	30	(89)	17	(143)	31	(83)	18	(97)	31	(70)	22
2	(100)	19	(68)	13	(78)	17	(83)	18	(57)	18	(73)	23
3	(22)	4	(37)	7	(41)	9	(37)	8	(20)	6	(16)	5
4 or more	(245)	47	(330)	63	(199)	43	(258)	56	(143)	45	(158)	50

$\chi^2 = 69.17$
$df = 3$
$p < .005$

$\chi^2 = 43.37$
$df = 3$
$p < .005$

$\chi^2 = 14.38$
$df = 3$
$p < .005$

Table 4

STUDENT PERCEPTIONS OF OWN POSITION IN A CLASSROOM FRIENDSHIP GROUP

OWN POSITION IN FRIENDSHIP GROUP	THREE CATEGORIES OF CLASSROOMS IN FALL AND SPRING											
	LABORATORY GROUP A				SEMINAR GROUP B				CONTROL GROUP C			
	FALL		SPRING		FALL		SPRING		FALL		SPRING	
	N	PER CENT	N	PER CENT	N	PER CENT	N	PER CENT	N	PER CENT	N	PER CENT
At center of large group	(96)	20	(120)	25	(48)	16	(51)	17	(55)	18	(81)	27
At periphery of large group	(120)	25	(97)	20	(72)	24	(66)	22	(74)	25	(66)	22
In a small group	(158)	33	(245)	51	(151)	50	(155)	51	(119)	40	(117)	39
Alone	(106)	22	(18)	4	(31)	10	(30)	10	(52)	17	(36)	12

$\chi^2 = 131.35$
$df = 3$
$p < .005$

$\chi^2 = 0.81$
$df = 3$
$p = NS$

$\chi^2 = 18.10$
$df = 3$
$p < .005$

Table 5

STUDENT PERCEPTIONS OF HOW OFTEN THEY HELP ONE ANOTHER WITH SCHOOLWORK

	THREE CATEGORIES OF CLASSROOMS IN FALL AND SPRING											
	LABORATORY GROUP A				SEMINAR GROUP B				CONTROL GROUP C			
	FALL		SPRING		FALL		SPRING		FALL		SPRING	
HOW OFTEN THEY HELP ONE ANOTHER	N	PER CENT	N	PER CENT	N	PER CENT	N	PER CENT	N	PER CENT	N	PER CENT
Almost always	(56)	11	(86)	17	(71)	15	(71)	15	(42)	13	(48)	15
Usually	(172)	34	(206)	41	(162)	34	(200)	42	(110)	34	(107)	33
Seldom	(187)	37	(171)	34	(157)	33	(162)	34	(113)	35	(120)	37
Almost never	(92)	18	(44)	8	(85)	18	(42)	9	(58)	18	(48)	15

$\chi^2 = 49.19$
$df = 3$
$p < .005$

$\chi^2 = 30.81$
$df = 3$
$p < .005$

$\chi^2 = 3.09$
$df = 3$
$p = NS$

Finally, the data in Table 5 indicated that the students in both the Group A and Group B classrooms increased during the school year in the degree to which they were helpful to one another with their school work. Students in the Group C classroom groups showed no difference between the fall and spring in helpfulness.

Project 2: Classroom Mental Health Consultation

In Project 2 skilled psychological consultants attempted to enhance teachers' capabilities for coping with group processes in the classroom. Our orientation was that through problem-oriented discussions with mental health specialists teachers would develop a better understanding of and be more skilled in working with the social-emotional aspects of classroom groups (Edelmann and Schmuck, 1967). Consultation sessions centered on the relationships of consultant to teachers, teachers to teachers, and of teachers to the children they taught. Since the project was carried out in metropolitan Philadelphia, some attention was given to increasing teachers' ability to work with groups of students from disadvantaged families.

Six highly trained consultants (two psychiatrists, two clinical psychologists, and two social workers) were employed for the project. The bias of the consultants was psychodynamic and interdisciplinary. Only the social workers, however, had had professional experiences in public schools.[1] The consultants were assigned one to a school for half a day each week for 15 weeks. Three consultants worked in schools with mostly middle-class children, while the others worked in schools with culturally disadvantaged youngsters. Forty upper elementary teachers received consultation. Three consultants worked with groups of six teachers each; the other consultants worked with five, eight, and nine teachers respectively.

Two additional schools, one middle-class and one lower-class, were included for comparison purposes. The 20 upper elementary teachers in these two schools received no consultation.

This project began during the fall of 1966 when pre-data were collected; consultation took place during the fall and winter months, and final data were collected in May 1967, three months after the consultations were completed.

Consultation Sessions

The consultants spent two hours each week in group discussions with the teachers. They also visited classrooms to make observations which would often culminate in individual conferences. The project plans called for both

1. The consultants received special training prior to and concurrent with their work with the teachers in the schools. Drs. Eli Bower (Hollister and Bower, 1967) and Ruth Newman (Newman, 1967) were responsible for much of this training. They discussed their respective approaches to school consultation and guided the six specialists through problematic situations that would arise during the consultations.

the group discussions and the individual conferences to center on teachers' own reactions to the classroom groups, especially to problem incidents involving several students. The consultants were to emphasize the development of trust in the group and to open up new pathways of behavior and new understandings of desired changes only after some trust had developed. Finally, they were to explore in depth how teachers might interact with students with interpersonal relations problems, low self-esteem, marked disinterest in learning, or recurrent daydreams and inattention.

The consultants wrote historical accounts of every meeting with teachers, whether in group discussions or individual conferences. Along with these detailed descriptions of each encounter with teachers, the consultants were asked to jot down at the close of each session any problems they were having in establishing themselves as helpful and to specify any changes they saw in the schools, especially changes in the teachers with whom they were consulting.

Analyses of the consultants' reports indicated that certain recurrent themes occurred during the 15 weeks. During the first several sessions, classroom group problems were viewed as resulting from forces outside the control of the teachers. The teachers primarily ventilated their antagonistic feelings toward the "impersonal and unhelpful central office," the "authoritarian principal," the "incompetent counselor," the "uninterested parents," or the "intransigent students." These parties were seen as limiting the level of effectiveness that could be expected of the teachers. Some teachers felt that membership in the consultation group was involuntary, feeling that a school counselor, parental group, or the principal had really organized the group. Others needed reassurance that the principal or central office personnel would not be involved directly in the consultation groups.

After the teachers had a chance to voice these feelings in a supportive atmosphere, without being sanctioned by the consultants, they were more likely to discuss problems present in their classrooms and to see themselves and their students as jointly involved in them. As classroom group or individual problems were brought up for discussion, the teachers looked to the consultants for the solutions. They expected the consultants to recommend concrete actions that could be taken to solve the problem. At times, they expected the consultant to direct the principal or central office administrators that certain students perceived as mentally unhealthy should be removed formally from the regular classroom and placed in special education classes. The consultants generally assumed the point of view that they could only help teachers find their own answers, that these answers would most likely involve the teachers' changing their own classroom behavior, and that they did not have the authority to remove youngsters from classes.

Toward the end of the 15-week period, the teachers talked more about their own insecurities, doubts, and lack of knowledge and skills. During this phase the teachers turned more to one another for sharing ideas on handling classroom group problems. They offered to meet with one another at other times during the week to share teaching practices. The consultants' role became less prominent as the teachers conversed more freely and openly about their own classroom problems.

Project 2: Data Collection

In addition to the consultants' anecdotal accounts, data were collected from the total group of 60 teachers early during the fall and again late in the spring, via four self-report questionnaires.

Three teachers' questionnaires focused on perceptual variables, measuring conceptions about self as teacher, ways of categorizing students, and conceptions of positive mental health in the classroom. These questionnaires were scored "blind" by raters.

The fourth questionnaire queried teachers on how they might handle a variety of problematic situations in the classroom. Each consultant scored all of these protocols on "effectiveness." The consultants did not know what teacher or school they were scoring, nor did they know whether they were scoring the fall or the spring data.

The consultants did not see any results of the four questionnaires until after the consultations were completed.

In measuring the teachers' self-concepts, they were asked to write down ten phrases which described themselves as teachers, and rate the positiveness or negativeness of each phrase. We anticipated that the consultations would lead to a more *balanced* view of oneself as a teacher. We thought that those teachers who viewed themselves in the fall as quite negative and insecure would gain a greater sense of competence and self-esteem from the consultation. On the other hand, we considered that those who saw themselves as solely positive and effective in the fall would begin to uncover some areas within themselves that required some improvement. Thus, the raters judged as more positive those self-concept patterns which became more balanced, containing both positive and negative attributes, or which changed from more negative to more positive, and judged as more negative those patterns which remained predominantly negative or defensively positive.

In the questionnaire on categorizing the students, teachers were given a set of cards with the name of a student on each card and the following instructions:

> In your mind, there are probably many ways in which the students can be seen as similar to and different from one another. Place these cards in piles in as many different ways as might occur in your thinking. Each time you place the cards into piles, you should have some main idea in mind and a descriptive title for each pile.
>
> For instance, in your mind, you might divide the class into boys and girls. Then you would sort the cards into two piles, the main idea is "sex difference" and the descriptive titles of the piles are "boys" and

"girls." Another division which might occur could be color of hair. Then "color of hair" would be the main idea, and "blondes," "brunettes," and "redheads," could be the descriptive titles.

We expected the teachers to develop in several ways as a consequence of the consultation. For one thing, we considered that teachers with consultation would use more main ideas having to do with emotional factors, attitudes, motivations, and interpersonal relations at the end of the school year. We expected more categories on topics such as anxiety, security, self-esteem, attitudes toward school, and peer relations. Further, we expected that the teachers who received consultation would increase the number of differentiations that they made under the main categories. We felt that the consultation would facilitate a more sophisticated and differentiated view of the students. We expected that the teachers might see their students more in terms of feelings but also as being increasingly different from one another.

The third questionnaire was aimed at measuring teachers' cognitive structures concerning "mental health" in the classroom. Each teacher wrote about his ideas of good mental health practices and conditions in the classroom by placing one idea each on a maximum of 25 small index cards. The teachers received the following directions:

> Let us suppose that the following situation occurs. A visiting teacher from a foreign country engages you in conversation about school practices in this country. Assume that your visitor knows very little about American teaching practices. He wants to know what you consider to be good mental health practices and conditions in the classroom. What sorts of things would you include in a list which he could refer to as he tries to learn about classroom mental health?
>
> Using these cards which have been provided, write one word, phrase, or sentence on each card which describes good classroom mental health practices or conditions. Use as few or as many cards as you need. A total of 25 cards is supplied.

Teachers were then asked to sort these cards into groups and subgroups. The range of groupings generally included physical properties of the room and school, physical properties of teachers or students, intellectual skills, personality characteristics including attitudes and motives, interpersonal relations, and group social relations, climate, and cohesiveness. We expected that after the consultation the teachers would emphasize students' attitudes, feelings, and motives, as well as classroom interpersonal relations and group climate. Although physical characteristics might be included, we viewed these as less central to effective classroom group processes. We further considered that the mental health categories would have more detailed subgroupings and that the teachers would relate these more directly to the students in their class.

The fourth questionnaire, titled "Classroom Situations," was made up of forty-four situations which were taken from actual classrooms and presented in the form of dialogues. The teachers received these directions:

Pretend you are the teacher in each situation (even if you have not met such a situation or would not have allowed it to develop). When the dialogue closes, write the exact words or nonverbal responses you would use at that point.

The students also were asked to complete four questionnaires in the fall and spring. One questionnaire measured students' perceptions concerning the informal group processes in the class. Each student answered 12 questions on how he saw others in the class behaving, with one of four answers: almost always, usually, seldom, or almost never. Some of the items were, "Help one another with their school work," "Laugh when someone misbehaves," and "Work well with one another." The second questionnaire measured attitudes toward school and self-esteem with incomplete sentence stems. Examples of items used to measure the former were: "Studying is _____," "Homework is _____," "Learning out of books is _____." Self-esteem was measured with stems such as "When I look at other boys and girls and then look at myself, I feel _____," "When I look in the mirror, I _____," and "My teacher thinks I am _____." The third questionnaire presented sociometric questions on friendship and helping relations, asking students to choose the four other students in the class whom they liked the most and the four who were most helpful to other students. They also estimated their own status in the group on being liked and helpful. The fourth questionnaire dealt with students' attitudes about academic work and school in general. The students were asked about such things as "how hard they saw themselves working," "whether the teacher really understands them," and "whether the students helped one another."

Results of Project 2

Consultants' Impressions

The consultants generally agreed that significant and positive changes occurred in many teachers as a consequence of the consultations. Perhaps the most striking change was in teachers' asking one another for help. Early in the year, many teachers reported that they were ashamed to ask for one another's assistance. The teachers were generally discouraged or indifferent about staff relations. But after the consultations many teachers had formed a strong group feeling, had a new sense of challenge and interest, and were using one another outside the sessions to talk over problems, trade materials, and respond to new ideas. Some teachers who had decided during the fall to give up teaching changed their minds as they noted how much support they felt from their colleagues.

The consultants also felt that another general direction of change in the teachers was toward a more differentiated examination of their standards and attitudes, with somewhat greater leeway for accepting a variety of student behaviors. One consultant noted that his teachers showed more interest and ability to deal with individual differences. Another commented that a number of students had been perceived by their teachers as being disturbed, and that during the course of consultations this was changed to perceiving the students as more energetic, restless, and child-like than disturbed. According to one consultant, because the teachers' behaviors toward these children changed, some classroom problems seemed to disappear.

Some teachers were seen as reaching a stage in which they could examine their own behavior as a factor in creating undesirable behavior in their students. Other teachers spoke less judgmentally of students and parents at the end of the consultation and instead were more likely to explore their own relationships to their students. Some began to sort out their own needs from those of the students, while others noted publicly that "problem students" often ceased being problems when a teacher extended special help, affection, and arranged for some success.

Questionnaire Data

Data collected from the teachers generally indicated positive and significant changes during the school year in their perceptions of self as teacher, their cognitions of mental health categories, and their views on how to work with problematic classroom situations. The data on categorizing students did not change greatly during the year. These data are summarized in Table 6. "Positive" and "negative" are defined according to the predictions described above.

In each case, except for the data on categorizing students, results showed probabilities less than .01. We can assume that these data indicate significant changes and therefore that the consultations altered many teachers' cognitions related to successful teaching.

However, an overview of the student results indicated that positive and significant changes did *not* occur in the consultation classes. The students' attitudes toward school and self did not improve in either the consultation or the comparison groups. The informal group processes appear to have remained about the same throughout the year, except for some evidence that helpfulness increased in the consultation groups.

The over-all results do, however, obscure some positive changes that occurred in a few classrooms. Out of the 40 consultation classes, six showed distinct improvement and these, interestingly, were all in only two schools. In these six classes, the friendship and helpfulness patterns became more diffuse over the course of the year. Moreover, significant changes occurred in the positive self-esteem of many of these students. In contrast with this, no changes whatsoever occurred in the students' attitudes toward school.

It appears that the cognitive and attitudinal changes which occurred in the teachers were *not* also accompanied by behavioral changes that made a difference in their classrooms. The teachers grew in their intellectual aware-

Table 6

SUMMARY OF TEACHERS' PERCEPTIONS OF SELF, STUDENTS, AND CLASSROOM PROCESSESS

FOUR VARIABLES OF TEACHERS' PERCEPTIONS FOR CONSULTATION AND COMPARISON GROUPS IN FALL AND SPRING

EVALUATION IN SPRING COMPARED WITH FALL	SELF-CONCEPT				CATEGORIZING STUDENTS				MENTAL HEALTH CATEGORIES				CLASSROOM SITUATIONS			
	CONSULTATION GROUP		COMPARISON GROUP		CONSULTATION GROUP		COMPARISON GROUP		CONSULTATION GROUP		COMPARISON GROUP		CONSULTATION GROUP		COMPARISON GROUP	
	N	PER CENT	N	PER CENT	N	PER CENT	N	PER CENT	N	PER CENT	N	PER CENT	N	PER CENT	N	PER CENT
More positive	14	35	2	10	5	12	0	0	15	38	0	0	19	48	3	15
No change	24	60	16	80	35	88	20	100	24	60	20	100	14	35	13	65
More negative	2	5	2	10	0	0	0	0	1	2	0	0	7	17	4	20
Probabilities*	$p < .01$				$p =$ NS				$p < .01$				$p < .01$			

* Fisher's Exact Test (Hays, 1963), applied because of the very small sample, requires a two-by-two contingency table; thus the data labeled "more negative" were dropped.

nesses about interpersonal relations in the classroom and in their willingness to explore new ways of handling them, but they did not in fact make major shifts in their classroom behavior. Any behavior changes that did occur, as reported by the consultants, were probably short-term and motivated out of desires to please the consultants. The group processes in the classrooms, by and large, remained unaffected by the consultations.

Project 3: Organizational Development Laboratory

In Project 3, we did not attempt to influence, directly, teachers' capabilities for working more effectively with classroom group processes. Rather, we assumed that the social relations of a school set the stage for classroom innovation and that more effective organizational processes support teacher innovativeness and performance in the classroom (Lippitt, *et al.*, 1966).

This project was aimed at improving school organizational processes in the short run so that classroom innovations might be made more easily in the long run. It employed an organizational training program to help a junior high school faculty to become more aware, open, analytic, and skillful about its interpersonal relationships, communication patterns, behavior norms, decision-making processes, and group problem-solving skills.

A six-day laboratory was held before the beginning of school, 1967, and involved the entire faculty—except for two with illnesses in their families—including the head custodian, head cook, and administrative secretary, making a total group of 54 participants. The laboratory staff was composed of five trainers. The laboratory was designed to help the staff discuss its interpersonal relations, identify and explore its communicative problems, and move toward tentative, working solutions through group problem solving. Several follow-up training sessions were also scheduled during the 1967-68 school year.

Laboratory for the Faculty

During the first two days of the laboratory the design called for a series of structured group exercises which were to lead the faculty into discussions about its own organizational processes. For instance, a "NASA Trip to the Moon" exercise was employed in which five groups of 10 or 11 persons formed to decide on those items that would be most important to carry on a fictitious 200-mile trip across the moon's surface. The underlying theme of this exercise concerned the efficient uses of individual resources in making group decisions. After the exercise was completed, discussions were commenced by the trainers with such questions as: "What were your reactions to the exercise?" "How did you feel?" "What were you thinking?" "How similar or different were your behaviors here from the way they usually are in school?" and "What implications does this exercise have for your staff?" These discussions were followed by a general assembly of the entire faculty in which staff members gave their reactions to what they learned during the exercise. Each group chose its own way to report back on what it had experienced. Some elected a spokesman, while others held a group discussion in front of the general assembly. These group processes also were discussed as they took place. The trainers attempted to support openness and the giving and receiving of helpful feedback during these sessions.

Subsequent sessions during the first two days were similar in form. They began with a structured activity, were followed by discussion in small groups about the activity, and ended with some sharing of various insights on organizational processes within the entire faculty. Some of the structured activities involved nonverbal cooperation, preparation of murals depicting psychological views of the school, planning and executing a complex puzzle requiring coordination, and a communication and feedback exercise in which staff members gave feedback to one another in variously sized groups and were required to indicate that they were "hearing" by paraphrasing what the other had just said. In all of these activities the faculty members regrouped each time, using the criterion of seeking out persons with whom they had communicated very little.

The remainder of the laboratory was spent in working through a six-stage problem-solving process. The staff was asked to choose "real" issues that were bothersome to the organizational functioning of the school. Three problems were identified as being the most significant: (1) a lack of role clarification, (2) low degrees of staff involvement in meetings, and (3) the nonuse of staff resources. While proceeding through the initial problem identification stage, several group formations and processes were employed that would be useful forms for the staff's operations during the school year.

After the three problems were identified, staff members volunteered to work jointly on one of them and proceeded through the problem-solving processes that involved five more steps: (1) further problem refinement and operationalization, (2) force-field diagnostic exercises, (3) brainstorming action alternatives to reduce restraining forces, (4) designing concrete plans of action, and (5) trying out the plan with a training activity involving the rest of the staff.

The three training activities designed by the problem-solving groups represented high points of the laboratory. The group that worked on *role clarification* felt that a lack of trust among the staff was one important restraining force keeping staff members from clarifying their roles. They carried out a variety of nonverbal exercises to explore feelings of trust in the total staff. Each of these was followed by discussion on its meanings for the organizational functioning of the faculty. The second group, on *staff involvement,* organized several small discussion groups and acted as outside observers. During these discussions, persons who had been talking a great deal during the last five-minute interval were asked to move back from the group by the observers and to stop talking. Others still in the group were told that those who were moved back were not to answer any questions asked of them. After only two persons were left, discussions were held in each group on "feelings toward involvement during staff meetings." The third group, involved with *using staff resources,* set up several small groups, each of which was a simulated mini-staff of a junior high school. A crisis was pictured in which no texts or materials were available, but youngsters were coming to school the next day. Each staff person was told to specialize in an area other than his own subject matter and to seek help from others in his group. The fictitious staffs were to construct a curriculum by using one another's resources. The whole faculty assembled at the end to discuss implications for their organizational functioning.

The laboratory ended with a "strength exercise" that was designed to raise members' self-esteem and contribute to group cohesiveness. The staff divided into small groups of seven or eight. Each staff member spent a few minutes reflecting alone on his own strengths as a staff member and the unique strengths of others in his group. The time spent alone was followed by a sharing of these "strength perceptions." No admissions or observations of weaknesses were allowed. Every group included each of its members in their discussion and then the entire faculty discussed meanings of the exercise.

Project 3: Data Collection

Faculty members were asked to complete several self-report questionnaires just prior to or during the laboratory. These were designed to measure the school's organizational climate, reactions to staff meetings, staff communication patterns, and perceptions of the principal. The research evaluation also called for some interviews and observations to be collected during the school year, as well as these same self-report questionnaires again in the spring. All the measures, whether they were questionnaires, interviews, or observations, were designed originally to center only on organizational processes. They did not include questions about classroom innovations.

Results of Project 3

Some early developments warrant inclusion here because of the light they shed on helping teachers improve classroom group processes. (See Schmuck and Runkel, in press, for more detail.)

We learned only inadvertently about the teachers' making use of experiences from the laboratory in their classrooms. The first signs came immediately after the laboratory when a one-page questionnaire was filled out by all faculty members on their reactions to the laboratory. Even though no question about classroom applications of the workshop was asked, seven teachers mentioned plans to make use of some laboratory experience in their classrooms.

A second indication came in some of the essays about the laboratory written by 21 teachers. All workshop participants had the opportunity of receiving two hours of university credit for active participation. Twenty-one teachers desired three credit hours and were required to prepare an essay on their laboratory experiences. Their assignment was to write about any changes, positive or negative, in the school's operation which they considered attributable to the laboratory. They were asked to complete the essay no later than six weeks after the end of the laboratory. Most papers came in about one month after it closed. We expected to receive analyses of the school's organizational functioning primarily. Many of the faculty members, however, wrote extended reviews of how the laboratory had positively influenced their classroom performances. Some were quite specific about having used, with their students, some of the group formations, techniques, or processes employed during the laboratory.

Finally, a third sign of classroom application came about six weeks after the laboratory closed when we visited the school to interview staff members about the faculty's organizational processes. Again, even though no question was asked formally in the interview about classroom innovations, 15 teachers mentioned using new group processes in their classrooms. With these unanticipated data, we added one question to the interview schedule for the next round of interviews. The question was, "Has the laboratory experience influenced your classroom teaching in any ways?" "If yes, in what ways?" Of the 20 teachers who were interviewed on the second round, 19 answered yes to the question.

The teachers' comments on "in what ways" the laboratory influenced their teaching divided into three categories. Some teachers mentioned only very general outcomes such as "a change in my general approach to students," a better atmosphere in my classroom," or "more attention to the feelings of the students." Another small group of teachers commented on specific attitude changes such as "I am more comfortable this year," "I am sensitive to students' feedback," or "I am more relaxed in letting the students discuss things." Eleven of the 19 teachers fitted into the third category. They mentioned specific group procedures that they actually were using in their classrooms such as "using small groups for projects," "using nonverbal exercises to depict feelings about the subject matter being studied," "using 'theatre in the round' or 'fishbowl' formations for having students observe one another," "using a paraphrasing exercise to point out how poor classroom communications are," "using the problem-solving sequence and techniques in social studies classes to learn more about social problems," and "using small groups for giving and receiving feedback about how the class is going." As far as we know, none of these practices was used by these teachers before the organizational development laboratory.

Discussion and Conclusions

The three interventions discussed above helped teachers, directly or indirectly, to work toward improving classroom group processes.

The organizational development laboratory for a school staff, described in Project 3, set the stage for staff members' unexpected attention to classroom group processes by encouraging them to experiment with innovative group procedures in the school organization. Training activities carried out during the laboratory presented group forms, techniques, and procedures that could be used just as appropriately in the classroom as at staff meetings. The laboratory was a living example of McLuhan's dictum that "the medium is the message" (McLuhan, 1964). A majority of the teachers tried new group processes in their classrooms that were directly patterned after their organizational laboratory experiences.

In Project 2, regular discussions about classroom processes with psychological consultants helped improve teachers' perceptions of self as teachers, their cognitions of mental health categories, and their views on how to work with problematic classroom situations. However, these cognitive and attitudinal changes were *not* accompanied by behavioral changes in the classroom. This is not surprising since verbal learning is quite different from skill learning. Persons do not learn to play baseball, to dance, or to give speeches by reading books or through discussions. Nor should a teacher be expected to improve the complex skills of classroom instruction through mere discussions. Discussions on classroom group problems, students' psychodynamics, and different approaches to teaching can be expected to assist a teacher to think, talk, or write more intelligently about the issues, but actual behavioral tryouts and experiences are necessary before new skills are used easily in the classroom.

A teacher development laboratory (Project 1) which included problem-solving techniques, sensitivity training, and role-play tryouts *did* lead to behavioral changes in the classroom. The sensitivity training and related human relations activities seemed to challenge teachers' cognitions of interpersonal relations, to lead teachers to introspect about their effects on others, to encourage exploration of values about teaching, and to develop colleague norms of support and helpfulness. The problem-solving procedures helped teachers think more systematically about new patterns of classroom behavior, and the role-play tryouts helped build psychological connections among new cognitions, attitudes, and behaviors.

Taken together, these interventions can fit well into integrated action programs that might be employed by school systems for improving classroom group processes. Two integrated programs of different durations can be mentioned here.

One would take place over an 18-month period. It would commence with an organizational development laboratory during the latter part of August, just prior to the beginning of the school year. Following this, teachers would be asked to volunteer for a program of consultation and training in classroom group processes. A psychological consultant, skilled in interpersonal relations theory and classroom processes, would work with them two hours each week for the entire academic year. Then, during the following summer, a teacher development laboratory would take place. Follow-up discussions could occur during the fall semester to help the teachers follow through on trying out new procedures and to reinforce continuously any insights or new skills developed during the previous year.

Another shorter program, lasting for only about six months, would be launched just two weeks before the beginning of school. A one-week organizational development laboratory would be followed by a second week's teacher development laboratory. This design would facilitate the translation of group processes found to be useful during the organizational laboratory into classroom innovations during the teacher development laboratory. Then, during the fall semester, follow-up discussions could be led by psychological consultants who would emphasize the problem-solving process and give support to teachers trying to implement their plans.

Many other action designs might be developed using these three basic interventions as the elements. We hope that behavioral scientists and educators will collaborate in trying some of them.

References

BRADFORD, L., BENNE, K. and GIBB, J.   *T-group theory and laboratory method.* New York: Wiley, 1964.

CHESLER, M. and FOX, R.   *Role-playing methods in the classroom.* Chicago: Science Research Associates, 1966.

COCH, L. and FRENCH, J. R. P., Jr.   Overcoming resistance to change. *Human Relations,* 1948, 1, 512-532.

EDELMANN, A. and SCHMUCK, R.   *Pilot study in exploring the use of mental health consultants to teachers of socially maladjusted pupils in regular classes.* Unpublished final report. Philadelphia, Pa.: Mental Health Association of Southeastern Pennsylvania, 1967.

FLANDERS, N. and HAVUMAKI, S.   The effect of teacher-pupil contacts involving praise on the sociometric choices of students. *Journal of Educational Psychology,* 1960, 51, 65-68.

FOX, R., LUSZKI, M. and SCHMUCK, R.   *Diagnosing classroom learning environments.* Chicago: Science Research Associates, 1966.

HAYS, W.   *Statistics for psychologists.* New York: Holt, Rinehart and Winston, 1963. Pp. 598-601.

HOLLISTER, W. and BOWER, E. (Eds.).   *Behavioral science frontiers in education.* New York: Wiley, 1967.

KAUFMAN, M., SCHMUCK, R. and LIPPITT, R.   *Creative practices developed by teachers for improving classroom atmospheres.* Document No. 14, Inter-Center Program on Children, Youth, and Family Life. Ann Arbor, Mich.: Institute for Social Research, 1963.

LIPPITT, R., BARAKAT, H., CHESLER, M., DENNERELL, D., FLANDERS, M., WORDEN, O. and SCHMUCK, R.   The teacher as innovator, seeker and sharer of new practices. In R. Miller (Ed.), *Perspectives on educational change.* New York: Appleton-Century-Crofts, 1967. Pp. 307-324.

McLUHAN, M.   *Understanding media.* New York: McGraw-Hill, 1964.

NEWMAN, R.   *Psychological consultation in the schools.* New York: Basic Books, 1967.

SCHMUCK, R.   Sociometric status and utilization of academic abilities. *Merrill-Palmer Quarterly,* 1962, 8, 165-172.

SCHMUCK, R.   Some relationships of peer liking patterns in the classroom to pupil attitudes and achievement. *School Review,* 1963, 71, 337-358.

SCHMUCK, R.   Some aspects of classroom social climate. *Psychology in the Schools,* 1966, 3 (1), 59-65.

SCHMUCK, R., CHESLER, M. and LIPPITT, R.   *Problem solving to improve classroom learning.* Chicago: Science Research Associates, 1966.

SCHMUCK, R. and RUNKEL, P.   Organizational training for a school faculty. Eugene, Ore.: Center for Advanced Study of Educational Administration, in press.

SCHMUCK, R. and VAN EGMOND, E.   Sex differences in the relationships of interpersonal perceptions to academic performance. *Psychology in the Schools,* 1965, 2 (1), 32-40.

Index of Persons

Aaron, D., 502, 521
Abbott, E., 44, 55
Adams, D.K., 122, 132
Adelson, J., 293, 305
Adkins, W., 414n
Adorno, T.W., 482, 488, 493, 499
Adrian, C.R., 243n, 268
Agger, R.E., 243n, 268
Aichorn, A., 44, 55
Alden, E., 141, 148
Alexander, C.N., 285, 301, 304
Allen, J., 247
Allen, K., 105, 119
Allinsmith, E., 402, 410
Allinsmith, W., 402, 411
Allport, F.H., 13, 42
Allport, G.W., 217, 223, 424, 433, 458, 467
Alpert, R., 58-75
Altbach, P., 502, 507, 522
Alter, R.D., 122
Andrews, J.D.W., 414n, 425, 433
Aneshansel, J., 217, 223
Aram, J., 458n
Argyle, M., 691-93, 705
Argyris, C., 311, 317, 693n, 705
Arnold, C.P., 105, 119
Aronfreed, J., 402, 410
Artley, A.S., 219, 223
Asch, S.E., 37, 42, 404, 407, 410, 420, 581
Ashmore, H.S., 215
Astin, A.W., 87, 91
Atkinson, J.W., 66, 75, 227-28, 233, 234,
    237, 358-59, 361, 365, 369, 416, 419,
    421, 433, 434, 461, 467
Ausubel, D.P., 617, 623
Avery, R.W., 658n, 670
Axelson, L.J., 233, 238

Babbitt, I., 59, 60, 65, 75
Back, K., 265, 268
Backman, C., 2, 6, 9, 169
Baer, D.M., 105, 119
Bailey, D.E., 122, 129, 133
Bales, R.F., 311n, 317, 405, 412, 631n,
    632n, 636
Bandura, A., 217, 223, 415, 428, 433
Banfield, E.C., 243n, 268
Bany, M.A., 150
Barakat, H., 734
Barker, L.S., 42
Barker, R.G., 5, 6, 11, 12-42, 138, 148
Barnard, C.I., 661, 670
Bartlett, F.C., 217, 223
Bass, B.M., 227, 237
Basset, R., 293, 304
Bauer, R.A., 424, 433
Becker, H.S., 87, 91, 313, 317, 556n, 567
Becker, W.C., 105-20

Beez, W.V., 327, 328-34
Belisle, E.L., 638, 655
Belknap, I., 666n, 670
Bell, D., 502, 521
Bell, G.D., 299, 305
Bell, T.H., 665, 670
Bendix, R., 284, 305, 616, 623
Benedict, R., 425, 433
Benjamin, L., 228, 238
Benne, K.D., 459, 467, 693n, 705
Bennis, W.G., 692n, 705, 734
Berelson, B., 416, 420, 423, 424, 426, 433
Berenda, R.W., 407, 410
Berger, B., 283, 305
Berlew, D.E., 459, 467
Bernstein, B., 170-72, 186
Bernstein, M., 691-705
Bettelheim, B., 600, 613
Biddle, B.J., 93, 599, 600-13
Bidwell, C.E., 586n, 598
Bijou, S.W., 105, 119
Bixby, F.L., 46, 56
Blake, R., 217, 219, 223
Blau, P.M., 625, 634-36, 640, 654
Blauner, R., 309n, 317
Block, J., 471, 483, 488
Bloom, R., 6
Bloom, B., 77, 92
Boehm, L., 400, 402, 410
Boocock, S.S., 335, 336-56
Bordua, D.J., 284, 299, 305
Borg, W.R., 215
Bovard, E.W., 226, 232, 237
Bower, E., 722n, 734
Bradford, L.P., 459, 467, 693n, 705, 734
Braham, M., 304, 305
Braly, K.W., 217, 223
Braungart, R.G., 504, 521
Breckenridge, S.P., 44, 55
Brehm, J.W., 465, 467
Bridges, E.M., 624, 625-36
Brim, O., 586n, 598
Brittain, C.V., 304, 305
Brogden, H.E., 66, 75
Bronfenbrenner, U., 319, 336n, 356, 389,
    390-412, 503, 521, 592n, 593, 598
Bronner, A., 44, 56
Brookover, W., 6
Brophy, J., 170n, 174, 184, 186
Brown, B., 170, 186
Brown, R.W., 421, 433, 466, 467
Browning, C.J., 639n, 654
Bruner, J.S., 577, 581, 598
Buchanan, P., 437n, 456
Buell, J.S., 105, 119
Bunker, D., 445n, 456
Burns, H.W., 585n, 598
Burris, R.W., 415, 433
Burton, R.V., 402; 411

Bushnell, J.H., 554
Butterworth, C.E., 284, 285, 303*n*, 305

Cahen, L.S., 328, 334
Callahan, R.E., 358*n*
Campbell, A., 354, 356, 639, 654
Campbell, D.T., 438*n*, 441, 456
Campbell, E.Q., 285, 301, 304
Caplan, G., 399, 411
Caplow, T., 310*n*, 317
Carlson, R.O., 616, 623, 656, *657-70*, 671, *672-89*, 706
Carr, H.A., 423
Carter, R.F., 584*n*, 598
Cartwright, D., 154, 167
Carville, D., 707*n*
Chall, J., 361, 368
Charters, W.W., Jr., 77*n*, 586*n*, 598, *638-55*
Chase, M., 6
Chesler, M., 707*n*, 711, 712, 734, 735
Child, I.L., 402, 412, 556, 567
Christie, R., 593, 598
Clapp, N.W., *44-56*
Clark, B.R., 336, 356
Clark, H.B., 222, 223
Clark, J.P., 309*n*, 317, 638, 639, 654
Clark, M.K., 222, 223
Cloward, R.A., 45, 55, 359, 369, 416, 434
Coch, L., 691, 705, 712, 734
Cohen, A.K., 399, 411, 553, 554
Cohen, A.R., 465, 467
Cohen, E.G., 284, 299, 305
Cohen, M., 229, 238
Coleman, J.S., 6, 151, 167, 188-202, 204, 206-9, 212-14, 269, *270-81*, 283-85, 293, 303*n*, 304, 335, *336-56*, 389, 553, 554, 615, 623
Collier, H.L., 227, 238
Collins, B.E., 624, 626, 636
Corwin, R.C., 309*n*, 317
Coser, L., 510, 521
Coser, R.L., 309*n*, 317
Crain, R.L., 240, 241-68
Criswell, J.H., 227, 228
Cronbach, L.J., 601, 613

Dale, E., 361, 368
D'Andrade, R.G., 419, 425, 427
Dann, S., 399, 411
Danzig, E., 414*n*
Davidson, K.S., 228, 239
Davis, A., 170, 186
Davis, J.A., 87, 91, 271*n*, 556*n*
Dean, D.G., 309*n*, 317, 638, 655
Dean, G.S., 91
De Charms, R., 357, *358-69*
Deese, J., 226, 238
De Fleur, L.B., 5, *371-88*
De Fleur, M.L., 5, *371-88*
Dennerell, D., 734
Denney, R., 358, 369
Denny, M.R., 629
Dennis, W., 217, 219, 223
Dentler, R.A., *189-98*, 293, 305
Derber, C., 501*n*
Deutsch, M., 170, 186
Devor, G., 5, 169, 319, *320-26*
Dewey, J., 311*n*, 510, 690
Dickson, W.J., 418, 434
Dittes, J.E., 227, 238

Divine, Father, 1
Doakes, J., 16
Douvan, E., 293, 305, 638, 655
Doyle, W.J., *625-36*
Drachkovitch, M.M., 309*n*, 317
Drucker, P., 336, 356
Duncan, O.D. 285, 305
Dyer, H.S., 199, *200-15*
Dymond, R.F., 414, 424, 434

Easterbrook, J.A., 226, 238
Ebel, R.L., 644, 655
Echelberger, E., 152, 167
Edelmann, A., 707*n*, 722, 734
Edwards, A.L., 217, 223
Eells, K., 170, 186
Eidell, T.L., 615, 618, 619, 621, 623
Eisenstadt, S.N., 399, 400, 411, 502, 507, 522
Ekstrom, R.B., 215
Elias, A., *44-56*
Elkins, D., 152, 168
Ellena, W.J., 93
Ellis, R.A., 284, 305
Ends, E.J., 427, 433
Epps, E.G., 233, 236, 238
Erikson, E.H., 487, 488, 503, 507, 522
Etzioni, A., 616, 617, 623
Eysenck, H.J., 414, 433
Ezekiel, R.S., 471, 484, 486, 488

Faigin, H., 399, 411
Farmer, M.E., 639*n*, 654
Feigenbaum, R., 5, *570-82*
Feitelson, D., 170*n*
Feldman, J., 271*n*
Ferry, W.H., 387*n*, 388
Feshbach, N.D., 5, 169, 319, *320-26*
Festinger, L., 265, 268, 419, 433, 465, 467, 571, 581
Feuer, L.S., 309*n*
Fiske, D.W., 441, 456
Flacks, R., 357, 500, *501-22, 524-54*
Flanders, N.A., 93, 734
Floro, G.K., 670
Floud, J., 284
Foskett, J.M., 584*n*, 598
Fox, R., 711, 712, 734
Frank, J., 419, 433
Freedman, M., 536, 553, 554
Freitag, G., 117, 120
French, E.G., 426, 433
French, J.R.P., Jr., 141, 148, 226, 227, 238, 691, 705, 712, 734
Frenkel-Brunswick, E., 482, 488
Freud, A., 399, 411
Freud, S., 405, 411, 427, 458, 510
Friedenberg, E.Z., 308, 317
Friedman, G.A., 359, 369
Friedman, N.S., 598
Friesen, W., *12-42*, 146, 148
Fromm, E., 616, 623
Fulenwider, M., 458*n*
Furstenberg, F.F., Jr., 285, 293, 297, 304, 305

Gage, N.L., 7, 77*n*, 601, 613
Gall, H.S., 367, 368
Gershon, E., 58*n*

Giacquinta, J.B., *691-705*
Gibb, J.R., 459, 467, 693*n*, 705, 734
Gilbert, D., 616, 623
Glazer, N., 358, 369
Glidewell, J.C., 632*n*, 636
Gnagey, W.J., 142-43, 148
Goffman, E., 311*n*, 317, 600, 613, 616, 623
Gold, M., 152, 168
Goldberg, B., 105*n*
Goldberg, M., 105*n*
Goldiamond, I., 458, 467
Goldman, M., 235, 238
Goldrich, D., 243*n*, 268
Goldsen, R.K., 503, 522, 553, 554
Goldston, J., 228, 238
Goode, W.J., 584*n*
Goodman, M.E., 217, 223
Goodman, P., 308, 379
Goodman, S.M., 203-4, 215
Gordon, C.W., 304, 305, 615, 623
Gottlieb, D., 282, 555, *556-67*
Gough, H.G., 493, 499
Gouldner, A.W., 650, 655, 658*n*, 661, 667*n*, 669, 670
Greenbaum, C., 231, 233, 238
Greenwald, H.J., 222, 223
Gregor, A.J., 217, 219, 222, 223
Greiner, L.E., 693*n*, 705
Griffith, J.C., 389, *458-67*, 468, 599
Gronlund, N., 151, 168
Gross, N., 583, 687, 689, 690, *691-705*, 706
Grossberg, J.M., 458, 467
Grusky, O., 661, 670
Guetzkow, H., 624, 626, 636
Gump, P., 5, 6, *12-42, 135-49*, 468
Gumpert, C., 327
Gumpert, P., 327
Gurin, G., 354, 356, 639, 654
Guskin, A., 2
Guskin, S., 2

Hadassah, D., 217, 223
Hagen, E.E., 357, 369
Haire, M., 399, 411
Hall, D., 458*n*
Haller, A.O., 151, 168, 284, 285, 303*n*, 305
Halpin, A.W., 644, 655
Halsey, A.H., 284, 305
Harding, J., 216
Harris, I., 235, 238
Harris, F.R., 105, 119
Harris, M.R., 483
Harris, T.M., 436*n*
Hart, B.M., 105, 119
Hart, H., 366, 369
Hartley, E.H., 319
Harvey, O.J., 121, *122-33*
Havighurst, R.J., 170, 186, 408, 412
Havumaki, S., 734
Hays, W., 168, 734
Healy, W., 44, 56
Heckhausen, H., 419, 433
Heider, F., 145, 148, 552, 554, 569, 570-71, 577, 579-81
Heinicke, C., 631*n*, 636
Heist, P., 87, 91, 526, 554
Henry, J., 308, 317
Herrick, V.E., 170, 186
Herriott, R.E., 283-85, 305, 584*n*, 598
Heslin, R.E., 122

Hess, R.D., 169, *170-87*, 319
Hill, C.M., 585*n*, 598
Hobbs, N., 470
Hoffman, M.L., *402-4*, 411
Hoffmeister, J.K., *122-33*
Holland, J.L., 87, 91
Hollingshead, A.B., 299, 305
Hollister, W., 722*n*, 734
Holt, J., 311*n*, 317
Hook, S., 309
Hopkins, T.K., 437*n*, 456
Hopson, J.A., 655
Horowitz, E., 227, 238
Horowitz, L., 217, 223
Horowitz, R.E., 217, 223
Houghton, L.J., 359, 369
Hovland, C.I., 417, 418, 420, 427, 433-34
Hoy, W.K., 614, *615-23*
Huizinga, J., 335
Hunt, D.E., 121, 133
Hutchinson, J.G., 293, 305
Hyman, H.H., 285, 305, 437*n*, 456

Ichheiser, G., 581
Irion, A.L., 423, 434
Irvine, E.E., 399, 411

Jackson, J.D., 174, 186
Jackson, P.W., 93, *94-103*
Jacob, P.E., 59, 66, 75, 503, 522
Jacobson, L., 328, 333, 334
Jacques, E., 693*n*, 705
Jahoda, M., 283, 305
James, W., 458
Janis, I.L., 417, 418, 434
Jenkins, D., 584*n*, 598
John, V., 170, 186
Johnson, C., 357, 369
Johnson, D.W., 2, 5, 150, 216, *217-23*, 436*n*, 456
Johnson, L.V., 150
Johnson, T.J., 5, *570-82*
Jonckheere, A.R., 499
Jones, E.E., 217, 223
Jones, R.G., 615, 618, 623
Josephson, E., 309*n*, 317
Josephson, M., 309*n*, 317

Kagan, J., 179, 181, 186
Kahl, J.A., 284, 295, 299, 303*n*, 305
Kahn, R.L., 581, 625, 636, 693*n*, 705
Kairov, I.A., 398, 411
Kandel, D., 282, *283-306*, 500, 583
Karon, B.P., 235, 238
Katz, D., 217, 223, 581, 625, 636, 693*n*, 705
Katz, E., 267, 268, 673, 684*n*, 689
Katz, I., 224, *225-38*
Kaufman, B., 309*n*, 317
Kaufman, M., 711, 734
Kausler, D.H., 419, 434, 426
Keislar, E., 152, 168
Keith, P.M., 625, 636
Kelly, G.A., 434
Kelly, H.H., 227, 238, 239, 406, 412, 417, 418, 434, 544, 582
Kendall, M.G., 288, 305
Kendall, P., 556*n*, 567
Keniston, K., 503, 506, 509, 522
Kennedy, W.A., 170, 186

Kerlinger, F., 6
Kerr, N., 105, 120
Kimball, B., 235, 238
Kinder, M.I., 117, 120
Kirk, H.D., 639n, 654
Kirk, J., 86, 91
Klinger, E., 57
Knapp, R.H., 60, 75
Knight, P.H., 339, 356
Knowles, E., 445n, 456
Knupfer, G., 354, 356
Koenig, K.E., 524n
Köhler, W., 154, 168
Kolb, D.A., 389, 414n, *458-67*, 468, 599
Korn, R., 45, 56
Korzybski, A., 434
Koser, L., 119, 120
Kounin, J.S., 134, *135-49*, 435, 468
Kozol, J., 308, 317
Krushchev, N., 397

Lahaderne, H.M., 93, *94-103*
Landreth, C., 217, 223
Lane, C., 284, 305
Lang, G.E., 387, 388
Lang, K., 387, 388
Lasch, C., 502, 510, 522
Lawrence, P.R., 309n, 317, 691, 705
Lawrence, W., 45, 56
Lazarsfeld, P.F., 240
Leavitt, H.J., 154, 168, 692n, 693, 705
Lee, F.J., 235, 238
Leites, N., 72, 75
Lesser, G.S., 170, 186, 282, *283-306*, 500, 583
Lev, J., 649n, 655
Levin, H., 402, 403, 412
Levine, J.M., 217, 223
Levinson, D.J., 482, 488, 616, 623
Lewin, K., 33, 42, 151, 168, 282, 404, 411, 693n, 705, 712
Lieberman, M., 646, 655
Lighthall, F.F., 228, 239
Lippitt, R., 151, 152, 168, 404, 411, 577, 582, 584n, 598, 711, 729, 734, 735
Lipset, S.M., 284, 305, 502, 507, 522, 593, 598, 667n, 670
Lit, J., 235
Litcher, J.H., 216, *217-23*, 357
Litwin, G., 414n
Lövaas, O.I., 117, 120
Lowell, E.L., 359, 369, 416, 434
Loyola, I., 427
Luszki, M., 711, 734

McArthur, C.C., 58n, 75
McClelland, D.C., 6, *58-75* 358-60, *367-69*, 413, *414-34*, 460, 461, 469, 488
Maccoby, E.E., 319, 402, 411
McConnell, T.R., 87, 91
McCorkle, L.W., 45, 46, 56
McDill, E.L., 283-85, 293, 303n, 305
McEachern, A., 583
McFee, A., 88, 91
McGee, R., 660n, 670
McGeoch, J.A., 423, 434
McGuffey, W.H., 361, 369
McKay, H.D., 45
McKelvey, W., 458n

McLuhan, M., 733, 734
McPherson, D.A., 217, 219, 222, 223
Madson, C.H., Jr., 105, 119
Mahan, D.J., *625-36*
Maher, T., 253
Makarenko, A.S., 390-92, 411-12
Mallery, D., 309n, 317
Mandler, G., 226
Mannheim, H., 56
Mannino, F.V., 299, 305
March, J., 151, 168
Marklund, S., 215
Martinez, J., 7
Marvick, D., 670
Marx, K., 309n, 637
Maslow, A., 469, 488
Mason, W.S., 583, 687, 689
Matza, D., 356
Mayer, M., 585n
Mayeske, G., 202
Melville, S.D., 202-4, 207, 208n, 215
Menzel, H., 684n, 689
Meredith, D., 458n
Merton, R.K., 555, 556n, 567, 622n, 623, 691, 705
Meyer, R., 170n, 186
Meyers, E., 285
Meyerson, L., 105, 120
Michael, J., 105, 120
Michael, J.A., 285, 306
Michael, S.K., 436n
Michaels, W.B., 91
Middleton, R., 309n, 318
Mierke, K., 419, 434
Miles, B., 7
Miles, M.B., 389, 435, *436-56*, 599, 693n, 705
Miles, R.E., 693n, 705
Miller, D.R., 402, 403, 412, 556, 567
Miller, R., 503, 522
Miller, W., 399, 412
Miller, W.E., 354, 356, 639, 654
Mills, D.L., 661, 670
Mischell, W., 482, 488
Mitchell, G.D., 639n, 654
Moeller, G.H., 357, *358-69*, 637, *638-55*
Mollenkopf, W.G., 202-4, 207, 208n
Monroe, M., 219, 223
Moore, W.E., 600, 613
Morgenstern, O., 335, 600, 613
Morland, J.K., 222, 223
Morrison, F., 399, 411
Morrow, W.R., 299, 306
Mort, P.R., 215
Moss, H.A., 181, 186
Murphy, G., 217, 223, 406, 412
Murphy, L.B., 406, 412
Murray, H., 76, 77
Murstein, B.I., 227, 238
Myrdal, G., 189, 198

Neugarten, B., 501n
Newcomb, T.M., 43, 151, 168, 285, 306, 406, 412, 503, 522, 523, *524-54*, 599
Newman, R., 722n, 734
Nielson, L., 105n
Norton, A.E., 146, 148
Novikova, L.E., 392, 412

Obradovic, S., 146, 149

Ohlin, L.E., 45, 55, 56
Olim, E.G., 170*n*, 174, 187
Oppenheim, D.B., 222, 223
Orne, M.T., 334, 420, 434
Osborne, K., 145, 149
Osgood, C.E., 66, 75, 571, 582
Owen, R., 308

Pace, R., 6, 76, *77-91*
Page, C.W., 427, 433
Parker, R.G., 365, 369
Parsons, T., 293, 306, 311*n*, 317, 405, 412,
   507, 508, 522, 617, 623
Passow, A.H., 584*n*, 598
Pearlin, L.I., 309*n*, 317, 638, 639, 655
Peck, R.F., 408, 412
Pervin, L.A., 91
Piaget, J., 386, 388
Pilnick, S., 43, *44-56*
Plager, E., 119, 120
Polansky, B.N., 577, 582
Polansky, N., 145, 149
Portes, A., 285, 305
Poshman, L.J., 217, 223
Powelson, H., 616, 623
Prather, M., *122-33*

Rabin, A.I., 399, 412
Radke, M.J., 217, 223, 227, 239
Ramsøy, N.R., 285, 306
Rankin, E.F., 602*n*, 613
Raven, B., 226, 227, 238
Reader, G., 556*n*, 567
Redl, F., 44, 56
Rehberg, R.A., 284, 306
Rhea, B., 307, *308-18*
Richards, J.M., Jr., 87, 92
Rickover, H., 585*n*
Riesman, D., 151, 168, 358, 359, 366, 367,
   409, 412
Riessman, F., 308, 317
Rigsby, L., 285
Riley, J.W., Jr., 642, 655, 673, 689
Riley, M.W., 304, 642, 655, 673, 689
Rindlisbacher, A., 368, 369
Roberts, S.O., 232, 236, 238
Robinson, H.M., 219, 223
Robinson, J.M., 232, 236, 238
Roethlisberger, F.J., 418, 434
Rogers, C.R., 414, 424, 427, 434
Rogoff, N., 92
Rokeach, M., 467
Rosen, B.C., 399, 412, 419, 427, 434
Rosen, M., 227, 239
Rosen, S., 577, 582
Rosenberg, M., 240, 503, 522, 554
Rosenberg, P., 227, 239, 240
Rosenberg, R., 309*n*, 317
Rosencranz, H.A., *600-13*
Rosenthal, D., 267, 268
Rosenthal, R., 327, 328, 333, 334, 419, 434
Ross, D.H., 675, 689
Rostow, W.W., 366-67, 369
Rousseau, J.J., 311*n*
Rubenstein, D.B., 117, 120
Rubin, I., 458*n*
Ruebush, B.K., 228, 239
Runkel, P., 707*n*, 731, 735
Russell, B., 201

Ryan, J.J., III, *135-49*, 468
Ryans, D.G., 598, 646*n*, 655

Safford, T., 7
St. John, N.H., 584*n*, 598
Sanford, R.N., 482, 488
Sarason, I.G., 226, 235, 239, 428, 434
Sarason, S.B., 228, 239
Saturen, S., 707*n*
Scarpitti, F.H., 56
Schachter, S., 265, 268
Schaeffer, B., 117, 120
Schanck, R.L., 600, 611-13
Schedler, P., 501*n*
Scheff, T.J., 657*n*, 670
Schein, E.H., 693*n*, 705
Schild, E., 335
Schmuck, R.A., 150, *151-68*, 389, 599,
   706, *707-35*
Schoggen, P., 14, 42
Schroder, H.M., 121, 133
Schwitzgebel, R., 460, 467
Scott, W.C., 585*n*, 598
Scott, W.R., 625, 634-36
Sears, P., 152, 168
Sears, R.R., 402, 412
Secord, P., 2, 6, 7, 9, 169
Seeman, M., 309*n*, 317, 638, 655, 665, 670
Sewell, W.H., 151, 168, 284, 299, 303*n*,
   306
Sexton, P.C., 584*n*, 598
Shah, V.P., 284, 299, 303*n*, 306
Shaw, C.R., 45, 56
Shaycoft, M.F., 205-6, 215
Sherif, C., 492, 499
Sherif, M., 492, 499
Shils, E.A., 311*n*, 317
Shipman, V.C., 169, *170-87*, 319
Shipton, J.M., 638, 655
Short, J.F., Jr., 399, 411
Sieber, S.D., *584-98*
Siegel, A.E., 491, *492-99*
Siegel, S., 363, 369, 376, 388, 491, *492-99*
Sigel, I.E., 181, 186
Simmons, D., 371, 386, 388
Simmons, J.B., 117, 120
Simon, H., 151, 168
Simpson, R.L., 283, 284, 306
Singer, D., 217, 223
Skinner, B.F., 104, 421, 426
Slavson, S., 44
Smith, A., 308
Smith, L.M., 93, 625, 636
Smith, M.B., 457, *469-89*
Spence, K.W., 226, 239
Spiegel, L.A., 582
Spiro, M.E., 399, 412
Spock, B., 390
Stein, M.I., 77, 92
Steinberg, L., 6, 7
Steiner, G.A., 416, 420, 423, 424, 426, 429,
   433
Stellwagon, G., 58*n*
Stendler, C.B., 371
Stephens, T.M., 6, 335
Stephenson, R.M., 56
Stern, G., 6, 76-78, 84*n*, 86
Stevenson, R., 14
Stinchcombe, A., 309*n*, 312*n*, 317, 504, 522

Stock, D., 437n, 456
Straus, M., 151, 168
Strauss, A., 556n, 567
Strauss, M.A., 359, 369
Strickland, L.H., 581, 582
Strodtbeck, F.L., 66, 75, 284, 306
Sturgeon, R., 105n
Sturr, J., 60, 75
Suchman, E., 503, 522, 554
Suci, G.J., 66, 75, 408
Sutherland, J., 227, 239
Svehla, G., 285, 306
Swados, H., 308
Swanson, B.E., 243n, 268
Swanson, G.E., 402, 403, 412, 503, 522,
    556, 567, 628n, 636

Tagiuri, R., 577, 581
Tannenbaum, F., 56
Tannenbaum, P.H., 66, 75, 571, 582
Taylor, J.A., 226, 239
Terrien, F.W., 661, 670
Thibaut, J.W., 227, 239, 406, 412, 582
Thistlethwaite, D.L., 83-84, 86, 87, 92
Thomas, D.R., 33, 105-20
Thomas, E.J., 600n
Thorndike, E.L., 327, 426
Thornton, G.R., 577, 582
Thrasher, F.M., 399, 412
Toby, J., 642, 655
Tomich, E., 600-13
Torrance, P., 6
Trager, H.G., 217, 223
Travers, R.M.W., 586, 598
Trow, D.B., 657n, 670
Trow, M., 87, 92, 503, 522, 553, 554
Tryon, R.C., 122, 129, 133
Tumin, M.M., 600, 613
Turner, A.N., 309n, 317
Turner, R.H., 285, 306
Twyman, J.P., 600-13
Tyler, R.W., 170, 186

Udy, S., Jr., 652, 655

Van de Riet, V., 170, 186
Van Egmond,E.,152, 168, 708, 735
Veblen, T., 522
Von Neumann, J., 335, 600, 613

Waite, R.R., 228, 239
Walker, A.M., 638, 655
Walker, H.M., 649n, 655

Wallace, W.L., 285, 306, 555
Wallen, N.E., 586, 598
Waller, W., 309n, 318, 586n, 598, 615, 618,
    623
Walters, R.H., 217, 223, 415, 428, 433
Waly, P., 236, 238
Ware, R., 122, 133
Warren, N., 283, 305
Warwick, D.P., 524-54
Washburne, C., 311n, 318
Watson, G., 8
Watson, J.M., 365, 369
Webb, E., 491
Weber, M., 358, 359, 369, 637
Webster, H., 536, 554
Weiby, M., 5, 570-82
Weinstein, E., 371, 381n, 388
Wendt, H.W., 60, 75
Westby, D.L., 284, 306
Wheeler,S., 600, 611-13
Whisler, T.L., 662n
Whitam, F.L., 436n
White, B.J., 122-33
White, J.C., Jr., 170, 186
White, R.K., 151, 168, 404, 411
White, R.W., 470, 488-89
Whiting, J.W.M., 402, 412
Whyte, W.F., 151, 168, 399, 409, 412
Whyte, W.H., 358, 369, 399, 409, 412
Wilder, D.E., 584-98
Willems, E., 12-42
Williams, O.P., 243n, 268
Williams, R.M., 503, 522, 554
Willower, D.J., 615, 618, 619, 621, 623
Wilson, A.B., 151,168,285, 299, 306
Wilson, J.Q., 243n, 268
Wineman, D., 44, 56
Winter, D.G., 10, 57, 58-75, 389, 414n
Winter, S.K., 457, 458-67, 468, 599
Winterbottom, M.R., 367, 369
Wiseman, F., 307
Withey, S., 151, 168
Wolf, M.M., 105, 119
Wolfenstein, M., 72, 75
Wright, C.R., 437n, 456
Wright, H.F., 42, 138, 148

Yarrow, M.R., 227, 235, 239

Zachs, J., 460, 467
Zander, A., 154, 167, 691, 705
Zientarski, D., 105n
Zimmerman, E., 105, 120
Zimmerman, J., 105, 120

Index of Subjects

Abilities, utilization of, 155, 158, 160-64, 167

Abstract and concrete teachers, study of effect on student performance by, 122-23
method, 123-27
results, 127-32

Achievement, academic:
adolescent subcultures and, 270-81
school characteristics and, 189-215

Achievement motive, 165, 358-59
developed, 415-29
summary, 429-33
readers used to measure:
discussion, 364-65, 367
hypotheses, 360
method, 360-63
results, 363-64
summary, 368

Adolescents (*see also* Students)
educational plans of, parental influence on, 283-86
method, 286-88
results, 288-303
summary, 303-4
subculture of, and academic achievement, 270-81

Adult-oriented child, 408

Advantaged, revolt of, 503-4

Affiliation motive, 165, 358-59
readers used to measure:
discussion, 365-68
hypotheses, 360
method, 361-63
results, 363-64
summary, 368

Affluent society, social priorities of, 169-70

Age and Occupations Test, 376-77, 386

Alienation of high school students, 309-12

Anti-authoritarianism as theme of student protest, 505

Anticipated comparison, effects of, 233-34

Anti-dogmatism as theme of student protest, 505

Antihumanitarianism in American private schools, 65

Anti-institutionalism as theme of student protest, 506-7

Appraisal-focus with desist-technique, 141-42

Approving behaviors, 112, 114, 116

Aspirations, 192-97, 272, 278-280, 282-306

Associative network, changes in, 74-75, 421-24

Attitude:
toward school, 155, 157, 161, 163-64, 167, 192-97
toward self, 155-56, 161-64, 167

Authoritarianism, 482
student protest and, 505

Authority in American private schools, 63-64

Behavior, human, 11 (*see also specific types of behavior*)
intra-individual, 13
scientific psychology and, 12-13
shaped, 44-46

Behavior settings:
K-21, 21
nonclass participation in, 25-32
forces, 33-40
method, 40-41
offerings, 26-27
use, 27-32
size of, 38
theory of, 21

Bi-racial situations, performance of Negroes in:
determinants of, 225-28
experimental evidence on, 228-36
summary of, 236-37

Bi-racial teams, performance of, 228-30

Bureaucratization and teachers' sense of power, 638-55
measure of, 642-44

Campus atmosphere, 77
consequences of, 81-85
differences between, 79-80
measuring, 85-90
similarities between, 78-79

Career-bound superintendents, 656, 658, 668, 669

Career game, 340

Career preference changes in graduate school, 558-65

Categorical-inferential conceptualization, 179-81

Causation, teacher's perception of, determinants and consequences of, 570-71
methods of study, 571-74
results and discussion of study for:
attribution of characteristics, 576-77
effectiveness, 575-76
expression of sentiment, 579-81
perception of causation, 577-79

Character education, Soviet methods of:
Makarenko and, 390-92
principles of, 398-99
family vs. collective, 399-405
group criticism and self-criticism, 407-10
group incentives, 405-7
socialization in school collective, 392-98

Citizenship education, 339

Civic elite, power of, and school desegregation, 241

Civil rights (*see* Desegregation)

Clarity of desist-technique, 138-41

Classical personal style developed in American private schools, study of:
  nature of education, 59-60
    antihumanitarianism, 65
    authority, 63-64
    cynicism, 64-65
    intellectual pressure, 60-61
    self-control, 61-63
  results of, 67-75
  testing procedure, 65-67
Classroom life:
  classroom management and desist-technique, 135
    influence of variables on results, 143-46
    variables operating at time of, 136-43
    videotape study, 146-48
  disruptive behavior, teachers' elimination of, 104-6
    implications, 118-19
    method, 106-11
    results, 111-18
  group processes in, improvement of, 707-35
  peer groups in, study of:
    hypotheses and results, 158-64
    implications for further study, 164-66
    methods, 155-58
    pupil attitudes and achievement, 150-55
    summary, 166-67
  teacher-student interaction, study of inequalities of, 94-95
    method, 95-96
    results, 96-103
  teachers' beliefs and behavior and student performance, study of, 122-23
    method, 123-27
    results, 127-32
Classroom studies:
  classroom management, 135-48
  effect of teachers' beliefs and behavior on learning of students, 122-32
  elimination of disruptive behavior, 105-19
  inequalities of teacher-pupil interaction, 94-103
  peer liking patterns and pupil attitudes and achievements, 151-67
  use of multi-ethnic reader, 217-23
Cognitive modes in children, socialization of, 170-71
  conceptualization, 179-81
  control systems, 172-74, 177-78
  maternal teaching styles, 181-86
  verbal codes, 171-76
Cognitive theory, 121
Coleman Report, critiques of, 189-215
Collective:
  family vs., 399-405
  school, socialization in 392-98
Collective-oriented personality, 409
College environments, 77
  consequences of, 81-85
  differences between, 78-79
  measuring of, 85-90
  similarities between, 78-79
Commitment:
  desist-technique and, 144-45
  for high school students, 313
Communication between parent and child on educational plans, 299-301

Communication between teachers and students: (*see also* Student-teacher interaction)
  behavior of teacher with disruptive students, study of:
    implications, 118-19
    method, 106-11
    results, 111-18
  concrete and abstract teachers' effect on student performance, study of, 122-23
    method, 123-27
    results, 127-32
  desist-technique, 135
    influence of variables on results, 143-46
    variables operating at time of, 136-43
    videotape study, 146-48
  inequalities of, study on, 94-95
    method, 95-96
    results, 96-103
Communication codes, 171-76
Community disaster game, 341-42
Community as theme of student protest, 505-6
Comparison, anticipated, effects of, 233-34
Competence, patterns of, and Peace Corps:
  general competence, 473-76
  personality patterns, 477-79
  prediction problems, 481-82
    authoritarianism, 482
    personal future, 484-86
    personality change, 484-86
    psychiatric ratings, 483-84
  role performance, patterns of, 476-77
Conceptualization, 179-81
  concrete-abstract modes of, 121
Concrete and abstract teachers, study of effect on student performance by, 122-23
  method, 123-27
  results, 127-32
Consultation, as teacher improvement strategy, 722-28
Content analysis, 370
  of children's readers, *358-369*
  of imaginative stories by private school students, 66-74
  of television, 371-73
    influence, 382-85
    measuring instrument, 373-81
    sample, 373
    summary and discussion, 385-88
Context, 14-18
Control, pupil, ideology of, 615-16
Control systems in family, 172-74, 177-78
Cosmopolitans, 656, 658
Criticism, group, and self-criticism, 407-10
Cultural orientation, measure of, 359-60
  use of readers for:
    discussion, 364-68
    hypotheses, 360
    method, 361-63
    results, 363-64
    summary, 368
Cultural deprivation, effects on child of, and social-status differences:
  cognitive modes and, 170-71
  communication modes and, 171-76
  conceptualization and, 179-81
  control systems and, 172-74, 177-78
  maternal teaching styles and, 181-86

Cultural values and motive acquisition
theory, 425-26
Curriculum, enforced, in secondary education, 337-38
Cynicism in American private schools, 64-65

Decision process in desegregation:
appearance of issue, 245
escalation and resolution, 246-47, 252-54
first civil rights actions, 246
introduction of new actors, 247-48
key response, 246, 250-52
rejection of demands, 246
Delinquency:
Essexfields program and, 46-49
alumni, 52
family contact, 52-53
formal structure, 50
implications, 54
informal structure, 50-52
research design, 55
transition to community, 53-54
social base of, 44-46
Demand characteristics, 327
Denial of hostility, 235
Deprivation, effects on child of, social-status
differences and:
cognitive modes and, 170-71
communication codes and, 171-76
conceptualization and, 179-81
control systems and, 172-74, 177-78
maternal teaching styles and, 181-86
Descriptive global conceptualization, 179-81
Descriptive part-whole conceptualization,
179-81
Desegregation:
attitudes, aspirations, future plans and,
192-97
facilities, staffs, services and, 190-91
school system acquiescence to, 241-42
acquiescence, 248-60
civil rights liberalism, 260-65
cohesion, 265-67
decision process, 245-48, 250-55
research design, 243-45
summary, 267-68
student achievement and, 191-98
Desist-technique, 135
influence of variables on results of:
commitment, 144-45
liking for teacher, 145-46
motivation, 143-44, 145
variables operating at time of:
clarity, firmness, roughness, 138-41
deviant's reaction and prestige, 142-43
punishing vs. reprimanding vs. ignoring,
137-38
task-focus vs. appraisal-focus, 141-42
threatening vs. supportive, 136-37
videotape study of, 146-48
Developmental theory, 39-40
Deviancy, 48-51 (*see also* Norms)
desist-technique and, 142-43
Dictatorialness of teachers, 122-23, 128,
131
Differentiation, hierarchical, effects of,
625-36
Disapproving behaviors, 114, 116-18
Discipline, 62-63
desist-technique, 135

influence of variables on results, 143-46
variables operating at time of, 136-43
videotape study, 146-48
social status, ethnicity and, 320
behavioral comparison, 324
dependent measures, 321
discussion, 326
experimental situation, 321
negative reinforcement, 323-24
positive reinforcement, 323
subjects, 320-21
teachers' behavior with disruptive students, study of:
implications, 118-19
method, 106-11
results, 111-18
Dogmatism and student protest, 505

Ecological environment, 13-14
structure of, 15-16
units of, 16-21
Education, character, Soviet methods of:
Makarenko and, 390-92
principles of, 398-99
family vs. collective, 399-405
group criticism and self-criticism,
407-10
group incentives, 405-7
socialization in school collective and,
392-98
Education, citizenship, 339
Education, secondary, 23-66, 270-281,
308-318, 336-37 (*see also* High
Schools)
as modified by socialization, 556-57
games with simulated environments and,
338-40
structural defects in, 337-38
Educational engineers, 8
Educational innovations, adoption of,
672-89
Educational opportunity, equality of,
189-90
in Northern urban schools:
attitudes, aspirations and future plans,
192-97
facilities, staffs, services, 190-91
student achievement, 191-98
school characteristics and pupil achievement and, 201-15
Educational settings, 3-4
organizational innovation and, 694-702
Efficiency and hierarchical differentiation,
625-36
Elaborated communication code, 171-76
Emotional reactions to test situations,
235-36
Employment and superintendents, 659-61
Environment:
behavior and, 11-12
structure, 15-16
units, 16-21
educational, 43
simulated, games with, 338-40
career game, 340
community disaster game, 341-42
legislative game, 341
results, 344-46
summary and discussion, 355-56
testing effects, 342-43

what is learned, 346-54
Environmental press, 76
  in colleges:
    consequences, 81-85
    differences, 79-80
    measuring, 85-90
    similarities, 78-79
  defined, 77
  determined, 78
Essexfields, delinquency treated at, 44-49
  alumni and, 52
  family contact and, 52-53
  formal structure of, 50
  implications of, 54
  informal structure of, 50-52
  research design of, 55
  transition to community and, 53-54
Expectancies, 327
  biased psychological reports, influence on
      teacher-student interaction of, 328
  conclusions, 324
  method, 329-32
  results and discussion, 332-34
Experience, early childhood, in socialization
  conceptualization and, 179-81
  control systems and, 172-74, 177-78
  maternal teaching styles and, 181-86
  verbal codes and, 171-76
Experience, effect on beginning teachers,
  615-23
"Experimenter bias" studies, 419

Facilities of schools, 190-91
Failure, threat of, 235
  to Negroes in bi-racial situation, 228
Family, 44 (*see also* Mothers)
  patterns of interaction of, 297-99
  vs. collective principle, 399-405
Firmness with desist-technique, 138-41
Forces towards participation in nonclass settings, 33-40
Future plans of students, 192-97, 282-306
  (*see also* Aspirations)

Games, 335
  with simulated environments, 338-40
    career game, 340
    community disaster game, 341-42
    legislative game, 341
    results, 344-46
    summary and discussion, 355-56
    testing effects of, 342-43
    what is learned, 346-54
General culture occupations, 374, 382-83
Goal-setting studies, 419
Grade levels and teaching styles, 589-91
Grades, 338
Graduate schools, study of socialization pro-
  cess in:
  career preference changes, 558-65
  faculty encouragement, 565-66
  frame of reference, 557
  sample of, 557-58
  summary of, 566-67
Great Britain, public schools in, 57
Greek model of education in American pri-
  vate schools, 59-60
Group affect, 158, 167
Group, classroom (*see* Classroom life)
Group criticism and self-criticism, 407-10

Group incentives, 405-7
Group norms and creative individualism,
    study of:
  adapting to community norms, 537
  change, directions of, 538-39
    variations, 539-45
  conclusion, 552-54
  consensus on community norms, 525-26
  interviews:
    individualism, 526-27, 535
    intellectuality, 528-29, 535-36
    unconventionality, 528-29, 535-36
  sanctions and community norms, 530-31
    negative sanctions, 531-32
    positive sanctions, 534-37
    typology of students, 532-34
  setting of, 524-25
  student types:
    norm acceptance, 546-49
    social structure, 549-52
  supporting data:
    adjective check list, 529
    self-descriptions, 530
Groups, reference:
  and motive acquisition, 429
  study of, 492-499

Hawthorne effect, 343, 418
"Hello-Goodbye" effect, 418-19
Hierarchical differentiation, effects
  of, 625-36
High schools,   308 (*see also* Education,
    secondary)
  alienation in, 309-12
  meaning in, 312-14
  methods for study of, 40-41
  powerlessness and paternalism in, 308-16
  size of:
    optimal, 41-42
    participation in nonclass settings and,
      25-48
Higher education, 77-91, 492-99, 501-22,
  524-54, 556-67 (*see also* Graduate
    schools)
  environmental press in, 76
  in colleges, 78-90
  defined, 77
  determined, 78
Hostility, denial of, 235
Humanitarianism:
  in American private schools, 65
  as value pattern of student activist, 517
Hypothetico-deductive method, 134

Ignoring behavior, as desist-technique,
  137-38
Incentives, group, 405-7
Individualism, creative, study of, 524-54
Induced threat in different racial environ-
  ments, 231-33
Influence and desist-technique, 141-42
Inner-directed character type, 358-60, 367,
  409
Innovations:
  educational:
    adoption of, 672-89
    social structure and, 684-89
  organizational, implementation of,
    691-705
Institutionalism and student protest, 506-7

Intellectual pressure in American private schools, 60-61
Intellectualism as value pattern of student activist, 516-17
Intellectuality, 528-29, 535-36
Intelligentsia, young, and radicalism, 501-3
Internat in Soviet socialization, 397-98
Intra-individual behavior, 13
Involvement in peer group, 154, 156, 162-64, 167
IQ instructions, in study of bi-racial performance, 232-33
IQ scores:
    and achievement, as function of classroom group structure, 151-68
    and performance, related to peer culture, 274-77
    in urban schools (verbal ability measure), 191, 206-8
    influence on teacher behavior and pupil performance, 328-34, 573
    teacher expectancies as influence on, 327, 328

K-21 behavior setting, 21
Knowledge, occupational, television as source of, study of, 371-72
    influence of, 382-85
    measuring instrument for, 373-75
        age, 376-77
        interviewing, 375
        sex, 378-79
        social class, 379-81
    purposes of, 372-73
    sample for, 373
    summary and discussion of, 385-88

Laboratory studies:
    hierarchical differentiation, effects of, on group productivity, efficiency and risk-taking, 625-36
    Negro performance in bi-racial situations, 225-37
    teachers' perception of causation, 570-82
Laboratories (training):
    organizational development, 729-31
    school principals, 437
    teacher development, 708-12
    to aid self-development, 459-60
Laboratory training, changes during and following, 436-37, 715-22, 731-32
    case studies of learning in, 446-55
Language use:
    cognitive modes, 170-71
    conceptualization, 179-81
    control systems, 172-74, 177-78
    maternal teaching styles, 181-86
    verbal codes, 171-76
Learning in classroom:
    games with simulated environments and, 338-40, 346-54
    peer groups and, study of:
        structural defects in, 337-38
Legislative game, 341
Liking status in peer group, 155-56, 159-64, 167
Liking structures, peer group, 150, 154, 156, 159-60, 164, 167

Maternal teaching behavior, 169
    cognitive modes and, 170-71
    conceptualization and, 179-81
    control systems and, 172-74, 177-78
    teaching styles and, 181-86
    verbal codes and, 171-76
Mathematics, educational innovations in, 675-83
Membership groups and reference groups, study of, 492-93
    discussion of, 496-99
    field experiment on, 493-95
    results, 494-96
    summary of, 499
Mental health in classroom, and peer groups, study of:
    hypothesis and results of, 158-64
    implications of, 164-66
    methods for, 155-58
    pupil attitudes and achievements and, 150-55
    summary of, 166-67
Mental health consultation, 722-29
Missionaries, 415-16
Moral purity:
    as theme for student protest, 505
    as value pattern of student activism, 517
Moral teachings, readers used to measure, study of:
    discussion of, 366-67
    hypotheses of, 360
    method of, 361-63
    results of, 363-64
    summary of, 368
Mothers:
    influence on educational plans of adolescent of, 283-86
        method, 286-88
        results, 288-303
        summary, 303-4
    teaching behavior of, 169
        cognitive modes, 170-71
        conceptualization, 179-81
        control systems, 172-74, 177-78
        teaching styles, 181-86
        verbal codes, 171-76
Motivation, 39 (*see also specific motivations*)
    desist-techniques and, 143-44, 145
    motive acquisition, theory of, 414-15
        basis, 415-29
        summary, 429-33
    secondary education and, 336-37
        games with simulated environments, 338-56
Multi-ethnic readers and attitudes towards Negroes, study of, 217-18
    discussion of, 221-23
    method of, 218-20
    results of, 220-21

Negative reinforcement, 107-8, 110-18, 185, 323-25
Negative sanctions, 531-32
Negroes: (*see also* Race)
    attitudes towards, and use of multi-ethnic readers, 217-18
    child discipline, study of, 320
    Coleman Report and, 189-215
    desegregation of (*see* Desegregation)

equal educational opportunity for, 188-215
performance in bi-racial situations of, 225-38
Nonclass settings, study of participation in, 25
    forces toward, 33-40
    method of, 40-41
    offerings of schools, 26-27
    students' use of, 27-32
Normative influence, 43
Norms:
    built at Essexfields, 47-49
    delinquency and, 45-46
    group, and creative individualism, study of:
        adapting to community norms, 537
        change, directions of, 538-45
        conclusion, 552-54
        consensus on community norms, 525-26
        interviews, 526-29, 535-37
        sanctions and community norms, 530-37
        setting, 524-25
        student types, 546-52
        supporting data, 529-30
North Carolina Advancement School, 57

Objectively-principled child, 409-10
Observation procedures:
    disruptive classroom behavior, 106-7
    effect of teachers' beliefs and behavior on student learning, 127
    teacher-pupil interaction, 95-96
Occupational knowledge, television as source of, study of, 371-72
    influence of, 382-85
    measuring instrument for, 373-75
    purposes of, 372-73
    sample for, 373
    summary and discussion of, 385-88
Occupations Test, 373-75
    age and, 376-77, 386
    interviewing with, 375
    sex and, 378-79
    social class and, 379-81
Operant conditioners, 415
Organizational development laboratory, 729
Organizational innovation:
    educational setting of, 694-702
    implementation of, 691-705
Organizations:
    and teachers' sense of power, 638-54
    bureaucratization measure, 642-44
    succession effects in, 657-64, 667-69
Other-directed person, 358-60, 367

Pacing, 426-27
Parental preference and professional role definition, 584-85
    conclusions of, 596-98
    consensus on, 594-96
    at different grade levels, 589-91
    methods, 585-89
    results, 589
    social position and, 591-94
Parents, influence on educational plans of adolescents by, 283-86
    method of, 286-88
    results, 288-303

summary, 303-4
Participation in nonclass settings, 25
    coding, 27-28
    forces toward, 33-40
    method, 40-41
    offerings for, 26-27
    students' use of, 27-32
Paternalism, institutional, in high schools, 314-16
Peace Corps study, 470-88
    competence, patterns of:
        general competence, 473-76
        personality patterns in field interviews, 477-79
    role performance, patterns of, 476-77
    prediction problems, 481-82
        authoritarianism, 482
        personal future, 484-86
        personality change, 486-88
        psychiatric ratings, 483-84
Peer group liking structure, 150, 154, 156, 159-60, 164, 167
Peer groups:
    delinquency and, 45-46
    influence on education plans of adolescents by, 283-86
        method, 286-88
        results, 288-303
        summary, 303-4
    involvement in, 154, 156, 162-64
    learning achievement and, 195-97
    liking status in, 155-56, 159-64, 167
    loyalty transfers and, 49, 51-52, 54
    pupil attitudes and achievements and, 150-54
        attitude towards school, 155
        attitude towards self, 155
        involvement in peer group, 154
        peer group liking structure, 154
        utilization of abilities, 155
Peer-oriented child, 408-9
Penetration into behavior settings, 29-33
Performance:
    in behavior settings, 30-33, 37
    of Negroes in bi-racial situations, 225-38
    of pupils, 328-34
    of superintendents, 656-70
    role, of Peace Corps trainees, 472-79, 481-86
Person-oriented appeal system, 172-74, 177-78
Personal contact occupations, 374, 382-83, 385
Personality change:
    character education in Soviet Union, 390-412
    motive acquisition, theory of, 414-15
        basis, 415-29
        summary, 429-33
    Peace Corps and, 486-88
Populism as theme of student protest, 505
Positive reinforcement, 107-8, 110-18, 185, 322-24
Positive sanctions, 534-37
Power:
    desist-technique and, 141-42
    teachers' sense of:
        bureaucratization and, 638-55
        measure of, 641-42
        organizations and, 652-54

Powerlessness of high school students, 314-16
Press, scales for measuring, 77-91
Prestige and desist-technique, 142-43
Prestige-suggestion studies, 418
Primary groups, 44
Private schools, St. Grottlesex studied:
 background of, 58-59
 nature of education at, 59-65
 results, 67-75
 testing procedure of, 65-67
Problem-solving, group, 625
 effects of hierarchical differentiation on, 625-36
 processes, 730
 techniques, 709-11
Productivity, group, and hierarchical differentiation, 625-36
Protest, student (*see* Student protest)
Psychological demands as environmental press, 77
Psychological reports, influence on student-teacher interaction of, 328
 conclusions, 324
 method, 329-32
 results and discussion, 332-34
Public schools, English, 57
 American schools patterned after, 59
Puerto Ricans, data in Coleman Report, 190-97, 202, 207
Punitiveness of teachers, 122-23, 128, 131

Race: (*see also* Negroes, Desegregation)
 attitudes, effect of multi-ethnic readers on, 217-224
 equal educational opportunity and, 188-215
 performance and, 224-39
 preferred teaching style and, 593-94
 social class and, in use of reinforcement, 320-26
Radicalism and young intelligentsia, 501-3
Readers:
 multi-ethnic, and attitudes toward Negroes, 217-18
 discussion, 221-23
 methods, 218-20
 results, 220-21
 used to measure cultural achievement orientation:
 discussion, 364-68
 hypotheses, 360
 method, 361-63
 results, 363-64
 summary, 368
 values expressed in, 358
Reality, perception of, 420, 424-25
Reference groups:
 membership groups and, 492-93
 discussion, 496-99
 field experiment, 493-95
 results, 494-96
 summary, 499
 motive acquisition and, 429
Reinforcement:
 by preschool children, 320-26
 positive, 322-24
 negative, 323-25
 criticism and praise by mothers, 185
 social, 104-5

teacher's approval and disapproval, 107-118
Relational-contextual conceptualization, 179-81
Reprimanding behavior with desist-technique, 137-38
Resourcefulness of teachers, 122-23, 128, 131
Restricted communication codes, 171-76
Risk-taking and hierarchical differentiation, 625-36
Role, 599
 consensus, 583
 definitions, professional, and parental preferences for teaching styles, 584-98
 occupational, as viewed by children, 370-81, 385-88
 TV influence on, 283-85
 performance by Peace Corps trainees, 472-79, 481-86
 social, as learned via socialization, 557
 teacher's, shared inaccuracies in, 600-13
Romanticism:
 as theme of student protest, 504
 as value pattern of student activist, 516
Roughness of desist-technique, 138-41

St. Grottlesex:
 nature of education at, 59-60
 antihumanitarianism, 65
 authority, 63-64
 cynicism, 64-65
 intellectual pressure, 60-61
 self-control, 61-63
 study of, 58-75
 results, 67-75
 testing procedure, 65-67
Sanctions and community norms, 530-31
 at Essexfields, 51-52
 negative sanctions, 531-32
 positive sanctions, 534-37
 typology of students, 532-34
School boards and desegregation, 241-42
 acquiescence, 248-60
 civil rights liberalism and, 260-65
 cohesion and, 265-67
 decision process and, 245-48, 250-55
 research design and, 243-45
 summary of, 267-68
Schools
 administration of, 198
 attitudes toward, 155, 157, 161, 163-64, 167, 192-97
 changing of, 671-735
 collective, socialization in, 392-98
 factors and equal educational opportunity, 200-15
 nonclass settings in, participation in, 25-32
 forces, 33-40
 method, 40-41
 offerings, 26-27
 use of behavior settings, 27-32
 organizational innovations and, 694-702
 private (*see* Private schools)
 size of, 24-25, 41-42
 superintendents of (*see* Superintendents)
Secondary education (*see* Education, secondary)

Self:
  attitudes toward, 155-56, 161-64, 167
Self-control:
  in American private schools, 61-63
  as value pattern of student activism, 517
Self-criticism and group criticism, 407-10
Self-direction, capacity for, study of,
    458-67
  discussion, 464-67
  procedure, 459-62
  results, 462-64
Self-oriented child, 408
Services of schools, 190-91
Sex differences:
  in basis for status achievement in high
    school, 272-74
  in effects of simulation games, 345-56
  in relation between peer rewards and ac-
    ademic performance, 274-77
  in role knowledge, 378-79, 386
  in teacher-pupil interaction, 99-102,
    320-26
  in use of reinforcement, 322, 324-25
Size of schools, 24-25, 38-42
Social facilitation, of Negroes in bi-racial sit-
    uations, 226-27
Social reinforcement (*see* Reinforcement)
Social structure:
  and educational innovations, 684-89
  of classroom group, 152-53, 154-66
Social threat to Negroes in bi-racial situa-
    tions, 252-26
Socialization, 556-57
  of cognitive modes in children, 170-71
    conceptualization, 179-81
    control systems, 172-74, 177-78
    maternal teaching styles, 181-86
    verbal codes, 171-76
  process of, in graduate schools, study of
    career preference changes, 558-65
    faculty encouragement, 565-66
    frame of reference, 557
    sample, 557-58
    summary, 566-67
  in school collective, 392-98
  of student activists, 511-12
  of teachers, 617-22
Society for the Psychological Study of
    Social Issues, 1
Socio-economic status:
  activism and, 512-13
  adolescents' educational plans and,
    294-97, 300-1
  cognitive modes and, 170-71
  concept utilization and, 179-81
  control systems and, 172-74, 177-78
  maternal teaching styles and, 181-86
  occupational knowledge and, 379-81
  preferred teaching style and, 591-94
  race and, in use of reinforcement, 320-26
  school performance and,
    in Coleman Report, 194-95, 206, 208-9,
      212-13
    in earlier studies, 203-4
  verbal codes and, 171-76
Sociometric status of students and achieve-
    ment, study of:
  hypothesis and results, 158-64
  implications, 164-66

summary, 166-67
Sophistication in American private schools,
    64-65
Soviet methods of character education:
  Makarenko and, 390-92
  principles of, 398-99
    family vs. collective, 399-405
    group criticism and self-criticism,
      407-10
    group incentives, 405-7
  socialization in school collective, 392-98
Status-oriented families, 172-74, 177-78
Stereotyped television roles, 384-85, 387
Structure:
  defects of, in secondary education, 337-38
  of classroom group, 152-66
  of ecological environment, 15-16
  social, among Superintendents, 684-89
Student press, 83
Student protest:
  advantaged, revolt of, 503-4
  conclusions re, 519-21
  radicalism and young intelligentsia, 501-3
  social change project and, 511-16
  social-psychological roots of, 507-11
  themes of, 504-7
  value patterns of, 516-19
Student-teacher interaction:
  behavior of teacher with disruptive stu-
    dents, study of:
    implications, 118-19
    method, 106-11
    results, 111-18
  desist-technique, 135
    influence of variables on results of,
      143-46
    variables operating at time of, 136-43
    videotape study of, 146-48
  faculty encouragement in graduate school,
    565-66
  inequalities of, study on, 94-95
    method, 95-96
    results, 96-103
  psychological reports, biased, influence
    on, 328-34
  role of, in secondary education, 338
  teachers' beliefs and behavior and student
    performance, study of, 122-32
Students:
  control of, 615-16
  in high school, 308-16
  measurement of behavior of, 123-24
  motivated and unmotivated, 336-56
  parents' influence on educational plans of,
    283-304
  peer groups, study of, 150-67
  performance of, and hierarchical dif-
    ferentiation, 625-36
  subcultures of, and academic achievement,
    270-81
Subcultures, adolescent, and academic
    achievement, 270-81
Success, probability of, for Negroes in bi-
    racial situation, 227, 234-35
Succession, school superintendents and,
    657-70
Superintendents:
  and adoption of innovations, 672-89
  employment of, 659-61

Superintendents: (cont.)
  succession and performance among, 657-70
Supportive behavior with desist-technique, 136-37

Task-focus with desist-technique, 141-42
Teacher development laboratory, 709-22
Teacher-pupil interaction (*see* Student-teacher interaction)
Teachers:
  abstract and concrete, study of effect on student performance by, 122-32
  achievement effect of, 196
  beginning, 615-23
  children as, 320-26
  classroom processes and, 707-35
  effectiveness of, 121
  mothers as, 169, 171-86
  power of, 638-55
  role of, shared inaccuracies in, 600-12
Teaching styles:
  of four-year-olds, 320-26
  parental preferences and professional role definition and, 584-98
Television as source for occupational knowledge, study of, 371-72
  influence of, 382-85
  measuring instrument, 373-81
  purposes of, 372-73
  sample, 373
  summary and discussion, 385-88

Television contact occupations, 374, 382-83
Test situations, emotional reactions to, 235-36
Threatening behavior with desist-technique, 136-37
Threats:
  failure, 235
  to Negroes in bi-racial situations, 225-26, 228, 231-33
Tradition-directed society, 359, 360
Training laboratory, study of, 436-56
  implications and conclusions, 455-56
  learning, case studies of, 446-47
    "late bloomer," 453-55
    quasi-learner, 450-53
    successful learner, 449-50
    unsuccessful learner, 447-48
  procedure, 437-41
  results, 441-46
  subjects, 437
Transfer-of-training research, 423-24

Unconventionality, 527-28, 536-37
Units of ecological environment, 16-21, 40
Utilization of abilities, 155, 158, 160-64, 167

Value patterns of student activists, 516-19
Value themes, in private school study, 68, 69-74
Values, cultural, motive acquisition theory and, 425-26
Verbal codes, 171-76
Videotape study of desist-technique, 146-48